SOLDIER LIFE

———————

MANY MUST FALL

TWO NARRATIVES OF THE CIVIL WAR

True histories of the 14th Iowa Infantry in camp and combat, told by the Wolf Creek Rangers of Tama County

Camp Pope Bookshop
2008

Press of the Camp Pope Bookshop
PO Box 2232
Iowa City, Iowa 52244
www.camppope.com

CONTENTS

Cover concept and design by Sara Kay Stoakes. Maps by J. A. McCann.

Front Cover Images, clockwise from top center:
Eleazar Stoakes on his farm; Peter Wilson; John Felter before enlisting; Four Soldiers of Company G (Thomas, Felter, Gallagher, Shanklin); John McKune; Felter gravesite at Crystal cemetery; John Gaston.

Back Cover Images, clockwise from top center:
Memorial Plaque, Herrick Chapel, Grinnell College campus; unidentified soldier; Veterans with flower baskets for the graves of their companions, Memorial Day 1908 Traer; unidentified soldier.

The photographs of the two unidentified soldiers were found unnamed inside an old family album owned by a descendant of one of the ten Wolf Creek Rangers featured in this book. Our hope is that they might be recognized and finally identified. We welcome any information from any reader who may know these men's names.

INTRODUCTION

Perhaps no other period in Iowa's history, or even in our Nation's history, held more momentous changes, saw more dramatic events, promised more opportunity, or threatened more dire consequences, than the decade from 1855 to 1865. One hundred and fifty years ago, pioneering families were leaving New York, Ohio, Pennsylvania and other eastern States, and began arriving in Iowa and other western territories in ever increasing numbers. Migration into the unsettled West had exploded.

The settlers came to central Iowa with their neighbors and friends and relatives to farm the rich, deep-soiled, abundantly watered, timber-laden farmland they found here. They chose their homesteads, dug wells, and built cabins from the trees they felled while clearing the prairie into fields, which were then tilled and made ready for planting their first crops. Their labor was incredibly difficult and their struggles just to survive were never-ending, but they had faith that their efforts today would reap higher benefits tomorrow. They were literally sowing the seeds of future harvests.

These resolute men and tireless women were building up completely new communities from the bare sod with their own backs and hands and hearts and minds far from any of the advantages and comforts they had left far behind them in the East, and they were made all the stronger for it. As they strove to re-shape the landscape, their experiences on the new land transformed them as well, molding them into a physically and mentally tough people who could face adversity with astonishing grit and courage. The remarkable resilience, stubborn self-reliance, and steadfast determination that these ordinary people learned through the everyday hardships of their pioneer experience would soon produce far reaching and long lasting fruits that would forever change the history of our country and the entire world.

In their daily quest to survive the twin adversities of danger and hardship, these hardy people were often sustained only by a fierce hope, knowing in their very core that things would someday be better if they only held their ground. Some families broke under pressure and fled back to the safety and diminished dreams of the East, but for those who remained, their simple refusal to yield became deeply ingrained into their character. For years they had faced calamity following calamity like a drumbeat, it would prove to be the best preparation possible for the awful ordeal of the Great Storm that was coming.

After years of continuous back-breaking work, struggle and tragedy, these frugal patient pioneers were finally seeing results. Epidemics had cut through their early communities like a scythe, swollen creeks and rivers had killed their livestock, ruined their plantings, drowned their children. They had faced the killing cold of winter, prairie fires, devastating storms, crop blights, pests and pestilence, and countless other dangers. They had made great sacrifices, endured debilitating hunger and hardships, but their great need had only made them inventive masters of the art of "make do or do without." These determined resourceful people had survived it all and were starting to see at last some of the hard-won prosperity that they had worked so long, so hard to enjoy. Their fledgling settlements were now progressing with good roads, permanent homes, well-stocked stores and productive mills. Towns were being platted, self-sufficient farms were producing a surplus of a variety of foods, and small manufacturing shops that made much-needed items such as pottery crocks, boots, nails and horseshoes had opened for business. As the 1850's faded into the 1860's, these families could foresee a brightening future as their crops flourished, their businesses expanded, and their lives grew better.

But instead of peace and prosperity, 1861 brought the horror of war to these Midwest pioneers. When the Southern states seceded from the Union and rebel forces fired on Fort Sumter in April, President Lincoln called for volunteers to meet the crisis and help put down the rebellion. Young Iowa men from the areas around the new Tama County villages like Buckingham, Toledo, Redman, and Irving stepped forward in large numbers to answer that urgent call. These little communities may have been spared the widespread destruction of property that the War brought to many other places, but the hopes and dreams and ambitions of individual families were put on hold for years while many of their best and brightest and most productive young men were pulled away from building their towns to defeat an enemy bent on destroying their Nation. The strength of the pioneers became the backbone of the soldiers they would become. Unfortunately for too many families, and for not a few towns, their dreams were shattered forever as the best of their sons and husbands and fathers were drained away, gone for years, some never to return.

Benjamin Franklin Thomas, called "Frank" by his family, was one of those young men who stepped forward, leaving his father's pottery shop in Buckingham to enlist with his two close friends, Peter Wilson and John Gaston, into the 14th Iowa Volunteer Infantry. Seven other close friends from the surrounding area soon joined them and a real life Fellowship was formed. They called themselves the Wolf Creek Rangers and their mission was to help defeat a real life enemy who threatened to undermine their very way of life and all the work they had so recently endured. On the day of their departure they were given a feast and were sent off with the prayers, and songs, and cheers of their community ringing in their ears. Not all of the members of the Fellowship would come home again.

Years later, at the beginning of a new century, B. F. Thomas, now a long-bearded grandfather with his wartime diaries and letters, sat down, like Tolkien's fictional Samwise, to put together a chronicle for his grandchildren of the real War as he and his fellows experienced it. In a time of peace and plenty, Thomas hoped that his grandchildren would not ever forget how this prosperity was secured, and what the cost had been. His book, *Soldier Life*, was privately published in limited numbers exactly one hundred years ago.

As a recent immigrant from Scotland, livestock breeder Peter Wilson perhaps felt an even deeper responsibility to his adopted country than did his native-born companions. He may have felt a more profound gratitude to the unique democracy that had so freely accepted him and gave his whole family a safe home far away from the endless petty strife of Europe with its rigid monarchies, confined social structures, and limited opportunities. The Wilsons appreciated, perhaps even better than their American-born neighbors, exactly what was at risk if the world's only democratic Nation should be dissolved. To the Wilson family especially, the potential consequences of a Union defeat were clear and terrible, and they later strongly felt that the magnitude of the accomplishment and the costs of the victory should never be forgotten.

Long afterwards, when the attack on Pearl Harbor sent a whole new generation of Iowans into yet another desperate, hard-fought struggle to defend our freedoms, members of the Wilson family gathered up letters Peter had written from the front lines to his family in Buckingham. They then allowed the State Historical Society of Iowa to publish his letters in their Journal. The *Letters of Peter Wilson* helped remind the World War Two generation of the sacrifices and hardships of their fathers, while serving to underline the vital importance of preserving these hard won freedoms for their own children.

The manuscripts of these two men have now been gathered here together for the first time in one volume, re-edited with new footnotes, and supplemented by previously unpublished letters written by other members of the Company to their own families. Letters and poems from these soldiers published in local area newspapers during the War have also been included in this volume of first-hand accounts. The guiding ideal that motivated the editing process was to adjust the text in small ways for an enhanced clarity that would allow the reader to become more easily and more fully immersed into the story told by the soldiers themselves.

Hopefully the written text, without the distractions of spelling problems and confusing abbreviations, can now be read as smoothly as if the men themselves were speaking directly to the reader. In a very small number of instances, offensive racially insulting terms have been slightly altered for the exact same reason spelling changes were made: to allow the reader to sink into the events behind the words without the distraction of modern thought patterns interfering with the flow of the events. A few of the supplemental letters published here for the first time were deliberately left closer to their original state with minimal punctuation for those readers wanting a feel of a "purer," less edited sense of the original writer. Copies of the original manuscripts can be found at the Traer Museum, or in the special collections of a few Iowa historical libraries.

The personalities of Thomas and Wilson and their companions shine out in these documents. Examples of their ardent patriotism, their complete faith in the rightness of their Cause, their abiding trust in God, their stoic bravery, and their willing acceptance of their uncertain fate are found on every page. Their endless curiosity about the crops and plants of the South, and their almost boyish fascination with the latest technologies and machines in their newly industrialized world are reminiscent of modern computer "geeks" marveling over the latest developments in our own era of electronics. Wonderful details emerge from their writings, some comic, some unforgettably tragic. Amusing anecdotes about drag-racing steamboats, cracker-stealing cows, and cross-dressing waiters are mingled the very next instant with tragic and heartbreaking stories of the deaths of their closest friends, which are in turn followed up by more mundane but extremely interesting details of their daily routine. Incredibly moving and memorable moments of pure poetry can be found in descriptions of the peace, beauty and stillness of a night before going into battle, or in the profound overwhelming joy of seeing their Flag flying on a train taking them to freedom.

As editors our only purpose is to honor these men, remember their sacrifices, and to keep their stories alive in their own words. We hope this new compilation book will re-awaken awareness about the heroic status of these ordinary family men, these farmers, potters and sawyers from Tama County, who courageously helped keep our nation strong and united at such great personal expense. They were modest men who came home from the battlefields to return to their mills, forges and farms. They knew they had accomplished something extraordinary, and were filled with pride at having completed a difficult task, but then they gathered up their tools, picked up their plows, and quietly began working to rebuild their lives.

The research into the experiences and lives of these men will not end with the publication of this book. Much additional material, including census information, documents from pension files, a full roster, and a list of burial sites, was not able to be included in this edition for various reasons. Hopefully, more first-hand accounts, letters, documents, and photographs might also surface in response to this book. We welcome hearing from all those who have more information to share about any of these soldiers. The Traer Museum will continue to compile additional documentation about all the soldiers of this Company and will make that updated material available to people seeking more information on the individual members of Company G, 14th Iowa Infantry.

THE TRAER HISTORICAL MUSEUM BOARD

SOLDIER LIFE

A Narrative of the Civil War

BY

B. F. THOMAS

Sergeant Company G, Fourteenth Regiment Iowa Volunteer Infantry

MARCH 6, 1907

PREFACE

During the Civil War I kept a diary in which I set down from day to day most of the events herein recorded. From this diary and the recollections inspired by its pages I have written this narrative of my experience as a volunteer soldier during that War, not primarily for general perusal, but for the purpose of leaving a true history of these events as seen by me, with my descendants.

THE AUTHOR

DEDICATED TO MY CHILDREN

"This was soldier life. The air is ever full of rumors and the next day they are contradicted by new rumors."
-- B. F. Thomas

TABLE OF CONTENTS

After supper Thomas Snelling and I took several canteens and went back a mile or more to a spring for fresh water. As we were going he told me he had a presentiment that he would be killed the next day. We talked of the battle we felt sure would be fought on the morrow. We slowly returned to camp.

Night had closed in upon us. The refulgent rays of the full moon poured through the branches of the leafless trees and cast long shadows upon the fallen leaves. No cloud obstructed the sparkle of the myriads of stars overhead. When we returned to camp the boys had rolled themselves in their blankets and nestled in the leaves, which were very plentiful, covering the ground in some places a foot deep. We too rolled in our blankets and sought rest.

Sleep refused to come at once. Everything was tranquil as if all the world was at peace. And yet within less than a mile of us was a hostile army encamped within guarded walls, awaiting an attack from us, and prepared to send death and destruction within our ranks. And we who were here lying asleep or awake in the mild moonlight only waiting for the morning light to assault their stronghold and conquer it if we could.

But as I lay awake my thoughts were not all on the morrow but they traveled through space to my own Iowa home and brought to view the loved faces and forms of those who were probably calmly sleeping, little dreaming of the great events that were so soon to transpire. And then I slept till the drums sounded reveille the next morning.

From *Soldier Life*

CHAPTER I

FROM HOME TO ST. LOUIS

School histories tell how the southern states were so incensed by the election to the Presidency of Abraham Lincoln, whom they styled an abolitionist, that they called conventions in all the south at which nearly all the slave-holding states passed ordinances of secession. Many men were gathered together in different southern localities and armed and drilled for military duty. The purpose of the south was to form a separate government and to accomplish this they seized all the public property located within their boundaries except Fort Sumter which was situated upon an island in Charleston harbor, and a fort at Pensacola, Florida. They repeatedly demanded the surrender of these remaining forts. Major Anderson who was in command at Fort Sumter obstinately refused. In the meantime the rebels had invested it with batteries and forts in such number and power that they claimed they were able to destroy it in a few hours.

The crisis came when upon April 12, 1861 the rebel forts and batteries opened fire upon Fort Sumter. All day long they sent shot and shell into the fort and all day long Major Anderson answered shot for shot and shell for shell. The next day the rebels under a flag of truce sent a boat to the fort and offered Major Anderson and his men free passage to the Union lines if they would surrender the fort. There had been a great breach made in the wall, and a fire had broken out and destroyed much of the inside work; thereupon Major Anderson agreed that if they were permitted to lower the flag themselves, firing a salute as it was lowered, and to march out with their arms, the flag flying and the band playing a national air, they would abandon the fort. These terms were agreed to and the fortress surrendered, but this incident did not close the struggle.

The firing upon Fort Sumter aroused the people of the north who till this time had hoped that the trouble could be settled without bloodshed. The President called for seventy-five thousand volunteers. It was but a few hours till many regiments were on their way for the protection of our nation's capital. Baltimore resisted the passage of Federal troops through her streets, and blood flowed upon her pavements. Many more regiments asked to be accepted than would fill the call. Congress assembled immediately and authorized the President to call for three hundred thousand men. The ink was scarcely dry upon this order when there came another call for three hundred thousand more. The south now occupied the territory in the east up to the south bank of the Potomac; along the south bank of the Ohio from Louisville to the Mississippi; up the west bank of the Mississippi even to St. Louis.

The disastrous battle of Bull Run was fought and lost in the east. Wilson's Creek, Blue Mills and Bellemont were fought and won in the west, and, if there was any difference, the prestige was with them. August had come and our government resolved to make Herculean efforts to crush the rebellion. For this purpose a call was made for more men.

Previous to this I had no thought of enlisting. Naturally I was not inclined to soldiering; but now it seemed to me it would be necessary for all young men situated as I was to enlist. Several of the young men of North Tama had gone to Waterloo, Vinton or Toledo and enlisted. A company had been raised at each of these towns. Up to this time there had been no war meetings nor any recruiting officers here in North Tama.

Early in September W. H. Stivers, a young attorney of Toledo, received a commission to recruit a company in Tama County. He opened his office in Toledo and soon made a visit to Buckingham. At his second visit he appointed an evening at which time he would hold a meeting there. I have not the date of this meeting but it must have been in the latter part of September, 1861. When he came he brought with him a young school teacher of Howard Township named William Gallagher whom he said he would like to have for First Lieutenant. There were probably half a dozen other recruits with him. Messrs. Stivers, Gallagher, Jaqua, Ames, Connell and others spoke at this meeting. After the speaking the call was made for volunteers. John Gaston, Peter Wilson and I had been talking of this matter for some days and now decided we would enlist. I wrote my name first; then Wilson and then Gaston. After each one wrote his name the crowd cheered loudly. It was indeed a very exciting time. Little did we know what the next three years were to bring us. No one thought we would be away more than a year. But as I look back now, after forty-five years have passed, I think if I had then known all I now know about it I should have gone just the same.

Stivers with his recruits went back to Toledo and left us at home saying he would call for us when ready to go to camp. A few days after this meeting he was up again and John R. Felter and John Espy McKune enlisted, also Robert and Mathew Clark who lived just north of Six Mile Grove.

We now learned that all our enlistments dated Sept. 9, 1861 which was the date of Stivers commission. All who enlisted prior to this time got that date. Our Company was called "Tama County Rangers". Our nominal officers were W. H. Stivers, Captain; William Gallagher, First Lieutenant; Simon F. Eccles, Second Lieutenant. Eccles was a school teacher from Redman in the east part of the county.

We remained at home till the 22nd day of October when we went to Toledo to join the Company. A number of our Buckingham friends went with us that far. When we arrived at Toledo the streets were full of people and they cheered us lustily and shook hands with us vigorously. After a time the Company was formed in line and marched to what was then the new Baptist church, where the ladies of Toledo had spread for us and our friends a bountiful dinner. Being soldiers, and very new soldiers at that, we assayed to demolish that dinner. But lo! we were filled full and the half had not disappeared. It is said, "The way to a man's heart is down his throat" and I believe it for certainly these ladies won our warmest regards by this generous dinner. But you will hear more of this farther on.

After dinner we were dismissed for thirty minutes to give opportunity for the friends to say their final words of good-bye. We of North Tama were sad spectators to the partings of our Toledo boys and their friends and relatives. Who of these boys departing were never to return? And who of these left behind would be gone when the boys would return again from the war? No one could tell. I remember especially the parting of Joe A. Shanklin and his sister. He was a tall, athletic young man just in his school life; she, two years his junior, a beautiful girl. As he pressed her to his heart and kissed her lips, both their eyes were full of tears and their voices were choked. But as they released each other their faces beamed with hope and patriotism, and as we passed from her sight she bravely waved her handkerchief to cheer him on his way.

In less than two months Joe came to me one evening all broken up. He had a letter from home carrying the sad intelligence that his sister had crossed the dark river of death. That night he and I walked in the darkness with locked arms. Little was spoken between us, but in the shadow of the night I felt my friend's struggle for mastery of himself in this time of his trouble. Two years after, Joe was shot dead at the battle of Pleasant Hill, Louisiana. He heard no voice of sympathy, nor felt a soothing hand. But before his death he had won the love and respect of his officers and comrades and had been promoted to a Lieutenancy.

From Toledo we went in lumber wagons to Marengo, which was then the nearest rail road station. The first night out we stopped at Irving. This was the home of a number of our boys. There were about fifty of us all told, and we were distributed among the citizens for lodging. I, with three others, was assigned to a family named Miles, just a man and wife. They were very loyal people, but Mr. Miles was quite despondent for he had just read that England was about to recognize the Confederacy and give them aid of ships and men. We did not believe it and therefore had no worry on that score.

Had breakfast at half past four and at daylight were off for Marengo, where we arrived about eleven o'clock the same morning. There was much enthusiasm manifested here as there was wherever we went. Great cheering and much hand shaking. We took dinner at the two hotels and some private houses. After dinner we marched out to the depot which is nearly a mile from town, and were ready to take the cars as soon as they came. Some of the Toledo ladies came with their friends this far, but from here all but the enlisted men returned.

Soon we were on the train and off for Davenport. Slow the train seemed to move and the trip was tedious indeed. I wonder if the recent partings and the continual deflection of the mind to other scenes had anything to do with ennui. Just before dark Captain Stivers handed out a large, mysterious looking box and upon its being opened we found it filled with "goodies" from the dinner table the ladies had furnished at Toledo. Our stomachs were again replenished and our hearts again softened and some eyes were dimmed by the memory of the kindness of those we had left behind. Dear ones left behind.

Finally we arrived at Davenport. Cheering, cheering, cheering on every side. Two other companies who came from the western part of the state were on the train with us. We were all dismounted from the cars and formed into line, and, headed by a brass band, marched out to Camp McClellan. This was a new camp about two miles from Davenport on the bank of the Mississippi River. When we arrived at camp we were immediately surrounded by the boys there who plied us with questions, "Where did you come from?" "What company is this?" "Is your company full?" and a thousand others that we knew nothing about.

After a time we were assigned to a barrack. These barracks were about seventy feet long and twenty-four feet wide; boarded up and down with rough boards; cracks battened; shingle roof; no ceiling; no plastering. In each end there were two doors situated at the corners. There was a passage along each side from door to door four feet in width; a partition through the center of the building from end to end: and then tiers of bunks one above the other with heads next the partition and feet next the passage.

This was our parlor, sitting room and dormitory. Our dining room was as big as all out-of-doors. The table was made by driving stakes into the ground; on top of these were nailed cross pieces and on these three boards were laid side by side and extending as long as the barrack. The heavens were above and the earth beneath. No chairs nor stools of any kind. The cattle of Iowa, today, have far warmer quarters than we had then, and fully as good feeding troughs.

The morning of October 24th the boom of the morning gun aroused us and we rushed out of the barracks to see what was the matter. Not far from our location we saw a flag pole with the Stars and Stripes floating from its top. Near it stood a small cannon. The smoke was still lazily ascending in the rays of the newly risen sun. We then learned that it was part of army regulations to raise the colors at sunrise and salute them by firing one shot from a cannon, the morning gun. At evening, when the last rays of the sun kiss the beautiful stripes and azure field and gilded stars, our noble flag is lowered and again the cannon gives forth its notice that the day has closed and the emblem of our nationality is furled.

When we rushed from the barracks we found the older companies all in line and the orderly sergeants calling the roll. As soon as the roll-call was over the companies were marched to the river to wash and then marched back to their tables and had their breakfast. We were hungry at once; but our table was bare the thought of breakfast. We soon learned that rations should have been issued us, but when our Captain went to the Commissary for them he was told that we were not legally known there and that we must report to headquarters down in the city. So Captain Stivers went to the city to give in his report. When it was received at headquarters he was given an order on the Quartermaster for rations for his men. When he found the Quartermaster, that officer in turn gave him an order on the Commissary. The Commissary being found issued the rations but there was no means of transporting them to camp. So Captain Stivers again found the Quartermaster and from him got an order on the Wagon Master for a wagon and team to transport the goods. Finally the government teamster drove into camp with his government mules hitched to his government wagon loaded with government rations for the government troops. The consequence was we were ready for breakfast just as the other companies were served their dinner. This was our first meal in Camp McClellan. We received our coffee in tin cups; our beef, beans or potatoes in tin plates; had white bread, but no cream for our coffee nor butter for our bread.

The rules of the camp were for us to arise at six o'clock A. M., answer to roll call, then march down to the river and wash our hands and faces in the mighty Mississippi. Just think of it, the Father of Waters for a wash bowl! Return to camp. Breakfast call. After breakfast, sick call and guard mount and then company drill for two hours. Then squad drill for another two hours. By this time we were ready for dinner. After dinner was company drill again, and at sunset dress parade.

Dress parade means the regiment formed in line of battle and then reviewed by the Colonel, its commanding officer. The company officers make their reports at this time and the official orders are issued. The regiment breaks into companies which march in review before the Colonel. At this time the evening gun is fired and the flag lowered.

The first call after breakfast is sick call. At this all the sick report to the surgeon's office and get their quinine. If too sick for duty they are excused by the doctor. Next following is guard mount. At this call the details of guards from the different companies are marched to the parade ground where they are apportioned to their respective stations. They are on for twenty-four hours, and are divided into three reliefs. Those of the first relief are placed at the several posts and are on duty two hours when they give place to the second relief which is on duty two hours. Then the third relief comes on duty two hours and is relieved in turn by the first. Each relief is on two hours and off four, four times in the twenty-four hours of the day. Then the new guard takes its place and the old returns to the companies. A regular line of guards surrounds the camp, and no one is permitted to leave camp without a pass from the commander, or the countersign.

There is much etiquette in the military. Think of the guard at the Colonel's office being obliged to stand upright constantly with his gun at "Shoulder arms" except when an officer passes. Then he must "Present arms" to the officer, who returns the salute by raising his right hand to the brim of his hat.

Oct. 24th. The flag was placed at half mast as a sign of mourning for the death of General Baker who was killed at Ball's Bluff.

Today our Company secured some men from Cedar County. This was in order to get enough men so we might be mustered into the service. In the consolidation of companies we got the Captain's office which went to W. H. Stivers. One of the other squads got the First Lieutenant, George Pemberton. We got the Second Lieutenant. William Gallagher, and First Sergeant, Simon F. Eccles. Story County got Second Sergeant, Addison Davis. The other minor offices went to our Company. Some of the men who belonged to the squads attached to us were not pleased with the arrangement or they were tired of soldiering and refused to join us. Adjutant General Baker then scored them very severely for their course and finally ordered them off the grounds. He then complimented us for our patriotic action and soldierly conduct. We were now assigned to the 13th Regiment Iowa Volunteers Infantry.

Friday, Oct. 25th. At nine o'clock at night the drums sound the "*Tatoo*". Then all lights must be extinguished and all be quiet in camp. But last night after all was still there came an order for all to "Turn out". After considerable noise and confusion we understood that there was a call for three companies to go to Fort Randal, Dakota Territory. Three companies were selected and started that night. They were afterward known as A, B and C of the 14th Regiment. We were all very glad that we were not taken, for they were to go there to guard the fort and would see no active duty. This was the first lesson we received on the sudden chances that might change the whole course of our service.

Lieutenant Gallagher took John Gaston and myself with him to Davenport today. We bought boots, shirts and such things as we thought we were in need of. John Gaston bought a small revolver.

Sunday, Oct. 27th. John Gaston and I got a pass to go to Camp "*Joe Holt*" in search of John Hopkins whom we supposed to be there. He had enlisted in a cavalry company that was now in this camp. When we got there we found he had been rejected for lack of size. Afterward he had cooked for some of the officers for sometime and had just gone to Atalissa to work on a farm for one of the officers. We were very sorry we did not see him, but glad that he had what seemed like a good place to work.

We got to our camp in time to attend religious services and were somewhat surprised when the whole service occupied just twenty-five minutes of time. As a rule our men were pretty rough. Much profane language was used, our own Mess being almost the only exception.

We were now building more barracks. Every man able to saw a board or drive a nail was called a carpenter and set to work. The weather was quite cool, especially the mornings. Ice frequently formed on still water. Many of the boys had severe colds and I could hardly see how we were to improve while in such open barracks. It was little warmer in barracks than out of doors. We had straw in our bunks and a double blanket each. So by sleeping two together we had one blanket below and three above us. We hoped to move south soon.

Several companies were mustered into the United States service today. So far we were only in the State service. Two men belonging to one of the companies mustered in refused to take the oath of allegiance. I do not know why. The mustering officers ordered them to leave the camp. As they started the soldiers hooted and hallooed at them, called them cowards, ran after them and threw mud on them, groaning and yelling at them till they were beyond their reach. I did not know what fate had in store for me, but I hoped I never would have the experience these men had that day. I would rather be shot than driven from camp as they were.

We had no tables now so we took our meals by answering to our names at roll call and taking our plate and tin cup and passing by the cook who gave us our bread and meat and coffee. Then sitting upon the ground we ate our dinner. We had had some potatoes but they were not good and our bread was not very plenty. We had moved into our new barracks though they were not finished yet.

Oct. 29th. The day was quite cold with drizzling rain and sharp gusts of wind. We huddled together as best we could to keep warm, for we had no stove in the barracks. Just as it began growing dark a more severe gust of wind blew the roof off the barracks in which the Benton County boys were. We called them into our barracks and shared our roof, our bunks and our blankets with them. This day and night was about the most disagreeable time we had had since coming here.

Oct. 30th. The rain was over and again we were at work finishing our barracks. The company in the barracks next ours was mustered into the United States service and two of their men refused to take the oath of allegiance. They were ordered to be drummed out of the camp. Thirty of their comrades formed a hollow square with the two men within. A martial band followed playing the "*Rogue's March*". They marched through the principal streets of our camp and to the main entrance. Then the officer in charge gave each of the "Rogues" a lusty kick and bade them "be gone". Poor fellows! The band then returned to their quarters playing "*Yankee Doodle*" with all the vim their instruments were capable of.

Friday, Nov. 1st Captain Stivers had been at Toledo for sometime trying to secure more recruits. About eleven o'clock last night we were awakened by the cry "The Captain has come, the Captain has come", and sure enough in he came, and several men with him. We climbed out of our bunks to see the Captain and the new recruits. I first met Dewitt C. Southwick and shook him heartily by the hand. Next I met Lemuel Kile, a man totally unfit for the service because of physical disability. The Captain called me to the door and there I met Eleazar Stoakes. This was truly a wonderful surprise to me. I had no thought of his coming. We had much to talk about and very little sleep that night. The barracks were nearly completed and we were out of lumber so could not work on them. We were quite comfortable now to what we had been.

Nov. 2nd. Captain Stivers told us to get ready to be sworn into the United States service. So we went, every man, Captain, cook and all, but when we got to the place where we were to be mustered the Adjutant ordered us to return to our quarters because we had not men enough to fill the Company to the minimum required. When we returned to the barracks some of our men said if we were not sworn into the 13th

Regiment they would return home. Others were willing to abide till the number could be secured. Captain Stivers came again and ordered us to march back to the parade ground. He said we were to be sworn in at once. We understood he had by some means got more men. So back we went to the parade ground and stayed there all the forenoon. By this means we drew no rations for the day, for rations are issued in the morning. About noon we were examined by the surgeons. There were four of them. They stood two on each side of the parade and we marched singly between them; holding our hands above our heads and moving our fingers. This was all the physical examination we ever had. I am told that in most camps they strip the soldier naked and carefully examine him in every respect. Four of our men were rejected, among whom was Lemuel Kile. We now had but seventy-two men and one lieutenant. The Captain could not be mustered till we secured eighty-three men. We were then sworn into the United States service on Saturday, November 2nd, 1861 to serve for the term of three years or during the war. We were then marched back to our barracks. It was long after noon, and no dinner and no rations to get dinner from. Just as we broke ranks a woman approached with two baskets filled with pies. Pies were in great demand and were soon at a premium. She sold out very quickly and our hunger was partially appeased.

Monday, Nov. 4, 1861. Last Saturday we were assured we were to be a company of the 13th Regiment. Today they told us the regiment was full without us and we should be Company C of the 14th Regiment. Company C is called Color Company because it has charge of the flag So they console us that while we failed to get a position in the 13th we would hold the post of honor in the 14th Regiment. Still there was much dissatisfaction among the boys because we lost our position in the 13th. We knew it was because we lacked men enough to fill the Company. The prospects ahead of us are always bright illusions. After we lose them we find they were simply glaring delusions.

Some of our men seriously talked of leaving our Company and joining some full company. Our men were improving much in their drill. For sometime I had been bothered much with neuralgia in my face, probably caused by so much exposure to damp and cold weather.

Since we had charge of the colors the boys seemed better satisfied. Lieutenant Pemberton was a soldier in the Mexican War, and wore a medal on his left breast given him by the State of New York for meritorious service. He was a good drill master and had charge of the Company most of the time. This gave him an excellent opportunity to gain the good will of the men, and I fear he made diligent use of it. There was now a talk of asking Stivers to resign and having Pemberton take his place. There was something about Pemberton I did not like, and I resolved I would do all I could to have Stivers remain.

Each regiment that was fully organized had dress parade by itself. But all the companies not included in these had dress parade together. Sometimes there were fifteen or twenty companies in this line, but very few of them had men enough to organize a full company. Sometimes several of these companies joined together, as we did some days ago, and formed one company. There had to be not less than 83 men nor more than 101 men in a company. As soon as ten companies had enough men to organize they were formed into a regiment and the other companies and squads formed the nucleus for a new regiment. It was in this way we were supposed to belong to the 13th Regiment and were dropped into the 14th where we were still striving to hold our own. Governor Kirkwood came and reviewed the 11th Regiment. He made a speech to them which was a very practical talk to men about to expose their lives for their country's cause. He then assured us that our Regiment would soon be fully organized, and that our uniforms and arms were ready for us and that we would soon follow the 11th Regiment to the front.

Thursday, Nov. 7th. The 11th Regiment commanded by Colonel Hare marched down to Davenport and paraded the principal streets and returned to camp at noon. It was one of the grandest sights I ever saw. Near a thousand men, all dressed exactly alike, in light blue uniforms, their hats with feathers flowing, bright brass trimmings on their hats, shoulders and belts, bright guns on their shoulders reflecting the refulgent rays of the sun. This with the music from ten fifes, ten snare drums and one base drum, the field officers on their horses dressed in what seemed the most gorgeous uniforms, and the silk flag and banner flying in the breeze, taken all together as a first view of real military life it sent a thrill through our nerves that we will never forget. Since this I have seen many regiments and armies of men, but never since have I felt the joy I did in seeing this my first regiment. And as I look back it seems to me they were the noblest looking men I ever saw.

Dewitt Southwick was asleep in his bunk when drill call sounded this afternoon. None of us knew where he was till we returned. The Colonel ordered him put upon double duty tomorrow as punishment. The boys laughed at him but he took it in good part. This evening a United States officer came into our barracks and arrested a man who joined us lately. The charge against him was desertion, he having belonged at that time to a company at Muscatine. We had no idea what would be done to him.

Captain Stivers left for home again this evening. He was after more recruits. Before going he told us that any of us that wanted to could have a furlough for a few days. So next morning John Gaston, Peter Wilson and I got furloughs and started for Long Grove where Wilson had an uncle, Mr. McCosh. We went afoot and on the road we passed for miles through a German settlement where no one could speak English, so were unable to inquire the way. We were lost and traveled quite a distance out of our way, but finally found the place and received a very royal welcome. It was very pleasant to us to sit at table again for our meals with our hats off and nice, clean white dishes filled with wholesome food. Golden butter and rich cream. We did not wipe our plates with our hands before putting our food upon them as we had fallen into the habit of doing in camp. The kind of treatment and rich food almost made us homesick, it was so different from camp life.

Stayed several days at McCosh's. Helped him finish corn picking and also attended a "Corn Picking Bee" to help a preacher named Hartsell pick his corn. Mr. Hartsell thought we were doing wrong in going to war because all war was wrong. Had a party at McCosh's the evening before we went away and had a very pleasant time.

Returned to Davenport and crossed on the bridge to the island where many years ago Colonel Davenport built a dwelling and blockhouse for defense against the Indians. Both these buildings were still standing. The blockhouse was built square, about thirty feet on each side. The second story was turned one-eighth around so the corners came above the sides of the first story. This enabled the whites to have a clear view in every direction from the fort. The first story was built of stone and the second of logs. There were loop holes for firing on all sides of the building. This old relic of the Indian war was very interesting to us.

We visited a cave in the side of the island. To reach the mouth of the cave we climbed down the bank, which was probably fifteen feet high, to the water several rods above the cave, and waded along on sunken rocks to the mouth of the cave. The entrance was very narrow. When inside we found ourselves in a circular room probably sixteen feet across. This room was fairly lighted by light admitted through the entrance. From the back of this room there was a hole extending farther which was so small that we could barely crawl through. When we got through we found ourselves in a room probably thirty feet long and ten feet wide, with roof ten or twelve feet high. In the back end of this room there was a hole extended through the roof to the surface of the ground through which some light came, so after we were in awhile we could see each other and also the walls. In the outer room were recorded the names of many visitors. By lighting matches we saw that there were also many names on the walls of the inner room, some of which were ladies. Whether they had crawled through this narrow passage and had written their own names or whether their names had been written by their friends we had no means of knowing. After viewing the cave for some time we retraced our way to the surface and soon after crossed the eastern arm of the river to Rock Island City. Spent some time there and then crossed on the ferry to Davenport and returned to camp.

"General" Wood of Buckingham had visited the boys during our absence and brought a letter for me from home. Just then I longed very much for a letter from a friend that lived near my home. She had given me a small Bible when I came away and I had sent her one in return from Davenport when I arrived there. May the principles contained in the Bible ever guide us throughout our lives.

Saturday, Nov. 16, 1861, the 11th Iowa Regiment started for St. Louis. As they left the camp and followed the winding road down the hill my heart was filled with joy and pride at seeing this body of noble looking men stepping off so firmly and fearlessly on their way to meet the enemies of their country. "Noble men! We expect to hear of noble deeds done by you when you reach the front." After the 11th Iowa had gone we moved into the barracks they had vacated. We were glad of the move for the location was much more pleasant. Several men were placed in the guard house for leaving camp on forged passes.

Monday, Nov. 18th. This morning we began drawing our uniforms and clothing. We each drew coats, hats, pants, shirts, drawers, socks and shoes. We did not get clothing here as at home. Our names were called, we stepped up to the desk and signed a receipt and the Quartermaster handed us each of the above named articles. Any one of the articles might be too large or too small. Therefore if the coats, pants, etc., were any one of them a misfit we went to trading with some one who might have the size we wanted. Sometimes it took several days to get the proper garments and man together. Sometimes it was necessary to make over some of the clothing in order to get a fit, but generally by judicious "swapping" all were suited. This trading was the source of much amusement for the boys. Sometimes one would call out "A pair of pants to trade 'sight-unseen.' " This challenge was accepted by a large man who perhaps got the smallest sized pair of pants and his plight created much merriment.

The weather was very changeable here. One day was a very mild, balmy day with perfect sunshine. Next morning we heard the rain on the roof before daylight, and it rained till evening, a dark, gloomy day.

A company of the 13th Iowa Regiment that came from Benton County was in the barrack just across the street from us. To this company belonged Buren R. Sherman and Ward Sherman, his brother, and some other boys we know well. They had a space in their barrack large enough to dance in and frequently had us over there to dance with them. A boy with a handkerchief tied around his arm represented a girl. One of our boys from Toledo, Josiah Luke, was about the best violinist I ever heard. He frequently made the music for us. Card playing was the principal pastime for the boys, but I did not play.

Thursday, Nov. 19th. The 13th Regiment received orders to go south tomorrow. We saw them on dress parade this evening and a fine lot of men they were, though I hardly thought them equal to the 11th Regiment. Colonel Crocker commands the 13th.

Nov. 20th. Our first episode of real military life occurred last night. As said before, the 13th Regiment was ordered to march today. Many of their men took the opportunity to run the guards and spend the night in a carousal in Davenport. Captain Stivers was officer of the day, which fact gave him command of the camp. When he learned of the boys escaping to the city he thought he would have some fun. He came to our barrack about eleven o'clock and called about ten of us to go with him. All our Mess and some others were called. When we got outside of camp he told us of the escapade and said we would go to the city and arrest every one of the boys we could find. It was a lively march we made of it. Soon we entered the city and the Captain took us to a place where he expected to find some of the boys. We entered a large room. There was a small counter in one corner and some bottles on the shelves along the wall. A woman presided behind the counter. There were a number of girls finely attired, playing cards or chatting with a number of soldiers and citizens. We compelled the soldiers to show their passes, which everyone did. From there we went to many other places of like character. At one house as we entered we saw some soldiers run up stairs. Stoakes and I followed them and when we got to the top of the stairs they ran into two of the bed rooms. I followed one and caught him. When we came out we saw that Stoakes had lost his man. He turned back into the bed room again and thrust his gun under the bed and the man called out that he would surrender. About this time my prisoner got mad and swore at us in a terrible manner. But he had to go just the same. These, with some the other boys caught, were marched back to camp and placed in the guard house. Captain Stivers and the boys enjoyed the night's adventure very much.

Letters from home quite abundant but not the one I most wanted. This morning I was detailed as Corporal of the Guard. It was the first time I had been on guard. The guard is composed of three reliefs and each relief was in charge of a sergeant and a corporal. The relief was mustered by the sergeant and numbered and he took their names and companies. The corporal then marched them to post No. 1. When he came near the post the sentry challenged. "Halt, who comes there?" "Relief guard." "Advance, relief, and give the countersign." The corporal then advanced while the guard kept him covered with the bayonet. The corporal leaned forward and whispered the countersign, which in this case was "Forsythe". Then the corporal placed relief No. 1 on this post. The retiring guard gave to the new guard any special instructions he might have. Then the relief passed on to the next post, the relieved guard marching behind the others. So they went around the entire camp till all the guards had been changed. This corporal was now on duty two hours. If there was any need of him the guard who needed him called out "Corporal of the guard, Post No. 4" or whatever his number was, and the corporal immediately went to that post to learn the occasion of the call.

One of the guards whom I had to relieve was an old Prussian Soldier. These old country soldiers held us American boys in utter contempt. The first time I relieved him he was very exact that I should advance just to the point of the bayonet and lean forward just right. The second time I relieved him he had been drinking. In spite of the best of care he struck me with the bayonet but it did not tear my clothes. The next visit to him would be the "Grand Rounds". That is, the "Officer of the Day" and the "Officer of the Guard" with some minor officers went sometime between eleven and two o'clock at night and visited every post to see that all was well. This night the "Grand Rounds" was led by Sergeant McMaken of Company K who was also Sergeant of my relief. I told him of the old Prussian and warned him of his condition. When he approached that post the Prussian was so far under the influence of liquor that he would have run his bayonet through the Sergeant if the other officers had not helped to overpower him. He was sent to the guard house to sober off.

We were now fully fitted out with our uniforms so we packed our citizen's clothing and sent it home. As the 13th Regiment filed out of camp and trailed along the road toward Davenport we all followed to the guard line and then stood watching it. What a grand display it was and how our hearts beat with patriotic fervor as we watched the men marching with steady tread, their silken banners waving in the breeze and drums beating. Gladly would we have gone with them then and there. "Hope our time to march will soon come." We had been organized into a regiment, or part of one, for some days. We had but seven companies. A, B and C of our regiment were the three Companies sent to Fort Randal some time before. We had the other seven companies, and we were Company G of the 14th Regiment Iowa Volunteers. Colonel William T. Shaw of Anamosa was our Colonel. He served in the Mexican War, seemed to be quite an old man. Was crippled so he walked quite lame. Swore like a sailor. The Lieutenant Colonel was William V. Lucas from Iowa City, brother-in-law to Governor Kirkwood. Our Major's name was Leonard, but we knew nothing of him but that he was also related to the Governor. Our Adjutant was V. N. Lynn of Davenport; Surgeon, George M. Staples of Dubuque; Chaplain, Reverend Heber. One Lieutenant of Company K, William Kirkwood, was a nephew of Governor Kirkwood. We were called "Kirkwood's pets". It was said that he was trying to have us sent to Fort Leavenworth to do post duty there. None of the officers or men except the Governor's relatives wanted to go to Fort Leavenworth. Colonel Shaw had been trying to get an order from Washington to send us to St. Louis, but the Governor so far had prevented it.

Nov. 22nd. Snowed some, and was quite cold. Drew our overcoats today. They came at a very opportune time. I hardly see how we could have got along without them.

Nov. 26th. General Baker, who was Adjutant General of the State, drove through the camp and told us to bank up the barracks and make them comfortable for we would remain here all winter. He said the Government at Washington had ordered him to send no more troops till further orders. This made us feel blue. To think of spending the winter here when we might as well be doing some good at the front.

This evening I was lying in my bunk reading when the Captain came to the door and called for me. I sprang to the floor and passed to the door when I was greatly surprised to meet John Hopkins. I was truly very glad to see him. He had heard that we were about to move down the river and came down from Wilton Junction to see us before we went. And he was just in time. For yesterday we had been told by the highest military authority in the state that we would remain in this camp till spring. Now, today, we received orders from Washington to be ready to march at once.

We were to leave at 3 o'clock p.m. on the steamer "Jennie Whipple". We got everything ready but just before starting a Captain Turner of the 16th Regiment came to our Captain and claimed we had a man of his company with us whom he demanded that we give up. Turner swore the man should not go out of the camp while he lived. He brought a number of his men to assist him. Our officers stepped between Captain Turner and the man he claimed and drew their swords and ordered the assailants away. Captain Turner claimed he furnished the man the clothes he had on and of course owned the man. The man admitted the matter of the clothes. One of our officers then took the man and caused him to strip the clothes all off and gave the clothing to Turner and bade him be gone which he and his men did at once. I had no doubt he was Captain Turner's man but Captain Stivers sorely needed him to make out his number and no doubt bribed him to come with us. It was a dear bargain to us, for he was really the worst man I ever knew. A gambler, liar, coward, and, I believe, murderer, and finally a deserter. It was a sorry hour for us when we triumphed over Captain Turner.

Four companies of our regiment, including ours, were marched down to Davenport to take the boat to St. Louis. When we arrived at the wharf the captain of the boat decided he would take only three companies, so our Company was ordered to return to the barracks. Many of our men procured liquor while in Davenport and by the time we again reached camp some were pretty drunk. The officers all went back to town and the boys raised a regular "jamboree" in camp. It was a dismal night we spent. No stove in which to make a fire to keep us warm. No food to eat and no officers to give the semblance of authority in keeping order, and many of the boys wild with liquor. Doubtless Camp McClellan never saw another night the equal of this.

Nov. 28th. This morning we arose early with shivering bodies and aching limbs with no prospect of any breakfast in camp. Many of the boys had run the guard during the night and were now in Davenport, still carousing and drinking. Finally Captain Shannon of Company E came to camp and found us without rations. He went to the Commissary and ordered him to issue rations to us at once. He enforced his order by interspersing many oaths and threats. The Commissary then proceeded to issue rations for us. The Commissary was following the letter of the law in withholding the rations, for he had no authority to issue them only on the written order of a commissioned officer. We received the rations and had a meal prepared but it was noon before this was accomplished.

After noon we again prepared to move south. When we remembered how grandly the Eleventh and Thirteenth Regiments had marched down the hill from the camp with their banners flying, and bands playing it was somewhat humiliating for us to go a part at a time with no grand display like they made. We had no government regimental colors, which consist of a silken flag of stars and stripes about six feet wide and nine feet long, and a blue silk banner the same size with a large eagle embroidered with gold thread upon each side, both flag and banner finished all round with a wide gold fringe. The three companies that went to Fort Randal took our colors with them. We had a cotton flag about two-thirds the size of the regulation flag that one of our companies had brought with it from home. So the difference between the display of the other two regiments and ours was very great.

At three o'clock p.m. we again left the camp for Davenport. That is, the four companies that were then there. We went to the depot and then waited till six o'clock p.m. when we took the cars for the south. Crossed the mighty Mississippi on the only bridge that then spanned that stream, and glided over the prairies of Illinois in the darkness of the night.

Morning light found us at Joliet. This journey was made in regular passenger cars, which I here mention because it was the last trip we had in passenger coaches till we were discharged. There were guards placed at each door of each car to prevent the boys getting out. Not that they feared desertion, but that they would all get off every time the train stopped and were likely to get hurt or left if allowed this liberty.

Passed through Bloomington and traveled over wide stretches of wild prairie country that seemed level as water. At a small place called Lincoln we stopped thirty minutes to allow another train to pass. Some of our boys climbed out of the car windows and went up town to get something to eat or drink. Rations were issued us while here. We were also let out to fill our canteens with water. With some others I went to a house and asked for water which was granted. Then a lady came out with a large plate of cakes and urged them on us "soldiers". Soon again we were on the train speeding over the prairies, though sometimes we passed through large tracts of timber. We expected to arrive at Springfield before night but six miles before reaching the city we came up with a freight train with one car derailed. It was after dark before they got it on again. Then we followed them slowly into Springfield.

Arrived at Alton about ten o'clock at night and immediately went aboard the steamboat for St. Louis. The boat would not start till morning, so we spread our blankets where we could about the deck and lay down to sleep. The name of the boat was *Meteor*. The next morning we were up stirring about early because we were cold and needed exercise. Racing, boxing and jumping soon took the chill off of us. But it was too cold for comfort. Started before sunrise, soon passed the mouth of the Missouri River with its great flood of muddy water pouring into the clear water of the Mississippi, and knew that our trip to St. Louis was ended.

FROM HOME TO ST. LOUIS - Notes:

-- Lieutenant Colonel Lucas of the 14th Iowa actually was **Edward W Lucas** 36 from Iowa City, son of the first Governor of Iowa, Robert Lucas. Edward Lucas was with the regiment at Shiloh. **William V Lucas** 27 was First Lieutenant of Company B. William and **James Lucas** 19 were from Waverly in Bremer County and both went with the three detached companies for service against the Sioux in the Dakotas. Long after the War William and James Lucas returned to the Dakotas where William was elected to the US Congress. Their cousin, **Parker Lucas** 18, also from Waverly, served with the 9th Iowa Cavalry. **Hiram Leonard** of Kossuth, Des Moines County, was appointed Major November 6, 1861 and resigned February 26, 1862. The Adjutant of the 14th Iowa was **Noah N Tyner**, " V. N. Lynn" is not found in the roster. The chaplain of record was **Samuel Benton** but he served only a very brief time; "Reverend Heber" has not been identified. In 1863 a sergeant of Company I, **Frederick F Kiner**, was promoted to chaplain. Kiner, 27 from Mount Pleasant, enlisted in October 1861 and later wrote about his experiences with the 14th Iowa in his book "*One Years' Soldiering*".
-- The officers' positions were frequently shuffled and re-shuffled as companies were consolidated and regiments formed in the early months of the War. Stiver's proud "*Tama County Rangers*" were blended into a larger regiment. When the dust settled, the officers of Company G 14th Iowa Volunteer Infantry were: **William H Stivers** of Toledo, Tama County Iowa, who was 31 years old in November 1861 when he was appointed Captain of Company G. Two months later in January 1862 he resigned his commission and returned home. **George Pemberton** 35 of Scott County was initially appointed First Lieutenant then moved up to Captain when Stivers left. However, a few months after Shiloh Pemberton soon followed Stiver's lead and resigned his own position in July 1862. **William Gallagher** 27 of Toledo, who eventually became the Captain of Company G, was promoted to First Lieutenant in January 1862 when Stivers quit and Pemberton moved up. The Sergeants, **Simon F Eccles** 27 of Redman and **Addison Davis** 21 of Nevada, eventually became Lieutenants.
-- **Joseph A Shanklin** 19 of Toledo was chosen Second Corporal. Shanklin's 17 year old sister Mary died November 9 1861. She was laid to rest in Toledo's Woodlawn cemetery. Tragically in a few short years she would be joined by three of her brothers.
-- Captain Shannon of Company E who forcefully demanded rations for hungry men was **Joseph O Shannon** 32 of Burlington. He would later be taken prisoner at Shiloh and suffer six months starvation in a Confederate POW camp. When he was finally released from the POW camp he was discharged for disability. **John H Turner** 34 of Muscatine was appointed Captain of Company E 16th Iowa Infantry February 1862. He was taken prisoner with many of his regiment at the battle of Atlanta July 22 1864. The officers were sent to POW camp at Macon Georgia, the privates to Andersonville. Turner lived to be discharged at the expiration of his three year term of service in March 1865 from Washington DC a few weeks before the assassination of the President. **William T McMaken** of Company K was a 30 year old sergeant from Middletown.
-- Born in Indiana, **Marcellus Monroe Crocker** moved to Burlington Iowa as a young teen with his family. Energetic, hard working and highly intelligent, Crocker's remarkable abilities caught the attention of U.S. Senator and General A. C. Dodge, who with U.S. Congressman Shepard Leffler helped Crocker secure an appointment to West Point. Unfortunately, the untimely death of Crocker's father made it necessary for him to leave the Academy before he could graduate. To support his mother and younger siblings, Crocker came home to go to work for a local judge. Under the judge he studied for the bar and in a few years he had

already became well known as one of the most successful lawyers in the State. When the rebels fired on Fort Sumter, however, Crocker again put aside his personal interests when he moved quickly to raise a company of volunteers. At first he was a company Captain in the 2nd Iowa Infantry, but quickly rose in rank to Major, then to Lieutenant Colonel of the same regiment, and finally to Colonel of the 13th Iowa Infantry. He distinguished himself for coolness and bravery during the battle of Shiloh and was rapidly promoted again to Brigadier General. At Corinth he commanded "Crocker's Iowa Brigade" which was composed of the Eleventh, Thirteenth, Fifteenth and Sixteenth Iowa regiments. Under his leadership it became one of the most successful brigades in the Army of the Tennessee. He was promoted again to Major General, and fought with distinction at the battles of Jackson and Champion's Hill, where he won praise from General Grant as one of the army's best division commanders. Suffering from fever Crocker came home on sick leave in 1863. The Republican State Convention was in session while he was in Des Moines, and there was a movement to nominate Crocker for Governor. He declined the honor with the remark: "If a soldier is worth anything he cannot be spared from the field; if he is worthless, he will not make a good Governor." He returned to command in north Georgia during Sherman's Atlanta Campaign, where his men became known as "Crocker's Greyhounds" for the pace they kept. Growing increasingly ill, it was discovered Crocker had tuberculosis. He offered to resign. Instead he was transferred to a command in New Mexico where it was hoped the climate would be beneficial to him. He attempted to return to combat in Nashville under General George H Thomas but in time his illness proved fatal. In August 1865 he passed away in Washington DC at the early age of thirty-five. He was buried in Des Moines, honored as one of Iowa's greatest heroes.

-- **Buren R Sherman** of Vinton, Benton County, and **Ward B Sherman** of Buckingham, Tama County, served with Company G of the 13th Iowa Infantry. Buren enlisted September 1861 and by February 1862 had risen from Second Sergeant to Sergeant-Major and then to Second Lieutenant. He was wounded in the thigh during the Shiloh battle and a week later was promoted Captain. He held that rank exactly a year and then resigned his commission on April 17 1863. His brother Ward enlisted the following day after Buren in September 1861 and served for two years with the 13th Iowa Infantry. In November 1863 Ward resigned to accept a promotion with the 9th Iowa Cavalry. After the War Ward Sherman became a very successful insurance man in Chicago. Buren Sherman became Governor of Iowa.

-- Violinist **Josiah H Luke** was the 20 year old son of a Toledo area farmer.

-- The four men who unsuccessfully tried to enlist November 2nd were Lemuel Kile, Chester Kellogg, David Palmer and Daniel Rayme. Two others, Patrick Boyle and Henry Rictor, were sent home on different dates. Lemuel Kile tried hard to enlist with the others from the Buckingham area. He was a close friend of all the Wolf Creek soldiers. BF Thomas was probably correct in thinking that Kile, who was clearly patriotic and well liked, was physically unfit to be a soldier; several others who knew Kile thought so as well. In February 1865, before the War was even over, Kile died at Buckingham at the age of 34. John S Hopkins of Buckingham was a close friend of BF Thomas and a close relative of Wilson and Stoakes. Mr. McCosh, Wilson's uncle who would open his house many times to the soldiers from North Tama, was David McCosh. "General" Alfred Wood of Buckingham was not a military man. He ran a sawmill and hauled logs with a team of oxen and was rarely seen without his whip. A forceful man with a natural air of command, a friend good naturedly teased him one day, "You carry that whip like a general carries his sword", and the name stuck so tight that his given name was all but forgotten.

-- Wilson and Gaston signed up together with BF Thomas; Felter and McKune signed up together; and then the Clark brothers, Rob and Mat; they were joined later by Stoakes and Southwick. When Edmund McClaury of Irving paired up with "Frank" Thomas the group of ten messmates from the Wolf Creek area was complete.

The following poem was written by Benjamin Franklin Thomas at Benton Barracks, St. Louis, Missouri and was printed in *The Iowa Transcript*, Tama County Iowa, Thursday Jan. 16, 1862

For The Transcript
TO MY FRIENDS

Dear brothers, I am thinking now
Of the time I went away;
Of the dark shades upon your brow
'Gainst which you strove but then 'twould stay.
Oh! I remember how it pained
And wrung your hearts to see me go,
But well you know our flag was stained,
And for it's sake that blood must flow.

Sweet sisters, I remember well,
When to my country's cause I came,
How your true hearts with anguish fell
At every mention of the same.
But now I know that you are proud;
And speak in praise of one that's gone,
And think with pleasure on the time
That you will meet him "on the lawn".

Dear father, age is coming on
And yet your son is far away;
The son you always kept at home
To be in age your rest and stay.
But then when young you always taught
Me to obey my country's laws.
You taught me that the noblest death
Was die if need be in her cause.

Oh! mother, yet I hear your sigh,
When I recall the time I came.
But Oh! you heard my country cry!
And mother say! am I to blame?
You know full well your father's blood
Was early for his country shed.
The same blood now runs in my veins;
Could I the rebel traitors dread?

My country's cause is just and right;
And she will triumph too ere long
For those who fight against their God
Are never, never very strong.
And mother, surely the same God,
Who now protects me as I roam,
Will give me strength to fight the foe
And lead me safely to my home.

FRANK THOMAS   Benton Barracks, Mo.

CHAPTER II

FROM ST. LOUIS TO FORT DONELSON

"Arrived at St. Louis about ten o'clock this 30th day of November, 1861."

We formed our battalion on the wharf and soon began our march through the narrow streets of the old French town of St. Louis. This part of the city was very dirty. At Fourth Street the newer part of the city begins and here the streets were much wider and cleaner. Here we saw the first street cars we had ever seen. A small car drawn by two mules and running on narrow flat iron rails. The citizens manifested much interest in us. In places they cheered us lustily. It was only a few months before that this city was in the hands of the rebels, and there was fighting in its streets.

It was a long distance from the landing to Benton Barracks and we were much fatigued when we arrived there. It was situated just back of the fair ground. In the fair ground, or gardens, as they were called, was a large amphitheater which would seat several thousand people, a fine race track, many beautiful flower beds and gardens, shrubbery, vases and statuary such as I have never seen before. The barracks were just back of this and contained probably eighty acres of perfectly level ground.

The ground was enclosed with a board fence ten feet high, boards set on end. Inside this fence first came stables and closets, then the cook houses and dining halls and then the barracks for the soldiers. These barracks extended on each side the entire length of the ground. In front of the barracks a porch extended the entire length about ten feet wide.

This was the form of the barracks. They were about thirty feet wide. At the end there were two rooms taken off for officers' quarters. Then the room the boys occupied was about sixty feet long. Then two more rooms for officers' quarters. Then a covered passage about twenty feet wide and then the next suite of rooms beginning with the officers' quarters, and so on. The doors in the officers' quarters opened into the covered passageway. There was no door from their rooms into the boys' barracks. There was a door in each side of the barrack in the center, one opening upon the porch in front and the other to the rear, for passage to the dining hall. In this dining hall were long wooden tables with long benches on either side. These tables were kept scrupulously clean and therefore we never needed table cloths. Hydrant water was plenty and large ranges were in the cook houses for cooking upon. All the space in front or between these two lines of barracks was open ground for parade and drill. There was a headquarters building at the head of this parade, two stories high and surmounted by a cupola and flag staff. From this cupola the bugle calls were sounded that divided our time. At a certain note the camp was aroused in the morning; then breakfast call; then sick call, when the sick went to interview the doctor. At another note the new guard was formed. At another we went upon drill, and at another were called from drill. At another we retired from the parade ground in the evening, and at the final note blew out our candles and went to bed. In the barrack was a row of bunks extending around the entire interior except where the doors were. They extended into the room about six feet and were three stories high. The first one about ten inches from the floor; the next enough above this to allow the occupants of the lower berths to sit upright, and the third one above this about the same height. They slanted a little toward the center of the room, and had some straw in them. We slept with our heads to the wall and our feet toward the center of the room. It is said there were about thirty thousand soldiers here at this time. The barracks were all full.

Sunday, Dec. 1, 1861 we had our first Grand Review and Inspection. All the troops belonging to the barracks were out, infantry, cavalry and artillery. We carried all our belongings with us. At inspection we were in line. Our knapsacks were unslung and laid in front of us and opened. This was so the inspecting officer could readily see the condition of everything. The knapsack contained our surplus clothing. The brass mountings, such as shoulder caps, buckles and buttons, had to be burnished as bright as if they were new. We had not drawn our guns yet but those who had guns and accouterments were required to have them burnished as bright as possible. They stood at shoulder arms with their steel ram-rods loose in the barrel of their guns. As the inspecting officer came to each one the soldier brought his gun down in front and tossed it from his right hand into the left hand of the officer in such a manner that the lock side was up. The officer snapped the hammer, then tossed the gun up and down so the ram-rod would jingle in the barrel. If it was all right he suddenly tossed it back with some force so that if it was not caught it would inflict a severe bruise upon the soldier. The principal thing with the gun was to have the outside so clean it would not soil the officer's white kid gloves, and the inside so clean the ram-rod would ring clear when it struck the bottom of the barrel as the officer tossed it up and down. But woe to the soldier that had soiled clothing, tarnished brasses, or rusty or unclean gun!

Then for review we put on our knapsacks and marched in column by companies by the reviewing officer who at this time was General Halleck. After the review we were marched to our quarters very tired men.

This evening two of the 3rd Iowa boys, who were encamped in the barracks directly across the parade ground from us, were playing at bayonet exercise when one of them playfully snapped his gun at the other, not knowing the gun was loaded; but it was and the boy was killed. The boy that killed him was nearly crazed.

Dec. 2nd, 1861. Was surprised to find about two inches of snow upon the ground this morning. Not very cold. Nevertheless, we did the usual amount of drilling. By sunset the snow was all gone.

Dec. 4th. Lieutenant Gallagher took our Company out about six miles in the country. Found plenty of persimmons which were excellent eating at this time. Before frost they are bitter, but after they have been frosted they are delicious. Talked with a number of citizens. Everyone claimed he was Union but his neighbors were all "Secesh". Many of our men were sick at this time. The surgeon had recommended that we pitch tents in the fair ground and live in them. This suited the boys very well.

Sunday, Dec. 8th, 1861. Inspection today. It seemed to be a custom in the army to have inspection and review every Sunday. Our inspection today was regimental, and not a congregation of all the camp as the last Sunday's was. Yet all the other organizations had their inspection. It had been quite wet for some days which made our parade ground very muddy.

Dec. 10th. We had officers' drill. There were only officers and sergeants. The space for companies was measured off and a sergeant placed at each end and a string stretched from one to the other. This was for training the officers in the movements without the bother of the men who were very awkward yet. Major Brodtbeck of the 12th Iowa was drill master. He was an old man and had been an officer in the German army. He was very precise in giving his orders and wanted them obeyed exactly. He got mad at the mistakes of some of the officers and told them the sergeants understood the commands better than they did. This pleased the sergeants.

Troops were leaving camp every day and new regiments coming in. It was a very busy life here. The 13th Iowa, Colonel Crocker, and a battalion of sharp-shooters went today. This morning one of the sharp-shooters was found outside the camp cut almost to pieces. It was learned that yesterday he had difficulty with a saloon keeper which led to a strife in which he was so badly hurt he died on his way to the barracks. The saloon keeper could not be found this morning. Sometime in the night our guards had been shot at by prowlers about camp. "Secesh" sympathizers we supposed.

One day a man in a buggy driving by the front gate called out "Hurrah for Jeff Davis!" The boys rushed by the guards and captured the man and took him to headquarters as a prisoner. I do not know what the commander did with him.

Dec. 13th. Again our Company took a trip of about seven miles into the country. Got plenty of persimmons. Ed McClaury, a boy from Irving, and my bunk-mate since we started, was very sick. Had a high fever and was out of his head part of the time. There were a number of the boys sick.

Sunday, Dec. 15th, 1861. Ed McClaury broke out with the measles today as also did some others of the boys. There were also some mumps in camp. Mat Clark had the mumps and was quite bad with them.

Two of our boys got into difficulty and came to blows. This was not very uncommon, but our Captain saw it and attempted to quiet them. One of our corporals, John Maholm, threatened to strike the Captain. He was reported to the Colonel and at dress parade that evening orders were read reducing Corporal John Maholm to the ranks. It was a very severe blow to Maholm and he seemed much dejected by it.

McClaury was very full of measles but was not nearly so sick as he had been nor as some of the other boys were. Leroy Bowen and Sam Jenks were taken to the hospital today. It was said the men of Company E were nearly all sick with either measles or mumps. There were more than a dozen of our Company confined to their bunks in barrack besides a number in the hospital.

There was a vague rumor that our piece of a regiment would be disbanded and the men put in other regiments to fill them up. But we intended not to be so treated. We will fight before we will be separated.

There was again a move to go into tents. When it had been proposed before, the weather got so wet it was thought best not to go, but now the weather was fine and the Colonel thought that all the well men had better go into tents and leave the barracks to the sick. John Felter now had the measles and I had to care for him and McClaury and others of our Company, so I could not go to the tents. But the other boys who were well could sleep there. Every well man had to drill every day, two hours in the morning in company drill, and two hours afternoon battalion drill. The boys grumbled a great deal but I know they were better off drilling thus than lying idle. Andrew Whalen was taken to the hospital today.

Dec. 19th. There were now four of us well men detailed to care for the sick in the barracks. Two of us had charge six hours and then the other two six hours. Two regiments left camp today. The 13th Missouri and the

8th Iowa, Colonel Geddis.

Just now our country was very much agitated over the demand of England for the surrender of Mason and Slidell, who were Confederate Emissaries taken from the English ship "Trent" by a United States man of war. The threat was war. We might be obliged to fight English soldiers as well as "Secesh" before we were through with this. But I had great faith in the good sense of our government to pull us through without war with England. Most of the sick were better but we had three new cases that were quite bad. We heard that two of our boys in the hospital were not expected to live.

Dec. 24th. Yesterday we had word that Leroy Bowen was dead. This was the first one to be called from our ranks. He was but a boy of seventeen years, full of hope and joy. It seems strange that one so full of life and energy should be the first to go. Several others were very sick.

This afternoon our Company marched to the hospital and got the body of Leroy Bowen and bore it to the cemetery and laid him in his lonely soldier's grave. It was marked "101". The column was broken, the portals of the future existence had opened and one had passed through. Doubtless many more would follow before the war was over. We bemoaned his sad fate. A willing soldier to battle for his country called away before he saw a foe or a battle. But his services with us were completed and he had gone where he will reap the reward for faithful duty here.

We had been vaccinated against smallpox. When it came John Maholm's turn the doctor scratched his arm and he fainted and fell off the chair. He was the corporal who was reduced to the ranks sometime ago, and he had not been well since, which, I suppose was the cause of his fainting. The smallpox was quite prevalent.

Surrounding the city of St. Louis there was a complete line of fortifications. These were composed of forts. As you approach them you first come to a ditch, probably eight feet deep and fifteen feet wide partly filled with water. Inside the ditch there were timbers about eight inches square driven in the ground side by side so they formed a solid wall probably six feet high. The tops of these timbers were sharpened to a point and near the outside surface of the ground there were loop-holes cut to enable the garrison without exposing themselves to fire on an enemy approaching. About four or five feet inside this wooden wall arose the fort proper. It was of earth and ten or twelve feet higher than the wooden wall. On top of this wall were large cannon planted that command the surrounding country. There was a bridge across the ditch so arranged with chains that it could be raised and when so raised it closed the passage way into the fort. These forts were placed some distance apart and all houses and other obstruction between or in front of them had been removed so that in case of attack they would have a clear view of the enemy. To us they looked very formidable indeed.

I had been relieved of duty caring for the sick. John Gaston was sick but was not considered dangerous. There were continually rumors of going south. Almost every man you met had a new rumor. Many believed the stories they told, some took delight in telling some exciting rumor just to see what effect it would have on the boys.

Dec. 25, 1861. "Merry Christmas!" was the word shouted from one to another as soon as we awoke this morning. The boys seemed but a merry family of children instead of sturdy soldiers. Yet I know many of them noted the difference between Christmas here and what it would have been at home. There was no drill nor inspection today. I did guard duty today instead of a private who was detailed but was too sick to go. There were still so many sick that duty came pretty heavy upon the well ones. Therefore they were not excused sometimes when they really were not fit to go. So this case was. So far we had not had guns. We had been promised them many times but failed to get them. We were to have them today sure but failed again. John Gaston had bronchitis. He was so very hoarse he could not speak except in very faint whisper. Hope he may be better soon. Received a letter from Miss Stoakes with her miniature enclosed. I was very glad to see even a resemblance of her fair face.

Saturday, Dec. 25th. Our guns came today and we took them out to try them. We fired about ten rounds each and they proved very poor fire arms. They were condemned by the inspecting officer and turned back to the Quartermaster. We hoped to get better guns.

Monday, December 30th. Joseph J. Alldredge was buried today. He had measles and they settled upon his lungs. It was strange any of the boys got over the measles the way they were exposed here. Alldredge's grave number is 139. Leroy Bowen's grave was No. 101, and he was buried December 24th. In the six days following there had been thirty-eight boys buried in that cemetery.

December 31st. We had general inspection today; kitchen, quarters, clothing, knapsacks, bedding and everything was thoroughly examined. If there was a button off the clothing or mud on the shoes we caught a scolding. Some were even punished, and probably deserved it.

This afternoon our guns were returned to us and we were ordered to make another trial. We were ordered by our officers to put in double loads and we fully obeyed orders. Out of the thirty-five guns in our squad, fifteen burst and one had the tube blown out. This will condemn the old guns for sure.

We had an institution with us not mentioned before. It was the regimental sutler. There was one with each regiment, and in camps like these barracks there was a larger institution called the post sutler. Our regimental sutler's name was D. A. Pete and he was a brother-in-law to Colonel Shaw. His profits must have been enormous, for he was practically without opposition, and was in it for the money he could make. He sold the boys on credit if they wished and many of them had availed themselves of the privilege. Now the sutler had come to the boys who owed him and asked them to sign an order on the paymaster to withhold enough of their pay to liquidate the sutler's claim. This the boys refused to do. They said they intended to pay their debts but did not want the stigma of being obliged to sign the money away before it came into their hands. This afternoon the Adjutant came and talked to the boys about the matter. He said they must sign the order or all who owed the sutler and would not sign should draw no pay. Then many of the men signed, but not all. I owed him nothing. We expected our pay the next Monday.

Jan. 3rd, 1862. Much rain and sleet and therefore much mud and no drill. I was again detailed to care for the sick. There were eight very sick boys in the barrack besides a number in the hospital. This refers to Company G only.

There was again a prevalent rumor that we were to be sent to Fort Leavenworth for garrison duty. The rumor said that Governor Kirkwood asked this as a personal favor of Secretary Cameron and he promised that we should go. The boys would have much preferred going down the river.

Jan. 5th, 1862. Rain and snow seemed to be the order of the weather for some time past. There was now about two inches of snow upon the ground, but the weather was very mild and the snow did not last long. Rumor now said we would start the next Wednesday for Fort Leavenworth. I still hoped it was not true. We all knew that Colonel Shaw would not go if he could help it. John Gaston was not able to go and I would be sorry to leave him here. Our boys had three fights among themselves today which was rather above the average. But fighting was quite frequent among them.

Jan. 7th. Last night another of our boys died. His name was Charles R. Whealen, from Story County. He was buried to-day and his grave number was 197, or 96 burials in thirteen days. John E. McKune and Eleazar Stoakes were both on the sick list, but neither very bad.

Weather cooler and therefore better. Again there was pressure brought to bear to compel us to take the condemned guns. But our officers said we must not take them. There was much ill feeling among the men about them. Casaday, Fingle and Jesperson, three men we got at Davenport, Casaday the one that Captain Turner claimed, had been drinking and causing much trouble of late. Today they had been down to St. Louis and when they returned brought three other men with them and asked that they might be substituted for them. Our Company officers did all they could to make the exchange but for some reason unknown to us the Colonel refused to exchange.

Jan. 15, 1862. Peter Wilson was taken sick yesterday. John Gaston sat up some today for the first time. This morning the mercury registered zero, by far the coldest it had been since we came here. Again we were given our guns. The same old Belgian muskets we had before. If we were to go to Leavenworth it made little difference what we had. Wooden guns would be almost as good as these. But we had not gone to Leavenworth yet.

Changed the detail for caring for the sick and I was again with the boys in the tents. John Gaston sat up some most every day. Most of the sick were able to go out to dinner with the Company. Today one of our men named Cheney had trouble with a cavalry officer. He was reported and ordered to be bucked and gagged. The bucking consists of sitting on the floor with the knees together and feet drawn near the body. The hands tied together and the arms spread and slipped over the knees until a gunbarrel can be stuck through over the arms and under the knees, securely locking the limbs and arms together. It is a very painful position. The gag was arranged by placing a bayonet across within the mouth and strings tied to each end and together behind the head. In this condition the man is unable to speak a word or move himself. Cheney was a good man and we felt it was no fault of his that he received this punishment. He was kept in this painful condition for about an hour.

Captain Shannon of Company E had been drinking for several days, and was a wild one when drunk. Yesterday our Major Leonard, who was a very strict temperance man, saw a wagon load of beer coming in at the gate. He called some of the boys to help him and they took hold of the wheels on one side and upset the wagon and spilled the beer on the ground. The next day Captain Shannon was officer of the day although pretty drunk. He was near the gate and saw a milk wagon coming in. He called the guards to help him and took the wagon by the wheels and upset it, spilling the milk on the ground. The driver sprang to his feet and rushed up to the Captain and demanded pay for his milk, saying he had a permit to sell milk in camp. He showed his permit to the Captain who snatched it from his hand and tore it to pieces. He then choked the milkman and told him to get out of the camp. The milkman reported the Captain to the commander of the post. I do not know what the outcome was. Shannon thought himself even with the Major.

The Major was very strict in regard to the beer matter and had watched the boys pretty closely. The boys had some empty beer kegs concealed about the barracks. When they saw the Major coming one of the boys would run out in sight of him with one of the kegs in his arms. The Major would at once rush in pursuit of him. They would dodge back and forth through the barrack. If the Major got too close the boy would toss the keg into one of the upper bunks and another boy would appear at a much greater distance with another keg which the old Major would think was the same one and would rapidly pursue it. He never succeeded in capturing one of the kegs. But he made much sport for the boys.

Jan. 18th. David Casaday was bucked and gagged today for insolence to the Commissary. No one pitied him. We all felt that he was a very bad man and would make us much trouble before we were through with him. The next day Casaday was in trouble again. He was placed on guard in the morning and soon hired another man to take his place and went into the city. He was found in a dive, drinking and gambling. He was arrested and brought back to camp. It was ordered that he should carry his gun and march back and forth in front of the barracks for six days.

Jan. 21st. Yesterday there was a call for a sergeant from our Company to go on prison guard. No sergeant being able, I was detailed to fill the place. There were a large number of prisoners held here, all from our own army. The roughest characters you will find anywhere. Many of them deserters. Among them was one who had belonged to the 13th Missouri, had deserted and joined the rebels, was wounded and captured, recognized, and now was pretty sure to be shot. He strenuously denied joining the rebels, but it seems he was captured fighting in their ranks.

Some of our men are much displeased with Captain Stivers' conduct. They were in favor of getting rid of Stivers' and having Pemberton for Captain. There was a petition circulated asking Stivers to resign which nearly all the boys signed. When presented to him he put it into his pocket and made no reply. He had been very anxious to go home for sometime but could not get a furlough. Today he again applied for a furlough and stated that he would tender his resignation if the furlough was not granted.

Jan. 25th. Captain Stivers' resignation has been accepted and we are now without a Captain. We petitioned Governor Kirkwood to appoint George Pemberton Captain, William Gallagher First Lieutenant, and Simon F. Eccles Second Lieutenant. There was a struggle for Orderly Sergeant. It laid between Davis, Gaston and Shanklin. There was some talk of giving us a lieutenant from outside our Company. Some of the Governor's relatives, I presume. We thought it would not be healthy to try that with us.

Jan. 29th. Captain Stivers left us yesterday. He said when he left he would be back again. But he did not come but sent for his trunk and went without a word of good-by to us.

Tried our guns again today. Some of them would not explode the caps. Others would after the second or third trial. While trying the guns there came a heavy rain and we returned as thoroughly wet as if we had been in the river.

There was some talk of sending us out along the railroad to guard some bridges. We would all like to have gone even with the old Belgian guns we had if nothing better could be secured. Three of our men were discharged today. S. Young, D. Arbuthnot and S. Jenks, because of disability. Many regiments are moving to the south now. Hoped our time would come soon.

February 1st. The sick have so far recovered that no one stays up at night with them. Regimental inspection yesterday. The Colonel scolded pretty severely, saying that none of our guns were as clean as they should be. They now require the inside of the gun to be so clean that when they jingle the ram-rod and then withdraw it, it will not stain their white kid gloves when the end was pressed against them. Also, the gun barrel must be bright and shiny. Not the least sign of rust or grease upon it. The brass all polished so it looks like new. Now it was lots of work to keep everything in such good condition when there was so much rain and mud as we had for the last month. Besides, drill twice a day kept us pretty busy.

Boys in the army are in some respects like boys at home. Some of them like to lie abed late in the morning. It was the custom in military camps to have the first roll call at daylight. We fell into line in front of our barracks and answered to our names and were then dismissed until after breakfast. Some of our boys would wait till the last minute and then come into line in their night clothes and as soon as dismissed go to bed again. The Colonel learning of this ordered that the men should come into ranks fully dressed, with cartridge box, haversack, canteen and gun, ready to go on duty if duty called; that no man should be admitted to the ranks after the orderly began calling the roll; after roll call the Company to drill for fifteen minutes, and a delinquent to he reported for punishment. It was pretty hard on the sleepy-heads and caused much merriment as well as much growling.

Joe Shanklin was detailed as corporal of the prison guard. He was busy helping the Orderly with his books and I was sent in his place. We gave up our guns again and expected others at once. Things looked lively and we expected to be moved.

February 4th. Drew new guns. They were much better guns than the ones we had and the boys were well pleased with them. The other guns were smooth bore and fired a round ball and three buckshot at a charge. These were rifled and fired the famous Minie ball. Orders came this evening to be ready to march at seven o'clock tomorrow morning. Some of the boys had too much liquor and were having a loud time. Gideon Hate was especially noisy. Lieutenant Gallagher told him to be quiet or he should be bucked and gagged. Gideon ordered him to do it if he dared, and in a very few moments the orders were carried out. Gideon soon had enough of it and by signs pleaded for mercy. It was still a very unpleasant sight to see a man bucked and gagged.

Was up at four o'clock next morning and started at seven. Took us about two hours to reach the landing and get aboard the boat. It was the large steamer "*Empress*". At two o'clock in the afternoon the boat started. Fingle, Breese and Powell were left by not coming to the boat in time. The boat was heavily loaded and there was much floating ice in the river which made our progress slow.

Our place on the boat was not in the cabin as passengers but on the boiler and upper decks. In the back part of the boiler deck were the mules and horses, and next was our Company's quarters. As we laid down to sleep there was but a small scantling between to keep the mules off of us.

I was detailed as sergeant of the guard. The duty of the guards was to stand at the cabin doors and prevent all but commissioned officers from going in. To guard the gangway when the boat was stopped at landings and to guard our own regimental stores that were stored on the forward deck. The boat tied up at dark fearing that we might run into range of a masked battery if going at night.

Sometime in the night some of our boys by some means got ashore and set fire to a large log cabin that stood there. As soon as this occurred the boat cast off from shore and followed its course down the river. It was said there were large bodies of rebels prowling about and they feared the fire would attract them and they would cause us trouble. At one time during the night all steam was shut off and all the lights extinguished and we floated noiselessly down the river. It was said this was done to pass an extremely dangerous point.

When we reached the mouth of the Ohio River the boat turned up that stream and came to landing at Cairo. There were many boats there and many of them were loaded with soldiers.

Just as we came to the landing we saw what was called a "turtle back" gunboat coming down the Ohio River with a rebel flag flying below the Stars and Stripes and firing a salute as she came. It landed just below our boat and so near that we could step from our boat onto it. Then we learned that this boat was one of the fleet that had captured Fort Henry the day before and the rebel flag they carried was the one they had captured with the fort. This boat laid very low in the water. The sides were built slanting from the water's edge upward and inward about eight feet. These slanting sides were covered with iron plates one inch thick laid on very heavy solid timber. The deck above this was level. One rebel shot, a very large one, had struck the boat fair in the center of the front. The iron plate was dented into the wood four inches but the iron was not broken and the shot glanced over the boat. One shot struck exactly upon the corner of the boat where the plates met. It tore up two of the plates and entered the boat but did no other damage. Many other shots struck the boat, but these were the most effective.

Soon our lines were cast off and we moved up the Ohio to the mouth of the Tennessee River and up that to Fort Henry where we landed. Here we saw some of the effects of battle. The pools of blood where men had been killed. Large holes torn in the ground where shells had exploded. One very large cannon, burst; a side split off at the breech. I think the slab of iron torn off was over four feet through and eight feet long. A rebel prisoner told us he was at the gun when it burst. They had put in a ten inch percussion shell and just as they fired it a shell from one of our guns struck exactly in the muzzle of their gun. Both shells exploded and it was too much for the gun. The same prisoner told me that the first shot he fired from the big gun struck one of our turtle backs fair in front and glanced from the iron plates into the air. He said he knew at once they were beaten.

Our army had landed several miles below the fort and marched up to surround the rebels and prevent their escape. But the gunboats began the battle before the army arrived and therefore the rebel army escaped. This army was under command of Brigadier General U. S. Grant, a man at this time practically unknown. Later his name became a household word, and is so to-day throughout the world.

We landed here February 8th and got our tents pitched and all our goods unloaded from the boat before night. There was a much more formidable fort on the Cumberland River about twelve miles from here which we were expected to attack and capture within a very short time.

February 10th. Some of us went out foraging to-day. We traveled a long ways and for sometime all the farms were guarded by Union cavalrymen who would not allow us to kill beef, pork nor chicken. Finally we found a nice heifer without a guard. We quickly killed and dressed her and took all we could carry of the meat. After traveling for a long time we came to a log cabin in which was a woman and a number of children. We asked for something to eat, for by this time we were very hungry. The woman told us she had nothing in the house but some hominy she was just boiling. She thought it was about done and invited us in. We entered the house and over a fire in the large fire place hung a great iron kettle nearly full of "hulled corn". Some of this she took up in a basin and set upon the table. Then she set plates and spoons and invited us to dinner. All at once she exclaimed, "I declare, I forgot to tell you 'uns the hominy is not salted and I have not a bit of salt in the house." We ate the hominy without salt and it seemed delicious, for we were very hungry. We asked the woman where her husband was and she answered that he had gone to help a neighbor that day. Doubtless he was with the rebel army at Fort Donelson. When taking our leave of her we gave her a generous piece of our beef for her and her children. I have often wondered what became of this woman and her six little children now located between two hostile armies and a severe battle pending, and only hominy without salt and some fresh beef, the best the country afforded.

Early the morning of the 12th of February we broke camp and started for Fort Donelson. The air was balmy as a May morning so we wore only our dress suits and carried a single blanket each. Our tents, overcoats and knapsacks were placed aboard one of the boats to be taken by water to Donelson. We had already heard many rumors of the great strength of the fort that we were soon to be pitted against. But our boys were all eager to press forward in their anxiety to be there in time.

The country we passed through was quite rolling, barren pine land. The soil was red as brick dust, and the timber was mostly pitch pine or yellow gum. As we approached the Cumberland the timber changed to beech, hickory, oak and walnut, and the soil was much darker in color. Before four o'clock in the evening we went into camp as we were near enough the fort for the time being. Had no tents to pitch. Built fires, made coffee and ate our hardtack and "sow belly".

After supper Thomas Snelling and I took several canteens and went back a mile or more to a spring for fresh water. As we were going he told me he had a presentiment that he would be killed the next day. I told him such thoughts came to everyone placed as we were; that he was no more likely to be killed than I or any other of the boys. That he should strive to banish such thoughts as much as possible. This and much more I said to him, and he seemed to cheer up. We talked of the battle we felt sure would be fought on the morrow. What a victory to us might mean not only to our army but to the government at Washington. We also discussed what defeat would mean to us and to our government. We slowly returned to camp. Night had closed in upon us. The refulgent rays of the full moon poured through the branches of the leafless trees and cast long shadows upon the fallen leaves. No cloud obstructed the sparkle of the myriads of stars overhead. When we returned to camp the boys had rolled themselves in their blankets and nestled in the leaves, which were very plentiful, covering the ground in some places a foot deep. We too rolled in our blankets and sought rest.

But sleep refused to come at once. Everything was tranquil as if all the world was at peace. And yet within less than a mile of us was a hostile army encamped within guarded walls, awaiting an attack from us, and prepared to send death and destruction within our ranks. And we who were here lying asleep or awake in the mild moonlight only waiting for the morning light to assault their stronghold and conquer it if we could. We fully believed we were right and justified in doing as we were doing. Did not they equally believe in the justness of their cause? And yet the only solution of the question was an appeal to the sword. But as I lay awake my thoughts were not all on the morrow but they traveled through space to my own Iowa home and brought to view the loved faces and forms of those who were probably calmly sleeping, little dreaming of the great events that were so soon to transpire. And then I slept till the drums sounded reveille the next morning.

FROM ST. LOUIS TO FORT DONELSON - Notes:

-- Swiss born Major **Samuel D Brodtbeck** 43 of Dubuque was the well respected and popular drill instructor. He had accepted his commission as major of the 12th Iowa in November 1861. After the cold, wet siege of Donelson he suffered badly from rheumatism and when most of the regiment was captured at Shiloh, he resigned his position with the Infantry but retained his rank to work directly for the Governor as his aide-de-camp. Brodtbeck's son **Otto Brodtbeck** 20 served three years with the 27th Iowa as Quartermaster Sergeant. Father and son died in the 1890's in Los Angeles where Otto was a very successful and well known real estate developer.
-- The accidental shooting victim of the 3rd Iowa was: **Luther Griggs** 21 of Cedar Falls. The roster says: "Accidentally killed by gun in hands of comrade December 2 1861 at Benton Barracks St. Louis Missouri." He is buried in Jefferson Barracks National Cemetery, St Louis.
-- **Leroy Bowen** 18 of Toledo died December 22 1861 of measles; **Joseph J Alldredge** 19 of Nevada died December 29 of lung fever; **Charles R Whealen** 18 of Marshall County died of lung fever January 6 1862;

Bowen and Alldredge are buried in Jefferson Barracks National Cemetery. Whealen's parents seem to have brought his body home for burial at Marietta cemetery in Marshall County. Leroy Bowen, the first man of the regiment to lose his life, was the son of David Bowen, a farmer near Toledo. Members of the Bowen family farmed in Tama County for fifty years after the War. The name Alldredge was spelled in the roster as"Aldridge", which is also the spelling BF Thomas used.

-- **Daniel Arbuthnot** 23 of Benton County was a stepbrother to Edmund McClaury. Daniel was discharged February 16 for disability but eventually recovered from his illness. He died in Pomona California in December 1919. **Samuel W Jenks** 19 of Story County was not discharged for disability according to official records but is listed as killed in action April 6 1862 at the Hornets' Nest during the Shiloh fight. Perhaps Thomas was thinking of a different Story County man, **Isaac Walker** 28 from Nevada, who was discharged for disability in December 1861. "S Young" cannot be identified with certainty in the records. **Elijah S Young** 38 is listed as discharged for disability in April 1862, the day before the Shiloh battle. He was released from Cincinnati where many had been hospitalized after Donelson; twenty years later he was still not fully recovered from chronic illness. **David S Young** 42 was listed as missing after the battle of Shiloh, presumed to be a prisoner of war; and was later discharged in April 1863. Both men were born in Ohio but were residents of Tama County when they enlisted. Elijah remained in Tama County the rest of his life, died in 1899, and is buried in Oak Hill Cemetery; David returned to Ohio where he died in 1908.

-- **Gideon Hate** was a 17 year old blacksmith from Toledo. Drinking liquor got him in trouble at the barracks; later, while on the march, wanting a drink of water would almost get him killed. **Alexander Cheney** was a 25 year old resident of Davenport born in Three Rivers Canada according to Captain Gallagher's records (the published roster says Cheney was a native of Germany). Cheney would later show amazing resilience after the battle of Shiloh. **Peter Jesperson**, who was born in Copenhagen Denmark, may have tried to enlist in Company B only to be rejected by the officers. Not one to be easily discouraged, it appears he showed up a week later and was admitted into Company G. Jesperson was 23 years old. The determination he showed in signing up may have come in handy later at Shiloh's Hornets' Nest. Thomas spelled it "Jasperson". The roster says Jesperson was from Burlington but other records show he was from Cedar County.

-- The three men who missed the boat apparently did catch up with the Company eventually. A few months after being left behind in the incident cited here, German born **Peter Fingle** 26 of Rock Island Illinois is listed as deserting on May 7 1862 from Corinth Tennessee. **William Breese** 22 of Tama County, who had been made a Corporal in December, perhaps caught a different boat a year later in February 1863 when he too deserted. **Leander Powell** 18 of Tama County was honorably discharged from Davenport February 5 1863. He lived many years in Leon Iowa where he died in 1907.

-- **John Maholm** 22 of Redman, Tama County, enlisted October 9 1861 as a Fourth Corporal. He was discharged April 25 1863 as a Private, from Benton Barracks, Missouri. The roster wrongly spells his name as "Mahlon". Troublesome David Casaday 20, who was bucked and gagged, enlisted November 23 1861 (from Scott County, according to BF Thomas; the published roster spelled his name Cassady, from Jefferson County). The variety of men and officers brought together as Company G to prepare for war at Benton Barracks struggled with death, disease, disability, drunkenness, desertion, and the disorderly. By the time they reached Donelson they had become a cohesive and formidable fighting unit.

Special note about the poem "*To My Friends*", page 11: BF Thomas' mother Lydia was the daughter of Hezekiah Phillips, who was born in Wales in 1756 and came to this country at age 9. When the Colonies declared their independence from Great Britain, Hezekiah enlisted at age 17 into Daniel Morgan's company of Virginia Sharpshooters. He was wounded in the shoulder December 31, 1775 during Benedict Arnold's bold nighttime assault on Quebec. Several years later, on January 17, 1781, BF Thomas' grandfather Phillips was wounded in the arm while again fighting under Morgan at the crucial battle of Cowpens in South Carolina.

CHAPTER III

FORT DONELSON TO SHILOH

February 13th was equal to a June day in Iowa. The birds sang, the squirrels chirped and the first beams of the sun touched the leafless branches of the noble beech trees and turned them into gold. All was peaceful and happy. No, not all. At sun-rise the morning gun was fired from the rebel fort and so still had been the air that the concussion seemed but a few rods away.

Poor Tom Snelling was not tranquil. Every movement indicated his stress of mind. He attempted to conceal the brass belt buckle and other brasses by turning the belts cross-wise, fearing the bright brass would be a target for the rebel marksmen. I talked to him of the beautiful morning and the prospect of the victory we would achieve that day. Not a word of his presentiment. Cheered him as best I could and felt that I had succeeded to some extent in eradicating the gloomy feeling from him.

We soon formed line of battle and moved forward to the brow of the hill when a single rifle shot, from the fort half a mile away and out of sight, came buzzing through the trees and cut the air just above our heads. I was surprised to see our Captain trying to screen himself behind a tree not six inches through. At first I thought he was just making fun, but when I saw his face I knew he was frightened. He claimed to be an old Mexican soldier, and, as I have said, wore a medal given him for bravery. But he was a coward and I knew it. We now advanced down the hill through the thick timber. The hill was a long gradual slope terminating in a narrow hollow through which wandered the shallow bed of a wet weather brook. We crossed this and came to where the rebels had felled all the timber with the tops toward us. We were now in plain sight of the breast works on top of the hill directly in front of us. It was impossible for an army to penetrate this mass of fallen timber, and as we hesitated a moment we received the heaviest fire I was ever subject to. The air seemed literally full of flying bullets, many of which struck in the leaves in front of us and threw them into the air so that for several feet above the ground the air was full of leaves. They screamed through the air above our heads and they ploughed through our ranks. At the first Tom Snelling was shot just below his right eye and killed instantly. We returned the fire as best as we could but all the advantage was with the rebels. They were behind breast works and were little exposed while we were in plain view of them.

We stood this for sometime when our Colonel ordered us to fall back into the edge of the standing timber and shelter ourselves behind the trees. This we did and from this point kept up a steady fire whenever the head of an enemy appeared over the breast works. At one time a rebel battery to our right opened fire on us. The first shot went far above us. About the third discharge struck among the men and they had us at their mercy, had not Birge's Sharp Shooters come up just at that time and soon silenced the battery. Birge's Sharp Shooters were men armed with the old home-made squirrel rifle. They wore a gray uniform and had a squirrel tail in their hats. They did not drill as we did but fought after the old Indian style. When the rebels loaded the guns at this battery they had to stand up and were exposed above the breast works. So when the sharp shooters came they killed every man that raised up to load the cannon and therefore silenced the battery. Only once was this battery used again during the battle. There was a change in alignment and a new regiment came behind the sharp shooters. Seeing the gray uniforms they thought them rebels and fired on them, killing one and wounding several. During the excitement this caused the rebels succeeded in loading and firing their cannon twice. Then they were silenced again.

In this first day's battle our regiment lost six killed. In our Company one was killed and several wounded. Ep McKune was struck by a ball upon the belt buckle. It bent the thick brass nearly double and knocked him down. The buckle evidently saved his life. A ball passed through Pope's cartridge box and the compact turned him a somersault.

By four o'clock it was raining pretty fast and turned to snow before dark. We now withdrew a short distance to get some rest and something to eat. We could not light fires for that would draw the fire of the rebel batteries. As night came on the boys lay down singly or in couples and covered themselves as best they could with their blankets. I crouched beneath a leaning tree and wrapping my blanket around me and my gun so as to keep the gun as dry as possible, I slept as well as could be expected. When daylight came I crawled out from my cover and found about four inches of snow upon the ground. Very few men were to be seen, but the little mounds of snow all over the ground as far as the eye could reach told me that I was in the midst of an army invisible because covered with snow. Each little mound covered one or two of the boys. Dress coats, blankets and snow for covering.

But we soon had a roaring fire started and the boys arose by scores until the woods were alive with men.

Soon the bright rays of the sun touched the snow laden bows of the forest trees which sparkled like crystals, and the rebel morning gun boomed just over the hill from us. We did not like its sound for it was a salute to the rebel flag that floated over the fort. The boys built many large brush fires and dried their clothes and warmed themselves at them.

All night long we had heard the rebels chopping timber inside their works; this morning shows what their labor was. Yesterday when they fired on us their heads were exposed over their breast works; now they have cut short chunks of wood and laid them across the top of the works and then laid long logs lengthwise of the works upon these blocks. This gave them an opening under the log for their guns to protrude and furnished protection for their heads. Some of them must have got sore heads there yesterday to cause them to think of this method of protection.

This morning we heard the gun-boats steaming up the river although the river is not in our sight. They steadily approached nearer and nearer and now a solitary shell from the rebel water battery just under the fort shrieks as it raises high in air and goes down the river a missile of death against our boats. Soon we heard the dull explosion of the shell down toward the noise of the approaching gun-boats. Another and another shell from the rebels and then the deep bellowing roar of one of the guns on the boat answers them. Gladly we hear the sound and follow the hiss of the shell as it speeds at its target and imbeds itself in the walls of the fort and then explodes with terrific force. How the woods rang with our cheers at this time. Cheer upon cheer.

Now both sides began firing heavily and the gun-boats gradually pushed ahead, up and up, nearer the fort. We felt something like Ivanhoe did when he was shut in the castle when Cour De Leon assailed the gate with his heavy battle ax. He heard the heavy blows dealt the gate by his friend but was unable to assist in his own delivery. So we heard the mighty battle fought near our sides but could do nothing to assist.

Steadily our boats ascend the river. They are now within reach of the smaller batteries on the main fort, which add the sharper crack of their guns to the mighty uproar. Suddenly our boats cease firing. Then the rebels cease firing also, and we hear them cheer and cheer. I think after this lapse of time that that cheer was the most direful sound I ever heard. It meant victory to the rebels and defeat to our boats. Later we learned that they shot through and through our boats which were obliged to retire or be sunk.

Thomas Snelling's body was still lying where he fell the day before and our Captain called for men to volunteer to get the body and bury it. As he came with the Story County men we expected them to go for him but no one volunteered so I said I would go for one. Then Addison Davis, Turner McLain and J. D. Williams said they would go. As soon as we approached into the open ground the rebels began firing upon us. We then ran to where he laid and picked him up and carried him back to the standing timber and took shelter behind trees till the firing slacked. Then we took him again and carried him back around the hill till we were out of sight of the fort. The fire upon us was very severe whenever we were in sight and it was marvelous that none of us were killed. We then got pick and shovel and dug a grave, and in the grave put small twigs of evergreens and laid his body on these. Upon him we laid another layer of evergreens and then covered him up with earth.

> "No useless coffin enclosed his breast
> Nor in sheet or shroud we wound him;
> He lay like a warrior taking his rest
> With his martial coat around him"

We then took our guns and fired three volleys over the grave. Thus we paid a last tribute to the first martyr in actual battle sacrificed from our Company.

> "And nothing will wreck if they let him sleep on
> In the grave where his comrades have laid him."

At night we heard that General Grant proposed to invest the fort and await reinforcements. We were ordered to hold our positions in the enemy's front and not let him escape through our lines. Since the gun-boats had been defeated it might be the rebels did not care to escape.

Saturday, February 15, 1862. This morning a battle began early on our extreme right. The rebels made an attempt to cut out and their cavalry could escape through the gap they made, but our infantry rallied and succeeded in checking their infantry. They received more reinforcements and drove our men back. At this time they could have gone out, but their commander flushed with his success at once concluded he could cut Grant's army in two and double our right wing upon itself and crush it. This he valiantly tried to do but failed, and soon found himself so hemmed in he was obliged to seek the fort again for safety.

This ended the battle on our right. There was very heavy loss on both sides.

Just after this General Smith, who was a very old man and had been General Grant's instructor at West Point, and was now commanding our division, asked permission of General Grant to take his division and attack the enemy at some distance to the left of our present position. The argument was that the rebel forces were concentrated on our right wing and they would be weak on our left.

The position chosen for the attack was one nearly barren of timber, where there would be less obstruction to oppose us. General Grant gave permission and immediately our brigade was in motion, for it was assigned to the lead. We moved by the left flank parallel to the rebel works till we came opposite the place selected for attack and then formed column of attack. First the grand old Second Iowa spread out its full length in front of their works. This regiment was under disgrace. It had been on provost duty at St. Louis and while there some of the boys destroyed some property in one of the public libraries. General Halleck who was in command of the department demanded that the culprits be surrendered for punishment. But this could not be done, for no one in authority knew who had done the work. So General Halleck relieved the regiment from provost duty and took their colors from them and sent them south. The boys were hot and just longed for the chance they had that day to wipe out the disgrace attached to them.

Twenty paces behind them went the Seventh Iowa and the Twenty-fifty Indiana. These were both very small regiments and together did not cover as much ground as the Second Iowa. Twenty paces back of these marched our regiment. Away the column went with guns at right shoulder shift. Up and up and faster and faster. Before we advanced in column and leaden hail began to drop among us, and faster and faster came the bullets. On went the boys in our lead. Not a gun was fired from our side but on and on they ran. I think we gained on those in front for I know when they went over the breast works we were close on their heels. Some of the rebels waited till our men sprang over the works, but most of them were seen running toward the next works sixty rods away. Some men were killed with the bayonet and some shot and some captured, but most of them escaped.

We were masters of the outer works. The rebels had a battery on the next works and at once they began shelling us. Some of our men had followed them half way across to the next works. There is no doubt if General Smith had had all of his division here at this time we could easily have captured the next line of works that evening.

When they began shelling our men the officers ordered us back outside the works to get the protection of the embankment. The rebels had gunners with this battery, for after we were outside the works they threw their shells so they passed about two feet above the works we were behind, and shell after shell burst just as they passed the works. We lay very close to the ground while this lasted, and it continued till dark.

During the cannonading some one told me Captain Pemberton was shot during the charge and was lying just outside the works. I went to him and he seemed unconscious. After awhile he told me he had been struck on the breast by a bullet. I was trying to open his clothes to see where he was wounded and he said it was a spent ball and did not go through his clothing. This might have been true and he be badly hurt. He then told me to go back to the Company and send Woodard to take care of him, and I knew he was not hurt, only a coward. I told the lieutenants so that night and they said they also knew it.

About this time General Smith and Colonel Lauman rode along our lines and told us that we had captured the key to the situation. They felt sure the rebels would try to recapture it before morning. We must hold our ground at all hazards. "Do not depend on the bullet; use the bayonet." were their parting words. During this time the snow had thawed away and in the evening we were in mud ankle deep. But before midnight we were walking over frozen ground again. As soon as it was dark some of us made a raid over to the abandoned rebel tents just inside the works. We were in search of provision. We found quantities of corn bread which was quite a treat to us. In one of the tents I found a young rebel who had been shot through the knee. He said he was very cold. We tore a section of the tent to make a stretcher and carried him back through our lines to our hospital. He was a Tennessean. I knew nothing more of him. When we got him to the hospital I tried to talk with him, but he was not inclined to talk. He was cold and sick from his wound and I do not blame him for not talking.

About midnight our Company cook with the help of some of our stragglers brought two camp kettles full of hot coffee for us to drink. It was very considerate of him and we were very thankful, for the night was cold and we had had no supper and no fires. Several times during the night stray shots were fired by the rebels and once the ball in a spent condition struck in the breast works where we were.

Sunday Morning, February 16, 1862. Before daylight we heard a bugle sound in the enemy's ranks. We supposed they were forming to make a charge. Again and again it sounded from time to time till it became light enough for us to see their works. There was a man standing on their works waving a white flag and the bugler beside him blowing the bugle. Lieutenant Logan of Company I and Sergeant Savage, who was our color sergeant, took our flag and went out to meet them. As soon as our men started the man with the white flag and one or two more started to meet them. They met between the lines and after a little parley all came to our lines. We soon learned that the rebel emissary had a message from General Buckner to General Grant. The messenger was given an escort and passed through our lines on his way to General Grant's headquarters, which were some three miles back of us. We had no idea what the message was. We supposed it might be a request for an armistice because it was Sunday and there were many dead to bury. After a long time the rebel emissary returned and our men conducted them half way back to their lines. Now the message was conveyed to General Buckner whose headquarters where at Dover, three miles up the river from where we were. After another anxious time the messenger again appeared and was again conducted within our lines and again returned.

It was noon and the warm sun was shining. We had captured the works the night before and stood in the trenches all night. No supper and no breakfast. Expecting at every moment we would be relieved by other troops so we might get something to eat and rest awhile. Just at noon the relief came and we marched down the hill toward our camp. When we reached the foot of the long hill an orderly came riding after us as fast as his horse could come. He gave his orders to Colonel Lauman who commanded our brigade and he read them aloud: "The fort has surrendered and Colonel Lauman's brigade of General Smith's division has post of honor and goes into the fort first." Oh, how we cheered! We were not hungry nor tired nor anything but just anxious to get into the fort as soon as our legs would carry us there. Immediately the orders were given to countermarch up the hill again. Back to the breastworks and over them again; then onward to the next line of works and over them. Here we came upon the first rebels. They were drawn up in line and as we approached they laid their guns on the ground in front of them. The butt of the gun at their feet and the muzzle directly in front. Regiment after regiment and thousands and thousands we passed in this manner. All with their guns grounded and their arms folded on their breasts. Finally we came to the entrance of the main fort. We had marched in our proper order, the Second Iowa in front, the Seventh next, then the Twenty-fifth Indiana and last of our brigade our regiment.

Just as our regiment was at the entrance of the fort an orderly came riding up and stated that the rebels were destroying the public property at Dover some two miles up the river. Our regiment was ordered up there to stop this. So we hastened through the mud and water, for the ground was thawed again by this time, to the town of Dover. There we found several wagon loads of flint lock guns, some ammunition and a large quantity of flour and meat but saw no evidence of an attempt to destroy any of it. There were broken vehicles and crippled horses scattered about the streets. In many of the houses were dead men who had been carried in from the battlefield by their friends. Some wounded men and many prisoners. Nearly all the houses were abandoned by their owners. No law. No order. No management by anyone. Soon our officers established a system of guards and order came out of chaos and all were comparatively quiet. Other troops came and relieved us and we were ordered back to the fort. Many of our boys gathered up whatever they thought might be useful in camp. Stoakes and I thought some of the flour that was so plentiful would come good, but as it was in barrels, and we were not able to carry a barrel, we knew not what to do. By chance we saw a trunk. We quickly emptied the clothing out and opened a barrel of flour and from its contents filled our trunk. This was the foundation of slap-jacks for many a day. This we carried easily between us.

We arrived at the fort after dark, wet, muddy, hungry and tired. Nor is it to be wondered at that we were hungry and tired for we had been busy day and night since Saturday noon, and very little to eat in the time. Cabins sufficient for our use had been reserved for us, which we now occupied. Just after we arrived in the fort the rain began to pour down. We sank down on the cabin floors and slept. How sweet to hear the rain on the roof and feel that you are safe from its drenching qualities. And if we awoke to consciousness during that night it was merely to murmur to ourselves, "Victory, victory", and sleep again, thankful the victory was ours and that we had a roof to shelter us from the rain. We knew we had a victory over the enemy but it was when we received papers from the North we began to appreciate what we had done. The whole North went wild over the news. The Iowa Legislature was in session at Des Moines. When the news was read to them many members made a motion to adjourn. One more thoughtful than the rest asked them to withdraw their motions till he could make one. Then he moved that the statutory liquor law be suspended for twenty-four hours. The Legislature then adjourned and "There was a sound of revelry" in Des Moines that night. So all over the Union States the rejoicing was great. Some of our wounded were sent to Cincinatti. Among them were some of the Second Iowa. These were pounced upon by the people and feted and feasted till it is a wonder they lived to tell the tale. Because of the victory won General Grant was made a Major General and Colonel Lauman a Brigadier General.

The next morning we found that some of our boys had the flat bottom of a large iron kettle, the top broken off just where it turns up to make the sides. There were three legs under this bottom about four inches long. We built a fire on the ground and when we had a good bunch of coals set this bottom on them. We mixed some of our flour with water so as to make a batter. This we poured upon our kettle bottom in patches and the product was most delightful pancakes. They might not taste as well at home as they did there. To add to our larder some of our boys captured a quantity of brown sugar. This we melted into syrup and ate with our pancakes. We called the pancakes "flap jacks".

The fort proper, in which we were now living, covered an irregular piece of ground of sixty or seventy acres. The walls of the fort occupy the top of a ridge that conforms to the bank of the river for some distance and then diverges to the south and then east and again north to the place of beginning. Not in a regular oblong square but in a zigzag way making many faces and angles in almost all directions. This ridge extended all the way round except at the southeast corner where the entrance was. This was on low ground. The ground enclosed was like a basin among the hills, lower than any of the surrounding walls except those at the entrance. The walls of the fort varied in height in different parts. Some places not more than eight feet high and at others probably more than twenty feet, that is inside measure. This was so the top would keep near a uniform level. Outside the walls were higher because the dirt of which they were composed was taken from outside forming a deep ditch. Near the top of the wall they had driven stakes and woven brush so as to hold the dirt placed outside of this in a perpendicular wall about three feet high for the men to stand behind to guard the works. Outside this woven fence was much dirt piled against the stakes and brush so that cannon balls could not penetrate. Inside this fence was a level walk from three to five feet wide. At the angles of the wall the walls were much wider and cannon were planted so they could fire over. The outside of the walls had been raked smooth, and all stones or blocks of wood removed leaving the face all smooth earth. In case a stone or chunk of wood was in the wall a cannon ball might strike it and throw it over the wall or itself glance over the wall. If it struck in fine earth it remained where it fell.

This was the fort proper. Between these walls and the river, over half way down the bluff was what was called water batteries. These were walls thrown up and large cannon mounted to command the river. There were two of these batteries and they were the guns that drove our gun boats back a few days before. Outside the fort were several lines of breastworks. One far outside that began above Dover and circled through the country and came to the river below the fort. It was at this outer line of works that both battles were fought.

The gathering up of arms and army stores and guarding prisoners and marching them to the boats busied us for several days. I frequently saw General Simon B. Buckner, the rebel general who was in command when the fort surrendered. He was a small man but walked and looked every inch a soldier.

The cabins occupied were very good shelter from the almost constant rain that we were having. The one next us had been struck by a shell from one of our boats during the battle. The shell came through the roof and exploded. It took out the opposite end of the cabin and tore half the roof off. It just showed us what a shell could do. One day while at the surgeon's office one of our men was brought in wounded. He had had a fuse that belonged to a spherical shell and had set fire to it. It had exploded close to his face and torn his right eye out so the eyeball laid on his cheek and hung by the cord. It had also torn his other cheek so he was a very sad sight. Now I had seen many dead and mutilated bodies as well as seriously wounded men and thought no such sight would move me, but when he was brought in I at once got sick at my stomach and went out and vomited. This was the only time this occurred. At the charge a few days before a man stopped me to ask if he was badly wounded. He turned the side of his head to me and I saw that a piece of shell had struck a glancing blow just back of the left ear. It had broken the skull and torn off a piece probably two inches square and left the brain covered only by the thin skin in which it is encased. I dared not tell him what I saw. I pointed to our hospital flag, probably a quarter of a mile away, and asked him if he thought he could go to it. He said certainly he could. I told him that was the hospital and go there. I never heard of him again.

We left Fort Donelson March 7, 1862, for the Tennessee River. I had been quite sick the last two days before we started and was really unfit to go, but did the best I could. About three o'clock in the afternoon I felt I could go no farther. I went into a fence corner to lie down and Dr. Staples saw me. He rode up to me and asked how I felt. I told him I could go no farther. He said the command was going into camp about three miles farther on and for me to lie down here and he would send an ambulance back for me. He rode away a short distance and then returned and told me he would give me something that would help me. He took a small gauge glass from his holster and poured probably two table spoons full of whiskey into it and told me to drink it, which I did and he rode away.

I laid down and in a few minutes my stomach began to cramp me. Soon it became so severe I thought it would surely kill me. I rolled on the grass and soon was wet with sweat from the misery I suffered. When the pain finally eased I fell asleep, and awoke just as the sun was setting. I started for camp where I arrived an hour later. The boys were surprised when I came in for the doctor had told them I was sick and he would send me to the hospital. By some means his ambulance had missed me. Probably picked up a load before it got as far out as I was.

I improved at once and in a few days was around again. The camp here was called Camp McClernand and was about five miles above Fort Henry and some distance from the river. There was a small stream flowing through a beautiful grass plot and there we placed our camp. There was one farm house here with a family living in it. Some of the officers boarded with them and others lived in their tents. We remained a week here with beautiful weather. But when we had orders to move the morning of March 14th the rain came pouring down in floods. There was a slack of rain soon after noon and we marched for the river. The road was very bad. Much of it through swamps where it had been built with "corduroy" bridges. Soon after starting, the rain came on again and to add to the trouble a company of rebels, we knew not how many, began firing upon our men whenever they could get within reach. Finally Company H went to meet them and after a sharp skirmish drove them away. Probably they were just feeling of us to see if we really were upon the move.

Came to the river about dark and went directly aboard our boat, the "*Autocrat*", wet, tired, hungry and cross. Our tents and equipage could not be loaded then so we did not start up the river till next morning about eleven o'clock. We then had everything aboard and steamed up the old Tennessee, but had not the least idea where we were going. The "*Autocrat*" was a very large boat and our regiment the only troops on her so we had plenty of room. Our Company was placed on the lower deck. We would have much preferred the upper deck, but had to take whatever was assigned us. Passed a railroad bridge which had been a handsome structure but now lay a wreck, destroyed by our gunboats. The result of ruthless war.

That night I lay awake just inside the wheelhouse on the boiler deck. I heard what I supposed to be the discharge of a cannon far away. But a few moments later came a crash in the wheelhouse just beside us. Timbers breaking and crashing and the wheel stopped. At first I thought it was a cannon shot and it had gone through the wheel. But on second thought I knew it could not be that for there was too short a time from the first sound to the second for the ball to come so far. The bells tingled and the engineers shut off steam and some men came down with lanterns and opened the wheelhouse. There was the cause of the disturbance. The wheel had struck a snag low in the water that gave the first sound like a cannon at a distance. Then the wheel caught the snag on one of its paddles and raised it so the end ran up through the wheel and tore out two of the paddles. The lower end of the tree, for it was a tree, was fast in the bottom of the river while the upper end was fast in the wheel. It took quite a lot of chopping as well as a good deal of swearing to get loose.

There was not much settlement along the river. Sometimes we did not see a house for miles. Arrived at Savannah Sunday morning March 16th, just one month from the capture of Fort Donelson. Peach trees were very plenty here and were in full bloom. I sent peach bloom in letters to Miss Stoakes and to Mrs. Jaqua. This was Mrs. Jaqua's birthday.

It was claimed that when the State of Tennessee voted on secession every vote in the precinct in which Savannah is situated was for the Union, and that the people were all for the Union yet. I hoped this was true. The people seemed glad to see us. While tied up here I heard that the Fifth Ohio Cavalry was on a boat just below us. John Slippy, who is my uncle by marriage, belonged to that regiment. I soon got leave to visit him, but when I came to their boat I found that he was with a squadron of their regiment that had gone on up the river. A soldier fell overboard from the "*Hiawatha*" today and was drowned. I saw him fall and saw him several times in the water but he sank before the boat reached him. He was a long distance from where I was. He belonged to the Thirteenth Iowa.

We frequently heard the name of Corinth, Mississippi, as the next place we might expect a battle. It was some fifteen or twenty miles from the river. It was claimed that Corinth was a much stronger place than Donelson. But we felt sure we would be able to capture it when the time should come.

This evening a boat came down the river and the cavalry squad my uncle belonged to was on it. I soon found him and we were glad to see each other. He says they had a little fight at Pittsburg Landing, a point twelve miles above here. The rebels ran away and our men now hold possession of the ground.

Tuesday, March 18, 1862. Last night orders were given for the boats to move up the river as soon as possible. The large drove of mules that belonged on our boat was on shore and could not be got on board at once so we did not get started as soon as the fleet generally. There were probably thirty transports along the river here at this time and more coming all the time. There were also several gunboats with us. The gunboats always anchor in midstream. The transports tie to shore.

The Eighth Iowa came up the river yesterday. They were fired into a short distance below here and one man was killed and one wounded.

We started March 19th and soon passed several other boats. The river was very full of water, so we crossed the rapids without trouble. Arrived at Pittsburg Landing and found all hurry and bustle. The bank or bluff is probably fifty feet high and very steep. It seems it would have been an excellent point to fortify. When we arrived here there were many boats ahead of us. They were tied along the shore for a long distance and other boats were tied outside these till there were several tiers of boats along shore. There were two boats between us and the shore, and very little goods had been unloaded from any of them yet. Some Ohio troops had just finished a road zig-zag and very steep up to the top of the bluff. Captain Shannon was officer of the day on our boat and he was considerably under the influence of liquor. He got our wagons together, loaded with our camp goods and ran them over the other boats by hand, then got the mules hitched to them and started them up the new road just finished. They were stopped by the men who had dug the road. Then Captain Shannon rode forward and told the Ohio men that he was officer of the day for the camp and that our regiment must land first. The Ohio officer demurred and he ordered them under arrest. He just got our wagons to the top of the bluff when the real officer of the day rode up. Shannon knew by the scarf that he wore that he was the officer of the day, but he was reckless and riding up to him ordered him to consider himself under arrest. But the Captain was not able to enforce his command and soon found himself under arrest. When Colonel Shaw learned that Captain Shannon was under arrest he went to the officer of the clay and apologized, saying he was very sorry for what had occurred; that Captain Shannon was drunk, and assured the officer if he would release the Captain he would see that he was taken care of and would cause no more trouble. Well, they released him and we awaited our turn to climb the hill. But if Captain Shannon had had his way for thirty minutes more we would have been on the brow of the hill with all our equipage. Captain Shannon was a case.

The same afternoon we got our goods all off the boat and marched out about half a mile from the river and made our camp. This whole country was covered with a heavy growth of timber. Where we were camped there was no undergrowth. All large, straight, tall trees, sugar, beech, oak, hickory, ash, and so forth. Beautiful trees. The ground back from the brow of the bluff was nearly level; very little rolling. Our regimental camp was laid out in order. Imagine our parade ground running east and west. On the south side imaginary streets to intersect the parade at right angles running south as far as needed. On each side of this street are our tents, the door of the tent next the street. The Company forms in line in this street and then marches out to its place on the parade ground. There was an alley back of our tents and between them and the next company's tents where we did our cooking, which was all done out of the tents.

The buds of the trees were swelling, and bursting. Birds were singing and squirrels playing in the swaying boughs and all nature was gay, for spring was here and the new life had begun to start forth and as far as nature goes everything was fulfilling its office of joyous gratitude to God. Not so with man. Here among the beauties of nature was congregated a large army fitted and equipped for a bloody contest. All the pomp and grandeur of war was displayed and we were now waiting only for a few more troops when we expected to advance upon Corinth and try the fortunes of war again with our enemy, confident of success because we were confident of the justness of our cause.

April 1st, 1862. "All Fools' Day", and so it proved to us. Our Colonel was not familiar with his men in any sense; held himself aloof; never made advances nor permitted any semblance of equality. Once while at Benton Barracks one of our men approached him and said: "How do you do, Colonel?" The Colonel never looked at him. The man walked around so he was facing him and approached again extending his hand: "Good morning, Colonel." The Colonel turned to a corporal saying, "Corporal, put that man in the guard house." Knowing him to be this kind of man we were completely surprised at this morning's episode. We were formed for drill and the regiment was in place on the parade ground. We had gone through some exercise with the manual of arms when the command was given to "Charge bayonets!" The officers were all in their places behind their companies and the Colonel behind them. Well, there came no command to halt and away we went into the woods. Soon the officers discovered the Colonel had slipped away from us and left us to ourselves. The officers then called the men back to the parade ground and formed as for dress parade. Everybody turned their caps with the tips to the rear. One of the captains took the Colonel's place now in front of us and a mock band with old tin pans marched back and forth in front of us, as our band should have done. Then the Lieutenant acting as adjutant called, "Eight corporals to the front and center," instead of "First sergeants," etc. When they arrived at the front he ordered them to report. Each corporal as his turn came laid his left hand on his right breast as the sergeants always did, and reported, "Company G, all badly fooled." When all had reported the adjutant turned and reported to the Captain, "All companies badly April fooled." We were then dismissed to our quarters. There was no more drilling that day and the Colonel capped the joke by giving notice that there would be no dress parade that evening as we had had one that day already.

April 2nd. Captain Pemberton, Lieutenants Gallagher and Eccles received their commissions today. There was much rejoicing among the men over the event. There were some promotions among the non-commission officers. Joe Shanklin became Orderly Sergeant, Addison Davis remained Second Sergeant, E. G. Oldroyd Third, George Walrath Four and A. H. Hazlett Fifth. Wilson was First Corporal; I was Second and Gaston Third.

April 3rd. Our division had grand review. This was on a much grander scale than the one we held at Benton Barracks. The men were much better drilled and made a finer appearance. It was held on an open piece of ground about three miles from our camp. All of General W. H. L. Wallace's command took part. At first the regiments were arranged in line of battle around the outside of the field facing inwards. The general officers including Grant, Wallace, Tuttle, Lauman and others we did not know, took their positions near the upper end of the field. Suddenly a battery of six guns entered the field at the lower end. They came at a swift gallop and went into position in front of the generals, unlimbered their guns and before we could realize what it meant, began firing a salute. They took the cartridges from the caissons, loaded the guns and fired gun after gun in as true sequence as the ticking of a clock or tolling of a bell in intervals of about two seconds. Thirteen shots were fired and they as quickly limbered up and galloped away. When one understands that when they unlimber the six horses that belong to each gun turned in the shortest possible time and space and stood with their heads toward the cannon, and when one is told that they turn so short and quickly that they seem nearly to lay flat on the ground one will agree they were well trained. Again they turn to limber up. Then the infantry opened ranks for inspection and laid out their opened knapsacks at their feet so that all the contents could be seen. The inspecting officer passed along the line viewing knapsacks, guns and accoutrements. After this inspection (there was an officer to each regiment) the knapsacks were put on again and the ranks closed and all the general officers rode around the field in a body. As they came to the head of each regiment the regiment's officer gave command "Present arms" and we stood so till they passed. After this the regiments formed column by company and marched in review clear around the field so they all passed in front of the officers.

It was a hard day's work. When we returned to camp the Colonel ordered "No dress parade this evening." He makes our life as comfortable as he can. Other regiments have a regimental camp guard and let no man leave camp without a pass from the Colonel. We never had this camp guard. If the boys got to straggling from camp he would order roll call every hour if necessary till he broke it up. If a man was absent from roll call two or three times he was punished, sometimes severely.

April 4th. It was Wilson's turn to go on guard but he was sick so I took his place. John Gaston was also sick so he was unfit for duty. The guard duty was at the landing guarding commissary stores. It rained quite hard about four o'clock this evening and hailed some. Just after the rain the long roll sounded in many of the regiments within hearing. We fell into line but were soon dismissed. We were told that one of our regiments had gone some distance from camp and was attacked by the enemy. After a sharp fight they fell back within our lines. Two days' rations were issued us that evening with orders to cook it that night and be ready to march in the morning.

Saturday, April 5, 1862. Everything quiet. No signs of marching. After the scare Friday night we have discussed the question why have we lain here three weeks upon the enemy's side of an impassable river and never thrown up a shovel full of dirt or chopped a tree for protection? This was grand ground to fortify, and a few days' work would make it almost impregnable.

FORT DONELSON TO SHILOH - Notes:

-- **Thomas Snelling** 26 of Nevada, Story County enlisted October 9 1861. He was killed in action February 13 1862 at Fort Donelson, Tennessee. The son of Alex and Agnes Snelling of Story County, Tom was born in Ohio but his burial place is unknown. Members of his family were still living in Nevada into the 1920s. The funeral verses quoted at Snelling's burial were taken from the Charles Wolfe poem, "Burial of Sir John Moore after Corunna". **Turner McLain** 19 of Nevada, Story County, and **Addison Davis** 21, also of Nevada, who risked their lives to regain Snelling's body, may have enlisted as partners along with Tom. They were all from the same area, enlisted and mustered the same day; it is possible they were all messmates and bunkmates. **JD Williams** who went on this recovery mission with BF Thomas and the Story County men was 19 and from Benton County. Davis, McLain and Williams would again show their grit under fire at Shiloh and beyond. McLain was promoted First Corporal July 1 1863. Davis was later promoted First Sergeant, and then Second Lieutenant. "Pope", who was knocked over by a rebel bullet during the battle, was **John A Pope** 22. Pope enlisted from Toledo October 10 1861.

-- There is no "Woodard" in Company G. The man Pemberton requested to come to his aid must have been **Rezin Woodward** 33 of Marshall County, or perhaps **Lorenzo Woodward** 21 of Story County. Both men enlisted the same day in October 1861, as did Charles Whealen who had been among the first to die at St. Louis. Whealen was a close neighbor to Rezin and his brothers James and Mortimer. **James Woodward** 25 served three years with 3rd Iowa Infantry while **Mortimer Woodward** enlisted in 1864 at age 23 for a 90 day term in the 44th Iowa. The Woodward brothers moved to Cloud County Kansas after the War; one family account states Rezin was wounded at Donelson. Rezin was honorably discharged for disability from the army hospital in Corinth a few months after the Shiloh battle. Whether Lorenzo Woodward was related to Rezin and his brothers isn't known. Lorenzo and another Story County soldier, **Eugene Wills**, a 17 year old fifer, who had also enlisted the same day as Lorenzo, could not be accounted for after the hard fighting at Shiloh had ended. They both were later listed as deserters but their true fate is unclear.

-- Lieutenant Logan and Sergeant Savage who met the Confederate truce party were **George H Logan** 28 of Bloomfield, Davis County who was appointed Second Lieutenant of Company I November 1861, and **Joel E Savage** 23 of Mount Pleasant, Henry County who enlisted into Company I October 1861. Both men were taken prisoner at Pittsburg Landing Tennessee. Both were exchanged with the officers on October 17 1862 at Aiken's Landing Virginia. Logan was later killed in action at Pleasant Hill while Savage lived to muster out with the regiment at Davenport in November 1864.

-- BF Thomas' uncle in the Ohio Cavalry, **John F Slippy**, lived in Perry Township near Wolf Creek with his wife Eveline and their children. He and Eveline later moved to Clarion Iowa but members of the family lived in Reinbeck and Waterloo long afterwards.

-- **John Gregg** of Company F of the 13th Iowa Infantry is said by the roster to have drowned on May 16, 1862 at Savannah Tennessee, just down river from Pittsburgh Landing. Gregg was born in Ohio and had enlisted at age 19 from Lisbon, Linn County in September 1861. Despite the wrong month, he is most likely the same soldier BF Thomas writes about above who fell from the "*Hiawatha*" on March 16, 1862. The soldier who was killed coming up the river was **Alexander Jennings** 18 from Marengo. The roster says he was born in Ohio, enlisted into Company G of the 8th Iowa in September 1861 and was killed on board the steamer "*War Eagle*" by guerrillas March 17, 1862. The companion who was wounded in the same incident with Jennings was probably Pennsylvania-born **Martin Gentzler** 22 of Company C of the 8th Iowa. Gentzler enlisted from Columbus City, Louisa County at age 22 and died of wounds received March 17, 1862.

-- **Joseph O Shannon** 32 of Burlington was appointed Captain of Company E November 1861. He too was captured at Pittsburg Landing and was discharged November 1862 a month after the officers' exchange at Aiken's Landing. See Chapter 1.

-- Third Sergeant **Elmer G Oldroyd** (Thomas spelled this name "Oldroid") was 25 years old and a Toledo resident. A letter he would soon write would become very important to the families of the Tama County men of Company G. Fourth Sergeant Walrath was **George A Walrath** 20 of Tama County; the name is wrongly spelled "Walroth" in the roster. In August 1862 he was discharged from Danville Mississippi for disability; before joining the Iowa 14th he had served a three month term in the 11th Illinois. After the War he was a Postmaster and Justice of the Peace at Blairsburg Iowa where he died in 1922. Walrath's obituary says he was wounded by a shell explosion at Shiloh; it was the cause of his disability discharge. Sent to the rear for treatment, the exploded shell may have spared him from a trip to a POW camp. Fifth Sergeant **Andrew H Hazlett** 24 from Shueyville, Johnson County later made the rank of Lieutenant.

-- Speaking of Donelson many years later, a Company K man, **James A Bridges** 18 of Kossuth, Des Moines County, said that he and the men with him had been forced to lie out in the rain and snow two nights. He said it became so cold that their hair and clothing froze to the ground. Terrible exposure and frostbite left many men unable to even walk and those were taken away downriver to hospitals. Another man estimated that more men were crippled or died from the exposure at Donelson than from the guns of the enemy. Bridges, who had enlisted in October 1861, was discharged as disabled in February 1863. He and the other hospitalized men missed the big fight at Pittsburg Landing.

CHAPTER IV

SHILOH

Early in the morning of April 6th we heard firing far distant on our right. For sometime we thought it was one of our divisions on review. But the firing increased and seemed to come nearer. Stoakes and I were washing dishes. We joked about the rebels coming in on us and wondered if they would let us alone till we got the dishes dried. We did not believe we were attacked. But before we finished the dishes the long roll sounded in the Second Iowa and the doleful sound was re-echoed by our own drums. Everything was hurry then. We began faintly to realize that the rebel army was upon us. We were soon in our accoutrements and took our haversacks and canteens with us but left everything else. Our knapsacks and blankets were left in our tents. The regiment was formed and marched some distance and joined the balance of our brigade which immediately took up its line of march that led toward the horrible roar in front. Gaston and Wilson would both go along though they were neither fit for duty.

Soon we began to meet stragglers and wounded men hastening toward the river. They told us all was lost, that a large rebel army had attacked us and was driving everything before it. That our army was then defeated and would be driven into the river. Still far in front we heard that terrible roar of infantry firing interspersed with the heavier discharge of cannon. On we went fast and faster. John Gaston gave out after running more than a mile. The last I saw of him he was leaning over a stump vomiting. Peter Wilson, though quite weak, kept up with us. The farther we went the more stragglers we met. The firing in our front had ceased though it was still severe on the flanks. When we had approached as near as our officers thought wise they selected their ground and formed line of battle and awaited the enemy's approach. The ground we occupied was clear of underbrush and was near the top of a slight ridge which ran parallel to our line. On the other side of this ridge, and immediately in our front, the ground was covered with a dense undergrowth. To our right and in front was an open field near the center of which stood a farm house. Along the top of the ridge was an old road which by wash and wear had become some-what sunken compared with the general face of the ridge. This was our line of defense. Oh, for a few hours' work with spades to throw up a breastwork! But there was no time for that now. On our right was the Twelfth Iowa. They occupied the open timber and faced the open field. To their right was the Seventh Iowa and again the Second Iowa. These four regiments composed our brigade which was commanded by Colonel Tuttle of the Second Iowa, and belonged to General W. H. L. Wallace's division. The Eighth Iowa was on our left but it belonged to General Prentiss' division.

As said before, when we occupied this position there was no fighting in front. It seemed we were put here to fill a gap. Very soon some men of Colonel Moore's Twenty-First Missouri regiment appeared in front of us. As they came through the bushes they seemed to be much frightened. They were scattered like skirmishers and said the rebels were coming in heavy columns. We could then hear the rebels coming but could not see them for the underbrush. Our Colonel asked the Missourians to lie down so we might fire over them but they came right on. He then ordered us to lie down and the Missourians went over us to the rear. As soon as they passed the Colonel ordered us to our feet. Our guns were loaded and our bayonets set before this. As soon as the Colonel thought the rebels were quite close he gave the command, "Ready" "Aim!" "Fire!" "Charge bayonets" and we plunged into the bushes after them. But only the dead and wounded remained. Those who were able had fled. Their flag had fallen and was captured not six rods from our lines. We retired to our position and for sometime all was quiet in our front. Then again we heard them coming. This time they knew where we were and came determined to drive us off. The battle raged for a long time but we held our ground and finally they were again put to rout.

Now a battery was brought to our support, so when the enemy came upon us again it helped greatly in repulsing them. There was also a battery with the Twelfth Iowa, but a rebel battery from across the field in their front got the range of it and throwing a stream of shells that burst just in front of the Union battery compelled it to leave the fields. The open field mentioned as being to our right caused us to have the heavier fighting. The rebels would not attempt to cross this field but deployed through the timber at the side of it. This brought them directly upon us. About this time General Prentiss on our left, moved his division to the right so that the Eighth Iowa regiment overlapped about half of our own regiment just in front of us. The rebels now came in force and our Colonel ordered us to lie down. The rebels pressed closer and closer, the little battery poured its grape and cannister into them with all its power. Colonel Geddis' Eighth Iowa gave them all that men were able to give, and finally when the enemy were so close they almost laid their hands upon our cannon the advance was stopped and they began to give way and soon were in full retreat.

Colonel Geddis had two horses killed under him directly in front of us, and several battery horses were killed. This seemed like the heaviest battle fought that day and we were unable to fire a gun. Again the Eighth Iowa regiment was moved to the left till it left a wide gap between them and us.

During all this time both wings of our army had been driven back. Steadily the noise of battle swung back on either side of us and still we held our ground. During the lull of battle we discussed the situation. It was the general opinion that our officers were using strategy. Our wings would fall back till the enemy formed a "V" cap outside of our lines. Then we would be reinforced and piercing their center would double up one of their wings in the bend of the river. But as the battle progressed and the wings went farther back we became anxious that reinforcements should soon come. But instead of reinforcements coming to us the rebels concentrated a large force on General Prentiss and hurled him back behind us. The line between him and Wallace was broken and a wide gap opened there through which a large body of the enemy threw themselves. This was about half past five o'clock in the evening. Then we saw the Second Iowa and the Seventh Iowa far away to our right going from us at a "double quick" toward the landing. We had no orders to retreat so we turned about and poured a heavy fire into the body of rebels that were now between us and the river. Bullets reached us from several directions and our men were falling fast. It is strange what a fatal effect a cross fire has. We now received orders to move to our right and rear to the Third Iowa camp. A few of us were among some fallen trees and in easy firing distance of the rebels, so we did not go at once but remained there firing as fast as we could load. Our major saw us and rode back and called us to come on as the regiment was going out there.

We were near the top of the ridge in front of the open field and as we ran we gained the top of the ridge and saw many rebel batteries planted on the field but not firing. While on the ridge we passed Cheney who was lying on his back with a bullet hole just above the right eye. We had no doubt he was dead, but our men told us when they found him two days later he was still alive and told who of us passed him there. I had stopped beside him and fired at the rebels and he told them so. We saw our regiment formed in line some distance from us and started to join them. As we crossed a hollow a large body of rebels were coming up on our left. They were in brush and we were on open ground. A worm fence was along the edge of the brush. When they came to the fence they saw us and we them. Our path was directly across their front and they raised their guns and fired upon us. They were so close we heard their guns click when they cocked them. The bullets flew thick all about us, but strange to say not one of us was shot. This squad was our own Mess and Sergeant Hazlett, and I take it we had a marvelous escape.

SHILOH - Notes:

-- The camp of the 14th Iowa was approximately 3 miles north of the old road where they ran to make their stand. Their tents were pitched in the area of the present day Iowa Monument near the Shiloh battlefield visitor's center. Another smaller monument along the old road marks the location where the Regiment formed their line of battle.

-- The line of defense these regiments drew up along the old road is today remembered as the "Hornets' Nest". By stubbornly holding their position through several waves of frontal attacks, the men of the Hornets' Nest delayed the rebel advance long enough for Grant and Sherman to organize a final line of defense with the rest of the scattered Union army. Their unflinching bravery bought Grant the time to bring up re-enforcements overnight and gave him a second chance to win a crucial victory the next day, thus perhaps saving not only Grant and Sherman's careers, but ultimately the entire outcome of the War itself.

-- Canadian born **Alexander Cheney** 25 enlisted November 1 1861. Severely wounded, at first thought killed in action, he was found alive by a burial squad after lying in the field two days. Cheney lived several days with this terrible head injury. For a time he even regained his powers of speech and described the battle and the friends who checked his body for signs of life. According to Captain Gallagher's records, Cheney died April 10 1862 (the published roster says July 10). Alexander Cheney is buried in Shiloh National Cemetery, Pittsburg Landing Tennessee, Section C Grave 7. See Chapter 2.

-- According to the published regimental roster, **Corporal Samuel W Jenks** of Story County was killed in action at Shiloh during the fight at the Hornets' Nest on the first day, April 6 1862. In Chapter 2 BF Thomas listed Jenks as discharged for illness in February but records at the National Archives, and Captain Gallagher's records confirm that Jenks was killed at Shiloh. Samuel was the 19 year old son of William and Aurelia Jenks of Lagrange County Indiana. Samuel's grave has not been identified; he is possibly buried in Shiloh National Cemetery as one of those designated "Unknown".

-- Four men from Company G were listed in the roster as wounded in battle at the Hornets' Nest. They were sent to the rear for first aid treatment and escaped capture with the rest of the regiment. They all recovered from their wounds. **Peter Jespersen** was badly wounded in the leg and discharged as disabled on September 9 1862. Jesperson, who lived in Cedar County when he enlisted, later farmed near Ashland Nebraska where he died in September 1906. **Jeremiah Mills** 25 of Tama County was shot in the hand at Shiloh. Mills re-enlisted in December 1863 and served until the end of the War. He became a carpenter in St. Louis where he died in 1904. **Henry Loomis** 21 of Tama County was wounded severely in the arm. Discharged for his wounds on August 25 1862, he later lived in Omaha Nebraska, dying there in June 1917. **Elmer Oldroyd** 25 of Toledo was shot across his scalp. When the fighting at Shiloh ended, he carefully went over the battlefield looking for all his missing companions. Sergeant Oldroyd then sent a letter to the Toledo newspaper with a carefully compiled list of the dead, wounded and captured from Company G for all their anxious families back home in Tama County waiting desperately for any word from the battleground.

-- **Francis Klein** 37 of Davenport was shot in the foot during the battle before being captured with the regiment and taken to the southern POW camps. He survived his time as a prisoner but was discharged in June 1863 from St. Louis. Klein was a stone mason in Rock Island Illinois for many years after the War.

-- **Robert Taylor** 41, a baker from Davenport, was shot in the thigh near the hip and was later sent by boat to a hospital at Camp Dennison at Cincinnati Ohio. According to pension records preserved at the National Archives, the ball was lodged against his thighbone and the wound became terribly infected. The ball was finally removed on June 1st but Taylor still continued to weaken. After several months in pain, he died at Dennison on July 11 1862 but the hospital failed to officially report his death in their records. His widow Eliza brought Robert's body home to Davenport for burial at Pine Hill Cemetery. The published roster says he was born in Tennessee but Captain Gallagher's company records say Taylor was born in Erie County, Pennsylvania.

-- On the same day that Robert Taylor died in Cincinatti, **John A Pope** died at Mound City Illinois. Pope, who had walked away after being bowled over by a rebel bullet at Donelson, and who survived the intense fight at Shiloh's Hornets' Nest, had been taken prisoner with the regiment at Shiloh. He lived through the rigors of the POW camp but was so debilitated that he needed to be hospitalized at Mound City Illinois after his release on parole. He died there of fever July 11 1862. Pope, messmate and friend of Sergeant AH Hazlett, was born in Vermont but was a salesman working in Toledo before the War.

-- Twenty year old **John L Martin** of Story County is buried in the Shiloh Battlefield National Cemetery. The company records and the roster say he died from disease at Shiloh a few weeks after the fight but some published sources list him as killed during the battle.

-- The men of "our mess" who had been firing from fallen trees and then miraculously escaped being killed at close range would have included all of BF Thomas' messmates except John Gaston who had been detailed to deliver powder to the Union batteries defending the Hornets' Nest.

CHAPTER V

PRISON LIFE

When we got to where the regiment was formed we saw that they had their guns stacked. We asked what it meant and they said we had surrendered and pointed to a solid column of rebels just beside us that we had not seen. We broke our guns rather than stack them. Although we had surrendered we were not free from rebel bullets, for troops coming in sight of us even at long distance would fire shots and sometimes volleys at us and a number of our men were killed and wounded here. The rebel officer in command told us to go into the tents that were standing here, so our uniforms would be hid and leave their men in sight. We did so but just after there came a heavy fire upon us, and one of the most dismal sounds in the world is bullets piercing the tents in which you are and no chance to see where they come from. We went out of the tents again. As I went through the door of the tent a bullet passed near my cheek and struck the man behind me in the head. He fell against me, I suppose dead. I do not know who he was.

There was a small man, a rebel captain, who had been acting like a little bantam rooster, strutting in front of his company and showing off his military airs. Just as we came out of the tents a spent ball struck this captain on the shin. It sounded like a hammer on a log. It hurt worse than if it had been at full force and gone through his leg. Well, he just howled with pain, and we "Yanks" roared and laughed. Yet I could not help pitying him for he certainly suffered severely.

Finally they got the firing stopped. About this time two of the rebel cavalry got the flag and banner belonging to the Twelfth Iowa. I have described these beautiful silk standards. They rode back and forth along a path through a puddle of water and mud and dragged these colors through the filth. We saw this depredation and were unable to lift a hand to redress the insult. Our own old cotton flag was torn to pieces and tramped into the mud. We were now formed into line and started off the field. I saw Robert Kirkpatrick of the Eighth Iowa whom I had known before we enlisted. He was wounded in the knee. I helped him along some distance and then fell in with some of his company who took care of him. Just as I got to my own Company again Lieutenant Gallagher asked me to help Adjutant Duncan of the Twelfth Iowa who was wounded in his head and quite dazed. A corporal of the Twelfth Iowa and myself half carried the Adjutant, one of us on either side with an arm around him and his arms over our shoulders. We were unable to keep up with the other prisoners and soon found they were out of our sight. We three prisoners with a rebel Lieutenant Colonel of the Fifty-fifth Tennessee named Reed and four rebel guards were alone.

Just as the dusk was deepening we heard a cannon from one of our gunboats fire a shot and soon after we heard the noise of the missile coming. Nearer and nearer it came and louder and louder the sound grew. We all stopped but the next instant the four rebel guards sought shelter behind the trees. The colonel and three prisoners stood still. Suddenly the shell burst about four rods from us and about three feet from the ground. It tore great limbs and flakes of bark from the trees and scattered leaves and dirt all over us but left us unharmed. It was probably because we were in the direct line of its path that we were saved. We were then probably four miles from the gun that threw the shell. Thus the second time that evening we had escaped from what seemed certain death.

Soon after this we came to a rebel hospital and the Colonel proposed that we leave the Adjutant there. The Adjutant made strenuous objections but we reasoned with him and finally he consented to stay. We had lost all trace of our men and the night was very dark except when we were among the rebel camp fires. We were following along a road that meandered along a small stream of water. Suddenly we heard a voice far up the bluff on the other side say, "Here, boys, we can get down." I knew the voice to be one of our boys and called, "Jack Moyer, is that you?" He answered and said they were camped on the high ground and some of the guards had brought a squad of them to get water. They came down and got the water and we climbed up with them to the camp. Colonel Reed told me he had felt very anxious to get us with our own men, because if we were long in prison it would be much better for us to be with our own Company. He also told us that he was a Cumberland Presbyterian minister and when the State of Tennessee voted on secession he had stumped the state for the Union. The State voted at three elections before secession carried. But when it once carried he belonged to the State and gave his services to the Confederacy. I knew his home was in Nashville. Often I have made inquiries in regard to him. About two years ago I learned that soon after the battle of Shiloh his regiment was mounted and attached to General Forrest; that he was at the massacre at Fort Pillow and was killed there.

We found our men camped in an old cotton field surrounded by their guard. They had built fires and were preparing coffee. After eating something we soon laid down to sleep. Nothing under us but the ground; nothing over us but the sky. But by and by there came a very heavy rain with an accompaniment of hail. It rained till the furrows between the cotton rows were full of water. There we stood in the mud and water about as forlorn a lot of men as ever breathed. After the rain ceased and the water sank away somewhat the rebel guards carried in rails for us to build fires with. They also brought us chunks of fire to start ours with. We could not lie down again till near morning the ground was so wet.

While standing around the fires Colonel Shaw came to us and asked where Captain Pemberton was. Now he had been with us when the battle began but was soon missing and we knew nothing of where he went. The Colonel said he knew he was a coward, and when we got out of this he would have him punished. He also said that Pemberton should never command the Company again.

We got some sleep before morning came. At the time we were captured we supposed our whole army was either captured or driven into the river. We had not heard a shot fired except a few from the gun that sent its shell so close to us after we started off the field.

Next morning we were drawn up in line around the field a few paces inside the line of guards for the purpose of being numbered and served with rations. As we stood there, not more than two rods from their line, some rebel cavalry rode to the commander and there was an exciting talk between them. When the word passed along their lines and all were much excited. They examined their guns and brought them to a "Ready." We saw our danger. They were frightened at something they had heard and were liable to fire on us at any moment. We knew, that in the state of mind they were, if one of them discharged his gun accidentally the others would all fire upon us and in the agitation it was strange this did not happen. There we faced each other for some minutes. There was a club as large as my arm and about four feet long lying on the ground between our lines and theirs. I thought if I escaped the first fire I would grab this club and with it make way through their lines and try to get to the river. But finally their officers became calm enough that they ordered their men to shoulder arms and then started us on our way to Corinth.

We knew afterwards that our men had begun driving their army back and this frightened these raw troops that had charge of us and produced the danger. I have always considered this one of the most dangerous places I ever was in. Now we began to learn that there was a very small number of our men captured. There was not over a thousand men with us and there probably had not been more than two thousand captured.

We were now hurried out on the road to Corinth and as we passed the road side it was literally covered with wounded rebels. Wounded in every conceivable manner. Some entirely helpless and some but slightly hurt. It seemed like in the next two hours we passed more than two thousand of them. Some of them taunted us as being the cause of their condition. I remember one man pointing to his companion and calling to us saying, "Are you not ashamed to do such work as this?" The man he pointed to had been shot in the mouth. The mouth was entirely destroyed and he was a ghastly sight indeed. I do not know why I associated him with a color bearer whom we fired at several times just after they had driven our wing back and got behind us. While firing at him he and his flag went down, but I do not know why he came into my mind when I saw this man. Neither do I know why, when many years after some men came here from Missouri with a drove of mules and stayed some days at Jonas Woods, one with a scarred face that showed his mouth had once been destroyed, I did not dare ask the man where he had received the wound. But I had no thought that either of them received his wound from me. Yet there was something strange in my feelings toward them. I think this morning's march through the ranks of the dead and wounded was one of the most gruesome times I ever saw. And what were we? Prisoners of war now on our way to a southern prison! At this time there was little known of the prisons in the south for there had been few prisoners, but we soon learned what it was to be prisoners.

The country over which we were marching was somewhat rolling but much of it was level and very swampy, so the roads were horrible. We thought if the rebels were being defeated they would not be able to save their artillery or baggage wagons. So we rejoiced to think they would lose all in the battle although we ourselves were prisoners. Passing quite a respectable farm house the family had gathered in the front yard to see us go by. The elderly matron, quite portly, remarked, "Well, Yanks, this is pretty good work our boys have done for a breakfast spell." One of our boys answered, "Mother, I hope before dinner you will have cause to change your mind."

We arrived at Corinth about five o'clock in the evening. As we marched down the middle of the street I saw standing in a door Adjutant Duncan, the man I had cared for the day before. He recognized me and saluted me. I never saw him after. Just after we captured Donelson three Tennesseeans joined Company H of our regiment. They said they were Union men and wanted to join the Union army. One named Roland was probably about twenty-eight years of age, the other two men mere boys of sixteen or eighteen years.

After marching through the streets of Corinth some distance we were halted and being very tired we all sat down together on the ground. One of the young recruits was beside me and Roland was probably four feet away. A man came along beside the column of prisoners and recognized Roland. He called him by name and ordered him to come out from among us. Roland's countenance never changed. He did not appear to know he was the man spoken to. The man said. "I will bring some one who will make you hear," and went away. He soon returned with an officer on horseback and several men and pointed out Roland. Twice the officer called him by name and ordered him to come out but still Roland seemed perfectly calm and undisturbed. Then the officer drew his revolver, cocked it, pointed it at Roland, called him a vile name and told him if he did not come instantly he would shoot him. Then Roland arose and went with them. We learned afterwards that he had formerly belonged in the rebel army but claimed he had been forced into their service but had always been a Union man. Next morning he was tried for desertion and condemned and shot. The boy that sat next me cowered down to the ground and was pale as cloth, and well might be. He was very close to the door of death. But they did not recognize him. I do not know where the third one was. We were told afterward that it was Roland's own brother that first recognized him. I think not because he called him Roland instead of calling him by his given name as a brother would.

We sat in the street till after dark. Those in front were being loaded into box cars to be sent south. Before dark it began to rain again and we soon were thoroughly wet. Peter Wilson was very sick and Stoakes and I took the best care of him we could, and that was but little. When we sat down he would lay down with his head in one of our laps. Sometime after dark we were moved down to the railroad track under a roof that was built on posts. No enclosure. There was a floor under this roof and there was more of us than could gather on the floor. By the way it was Captain Shannon that succeeded in getting us under this roof. Soon Wilson begged so hard to lie down that I got down with him and held him in a sitting posture with his head on my breast. I knew nothing more till I awoke in a very cramped condition, to find that the body of men who had been crowded together in a standing position had all lain down. They were piled on me so it was sometime before I could extricate myself. When I got loose I felt among the faces till I found Wilson had managed to get his head above the bodies that had lain on him. So we slept till near morning when we were aroused and marched into box cars. This was much more comfortable as we were not near so much crowded. We were aboard the cars but did not start south till after daylight Tuesday morning, April 8th, when we started for Memphis. This morning the rumor of the defeat of the rebel army was confirmed. We also heard that Island Number Ten was captured. This heartened the boys very much.

Arrived at Memphis after dark. Thousands of citizens gathered around us, some to comfort and cheer us and others to chafe and revile us. Soon they began to unload and march us down the street and again the rain poured down on us. It was ten o'clock before our car was unloaded. We marched slowly through rain and slush stopping sometimes, we knew not why, and then moving on again. At every stop Wilson would beg us to let him lie down. But Stoakes and I supported him between us as best we could. Finally we came to a large warehouse on the wharf into which we were ushered for the present. Our boys were in the third story. As soon as we were in our quarters we sank upon the floor and were asleep at once. About two o'clock in the morning we were aroused to receive our suppers which consisted of pork and crackers; nothing to drink.

In the morning we discovered that we were in a large room probably thirty feet wide and more than a hundred feet long. Just beside it was another room of like dimension. On each of the two floors below us were rooms of like size and were all occupied by our men. There was no furniture and no convenience, only the bare walls and floor, but we had plenty of room. The next morning the surgeons came and examined the sick. They sent Wilson to the hospital. He was very sick and despondent and we feared we would never see him again. We wished they could have left him with us that we might cheer him up and care for him. But the surgeon thought best to send him to the hospital. The surgeon seemed much interested in him and had a very kindly disposition. Several other men were sent to the hospital but none of our Company but Wilson and Grubbs.

Next day all the commissioned officers were taken from us. It was the severest thing that had happened us so far. The boys were quite despondent because of it. Then a surgeon came into our room and told us he was going through the lines and would carry letters for us; to write short letters home so they would not be too much bother to the officers, to whom they had to be submitted, to read, and he would take them and mail them when he got to where the United States Mail could be reached. Several of the boys and myself took this opportunity to write home. My letter did not reach home for nearly two months. I never knew why.

We fell into line four times that day under orders to go farther south, but after waiting sometime were again dismissed. It was supposed that when orders came for us to go they took all they could take on the train from those in the lower rooms and we waited another train.

I neglected to state that in the room we occupied there were some large tarpaulins which they had been painting there when we came. They were pieces of heavy canvas twenty by thirty feet square heavily painted and were for use on the wharves to spread over goods and merchandise, to protect them from the weather while there. When we had once or twice been called into line to go out and the rain was pouring, with our thin blouses and no overcoats, we looked upon these tarpaulins as something especially sent for our benefit.

So we cut them into pieces five or six feet square so as to use them as blankets and thus when called into line again all the men in our room were provided with water-proof blankets. Still we did not go south. Next day a man came into our room looking for his tarpaulins. We knew not what he wanted and for sometime we thought him crazy. He first turned very pale and then very red. He tried to talk but stammered incoherently. After sometime he managed to inform us that these were his tarpaulins. He began to insist that we must pay for them. One of our boys told him that when we left our camp we came away in a hurry and neglected to bring our loose change with us. Then he began to realize that we were war prisoners and were beyond his power to collect from. He told us there were several thousand dollars worth of the tarpaulins and he would compel the United States to pay him for them. This caused a general laugh. Then he said if we attempted to carry the pieces off he would have those taking them separated from the others and punished. When we went the next day most of the boys left their tarpaulins for fear of this threat. But it was raining hard and some of us could not resist spreading them over our shoulders as we went out. We saw nothing of the owner nor did we abandon the blankets till we got to Nashville two months later and drew new woolen blankets.

April 10th. General Price's army came up the river on boats and landed here and took the cars for Corinth. We were in plain view of the landing as our prison house was the first building next from it. If General Curtis, who had been pitted against General Price in Arkansas, had only known what we then knew he might have crossed the river and have walked into Memphis almost unopposed. Many visitors came to see us. Frequently they whispered to us aside so the guards would not hear, that they were Union men and as far as possible gave us the news. Some slipped the daily paper into our hands. We never knew whether to believe their professions of Unionism or not, but we were always glad to get their papers. They told us there were several small battles fought after Shiloh but that the rebels succeeded in reaching Corinth without serious loss. It was here we first learned that the rebel general, Albert Sidney Johnston, had been killed at Shiloh. We also learned that our own General W. H. L. Wallace had been killed there.

There were guards placed about the room to keep order and at the stairway to prevent us passing up or down. They permitted about three boys at a time to take a number of canteens and go down to a hydrant for water. There was a line of guards around the lot the building stood on and we were not allowed to go off the lot. There was a shed on the lot in which a number of hogsheads were stored. By some means one of our boys learned that these hogsheads contained molasses. He cut a hole through with his knife and filled his canteen then plugged the hole up again. The news soon spread all through the building and the molasses flowed freely so that nearly all the canteens were soon filled with it.

There was a rope doubled over a large pulley near the ceiling in our room that passed down through trap doors in each floor to the basement. Our boys managed to raise the trap door and began what they called our exchange of prisoners. That is, if a boy on the third floor belonged to a regiment or company that was mostly on one of the other floors he grasped the rope and the boys passed him to the proper floor. By this means many of the boys who had been entirely alone before were placed with their friends. But this worked so well that they finally raised the trap into the basement and some of them went down there to explore the regions. They soon came back with two boxes of cigars each. They said there was a large quantity of cigars stored in the basement. While we remained there the boys had plenty of cigars to smoke. This was all done on the sly so the guards did not see it, but sometimes we thought the guards knew what was going on and did not care just so we did not escape.

There was a rebel gunboat anchored midstream in front of our prison. It was the pleasure of the rebels when they were going through the drill to aim the cannon at our windows. They went through every motion of loading and firing and probably at every imaginary shot claimed they killed a score of "Yanks". The gunboats here were not nearly the equal of ours, so we sincerely wished they might soon meet and settle matters between themselves.

Sunday, April 13th. Just one week today since the battle and our capture. How much had taken place and how long the time seemed since then. At two o'clock this afternoon we marched through the rain to the railroad and got on the cars to go south. Tried to learn something of Wilson from the citizens we passed but could not. We went onto flat cars that had standards at the sides and slats nailed on the standards. They also had canvas on for shade, and boards across with their ends on the slats for seats. About two miles out we came up with another train that had two cars off the track. It took till dark to get them on and then we started again.

Monday came to Canton, Mississippi, and stopped awhile. Talked some with the citizens who came to the cars to talk with us. All seemed to be very strong "secesh" and some were quite combative, at least in talk. We arrived at Jackson about two o'clock in the afternoon and got some supplies from a large hotel near the depot. Could not see much of the city where we were. We stayed here till after dark and then started as we supposed for Mobile. But before starting we were taken from the rebuilt flat cars and put into tight box cars which were uncomfortably warm. After suffering sometime for air our boys punched some of the boards off the end of the car and that gave us better ventilation. After a two hours run our engine broke down and we did not start again till after daylight next morning. The country was covered with a heavy growth of pitch pine. The soil was red as brick dust and very gravelly, and in some places stony. Several hundred miles south made a great change in the vegetation. Here fields of rye were nicely headed out. At home they were probably just sowing wheat and oats.

Arrived at Mobile at three o'clock in the morning April 16, 1862. We were taken from the cars and marched some distance through the streets to a large cotton shed in which we were placed. There were probably a thousand of us in this building which was probably one hundred and fifty feet long and ninety wide. It was enclosed on all sides with a brick wall about twelve feet high. From this wall on each side a shed roof covered about one third across the building, leaving a third in the center without a roof. At each end were double doors twenty feet wide. There was a floor under the roof but the part that was not covered was paved with broken shells. There was a hydrant inside the building.

We were guarded by Prussian soldiers. They said they were "consular guards" hired to guard us, and that they had no sympathy with the south but that the country that had seceded was too large to ever be conquered. They tried to treat us kindly. In the morning the provost marshal visited us. One of our men in talking used language that the provost considered an insult, and he had him in irons at once. We thought he only wanted to show his authority.

The first morning we were there when the rebels issued us rations. They rolled a large hogshead filled with crackers into our pen and left them with us to divide. We were not organized in any manner and as soon as the hogshead was opened the boys made a rush for the crackers. Many of the boys were trampled under foot by their eager companions. We had a small boy with us who enlisted as a musician. He was eighteen years old but no larger than an ordinary boy of twelve. Several of us worked our way with him as near the hogshead as possible and then tossed him over the men's heads into the hogshead. It was a good throw and instantly he was tossing great hands full of the crackers to every Company G man within reach. By this means we secured our full share. Some of the boys had black eyes or bloody noses after this scrap over the crackers. It was strange that there were no limbs broken and no one killed. After this we formed into companies and appointed officers who divided the rations as they should be done.

The weather was very warm, in fact, excessively hot, and the peculiar form of our pen made it worse. The sunshine poured in at the wide space between the two shed roofs and there was no means of getting a circulation of air. The men divested themselves of all but the scantiest raiment and then lay panting in the shady side of the pen. At night the air was much cooler. The water in the hydrant was pure but quite warm.

One day a planter from some distance up the Alabama River came in to see us. Said he was raised in Pennsylvania. Came south forty years ago to teach school. After teaching sometime found he could make more money as overseer of a cotton plantation. This led him to purchase negroes for himself and his possessions had gradually grown until at that time he owned a large plantation and more than one hundred slaves. He was of medium height, rather thick set, with a bald head and jovial countenance, probably sixty years of age. In Iowa he would have rated as a very ordinary looking man. He told us that the rebel general, McGruder, and General McClellan were then engaged in a great battle and he felt sure the rebels would be victorious and in his opinion that would close the war. We did not believe General McClellan would be whipped nor if he were would it close the war. The planter was quite jolly. Sat in the shade with his hat in one hand and a large bandanna handkerchief in the other with which he would frequently mop his bald head. Said when he heard we were there he hoped he would find some of his Pennsylvania friends among us. There were many other visitors but I describe this one because he was a sample of many men who had gone south to teach school and had then become planters themselves.

Here we received a number of large "Dutch ovens", large iron kettles with flat bottoms set on legs. The kettles were about fourteen inches across, eight inches deep and had covers with a flange about one and one-half inches high, so when the oven was placed on the coals to bake in, it was also covered over the top with coals. It made a very good oven in which to bake corn bread or roast meat, that is, if we only had the meal and meat. I remember seeing my mother often bake biscuits in just such an oven when I was a small child. We also got some spiders, tin plates, knives and forks and tin cups. There were four men to a set of plate, knife and fork and cup. There were a very few tin spoons among us.

April 19, 1862. Were ordered to bake our meal into "johnny cake" and be ready to leave at six o'clock that evening. Were sorry we could not go by daylight so we might see something of the city and bay. But our journey, our means of travel and time of going were not of our choosing. Robert Clark became very sick and today was taken to a hospital. It was sad to think of leaving him here among strangers and enemies. We learned two months later that he died a few days after he was taken to the hospital. This was the first death in our own Mess. He and his brother Mat lived just north of Six Mile Grove in Black Hawk County. Robert was working at Toledo and joined our Company there. Then he went home on a visit and brought Mat back with him. We were told we were to go up the river, some said to Tuscaloosa, but we knew nothing about it.

About seven o'clock nearly four hundred of us were taken out of the pen and marched to the river where we were placed aboard the steamer "*St. Charles*" and in a few minutes started up the river. By the light of the pitch torches on the landing we observed that the boats lay some with the prow one way and some the other, which indicated we were on tide water, for in flowing water the boats always tie up with the prow up stream. We were all placed on the boiler deck and not permitted to go above to the cabin. Talked with one of the engineers. All the boat hands were colored men and he was a light mulatto. He said he hoped the war would last till the colored race were freed. He spoke harshly of Lincoln because he had refused to enlist and arm the negro. Of course our talk was not in the presence of any of the guards. I formed acquaintance with one of the guards, a citizen of Mobile. He said if he had known me while at Mobile he would have taken me out to see the city for he said a few of our boys had been taken out by some of the citizens.

The Alabama River lays deep in the ground. That is, the banks rise high on either side and there is almost no bottom land along the river. The banks are very steep and from fifty to a hundred feet high. From the boat we only saw the bluffs and sometimes a house near the edge of the bluff. Occasionally there was a landing and from it a narrow railroad track ran up the bluff, at the top was a capstan and a mule. Freight was loaded on a small car, half as large as a common wagon box, then by means of a long rope attached to the car and capstan the mule elevated it to the top.

As we glided up the river the morning came upon us in a dense fog; but when the fog cleared away we saw the trees that grew along the river bank covered with trailing gray moss. It had a weird appearance. Sometimes it was a few inches long and sometimes many feet long, probably twenty-five feet of gray veil gently swaying in the breeze. There was so much of this growth in places that it gave the scenery a very somber appearance.

April 21st. We arrived at Cahaba, Alabama, and were immediately landed and the boat went on up the river. The bluff was before us, the river behind and a strip of level ground probably two rods wide our standing room. But there was a guide to pilot us and following him in a tortuous course we finally emerged upon the top of the bluff where we found the village. Then we were marched some distance to a new brick warehouse but partially finished. The walls were built and part of the roof and floor. The balance of the building was floored with the ground and roofed with the sky. No windows or doors, and into this building we were marched and this was our prison for nearly two weeks. The building was probably eighty by one hundred and fifty feet. In front was a large door twenty feet wide. The spaces for windows were high up from the ground. There were guards at the door and windows.

Instead of the warm weather we had been having at Mobile we had quite cool weather here. It rained as we came up the river and then turned cold like it does in Iowa. The next day the men we left in Mobile came and joined us. We learned that the reason we were sent out of Mobile in such haste was that the Union gunboats were near there and they might make an attack at any time. There was no provision made for rations here. They gave us what they had but it was entirely insufficient for the sustenance of the men. Cahaba was a small town of not more than six or eight hundred inhabitants. The citizens learned of our condition and sent in some provision. One good old lady came to the door with a plate of beans for us. A plate of beans to feed a thousand men! Think of it! But she did what she could.

April 23rd. We received some small barrels of corned beef from Mobile. They issued a barrel of this meat and when the head was removed from the barrel the meat stank so we had to remove it from the building. Several other barrels proved as bad but finally we secured one we were able to eat. We boiled this meat in our large iron kettles and with our corn bread we lived fairly well. We got no salt except what was in the meat barrels, but this did pretty well. This was the first time in my life when I anxiously awaited my breakfast, knowing when it came it would be a small piece of corn bread and small piece of beef and no coffee or warm drink. One of our boys saw a paper drop from the pocket of one of the guards and managed to secure it and we had it to read. There had been some fighting about Corinth and also some upon the Potomac. But the item that most interested us was that our government had refused to exchange prisoners and the rebel officers thought they had best parole us. We would much prefer to be exchanged.

When we first came here a guard would take three or four of us with canteens out along the street about three blocks to an artesian well to get water. The well was finished with a top something like a hydrant. The spout came out of the stock and turned down so the stream fell into a large stone basin larger than a common wash tub. The stream was probably two inches thick and came with such force that the water seemed to boil in the tub. As it came from the ground it was much too warm to drink but by filling our canteens and wetting the cloth that covered them and then hanging them in the air the water soon got cool. After we were here a few days they conducted this water that flowed from the well along the gutter beside the street, into our prison. It flowed in a board trough and near the center of the pen they sunk barrels into the ground so the top was a little above the surface of the ground. The water first flowed into one and from it into the next, so we always had plenty. We used the last barrel for a bath tub and it had customers nearly all the time. Our fires were built upon the ground and of course we had to have many of them to accommodate those who were cooking. The wood they gave us was pitch pine and the smoke was heavy and black. Many of the men got sore eyes because of the smoke.

The men naturally gathered about the large door-way where they could see out, and sometimes crowded pretty close to the guards. The guards repeatedly threatened to shoot if they did not keep back. The boys had always replied that if they shot one of our men we would kill the man that did it. One day there was a shot at the door. The gun was discharged accidentally and no one was injured, but the boys a little way back thought of course they had shot one of our men. The excitement was tremendous. I chanced to be near enough the door to know the cause of the discharge, but we could not make those farther back hear us; for some minutes it seemed the boys would demolish everything. But when they learned the truth the excitement soon quieted and order was restored, but I never saw whiter men than the guards at the door.

One day when idleness ruled the house and many of the prisoners and some of the guards were asleep, suddenly we were aroused by the shrill screaming of a fife delivering the inspiring notes of "Yankee Doodle" to the somnolent air. In an instant guards and prisoners were aroused. Cheer upon cheer came from the prisoners; deep guttural oaths from the guards. A rebel captain and half dozen armed guards came in to arrest the bold musician, but neither fife nor fifer could be found. At intervals for several days we were regaled with the notes of this beloved national air and again and again was the capture attempted and always with failure. Some said the fifer made his instrument out of a piece of cane pole; others said it was a fife he had kept concealed. Which was the true story we never knew. We never saw the fife nor fifer, but are very thankful to him for the happy diversion he gave us.

We often discussed the chance of getting to our lines if we cut out of prison and carefully advised what would be the best course to take, learned all that each one remembered of the geography of Alabama, and tried to fix in our minds a map of the country between this and our lines. With all the care the rebels had taken to search us when captured, we found there were eight revolvers concealed among the prisoners. We had no fear but we could easily overcome all the troops here guarding us, but the distance to our lines was too great for us to attempt to escape in a body. They would intercept us with mounted men and overpower us. If we separated it would be impossible for individuals to make the long march alone. So we abandoned the idea of trying to escape from Cahaba.

April 28th. We were told by a citizen that New Orleans had fallen into our hands. Hoped it was true but felt uncertain. Our rations were much better than when we first came here. Several of our boys were sick. We ascribed it to the close confinement and spoiled meat. Espy McKune was sick and we feared he would have a spell of the fever. He was taken to the hospital.

May 1st. We had four days rations issued to us with orders to cook the same and to be ready to move. I was quite unwell myself but not so as to go to the hospital. Gradually the impression was given out that we were to go to our lines and be paroled or exchanged. The boys generally believed this and were in excellent spirits. McKune was not able to go with us and we were all very sorry for that. It seemed hard to leave him among strangers, but there was no help for it. It was so we had left Wilson and Grubbs at Memphis, and Clark at Mobile. Now we had been ordered to take our "Dutch ovens" and kettles with us. That cast a shadow of doubt over our vision of liberty. Why should we take them with us if we were going to be exchanged?

Friday, May 2nd. We were awakened at half past three in the morning so as to be ready to take the boat when it came, and were aboard the boat and left Cahaba at sunrise. Passed Selma at eight o'clock. This was a large town on the left bank of the river. It was the county seat of Dallas County and did quite a little manufacturing. There was a foundry there that cast rebel cannon. Our officers were confined there in prison. The city was nearer on a level with the river banks so we saw a good part of it. Saw rebel soldiers but did not see what we believed to be the prison in which our officers were held. How glad we would have been to meet the officers again. From Selma to Montgomery the river passage was between high bluffs with very little bottom land. The gray moss was prevalent upon the trees and the long trailing festoons were either graceful streamers or mourning veils according to the feelings of the observer. The mistletoe was also very plentiful on the trees. There is no growth in the north like it. It is a small shrub that grows from the sap of another tree. It must start from a seed that gets hold in some manner. The root is like a small onion bulb and is set solid in the sap wood of the tree. They seem to have grown in harmony. While you can easily trace the bulb shape of the mistletoe you can also trace the growth of the tree around it and yet in one solid mass. It flourishes on the oak and sycamore and many other varieties of trees. The bush that grows from this is sometimes as large as and in shape of a bushel basket, though they are mostly smaller. They are an evergreen though they grow on all kinds of trees and invariably kill the tree they grow on. They are therefore sometimes likened to sin that fastens upon the soul of man; something hard to get rid of and certain to kill if not eliminated.

Arrived at Montgomery at half past six the same evening. At half past eight we were taken off the boat and taken to the amphitheater of the fair ground where we slept through the night and had breakfast next morning.

Saturday morning, May 3rd. We were put in box cars and started east. There were no guards in the cars with us but were all on a passenger car on the rear end of the train. They still tried to have us believe we were going to our lines. They remarked several times in our hearing: "There is no danger of their trying to escape when they are traveling as fast as possible to their lines." Three of our boys were so sick they were left at Montgomery -- McLain, Miller and Fitch. We were now traveling on the Montgomery & West Point railway. Passed several small towns and at last came to a junction where we were taken on the southern branch. This most thoroughly convinced us that we were not to be exchanged. Crossed the Chattahoochee River and soon arrived at Columbus. We were now in Georgia. We changed cars there and took the road that leads to Macon, Georgia.

We stayed at Columbus several hours. There was a large camp of rebel recruits there. After we were again in the cars an officer of our guards walked along on top of the cars and told the rebels they might come and talk to us if they would talk civilly. We were in cattle cars with boards placed crosswise for seats, the open sides giving excellent opportunity to see out. A large number of the rebels came to the side of the cars to talk with us. One man about my age was sitting on his satchel when given privilege to talk. He came directly to me and asked me how long I thought the war might last. I told him I thought there would be two more heavy battles fought, one near Richmond and the other at Corinth: that we would likely win both and if so that would close the war. He then told me he was a conscript; that he had been married but three weeks and was very sorry to be in the army; that he hoped my prediction would be fulfilled and the war be over. He asked if there were any Masons with us. By that I thought he was a Mason. We talked for sometime and shook hands when we parted. He said, "I have no doubt we might have been warm friends had we known each other in time of peace, but now if we meet again it will be as enemies and each will likely do his duty by the other if we so meet." I heartily endorsed the sentiment and cordially wished him a speedy return to his young bride. "Who knows whether we will meet again and what manner of meeting it may be?"

Another man asked, "What uniform do you use for your riflemen?" I asked him what he meant. He said he had been in the Mexican War. There the infantry wore a blue uniform and riflemen a gray. The Confederates wore the gray now and what did our riflemen use? I then told him our tactics were changed so that all our infantry men drilled and wore uniforms alike. We were all riflemen. But this was the first I knew the rebels had stolen our gray uniform. The First Iowa Infantry had been uniformed in gray and it was beautiful. But if it had become a symbol of rebellion it had lost all its beauty for me. The uniform we had seen thus far had been butternut.

Left Columbus about ten o'clock in the morning and traveled all day and the next day.

Sunday morning, May 4th. We arrived at Macon, Georgia, just four weeks from the day we were captured. Indeed it seemed like four months instead of four weeks. Remained on the cars till ten o'clock. Macon was a large city and it being Sunday there were many idlers about, so the word spread fast and thousands of people came to see us. Many questions were asked us. Some wise and some silly. Some kindly and some manifesting much bitterness of feeling. One young man asked "Don't you think this is a foolish war?" "Yes." He was astonished at first, then repeated, "Don't you think it foolish in your government to try to coerce the southern states to stay in the Union?" "No! We think the foolishness is in the southern states attempting to secede from as good a government as the United States." Then his wrath arose. "I hope I may soon meet you in battle." "Well, your wish may soon be gratified if you will only withdraw yourself from your company of home guards where there is no danger and enlist in your active army and go to the front." This caused a shout of laughter from the citizens for the shot had hit. He was a member of the home guards. We knew but little about the geography of our own country at that time. To illustrate: Two nicely dressed gentlemen with canes and silk hats approached. One asked, "Where do you come from?" "Iowa." He turned to his companion and said, "He means Ohio." Then to us, "Cincinnati is in Iowa, is it not?" The reply, "See here my short haired friend, you must not think we are all blamed fools just because you are. We came from Iowa the brightest young State in the Union, and we are not ashamed of it."

At ten o'clock we were taken from the cars and marched to the border of the city and placed in the fair grounds. They had named it "Camp Oglethorpe". The grounds were enclosed with a tight board fence about eight feet high. There were several buildings within the enclosure which were utilized as hospitals and for commissary storage. There was a long row of cattle and hog sheds, boarded up on the back part and with board roof, open in front. These were occupied as sleeping quarters. But many of the men had not even the board roof but slept on the open ground. Now when you remember we had no coats, only thin blouses and no blankets except those men who brought away the tarpaulins from Memphis, you will understand we were not reveling in luxury as far as sleeping arrangements were concerned. But much of the ground was covered with grass and there were many thick shade trees growing here and there so things were not so bad as they might have been. There was a small stream of water running across one corner of the ground that gave us plenty of pretty good water for use. At noon Sunday they served a loaf of bread to each of us. This was the first light bread we struck in the Confederacy.

Two crackers for supper and one for breakfast was what had been furnished each of us up to that time. We had now drawn what the rebel commissary called "hams of bacon". But it came off of the wrong end of the hog to be called a ham in Iowa. It was what we call jowls. The lower jaw of the hog pickled and smoked. But it was smoked meat and the first we had seen in the south. They also gave us soap, candles, sugar, etc. Well this was a change. Lots of open air, clear water and a variety to eat if not in very large quantity. This morning we succeeded in getting a paper. It was the first we had had for sometime. It gave a terrible account of the battle below New Orleans. The whole rebel fleet was lost. It claimed great barbarity on the part of our officers.

Today they formed us into companies of one hundred men each. These companies had to fall into line at eight o'clock in the morning and six o'clock in the evening for roll call. At morning roll call was brought out our pots and kettles for inspection. It was ordered that at morning roll call we must have everything including pots, kettles, dishes, cups, spoons, knives and forks and also our hands and faces bright and clean and hair combed and brushed. The major did the inspecting himself and was pretty severe on some for their dirty hands. The next morning he sent word to the sergeant to do the inspecting. It was done very thoroughly and with considerable amusement connected with it.

Orders were read that no outsiders would be allowed to converse with the prisoners, that we were not to be allowed papers, books or any means of learning the news. This seemed like shutting out the sunlight. Major Hardee, a nephew of General Hardee who wrote the book on tactics, was in command here. The mayor of the city sent us enough white bread for our dinners one day. Many thanks. Three of our men had been taken to the hospital already. One, John D. Williams, was very sick. The rebels had been firing a salute. They told us it was in honor of the capture of General Mitchel's division of our army. We had no means of contradicting or verifying it. The Commissary told us he had ordered ten thousand pounds of straw for us to lie on. It was to be here the next day. We were afraid he lied about it.

Just at roll call that evening it rained on us very hard for a quarter of an hour. It not only soaked our clothing but wet the ground so we did not know where we were to sleep. It turned pretty cold after the rain, much like it might at this time of year in Iowa.

The prisoners in camp here were divided into two brigades. The first was composed of all soldiers not from Iowa and the second was all Iowa boys. The first brigade was called out to drill this evening at four o'clock and drilled for two hours. Major Hardee drilled them himself. Some say it was done at the request of their sergeant major. We hoped they would not attempt to drill the second brigade, for while drilling is well enough, being forced to do it when a prisoner is another thing. I did not believe the Iowa boys would be forced to do it.

And now a rumor was rife that the non-commissioned officers were to be separated from the privates and kept in close confinement. This if carried out would have been very silly of them as well as a very sad matter for us. Our boys tried to persuade us to cut off the chevrons from our sleeves so we would not be known. The chevrons were given us by our government and we would not part with them in this manner. Some straw came to be put into the hospital but none for us. One of the boys heard the major tell some lady visitors that we would all be paroled soon. It may be he told this on purpose for our men to hear and thought we would be more tractable, for there was considerable complaint about the way we were housed and fed. We were the first prisoners brought here and for a time a novelty. During this time we were treated very well and fed pretty well, but this novelty had worn off already and we fared pretty hard so far as rations go, and practically had no beds, not even straw to lie on.

May 8th. It was so cold last night that John Felter and I went to the hospital building and laid close against the wall, outside, of course. It was warmer there than sleeping out in the open air, or in our shed. Next day we got some old lumber and put a rough floor in our shed. The boys told some wonderful stories about the "Gray backs". It was reported that one of our boys while asleep upon the lawn was seen to be slowly moving along the ground. Upon examination it was discovered that the colony of "Gray backs" under him had all started in the same direction and so carried his body along on their backs. This is a mild sample of their stories. To say the least the "Gray back" was the most numerous thing in the camp.

Where the Confederacy got all the jowls they had been feeding us was a mystery. They must have been near the bottom of the lot, for they were often spoiled and wormy now. The order for the guards not to converse with us was a dead letter. They brought tobacco for our boys and sometimes slips of newspapers or gave us an item of news orally. The news they gave us of our army was always of its reverses and not of its victories. Ten new prisoners were brought into camp. They had been captured near Huntsville, Alabama. They told us much in regard to army movements that was new. From their report the war had not been as successful as we had hoped for. Still on the whole the Union was gaining but the Confederacy was much stronger than we had supposed.

We drew both flour and meal today. The flour we exchanged with a baker, who came in for that purpose, for light bread. The meal we made into mush and then fried it for breakfast. This was excellent but there was never more than half enough of it. Major Hardee told Joe Burright that he had written their war department about having us paroled and he hoped to have an order in a few days to set us free. We were in hopes this might be true.

One evening some straw was brought in and Southwick secured a large armful which he kindly divided with us. Southwick and Stoakes bunked together and Felter and I. The straw made quite an improvement in the sleeping arrangements. But when a few evenings later a candle was knocked over in the straw it was all in a blaze before anything could be done to save it. The shed caught fire but was soon extinguished. It caused quite an excitement for the time.

Every day the boys played base ball. It is quite an exciting game and gave plenty of exercise. Many of our boys had become excellent players. Some pitched quoits and some marked off checker boards on the ground and played checkers. The drilling the major tried to install a few days before proved a complete failure.

Saturday, May 10th. The first brigade was ordered to fall into line and when so formed officers passed along the line taking the name, company and regiment and state of every man as they passed. This the order said was done for a special purpose. It seemed strange this was not done sooner and yet we could not help but place a special significance upon its being done then. Did it mean preparation for exchange? It took a good part of the day to make up the roll of the first brigade and there was nothing further done. The second brigade felt quite uneasy fearing something was coming to the first which the second would not be permitted to enjoy.

The beef issued us in lieu of the jowls was even worse than any we had before. So by some means our Commissary managed to exchange it with some outsiders for cabbage and tobacco. The beef was so badly spoiled we could not eat it and we could eat the cabbage and some of our boys could chew the tobacco. What anybody wanted with the beef was a mystery to us. About one hundred and fifty secesh soldiers marched into our camp today and pitched tents on the south side of the grounds. What they were here for we knew not. Some thought they had come to guard us to our lines. There was a thought of freedom in almost every movement made. I had no idea what they should camp inside our camp for, but here they were. At roll call this evening it was announced that there would be preaching in camp tomorrow evening at five o'clock. This was the first effort they had made for our spiritual welfare. For dinner today we cooked a half head of cabbage. There were seven in our Mess and we had a feast and it was splendid for sure.

Sunday, May 11th. We had been here but one week but it seemed like a month. It seemed like they fed us on wormy jowls for two weeks and spoiled beef for two weeks more, but facts are facts and we had been here but one week. Nothing of importance occurred till time for religious service. Then nearly all the prisoners assembled in front of the hospital and a minister from the city presided. After singing a hymn he offered a most excellent prayer. He prayed the Lord to care for our distracted country, not countries; for special blessings upon the friends and relatives of the prisoners: that the now severed families might soon be reunited in happy homes; for all rulers over the people, naming presidents, kings and magistrates. The text he chose was from St. John, Sixth Chapter and Sixty-eighth Verse: "Lord, to whom shall we go? Thou hast the words of eternal life." The first point he made was: go where you will, you will find in the people you meet traces of religious belief. Second, the difference between true religion and that of the heathen. Third, the manner of getting true religion. Fourth, the benefits religion gives during life and its greater benefit at death. Fifth, a very earnest appeal to everyone to embrace Christianity at the earliest possible moment. The discourse was very good and was well delivered. The last prayer was offered by another man and was worded very kindly and courteously in our behalf. He especially desired blessings upon the friends who mourned our absence, and earnestly asked that the war might soon be brought to a close so that all might go to their homes in peace. The boys were generally well pleased with the meeting. It seemed strange that this was the only religious service we had while in prison. I wonder if our preachers ever preached to the rebel prisoners in the north.

Monday, May 12th. Yesterday, forgetting it was Sunday morning, we traded meat to a man who was to bring us milk in place of it this morning. But alas! no milk came. We did not lose much for the meat was absolutely spoiled. Now it may be the man ate the meat yesterday and it killed him and in that case he was unable to bring us the milk. Or it might have made him so sick he was unable to milk the cows. Whatever the cause, we got no milk. These people must be awfully hungry for meat to eat such as we have been trading them.

Today nine marines from the gunboat "*Sumter*" were brought into our prison. They had been out on a pleasure excursion, lost their way and were captured. Six officers were captured with them but were sent to some other prison. These men were pretty hard cases. This evening Felter and I were at the doctor's office. There we heard the Quartermaster contracting for wood to be delivered along all summer. This looked to us as though we might stay here all summer. It seemed to me that I had now lost the last spark of hope that we would be paroled or exchanged. But in talking with them I found Felter, Hazlett and others still had hopes we would get out soon. I had been quite unwell for some days, some fever and no appetite. Also a very sore mouth. Each night I had night sweats and my head was stopped up with cold. I now had some medicine from the doctor and hoped I might soon be better. Our boys got some milk tonight. The old man offered only a quart of milk for about seven pounds of spoiled meat, but when they went to the boy that was measuring out the milk they told him it was two quarts we were to have and he gave it to them. It is claimed that all means are fair in war. One of the boys was still arguing with the old man for more milk and finally the old man gave him a quart of sour milk.

May 18th. We got news by our private line that Norfolk had been captured and the rebel ram "*Merrimac*" was burned to keep her from falling into Federal hands. Also that the rebel army at Corinth was entirely surrounded and must capitulate. All very good news. It put new life into us to get such news. I talked with a man who was on board the "*Merrimac*" during its battle with the "*Monitor*". It was no use to tell him the "*Monitor*" had only two guns. He knew it had at least a half dozen. No two guns could fire as fast as the "*Monitor*" did. But it only had two guns.

Our division now gave their names and description as the other division had a few days before. Had not drawn as much rations for the last three days as we had before. Did not know what it meant.

May 14th, 1862. My mouth was now very sore as it had been for sometime. Went to the doctor again today. He gave me more medicine but said it would be some time before it got well. Was in very good health otherwise. There was some talk among the boys of taking an oath never to bear arms against the Confederacy. The rebels were urging the boys to this because they told us our government had abandoned us and refused to exchange for us. It was rumored that some of our men would accept these terms. I was sure none of the Iowa boys would accept this offer. We were told this morning that there were five of our men lying dead in the hospital. There was only one from Company G in the hospital and he was very sick, John D. Williams.

The middle of May found us still prisoners and without hope of release. "What will the future be?" Yesterday another body of about three hundred secesh came into camp. They had no arms, only knapsacks, haversacks and canteens. Next morning some of the new troops were on guard. This meant the men who had guarded us were going to the front and these raw recruits were to take their places. This morning the rumor spread through the prison that Richmond was captured with an army of prisoners. We cheered lustily, but did not believe the story. It made us feel good to cheer at such news although the rumor had been repeated so often it was stale.

My weight by the commissary scales was one hundred and forty-nine. I knew that was wrong. I never weighed more than one hundred and forty-five and I was much lighter now than usual. The scales were doctored to make our rations hold out. We received notice today we would get no more bread for two days, claiming we had overdrawn our allowance. There was no help for it. It was a matter that could not be arbitrated nor even debated. Their word was law unto us. The Commissary or the baker had cheated us and we were the sufferers.

There was a funeral service held over the five who died last night. I was too unwell to go, but those who went spoke highly of the sermon.

May 16th. Three more men died in the hospital last night. This was getting to an alarming stage. At this rate there would soon be none left to either parole or exchange. Last night one of the guards challenged what he supposed to be a prisoner approaching the line. The object did not halt and the guard fired at it. The corporal of the guard came and the sentry told him he had shot a prisoner. But the corporal could not find the body. This morning the officers felt sure some of our men had escaped. Therefore they called us into line and had the roll called twice. This did not satisfy them so they put us all on one side of a line and caused each man to cross to the other side as his name was called. But the boys crowded so close to the line to see what was going on that some must have gone back unobserved for it was said the tally showed four more than they thought they had. However this may be, our boys were pretty sure two or more of our men passed their lines last night.

May 17th. Three more men dead in the hospital this morning. The wonderful mortality was not so strange after all. These men inhaled the seeds of death while in the prison pen at Cahaba. The foul meat that had been served us here but added to their trouble. It was not strange so many died. It was more strange so many of us lived. When captured I had but fifteen cents in money. Five cents of that I gave for a small cup of milk while at Cahaba. Today I bought two Confederate postage stamps at five cents each. With one stamp I sent one letter to the surgeon in charge of the prison hospital at Cahaba to learn what had become of Espy McKune, and the other stamp I enclosed that he might send his reply. This letter I handed unsealed to Major Rylander who was in command here. He read the letter and consented to its going on its mission. It looked to us that we might be moved from here and that soon and it might be to our own lines. So I was anxious to get word from McKune if possible before we moved. We hoped to hear of his recovery.

May 18th. There was much excitement in camp. Major Rylander told us that our government absolutely refused to exchange prisoners and the Confederate government would not parole us. Therefore he asked us all to sign a paper stating that if it was impossible for him to get us a parole we would then take the oath not to bear arms against the Confederacy again. Many of our boys were willing to do this. They argued that at the present death rate we would soon all be dead and therefore of no account to our country, while by taking the oath we could go home and be a help in civil life at least. None of our Mess will sign any such paper. We had enlisted for three years service and the emergency, though great, was not sufficient cause for breaking our oath to our country. We were doing all we could with the other boys to prevent their signing this paper. The future was not bright and many were very homesick, therefore could be led to do what they would not think of doing under other circumstances. Fifteen of ours boys were so excited over the matter that they signed their names to a blank sheet of paper and gave it to the major to fill out with any kind of oath he pleased if he would only let them go home. The majority of the boys were firm in refusing to take the oath they asked, and unless we all took the oath they would give it to none. One of the men who guarded us on the boat from Mobile to Cahaba was here today. We recognized each other at once and enjoyed some conversation together. Was unable to get any news from him although he was very friendly.

May 19th. Major told our boys again that there was not the least chance for getting us paroled. This was as he believed it but we hoped something would turn up to our advantage. It did seem hard that we should be held here to starve and to die as prisoners on the technical point that to exchange prisoners with the Confederacy would be recognizing their belligerency. They are belligerent and that we know. It seems if our officers in the field had exchanged us it would have been justified but our government must not do so. If this policy had been continued it would have caused the death of thousands of our soldiers. But the government at Washington knew best and we loyally abode by its decisions. We began to have hopes the government might push an army through the south and thus relieve us. We also learned that Governor Brown of Georgia refused to allow the Confederacy to conscript men in his state, on the ground that the government had no authority to compel people of a state to go to war against their choice. State rights carried out. So we were likely to have a counter rebellion in Georgia.

May 20th, 1862. This morning we were called into line to listen to orders. The major read the following order "All prisoners captured at Shiloh, except commissioned and noncommissioned officers, shall be at once paroled not to bear arms against the Confederacy until legally exchanged. The officers to be held as hostages for the fulfillment of the parole by the privates. By order of General G. T. Beauregard." This order he assumed to issue because he was in command when we were captured. We were his prisoners. This did for the men what we wanted but it left all officers, and I was one, as hostages. Well, I resolved I would escape if possible. If I failed I failed, nevertheless I would try. My chevrons I had worn and when we were threatened with punishment as non-commissioned officers I still felt proud of them and thought I never would part with them. But now I removed them from my blouse and intended to try to pass as a private soldier. If I had escaped through the prison guard and could get a citizen's suit of clothes I certainly would put off my uniform and don the citizen's suit. It seemed to me the cases were alike. If I could get out of this I intended to go.

That afternoon we were formed into line and passed the mustering officers. They made what was called a complete description roll of us, taking the name, regiment, company, state, age, place of birth, occupation, height, color of hair, eyes, etc. As it neared my turn they asked every man if he was a private. But when it came to me I was asked the other questions but not that one. It made no difference for I intended to say I was a private for I had fully resigned my position when I removed my chevrons that morning. I was not alone in this. A number of our non-commissioned officers did the same thing. Sergeant McMaken of Company K, a very dear friend of mine, would not do it. He said he could not act a lie even to save his life. He was glad I went but he could not do it. There were a number of others who did not go. When asked if he escaped the guard would he use a citizen's suit if he could get it, he said he certainly would, but thought this was different. Many of the men thought the major had us marked and would take us out before we got out of the grounds. But we resolved to go out as far as we could.

May 21st. Finished the descriptive roll and were copying it into other books. It was said we were to go next Friday. The camp was always full of rumors. This evening the great rumor was that the Confederate government had countermanded the order of General Beauregard to parole us. This made many of the boys who were so elated this morning very blue tonight.

May 22nd. Yesterday evening we drew at the rate of a loaf of bread to seven men to last twenty-four hours. This was scant enough for one meal. We had a little rice upon which we could make one meal and had no knowledge of how the third meal was to be provided.

Friday, May 23rd. 1862. Today we were called into line and told they had lost a part of the rolls they had made so we would have to be mustered again. It seemed that some of our boys, probably a non-commissioned officer, had stolen the rolls and destroyed them, or the officers did it themselves so that more of the officers would enroll. Let that be as it may, we again passed muster and many who had stood aloof before were now anxious to enroll, among them my friend McMaken.

This time the rolls were completed and we were told to be ready to start at five o'clock tomorrow morning. Bright and early we were all ready to go but were not called till six o'clock in the morning, May 24th. 1862. As we approached the gate we were halted in squads of ten or twelve and raised our right hands and repeated after an officer the following oath: "*You and each of you do solemnly swear that you will not take up arms against the Confederate States of America, nor aid in conspiring against them in any manner until you are exchanged or otherwise honorably discharged from this obligation.*" This was nothing but a straight parole and we took it willingly. Then we passed through the gate on our way to liberty.

Soon we were in box cars and speeding to the north. There was not a man challenged or sent back but everyone that tried went out. There were over fifty more names on the second roll than were on the one lost or stolen. At eight o'clock we were on our way to Chattanooga, near which city it was expected we would meet our men. Passed through Jonesboro and arrived at Atlanta at one o'clock in the afternoon. Soon another train came in with paroled prisoners from Tuscaloosa. Jack Moyer, one of our Company, was on this train. They would not let him come on our train, but we talked with him. His suffering had been much worse than ours. He was quite weak and looked half starved. Left Atlanta at seven o'clock in the evening. The cars were so crowded they were very uncomfortable. Not room to lie down. It was very tiresome and the road being very rough made it still more distressing. It was a mountainous country and we passed through many tunnels and over many bridges, all of which were guarded by rebel soldiers. This would indicate we were nearing our lines.

Sunday morning, May 25th. We were still among the mountains. Saw many large vineyards planted on the steep hill sides. Also orchards of peaches, apples and pears. This fruit growing was very extensive here. Arrived at Chattanooga at eight o'clock this morning. Remained on the cars about an hour, then we were run out of town to a cotton shed and disembarked. They carefully counted us and held us somewhat loosely under guard.

Chattanooga was situated in the valley of the Tennessee. The ground was pretty rolling where the city was built but the place we were taken to was quite flat. From where we were the ground stretches off in a level plain to the foot of the Lookout Mountain. They claim this mountain rises three thousand feet above the plain, but from where we were it looked like a high ridge with no semblance of a mountain peak. The side next us was covered with timber to near the top where there seems to be a perpendicular face of rock to the top. This rock face we learn was from fifty to several hundred feet high. In the timber on the mountain side you see numerous white houses nestling among the green trees which adds much to the appearance.

This afternoon twenty-eight men were set apart as cooks for the prisoners. At five o'clock in the afternoon they called the roll and gave us very sad bread and very good beef. From this our cooks managed to prepare us a very good supper. Here a man joined us who had been left at Memphis, sick. He told us Wilson was a very sick man but when he left there three weeks before he was getting better. Also a man who had been left at Mobile told us that Robert Clark died soon after we left there. This was the first one to die from among the boys of North Tama. Some of our boys saw McKune on another train at Atlanta and talked with him. He was in pretty good health. I never received an answer to the letter I wrote the hospital surgeon about him. Probably the surgeon knew he was about to be paroled. We now hoped to have him with us in a few days, at least as soon as we got to our lines.

Monday, May 26th. Called into line at seven o'clock and drew what they called a half ration. That was half as much as was allotted as a ration and about two hundred of us were marched back through the city to the river and went aboard the steamer "*Point Rock*". We were told we were to go down the river to some point where a bridge had been destroyed. There we were to be landed on the north side of the river and the boat was to ferry the rest of our boys across the river, they to be sent there by railroad. As soon as we left the city we swung around the foot of Lookout Mountain over what was called Moccasin Bend. We had a much better view of the mountain than from the camp. The side next the river was one abrupt rise of nearly three thousand feet and as near perpendicular as possible. Soon we came to the shoals or rapids. The river has a great fall here and the water runs very rapidly. There are many large rocks in the stream and it was somewhat difficult to steer the boat clear of them. At one time we ran so close between two large rocks, one of them entirely submerged, that the water recoiled in a great wave over the boiler deck. It certainly was dangerous boating. The Tennessee is a beautiful river and the mountain scenery is grand. The river seems to have cut its way through this ridge of mountains, forming a deep channel very tortuous and with a very swift current. On the mountain sides there was sometimes a little farm opened and a house built. Sometimes high up among the clouds and again near the water's edge. Very little level or bottom land. Oak, ash, hickory, maple, pine and sycamore timber gave the landscape a variety of shades and colors, and as the mountain ranges arose one above the other the scenery was picturesque and grand.

After traveling down the river about four hours we came to a more level country. The river was much wider and not nearly so rapid. Passed Bridgeport in the evening. The bridge here had been destroyed. This was not the place we were to land, for we passed by and traveled probably thirty miles farther down the river and then the boat tied up for the night. The boatman told us we were not far from a place called Bellefont. We went ashore to sleep. Some of us found an old wagon box and slept in it. It was a very comfortable bed after what we had been having.

Called on board early next morning and started up stream again. Ran about three miles and came to an island in the middle of the river and were landed on this island and the boat went down the river again. They said they went to meet some of our officers who were coming to receive us. They would be back by eleven o'clock. The island was nearly a mile long and narrow. There was some cultivated land on it but it was mostly heavy timbered, the trees festooned with gray moss. Some part was covered with cane reeds as thick on the ground as they could stand and ten to thirty feet high. There was some corn in a rail pen which the boys parched in two large dripping pans they got from the boat. This parched corn in a sense satisfied our hunger. Remember we left Chattanooga the day before with but a half ration. We were on the island this day and the next day we arrived in our lines in the evening. Three days on a half day's ration.

The boat came back after noon with no news from the Union lines. Soon after we saw some men come to the bank on the north side of the river who called to us. We got aboard the boat and went across to them. They were some of our men who had left us when landed below, the day before, and a lieutenant from General Mitchel's division, which was now at Huntsville, Alabama. To say we were glad to see this man would be putting it mildly. Everybody wanted to shake hands with him and ask him a hundred questions. He said he had a squad of men on the railroad about six miles from here; that he heard we were here and came over to see us. He also said that General Mitchel knew we were coming and would send cars to carry us to Huntsville. The cars would probably be here tomorrow morning. There was but six miles for us to march and we would be with our men. Many of the boys wanted to go at once to the railroad but this the guards would not permit until our officers were there to receive us. It seemed that neither army occupied this territory but small parties of each traversed it occasionally. Some coffee and parched corn for supper. Not much hungry for food only hungry to get to our lines at once.

It was cold at night on the river bank and we had no blankets and scant clothing, and some one proposed we climb up the mountain to a higher and warmer climate. So a number of us ascended the mountain and when we found a nice level plateau covered with a growth of young cedar trees we lay down and slept comfortably till morning. When we got back to the other boys next morning McClaury had some hard-tack and Stoakes some corn bread. Upon this we made our breakfast.

Soon the boys began striking out for Bellefont. A few at first, then more and more till finally we were all on the move. There were some rebel officers and a few of the guards went with us to transfer us to our officers where we met them and get proper receipts for us. The town of Bellefont was about three miles from the river and it was three more to the station on the railroad of the same name. The people of the town heard we were coming and were in a starving condition. They sent word throughout the adjacent country last night to have people bring in what eatables they could and many of the citizens of the town were up all night cooking and preparing for us. In the morning when the first of our boys arrived at the town they found plenty of eatables, but by the time we arrived the place was pretty well cleaned out. One lady gave McClaury her last cup of coffee and others of us a small piece of bread and butter each. She said it was all she had but there was more farther on in town. We went on to where they were dividing some more rations among the boys. Here they gave us a small piece of bread and pork, each very small. An ordinarily hungry man could have eaten what they gave to ten or fifteen of us. While the people of the town were rank secesh they did the very best they could to supply our wants. They were also very kind in their language to us. We then went on to the railroad station. There was no train there so there was nothing for us to do but wait. The depot had been burned some time before and there was only a farm house standing near.

Waiting was monotonous and when the sun had long passed the meridian and still no cars, the boys began to manifest a restlessness. There were a number of shoats weighing sixty or seventy pounds each running about where we were and one of the boys caught one of the shoats and killed it. In a few minutes it was nicely dressed and hung on the limb of a tree. Then the boys gathered wood and built fires. There were large pieces of sheet iron about five by eight feet that had been burned in the depot building and were much crinkled. They laid two of these upon the fires. Soon every depression in this iron became a little frying pan containing a bit of fresh pork which was being nicely browned in its own grease. Probably this was as convenient a frying pan as was ever produced in a time of emergency. The frying and eating did not cease until several of the pigs yielded up their bodies to sustain the Union cause.

Near evening we heard the low rumble of the approaching train and after awhile a far distant whistle. Again the noise of the train coming nearer. It was wonderful how among the hills and valleys the sound would sometimes seem so near and again die out till you heard nothing. Again a sharp whistle near the headland of the valley and every voice was hushed and every eye was strained on the point where the rails turned about the jutting hill and were lost to view. The sound of the train drew near the point where all our attention was centered. With another wild shriek of its whistle the locomotive burst into view. The sun was low in the west as the locomotive came into view in the northeast, half a mile away. On one bow floated a small white flag; on the other, our own flag, the beautiful Stars and Stripes. As they struck the sunlight all the beauty of the flag was brought to view. At the first sight the boys made no sound of joy. Men leaned forward and stretched out both hands as if to grasp its resplendent folds. For a time all was still as death and then a mighty shout of joy from every throat of these who wore the blue. Shout on shout and cheer on cheer till it made the very mountains quake. Men hugged each other, pounded each other, wrestled with each other; turned summersets and hand springs and in every conceivable way manifested their joy. You will remember the last American flag we had seen was the one the rebel soldiers were dragging in the mud at Shiloh two months before this. This was its spirit resurrected coming to give us freedom from the jaws of death. When the train rolled up to our ground and stopped the boys overpowered each other to touch the flag, to hug the fireman and engineer and every man aboard the train. But quiet was restored, the roll was called and as each man answered to his name he marched over to the Union side of the lines a free man.

PRISON LIFE - Notes:

-- The Tennessee born volunteer who was executed by the rebels at Corinth, was **William C Roland** of Lawrenceburg Tennessee, a town east of the Shiloh battlefield. In the roster of Company H he is listed as "Rolan". The roster says he was "Killed in action April 6 1862 Shiloh Tennessee". His two companions, both born in Tennessee, both of Lawrenceburg, and who both enlisted into Company H, were: **George W Shaffer** (Chaffer) 18 and **Samuel Simon Todd** 21. As Grant's army assembled at Pittsburg Landing, Union loyalists in the area came in to volunteer to aid the effort to put down the rebellion. As Southern men enlisting into the Union army, they faced much greater risks if captured than their companions from Iowa. All three of these brave and loyal men enlisted into the 14th Iowa on March 28 1862 a week before the Shiloh battle. Shaffer and Todd were listed as missing in action; both men survived their time as prisoners of war. Shaffer later mustered out with the regiment November 1864 at Davenport Iowa while Todd continued to serve in the 14th's Residuary Battalion until late March 1865. With the Union restored both men returned to Lawrenceburg to farm.
-- The Lieutenant Colonel of the Confederate 55th Tennessee was Wiley M Reed who later assumed command of the 5th Mississippi under Forrest; Reed (Thomas spelled this name "Reade" and "Reede") was killed during the April 1864 battle at Fort Pillow.
-- The two wounded men from Iowa who BF Thomas helped were probably **Corporal Robert H Kirkpatrick** 21 of Vinton, and **Adjutant Nathaniel E Duncan** 25 of Dubuque. Kirkpatrick enlisted into Company B, 8th Iowa Infantry and was wounded and captured at Shiloh April 6 1862. He survived the POW experience and served until 1864. Duncan was appointed Adjutant of the 12th Iowa, was missing in battle April 6 1862 at Shiloh, and mustered out November 1864.
-- **William T McMaken** 30 of Company K from Middleton survived the War and mustered out with the regiment. See Chapter 1
-- Among those men who died just prior to the parole were 18 year old **Burtis M Gard** of Company H and **Hiram Turner** 24 of Company I. Gard, who was from Wyoming, Jones County, died on May 15, while Turner, from Agency, Wapello County, died on May 19.
-- The unnamed Company G boy in the cracker barrel at Mobile may have been **James Fox** 17 of Toledo. He enlisted as a drummer and was the shortest man in the regiment at five foot two. He had dark hair, dark eyes and had a dark complexion. As small as he was, he survived the winter illnesses, the marching, the fierce fight at Shiloh, the rigors of captivity in Georgia, and served out his full three year term of service. He seems to have been resourceful, energetic and a hard worker, skilled at making harnesses and saddles, and later as a wheelwright, carpenter and blacksmith. At both Benton Barracks and Columbus Kentucky Fox temporarily

left his company duties to be employed by the Post Quartermasters who were then reluctant to allow him to return to normal duty. The roster states that James Fox was born in Maine, but so far no other records have been found on him, both before or after his time as a soldier, hinting perhaps that he had enlisted underage without his parents' permission under an assumed name. Perhaps that is also why Thomas does not name him here, keeping his friend's secret.

-- **Martin Grubbs** 18 from Tama County survived this period of captivity after Shiloh. Despite chronic illness he stayed with the Company afterwards but died in November 1864 just ten days before his three year term of service was to end. He is buried in Jefferson Barracks National Cemetery St. Louis. **Robert Fitch** 18 of Redman, Tama County, was a neighbor of Jacob Overturf and Lieutenant Eccles. Robert survived his time as a POW but was discharged in December 1862 debilitated by lingering illness. **Jackson R Moyer** 19 of Tama County and **Turner McLain** 19 of Nevada both lived to muster out with the regiment in November 1864 at the end of their three years. **Joseph Burright** 28 and his brothers **Stewart Burright** 26 and **Cornelius Burright** 19, all from Tama County, had enlisted together as musicians in October 1861; all three served until November 1864 but only Joseph was captured at Shiloh.

-- **David Miller** 20 of Toledo died May 27 1862 at Montgomery, Alabama while still being held as a POW. Hospitalized at Montgomery, he must have been too ill to leave with the others. He died within a day or two after the others departed to go north. The location of David's grave is not known; Miller and Robert Clark may both be buried in Andersonville National Cemetery marked as "Unknown".

-- **John D Williams** 19 of Benton County, died at Macon Georgia of pneumonia the same day David Miller died on May 27 1862, and under the same circumstances as a POW. He seems to have been left behind while the rest were paroled. He may have been too sick to even attempt parole. Williams was one of the men at Donelson who bravely volunteered to retrieve the body of Tom Snelling despite the heavy enemy fire. He is buried in Andersonville National Cemetery, Site 13258.

-- The first of the ten messmates to die, **Robert Clark**, died of illness, as a POW, in Mobile Alabama probably on May 5 1862. Some sources say May 15. His true burial place is unknown but his name appears on a headstone shared with his parents at LaPorte City Iowa.

CHAPTER VI

HOMEWARD BOUND

When all were accounted for our officers gave a receipt for the number checked off and we boarded the flat cars and soon were on our way to Huntsville. The train was heavily loaded and frequently came to grades where the locomotive failed to pull it. Then we on the flat cars would get off and push the train over the grade. This was repeated several times. We seemed to crawl along so slow and were in such a hurry. Soon we came to where the bridges and water tanks were guarded which taught us we were now within the Union lines. The troops scattered here as guards were of the Tenth Wisconsin.

Arrived at Huntsville at seven o'clock in the evening, May 28th. Did not leave the cars for sometime after our arrival. Then we were formed into line and marched into the city. They would march to an empty building and take from the head of the column as many as the building would hold, then march the remainder to another building. This was done several times and as we were near the rear end of the column we were marched and countermarched till we were tired. So when we came to a smooth flagstone pavement beside a house and sheltered by large catalpa trees we laid down on the smooth stones and slept there till morning. We were somewhat disturbed by citizens awaking us and admonishing us to get in some place or we would catch our death of cold sleeping in the open air. Little they knew that this was the most comfortable place we had slept in for two months.

Southwick and McClaury were both quite sick when we arrived here and were taken directly to the hospital.

Huntsville was a city of about six thousand people. It was built upon high rolling ground and had many very substantial buildings, and much manufacturing was done. There was a very large spring gushing out of the rocks at the foot of a bluff some fifty feet below the level of the city. Two rods from the bluff was a dam four feet high where was situated a hydraulic ram that forced the water up the bluff and into the third story of the houses for the city's use. The stream that flowed to waste over the dam was two rods wide and twenty inches deep and flowed very swiftly.

Thursday, May 29th, 1862. This morning we were collected in the court house square and full rations issued to us. In fact the rations were set out and each one helped himself to what he wanted. Just think of it. All we could eat and all we could carry away. After breakfast we were marched off in squads of about sixty men each and each squad taken to a separate regiment for them to care for during our stay here. About this time we missed Stoakes. He had gone no one knew where. Our squad was sent quite a distance out of the city to the Third Ohio regiment to dwell with them. When we arrived at their camp there sat Stoakes among them. One company of the Third Ohio was raised at Stoakes' old home in Ohio. He chanced to meet one of the boys he knew in the city and went to camp with him, and chance sent us to the same camp to tarry. They received us very kindly and made everything pleasant for us as best they could.

May 30th. Felter and I went to the city to learn how our sick boys were. Southwick was quite bad. He could keep nothing on his stomach and looked very pale and thin. McClaury was better. Felter and I took dinner at the hospital. I noticed we could still appreciate a good dinner. The male citizens of Huntsville were at home. In most towns they all left when our troops came. While they were here they were also almost unanimously secesh. There was much wealth here and it was a fair country to look upon. When we arrived at camp we found we had orders to be at the depot at four o'clock in the morning. The Third Ohio boys cooked our food at night so we might be prepared to go in the morning. They are splendid fellows. They entered the service before we did and have marched more than two thousand miles and have never been in battle, while we have scarcely marched any and have fought two heavy battles and spent two months in prison. Soon after this the Third Ohio was in the battle of Perryville, Kentucky, and lost many of their men.

Did not get to the depot till five o'clock and were then two hours too early. Several trains were there with engines fired up and we supposed we were going on the cars. But about seven o'clock we were ordered into line and stood in the hot sun for an hour and a half and then started on foot for Nashville. We now learned what to us was a very sad piece of news. When we came to Chattanooga General Mitchel was at Nashville. The rebels sent word to Huntsville that we were there on parole and wished to be received into our lines. The officer in command ordered that we be received. But General Mitchel came back to Huntsville before all our men were transferred and immediately rejected the agreement. So the rest of the paroled men, including McKune, were returned to Macon, Georgia. The excuse he gave was that he was about to make an advance upon Chattanooga and if he received the paroled prisoners they would consume his supplies and thereby frustrate his plans. It was an act of kindness in the rebel General Beauregard to parole us when his government would not release us. It was a most heartless act in General Mitchel to reject the men when they were at his lines to be received. McKune died soon after being returned to Macon. But such also would have been our fate had General Mitchel been at Huntsville one day sooner. It was current among his men that he cared for their lives not a straw so he could gratify his own ambition.

So we started on the long tramp from Huntsville across the state to Nashville. We were not alone. The Tenth Ohio under command of Colonel Moore of Cincinnati was with us as guards for a long wagon train, one hundred and eighty-six wagons, loaded with cotton bales. The sick and starved boys walked and the cotton was hauled. General Mitchel made his boasts that he captured enough cotton to pay the expense of his command. This he did at the expense of the lives of his men. Men's lives counted as nothing to him. Bales of cotton represented money.

My eyes had been very sore for sometime. One of the boys always walked with me to guide me as I could hardly see to walk.

The first day we marched about seventeen miles and camped on the banks of a small stream which furnished good water. Sunday morning the bugle sounded at half past one o'clock and we started to march at half past three. Colonel Moore had a great fear of being attacked by General Morgan at the crossing of Elk River. But we passed it safely. At Elkton we struck an excellent graveled pike. The country we had passed over was broken and the road rough, uneven and stony. But this turnpike was splendid for marching. We understood this pike led to Columbia, Tennessee. This afternoon our protectors were badly frightened at some cavalry they saw at a distance. But before they got the train corralled so as to resist the attack they discovered the cavalry to be a scouting party sent out by our men at Pulaski. We marched till eight o'clock in the evening and camped within three miles of Pulaski, having marched seventeen hours. Our boys were not used to this and got very tired and sore.

It rained some during the night and next morning the bugle sounded at two o'clock but we did not march till five. Stoakes, Felter and I started ahead of the column and after we had gone the order was given for all who were sick and unable to walk to get into the wagons. Of course we did not have the order. Soon we reached Pulaski where the soldiers gave us a hearty welcome. Their band came out and played several patriotic airs and everything was done to make us welcome. When we knew there were many of our boys riding in the wagons, Stoakes asked the wagon master if I might ride. He said he had given orders for all unable to walk to get in the wagons that morning and if I did not avail myself of the privilege at that time it was now too late. So we trudged along some two or three miles and I told the boys I could go no farther, for them to go on and I would go back to Pulaski and stay there till my eyes got better. As we talked a teamster stopped and asked what the matter was. They told him and he said to get right into his wagon. I told him I might get him into trouble because of what the wagon master said at Pulaski. But he said to get right in and be still and the wagon master would not know but that I got on in the morning. So the boys helped me up into the big wagon where I rode the rest of the day.

In the evening the boys came for me and took me to where they had camped. The camp was in a beautiful beech grove. The largest beech trees I ever saw and the most perfect. There was some rain in the evening. In the night there came a very heavy rain. The beech trees made so complete a shelter that it rained quite awhile before the water came through the branches and leaves, but when it came through it poured down in torrents. The ground we were camped on was nearly level and was soon covered with water. Poor exhausted men. Some stood shivering in the rain; others more exhausted lying even in the water. We probably suffered as much that night as we ever did during the service. There was no shelter or protection for us. One man died during the storm. When the storm subsided, we, wet and chilled to the bone, tried to start fires again, for the fires had been extinguished by the rain. After much maneuvering the fires were again ablaze and we gathered about them to dry our clothes and warm our bodies. We were probably as forlorn a set of creatures as was ever seen.

After breakfast we marched to Columbia, a distance of eight miles. We had marched from Huntsville to Columbia in just about three days, and the distance is eighty miles. Not hard marching for men in good condition, but very severe on us. Colonel Moore made a short speech to us before leaving. He congratulated us on the speed we made in our march and invited us if ever we came to Cincinnati to call upon him. But our feelings toward him were not of a pleasant nature. We felt that we had not been treated with the consideration men should receive in the condition we were in. We were sure we had seen all of him we wanted to see.

Took the cars here in the evening and went to Nashville. When we arrived there they took us to the fair ground and gave us the amphitheater for quarters. It was a very open building. In fact, only the floor and roof. Remained several days in the fair ground. Plenty of spring water and good rations. Then we were moved to an open field some distance south of the city, and occupied tents. We received rations and clothing but were closely guarded in our camp. Difficult to get passes to the city.

Stoakes, Felter and I got a pass one day and spent the day sight seeing. Saw the house President James K. Polk had lived in. He is buried in the front lawn where a handsome monument is erected to his memory. We were invited into the lawn to see the grave. While there his widow came from the house to go to her carriage. She very kindly saluted us as she passed. The lawn was not large but contained many beautiful evergreens, foliage, trees, plants, flowers and statuary. A sparkling fountain adds much to the beauty of the landscape. Visited the State House and there saw Governor Andrew Johnson who was afterward President of the United States. He was in the Governor's room and was entertaining visitors.

Met an old citizen on the street who talked to us and something of a crowd that gathered about. He was a Union man. He said, "The day will come when Lincoln's name will he held in equal reverence with that of Washington." It did us good to hear the old man talk so loyally when we knew a large majority of the people there were secesh. The old gentleman took us to a restaurant and treated us to a dinner. We knew not his name but he was a noble patriot.

In camp our boys were very ill natured. Suppose it was because of the starvation we had had and the treatment we were having. Fights were of very frequent occurrence with them. The smallest grievance produces a combat. They hurt each other but little, and a fight did not leave them bitter enemies. There was much stress used by the authorities to induce us to enlist in a Tennessee regiment. They told us our parole made no difference. That it was obtained of us by coercion and therefore was not binding. That we never would be recognized in case we were captured again. They seemed to forget that there was no chance of our being exchanged or paroled had it not been for the kindness of heart of General Beauregard. That in accepting his kindness we took the oath of parole and in honor to ourselves must stand by our contract. As soon as President Lincoln knew we were paroled he sent orders for us to go home and stay till we were exchanged. This order the authorities here had ignored and held us virtually as prisoners. We had tried to get news of our condition to the Adjutant General of Iowa, General Baker, but supposed we had failed. If he had known how matters were he would have made things howl. We had been here now near twenty days and there was not as much chance of getting away as when we first came.

June 19th. Felter and I were down to the city again and went down to the wharf to see what chance there was of getting away on a boat unobserved by guards. We found the little steamer "*Hazel Dell*" would start down the river the next day. Asked the captain if he would carry us down to Smithland, which was at the mouth of the Cumberland. We offered him a silver watch to carry the three of us there. He said he did not want the watch. We were disappointed for we had not a cent of money to offer him. As we turned away another man proposed to take the watch and pay our fare to Smithland. We had told them who we were and why we were going and that we would have to avoid the provost guards. The captain said he would start at noon the next day; for us to come on some time in the forenoon and conceal ourselves among the freight till the boat started. Well, we went back to camp full of joy at the prospect of going home. But when we laid our plan before Stoakes he refused to go. He thought we had better wait till they sent us home. But after much coaxing he finally concluded to go with us for we would not go without him.

We slipped away from camp and went to the city next morning and concealed ourselves on the boat. At noon the boat pushed out from shore and started down the river. As soon as the motion of the boat assured us we were off we came out to see the sights. We passed the city limits and came to where a railroad bridge had been destroyed. The pier that stood near the middle of the river was torn down something like a foot below the surface of the water. There was a dredge boat working in the river some distance above this pier. Our boat passed the dredge and then attempted to cross the other side of the pier. For some cause the turn was not made soon enough and the prow of the boat struck the sunken pier with full force. The shock nearly threw us off our feet and the deck waved like water. The boat struck fast on the rocks and all the power of reversed wheels and prod poles would not start her off. They then took a large rope to the north bank of the river and fastened it to a tree and with the capstan of the boat driven by a donkey engine tried to pull her off. At ten o'clock they were still working with the capstan and the boat still lay on the rocks.

We went to bed and the next morning awoke to find our boat tied up at the wharf we left the day before at noon. The hull of the boat was damaged so it must be repaired before proceeding down the river. We kept ourselves in close quarters till the boat was repaired and started again, which was near evening the same day. Our plan was to land at Smithland, cross to the Illinois side of the Ohio and walk to the Illinois Central Railroad which we thought to be not more than twenty miles. When we reached the railroad we expected to sell the other watch we had for enough money to carry us to Clinton, Iowa, to General Baker's presence. We understood that soldiers traveled at half fare. The Cumberland River was very low and although our little boat drew but twenty-six inches of water, she was on a sand bar more than half the time. In fact, at times when the boat was stuck near the shore we left her and went in search of blackberries, knowing if she got off the bar she was on she would soon stick again.

I became acquainted with a passenger who had been to Nashville to see after a wounded nephew. The man lived near where I was born in Ohio and knew many of my relatives there. As we neared Smithland he asked me how we were off for money, because I had told him we had just come out of prison. I told him the whole story. We had no money. Had two watches when we started. Gave one to pay our passage to Smithland and thought the other would pay our way at half rates to Clinton. The watch was easily worth twenty-five dollars. The next day he broached the matter to me again. Said we could not sell the watch for enough money to get to Iowa but he would loan us sufficient to get to Clinton. Asked how much I thought we needed. I thought ten dollars in addition to the watch would do, but he said it was not enough and gave me twenty dollars and said he thought I had better take more yet. But I felt sure this was plenty.

We were over three days going from Nashville to the mouth of the river when we should have done it in less than one. We passed Fort Donelson and were surprised to see everything in such good repair. When we were there before the river was very high, and now it was very low. It did not look like the same stream. The water battery was far up the side of the bluff and the fort itself seemed much higher than it was when we were there before. The Stripes and Stars floated from the flag staff. We gave a hearty cheer at sight of the old fort. Just below the fort was a line of barges across the river filled with stone and sunk so as to prevent the passage of a boat. It seemed to us the river was too high for this to have obstructed our gunboats at the time of the battle. But this may have partly aided the rebels in repulsing them. One of the barges had been swung around so as to let boats pass between. This we suppose was done after the fort was captured.

At Smithland we bade the captain goodbye and also Mr. Murray who had so kindly befriended us. We started down the river. After going some distance we employed a man with a skiff to carry us across to the Illinois side of the river. We had drawn extra clothing at Nashville and gave this man a pair of pants to carry us over. When we started he laid two guns by his side. He said he had an enemy on the other side who said he should never come ashore there again. So he took his guns along to enforce a landing if necessary. But no enemy appeared and we landed in safety. We then started for the railroad. But whatever road we took we soon found it was either taking us to Golconda, a town on the Ohio above Smithland, or to Metropolis, a town on the Ohio below Smithland. We could not account for every road leading to the Ohio River till we stopped at a farm house where they told us we were in a great bend of the river and would pass through a neck between Golconda and Metropolis and that the two towns were not far apart, but one above the other below us on the same river. We would have been much nearer the railroad had we remained on the boat till we came to Golconda. When asked how far it was to the railroad we were told it was fully sixty miles. The people were very kind to us and invited us to stay over night with them, which we did.

Next morning Felter was quite sick so we were unable to move till afternoon. Our marching was slow but we kept it up that afternoon and the next day. In the evening Felter was much worse and next morning we were obliged to employ a man to take his team and wagon and carry us to the railroad. It was about thirty miles to the railroad and we gave him the other watch and he was to give us ten dollars to boot. He left the watch at home and when we got to the railroad he had no money to pay us the boot so the watch went to pay the trip. When we arrived at the station the agent could not sell us tickets at half rates. No agent north of Cairo had that power. We were forty miles from Cairo. We consulted and decided we would save some money by buying tickets back to Cairo and there getting half rates out again. There was also a chance of getting a boat and going up the Mississippi River which would be much cheaper. So we went to Cairo. At Cairo we found all traffic on the river closed. They said there might be a boat next day and might not be one for a week or more.

We saw notices posted everywhere that no person was allowed to leave the city without a pass from the provost marshal. So we went to the provost for passes. We intended telling the provost who we were and how we came to be there and taking our chances on being detained because we had no furloughs. But when we went in to his office I stepped up to the desk and asked for three passes to carry us to Toledo, Iowa. He was writing at the time and without looking up asked if either one was a non-commissioned officer. I told him I was a corporal. He asked my name, and wrote: "Pass Corporal B. F. Thomas and two men to Toledo, Iowa." He asked no questions and I volunteered no information. We went to the ticket office and I fell into line to take turns in getting tickets. There was a soldier two or three ahead of me who laid down his papers and they gave him a ticket without his giving money. I immediately left the line and followed this man. As soon as I could I addressed him and told him what I had seen and asked how he got such a pass. He asked to see my pass. I showed it to him and he said I should have asked for a pass with transportation. I asked where he got his and he said of the provost. So back to the provost I went and told him I wanted passes with transportation. He looked up at me from where he sat at the desk and said, "If you get a pass with transportation we must charge the transportation on your furlough and you will pay it the next time you draw pay. It will make you more bother and save you nothing." As soon as he mentioned furlough I knew all about it and thanking him bade him good day. I went back to the boys and told them what had occurred. Then I went to the ticket window and laid out all our money and told the agent to give us tickets as far up the road as that would reach. He made some figures and gave us the tickets and soon we were on the cars, but before starting the guards came in and examined everybody's pass.

Going up the road Felter told us if we had tickets one station farther we would be at Sublette, and Dr. Adams, who owned land near father Felter's, lived there, and father Felter was his agent. If we could get there we could get means to go home. We told the conductor and he told us to stay on the train till we came to Sublette. The doctor was very glad to see us when he found out who we were and had us take dinner with him and furnished us plenty of money to carry us home.

Arrived at Clinton just at sunrise Sunday morning, June 29, 1862. Inquired for General Baker's office. No one in at this early hour. Found one of his clerks at the hotel. He directed us to General Baker's residence. He lived on top the bluff just out of the city. Arrived at his house and found him sitting on a lawn chair in his front yard. Saluted him and began to tell our story. Only began when he jumped to his feet and grasped us warmly by the hands and gave us a rousing welcome. Then he had us tell him all about how matters were with the boys at Nashville. When we told him how they tried to have us enlist in Tennessee regiments he stamped and swore like a mad-man. He said he had begun to suspect something of the kind because even after he had secured orders from the Secretary of War to have us sent to Iowa we failed to come. Now, he said, that he knew their game he would see to it that the boys were sent home at once. We talked with him an hour or more, then he wrote a note to give the clerk at the office. The note directed him to take us to the hotel, get our breakfast, keep us there till Monday morning, (there was no train leaving there on Sunday) and then give us free passes home. He told us to go home and stay there till he sent us word to come back. Sunday was spent eating and resting, and Monday morning's train found us ready and very willing to go home. Yes, Home, with a big H.

The North Western Railroad was only finished as far as Otter Creek, so that was as far as the train carried us. Stayed over night with a large farmer there and next day went to Toledo. There we learned that Felter's younger brother Chester had died while we were in prison. We also learned that Wilson was out and with our troops at Corinth. But Toledo was too near home for us to tarry long there. The same evening we arrived at home and were very joyously received. There was little sleep that night; there was too much to talk about. Oh, how glad we were to be at home once more.

While at home we learned that Gaston was discharged and on his way home. He did not arrive when expected and some days after Hugh Gaston, his brother, received a letter from a party in Dubuque saying John Gaston died there. Mr. Gaston went to Dubuque to bring the body, and Sprole, Stoakes, Felter, Hopkins and I went to Waterloo to meet him there. When Gaston got to Dubuque he found John had been decently buried and thought not best to remove him at present. This is the second of our Mess that had died. Ed McClaury, my bunk mate, came home sick and soon after died, making the third of our Mess gone. Sometime after we got word that Espy McKune after returning to Macon, Georgia, prison, died. The date was unknown. This was the fourth death among our number. Soon after we arrived at home Wilson came home from Corinth on sick furlough. Stoakes and I went to see him and found him able to sit up and eat dinner with us. We were overjoyed to see each other and enjoyed the day in visiting with him.

About two weeks after we left our boys at Nashville they were sent to Cairo, Illinois. General Strong was in command there and he said it was of no use to retain the boys in service when they were on parole, so he ordered them to make out muster roll to be discharged. The rolls were almost finished when he received orders to send the boys to St. Louis. A day or two delay and our boys would have been discharged and we three still in the service. The President's order to send the paroled prisoners home was modified to sending them to St. Louis to remain in Benton Barracks till exchanged.

We were not the only ones of the boys who left Nashville without leave. Several others of our Company and many of the regiment skipped out before they were sent to Cairo. But we were the only ones we knew of who reported to General Baker at Clinton.

HOMEWARD BOUND -Notes:

-- "Sore eyes", which affected Frank Thomas, seems to have been a common complaint, like the chronic diarrhea (often called "flux") that plagued many of the men, even years after the War. It may have been conjunctivitis or "Pink eye" which is highly contagious. Chronic diarrhea was one of the most common causes of death during the War. It was often caused by the persistent exposure to parasites and bacteria like Salmonella and E. coli frequently found in spoiled or ill-prepared food and contaminated water; it was frequently a symptom of another disease like dysentery and cholera. It quickly brought on severe dehydration and the men often simply wasted away unable to gain ground against anemia and malnutrition. It killed Gaston and McClaury and many of the others. Many soldiers suffered from the "Ague" or malaria. Many medical problems were described using terms not much in use today; "Quinsy" was tonsillitis, "Camp fever" was typhus or typhoid, and "Brain fever" was usually encephalitis; "Consumption" was tuberculosis. Mumps and measles were very serious diseases common in the barracks and both could easily be fatal. All of these were highly communicable. Large percentages of the men quietly suffered from these illnesses and still marched many miles a day doing their duty until they reached a state where they were unable to continue and were too debilitated to easily recover. Unsterile conditions when treating wounds or injuries was epidemic, causing terrible infections; "Mortification" was gangrene, and very dangerous, as was "Erysipelas" a very common infectious skin and tissue disease.

-- Bad water, terrible sanitary conditions, and unsuitable food preparation were rampant but not only in the prison camps. As seen in Chapter 2, things were not always better, even in the soldiers' own barracks and posts, or in any other places where the men were camped in close quarters in large numbers, with so many of them already suffering from contagious or easily-spread maladies.

-- Another common illness among the soldiers was "Lung fever" or pneumonia, which is thought to have been the cause of death for Robert Clark. Living outdoors, marching and sleeping often in bad weather and in wet or damp clothes, left many of the men, already in weakened condition, very vulnerable to pneumonia. It was often fatal, and not just to soldiers. As noted above, John Felter's 19 year old brother Chester P Felter died May 8 1862. He is buried in Crystal cemetery in Tama County Iowa; his death was caused by "lung fever".

-- The Union General named Mitchel, who heartlessly sent a trainload of starved and sick Union soldiers away from safety at Huntsville back into rebel captivity, while forcing another group of hungry and very weak paroled Union soldiers to walk to Nashville, is Ormsby MacKnight Mitchel. While some say he was only following orders from Secretary of War Stanton, there is no question his decisions needlessly cost loyal and brave men their lives. Certainly John McKune and several others died as a result of Mitchel's incredible and callous disregard. Ironically, Mitchel himself died of yellow fever just a few months later in October 1862, just two weeks after Edmund McClaury died.

-- Colonel Moore of Ohio, who guarded Mitchel's lucrative cotton train, may have been Lt. Colonel Robert M Moore, who had been promoted from Captain of Company D, 10th Ohio Volunteers, in January 1862. He resigned his commission in March 1863.

-- The Illinois doctor who generously aided Thomas, Felter, and Stoakes because of his friendship with Felter's father may have been Dr. Richard F Adams, a physician residing in Amboy Illinois in 1860.

-- **General Nathaniel Bradley Baker**, who had been Governor of New Hampshire before migrating to Iowa, was the Adjutant General of Iowa. From the very first day, Baker had been working tirelessly to obtain the release of the Iowa prisoners taken at Shiloh and to have them brought home. His wartime correspondence is preserved in the library of the Iowa Historical Museum in Des Moines. Several letters, dated after this extraordinary June 29 front-lawn meeting with the three "runaway" parolees, were immediately sent out by Baker to various western posts and hospitals seeking news about the newly released Iowans and strongly asking for their immediate return to the State. The urgent messages were all similar to this one sent out July 1, addressed to the "Commandant, St. Louis Mo.": *"Sir, I desire that if any Iowa soldiers who were prisoners (at Nashville or any other point) and cannot be exchanged and who are now on parole be sent to Davenport with directions to Capt. H.B. Hendershott 2nd Artillery to give them furloughs until exchanged. Other soldiers of other states have had this favor. Give it to us. Very Resp'y Y'r Ob't Serv't, N.B. Baker, Adjt. Genl. of Iowa"*.

-- **John Gaston**, detailed to deliver ammunition during the Shiloh battle, escaped being taken prisoner with the rest of his companions. Still very ill after the battle, he was hospitalized for a time at Corinth. When he was finally sent home in July, almost two months after the prisoners had been released, he got as far as Dubuque by riverboat but could go no further. He died July 21 1862, (some sources say it was July 22). He was the second of BF Thomas' messmates to die. Gaston is buried in Linwood Cemetery in Dubuque. Before the War John Gaston worked as a sawyer in his brother Hugh's lumber mill at West Union near today's town of Traer. Sprole is William Sprole, Hugh Gaston's 30 year old hired man who later became a successful farmer in his own right. Hopkins was John S Hopkins, 18 year old son of Martha Stoakes and her first husband. Martha later married Peter Wilson's father John.

-- **John E McKune** died August 9 1862, still a POW at Macon Georgia; he is buried near JD Williams at Andersonville National Cemetery, Site 13075. Thomas' account of the order of his friends' deaths is mistaken; John "Ep" McKune was actually the third messmate to die. During their time in captivity, many of the men spent their time carving jewelry, or small toys, or even chess pieces, out of bones left over from meat when it was provided. Some men bartered their creations to trade for milk or vegetables, or postage stamps and paper, from their guards, or from curious citizens who came to gape at the Yankee prisoners. Before his death John McKune somehow managed to carve, and safely send home, a small ring for his three year old niece, Abbie, the only daughter of his sister Augusta McKune Wood. Abbie kept her Uncle's precious gift the rest of her life and it has now passed into the hands of her great-grandson, Tom L Sawyer.

-- **Edmund McClaury**, hospitalized at Huntsville while the other paroled prisoners were either returned to captivity or forced to walk to Nashville, somehow made it back home to be with his family, possibly owing to the intervention of General Baker. Despite all the prayers and care of his family, he grew steadily weaker and never recovered his health. He died at home October 14 1862 and was the fifth of this group to die.

The following poem, written during the time BF Thomas was home on parole, is dated ten days after the death of **John Gaston** in Dubuque Iowa and appeared in *The Vinton Eagle*, Vinton, Iowa, Wednesday, August 6, 1862

For the Eagle

LINES
Written on the Death of John Gaston,
By a Fellow Soldier.

Oh! is it true that he is dead,
That he has passed from earth away?
The mind that light upon us shed,
Alas! has left its home of clay,
He went so nobly to the fight,
He battled bravely for our land,
For well he knew our cause was right,
And with the cause he'd fall or stand.

The rebel bullets did not do
The hellish work on which 'twas sent;
He passed the battles safely through,
Then started home, but life was spent --
For sickness long had bound her chain
Upon his noble, manly form;
He strove, alas, it was in vain,
To reach home's fireside so warm.

In honor he gets his discharge,
He starts to visit friends so dear,
His noble heart does now enlarge
Because his friends and home are near.
Alas! that home he'll never see;
Death meets and bids his victim stay.
No friend is near to bend the hand --
'Mid those unknown he passed away.

Alas! 'tis hard to give him up --
To know he sleeps within the grave.
The bitter drop within the cup,
No friendly hand was near to save.
Why does "Red Tape" have such a range?
Why so much sin 'gainst earth and heaven
To give to *officers* the power
To crush the life that God has given?

Had but a furlough *once* been given,
And he gone home to friendships care,
The chains of death would have been riven
And he in health been with us here.
His soul, alas, has left its clay
And gone to God from whence it came,
May God but justly judge, this day,
The officers that are to blame.

T.
Buckingham, Iowa, Aug. 1st, 1862.

CHAPTER VII

PAROLE CAMP

August first the President issued a proclamation ordering all the paroled prisoners who had gone home without leave to return to Benton Barracks on or before August 20th. In obeyance to this order Stoakes, Felter and I started for St. Louis August 11th. Wilson was unable to go with us. Went to Clinton and reported to General Baker who recognized us at once and congratulated us on improved appearance. Were joined there by many others of our boys and went together to St. Louis where we arrived August 17th. Found the boys all pretty well except Southwick who was sick in the hospital. Went to the hospital next morning to see him. He was very low. Surgeon said he would not live but a day or two. He was rational and very glad to see us. We had brought a letter from a lady friend, and as he was too weak to read, I read it to him. He understood what I read very well and was glad to hear it. He knew he would die soon and talked to us about it. Left him as comfortable as he could be made and promised to come again next day. When the time came to admit visitors next morning we were there, but too late to see him again. He died during the night. He was the fifth to die of our Mess of ten. Strange as it may seem, one had died out of each bunk leaving the five of us each with bunkmate gone. Remember we were mustered into the service November 2, 1861, and half our Mess were dead August 19, 1862. The time expired was eight months and seventeen days.

Received our pay August 31st. There was five months pay due us which we received. We were on parole and therefore did not do any guard duty. We had no officers with us, therefore did not drill. All that we did was draw rations, eat and sleep. As for pastime, some of us read or played chess, but most of the boys put in all their time playing cards. Having no officers with us there was no chance to get furloughs. The officers in command of the camp had hinted pretty broadly that we would not be followed if we went home. We frequently got passes for a day in St. Louis and some were using these passes to get out of camp and then skip for home. No doubt they were better off at home than here until they were exchanged. So it was not strange that at one time all but eight of our Company went home as soon as they got their pay. The three of us who had been at home earlier remained here. During September we lived the laziest life it was possible for men to live. Frequently we got passes to St. Louis and attended the theater or visited public libraries or the parks and gardens. The Mercantile library was an especially pleasant resort. It had the most extensive collection of books I ever saw, besides much fine statuary. The librarian was always very courteous to us.

In the barracks we wrote letters, poetry, history and fiction, sometimes several writing at once on some given subject. Again we taught each other in branches of learning wherein we may have been deficient. One boy who had nearly no advantages of school I put through Ray's Third Part Arithmetic, and nearly through analytical grammar. At the battle of Pleasant Hill the boy was captured and held fourteen months in prison. While there he mastered algebra and other higher branches of learning. Today he is one of the foremost lawyers in Butte City, Montana. Many of our boys received great benefit from the studies they pursued while lying at Benton Barracks. Most of them, however, spent their whole time card playing, and sometimes at much worse than that.

Wilson joined us September 4th. His furlough expired sometime before but he had been unable to come. I went with him to the commander and he reported his condition and the Colonel said he had done right.

For sometime I acted as hospital steward for our regiment. Our assistant surgeon, Dr. Pierce of Cedar Falls, had charge of us. He came each morning at sick call and prescribed for all that were able to come to his office. Then he visited those sick in the barracks and gave them whatever treatment he thought they would need. If they were very bad he ordered them sent to the hospital. After this morning call he returned to the city and we saw him no more till next morning.

I filled the prescriptions he ordered and stayed in the office and gave medicine to those who came after the doctor had gone. He had given me directions so I knew pretty well what medicines to use in emergencies. He used me well and seemed to have full confidence in me. I thought very well of him. He was honest and kind.

During October the weather grew colder and October 25th we had two inches of snow followed by a hard freeze. Very cold weather for that climate at that time of year.

Saturday, November 1, 1862. Colonel Shaw came to camp to see us. He was just out of prison and came to see us before he went home. He shook hands with everybody and seemed very glad to see us. I am sure we were all very glad to see him again. He told us that our second lieutenant, Simon F. Eccles, died at Selma, Alabama. Our officers and the boys we left in prison were now all out. The officers went home to see their relatives and would come back sometime soon. The Colonel was quite sanguine he would have us sent to Davenport to recruit and reorganize our regiment. The boys of our regiment who were not captured were then at Camp McClellan.

The Colonel left us next day to make a short visit home. The boys of the Twelfth Iowa who had just been paroled came a few days later. They looked pretty bad and certainly had had a very hard time of it in their prison life. Stoakes had been sick for sometime. We urged him to ask for a discharge but he still thought he would get well. We had become quite uneasy about him but finally he concluded to apply for a discharge. At this time Dr. Pierce had been relieved and Dr. Irwin of Keokuk, surgeon of the Eighth Iowa, was in charge. I had not been acting as hospital steward since Dr. Pierce had left.

November 8th. Stoakes got word his discharge papers had been sent to the commander for his signature, and just one week later they were returned duly signed. He now drew his pay and prepared to start home. Felter and I concluded to go home with him, so we went, Stoakes with his discharge and Felter and I on what was called "French furlough", that is, an imaginary furlough. We took passage on a steamboat to Davenport and from there to Marengo by rail. Arrived at Marengo a little after noon and ordered dinner at the hotel. While eating, a number of the citizens gathered in the dining room talking to us and asking questions about the service. All at once a smart Alec bethought himself that probably we had no furloughs and therefore were deserters. The more he talked the more he became convinced that we surely were deserters. We heard all he said but made no answer. Soon others began to agree with him and thought we should be arrested and taken before the provost marshal. About the time we finished our dinners the talk became quite noisy. We arose from the table and held to our chairs to be ready if need be for defense. We told them who we were and how we came to be there as we were; that we were going home till we were exchanged; that we had traveled a long way and were now nearly home; that we had a right to go home by verbal leave of our officers, and finally, there were not men enough in Marengo to stop us. Then came a hearty cheer from a large majority of the crowd and immediately the war cloud disappeared. We walked out of the hotel to where the stage stood waiting to take us to Blairstown, but before getting in every man wanted to shake hands with us. Even the smart Alec said he knew we were all right but he just raised the question to see what we would say. We mounted the stage and started. The last we saw of the Marengo men they were waving their hats and cheering.

From Blairstown we took the cars again to Toledo and the next day drove home. Do you know what that word "home" means? If you have always lived in the best home on earth you cannot realize its meaning. It is necessary to bear some of the crosses, some of the trials, some of the hardships and deceptions, some of the ingratitude and some of the false friendships of the world before you can fully realize what home, with parents, brothers, sisters and true friendship, is. If you have borne only a part of these trials you may appreciate something of our feelings at this home coming. Before the war began Felter was engaged to my youngest sister, Rebecca, and I was engaged to Stoakes' sister, Sarah, so our home coming was something of a general rejoicing throughout all three families.

During our stay this time John and Rebecca concluded they would consummate their engagement by getting married. December 10, 1862, they were married. Sarah thought she would prefer to wait till the war closed or my time of enlistment expired. Were it not for Stoakes' ill health this would have been a very happy time, I assure you.

Again we received orders to return to St. Louis by December 25th. Mat Clark lived just north of Six Mile Grove and he too was home. He came to our house December 20th and he and I went to Felter's the next day. There we found Felter too sick to return with us. Stayed over night there and next morning Clark and I went to Toledo. There we found a number of our boys ready to go to St. Louis. Took the train at Tama City and arrived at Cedar Rapids in time to get conveyances to carry us to Iowa City. There were over thirty of our Company along. Lieutenant Gallagher was with us. He came home as soon as he was out of prison, therefore was at home before we came. During this stay he was married to Miss Mary Crawford December 2nd, 1862.

Stayed over night at Iowa City at the Crummie house. The boys felt lively and cut up all the tricks they could think of. There were two large bedrooms with a door between. In each of these were four beds. The boys that stayed in these rooms scarcely slept a wink. It is not likely the people of the Crummie house will ever forget that night. Clark and I had a room to ourselves. Only a little more than a year before we had gone to Davenport with ten able men in our Mess; now but two of us were returning to our duty. Five dead, one discharged and still sick, another at home sick and one at St. Louis.

Monday evening found us at Davenport. Rumor said our regiment had orders to come to Davenport to recruit. Our orders were to go to St. Louis, so Tuesday morning, we boarded the cars and crossed the river into Illinois. Passed through LaSalle, Bloomington and Sandoval to St. Louis. This being Christmas day we stopped at one of the hotels and had an excellent dinner.

Arrived at Benton Barracks at two o'clock in the afternoon December 25th, 1862. The few boys that were left here were very glad to see us. They said it was the best Christmas present they ever had.

PAROLE CAMP - Notes:

-- The roster of the 8th Iowa Infantry says that **James Irwin** 25, a resident of Marion, Linn County, served as surgeon from September 1861 to April 1863.

-- The "boy" BF Thomas tutored in mathematics and grammar must have been 18 year old **Joel S Shropshire** of Tipton, Cedar County. Obviously ambitious and determined, and as well as brave and just plain tough, qualities most of these men shared, Joel did become a lawyer in Butte Montana years after serving through his full three year enlistment. During those three years he survived both the fierce fights at Shiloh and Pleasant Hill and endured the months of harsh treatment at the two prison camps of Macon Georgia and Tyler Texas. Looking closely through Captain Gallagher's records, it appears that after their time in the prison camp, men who had signed their names with an "X" before Shiloh had learned to write after Shiloh, or at least learned to sign their own names.

-- **Lieutenant Simon Eccles** died as a POW August 26 1862 at Madison Georgia. The privates were paroled May 24, except those who refused to sign the parole oath, who were too sick to leave with the others, or who had been sent back by Mitchel. The officers remained in prison for several more months. They were finally released along with any remaining privates in an exchange of prisoners at Aiken's Landing Virginia October 17 1862.

-- **Dewitt Southwick**, hospitalized with McClaury in Huntsville in late May, was later transferred to the hospital at St. Louis were he died August 19 1862, ten days after McKune died in Macon. Dewitt's death was the fourth from their group of ten. McClaury died two months later at home. Dewitt Southwick is buried in Jefferson Barracks National Cemetery in St. Louis.

-- After one year in service, in a three-year enlistment, by Christmas 1862 Mat Clark and BF Thomas were the only two of their Wolf Creek group still fit to return to duty. Robert Clark, John Gaston, John McKune, Dewitt Southwick and Edmund McClaury were dead. Eleazar Stoakes was discharged and ill at home; John Felter also was home sick in Iowa and unable to return to duty in time with the others; and in St. Louis, Peter Wilson may have been too ill to even go home on leave. The two years that still lay ahead must have looked very grim.

The following poem is dated a month after BF Thomas visited with Dewitt Southwick who was gravely ill at the hospital in St. Louis. It was published in *The Vinton Eagle*, Vinton, Benton Coounty, Iowa Wednesday, November 12, 1862.

POETRY
For the Eagle

THE DYING SOLDIER

Comrade, for me bear a message
To my friends now far away.
Listen closely to each passage
There is much that I would say;
For each word as now I speak it,
As my lips grow pale and cold,
Is, to those to whom you take it,
Dearer far than gems of gold.

When you meet my sister; comrade,
Gently break to her the word;
Though among the dead I'm numbered,
Tell her what you here have heard.
Tell her that my heart was cheerful;
For, in youth, 'twas taught by her
To be neither sad nor fearful,
When death's portals opened near.

Tell my father that my pillow
Was my gun upon the field,
Where the foe swayed like a billow
By our men compelled to yield.
Tell him that the love he taught me,
For my country's flag to know,
Early, to the grave has brought me,
Though we triumphed o'er the foe;

That my life has not been wasted,
Though my veins were drained of blood,
Death, the bitter cup is tasted
Tasted for my country's good.
Tell him not to mourn the soldier
Who now sleeps so far away;
Though his body now does moulder
Yet his soul with God doth stay.

Tell my mother, and be careful,
Kind and gentle as you can;
For I fear the news so fearful
Soon will snap life's slender strand --
Tell her that her son when dying
Lying, bleeding on the sod --
On his heart kept closely lying,
His loved book -- "The Word of God".

Tell her that she well had taught me
How our Lord for sinners died;
My own Savior now has bought me --
Soon he'll seat me by his side
Comrade, comrade, quick, I perish!!
Bathe again my fevered brow
Life is short- I can but cherish
Those few moments left me now.

Listen, friend, there is another --
Her again I ne'er will see:
I to her was more than brother --
She was more than life to me.
Tell her that when I was dying,
Her own miniature, so dear,
Was beside my bible lying
When I'm gone give them to her.

Here this letter -- take it to her --
Take it to the whole household
God alone I know can soothe her
When my lips are pale and cold.
Tell them all that I was cheerful
For in Freedom's cause I fell
Death approaches -- don't be fearful --
Comrade, once again, farewell.

FRANK
Benton Barracks Mo., Sept. 16th 1862.

CHAPTER VIII

TRIP TO ROLLA

December 29th. We were informed by our officers that we had been exchanged and therefore were again fitted for active duty. This I believed to be true, but some of our boys insisted we should have something more than merely our officers' word for it. Our officers were in the same danger we were, and would not go into action if they were not exchanged. I felt sure we were exchanged.

Received our guns. They were similar to the guns we had before the surrender. It was the custom to pay the soldiers every two months, but circumstances often prevent, so it was sometimes four or six months between times of payment. Our pay would be due the first of the month and we expected we would be paid before we went away. We were mustered ready for pay but for some cause unknown to us the first of the month passed and no pay came. Some snow and cold weather but not as cold as it was in Iowa.

January 10, 1863. Drew cartridges and had orders to be ready at any moment to go to Rolla, Missouri, to help the troops there defend the town against the approach of rebel General Price.

Sunday, January 11th. At three o'clock in the afternoon received orders to march to the depot to take the cars for Rolla. Arrived at the depot about seven o'clock and did not get aboard the cars till after ten. Many of the boys visited the saloons in the neighborhood pretty frequently and when we boarded the box cars these boys were pretty full of ardent spirits. The door of the car in which our Company rode was fitted with a spring lock and when we were in the door was shoved shut and locked so we could not get it open. The road was rough, the train ran fast, we had no seats but lay on the floor of the car, nor had we any lights in the car and it was a dark night. Pandemonium reigned. Drunken men swearing and fighting; other drunken men vomiting; others having a grand carousal. Singing, swearing, shouting. Can you imagine what this was to sober respectable men? Taking it all in all it was the worst ride I ever had in my somewhat eventful life. For two hours we were locked in the car. But while stopping for the engine to take water we made our troubles known to the outsiders and they opened the door for us. How grateful were we for the cold fresh air that came in at the newly opened door.

Arrived at Rolla about seven o'clock next morning. There was five inches of snow on the ground. Marched out about a mile from town and pitched our tents. They were the small wedge tents, about six feet square on the ground and came to a comb or wedge about six feet high. We were much crowded, being compelled to sleep five or six in a tent. We suffered much from the cold. There were plenty of Sibley tents large enough to hold eighteen men comfortable in each, and had sheet iron stoves to heat them. But Colonel Stone, an Iowa man, and afterwards Governor of this State, who was in command then, would not let us have these because we did not belong to his division. Just think of it! He an Iowa man refusing to let us have tents and stoves when we came to help him repel a rebel attack upon this town. I hope you will sympathize with me when I say he never received my vote when he was elected Governor some years after.

After much suffering and no signs of our enemy coming we got orders January 20th to return to Benton Barracks. Went to the depot at eleven o'clock in the morning and the train did not come for us till seven in the evening. During this time many of the boys took the opportunity to loot the saloons and stores. They stole cigars by the box and handful. I saw a box of plug tobacco drop off the shelf at the back end of a store and gradually move along the floor to the door where a man carried it off. What moved it? The room was full of soldiers and one foot would push it and another would push it till it reached the door. It was a shame but the boys claimed they must have something to pay them for the suffering they had endured in defending the city from an imaginary foe. Started from Rolla about eight o'clock in the evening and arrived at St. Louis about ten o'clock next morning. We then marched to Benton Barracks.

January 28th. Received our pay. I received fifty-two dollars for my last four months' wages. The boys were having a high time as they always do when they draw their pay. Many of them owe money to a comrade who has loaned them when they were out of money. A great many got to gambling as soon as they received their pay; some of them got passes to the city and spent their money there, and some quietly sent the most of their money home. There was but little saved out of thirteen dollars per month and yet some of the boys saved nearly all of it. Besides the thirteen dollars per month there was an allowance of forty-two dollars per year for clothing. Government sold us clothing at a reasonable price and if we did not draw forty-two dollars' worth in the year we received the cash balance. If we over-drew, the cash went the other way. Some of our boys bought clothing of their comrades, where money was scarce, at a much reduced rate, which would add to his money surplus for clothing.

January 30th. Companies G and H were ordered to Carondelet to guard the navy yard there, where they were building five large gunboats. This detachment was under command of Captain Warner who was captain of Company H.

Carondelet was seven miles below St. Louis on the river bank. There were several hundred men there at work and the place was very noisy. Many of the men were fastening armor upon the sides of the boats. The iron plates were about seven feet long and three wide and one inch thick. These plates were passed through an edging machine that makes the plates just the right size. The plane takes a shaving off the iron plate as easily as an ordinary plane would take one off a wooden board. The plane was permanent and the plate moved. Next they punch a number of one inch holes along the edge of these plates. Bolts are put through these holes to fasten the plates to the timbers. These holes are punched by great power punches. The plate lies on an iron table and the punch comes down exactly over a hole of like size in the table. The plate moves to the right position and the punch descends slowly and steadily seeming to pass through the iron easily, but when it cuts through, the whole plate jumps, showing the immense pressure on the punch. These plates were laid on solid woodwork at least two feet thick. This would withstand all common cannon shot but when struck by ten or twelve inch shot they are likely to penetrate them. There were at the Mercantile Library in St. Louis samples of plates that have been in action. Some of them were pierced clear through, but more were badly dented but not broken through. When they were laying these plates upon the sides of the boats and probably five hundred men driving the bolts through with sledges you need not expect to hear the sound of a human voice let the mouth be ever so close to your ear. This was the music we had for ten hours in the day and seven days in the week, for the government was in a great hurry for these boats.

As soon as we knew we were exchanged Lieutenant Gallagher was appointed Captain. That left both lieutenancies vacant. The boys were anxious we should hold an election to fill these vacancies. In case we held an election A. H. Hazlett was sure of the first place, and I of the second. Joe Shanklin was the Captain's choice for first place. He was a splendid man and a very warm friend of mine but the boys were almost unanimous for the above ticket. There was considerable discussion at times and there was no telling when the matter would be disposed of. I was sure I would like the commission if I got it through the choice of my comrades.

While at Carondelet we had much more liberty than was usually granted to soldiers. The boys were on duty about every other day. The day they were off they could have passes to St. Louis if they wished. One day Felter and I got passes to St. Louis, good till six o'clock in the evening February 4th. When we got there we found the city billed for "Coleen Bawn" at the theatre. We wanted to see this play so we changed our pass to read "Till six o'clock p.m. February 5th". We enjoyed the city very much, again visiting the Mercantile Library and the Zoo Gardens, and in the evening going to the provost for a pass, as we would have to have a provost pass at night. The clerk in dating it caused it to end at midnight. We told him we were going to the theatre and might not get to the hotel in time. He erased the date with a scratch and made it read till midnight the next night. We told him we were afraid the guards would not pass us because the date had been changed, which was often done by the boys themselves. He said it was all right and we would have no trouble. We went to the theatre where "Coleen Bawn" was played by Mr. and Mrs. Florence. The playing was fine and the plot splendid. The after piece was a very laughable farce, "Thrice Married".

Theatre over we had supper at a restaurant and started to the hotel to stay over night. Soon we met the provost guard. I passed without challenge, but they stopped Felter and demanded his pass. He showed them the provost pass and they at once detected the change of date. He explained to them but they only laughed at him. My first thought was to go to the hotel where Colonel Shaw stayed and have him get Felter released. But when they started with him to the guard house I spoke to them and told them the pass was genuine and that I had the camp pass it was issued on. When I showed them this they released him saying that my pass was all right. That was, the genuine provost pass would have sent us to the guard house while the pass we had changed saved us the disgrace. When released by the provost guard we went to the Randal house and stayed over night.

When we arrived at camp next day our detachment had orders to return to Benton Barracks. We would have much preferred to remain here but we were not to choose our place of service but to go at the word of command. William Breese and David Casaday deserted us here. They were both men of very bad habits and disagreeable to deal with. We were glad they were gone and hoped never to see them again. Returned to Benton Barracks and found the other companies of our regiment expecting to go down the river at once. Suppose that was the reason we were called in.

Snow five inches deep February 7th, and pretty cold. Next day snow all melted off and formed mud nearly as deep as the snow had been. It seemed there was a change of plan and we were remaining here. One day one of our boys was punished for some misdemeanor. His knapsack was filled with brick and he carried it marching about twenty paces back and forth. This was the first time we ever saw this punishment inflicted.

The load became very heavy as time passed. Several times since we came out of prison we had been mustered for commutation of rations. That is, to draw pay for the rations we did not draw while in prisons. This day we were mustered again but we doubted if we ever received our pay. It seemed it was the law to pay soldiers the value of rations they were entitled to and did not draw.

Sometime before there were notices published that at the Sub-Treasury in St. Louis on February 16, 1863, the government would exchange, with everyone who applied, the sum of fifteen dollars in postal currency (that is, notes of three, five, ten, fifteen, twenty-five and fifty cent denomination) for fifteen dollars in bills. The country was much in need of small change as all the silver had been retired. Many merchants had issued such notes of their own which were only good in their locality. Felter and I went to the city and each got fifteen dollars worth of this currency (they only let each one have fifteen dollars, no more nor less) to send home to help our people out. We sent the currency by the American Express Company. This was the first currency issued here but it became very common later. The boys were generally in good health and rather anxious to go down the river again.

February 22nd all the soldiers in Benton Barracks went to St. Louis to celebrate Washington's birthday. The manner of celebrating was to march about six miles down the street to General Curtis' headquarters and pass in review before him and then march back again to the barracks. It began snowing about the time we started back and when we arrived at the barracks we were wet through and very cold for by this time there was a regular blizzard blowing.

The next morning was quite cold but clear with bright sunshine. That day we received our regimental colors. They were the first colors we ever had for, as said before, the companies that went to Fort Randal got the colors belonging to the regiment. The beautiful silk flag and banner have been described before. They are a royal stand of colors. Upon the stripes of the flag in letters of gold were the words "14th Regiment Iowa Infantry Volunteers", and the names "Fort Donelson" and "Shiloh", the battles the regiment had been engaged in. We were proud of our flag.

Our Major resigned before the battle of Shiloh and Governor Kirkwood appointed his nephew, William Kirkwood, who was second lieutenant of Company K, to fill the vacancy. Jumping him over nearly all the other officers in the regiment, this made the officers mad. Captain Emerson of Company D and Captain Shannon of Company E resigned their commissions. Before their resignations could be accepted they were both captured with the regiment at Shiloh. They were in prison when their resignations were accepted and when they came home were mustered out of service. Now Major Kirkwood joined us for the first time since his promotion.

TRIP TO ROLLA - Notes:

-- Colonel Stone of the 22nd Iowa was **William Milo Stone**, 33, of Knoxville. Several months after these events (rather than "some years after") Stone resigned his commission as Colonel and was the successful Republican candidate for governor in the election of November 1863, serving from January 1864 to January 1868, after winning a second term in November 1865. He is said to been one of the founders of the Republican Party and to have become a personal friend and supporter of Abraham Lincoln; he is also said to have been in the audience at Ford's theater the night Lincoln was shot. As Major of the 3rd Iowa, Stone had his horse shot from under him at Shiloh and was taken prisoner of war the same day as Colonel Shaw and the 14th Iowa were taken. Stone's opponent was **Colonel James M Tuttle** who had bravely lead the Iowa troops in the charge on Fort Donelson, his 2nd Iowa being the first regiment inside the breastworks. At Shiloh, he commanded the brigade that included the 14th Iowa during the defense at the Hornets' Nest. Just prior to the surrender, Tuttle and his 2nd Iowa Infantry passed through the blistering crossfire that killed General William Wallace. The door to freedom for the other men of the Hornets' Nest was finally slammed shut by the encircling enemy forces. Tuttle and the 2nd were not taken prisoner at Shiloh but vigorously participated in the next day's fight that drove the rebel army off in defeat. Tuttle was an unquestioned hero to the Iowa troops but politically, as a Democrat during the War, he had little chance of winning the election.

-- General **Samuel Ryan Curtis**, who graduated top in his class at West Point and served with distinction during the Mexican war, resigned his seat in the US Congress to take command of the 2nd Iowa Infantry. A staunch abolitionist, the former mayor of Keokuk Iowa was quickly promoted and became one of the most successful generals in the Union army with important victories at Pea Ridge, Westport, and elsewhere that pushed rebel armies out of Arkansas and Missouri. General Curtis died a year after the War ended and was buried in Keokuk.

-- **William Kirkwood** 26 of Johnson County, the Governor's nephew, was appointed First Lieutenant of Company K in November 1861. Kirkwood was promoted to Major in September 1862 but resigned his position the following March (see Chapters 1 and 10). **Edgar A Warner** 31 of Waubeek, Linn County was appointed Captain of Company H in November 1861. He was taken prisoner at Shiloh and in March 1863 was promoted to Major, taking Kirkwood's place. Warner mustered out with the regiment in November 1864. **Richard D Emerson** 36 of Salem, Henry County, was appointed Captain of Company D in November 1861. He was listed as missing in action at Shiloh and his resignation was accepted immediately after the battle.

-- William Breese seems to have caught a boat going upriver this time. If officers found combat too overwhelming or stressful, they could resign and return home. Not so with enlisted men. Officers were also able to leave for trivial political reasons or in protest over another's promotion. Enlisted men who left risked stiff penalties, even death, especially if they ran during combat. Company G had a remarkably low desertion rate. Five men, who all had been willing volunteers, fled soon after the battle of Shiloh, one of the bloodiest and fiercest fights of the War, and where almost their whole company was taken prisoner. Two others left months later in February 1863, a month after the announcement of the Emancipation Proclamation, a controversial decision that at first seemed to provoke many desertions. But perhaps these two were simply unfit for military service. The roster says Breese deserted February 10 1863 from St. Louis Missouri. The roster also says that deserter David Casaday was apprehended after a short time and was restored to duty this same month, February 1863. See Chapter 2.

CHAPTER IX

HOW I WAS NOT MADE A LIEUTENANT

Major Kirkwood brought an order from Governor Kirkwood to our Captain authorizing us to choose two lieutenants by ballot. By this time Hazlett became fearful he might miss his place by election, and unknown to me he bargained with the Captain to defeat me. The Captain gave notice that we would hold the election March 12, 1863. When we were called into line to vote he told us we were at present only entitled to one lieutenant because of the small number of men. Therefore we would elect but one now and the other later. The ballots cast were nineteen for Hazlett, nine for Shanklin and seven for Davis. The seven for Davis were cast by proxy by the seven men of our Company in the Union Brigade at Davenport, the men who had not been captured at Shiloh. I felt at once I had been tricked by the man I had caused to be nominated. If it had not been sprung at the last moment and under a false guise, the boys would have given me their votes instead of giving them to Hazlett. Captain Gallagher and Shanklin were friends before they went into the service. They spent six months in prison together so I did not blame the Captain for preferring Shanklin to me. I also well knew he would have preferred me to Hazlett. But Hazlett through influence he had with the Governor had his promise that we should hold an election to fill the place, and so we did. As said before, Shanklin and I were warm friends although rivals for the place, while Hazlett owed it to my friends that he stood any chance to get the place he sought. Hazlett's and Shanklin's recommendations were sent in together to the Governor and their commissions came back together.

Lieutenant Colonel Lucas and Colonel Shaw did not agree very well. Neither did the soldiering agree with Colonel Lucas, therefore Lucas resigned. That we were expecting orders to go down the river again may not have had anything to do with it, we did not know, but when he resigned Captain Newbold of Company F was recommended for the place. He was one of the best officers we had. Not only a bright, brave man, but also an excellent Christian, as well.

March 24th I was again detailed to act as hospital steward. However, it was only temporary. The real hospital steward, who was with the Union Brigade, would take his place when the brigade joined us.

This Union Brigade was composed of men of different regiments of our division who were not captured at Shiloh. They were formed into a regiment called the Union Brigade and commanded by Colonel Lynch of the Fifty-eighth Illinois regiment. When our officers came out of prison the boys belonging to Iowa regiments were sent to Davenport, expecting that all these regiments would be sent there to reorganize. We were now daily expecting them to join us. Dr. Pierce had resigned and Dr. Stephens of Montour, Iowa had been appointed to fill the place of assistant surgeon of our regiment. He was here and had taken charge of the sick of the regiment.

March 28th. A detail of one captain, two lieutenants and seventy-five men was called from our regiment for a secret expedition. Most of our Company were in this detail. They started next morning. The rumor was they were to go to Vicksburg for scout work, but no one knew. We knew they went aboard a boat and down the river.

March 31st. The men of the Union Brigade joined us and we had orders to be ready at once to go to Helena, Arkansas.

April 2nd. Again have peremptory orders to start south tomorrow morning.

April 4th. Still in the barracks. Our boys came back this evening from their secret expedition. They had been to Memphis and were guarding a paymaster and his money. They had some startling adventures. The money, greenbacks, was in a heavy oak box set on the cabin deck in front of the cabin, and three guards were about it all the time. It was known to be loaded with money. When the box was moved to take it on shore at Memphis they discovered that someone had cut a hole from the boiler deck ceiling through the cabin deck and nearly through the bottom of the oak box containing the money. No one it seems knew who did the cutting or when it was done, but with a few more strokes he would have had a hat full of money.

Drew our pay April 2nd, 1863. It was almost a sure prediction of a wild night following pay day. Some of our men knew nothing but rowdyism. It seems so useless if not wicked to throw away every opportunity for usefulness into selfish orgie.

April 5th. Again exchanged our guns. This time we got Enfield rifles. They are of English manufacture and are a very good gun. We remember at Fort Donelson many of the rebels were armed with double barrel shot guns, although some had excellent rifles. At Shiloh we knew the difference as soon as we were under fire. There they had this same English Enfield rifle. For England furnished the rebels with much of their munitions of war during the early part of the rebellion. Not the English government but British subjects and British factories. Now we too received English guns.

April 10, 1863. Early this morning we were up and had our breakfast and soon after formed line and marched to the city and to the steam boat landing as we supposed to go to Memphis. But when we arrived at the landing the order was countermanded because of want of transportation, and we were marched back to the barracks again. You will notice that for more than a month we had been expecting to go down the river.

HOW I WAS NOT MADE A LIEUTENANT - Notes:

-- The men of the company were able to select their own corporals, sergeants and lieutenants from among their own members. Naturally the men would tend to vote for those they knew best, their closest neighbors and friends, and messmates, although a man might win more universal support by distinguishing himself in battle, or by earning the trust of the other men outside his own smaller group. Letters home most often refer to those men from the immediate neighborhood that their families would know best, and that might also reflect which men were grouped together as messmates. Within Company G the men often referred to themselves and others in geographical terms such as the "Wolf Creek boys", or the "Salt Creek boys" etc meaning their own small close-knit neighborhood clique. Shanklin wrote to his father about the men from Toledo; such groups made probable messmates.

-- Groups of messmates might act as temporary voting blocs to nominate their fellows, and they would form coalitions with other messgroups to put each other's candidates over the top. The men from Story County would most likely have messed together and voted together. Men like Hazlett, whose home county was not well represented within the Company numerically, might join together with other men of the Company who had not been long term residents of their counties and therefore more or less unaligned. These men who were more or less unaffiliated with the other neighborhood factions would then gain significant political power when banded together. It wasn't a firm system however, as Edmund McClaury from the Irving area on the eastern edge of Tama county was geographically a "Salt Creek boy" like those from Redman, especially since Salt Creek flowed past part of his family property. However, he clearly was aligned with Thomas, Wilson, Stoakes, Felter and McKune and the others from Wolf Creek in today's Traer area. Perhaps they had been his close friends before the War. All in all this system made for interesting political shuffling and bargaining with diverse groups working together cooperatively in their voting, but it also could create personal rivalries and jealousies.

-- **Doctor George McLellan Staples** from Dubuque was 34 years old in November 1861 when he was appointed Company Surgeon 1861. Born in Maine, he was a graduate of Harvard Medical School in 1855 before establishing his practice at Dubuque in 1856. Before the outbreak of war he raised a company of pioneers and capitalist investors to establish a settlement in the Dakota Territory at today's Sioux Falls South Dakota. He hoped to make a fortune in real estate speculation but gave up the enterprise to serve his country. At the Donelson fight he was a field surgeon caring for dozens of terribly injured men. At Shiloh he was made Surgeon-in-Chief of WHL Wallace's Division and personally provided direct care for more than 700 severely wounded soldiers in the field. After the siege of Corinth he applied for a leave of absence from sheer exhaustion. A few months later Dr. Staples was back at the front at Columbus Kentucky where he served as the Medical Director of the Sixth Division, Sixteenth Army Corps on the personal staff of General AJ Smith. Under Smith, Staples served at the Vicksburg campaign with Sherman, the Red River campaign with Banks, and the Missouri campaign against Price, personally attending to the battle wounds of hundreds of men in the field under the worst conditions. Staples received the highest praise and warm friendship of General Banks and was promoted to Brevet Lieutenant Colonel by President Lincoln for his service. He mustered out with the 14th Iowa Regiment in November 1864 and then quietly returned to his medical office in Dubuque. In July 1862, during his too short leave of absence from the front, utterly exhausted from his harrowing experiences in the field, Harvard educated Dr. Staples still found the heart to personally attend to the dying John Gaston and then generously arranged for the funeral services at John's burial.

-- Staples' assistants serving the 14th Iowa were Pierce and Stevens. **Doctor Samuel Newell Pierce** 29 of Cedar Falls was appointed Assistant Surgeon October 1861 and resigned April 1863 according to dates in the published roster; BF Thomas served as hospital steward under Pierce. **Doctor John H Stevens** 26 of Butlerville [Montour] Tama County was appointed Assistant Surgeon August 1862. Stevens mustered out with the regiment at Davenport November 1864.

CHAPTER X

CAIRO

The next day at noon we started again. When we arrived at the river we found the steamer "*Champion*" ready for us and we at once marched aboard of her. At four o'clock the boat shoved off from the landing and once more we were bound for down the river. Colonel Shaw did not go with us. He was Chief of Court Martial at St. Louis. Lieutenant Colonel Newbold was in command. Hazlett was accidentally left when we came away. We saw him running after the boat was near the middle of the river. He followed down the river some distance and probably thought the boat would land for him, but it steadily plied its course down the river. Colonel Newbold did not like Hazlett's carelessness and would probably reprimand him when he joined us again.

Arrived at Cairo next day. The Thirty-fifth Iowa was here doing guard duty. The boys told us we were to relieve them and they were to go down the river. We did not believe it, but next morning we were ordered to disembark and soon we were ashore and relieved the Thirty-fifth Iowa from post duty here. The boys did not like that. They would be on duty every other day as it took about a hundred men for each day's duty. The boys would rather be out where they would be marching every day than doing post duty. General Buford was in command here. He was an old banker from Rock Island, Illinois, and the man the Buford Plow was named after many years after the war. No military man himself but aped the true military man in many ways. He assumed to be very strict in military etiquette. He compelled Colonel Newbold to keep a headquarters guard at his door all the time, a thing our regiment never knew before. He gave orders that when he was either walking or riding along the street the soldiers should gather in squads at his approach, line up and salute him. If a single soldier saw him coming he must stand at attention and salute him as he passed. Now this was all strictly according to discipline but was very seldom enforced in military camps.

April 13, 1863. We have had a romance and a sad tragedy since leaving St. Louis. Captain Crane of Company H who was Colonel Shaw's wife's brother, a young lawyer of much promise, and a man loved and respected by everybody, brought with him from St. Louis a waiter boy. He took care of the Captain's things; brushed his clothes, polished his brass ornaments, blacked his boots, cared for the quarters and such other menial service as waiter boys were wont to do. He was quite a bright boy. Played cards, smoked and swore after the usual approved manner. As we came down the river there arose a rumor that Charlie Townsend, as the boy was called, was a girl in disguise. It was barely rumored but not talked much. After we were on duty here the Captain went to the theatre and took Charlie along. A detective arrested the boy as a spy, claiming it was a girl in boy's attire. Before the provost marshal the Captain admitted the person was a girl and promised if released he would send her home to St. Louis. The next day Charlie Townsend was still in camp the same jolly boy he had been before. Colonel Newbold heard the story, probably from the provost marshal. He came to Captain Crane's office where he and the boy were playing cards. The Colonel told the Captain the waiter must at once be returned to St. Louis. After some talk the Captain agreed to send her away and he and the Colonel left the office together. As soon as the door closed they heard the report of a revolver within and rushing back they found the girl lying upon the floor with a bullet hole in her breast. Life had fled before they reached her, and nothing but the body of the erring one was there.

The Captain's remorse was terrible. He was determined to take his own life and it was all the Colonel and others that rushed in could do to prevent it. He was immediately placed under arrest. The girl, it was said, belonged to one of the best families in St. Louis. Her people were wealthy and she had a fine education. She had become acquainted with the Captain and soon they were infatuated with each other. Rather than be separated from him she chose to go with him in disguise. There was only one end to this course and it came suddenly. It cast a heavy gloom over the whole regiment. Colonel Shaw resigned his detail as Chief of Court Martial at St. Louis and took command of the regiment. This he did to shield the Captain from punishment. The Captain was under arrest for some time and finally released without any charges being preferred against him.

April 15th. The promotion of non-commissioned officers was announced. Addison Davis was Second Sergeant; Charles Ford, Third; Peter Wilson, Fourth; and I, Fifth. Felter was Corporal.

Sunday, April 19th. There were orders for a detail of thirty men for scout service. Wilson and Felter were both on this detail. They returned next evening. They had been to Jonesboro, Illinois, to quell a copperhead insurrection. They brought about a dozen prisoners with them.

April 21st. Again a detail was called to go to Jonesboro. After our boys came away the other day the copperheads had a grand pow-wow and threatened the Union men so they feared for their lives and fled. Our boys will go back today and quell them this time so they will remain quiet for awhile at least. When they returned this time they felt assured they would not be called soon again. They said there was a strong secesh feeling throughout southern Illinois. Many of the citizens were outspoken rebels and many more were so at heart but concealed their sentiments when our men were there for lack of courage. About Jonesboro it was not safe for a Union man to express his opinions. How widespread this feeling was was hard to tell. Southern Illinois was settled mostly from Kentucky and Tennessee and you could hardly expect anything but southern sympathy to exist there. We met much of this feeling the time we came from Nashville and crossed part of southern Illinois. I remember hearing one young lady say she had a brother in the Union army and she hoped the first shot fired would go through his heart.

Saturday, April 25th. There was a rumor that the rebel General Marmaduke was approaching Cape Girardeau, a town in Missouri about sixty miles above here on the river. Orders were given that no man should leave camp as we might be sent up there any moment. Many boats passed Saturday night and Sunday morning loaded with troops for Cape Girardeau. The orders had been for sometime that all boats passing Cairo must come to the landing and report. Cairo is not exactly on the point between the two rivers but about a mile above the point on the north bank of the Ohio River. Boats passing up the Mississippi need not come nearer than two miles of Cairo. Many of these boats carrying troops in the great hurry to get to Cape Girardeau passed along the other bank of the Mississippi, but the fort just below town called them to halt by firing a shot across their bows. The officer in command at the fort was much perplexed by the problem. He knew the emergency at Cape Girardeau but his orders were to fire upon any boat passing without reporting. Suppose by some means the rebels might get boats and be sending troops to assist General Marmaduke. His orders were to stop all boats and compel them to report. And this he did.

Sunday morning I was ordered to take thirty men aboard a steamer and proceed up the Ohio River twenty miles to a woodyard and bring down a number of cords of wood for use in camp. Soon after we started we could distinctly hear the cannon firing at Cape Girardeau and we knew the battle was on. We got our wood and arrived at Cairo after dark that evening. The noise of battle ceased sometime after noon but we had no means of knowing the result of the fight. The next morning the boats began to come back loaded with our troops. They said the rebels had been badly defeated and were in full retreat. It was after this battle that General Marmaduke was quoted as saying: "I do hope to some day meet a federal force so small I may be able to defeat it."

May 9th. Companies E and F were sent to Jonesboro today. It seemed there had been some trouble there ever since our boys were up before and it was worse at this time, so the two companies were sent there to quiet them. There was a powder boat tied to the Illinois shore of the Ohio River about ten miles above Cairo. Twenty men under a sergeant went there to guard this boat. They took three days' rations and stayed there during that time. A tug boat took the men up there and brought the relieved guard back again. While my position as Commissary Sergeant for the Company released me from guard duty, I gladly accepted the offer of going in command of this squad for three days. We started about one o'clock in the afternoon. The water was smooth and clear. The river was very wide and without much current. The day was beautiful and the ride was delightful. We landed at the boat on the river bank in a grand grove of oak timber. The ground was covered with grass and a beautiful spring of cool water was only a few rods back from the bank. The relieved guard gave us our instructions. We were to keep off all parties whether suspicious or not. Allow no one to come near our camp. If attacked from the land side we had good protection behind the river bank. If from the river, we had the boat itself to protect us. None of the men should leave the ground at any time. During the day we were all on duty as it were. At night a guard was placed at each end of the boat and one on shore and the others slept. The boat itself was a large, flat boat. The gunwales were about three feet above the water and there was a narrow deck the entire length on each side at this height. At each end this deck extended back about twelve feet. There the boat house arose probably eight feet high and covered all the boat except the decks just described. There was a custodian in charge of the powder to serve it out on orders, but he had nothing to do with the guards.

We read, fished, played games and went in swimming. The time passed quickly away and our three days were up and the relief came. All the time we were there it looked to me like a very careless piece of business, as near as we could learn we were ten miles from the nearest help. We had a large quantity of powder on the boat. Doubtless this was known to the rebels, also the number of men guarding it. Easily a hundred men might have been landed above us and marched down on us. That we would have given them a warm reception was true, but by coming at night they might have rushed us and easily overpowered us and burned the boat. I said nothing of this to the boys but was very glad when I saw the tug boat coming with the relief.

While there a steamboat came and carried a great quantity of powder down the river. Several boats passed without stopping. One lone man was passing in a row boat when one of our men raised his gun and ordered him to come ashore. At first he paid no attention to the order, but when it was repeated with emphasis he turned toward us. I ordered the soldier to order him off again, which he did, and the man went on down the river. I never heard of any attempt to capture this powder boat but wonder why it was not done.

Now for a fish story. Soon after we came to Cairo our boys bought a boat large enough to carry eight of us at once. They also bought a line large enough to make a troll line about four hundred feet long. To this line they fastened short lines and hooks. To bait all these hooks took lots of bait. To get this we would get a piece of fresh beef as large as your hand, take this and a pail to some ponds above the city. With a string, tied to the meat we would drop it into the water and raise it out immediately. From it would be suspended one or more, sometimes a half dozen, crawfish. Quickly holding this above the pail the crawfish would drop off into the pail. In this manner we would soon have half a pail of crawfish. They put a crawfish on each hook and stretched the line in the slack water of the river and left it over night. Next morning they would go with the boat, beginning at one end of the line would raise it and take off the fish and re-bait it and drop it back. Soon we had more fish than we could use. As Commissary Sergeant I had charge of the provisions. I sold the beef we drew and did not use because of having plenty of fish. Also the surplus fish, and soon had money enough to pay for our boat, line, hooks and everything. Then as we still sold the surplus we bought pie and cake, etc. One day I noticed a half barrel of eggs that looked quite enticing. Fifty cents per dozen seemed cheap then, so after testing several and finding them very clear and bright inside I bought them thinking to give the boys a nice treat. But when we had a great lot of them fried we found them so musty we were unable to eat them. Those we had not broken we carried back and sold to the grocer again.

May 21, 1863. Received our pay. I received sergeant's pay from the 8th of April, receiving twenty-nine dollars in all. Had drawn about twenty dollars worth of clothing since September last, so there was about eight dollars due me on clothing account.

One evening Lieutenant Shanklin asked me to take a walk with him. We walked up the levee back of the city till we were entirely by ourselves. There had been nothing said by either of us for sometime when he suddenly turned to me and asked, "Frank, do you have hard feelings toward me in regard to the lieutenancy?" I answered that I did not blame him in the least for what was done; that he was worthy of the place and while there was dishonorable work done at the time to beat me, I felt sure he was not the guilty party. He said he did not approve of the course the Captain and Hazlett took in the matter and he hoped it would not make any ill feeling between us. I assured him it would not. The sequel will come farther on. I was glad to have this talk with him and re-establish the old friendship between us again, for I believed him to be a noble man.

May 24th. General Baker, Adjutant General of Iowa, the Governor of Wisconsin and other notables visited us. General Baker made us quite a speech. Among other things he told us of how Iowa received the news of the capture of Fort Donelson. How the legislature suspended the liquor law for twenty-four hours, and then adjourned. How the news was spread from town to town and home to home. Bonfires and illuminations were the order of the nights for sometime. Again he pictured to us the gloom that settled over Iowa when the news came of the battle of Shiloh, and of the severe fighting, the heavy loss and final capture of the Iowa Brigade to which we belonged. He was a fine speaker and paid us many pretty compliments. The Governor of Wisconsin also spoke to us and some ladies and gentlemen among them sang us some patriotic songs. Governor Kirkwood was along but was too sick to leave the boat.

Today we received commutation for rations not drawn while in prison. I received eight dollars and seventy cents for nearly two months' rations. Major Kirkwood resigned and Captain Warner of Company H was appointed Major in his place.

June 6th. General Vandevere's division came down the river and halted there for sometime and then proceeded down the river. General Vandevere and General Leffingwell held a political debate at Buckingham in the fall of 1860. Vandevere was a Republican and a very candid, earnest speaker. As he spoke he drew the sleeves of his linen coat over his hands till the hands were entirely concealed in the sleeves. Leffingwell, a Democrat and also a very able speaker, was much more lively. Full of fun as he could be, he pushed his fists through his hands and thus pushed his linen coat sleeves above his elbows. At that time they were both judges and personally were friends. It was the most logical debate I ever heard. At the same meeting Tom Drummond of Vinton, editor of the Vinton Eagle, and J. B. Dorr of Dubuque, editor of the Dubuque Herald, both prominent in state politics were there. Vandevere and Drummond were guests at my father's house that night and I saw much of them. At this time there were only two congressional districts in the state and Vandevere and Leffingwell were the opposing candidates in this the second district. Vandevere was elected and Drummond was elected to the state senate. The war came on and Vandevere and Leffingwell both went as colonels of Iowa regiments and both soon became generals. Drummond went as a lieutenant in the regular army and was in the first battle of Bull Run and his company was one of very few that came off the field in good order. Dorr went as Major of the Twelfth Iowa, was captured with us at Shiloh and escaped at the same time I did by representing himself as a private while a private remained in his place. Now General Vandevere's division was on its way to partake in the siege of Vicksburg.

June 7th. Fifty recruits joined us. They were to be known as Company C of our regiment. The three companies that went to Fort Randal had been detached from us and we were to have three new companies. Company C only having fifty men was not to have a captain then but would have when they recruit men enough.

June 8th. General Burnside's corps was coming down the Ohio River and going on down the Mississippi. This great number of troops going down the river means a contest for the supremacy at Vicksburg and an open river to the Gulf. It was a grand sight to see an army passing on board the boats. Nearly every regiment had a brass band with it and as they came near a city they poured forth patriotic music in great abundance.

CAIRO - Notes:

-- **William W Kirkwood**, whose appointment as Major was controversial, was a nephew of Iowa Governor Samuel J Kirkwood. William resigned March 4, 1863. His replacement was Edgar Warner. See Chapter 8

-- **Joseph Houseman Newbold** 25 of Hillsboro, Henry County, was appointed Captain of Company F when the 14th Iowa regiment was formed November 1861. He was taken prisoner April 6 1862 during the battle of Shiloh. As an officer he was held many months as a prisoner of war but with the release of the officers from captivity the regiment was reformed. In March 1863 Newbold was promoted Lieutenant Colonel. He commanded the regiment in Shaw's absence. Newbold was killed in action at the battle of Pleasant Hill Louisiana on April 9 1864, riding a captured war horse owned by former president Zachary Taylor, whose son Richard Taylor was commanding the rebel forces at Pleasant Hill. Captain Warren C Jones, who took over command of the 14th when Newbold was killed, brought the famous horse home to Mount Pleasant after the War. Newbold's brother **Cyrus Newbold** 19 had attempted to enlist with him in 1861 into the 14th Iowa but was not accepted for health reasons. In August 1862, two other brothers enlisted into Company C of the 25th Iowa Infantry; **Jacob Newbold** 22 was wounded in Louisiana and discharged the following year; **Joshua Newbold** 32 was appointed Captain of Company C; in 1877 he became Governor of the State of Iowa.

-- Captain Crane is **LeRoy A Crane** 22 of Anamosa. In 1860 Leroy lived with his parents next door to William T Shaw who became Colonel of the 14th Infantry Regiment of Iowa Volunteers. Shaw's wife Helen Crane was Leroy's older sister. Crane was elected Second Lieutenant of Company H November 1861 when the regiment formed. Crane was captured with the regiment at Shiloh, and held with the officers until October 1862; he was then promoted to Captain March 1863 when the regiment was reformed. Crane survived the War and mustered out with the regiment November 16 1864 at Davenport, Iowa. BF Thomas spelled the name as "Craine". This sad tale of a girl committing suicide in the camp of the 14th Iowa was even reported in the Jonesboro newspaper. Thomas spelled it "Jonesborough".

-- **Colonel William Tuckerman Shaw** 40 of Anamosa Iowa was born in Maine, the son of William Nicholas Shaw and Nancy Stevens. His grandfather had been an officer during the Revolution, serving as an aide to General Knox. William T Shaw taught schools in Indiana and Kentucky before enlisting into the army during the Mexican War, where he fought at the battle of Buena Vista. After that war, Shaw lived in the Indian Territory for a time, then he left for California during the Gold Rush of '49. His success in the mines is unknown but within a few years he was living on a farm at Anamosa Iowa, speculating in real estate, building commercial buildings in town, founding a bank and a railroad, and investing in many capitalist ventures.

-- When the Civil War broke out he was commissioned Colonel of the 14th Iowa Regiment and was praised widely as a brave and daring officer, and a fine commander. He was captured with his regiment at Shiloh and held captive six months until October 1862. Major-General AJ Smith praised him highly as a commander of skill and courage and later gave him command of a division. Some thought Shaw would be made a general but his outspoken criticism of the performances of his superior officers at Shiloh and at Red River halted his career advancement. He was described as tall and sparely built with a nervous, energetic temperament.

-- Colonel William Tuckerman Shaw of the 14th Iowa, was first cousin to Boston's Francis George Shaw, their fathers were brothers. A staunch abolitionist, Francis George Shaw was the father of **Robert Gould Shaw**, the Colonel of the famous 54th Massachusetts Infantry, the first "colored" regiment in the Union army. It was 26 year old Colonel Robert Gould Shaw, with his regiment of free black men, who was killed leading his men in the assault on Fort Wagner, South Carolina on July 17 1863. Their incredible bravery at Fort Wagner has been forever immortalized on a famous monument in Boston, and more recently in the movie *Glory*.

CHAPTER XI

COLUMBUS, KENTUCKY

June 16th. We received orders to be ready to leave Cairo at six o'clock in the morning, and at that time Companies E, F, G, H and I went aboard the steamer "*United States*" and were taken to Columbus, Kentucky, twenty miles below Cairo. We did not understand what the purpose of this move was. In the evening one hundred men were detailed to go on picket.

June 18th. We had relieved the troops who were here and were stationed here for guard duty. The city was located on the bank of the river and extended back probably twenty rods to the bluff. This bluff was probably three hundred feet high and came to the river just above the city. On this point Fort Halleck was located. It was high above the water and commanded a long view of the river as you looked up stream. It was built by the rebels. They had a huge chain, with links a foot long and made of two inch round iron, anchored in the bluff and then carried across the river for more than a mile and fastened there. It was their purpose that this chain would prevent our gunboats from passing down the river, and hold them under close fire till they could sink them. But sometime before the boats went down a lot of drift caught against the chain and broke it. A piece of chain about fifteen feet long was still fast in the bluff. Each link had a cast core that filled the center to keep them from crushing. Upon this cast core were the words "*Washington Navy Yard*". That would indicate the chain had been made at the navy yard at Washington. We were told this was the same chain that General Jackson had used at New Orleans to prevent the British boats from ascending the river. There was a stairway dug in the face of the bluff from the fort to the river. It zigzagged back and forth to give a more gradual incline, for the face of the bluff was nearly perpendicular, and was dug deep so as to cover those passing from view from the river. On the land side were heavy earthen walls. There were barracks, a powder magazine and officers' quarters in the fort. Many heavy guns were mounted upon the angles of the walls.

The second day we were there there was a scare. The report that a body of rebels were approaching to try to capture the fort caused us to do our guard duty diligently, and also for the men in the fort to lie with their arms in their hands. In fact we were aroused about two o'clock at night and manned the works expecting the rebels to come. But daylight came and no rebels. There was a negro regiment here camped just outside the fort. This was the first negro troops we had seen. They did not make a very good appearance. There was less than a thousand of them. Casaday was returned to us here without trial. We were all very sorry for that for we felt sure he would give us more trouble.

June 19th. Twenty men of the One Hundred Twenty-Eighth Illinois were put into our Company and the same number in Company H. They told us it was only for while we were here, but we feared it would be a permanent arrangement. It would be unfair for them as well as for us to have them remain with us. There were twenty men and a sergeant from our Company on picket today.

June 21st. We were joined by the companies we had left at Cairo, also by the new Companies A and B. Now we had a regiment of ten companies the first time since we enlisted. We had considerable sport with the men of the new companies. Everything was new to them. The boys led them into some very amusing, predicaments. Davis and McLain had been at home on furlough and now returned.

June 24th. Detailed on picket. Went about two miles on the road to Union City. There were twenty men, three corporals, one sergeant and one lieutenant. Lieutenant Burke of Company H was in command. Established the post in a secure place with three vidette posts, one in front and one on either flank some distance from the main post. Stationed one man on duty at each vidette post. We all understood the rebels were prowling about our lines and might attack us at any time. There were cavalry scouts outside of the picket line. They sometimes encountered small bodies of rebel cavalry and sometimes had pretty sharp skirmishes with them. Sometimes the rebels were strong enough to drive our cavalry inside the picket line, and once they drove cavalry and pickets into camp. Today there was such a dash made but after a sharp skirmish they fell back. The bullets flew thick for awhile but luckily none of our men were injured. Suddenly we heard the horses coming on the run and by the time we rallied into position our cavalry passed us. The next instant the rebels came into view down the road and we gave them a volley. They came on and received a second volley when they fled to shelter and returned our fire, but with their horses they were too much exposed to our fire and very soon mounted and scurried away. After this everything was quiet till we were relieved the next morning.

Before the skirmish a wagon load of beer in kegs came in and the boys stopped the driver and questioned him in regard to what of the enemy he had seen as he came. While talking to him in front two of the boys lifted a keg of beer out of the back end of the wagon and rolled it into the bushes. The man drove off none the wiser. Neither the lieutenant nor I drank beer. The boys were quite moderate with the beer drinking. The man came back in the evening and told us he had lost a keg out of the wagon somewhere and asked if we had seen it. The lieutenant and I answered not a word but the boys were loud in the declaration of ignorance. After he was gone the lieutenant urged that we should pay the man for the beer but the boys would not hear to any such thing.

June 30th. Had review under Colonel Messmore of the Thirty-first Wisconsin, and had an awful time of it. Marched about a mile from the fort and had just formed into line when it began to rain. Soon it was pouring down in great shape. There we stood till the reviewing officers passed us and then we marched in review before them. The rain was dreadful. The slush and water was awful and the whole proceeding was very foolish. The idea of marching out for review in the face of a storm like that! It was Colonel Messmore who did it.

July 1st. Casaday knocked a man down and robbed him in the streets of the city last night and was arrested for it today. Peter Fingle deserted at Shiloh but afterward joined the boys in the Union Brigade. Soon he deserted them and was not seen again till we came to Columbus. Here we found him dressed in citizen's clothing and at work. He was put under arrest and was soon to be tried for desertion. He was in a sense a bad man but not to be compared to Casaday. He enlisted with us at Davenport and was enlisted when drunk and when sobered did not want to go. We all felt sorry for him for we feared he would be severely punished.

July 4th, 1863. We had what we were led to believe would be a grand celebration today. It was to be a celebration by the civilians and military combined and to end in a grand barbecue furnished by the citizens. The citizens had prepared a place about three miles below the city. They would have a number of Kentucky men for speakers among whom were Judge Bullock, Senator Grover and several other notables. We marched down with our arms and accouterments and soon after we arrived the meeting was called to order. We noticed there were but few citizens there and what there were were mostly running stands for the sale of refreshments.

There seemed to be no preparation for a banquet. Senator Doolittle of Wisconsin was the first man called upon to speak but he had not come down from the city. General Asboth, who was in command at Columbus, was called upon and responded with a short speech. He was a German officer and spoke very broken English. After Asboth came Judge Bullock of Kentucky. He spoke but a short time and then read several letters of regrets from Kentuckians who were unable to come. Some singing followed and we were dismissed for dinner. Then the officers learned there was no dinner prepared for us. Colonel Messmore mounted the stand and called the soldiers about him. He said the city had promised us a splendid dinner but now excused that they had not time to prepare it. They had time to fix their booths and stalls where they might sell their beer, lemonade and cakes at exorbitant prices, and their large dance floor to attract the soldier and delude him out of his money, but showed no social or patriotic feeling. He asked the soldiers to all fall in in their regular order and march quietly back to camp where we had plenty of hard tack and coffee free. He asked the citizens to form in line and march back with us and partake of our frugal fare. He said we had been imposed upon and not one cent of our money would go into the booths of the citizens. There were probably a dozen ladies, officers' wives, with us, and when Messmore closed they sang the old song which closes with the words:

*"Though the streams were as clear
And the stars shone as bright
Yet it was not my own native land."*

And how the boys did cheer. We were strangers and they tried to take us in. We marched back to the fort and had our dinners and were very well content with our lot. In the evening all the boys so inclined went to the city and had a drinking frolic. Hazlett was quite drunk which brought him into trouble with Colonel Newbold.

July 7th. This evening the news came that Vicksburg had surrendered. Heard none of the particulars yet. Could see the light of the illumination at Cairo. The news was sufficient to set our boys wild. Nearly all went to the city to spend the night in revelry. I want to say right here that none of our Mess partook of these debauches. We learned next morning that the boys did much mischief in the city. They came home howling and swearing at all hours of the night and even till after sun-up the next morning.

The next morning the news of the fall of Vicksburg was confirmed. They claimed twenty-five thousand prisoners were taken. Fired a salute from the fort at noon and illuminated at night.

Saturday, July 11th. Last night we had one of our many scares. The long roll sounded and we fell into line.

Were told the Thirty-Second Iowa had gone to Union City and the rebels had attacked them and driven them back. It was supposed the rebels were following them up in force and would soon be here and attack the fort. But the day passed without event and the excitement subsided.

At eleven o'clock the next night we were called out again and half of each regiment was ordered out to guard the works; that is, stand at the breast works ready to repulse attack, the other half to return to the barracks to sleep. Our Company was one among the guards. The Company was divided into two platoons and one stood up while the other laid down to rest. The platoon on duty was ordered to stand on top of the breast works and the other platoon lay down just behind the works. We spent the night and next day thus, relieving each other at intervals. The next evening we were relieved and the other half of the regiment took the place for twenty-four hours.

This morning the Thirty-Second Iowa returned. They had three killed and nine wounded. They reported the rebels about nine miles from us. We thought General Asboth was very badly scared. We did not believe the rebels would attack us here behind breastworks. They might come nearer and harass us some but would never come to battle here. I was in command of the post guard or the guard that guards the fort and magazine today. It would have been a good day for the rebels to make an attack upon us, for in the morning the fog was so thick you could not see a man four rods from you. Towards noon the fog cleared and the sun came out. But the rebels failed to come.

July 14th. The excitement had quieted down somewhat till about midnight we were called out and told the rebels were above us on the river between here and Cairo and would compel us to come out and fight them. The next day passed without any news of the rebels.

July 16th. A detachment consisting of two regiments of infantry, two pieces of artillery and two squadrons of cavalry were sent out to Clinton to learn what they could of the enemy. They returned in three days and reported the country clear of rebels about Clinton.

Edgar Dykeman, one of our Company who was from Redman, died July 19th. His death was very sudden, he being sick only two days. He was one of the best boys we had.

Last night our whole Company was sent to town to guard the depot. The whole attention of the command was centered on the rebels outside our lines and now it was feared some enemy might fire the depot and destroy the immense amount of stores it contained. This had been done in other places and we were trying to guard against it here. Probably our officers had heard something to put them on their guard. So each night for sometime a company was sent to the depot to guard it from harm. Company H went to Union City today and returned this evening. They said the people reported about eleven thousand secesh at Jackson ready to march on this place.

Dykeman was buried July 20th. On picket at the railroad again. Had a very severe storm of lightning, wind and rain. The lightning was almost a continual illumination and the thunder rolled continuously while the rain poured down in torrents.

July 27th. On guard again at the same place. Everything seems quiet again. Heard today that the body of rebels that had been hovering around us made an attack on the works at Hickman and were defeated with severe loss.

There had been another promotion of sergeants in our Company. Davis to First; Ford Second; Wilson Third; I Fourth and Hoeffer Fifth Sergeant. The Corporals were all advanced. Felter First; Henry Williams Second; Luke Third and McLain Fourth. Last Sunday the Illinois men who had been with us for some time were sent to Island No. 10 to join their regiments.

July 30th. Received our pay for May and June. I drew thirty-four dollars, for sergeants were receiving seventeen dollars per month and privates thirteen.

My left arm was badly poisoned. I caught it from ivy I came in contact with while on fatigue duty. The arm was swollen to twice the normal size and yet I was detailed to go on guard and the surgeon would not excuse me. I was mad at once and told him he was entirely too severe on the men. He bade me beware of speaking so to an officer. I was walking away from him and replied that I did not fear him for everybody knew what I said was true. He then ordered me to come back and let him examine my arm again. I told him he had passed upon it once and that was sufficient. I went on to my tent expecting to be arrested, but I never heard anything of it after. I was hasty.

Three weeks afterward our hospital steward resigned and I wanted the place. I thought my chances were entirely thrown away, but I went to the surgeon and made application. He told me the place was promised to another man, though if he had known I would accept it he would rather have had me as I had served sometime in that position and part of the time under himself. He talked very pleasantly for nearly an hour and never referred to my quick temper.

A man was drummed out of camp. He belonged to Company A, Fifty-Second Indiana. The crime was desertion and the sentence that he be drummed out of camp and then sent to the penitentiary at Alton to serve out his unexpired time. The army was formed into a hollow square. The officer in charge and the prisoner inside. The officer read the sentence and then the prisoner was marched across the square followed by the band playing the "Rogue's March". Then he was marched to the entrance of the fort and sent away to prison. The band returned playing "Yankee Doodle".

August 5, 1863. The steamer "Ruth", one of the largest boats on the river, burned last night just above here. When she was discovered to be on fire they attempted to run her ashore but she struck a sand bar near the middle of the stream and was consumed. The report says some thirty people lost their lives there. The light from the burning boat made it quite light where we were. She was loaded with beef cattle for the army and they were all lost.

Drummed another man out of camp today. He belonged to Company E of the Fifty-Second Indiana. The crime was firing a shot through his captain's tent with intent to kill the captain. His sentence, to be drummed out of the camp and then serve three years in the penitentiary at Alton. The sentence was executed in the same manner the one was a few days previous.

August 14th. Felter and I were on picket together at the railroad, I as sergeant and Felter as corporal. Near noon we went to a farm house some distance outside the lines and found it was the home of a Union family formerly from Indiana. They cordially invited us to remain with them for dinner and we as cordially accepted. The dinner was excellent and the hospitality cheerfully given. When we started back they insisted on our coming again, which we promised to do. It was very pleasant to us to be treated so kindly by these good hearted people.

August 16th. Felter and I were again on guard together. This time in the city. It was Wilson's and Williams' turn on guard but both of them were sick so we went in their places. The weather was very warm and the boys complained very much at standing in the hot sunshine. During the night Felter had something like a congestive chill followed by a spasm. I sent for an ambulance and had him taken to a hospital. Next day he returned to camp and soon seemed as well as ever.

August 18th. Mat Clark was quite sick. Threatened with some kind of fever. While the weather had been quite warm the heat still increased till it became excessively hot. Too hot to be on duty but that did not excuse us, and I was on guard again. Many of our boys were now sick. There was a talk of moving us out of the fort into tents.

August 20th. On picket again today at the station below town on the river bank called "Number Seven". Captain Crane officer of the day and Lieutenant Shanklin officer of the guard. Shanklin was taken violently sick and sent to the hospital. When it came time to go the grand rounds at midnight Captain Crane said it was too dark and he would not go. I was fearful he might get into trouble and told him so. He then told me to take his horse and go myself. I mounted the horse and took one man with me and started. I soon was very sorry I started for we really could see nothing it was so dark. However, the horse followed the path readily. The man followed me on foot. When we came to a post and were halted the man passed around my horse and answered the challenge. When we passed the post he again fell in behind the horse. The picket line must have been six miles long and it took us over two hours to make the grand rounds, but we did it. The picket line was changed the next day and many of the posts discontinued.

Augusts 24th. On post guard today. Guard mount was held inside the fort and our division marched down to the city. About noon there came the most severe wind storm we ever experienced there. There was no rain but the wind blew so hard we could hardly stand up against it. The dust flew so thick it almost stifled us. This lasted more than an hour and was blowing quite hard yet in the evening. Just before dark I was taken quite sick and soon grew so bad the lieutenant sent two men to take me to our quarters. The doctor came to me at once and prescribed for me. The next day I had a high fever all day and next day the same condition prevailed. But the third day the fever left me and I soon grew much better.

Wilson had the ague and shook regularly every other day. Felter had some stomach complaint and he and Wilson were about to get a sick furlough and go home for thirty days. This would leave Clark and I alone again.

August 31st. On post guard again today. Lieutenant Dodds of Company F was our officer. He was very easy on the boys and in the morning all had gone to camp but those on guard. It was too bad to expose him to censure in this manner. Nothing came of it, however, but if the officer who came to relieve us had been strict we would have had to fall into line to receive him and there was only Lieutenant Dodds and myself to do this.

I felt almost as well as ever again. One night our boys went out about three miles to cut down a bee tree that they had discovered sometime before. They got about a pail full of honey and many stings. Besides they got their clothing so full of a burr, about the size of a wild buckwheat grain, that was so tenacious in holding on, that their clothing was almost ruined.

Company F sent in some furloughs for the signature of the officers and they were returned without signing.

We supposed by this that no more furloughs would be granted till some that were out would have returned. The rule was one furlough for each company and as many sick furloughs as the surgeon said should go.

Sometime ago there was a family consisting of a man, his wife and five children murdered near Island Number Ten. A number of negroes were accused of the crime. It was said one of the negroes took a babe by the feet and kicked its head till he kicked the child's brains out. It was a most brutal affair. A number of negroes were arrested and brought here for trial by military court martial. Nine of them were sentenced to be hanged. September 4, 1863 was the day set to hang the first three of them. The gallows were erected about a mile south of the city. All the troops off duty were marched out to witness the execution. The three negroes were led upon the scaffold and then a negro preacher standing on the scaffold with them made a long prayer. After the prayer the sentence was read. Then the preacher shook hands with them and bade them goodbye. By this time one of the negroes was quaking as with the ague. The ropes were adjusted about their necks and the white caps pulled down over their faces. Then the word was given and all three dropped about seven feet.

One seemed to die without a tremor, but the other two struggled for what seemed to be a long time before they died. To many of the spectators it was entertaining, and to some, amusing. One young lady on horseback near where I was tittered and laughed, saying, "Isn't it funny to see them dance on air?" To me it was a very solemn sight. Three men deliberately put to death with thousands gathered around to witness the sight. I never want to witness another such a scene.

Corporal Hoeffer came back from furlough last night. Felter received his sick furlough last night and started home. Went to Cairo on the steamer "*Jennie Hubbs*". Thirteen out of our regiment were furloughed.

There was much talk of our regiment being sent away from here soon. General Asboth had been removed and General A. J. Smith had taken command. Asboth was a foreigner and Smith an American. He looked like rather a hard working farmer, but they said he was a great fighter.

On picket at the spring, now called "*Number Nine*". Each post had one sergeant, two corporals and seven men, except our post which had five. Captain Gallagher had been away for sometime. He was on detail with the court martial. Lieutenant Hazlett told us the order for no more furloughs had been changed and he had made out applications for Wilson and I to go home. I did not believe they would be granted but we would soon know.

September 10, 1863. Moved out of the fort today. We were in tents in an old apple orchard, near the gibbet where the negroes were hanged. Conveniences were much better in the fort, but it would be much healthier in the tents. The most unpleasant thing here was the water which was so far away it had to be hauled to us in barrels and was warm and brackish. It was beautiful ground, slightly rolling, covered with grass and shaded by the large apple trees. A circus on exhibition near the city took in pretty nearly every boy that was off duty. It performed two days and nearly cleaned the boys out of cash.

September 13th. I had a hard chill followed by fever. The weather had been hot for some days but a little shower of rain followed by a north wind cooled the air so it was quite comfortable. Had another chill followed with fever the next day. Wilson received his furlough September 14th and started home. Clark and I were the only two of our Mess left here. We had two tents of the wedge-tent pattern, each covering about six feet square of ground. One tent we used as our parlor. In it we had a bunk long enough for four men to sit on side by side. In front of this tent we had a floor laid as a kind of open porch, the floor about three by six feet. At one end of this floor we sawed a notch out of the end of the board for a boot jack. When a comrade called upon us he very decorously stepped up to our boot jack and pulled his boots before he entered the parlor. In the other tent we had our bed. This was formed by driving four crotches in the ground so the fork was about a foot above ground. Lengthwise on these we had two poles laid and cross-wise on these poles we laid barrel staves with the hollow side up. Upon these staves we spread our blankets double and another blanket we pulled over us when we needed it. But so far the weather had been so warm we had not needed it. The only drawback to this bed was it made the occupants sleep close together. On the other hand, no one ever rolled out of this bed while asleep. It was much pleasanter than sleeping on the ground.

September 16th. On post guard today. Had a chill followed by a fever in the afternoon and was sent to camp by the lieutenant. Sergeant Morton and Corporal Root of Company F were also relieved because of the ague.

The next morning I went on sick call to the surgeon and he gave me some more quinine. It was a common remark among the boys that "If a man had his leg shot off the doctor would give him quinine." But I think quinine was what we needed in about every case because of the malaria. The doctor said I must not go on duty again till I was better. That was about the way I felt about it too. He said I must attend roll call and dress parade but not do guard duty or drill.

September 19th. Yesterday Sergeant Ford went to the Colonel and told him he had a chance for promotion to a commission in a new regiment if he could get home. The Colonel gave him a blank application for a furlough and told him to have the company commander sign it and he would approve it and thought the furlough would be granted. I thought it very doubtful. At dress parade the order was given to clean up our guns ready to turn them back and draw Springfield rifles.

Yesterday was my day for a chill but I escaped it. I had been taking large doses of quinine and think it about time I was receiving some returns for it.

September 20th. Charlie Ford received his furlough for twenty days and started for home this morning. I was glad he succeeded; feared he would not. Great excitement about going away, some thought to join General Rosecrans. This morning a larger detail of men was called for guard so as to relieve the Thirty-First Wisconsin who were ordered to Louisville. This regiment was composed of drafted men or substitutes and was the worst lot of grumblers I ever met. They felt pretty sure they were not mustered into the service legally and would not be surprised to get an order at any time to be mustered out and sent home. This camp was continually rife with rumors of discharges coming.

Colonel Messmore in command was a shrewd lawyer and I believed would be a good fighter. His time soon came for the regiment went to Louisville and from there to Perryville in time to take an active part in that battle. They lost a number of their men there. What their career was after this I know not. Colonel Messmore died in 1904 at Los Angeles, California.

There was a military prison in Columbus where there were a number of prisoners. Mostly citizens, but also some secesh and some Union soldiers such as Fingle as mentioned before. There was a captain who had constant charge of this prison. He remained at the prison office all the time. He had a negro boy about twelve years of age as office boy. One day this boy got quite drunk. There was a rebel captain in prison named Captain Cushman. The boy knew the captain before the war, and for some cause hated him. He would slip out his captain's sword and revolver and stagger toward the prison door. The captain would say, "Here, Tom, where are you going?" "Captain, I am only going in to kill Captain Cushman." Then the captain would take the weapons from him and bade him lie down and be quiet. But soon he was up and off again and always to kill Captain Cushman. It caused a good deal of merriment among the guard.

We drilled one hour in the forenoon every day to keep us in practice. Many of the trees in the orchard in which we were camped came in bloom. It was a strange sight to see the trees white with bloom in the fall of the year. Some of the boys felt superstitious. They said our camp was in the orchard. The gibbet where the negroes were hung was close by. The apple trees were in bloom out of season and this must portend evil to us. I had no fears because of all this.

September 30th. But something did happen to us last night sure enough. We mess now in full company and John B. Edwards was our cook. He was probably thirty-five years of age and the boys all familiarly call him "Pap". He had a large Sibley tent in which he kept his commissary stores. For several nights a cow had broken in the tent each night, probably for the salt, but she ate our crackers, hominy, etc. She had always managed to escape without injury to herself. Pap was mad and the boys strongly sympathetic with him. The situation was thoroughly discussed yesterday evening and the decision was that Pap was to stay in the tent and watch till the cow came and then shoot her with a load of salt. Larue loaded the gun; put in the powder then some paper, then a handful of salt and a little more paper. The salt was a little damp and Larue in his zeal rammed it down solid. He said afterward there was over four inches of ammunition in the gun. It was expected when Pap heard the cow coming he would come out of the tent, and when the cow started to run he would fire the salt into her side or quarters. But Pap must have fallen asleep, for he said the first thing he knew the cow had her head inside the tent. He placed the muzzle of the gun within a few inches of her face and pulled the trigger. The recoil of the gun threw him backwards so he fell through the other side of the tent. We heard what seemed to he a terrible clap of thunder followed by a tremor of the earth like when a heavy body falls and were out in a trice. Pap was lifting himself from back of the tent and in front lay the cow with her head in at the door. She was still kicking when we discovered her but soon lay perfectly quiet. Yes, dead. The wet salt packed solid had crushed her skull although it had not broken the skin. What was to be done? The wisest council prevailed. We would skin the cow and carefully dress the meat and turn it over to the Quartermaster and have him find the owner and pay for the cow. All went to work with a will and soon the quarters of the brute were hanging from the limbs of the apple trees.

In the morning a delegation of the boys went to the Quartermaster and told the story of our troubles. But instead of taking the beef off our hands he turned against us. He called us worse names than we ever dreamed could be legally applied to men who wore the blue. Said our Company were the worst sons of Satan in the regiment: that we were always getting into difficulty and he would have nothing to do with the matter but we might take care of ourselves. The next best thing to do was to make common cause with the other companies of the regiment. So we divided the beef into nice messes and took part to each of the other companies, not forgetting the officers. Telling the story without color or blemish and hinting that it would be difficult to find a man that had seen a brindle cow with crooked horns or a cow of any other color about our camp. The boys and officers had a hearty laugh over it and accepted our offering. Two of us went to Colonel Newbold and told him the whole story. At first he was very angry, but finally said the Quartermaster should have accepted our offer, but as he had not done so he himself would take no notice of the matter unless compelled to. If the owner came for the cow he supposed we would have to pay for her unless we could prove the owner was a secesh. We told him we had no knowledge of whom the owner was but felt sure he was secesh for no Union man would allow his cow to steal the rations from a poor soldier. The colonel laughed and we went back to our tents feeling much better.

Did this happen because the gibbet stood close by and the apple trees came in bloom in the fall? Who can tell? We never heard who was owner of the cow nor did we make special inquiry. At home we had been taught that salt cured meat, but here it killed instead of cured unless you would take the position that it first killed and then cured, for the cow never bothered our rations again. Sometimes the boys of the other companies would remark to each other when they knew the Quartermaster would overhear: "Don't you wish we could get some more good beef like that Company G gave us?".

Friday, October 2nd, 1863. Last night some prisoners from the military prison were discovered in a tunnel they had dug from their prison room to the street. The prison was surrounded by an open court which was enclosed by a tight board fence ten feet high. The nearest the building comes to this fence is about fifteen feet on the east side. There were three guards inside the prison with the prisoners, six between the building and the fence and more than a dozen posted at intervals outside the fence. During the day the prisoners had the freedom of the court but at night they were confined to the building. There were a few desperadoes confined in cells and were not allowed out at any time.

For some days the guards had noticed the frequent visits of the prisoners to the pump, which stood in the court, to fill their canteens, taking the water into the building. This caused our men to be more alert to learn what so much water was used for. The thought always follows any unusual occurrence that they are scheming an escape. Their work was kept concealed till last night when one of the guards outside the fence saw as he made the turn at the end of his beat the head of a man quickly disappear in the street in front of him. Startled as he was he managed to give the alarm. The guards off duty rushed out and there they discovered a hole in the ground large enough to admit a man's body. The guard had discovered the first man that attempted to escape, and he seeing the guard dropped back hoping he had not been seen, and intending as soon as the guard passed to make good his escape. If he had sprung out the chances were good he might have escaped and in the excitement several others might also have escaped. But now the game was up.

Along both sides of the building inside were bunks erected one above the other. The lower one had simply a board about eight inches high in front and the bedding lay on the floor. The next bunk above was just high enough that a man could sit upright in the lower bunk and his head would touch the floor on the next bunk above him. So likewise was the distance to the third bunk. In front of one of these lower bunks the prisoners had a bench upon which they sat to play cards. The game was always interesting and a crowd gathered about to see it. This was the blind used to throw our guards off the track. In this bunk so screened they had removed some of the floor and here began their tunnel. Soon they filled all the space under the building with dirt, then resorted to the use of water to make the dirt into adhesive clay so as to make it into balls as large as a man's head which they secretly carried to other bunks and secreted them under their blankets. For some days they had been watched very closely but were not discovered till they made their appearance on the street. I can readily imagine the chagrin of the poor fellows who had worked so faithfully under so many disadvantages to secure their freedom and found a total failure at the moment when success seemed certain. Is not liberty a great boon that men will sacrifice so much to gain it? After all was quiet again the captain of the prison placed twelve of the leaders in the attempt to escape in irons and close confinement. The only way to keep prisoners safe is to iron them.

Again I was on the sick list. Stomach trouble, biliousness and one day a severe shake like the ague. I was compelled to get an overcoat and it was only the seventh day of October. It had been very dry for some time but at last we had a heavy rain.

October 9th. Three more of the negroes were hanged. They were of the same lot as those hung here before. As they were being conducted to the scaffold they were singing in a low tone. We could not hear the words they were singing. After mounting the scaffold a negro preacher offered a short prayer. As soon as he finished and bade them goodbye they began singing again much louder than before. The ropes were adjusted and the white caps drawn down over their faces and still the singing continued till the drop fell. In twenty-five minutes they were pronounced dead. It was not a pleasant sight to see the hanging of human beings although they may be ever so hard criminals. I resolved if possible not to witness the sight again.

October 10th. On post guard today. The captain thought the prisoners were again digging a tunnel but was unable to locate it. They were being watched very closely. We now understood that Captain Cushman, who was supposed to be locked in a cell alone, was the leader of the last attempt to get out. By some means he had secured egress from his cell and was the leader in the tunnel work. If he had been at the exit when discovered he would have made his escape beyond doubt. He was placed in heavy irons as well as in a lone cell.

October 12, 1863. By the laws of Iowa the soldiers from the State had a right to vote wherever they may be on election day. Therefore our State election being held this day we had the polls opened in our camp. The governors, William M. Stone had 259 votes and General Tuttle had 87 votes. Stone would have had nearly every one had it not been for the treatment he gave us last winter at Rolla, Missouri.

October 15th. Peter Wilson returned from furlough. He must have enjoyed himself while at home. He looked splendid and I was very glad to see him. He had much to tell us about the friends at home.

On picket. A sergeant has charge of half the pickets now the same as a lieutenant had a short time ago. There was a small body of rebels along our front all day. Some pretty sharp skirmishing. Set a trap for them and tried to draw them into it but they were too sharp for that. There will be cavalry used tomorrow if they are still here.

October 17th. Cavalry out all day yesterday and chased a small body of mounted rebels toward Union City. Considerable skirmishing but no lives lost. Think they will bother us no more.

John Felter came back from furlough. He did not look well and was not fit for service.

October 18th. General Grant passed up the river. When the steamer came opposite the fort a salute was fired. We also heard the salute fired when he passed Cairo.

October 23rd. On post guard. Rained all day very hard and nearly all my men were wet through. It is quite cold. Overcoats are a necessity. Found a pocketbook containing over fifty dollars in the bunk I occupied in the guard quarters. When I returned to camp I called upon a sergeant of Company B who had occupied the bunk before I did and who I correctly supposed was the owner of the pocketbook. Returned it to him and enjoyed his surprise for he did know where he had lost it and supposed it lost beyond recovery.

October 24th. Froze hard last night. Ice half an inch thick. Colonel Newbold was determined to make us proficient in drill and therefore drilled us every day. The boys growled but knew it was better for them.

October 25th. Had regimental inspection by Colonel Newbold. Inspection made us a lot of work but was better for us. Without it many of our arms and accouterments, not to say clothing also, would be unfit for use. Colonel Newbold blended kindness with firmness. Many of the boys complained of his rigorous treatment and yet they loved him.

George Heimlich, a less than half witted man from below Toledo, who had been with us from the first, had been in the guard house for sometime. The charge against him was sleeping when on guard. He now received his sentence, which was to forfeit three months' pay and to labor three months on the works at Fort Quinby. It seemed pretty severe on one who was so irresponsible that he never should have been received into the service. Had very stormy weather for some days with heavy rain, after which it had turned very cool.

November 4th. There was another scare. That evening our picket guard was doubled and at four o'clock four companies were ordered under arms and in marching order ready to go at a moment's notice. Our Company was one of the four. We had no knowledge of what frightened the officers, but the next day all was quiet as usual. We had moved back from the orchard to the fort and now there was talk that we might build cabins on the edge of the bluff between the fort and the city. Probably we would winter here.

November 5th. There was a large detail, of which I was one, to go up the river about five miles and cut timber to build cabins. A number of teams went with us and we cut large cypress trees and then cut them into logs eighteen feet long. These were hauled to the fort. Cypress was the most wonderful timber I ever saw. Some of these logs were three feet through and from that down to eighteen inches and eighteen feet long. We easily split them into slabs about eight inches thick. Many of the slabs were nearly as smooth as if they had been planed. These were notched at the ends to fit each other and then built into the wall edgewise and they made handsome walls. We cut and hauled timber for two weeks. Some of the men remained in camp and erected the cabins. So the work went briskly on. For the roof we cut special pieces of cypress four feet long and split them into "shakes". These made a splendid roof. Government furnished lumber for doors and floors. Also one six-light window for each cabin. Our cabins finished we moved in and enjoyed the comfort of very commodious quarters. The ingenious boys then made many cupboards, shelves, stools, benches, etc., out of this beautiful cypress timber.

November 16. Fingle, the deserter who had been in prison for a long time, received sentence. He was to be shot the fourth of December next. The sentence was read to us at dress parade. It made quite a sensation among the boys. There was nothing else talked of that evening and I do not believe there was much sleep among them that night. Every one was sorry that this should happen to one of our Company. Casaday, our wicked man, and as bad a deserter as Fingle, was released and returned to his Company without even a trial. Every one thought he should have received the death sentence instead of Fingle. We had no idea why this sentence should be passed on Fingle and not on Casaday.

November 20. Post guard. Orders very strict. Must keep the relief that was off duty here all the time. This was to guard against surprise. Fingle was confined in a cell alone. There was a small grated window on the side next the court. As I was passing he saw me and called to me. I knew it was against the rules for anyone to talk to a sentenced man, but the captain of the prison told me to go and talk to him. This I did. He was as might be expected, very much down-hearted. I tried to cheer him up but there was but little to say to a man who was doomed to death in two weeks that would cheer him up. He was very anxious for a reprieve or a stay of execution. I promised to do what I could for him but knew I was helpless for any advantage to him. Upon invitation of the commander, took dinner at the Soldiers' Home. They served a very good dinner and had everything in good order then.

November 25th. When I came from on guard this morning I found a box of "goodies" sent from home. If those who sent the treat could have seen the boys enjoy the contents of the box I am sure they would have been amply rewarded. The good things were passed from man to man till everyone in the Company partook of some of them. You should have heard the complimentary remarks made during the feast. Well we did enjoy it and all felt very thankful to the donors for their kind remembrance of us.

Captain Gallagher went home on recruiting service.

December 1st. On picket guard far out of the city. During the night saw there was a large fire in the city. Next morning heard that the prison and several other buildings had burned. The fire originated from the stove in the prison. Two of our Company boys were on guard at the prison gate. The prisoners were let out into the court. They were very much frightened and tried to pass the gate, but our boys held them back till the guards formed their lines in the street and then let the prisoners into this living pen. Then guards and prisoners marched down the street in this form till they came to the city hall and then they put every prisoner in there in safety. All the prisoners confined in cells were taken by another company of guards and placed in jails. Not one of the prisoners escaped. This would make guard duty much heavier for it took many more guards now than it did before the fire. Had inspection by a little captain from the regular army. He examined everything very carefully and at last complimented us on our good condition and soldierly conduct.

December 2nd. Received orders for a detail of one captain, two sergeants, two corporals and thirty men from our regiment to convey prisoners to Indianapolis, Indiana. There were seventy-six prisoners. Captain Crane of Company H was detailed as captain. I and a sergeant from Company B as sergeants. The men came from several of the companies. We marched down to the city hall and stacked our arms in a room along side the hall. While I was outside the captain of the prison began calling the names of the prisoners who were to go and had them pass into the room our men were in. Captain Crane was engaged in supervising the delivery of the prisoners. When I entered the room I saw our men along one side of the room and a greater number of rebels on the other side and the loaded guns stacked between. I quickly stepped forward and called the men to "Attention!" and to "Take arms." Quick as thought they were in their places and their guns were in their hands. Instantly they all saw the danger we had passed. By the glowering brows and low whispers of the prisoners we knew the movement had barely saved us of a battle if not a tragedy in that hall. All is well that ends well.

Soon had the prisoners transferred to us and marched them aboard the steamer boat "Crawford", and were on our way to Cairo. From Cairo we went by railroad first to Mattoon where we changed cars to the Terre Haute and Richmond road and arrived safe at Indianapolis at five o'clock Friday morning. From the depot we marched through the city to the prisoners' camp. The prison was in the old fair ground. It reminded us of our old prison at Macon, Georgia.

The prisoners were counted and delivered to the keeper of the prison. Then we marched back to the city. Captain Crane told us we were to go to the Soldiers' Home and rest one day before we started back to Columbus. He said he would stay at a hotel. We marched out south of the city some distance to the Home. There was a line of guards around the Home but they did not interfere with us and we marched into the yard in front of the house and I went in and reported to the commanding officer of the house. He gave us in charge of a man who conducted us to a small brick building some distance from the house and told us to leave our arms and accouterments in there. As soon as we had deposited our guns the man locked the building and told us where to find water to wash and prepare for breakfast. After washing we waited more than one hour for breakfast. When it was finally announced we were conducted into a large room and seated on long benches around a naked board table. Upon the table were soggy baked potatoes, one to the man; strong black coffee, no cream, strong black molasses, and very strong, if not black, butter, and heavy bread. We went into the room hungry but our appetites failed us when we saw the bill of fare. We ate but little and arose from the table and started for the city but when we came to the line of guards they halted us. We told them we were going to the city. They said we could not pass without permission from the commander.

We went back to his office and asked for passes to the city. He said he could only issue passes on the order of a commissioned officer. We told him our captain had gone to a hotel and knew nothing of their rules. If we could get to him he would give us the order. I then told him that I was a senior sergeant and asked if he would let us out on my order, but this he declined to do. We asked that he deliver us our arms and let us go and we would take care of ourselves. He answered that we would have to have an order from a commissioned officer to secure our arms. We got hot about this time. I picked up an axe and started out. He asked what I intended to do with the axe. I told him I was going to batter the armory door to pieces so we could get our guns.

We all started for the armory. He called again but we went on. Then he came after us and asked me if I was actually in command of these men. I told him he knew very well that I brought them there and had charge of them and he could see how readily they obeyed me. Then he said for us to come back to the office and he would give us passes. I told him I was only a sergeant and he had no authority to issue passes without an officer's order. He said it made no difference if I was in command I could give the order. We went back to the office and he wrote an order to pass me and my men to the city to return by six o'clock in the evening. I read the order and handed it back and told him we wanted our guns. He asked what was the matter with the pass. I told him we wanted to see the city and probably would be scattered so that one pass would not do for all of us; that some might want to attend the theater that night and some would go to a war meeting where Governor Morton was to speak. What we must have was individual passes so each could take his own course and come back when we got ready. He sat still looking at me for some minutes, then he said, "Come with me." He led us out to the guard line and told the guards to let us pass as we pleased to the city.

Visited the State House and State Library where were exhibited many trophies of the war. Went to a hotel and had a square meal for dinner. In the evening there was the finest display of fireworks I ever saw. And then followed a great war meeting in the State House at which Governor Morton made one of his very characteristic speeches. Among other things he said: "In one year from this time you will not find a man in Indiana who had not been in the army but who will claim he tried to enlist and was rejected." "That everyone will claim that they were in favor of putting down the rebellion." Several other men made fine speeches and many men enlisted.

After the meeting I went to the theater and after that found a hotel with a good bed. Slept sound and long for we had not had any regular sleep since leaving Columbus. Up late next morning. After a fine breakfast walked out upon the street and soon met Captain Crane who ordered me to get the men together and be at the depot ready to take the eleven o'clock forenoon train.

I soon met the other sergeant and we gathered up the men and marched out to the Soldiers' Home for our guns and found not one of our boys had been back there after we left yesterday morning. They did not seem to feel at home there. We learned that the regiment that did the guard duty there and about the city had been in the service over two years and had not left the city yet. We almost wished the commander had let us capture our guns yesterday morning so we might have tried the mettle of the guards on a bayonet charge.

Indianapolis had a Union depot through which all its railroads ran. This was the only city at that time with such a depot. In due time our train came and we left Indiana's capitol.

Arrived at Centralia at nine o'clock in the evening and changed cars. Laid over four hours. The night was dark and one of our boys, Bartholomew of Company I, stepped off the sidewalk into a hole six feet deep. He fell on some timbers and was instantly killed. We were all very sorry. We carried the body to the train and took it back to Columbus with us. Then the officers of the Company sent the body home under escort of one of his comrades. He was a fine young man and all who knew him thought much of him.

At Cairo they had a number of deserters they wished to send to Louisville. They telegraphed General Smith to order us to take them there but he would not and we were glad for we had had enough of that kind of work. Arrived at Columbus and found everything in good order. Was glad to get back.

December 11, 1863. For two days troops have been disembarking from boats coming from up the river until there was quite an army there. We did not know where they were to go but expected when they moved we would go with them. Colonel Newbold had given orders to have everything ready to march at a moment's notice. The weather was warm with much drizzling rain.

December 16. On post guard. Rained pretty hard in the evening and continued raining all night. The army that had accumulated had marched south with General A. J. Smith in command. Did not know what the object was, but when General Smith strikes he aims at some one and they are pretty likely to get hit.

Small bodies of mounted rebels have harassed us for some time. They seldom get close enough to exchange shots but are always bobbing up in unexpected places. We were ever prepared for an attack. Sometimes they drove our pickets in and captured what they could in the tussle. It was supposed that General Smith would attempt to crush the larger body of rebels that these small parties radiated from and if possible break up this continual strife. The 25th Missouri had orders to go to Union City and occupy the place till further ordered.

December 19, 1863. Fingle escaped from prison. His death sentence had been extended for thirty days and he was in close confinement. When his cell was discovered empty, parties were at once sent in pursuit of him. After a long search they found him concealed among some logs and brush near the picket line. He was unable to get his chains off and of course could make no headway with chains on his ankles and wrists. We were all sorry he did not get away.

The headquarters of this division were moved to Union City. This was about the first we knew anything about Army Corps. We understand we belong to the Sixteenth Army Corps and are in Second Brigade and Third Division of that Corps. Colonel Scott of the 32nd Iowa was now in command at Columbus.

On picket with Lieutenant Dodds as officer of the guard. He became so sick we sent him to his quarters. I and the other sergeants went the grand rounds on foot. We had some fun surprising some of the guards. We were a little earlier than they expected and were both on foot so they did not hear us till we were right with them. Weather quite cool; in fact, it was cold.

December 21, 1863. I was doing some tailor work, making pockets in Wilson's overcoat, when Lieutenant Shanklin came into the barrack and asked me to take a walk with him. As soon as we were out of hearing of the others he asked if I would like to go home. I told him I would like very much to go if I could be spared but that the one furlough due our Company was in use. He then told me the intention was for our regiment to remain here all winter; that there was a detail of officers to go home recruiting. There was one to go from our Company and he had chosen me to go. The boat would go in half an hour and he asked me if I could be ready. I told him I thought I could. I gathered up my things and bade the boys goodbye, then went to the officers' quarters and thanked Lieutenant Shanklin for the detail and bade him goodbye. He squeezed my hand for a moment and I knew by his look that he felt in a sense he was repaying me for the loss of the commission a year ago. And it was our last farewell, for our regiment did go down the river with General Smith and Shanklin was killed on Red River. Doubtless giving me the detail saved my life, for in the battle on Pleasant Hill our Company was nearly destroyed.

COLUMBUS, KENTUCKY - Notes:

-- A death sentence could be imposed especially if the charge was cowardice or deserting under fire in the face of the enemy. The published roster states that Fingle was reported as a deserter from Corinth a month after Shiloh. From the roster, two other men, **John Evans** 20 and **Thomas Jorden** 18, both of Story County, seem to have left Corinth at the same time with Fingle. Until they each had faced the stress of combat, even for seemingly eager volunteers, it was impossible to predict who would measure up. No one could have predicted Shiloh; the ferocity of the fight surprised even Grant. For more on Fingle and Casaday: See Chapters 2 and 8
-- Governor Stone: See Chapter 8.
-- The rebel prisoner "Captain Cushman" was probably Captain Albert W Cushman of the 12th Tennessee Cavalry.
-- Colonel Messmore of the 31st Wisconsin was **Isaac E Messmore**, a lawyer and circuit judge from LaCrosse. He had graduated from law school in Richmond, Virginia before the War and later became an influential newspaper editor in Grand Rapids Michigan.
-- **John Scott** of Nevada, Story County, a Lieutenant Colonel of the 3rd Iowa Infantry, was appointed Colonel of the 32nd Infantry in August 1862 at age 38. He resigned May 27, 1864.
-- **Robert Bartholomew** 18 of Ashland, Wapello County, enlisted October 1861 in Company I of the 14th Iowa. Captured at Shiloh, he survived being held as a POW but was killed December 5 1863 at Centralia Illinois in the accident described above. He was buried in Ashland Cemetery.
-- **Lieutenant Orville Burke** 31 of Anamosa, Jones County, nativity Ohio, enlisted October 1861 as First Sergeant of Company H. He was taken prisoner at Shiloh. By March 1863 he had risen in rank to First Lieutenant. He mustered out with the regiment in November 1864 at Davenport. BF Thomas spelled the name "Burk".
-- **Lieutenant William H Dodds** 23 of Gainesboro, Van Buren County, was promoted to Second Lieutenant of Company F just a week before being taken prisoner with the regiment during the Shiloh fight. As an officer he was held prisoner until exchanged and was not paroled with the privates. A year later in March 1863, after serving six months in rebel POW camp, he was made First Lieutenant. Thomas spelled the name "Dodd".
William W Morton 21 of Oxford, Johnson County, also of Company F, was promoted Third Sergeant January 1863. Canadian born **Elisha W Root** 21 of Salem, Henry County, became Third Sergeant of Company D November 1863. All three men enlisted in October 1861, all three were taken prisoner at Shiloh, and all finished their three-year term.
-- **John B Edwards**, the cook called "Pap", was recorded as aged 30 when he enlisted in October 1861.

Edwards is buried in Buckingham Cemetery near Traer. **James M Larue** 18, who helped Pap "salt" the cow, enlisted from Benton County. Years after the War Larue owned ranches, first in Wyoming and later in California, where he raised and maybe salted a great deal of beef. He died at home on his ranch in Sonoma County California in 1912. Various census records and his age given at death seem to indicate he actually was born in 1847, making him around 14 when he enlisted. He was described as 5 foot 8 at enlistment, and in later years as 5 foot 9 and a half inches, which tends to show that he was still growing when he enlisted.

-- "Williams" who was too ill for guard duty with Peter Wilson is **Henry H Williams** 32 of Irving who was made Fourth Corporal April 1863 and Third Corporal July 1863. "Hoeffer" is **William C Hoeffer** 21 of Benton County who rose in rank to First Corporal on April 12 1863 and became Fifth Sergeant July 1 1863. The published roster spelled this name as "Hafer". One US Census spelled it "Hayford", but William himself used Hoeffer when applying for his pension, so BF Thomas probably had it correct. **George Heimlich** 27 of Tama County, who was caught sleeping on duty, was born in Germany; it is possible he may have understood German more easily than English instead of being simply "dimwitted". All four men had enlisted in October 1861 and mustered out with the regiment in November 1864 after serving their full three years. Larue and Williams had been taken prisoner with the regiment at Shiloh and endured the POW camp, but where Hoeffer and Heimlich were at the time of the Shiloh battle is unknown.

-- **Charles Ford** 21 of Tipton, Cedar County enlisted October 1861. He was not captured with the regiment at Shiloh and was promoted to Second Sergeant July 1863. His transfer to another company for promotion seems not to have succeeded because he was still with Company G when he was wounded in the right shoulder April 9 1864 at Pleasant Hill, Louisiana. He mustered out in November 1864 with the 14th.

-- "One of our best", **Edgar Dykeman** 24 of Redman village Tama County, had survived both the battle of Shiloh and the prison camps that followed, but he was still suffering from the chronic illness that had already killed many of his fellow soldiers. He died July 19 1863 and was buried in Columbus Kentucky. Sadly, just a few days earlier, on July 8 1863, his 35 year old brother **Simon Dykeman** of Company E 24th Iowa Infantry died in St. Louis. Simon, also from Redman, had enlisted with several other Buckingham area men August 1862. He is buried in Jefferson Barracks National Cemetery Section 6 Grave 40.

CHAPTER XII

HOME AGAIN

When I arrived at the boat I found Captain Campbell of Company K and Lieutenant Moorehead of Company I and six men all going to Davenport. The Steamer "*Minnehaha*" carried us to Cairo. Remained there till three o'clock next morning. Got a piece of ham, a little bread and a small cup of coffee for fifty cents. When we went to the railroad agent for tickets he refused to issue tickets on our order for transportation. Captain Campbell and Lieutenant Moorehead tried to explain the matter to him but he would not listen to anything. Captain Campbell got mad and ordered us to get aboard the train, which we did with alacrity. When the conductor came for our tickets Captain Campbell showed him our transportation and told him how the station agent would not give us tickets. He said to go on to Centralia, and the agent there would give us tickets. We arrived at Centralia at nine o'clock in the morning, December 22nd, and the agent gave us tickets without a word. Did not leave Centralia till one o'clock in the afternoon and arrived at Davenport at eight o'clock next morning. Went to the Pennsylvania House for breakfast and then went to headquarters and reported. The commander assigned us to our territory for recruiting.

My orders were to report to Captain William Gallagher at Toledo, Iowa. Drew a dress coat and got my transportation to Toledo and started at four o'clock in the afternoon. Arrived at Iowa City at nine o'clock and stopped at the Crummie House. Found the clerk of the hotel was a discharged soldier from Company F of my regiment. He was very glad to see me and although the house was crowded and I in late he managed so I had the best bed in the house. Had a splendid breakfast and took the train at ten o'clock for Marengo. I did not mention the fact to the people of the Crummie House that I was one of the boys that spent a wild night in their House a year before.

Arrived at Marengo at noon. Got dinner and took stage for Blairstown. Mr. Howe, a brother of Mrs. T. S. Talmage, Miss Shields whose father I knew at Vinton, and whose brother I knew in the Thirteenth Iowa, and a Miss Hutchinson of Iowa City, a friend of Miss Shields, were in the stage with me. They were all students at the State University. We had a very pleasant time by the way. Mr. Howe afterwards became a preacher and preached at the Converse school house in Clark Township.

Arrived at Blairstown at three o'clock in the afternoon and at six o'clock took the train for Iuka, as the station now called Tama was then known, where we arrived at nine o'clock in the evening. Took stage to Toledo and stopped at the Cary House. Samuel Chambers, a man who had belonged to our Company and been discharged, was there. He had re-enlisted under Captain Gallagher and was acting as clerk in his office. Captain Gallagher was out at his father's farm twelve miles from Toledo.

There had been a teachers' institute, or as they are now called, a teachers' normal at Toledo that closed the night I came. Several teachers were there from North Tama and would be going home next morning. So I had no difficulty getting a ride with them out as far as Mr. Gallagher's. I left the load of teachers about a mile east of the Gallagher farm and walked over to the place. When I arrived there I found a large assembly of people. It was Christmas day and they were having a family gathering and dinner. I reported to the Captain and asked permission to go home. But he gave very peremptory orders for me to remain where I was till after partaking of their dinner. I tried to excuse myself on the ground of the lateness of the hour and the long distance I had to tramp, but I was obliged to stay. Turkey for dinner! Who could resist? After dinner I started for home where I arrived just after dark. Expected to surprise my parents but one of the school marms gave them word that I was coming. I knocked at the door and when my mother opened it I asked if I could stay over night, disguising my voice as best I could. But she knew me and had me in her arms in an instant. It was a warm greeting I received, such as one as only loving parents can give to their children.

For some days I recruited myself more than the embryo soldiers of the neighborhood. There were so many to see and every place I went they had such good victuals that I grew fat and lazy. What a happy time I had at her home across the creek.

December 29th. Captain Gallagher and I held a war meeting at Crystal school house and secured two recruits, Jonathan Morton and William Wade. The school house was full of people. Captain Gallagher did the talking and he was good at it. At first call the two boys came forward and signed the papers. It did me good to see them come. Next morning Captain Gallagher told me to go home again and look about the northern part of the county for prospects of recruits and if I needed him he would come up.

December 31st. The wind blew like a hurricane and the thermometer was fifteen degrees below zero. The loose snow filled the air so it was impossible to be out long at a time.

Friday, January 1, 1864. The mercury registered twenty-five degrees below zero and the wind blew just as hard as ever. In all our experience in Iowa we never knew the wind to blow so hard with the mercury so low. There was much suffering among the stock and we even feared much there might be loss of human life. There was to have been a dance at J. C. Wood's, but while the wind quieted down at sunset it was too cold and there was no dance that night. The next morning the mercury marked thirty below zero but no wind. It seemed not nearly so cold.

Monday, January 4, 1864. John R. Thomas and George Shiner came to our house and enlisted. They were both married men and had families of small children depending on them. While I could not refuse to take them, I was very sorry to see them enlist. John was my only brother, two years older than I and not as robust and hearty as I could wish he was. The weather had moderated so the mercury was only three below zero. We heard that Mr. McKune lost all his cattle last Friday night. The wind was so strong it blew through their straw shed and they left it and went down into the southeast corner of the lot and there froze to death. I saw them sometime afterward. They stood in snow up to their bellies frozen standing on their feet. It was a pity for McKune.

We learned there was to be a draft in a few days. Everybody was dreading it. Men in a township raised money and hired recruits to go so as to prevent a draft. Each township was credited with the men that had enlisted from it and if they equaled its apportionment they did not have to submit to the draft, but if the number credited fell short of their apportionment then the draft came. A man enlisting could assign himself to any township he wished notwithstanding it may not have been his residence. This left men open in the market for the highest bidder. It also caused some hard feelings.

January 6, 1864. At Toledo. A cold and windy day. Draft had been postponed for twenty days. Met a civilian recruiting officer who was also a preacher named Swearingin. He was hot because we were detailed to come home recruiting. Said we were paid for fighting and had no right to come home and interfere with his local business. Well, I laughed at him. Told him he had been recruiting a year and we had more recruits in ten days than he ever had; that he was mad because he was to get fifteen dollars a head for all the recruits he procured and we were enlisting them at the expense of our time, or seventeen dollars per month; that the men preferred to enlist with us and he had better quit. He said he would see that we were called to our duty. Captain Schaffer of the Twenty-Eighth Iowa was also home recruiting.

January 7th. Got a recruit in Toledo. His name was George Bates. He was a single man nineteen years of age and six feet two in height.

January 8th. Got another recruit. Walked eight miles through the snow to get him. His name was William Leach. He had a wife and several children. His wife cried hard and I was very sorry for her. She said he was getting himself into trouble and she did not want him to go. Eighteen months after when she heard her husband was coming home she ran away with another man leaving Mr. Leach some of the children.

January 9th. Went to George Shiner's sale. His property sold well. Went to West Union to singing school that evening where I had some talk with Elijah Gallion about enlisting. He was a beau to Rachel Felter and some thought they were engaged. Gallion said he had talked so much about enlisting that he had the headache. After singing Reverend Messer preached a sermon. The weather was quite pleasant.

January 13th. Bought six acres of timber of Jaqua. Paid him one hundred and seventy dollars for it. Helped father butcher. Killed three nice hogs. We also killed one for Jaqua.

Monday, January 18th. Started to Toledo with my recruits. When we arrived at Morton's in Crystal we got word the Captain did not intend to send any more men till next Wednesday. Returned home and received a letter from Captain Gallagher instructing me to report at his office in Toledo at once and have the recruits follow the next day.

Thursday, January 21st. Came to Toledo last Monday expecting to take the recruits to Davenport Wednesday but there was a change of time on the railroad and we did not start. Secured two recruits after I went to Toledo. Joe McRoberts and Philemon Willey. Their parents lived about ten miles north of Toledo. Both were very sturdy, able young men. I now had twenty-three recruits to take to Davenport, nineteen for our Company and four for Captain Shaffer's company of the Twenty-Eighth regiment.

Left Toledo at nine o'clock in the morning January 21st, and took the train at Iuka at ten-thirty. Arrived at Blairstown at noon and hired three teams with sleds to take us to Marengo. Arrived there too late to get dinner. Went to the depot which was nearly a mile out of town in time for the four o'clock train, but when the train came it was so crowded they refused to let us get on so we were obliged to go back to Marengo and wait till the next day. We had supper and lodging by dividing between the two hotels as neither one was large enough to keep us all, and I had to pay the hotel bill out of my own pocket. Some of the men got too much liquor and became quite troublesome before we got them to retire. How much trouble liquor makes when men are on such expeditions as we were. I had no use for the stuff and never indulged in a single drop.

January 22nd. At ten o'clock we were all aboard the cars for Davenport. We were in a passenger coach attached to the rear end of a freight train. There were none in the car but our own boys. The boys were somewhat wild and up to all kinds of tricks. They climbed upon the box cars in front of us and ran along the train on top of the cars. When going up grade and the motion was very slow I saw several of them off walking along behind the train. Just boys, nothing more. I was fearful some of them might get hurt or left when off walking, but all came through safe. One of Captain Shaffer's men got too much liquor and became very troublesome. He was about twenty-eight years of age and as the liquor took effect on him he became quite quarrelsome. I finally got him into a seat and sat down beside him and would not let him out. I discovered he had a bottle in his pocket from which he had been replenishing his ill temper. I succeeded in getting it away from him and tossed it out of the car window. It was all I could do to keep him in the seat. After some time Joe McRoberts came and asked if I wanted him to relieve me for a time. So he took my place and kept the man quiet till he fell asleep.

Arrived at Davenport at five o'clock that evening and took the recruits out to Camp McClellan and turned them over to the commander. Saw they had good quarters, rations and blankets and bade them goodbye and went back to the Pennsylvania House and stayed all night. Reported to the recruiting officer in the morning and started for home at eight o'clock. Arrived at Marengo at noon. Crossed to Blairstown and took the train to Iuka and arrived at Toledo at nine o'clock in the evening. Went to the hotel where I found George Klingaman who was going to Buckingham in the morning. Went with him and arrived at home at three o'clock Sunday afternoon, January 24th, just in time to get some dinner and take a horseback ride across the creek to see Miss Stoakes with whom I spent the evening very agreeably, nor was this the first nor near the first nor last evening I spent with her while at home.

Felter wrote me that Fingle again escaped from prison. This time he succeeded in getting his chains off and then escaped the guard. I was really glad to hear this. None of the boys wanted him shot. All must be glad he escaped.

Sunday, January 31. The weather had been beautiful and mild for the last two weeks. The snow had all gone and up till now had been very warm for the season. But now it was snowing again and growing colder. Received letters from the boys in the regiment in which they say they have everything packed and expect to go south at a moment's notice. Hoped to join them before they went. Did not like the idea of the regiment going into active duty and I at home. Through friends I had had an offer from the Governor of a lieutenancy in one of the new regiments forming, but declined. Would rather finish my service with the old regiment than hold a commission in a new one.

February 6th. Received the bounty money sent me by John Thomas, George Shiner and William Leach and paid it over to their families. The President had issued another call for three hundred thousand volunteers. I feared there would be drafting done under this call.

February 9th. Jaqua and I surveyed my purchase of timber land. When we ran the lines we found it contained seven and a half acres and I paid him two hundred and five dollars for it. One very pleasant day Rebecca and I went to Nelson Felter's on a visit and the next Saturday evening went to West Union to a singing school.

February 15th, 1864 was a very stormy day and turned quite cool in the evening. The next morning the mercury was twelve degrees below zero. Rachel Felter and Elijah Gallion were married the evening of February 16th. He had enlisted and was going with us.

February 19th. Had a cotillion party at Q. D. Hartshorn's and it was a splendid time as we always had at the Hartshorn home.

February 22nd. Took Preston Greenleaf to Toledo. He had enlisted with me several days before.

February 26th. Henry Crowhurst enlisted with me. He wished to be assigned to Company E of the Twelfth Iowa because he had a brother in that company.

March 3rd. Went to Toledo with Lee Graham. Neither Captain Gallagher or Sam Chambers were there. Came home next day with James Camery and came by Gallagher's. The Captain took a copy of my order of detail and placed it on the muster roll and expected to draw our pay.

March 5th. Went with J. P. Wood to Six Mile Grove to help view and locate a road. Took dinner at Mr. Crowhurst's. They are very pleasant and hospitable people and made us welcome to a very nice dinner.

March 6th. This was my birthday and I was twenty-seven years of age. Yesterday was cold and I was out all day and chilled through, so I was quite sick. There was a baptizing at Hayward's bridge. Pretty cold I should think, for immersing.

I had bargained with J. P. Wood for a small farm. It laid between father's home and J. C. Wood's farm and contained sixty-three and a half acres. It was a very nice piece of ground and suited me very well. I paid ten dollars per acre for it.

Monday, March 28th. There was a baptizing at Klingaman's mill yesterday. Lemuel Kile was immersed. The thermometer was at zero in the morning and the water was very cold. I felt sorry for Kile but suppose it was right to follow the dictates of conscience. Sam Chambers had been spending some days with me.

The President had issued another call for two hundred thousand men to be raised by April 15th.

Miss Stoakes, Miss Messer, John Hopkins and I drove to Toledo March 23rd. Had our photos taken and took in the sights of the city. Drove home the same evening. Received my pay for four months, sixty-eight dollars.

March 29th. There was another snow storm. Three inches of snow on the ground. The next afternoon assisted at a turkey roast at Mrs. Cope's. Had a splendid time. John Hopkins had been waiting on Miss Messer for sometime and had made up his mind to marry her at once, but his mother wanted them to wait awhile. I then persuaded him to wait till I got home next fall and both get married at once. This he agreed to do.

March 30th. Had a very severe chill today. Shook like an ague fit for some time.

April lst. Another shake. Ague sure this time. Had taken heavy doses of quinine and hoped I had broken the ague.

April 8th. A light chill again followed by high fever and quite sick all night.

April 9th. Received orders to report at Toledo to return to my regiment.

April 11th. Rained all day so I did not go to Toledo. Received another letter from Captain Gallagher stating that he would start for Davenport next Thursday and wanted I should come Tuesday.

Left home early Tuesday morning. Father brought Mrs. Addie Wambaugh and her babe and myself down. I felt quite lonesome in the afternoon. Father had gone back, Captain Gallagher had not come yet and I was alone. As I wandered the streets I chanced to meet Mrs. Wambaugh and she invited me to spend the evening with the Morehouse family with whom she was staying. Mrs. Morehouse and Mrs. Wambaugh were sisters. Mr. Morehouse gave a very interesting account of his early life as a canal boat-man. I spent a very pleasant evening with this hospitable family.

April 14th. Left Toledo this morning at eleven o'clock. Made connections at Blairstown and Marengo and arrived at Davenport at nine o'clock the same evening. The Pennsylvania House was full and no chance for us to get lodging there so we went to the Scott House and got good rooms and had a good breakfast.

April 16th. Settled with Colonel Grier for my recruits account. The order was changed toward the last of our work so we got fifteen dollars each for several of the last recruits. He would not allow for the money I paid out to keep the recruits over night at Marengo the time I brought them down and was left there. With the allowance of forty-five dollars for these recruits I had about twenty dollars left over paying the expense. This was better than I expected.

In the afternoon met Mr. McCosh on the street and he would have me and Chambers go out to his place for a day. The people gave us a hearty welcome. Spent the Sabbath with them and their friends. Attended church twice. In the forenoon a young man named Barclay preached. He had scarcely opened his subject when he broke completely down. He hesitated and stammered a few sentences then he stretched forth his hands and exclaimed, "Oh, will you all please pray for me that I may succeed!" Then he was silent for a time and began again and preached a very creditable sermon.

Miss Brownlie, Mrs. McCosh's sister, came home with us and stayed for dinner and went to meeting with us in the afternoon. I understood there was a very close friendship between her and our comrade Peter Wilson. We promised to go to Brownlie's the next day for dinner. Tuesday took dinner with the Brownlies and spent the afternoon there. In the evening Miss Brownlie went with us to the McCosh home and soon after about a dozen couples of young folks dropped in and we had a very pleasant time till midnight when all wished us good-bye and returned to their homes. It was all very pleasant to us. Next morning Mr. McCosh took us to Davenport in his new carriage. This visit is still recalled as one of the brightest and best visits I ever enjoyed.

Reported to the captain and was informed that we would not leave Davenport before Thursday. Am sorry we cannot go down the river at once. We stopped at the Davenport House but changed to the Pennsylvania as it seemed more like home there.

April 21st. Started to St. Louis on the railroad. Would much rather have gone by boat but we were not choosers. Yesterday thought we were to go to St. Louis but found out we were to go on to Cairo. This was soldier life. The air is ever full of rumors and the next day they are contradicted by new rumors.

Left Davenport at eight o'clock this morning and arrived at LaSalle at noon. Had a severe chill this forenoon which showed I was not free from the ague yet. Left LaSalle at half past two o'clock on the Illinois Central railway and arrived at Centralia at eight o'clock in the evening and at Cairo at ten o'clock next morning. It had been raining since midnight. When we arrived at Cairo I was quite sick and went to the Soldiers' Home and went to bed. This Home was a nice place and well kept.

Saw Dick Boyd of Company H and Chambers saw James Fox of our Company. Our division wagon train just arrived. We were told the division was on its way up the river. Went aboard the boat "Liberty Number Two" at five o'clock in the evening preparatory to moving down the river. Left Cairo about one o'clock that night. Passed Columbus before daylight. Hickman at seven o'clock in the morning. Island Number Ten at nine o'clock. The island was much higher than the river banks on either side. It must be twenty-five feet above the water now. It was good ground to fortify and ought to have stood a long siege. Soon after passing the island we were hailed from the Arkansas shore by some men who carried a white flag but the captain of the boat feared an ambuscade and would not stop. Rebel bushwhackers were quite plentiful along the river. There were about three hundred and fifty soldiers on the boat. Very few had arms. They were men returning from furlough or from special duty like ourselves. Had a severe chill followed by fever this afternoon. Very hard rain today. Captain Gallagher was not with us. He must have stayed at Cairo.

Passed Fort Pillow, which the rebels under General Forrest had captured but a few days before and massacred the garrison because they had negro troops with them. Lieutenant Dillman of Toledo was among the killed. The rebels were still there and hailed us as we passed but did not fire on us. Lieutenant Colonel Reed of the rebel army and the man who had charge of me just after I was captured at Shiloh, was with General Forrest and was killed here at this battle.

I will now say that our regiment left Columbus along with General Smith's army over a month before this. They went down the river to Vicksburg and joined General Sherman's army on its march to Meridian. When they returned to Vicksburg General Smith's men were loaned to General Banks to assist him in his Red River expedition. They were to be gone on this trip three weeks and then join General Sherman on his march to the sea. This expedition was very poorly managed and General Bank's army was badly defeated at Sabine Crossroads and would have been destroyed had not General Smith's army met the victorious rebels the next day at Pleasant Hill and defeated them. The loss to our regiment at this time was very severe, our Company losing more than half their number in the battle of Pleasant Hill. The regiment was in five battles while up Red River. I will give more account of these as I go on with the narration. The time the men were to stay with General Banks was long over due and they were expected to come up the river very soon. For this reason they did not send us down the river.

We arrived at Memphis April 24th, 1864 just after midnight. Stayed on the boat till morning. Ordered to disembark and remain here till our division arrived. We were told it had orders to go to Cairo and join General Sherman on his march to the sea. We left the boat at ten o'clock in the morning and went to Fort Pickering to stay till our regiment came. Fort Pickering was situated upon the river bluff just below the city. We had very comfortable quarters. There were six of us together. One of the Second Jersey cavalry and one of the Tenth Missouri infantry, and Chambers, Helm, Walt and myself of our regiment.

Saw Sergeant Rhodes and N. Elliott in the city. They went home recruiting at the time I did. They had been as far down as Vicksburg and were returned here. George Helm was very sick.

The next morning at ten o'clock an orderly came in and called for all who belonged to the Third Division, Sixteenth Army Corps. We stepped out and he said we were ordered to return to Cairo and there wait for our division. We went to the landing and were ordered aboard the steamer "Belle Memphis" which was bound for Cairo. Captain Gallagher was on this boat. He had been farther down the river and was on his way to Cairo.

April 26th. Left Memphis at five o'clock in the evening the twenty-fifth. The "Liberty Number Two", upon which we came down, left a few minutes later. At one o'clock at night we were stopped by a gun boat and ordered to take on a lot of freight. While loading this the "Liberty Number Two" passed us and we saw her no more. Were passing New Madrid at noon when they fired a cannon shot across our bows as a call for us to stop, which we did. They had four prisoners they wished us to take to Cairo. They belonged to the notorious bushwhacker, General Rhoddy.

Arrived at Cairo at eight o'clock this evening. Went to the Soldiers' Home for supper and lodging. The next day we were ordered down the river again but this time only to Columbus. We were told the Third Division Sixteenth Army Corps was to report there. Took steamer and went to Columbus. Preston Greenleaf, one of my recruits, was there and had been there for sometime. Rained hard just as we arrived and of course we all got very wet. Cornelius Joor, who once belonged to our Company and was discharged and afterward enlisted in the Thirty-Second Iowa, was there. He said he lost his hat at the battle of Shiloh and he wanted us to get another one from the government for him. He was in earnest but we could not help laughing at him. Most of the men that came on the boat with us stayed under a shed down by the wharf, but Helm and I were both sick so we went to the Soldiers' Home and stayed over night. The next afternoon we moved into an old building known as the Railroad House. Five of us had a room about eight by ten and lived very comfortably. Garden truck was very plentiful on the market and in the gardens. Fruit trees in bloom. I heard that Runyon of Company F was in the fort. Runyon was my favorite antagonist at chess. So I climbed the bluff to meet him once more, but was disappointed as he had gone down the river a few days before. I had but eight dollars which must last till I get to the Company.

Today we got the first list of the casualties in our Company at the battle of Pleasant Hill. Lieutenants Hazlett and Shanklin both killed. (Hazlett was captured, not killed.) Three privates killed, names not given. Wounded were Ford, Isaac Davis, John Edwards and fifteen privates. The missing were Wilson, Shropshire and three others. Our Company is reported to have gone into battle with forty-seven men and lost twenty-eight.

There was a deep, sad mystery to us. Who are the dead? Who the wounded? Oh, how anxious I was to get to the regiment. We got no letters from anyone. Letters directed to us went to the regiment. We had no word from home or the regiment since leaving home. Only newspaper accounts and they so meager and unreliable. No one knows the sadness of this time of no communication with the outside world.

The New York Tribune gave the story of "How the Fourteenth Iowa Repulsed a Cavalry Charge." I will give this as near as I can recall it. "After three charges of rebel infantry had been repulsed the brigade was for sometime exposed to a heavy artillery fire from several rebel batteries. It was during this fire they lost the great number of men killed and wounded. Then they saw a large body of cavalry deploying cross the open prairie from behind a body of timber. As soon as they were fully developed they moved by left flank and advanced in line of battle. First at a trot and then at a canter and as they came nearer they rode at a furious gallop. The first patter of the horses' feet was like distant thunder, but when they came nearer it was like the awful roar of Niagara. The artillery ceased firing and our men arose to their feet ready to receive the cavalry charge. No raw troops could have stood against this avalanche that was being hurled against them. Only true veterans who knew the value of discipline could stand firm. Colonel Shaw rode along the line telling the men to stand firm and hold their fire till he gave the command. Now the cavalry sabers are out swinging about the riders' heads, glinting in the sun's full rays. Can our men withstand them? Yes; they knew each other and knew there would be no break in their lines. On they came. Now hear the rebel yell. Yell upon yell and echo upon echo. Surely now the men in blue will quail and give way. But calmly and coolly the line in blue stood before the blast. "Ready" came the voice of the Colonel, and every gun came to the soldiers' breasts. "Aim!" and every gun as one gun came to the soldiers' shoulders and his eye followed the barrel to the breast of an enemy. The rebel column was not twenty paces away. "Fire!" Oh, can it be possible? The proud Texas cavalry that but this moment was swinging and yelling like mad in confidence of victory was scattered and torn. Not a regiment; not a company, and very few men rode away. Some fell within our lines. Many horses, riderless, recoiled in front of our men, but the formation of regiment and company was gone and our brigade with the old Fourteenth Iowa in its center stood firm in their places, grand veterans that they were. No pen can do justice to their valiant courage manifested this day. No tongue can sufficiently laud their victory. Only those who saw this mighty dash of war and witnessed the complete overthrow of the rebels will ever appreciate the grandeur of their achievement."

I cannot describe my feelings when reading this account of our men's noble deeds. It made me much more anxious to see them.

May 5th. Churchill of Company B and Peyton of Company H joined us. Chambers had the ague. We had moved from the Railroad House into the barracks we built here last fall. The weather was quite warm. Even most too warm for comfort. Helm was still quite sick. As soon as Chambers was better he got a detail in the medical department.

Got a letter from Captain Gallagher. It was written from Cairo and was a week old when I received it. Said he was sick and was trying for a furlough to go home. A few days after I learned he had succeeded and had gone home. I was glad of it but I would much rather have gone to the regiment than go home.

May 9th. We heard that all the mail for the Third Division of the Sixteenth Army Corps was held at Cairo till the division came up the river. There was a captain of the Thirty-Second Iowa here who was going to Cairo to try to get the privilege of looking over the mail and bring us what was for us here. The morrow brought disappointment. They would not let him look over the mail matter. It seemed too bad to be so near the letters we wanted so much and not be allowed to get them. Probably there were a large quantity and it would not be practical to allow them to be handled. It was much worse on the recruits than it was on the old soldiers, for we were more used to disappointments by this time, but they are at the beginning of theirs. I wrote home two or three times each week. Helm was worse and they took him to the Soldiers' Home where he would have better quarters and get better care.

May 13th. Colonel Moore of the Twenty-First Missouri was here. He belonged to our brigade. I went to him and asked if he could get me a pass to Cairo. I heard there was a great demand for carpenters there and thought I might as well work and earn some money as to lie here idle. He said he was going there himself and would take me with him. He advised me not to go there to work for he felt sure we would be sent down the river soon. When we arrived at Cairo I searched the hospitals and all likely places for some of our men but could not find anyone I knew. At four o'clock in the afternoon the steamer "Convoy" left for Columbus and we were not at the wharf and so were left at Cairo. At seven o'clock we went aboard the "Belle St. Louis" and were soon at Columbus. Carmine of Company F had me bring him two barrels of apples and some cakes and nuts from Cairo. He was running a stand and sold apples, cakes, candy, cigars, etc. He said he was making four or five dollars a day at it. He wanted me to join him at this but I had not the tact. In fact I feared he would get into trouble about it.

May 14th. Had grand review under General Prince, but I had the ague and was excused from taking part.

May 15th. Colonel Lawrence who was in command here chanced to observe Carmine at his fruit stand and questioned him as to who he was and by what authority he was keeping a stand. When answered that he had no authority he at once ordered him under arrest. He intended to have him court-martialed and made an example of. I went to Colonel Moore and explained the matter to him and he went to Colonel Lawrence and secured Carmine's release. Probably he succeeded because it was thought we would be sent down the river in a few days. It was a narrow escape for Carmine.

May 17th. Orders came at ten o'clock this morning to be ready to move down the river. Just after noon went aboard the steamer "*Hannibal*" and started for Vicksburg. Helm was better and able to go with us.

May 18th. Arrived at Memphis at seven o'clock this morning. Saw Sergeant Parmenter of Company B on shore and called to him. He had been wounded at Pleasant Hill and was here at a hospital. Asked about our boys and especially about my brother. He said he thought John was dead but was not sure. Said Isaac Davis of my Company was here in hospital and he would go and bring him for he would know. Soon he returned with Davis who confirmed the death of my brother. John caught a heavy cold at the battle of Fort DeRussy which settled on his lungs, but he kept with the Company till they arrived at Alexandria where it culminated in pneumonia. He was placed on board the hospital boat "*Cheauteau*" and died about as soon as he was transferred to the boat April 9, 1864. He with two others was buried on the river bank at Fort DeRussy. It was the saddest news of my life up to that time. My only brother enlisted in good health and so soon to be taken away. It was a severe shock to me. Why should he be taken when he had a wife and three children depending upon him, and I left who had no one to care for?

Left Memphis about midnight. Passed Helena about seven o'clock next morning. Lieutenant Rogers, who had been a sergeant in Company I, was here a captain of colored troops. He was well pleased with his position. Passed the mouth of the White River at noon and that of the Arkansas about an hour later. These two large streams flow into the Mississippi but a few miles apart and both on the west side. All the land surveys of Missouri, Iowa, Minnesota and several other states start from a line drawn due north from the center of the mouth of the White River. This line is called the Fifth Principal Meridian. At the mouth of the Arkansas was the city of Napoleon. This city was famed in years gone by as one of the worst gambling holes in the United States. It was the home of gamblers and roughs of all types. Today it seems quite an insignificant and dilapidated village.

May 30th. Arrived at Vicksburg at five o'clock in the evening. This is a noted historical city. It was the main point of defense on the lower river and here General Grant dug his canal across a neck of land in order to pass beyond the reach of the rebel batteries, but he failed to carry his boats through and finally was compelled to run his boats by the rebel batteries. Here were the months of siege and the many heavy battles fought for the possession of this red clay bluff And here finally surrendered General Pemberton with his rebel army of twenty thousand men after a resistance almost unparalleled and after sustaining hardships almost beyond human strength to endure. When Vicksburg fell the last link of the chain that bound the waters of the Mississippi was broken and our boats sailed from the gulf to the twin cities in Minnesota. And here we were on the boat gazing at the city on the bluff side. In many places we could see the destruction that our shells had wrought among the buildings of the city.

Nobody seemed to know anything of where our division was. At six o'clock went steaming down the river to find General Smith's army. It was a splendid night. Calm, clear and bright moonlight. The river was wide and flowed silently onward without a ripple to mark its course. As the boat glided over the bosom of the still water we saw the long trailing gray moss hanging from the boughs of the trees so near the water's brink. The foliage of the trees was so heavy that the shadow on the shore was like midnight darkness while the river under the rays of the moon looked like burnished silver. All was still but the hoarse coughing of the steam pipes as the steam escaped and the thud, thud, thud of the paddles of the wheel as they struck the water. All was so peaceful and quiet that it seemed that man only was out of harmony with God. On we went to meet the broken and defeated army of General Banks and heroic veterans of General Smith. Oh, how the varying emotions chased each other through my breast as I watched the silent water and the trailing moss. Whom will we meet and who are among the dead and who maimed and crippled and who languishing in prison? And the friends at home, what did they know of the loss on this ill-fated expedition? Ah, there was mourning in the hearts of those at home.

May 21st. We arrived at the mouth of the Red River at seven o'clock in the morning. This was the place where the old Spanish explorer, Fernando DeSoto, died. It was said he plunged into every stagnant pool and spring and brook from the coast of Florida to the west bank of the Mississippi hoping to attain eternal youth which tradition of the Indians ascribed to the powers of the unknown spring. If he attained eternal youth it came to him after he crossed the river of death for he died here and his followers took his body in a canoe in the still hour of midnight and paddled to the middle of the river and sank the body in the turbulent waters. This was to keep his red enemies from mutilating his body.

Here our boat was gracefully circling over the same water to come to a landing place, and here was the fleet of boats belonging to our division. As we approached the landing we saw a column of men marching down on the levee of the Red River. Nearer and nearer they came and when we landed we learned that it was our own division just coming to the river as we came to the landing. Our brigade was the rear one of the division and would not be in for sometime. We learned that our regimental headquarters were on the steamer "Ewing". Found the steamer and were soon on board. Morton and Ford were both on the boat, Morton wounded and Ford sick. Our regiment came into camp at noon but we did not find them till about two o'clock in the afternoon. Just five months to a day since I left them to go home recruiting, and oh, so much has transpired in the time. So many of our boys dead or in prison or sent to hospital because of wounds or sickness. How tired and worn the boys looked. I never saw them so jaded. Over two thirds of our Company was lost on this Red River expedition. Not a commissioned officer left with the Company. Only two sergeants. It was a sad meeting. The boys all gathered around me to shake hands again and again. Each one tried to tell me of the hardships and losses they had sustained. It seemed to relieve them to tell their suffering to me. Here I learned the full particulars of the death of my brother, also of Colonel Newbold and Lieutenant Shanklin, as well as the other men we lost. The report of Lieutenant Hazlett's death was a mistake. He was captured with Wilson, Shropshire and a number of others. The prisoners captured on this expedition were sent to Tyler, Texas, and held there as prisoners till the war closed, fourteen months afterward. I received a handful of letters the boys had saved for me. I assure you these I enjoyed very much. There must be many more waiting for us at Cairo. I had many letters to write.

May 22, 1864. Went aboard the steamer "Ewing" at seven o'clock, but first carried on board a large quantity of fence rails which were used for fuel under the boilers. Then we started up the river. There were about twenty boats in the fleet all of which were under way at the time or soon after we were. While the river was wide and rather sluggish the progress was very slow as we moved up stream. Casaday and Tibbits were ironed and taken away by the provost marshal before we started. The charge against them was desertion.

Arrived at Vicksburg May 24th, or rather during the night before. We were twelve hours going down from Vicksburg to the mouth of Red River and thirty-six hours coming back. Went on shore about eleven o'clock and camped in a plowed field about a mile below the city. George Shiner was quite sick and remained on the boat. The next day met Major Tom Free and Chaplain Edwards. They were men I knew at Toledo before the war and had been soldiering in the Tenth Iowa but were now officers in a negro regiment. Major Free offered me a captain's commission in his regiment if I would go with them, but I declined. I wished to serve my time out with Company G of the old Fourteenth Iowa. It was kind of the Major to make the offer but I could not accept.

Felter and I went to the city and looked the ground over where the shells from our mortar boats had done their work. One shell had gone through the court house tearing a large rent through each wall. We also saw the caves the citizens had dug in the hills into which they fled for safety in time of battle. Vicksburg was practically destroyed.

May 27th. Had orders to be ready to move at any moment, but later we heard that another brigade had gone in the place we expected to occupy. If so, we were to remain here till the army went.

May 29, 1864. Casaday had been in irons and closely guarded on the steamer "Ewing", but last night he escaped and nothing was known of where he had gone. Hull was put under arrest for letting Casaday escape, though probably some of the officers knew more about it than Hull did.

May 31st. Captain Gallagher came down the river and took command of the Company at once. Lieutenant Burke of Company H had been in command since our lieutenants were killed or captured.

June 3rd. Drilled and had dress parade. This was the first dress parade we had since we returned to the regiment. Had orders to be ready to go up the river at an hour's notice. Went aboard the boat at eight o'clock in the morning. Pretty hard rain and everybody wet. A rumor that the rebels had a battery at the mouth of White River and kept all boats from passing. A boat came down this evening with holes through her smoke stacks where cannon balls had passed through. She brought our mail and I received letters that gave me much joy.

June 5th. Started up the river at one o'clock in the afternoon. As we passed the city we had an excellent view of it and vicinity with the extensive fortifications around it. It certainly was a very strong point to fortify, and was well fortified. Crossed the mouth of Grant's Canal and of the Yazoo River soon after leaving Vicksburg and Millikens at five o'clock. Casaday was seen on the steamer "Leviathan" but when officers went there to arrest him he could not be found. There were twenty-one boats that pushed their way up the river with us.

June 4th 1864. Casaday was captured aboard the "Leviathan" and was again in chains and irons. Next day arrived at a point about twenty-five miles below Columbus, Arkansas, at four o' clock in the afternoon and received orders to disembark. Drew two days rations and were soon ashore. Landed in a low swampy place covered with heavy timbers and underbrush and vines. Dark as pitch and drizzling rain. We lay in this swamp waiting for daylight. Some distance above us was a great bend where the river made thirty miles in a circle and came back within six miles of itself. On this narrow neck of land the rebels had a battery. If a boat passed down the river the battery met it at the upper end of the bend and fired upon it as long as it was within reach. As it passed down the river the battery crossed to the other side of the neck and fired upon the boat again. We were sent here and landed just below this point and hoped to surprise this battery and coop it in the bend of the river and capture it. It was said General Chalmers was in command here.

We started next morning as soon as it was light enough to see how to proceed. Soon it began to rain hard. Plodded along through mud and water and vines and brush hardly knowing whether we were going in the right direction or not. In less than an hour from the time we started our advance was fired upon by the rebel skirmish line. Then we knew General Chalmers had not been surprised and would not be caught in the bend of the river. We pressed the skirmishers back but they grew stronger and more stubborn. Finally they opened fire on us with a single cannon. One of our rifled Parrot guns was advanced to a good position and soon silenced their gun. But their skirmishers kept steadily at their work and we kept driving them slowly back. Twice their stand was so stubborn that our brigade formed line of battle when the rebels would give way and retreat. Near noon we emerged from the timber upon open ground beside a large body of water called Lake Chicot. We saw their battery planted about a mile from us in the edge of timber on the bank of the lake. Our skirmishers did not attempt to cross this open ground as they could see the rebel's line of battle stretching off to our left in the timber from their battery at the lake. They seemed determined to give us battle. One of our batteries was planted on the lake shore and shots were at once exchanged between them and the rebels without much execution. Our brigade was now deployed in line of battle with our right resting on the lake shore. We were on the open ground which was level till it came to the timber in which the rebels were where there was a considerable raise. This gave them much the advantage.

When we were fully formed and ready to advance there was a clash of authority between Colonel Shaw and Colonel Moore of the Twenty-First Missouri, each one claiming that he was the superior officer and was in command of the division. Colonel Shaw had been in command of the Third Division of the Sixteenth Army Corps and Colonel Moore had been at home and came down the river at the time I had. We knew nothing of the trouble between them till as spoken of here. If Colonel Shaw was senior officer Colonel Moore would be in command of the First Brigade and under Colonel Shaw. If Colonel Moore was senior then he could command the division and Colonel Shaw would command the Second Brigade. We never knew why General Smith did not decide who was the senior of the two but he did not and the matter came to a crisis when each one tried to give the other orders in the face of battle with the enemy. Hot words were passed between them, and finally Colonel Shaw turned to his orderly and told him to report to General Smith that he (Colonel Shaw) was too sick for duty. He turned his horse and rode off the field. This left Colonel Moore in command of the division. He then rode up to us and told us we were brave veterans and had done many noble deeds and that he would give us the opportunity to gain new laurels. "Fourteenth Iowa advance and capture that rebel battery." At this time the rebel battery was giving us a severe fire of grape and shell. We felt more like tramping Colonel Moore under foot than going under his lead into battle to win honors for him. But Captain Campbell who was then in command of our regiment sprang forward waving his sword and commanded "Forward! Guard Right! Double quick march!" And away we went after the rebel battery. The Fourteenth in the lead and the balance of the brigade following.

The rebel artillery and infantry gave us the hottest reception of which they were able while we fired not a shot only charged upon them and supposed we would soon be upon them with the bayonet. But when we came near the edge of the timber in which the rebels were covered we found a wide and deep stream of water between us and them. Then we fired volley after volley upon them and they fled in a very short time. And because of the raised ground they had been on they were soon out of our sight. Then Colonel Gilbert, who was in command of our brigade, called the men to gather the fence rails that were in a worm fence along the stream of water and fill the stream with them so as to make a bridge of them to cross upon. This was soon done, and in a few minutes some of our men and a battery of two guns were across and the battery was shelling the retreating enemy, our guns occupying the ridge the rebel battery had been planted on a few minutes before. When the third gun started over the rail bridge the wheels sank deep in the earth and when they struck the rails pushed them in a heap in front of them so that it was impossible for the wheels to raise over the rails. The muzzle of the cannon was in the water. It had the appearance of a permanent disaster. But the men took the bulk of rails away from in front of the wheels and placed pries so as to raise the cannon carriage. The drivers shouted at the horses and the wheels arose upon the obstacle and the stream was crossed. Soon our brigade was across and in hot pursuit of the enemy skirmishing with them and shelling them at every opportunity.

About six miles farther we came to a village called Lake City. Here the rebels took the road that ran directly away from the lake and we followed them no farther. We camped here for the night. The water of the lake was very clear and cool and was full of small fish. Whenever we dipped a pail of water we would dip up a number of fish from two to four inches long. It had rained nearly all day and we were wet and tired. We soon had great fires burning and supper cooking. There were few citizens in this town. Suppose most of the men were with General Chalmers. We had but little conversation with these who were here. Had a comfortable night's rest and in the morning took a look about the city. There were probably about two hundred inhabitants here when they were at home. It was the county seat of Marion county, Arkansas. The city was built upon the sloping bank of the lake and was a beautiful place. On the lake they had a commodious boat house and a number of pleasure boats. It had the appearance of being inhabited by a pleasure loving people. They certainly had many facilities for enjoying themselves. We opened the jail but found no one in it.

Yesterday our division was in front of the Second Division, a part of which was with us. Our brigade was also in front so our regiment was next to the front. The next day everything goes to the rear that had been in front. The regiment in front of us went to the rear of the brigade. The brigade went to the rear of the division and the division went to the rear of the army. Yesterday there was but one regiment in front of us, and today we are the front regiment in the rear brigade.

We left Lake City about eight o'clock next morning. It was a beautiful day, bright with sunshine and the road we were on was a good one. It was some eight or ten miles to the river. We followed along the bank of the lake about five miles farther and then struck for the river where we arrived at noon and found our boats awaiting us. They had come up the river from where we left them and had just arrived. As soon as the batteries were loaded on the boats we began to go aboard. Then the rebels came up behind the levee and began firing on us. They were behind the levee and we were in plain view. We returned the fire as best we could but soon it developed into a pretty lively little battle. It began to rain again but the rain did not interfere with the skirmishing.

The gunboat "Choctaw" was lying just above the fleet anchored in midstream. She raised her anchor and drifted down past the fleet and dropped anchor again. I saw what was coming and clambered upon the wheel house to see the fight. As the boat swung around with broadside to the bank she fired with her ten-inch guns. The concussion was very great. In fact so great it stopped my watch the first shot. I saw large oak trees cut off thirty feet from the ground, the top so completely cut loose that they fell straight down the trunk of the tree. It seemed the object of the gunners was to fell the trees upon the men who were concealed behind the levee. Not a shot was fired from the rebels after the gunboat opened fire. And now another sight came to view. We were about four miles above Columbia, a town of about eight hundred inhabitants on the bank of the river. The river curved so the town was in plain sight across the water. Suddenly in the gathering twilight we saw a blaze spring from a house in town. Another and others following, soon the whole town was ablaze. It lighted the whole country and burned till long in the night. This was done in retaliation for the battery firing on our boats. While it was probably not the citizens of Columbia who fired on the boats it was those who were in strong sympathy with them and they harbored them in their homes. When the rebels understood that if they did such work as firing upon passing boats our men would make reprisal on the community in which the deed was done, they would hesitate to bring down the wrath of the Federals upon their friends. It was an awful sight to see a city burn and know the whole community was without shelter. But this was war. In the battle yesterday we called the battle of Lake Chicot we lost over thirty killed and more than twice as many wounded.

June 8th. Our mail was brought and distributed to us this morning. I received two letters from father, one from each of my sisters and two from a friend who was very dear to me. I cannot express my joy upon the receipt of these letters.

The fleet started up the river at four o'clock in the morning. Passed Napoleon in the evening. Nearly out of fuel. Tried to get wood at the mouth of White River but failed. Finally captured a rail fence which we carried aboard the boat for use under the boilers. Rails make excellent fuel. There was nothing better for a rousing camp fire than good oak or chestnut rails. They also make good steamboat fuel.

June 9th. We had a hard rain in the afternoon. The wind blew so hard the pilot could not hold the boat against it. Several of the boats were blown ashore and tied up till the storm was over.

Arrived at Memphis at nine o'clock in the morning, June 10th. We soon were off the boat but did not leave the landing till after two o'clock in the afternoon. Saw many of the Forty-Fourth and Forty-Fifth Iowa regiments. They were on duty here. They were enlisted for only one hundred days. It seems the governors of many of the states assembled at Washington and proposed to the President that he make a call for six hundred thousand men for one hundred days; relieve all the old soldiers now on duty at such places as Memphis with these recruits; send the soldiers to the front and crush the Rebellion in one hundred days. Upon this suggestion the President made this call.

In the afternoon we marched out about two and a half miles from the landing and camped beside Elmwood cemetery. As we marched through the streets of the city the weather being very warm, many of the citizens came out with pails of cool, fresh water for us to drink. They were very kind to us and we fully appreciated their kindness.

The next day I was quite sick. My stomach was out of order. Probably some indiscretion in eating for which I must pay in suffering. Seth Crowhurst visited me. He belonged to the Twelfth Iowa and was a brother to the Henry Crowhurst whom I enlisted while at home. He said Henry was doing well. They were camped here for sometime awaiting the coming of the division.

Colonel Shaw started home on furlough. Colonel Moore was still in command of the division. It was rumored the fleet was chartered till the 25th of July and that led many of the boys to believe we would soon proceed up the river and then join General Sherman at Chattanooga. We hoped this was true.

About ten o'clock in the morning we got orders to be ready to march with three days' rations. We waited till night expecting to be called to arms at any moment, but did not get such orders. There was something that was greatly exciting the higher officers here, we knew not what. Gallion, Lefler and Cunningham came to the Company. They just came down from Cairo.

June 15th. Last night a man named Engle lectured to the regiment in behalf of the Soldiers' Orphans' Asylum, which was about to be established at Davenport, Iowa. After the lecture a paper was passed to each company for contribution. Our Company gave three hundred and seventeen dollars, and the regiment gave three thousand two hundred dollars. We were surprised and pleased with this.

The cause of the commotion among our officers at last manifested itself. General Sturges had made a raid into Mississippi with about eight thousand men. When near Guntown, about a hundred miles southeast of here, he was drawn into an ambuscade and the surprise was so complete his army was stampeded. The rebels shot or sabered many of our men. The slaughter was terrible. Sturges' men came back in a mob instead of an army. No order and no discipline but every man for himself. It really was a wonder they were not all killed or captured. Some of the poor fellows came into our camp last night so scared they were afraid of their shadows. Half starved and deathly tired. Poor fellows, we did all we could for them.

June 16th. Was sergeant of the guard yesterday. Part of our duty was guarding four prisoners of whom Casaday was one. Casaday had heavy irons on his wrists and ankles, so heavy that he walked with difficulty and very slowly. The prisoners were kept in a tent with two guards over them. About one o'clock at night I heard one of the guards call "Halt! Halt!" I jumped to my feet and rushed out of the guard tent and met the corporal on duty running to inform me that Casaday had escaped. He said Casaday had asked to be taken to the vault and he ordered one of the guards to go with him. They had not gone far from the tent till he heard the challenge and rushed forth to find Casaday gone. The guard said they were walking slowly down the path when suddenly Casaday's chains dropped from him and he sprang away from him and leaped over the fence into the cemetery and was gone. I questioned the guard closely but he stuck to his story. When asked why he had not shot Casaday he answered that his gun was not loaded. I felt sure the guard had let him escape on purpose. I remembered I had seen the same man, who was a stranger to me, walk out into the cemetery yesterday with a pair of boots in his hand. It at once flashed upon my mind that these boots were for Casaday. I asked him if he had not taken a pair of boots into the cemetery yesterday. He said he had taken a pair of boots through the cemetery to a shoemaker to have them repaired. I had been examining the chains and found the shackles all unlocked. I took the chains and went to Major Warner's tent. The Major was provost marshal for the division. He had heard the alarm and was in front of his tent in his night clothes. I told him Casaday had escaped and asked him who had the keys to the chains. He said they were somewhere about the tent. I told him about the guard carrying the boots into the cemetery and proposed he be put under arrest and the matter investigated. Then he said, "Sergeant, make no fuss about this. If he had not escaped he would have been shot in a few days. We are all glad he is gone." Well! Then the officers were privy to the escape. I too was glad he was gone but sorry he escaped when under my personal supervision. I am glad to say it was the last we ever saw or heard of Casaday.

June 22, 1864. Was in the city yesterday. Saw "Pap" Edwards. He was sent here to the hospital sometime ago. He was now able to be out on the street some. He told me that Mat Clark was here in hospital and quite sick. I went with him to the hospital and visited awhile with Clark. He was sick but I hoped would be better in a few days. Felter and I were the only men of our Mess in camp now. Today the boys received their pay. As I was not with them when they were mustered I got no pay, but would get mine next pay day.

HOME AGAIN - Notes:

-- **William J Campbell** of Des Moines County was appointed Captain of Company K September 1861. The roster record says he was only 22 yet he not only was Captain of Company K but he commanded the whole regiment in several engagements with the enemy, including Tupelo and Towncreek. He was captured at Shiloh and held POW many months. **John M Moorehead** 24 of Mount Pleasant, Henry County was appointed First Lieutenant of Company I November 1861. Both men mustered out November 1864 at Davenport when the regiment was dissolved after three year's service.

-- **John C Shields** 20 of Vinton, whose sister shared a coach with BF Thomas, enlisted September 1861 into Company G of the 13th Iowa Infantry, serving with the Sherman brothers named in Chapter 1. Shields eventually became Regimental Drum Major. Wounded July 22, 1864, near Atlanta Georgia, he mustered out in July 1865, from Louisville Kentucky.

-- John E McKune's father was John W McKune, whose cattle were frozen in the severe winter storm just a few months after his son's death at Macon. "The Iowa Transcript", the newspaper of Toledo Iowa, reported on January 14 1864: " *We learn that during the late storm some of our citizens lost more or less stock. Mr McKune, of Crystal township, we are informed had seven head of cattle frozen to death. This is the largest number lost by one man that we have heard of. In various parts of the county however some cattle hogs and sheep were killed by the storm and frost of the last day of 63 and the first of 64. People are quite unanimous in declaring they never saw as piercing and driving a storm in their lives as the one on the 31st ult. Many snow banks were so compacted that they would bear up a team and wagon.* "

-- "Captain Shaffer", who also came home to recruit, was most likely **Theodore Schaeffer**, 35 of Toledo, born in Pennsylvania. He was appointed First Lieutenant of Company F of the 28th Iowa in August 1862. Promoted Captain in January 1864, he mustered out July 1865 from Savannah Georgia. He later served as Tama County Treasurer.

-- The Crowhurst brothers of the 12th Iowa Infantry Company E were **Seth J Crowhurst** 21 and **Henry H Crowhurst** 18. Seth had enlisted in October 1861 and was wounded February 15 1862 in the Donelson fight. In April 1862 Seth was taken prisoner at the Hornets' Nest of Shiloh. He re-enlisted late in the War, was promoted to Fourth Sergeant and mustered out from Memphis in January 1866. Henry, recruited by BF Thomas on February 26 1864, was wounded severely in the leg at Towncreek, Tupelo Mississippi July 14 1864. Henry died from those wounds August 3rd and is buried in Mississippi River National Cemetery, Memphis, Section 2 Grave 466.

-- **Richard M Boyd** 18 of Marion enlisted October 1861 and mustered out November 1864. The roster makes no mention of Shiloh or Pleasant Hill but does say he was promoted Third Corporal of Company H April in 1863. **Elias C Churchill** 35 of Tripoli, enlisted August 1862 into Company B. He reached Fifth Corporal in July 1864 and mustered out the following November with the regiment. "Peyton of Company H" might be **Absolom Peyton** 25 or **Micaiah H Peyton** 22 both from Company H who enlisted the same day in October 1861, Absolom from Buchanan County and Micaiah from Lucas County. Both men mustered out in November 1864 with the regiment but Micaiah was listed as missing in action (probably taken prisoner with the rest of the regiment and sent to POW camp) at Shiloh; he was later made Sixth Corporal of Company H May 1864. Perhaps Frank Thomas had become well acquainted with Micaiah at Macon's Camp Oglethorpe during his time as a POW. The roster for Company H spells their name as "Paton".

-- Lieutenant Dillman was probably **Sylvester S Dillman** 34 of Toledo of Company E 24th Iowa Infantry who was killed September 19 1864 at the battle of Winchester Virginia, not at the Fort Pillow Massacre, which occurred in Tennessee April 12 1864. Dillman enlisted August 1862 as a 2nd Lieutenant and was later promoted to 1st Lieutenant. He had been wounded at the battle of Champion Hill May 16 1863 before he was killed in action at Winchester. The Confederate Lieutenant Colonel who was mortally wounded leading his rebel regiment in the assault on Fort Pillow was Wiley M Reed. Reed, widely praised as a brave and gallant officer, was shot in three places. See Chapter 5.

-- Sergeant Rhodes may have been **Isaac N Rhodes** 25 of Mount Pleasant, Henry County. Isaac enlisted as a Sergeant in Company I in October 1861 with his brothers **Milton Rhodes** 23 and **Wesley Rhodes** 19, both of Mount Pleasant. Milton enlisted as a Sergeant; Wesley enlisted as a Fifer. At Shiloh Wesley was wounded in the head while Isaac and Milton were taken prisoner and sent to Georgia's Camp Oglethorpe. In June 1862 Isaac and Milton and two other prisoners escaped the POW camp at Macon Georgia, stole a small boat and managed to slip down the Ocmulgee river to the Atlantic coast near Wolf Island. From there they managed to reach a Union ship patrolling nearby. It was a daring and wonderful escape and a matter of great pride for everyone in the regiment. Wesley survived his wound and mustered out with the regiment in Davenport. Isaac moved up in rank to Second Lieutenant before he too mustered out with the regiment. Milton was discharged from the regiment in August 1863 to accept a promotion to Captain of the 4th Regiment Arkansas Colored

Infantry Regiment at Duval's Bluff Arkansas. Sergeant Rhodes' recruiting companion was **Nathan Elliot** who was a Drummer from Salem. Elliot enlisted into Company I October 1861 at age 18. He served his full three-year term of service mustering out with the regiment November 1864 at Davenport.

-- "Carmine of Company F" who ran the black market grocery store may have been **Pearson Carmean** 28 of Company K. Pearson and his brother **Joshua Carmean** 25 were both of Kossuth, Des Moines County. Both brothers enlisted October 1861. Joshua was discharged for disability in April 1863 but Pearson, who was a corporal, served the entire three-year term with the regiment.

-- Colonel Moore of the 21st Missouri, who rescued Carmean and later quarreled with Colonel Shaw over command, was **Colonel David Moore** from Wooster Ohio who served from 1862 to 1865 and lost a leg from wounds received during the Shiloh battle.

-- "Walt", who shared the quarters with BF Thomas, Chambers and Helm, may have been **John Walt** 19 of Johnson County who enlisted in March 1864, or **William Walt** of Shueyville who was 19 when he enlisted October 1861. William had been listed as wounded and missing April 6 1862 after Shiloh, so perhaps Thomas had known him from the early days at Benton Barracks and the POW camps. Both John and William Walt were from Company F and both lived to see peace restored. BF Thomas' favorite chess foe was **John M Runyon** 29 of Shueyville, who enlisted in Company F October 1861 and mustered out November 1864 at Davenport.

-- **Elliot S Rogers** of Company D from Salem, Henry County, enlisted at age 21 in October 1861 as a Third Sergeant. He was promoted to First Sergeant two weeks before the Shiloh battle where he was taken prisoner. After his release he became a Hospital Steward in May 1863 but in August he was discharged to accept an officer's commission with the Arkansas Colored Infantry. BF Thomas misidentified the Company as "I". **Thomas S Free** from Toledo was 22 in July 1861 when he enlisted as a private in Company C of the 10th Iowa Infantry. By War's end he was a Major. He returned to Toledo and in time became a lawyer, the County Auditor, and a Judge, and one of the best known men of the area. In 1875 he was appointed the Agent of the United States for the Sac and Fox [Mesquakie] Settlement. Free's companion mentioned above was Reverend George G Edwards, pastor of the Baptist church in Toledo.

-- **Samuel H Chambers** and his friend **Samuel Bryson Betts** were 25 when they enlisted into the 14th's Company G in October 1861 from Tipton, Cedar County. Chambers was discharged for disability, in February 1863, but returned to duty when he re-enlisted the following December. He mustered out with the Residuary Battalion in August 1865. Chambers moved to Fox Lake Wisconsin after the War. Betts was also discharged for disability, in October 1863 from the military hospital at Keokuk. He returned home to Tipton where he remained the rest of his life. Both Chambers and Betts had brothers (**Thomas L Chambers** 32, and **James C Betts** 20) who enlisted from Tipton into Company B of the 24th Iowa Infantry in 1862.

-- **George Helm** 17 of Tama County, another roommate with Chambers and BF Thomas at Fort Pickering, enlisted into Company G on March 31 1864 and reported for duty April 9 1864, the same day of the battle at Pleasant Hill Louisiana. He recovered from this illness. Both Chambers and Helm served until the end of War in 1865. Afterwards Chambers settled in Fox Lake Wisconsin and Helm went to Washington Iowa.

-- **Cornelius Joor**, who was hoping for a new hat, was a 38 year old married farmer from Nevada, Story County who had been born in Holland. He enlisted October 1861 in the 14th Iowa and had been with those taken prisoner at the Hornets' Nest. Joor made it through the POW camps but he was not well and his recovery was slow. By December 1862 he was discharged from St. Louis for disability. He later enlisted into the 32nd Iowa Infantry Regiment, Company K, but in February 1864 he transferred to Company E of the 8th Iowa Infantry. Serving with the 8th under Geddes until April 1866 when he finally mustered out at Selma Alabama, Joor participated in campaigns around Meridan and Jackson Mississippi and in the defense of Memphis. After the War he returned to Story County farming for years near Nevada and later near Maxwell where his son Peter Joor was a medical doctor. Cornelius Joor is buried in Pleasant Run cemetery southeast of Nevada.

-- Casaday's guard was **Charles Hull**. Hull was a new recruit, enlisting from Muscatine Iowa in February 1864, aged 23. Two months later he was wounded severely in his right arm on July 14 1864 at Tupelo Mississippi. He later served with the Residuary Battalion, and discharged honorably in August 1865. Hull spent the rest of his life farming near Atlas Michigan. See Chapters 2, 8 and 11 for more on Casaday. **Alvaro W Tibbits** (The roster spells it "Tibbetts") 21 of Castle Grove, Jones County, enlisted into Company H October 1861. He was wounded in the right hand at Shiloh April 6 1862. The roster says he deserted July 29 1864 from Memphis Tennessee, two months short of his full three years.

-- **Joseph W McRoberts** 30 of Toledo enlisted January 2 1864; English born **William Leach** 34 of Buckingham enlisted January 4; **Philemon B Willey** 30 of Toledo enlisted January 5; **Harper S Cunningham** 18 of Tama County enlisted February 2; **Preston E Greenleaf** 18 of Tama County enlisted February 10. All of these men served to the end of the War with the Residuary Battalion. After the War Joe McRoberts farmed in Tama County for two decades before moving his family to Woonsocket South Dakota. William Leach went with two of his sons to farm near Fredonia Kansas. Philemon Willey, whose sister was married to McRoberts' brother, moved to Chicago. Harper Cunningham became a lawyer, opening an office in Guthrie Oklahoma. In time he became the Attorney General of the State of Oklahoma. Upon his retirement from the Attorney General's office, Cunningham moved to New Mexico. An active Freemason in Santa Fe, he was instrumental in the construction of the beautiful Masonic Temple there where he and his wife are now entombed. Preston Greenleaf took a job working for the railroad. During the freezing cold and rainy pre-dawn hours of October 18 1868, Preston was crushed to death in a terrible accident in the Waterloo railyard.

-- **Elijah Gallion** 21 of Tama County, enlisted February 18. A month after the June 10 entry in Thomas' diary above, Elijah was wounded slightly in the hand on July 15 1864 near Tupelo Mississippi; the end of his little finger was shot off. As BF Thomas noted here, before Elijah left for the War he married John R Felter's sister Rachel. He also continued to serve in the Residuary Battalion after the Regiment mustered out in November 1864. After the War he made his living selling nursery stock to Tama County farmers who wanted to plant a variety of fruit bearing trees and flowering shrubs. Elijah, Rachel and their children are buried in Woodlawn cemetery in Toledo.

-- **William Wade**, who was recruited by BF Thomas December 29 1863 with **Jonathon Morton**, died of fever April 1 1864 in New Orleans where he is thought to be buried. Wade and Morton were both 25 and from Crystal, Tama County, close neighbors to the Felter and McKune families. Jonathan Morton, who was wounded in the thigh, had at first mistakenly been reported taken prisoner at Pleasant Hill. Morton died at home within a few months after the end of the War.

-- Thomas says three privates of Company G were killed at Pleasant Hill, "names not given". Killed in action were Lt. Shanklin of Toledo and the unnamed privates **John F Shumaker** 33 and **Henry Spangler** 27 both of Nevada Iowa. Both men had enlisted in January 1864 three months before the battle with their friend private **Sephman F Martin** 29 also of Nevada who was mortally wounded and died later that same day. Unnamed by Thomas above were privates **Enos Kern** 21 of Toledo and **William Heath** 21 of Buckingham, who were also terribly wounded and died soon after the battle. Kern had enlisted in January 1864 but Heath had been with the Company since October 1861 and had been one of the men taken prisoner at Shiloh. Thomas then mentions "Wilson, Shropshire and three others" were missing, but there were more men taken POW from Company G than just those five. Two of these unnamed prisoners, privates **Daniel C Vail** 29 of Nevada and **William S Townsend** 18 of Toledo, died at prison camp in Texas. Both Vail and Townsend are buried in the national cemetery at Alexandria Louisiana.

-- Thomas names several wounded men. Big **George W Bates** 21 of Toledo was badly wounded in the knee at Pleasant Hill. "Pap", John B Edwards, of Tama County, had also been wounded at the battle, as was **Charles Ford** 21 of Tipton, Cedar County. Also severely wounded at Pleasant Hill was Addison Davis' younger brother **Isaac Davis** 19 of Nevada, Story County, who gave BF Thomas the sad details of his brother John's death. All of these men survived their injuries and the War.

-- **Sergeant William W Parmenter** 25 of Company B, who was the first to tell of John R Thomas' death, was from Waverly when he enlisted August 1862 a few months after Shiloh. Parmenter was wounded "dangerously" in the left shoulder at Pleasant Hill but recovered from his wounds and mustered out with the regiment in 1864. Two days after the battle at Pleasant Hill he was promoted to First Sergeant.

-- **George W Shiner** 28 of Buckingham, who enlisted with John R Thomas on January 1 1864, successfully served to the end of the War in the Residuary Battalion. Afterwards he farmed for a time in Missouri before moving to the Salt Lake City area. Shiner raised a large family and lived until October 1918. He is buried in Castle Dale Utah. Shiner's brother-in-law, Canadian born **James Lefler** 19, also of Tama County, enlisted on January 26. He went south into combat with the Regiment and later served in the Residuary Battallion with Shiner. When the War was over Lefler farmed near Fairmont Nebraska, where members of his family still reside.

-- **John R Thomas**, 27 year old brother of BF Thomas, from Buckingham, was a married cabinetmaker with three small children. According to an official roster he died aboard the Steamer "*South Western*" on April 13 1864. Although his body was initially buried on the bank of the Mississippi near Fort DeRussy, his name appears on a monument shared with his parents and sister at Buckingham cemetery near Traer. His actual final resting place is unclear.

CHAPTER XIII

FIRST MISSISSIPPI RAID

June 23rd. Received orders early this morning to be ready to march at eight o'clock in the morning. Packed all our things but the clothes we wore, and wore blouses rather than coats, and sent them to the city to be stored till we returned. Carried besides our guns and accoutrements a canteen, haversack, rubber blanket or a piece of canvas five by six feet square called a dog tent. We were probably in the lightest marching condition we could be and have any protection from the weather. For cooking utensils we each had a quart tin fruit can with the top melted off and a wire bale to carry it with. This to make coffee or boil meat in. We also had a half canteen, that is, a canteen with the seam melted so the disks came apart. This was the frying pan. The blanket or canvas was rolled into a roll and the two ends tied together with a string and hung over one shoulder and under the other arm. This was but a slight encumbrance.

Sometime ago the government offered four hundred dollars bounty to any man who had served two years or more in the army and would re-enlist. They were also to have a "veteran furlough", for these men were to be known as "Veterans". Very few of our men accepted this offer, but what did were now given their furloughs. Captain Jones of Company I, Addison Davis, Josiah Luke, Jerry Mills and a few others of our Company went as veterans and were furloughed now.

We did not get started that day but marched at six o'clock the next morning. We left the old camp and marched down to the city to the depot and then waited for a train. Two train loads of soldiers went out before we did. It looked like we were going out to redress the wrong done to General Sturges and his men. If so they would find General Smith quite a different character to General Sturges. A train of flat cars came in and we were ordered to get on board. After we were on the cars they still remained standing in the yards. The sun was very hot for it was now about eleven o'clock and we were in the full glare of the sun and surrounded by buildings. Leach was sitting on the edge of a car with his feet off the side when he suddenly became unconscious and fell to the ground. He was taken up and placed in an ambulance and sent to the hospital. I supposed it was sunstroke that ailed him.

We started at noon and went thirty-eight miles to the end of the road as it was used at that time. Arrived there at half past three o'clock in the afternoon. Marched a mile or so farther and went into camp on the bank of Wolf River. Next morning fell into line again and marched to the south side of the railroad about a mile farther down and camped again. We were about half a mile from the river and about the same distance from the railroad.

Colonel Moore of the Twenty-First Missouri now commanded the division and Colonel Gilbert of the Twenty-Seventh Iowa commanded the brigade. Colonel Shaw was in Memphis Chief of Court Martial.

We were having a very hot spell of weather. Sunday we had grand review, but I escaped by being on guard. Orders were given to be ready to march at five o'clock the next morning. Charles Ford went to Memphis to get the Company's books. This left me acting orderly sergeant till he gets back, which was but two days later.

Monday, June 27th. Awoke by reveille at half past three o'clock. Breakfast was soon prepared and eaten. The boys mostly messed two and two but sometimes one cooked alone and sometimes several went together. Felter and I messed together.

We were on the march before six o'clock. It was sultry hot and the boys marched too fast. Some gave out before they had gone five miles. When we crossed Wolf River orders were given to fill every canteen for we would get no more water till night. But this was a mistake for just after noon we came to a large pond of water that was covered with a thick green scum. The water when the scum was pushed away was thick clouded like dirty soap suds. It was quite warm to the hand and yet some of the boys tried to drink it. But these that did drink it soon threw it up again. I was not so much of a water drinker and had plenty in my canteen yet. Soon after leaving the pond I became too hot and was compelled to fall out and lie down for awhile; but after resting I was so refreshed that I was able to overtake my Company again. When we went into camp that evening there were very small regiments.

The One Hundred Twenty-Eighth New York had only six men with the colors. The next morning we heard that a number of men had died on the march from overheat. The New York regiment lost five men. The place we were camped next was a beautiful spot of ground covered with tall trees and luxuriant grass but was quite a distance from water. The weather continued very hot. Sergeant Ford came and assumed the duties of orderly sergeant. We were still near the railroad and again a train came out as far as our camp. That night all of our regiment and the Twenty-First Missouri was called to fatigue duty. That is to work. Our regiment unloaded eight hundred sacks of oats from the cars and built them into a huge stack.

Mustered for pay. We may not get our pay for sometime. In fact we do not want it if we are going out on a raid.

July 1, 1864. As I was coming from the railroad today I saw a man who had a large cheese. When I first saw him he was marking it off into sections. These sections were about one inch thick at the rind and came to an edge at the center. He proposed to sell these at one dollar each. It was a big price but as soon as he cut them off they sold and I believe he could have sold one or two more cheese if he had had them. I secured one piece for a treat to some of our boys.

Monday, July 4th, 1864. Fired a salute of thirty-four guns this morning. Not to waste ammunition the officers ordered them loaded with ball or shell and pointed them across the county where the rebel marauders might be. Orders this evening to be ready to march at an early hour tomorrow morning.

Captain Campbell of Company K received a letter from Colonel Shaw in which he stated that he was doing all he could to prevent our brigade from going any farther. We did not know why he did this but it was probably because of the trouble between him and Colonel Moore.

The next morning we were ordered to police the grounds; that was to cut brush and use them as brooms and sweep the ground and clean up. By this the boys thought the Colonel had succeeded in stopping our advance, but in the afternoon we were ordered to be ready to march at four o'clock and we were in line and on the march before five o'clock. Sprinkled on us pretty freely just after we started and there was a hard rain not far north of us. Passed over roads where it had rained hard a short time previous. Camped at nine o'clock about three miles southeast of Grand Junction. Didn't understand why we made this march at this time of day but supposed the commander had his reasons for it.

July 6th. Reveille before three o'clock and were ready to march before four but did not march till six o'clock. The First Division was in front and our brigade was in front of our division. Our division (Third Division Sixteenth Army Corps) was composed of three brigades and each brigade had four regiments. Ours was the Second Brigade and the First Regiment. The First Division had but two brigades here, the balance of the First Division was with the Sixteenth Army Corps with General Sherman. General Joe Mower was in command of these two brigades of the First Division. We also had two divisions of cavalry. The first was commanded by General Hatch and the second by General Grierson. Besides these we had parts of two batteries, the Third and Ninth Indiana.

We marched about twelve miles today. At eleven o'clock the head of column stopped and remained there for about two hours. Near us was a house and in the front yard were several stands of bees. Our boys tried to get the honey but were repulsed by the stings of the bees. A raw recruit with us looked on for sometime and enjoyed the repeated defeats of the boys. All at once he climbed the fence and walked deliberately up to one of the hives, which was merely a square box, lifted it up and turned it upside down and took out what honey he wanted and came away unstung. How the boys cheered him. It was a joke on the old veterans for this green recruit to teach them new tricks.

Marched till six o'clock and camped. I was again on headquarters guard. I had charge of the guard all night with no relief. Made my couch beside Colonel Moore's tent and as a number of officers had gathered there after night I must say I heard some of the most wonderful stories I ever heard told. The story telling and drinking was kept up till after midnight.

July 7th. Reveille sounded at half past two and we were to march at four but did not get away till five. Third Division in front and our brigade in the middle and our regiment in the rear of the brigade. Took no rest at noon. Very hot weather. Some skirmishing reported but saw none of it.

Felter gave out soon after noon and we had to leave him. Got him into a fence corner in the shade of a tree and told him to stay there till the ambulance came for him. That I would have the doctor send for him as soon as we went into camp. Marched till eight o'clock before we camped. Before we were settled our Company was ordered to go on picket duty. I went to where I saw the doctor's tent and told him about Felter. He said he would send the first ambulance that came in after him. We then marched out some distance and deployed as pickets. No fire; no supper; no sleep, although I had slept very little the night before; and the promise of a hard day's march before us next day. To say the least the situation was not pleasant. We understood we were but four miles from Ripley and it was expected that General Forrest would make a stand there. We expected a skirmish if not a battle the next day.

July 8th, 1864. Not as bad on picket last night as we expected it would be. During the night the air became quite cool and we were not disturbed so most of us got a good, long sleep. We went back to camp this morning for breakfast and found Felter there. He said when I left him he soon sank to sleep and slept till nearly sundown. When he awoke he was much refreshed and started for camp. About ten o'clock he met the ambulance coming after him but was then in sight of the camp fires. He was able to march again today.

First Division in front and our brigade in the rear of the Third Division. The head of column started at four o'clock but we did not get off till about six. Marched a short distance and were halted for fully an hour, then moved on again and passed through Ripley without any opposition, at about eleven o'clock in the forenoon. Ripley had less than a thousand inhabitants but was a very pretty place.

The weather was very hot. In fact too hot for men to be exposed to the sunshine. Went into camp about three o'clock that afternoon. The country is broken and covered with a heavy growth of timber. There are not many improved farms along our line of march.

July 9th. Last night our brigade passed to the front and our regiment was second in the brigade. These marching in the front brigade had much the easiest marching. They started about four o'clock while the air was cool, if it ever got cool, and went into camp early. Those in the rear did not start till the sun was well up in the sky and everything was growing hot. Then they had all the halts that are made by the train or the batteries in crossing bad places. A small halt of ten minutes with those near the front was multiplied till those in the rear were stopped an hour. Then they were hurried to make up the time they had lost. This made hard work. The standing order was for the reveille to sound at two and the head column to march at four. If it was a very hot day or the marching bad the head of column goes into camp at eleven or twelve o'clock if they find good camping ground. But the rear guard seldom gets into camp till after dark and sometimes not till ten o'clock at night. This was what an army of fifteen thousand men would do, for that was about our number. So we were glad to be so near the head of column for this day's march.

Our camp was about six miles southeast of Ripley. We were not marching very far each day because the weather was absolutely too hot for hard marching. We started promptly at four o'clock this morning and came to the Tallahatchie River about ten o'clock. The bridge over the river had been burned but we crossed on the timbers as they lay on the waters with some addition of logs and brush. It would be a surprise to civilians to see what shabby bridges are sufficient for an army to cross over on.

Camped on the south bank of the river. Our boys took this opportunity to wash their clothes and soon the river was full of boys washing their clothing. You will remember we had but the suit we wore. When the clothing was washed sufficiently clean we wrung them as dry as we could and then put them on. They dried as well on our bodies as if hung on the bushes and we could go about our work while they were drying.

For some days our boys had been afflicted by a little mite called a "jigger". It was a very small, bright red insect that burrows in the human skin. Its choice location was between the shoulder blades. I do not know how it learned that that one spot of the human body was out of reach of the hands, but there it located and there it stayed in spite of its victims' efforts to remove it. Before they are disturbed you can see them with the naked eye, but as you scratch or rub the skin it becomes red and the insect was concealed, being the same color. Some one told us to scour with fine sand and it would cut them off so while in the river we scoured each other to remove them. It was amusing to see a long row of men each rubbing his file leader's back with sand. I did not mean to say the jiggers were only on our backs, for they were all over our bodies and limbs but on the back was the worst place and they were out of our reach.

There had been a small town on the south side of the river called New Albany, but the buildings had all been burned. We had no knowledge who did it but it was done sometime before. Today we heard that as the negro troops passed through Ripley they were fired upon by parties concealed in some of the houses and that they in return set fire to the town and burned it to the ground. Hoped this was one of the false rumors we had so many of. There was too much property destroyed from necessity without being obliged to fire as nice and seemingly as quiet a place as Ripley.

July 10th, 1864. The First Division was in front today. Had a hard rain yesterday evening which made the air cooler. Besides, there was a strong breeze blowing. Marched steadily till after noon when the front was halted by skirmishers. We had descended to low ground, or rather were following along a small stream of water with hills on either side. The timber was so dense the rays of the sun could not penetrate their foliage. It was a dark and gloomy place. In this we were halted while the First Division ahead of us felt its way to higher ground. It was in such a deep ravine these same rebels had ambushed General Sturges only a few weeks before. As we sat on the ground waiting for an order to advance not one of us but felt the stress of fear that we might also be in a trap. For an hour we sat there without a word from the front when suddenly we heard a cannon far in front of us followed by the discharge of two not a half a mile away. Then there was lively cannonading for a short space of time and all was still again. At the first cannon shot every man was on his feet and in his place. When the firing ceased the column soon began to move forward and we came to where we ascended to the higher land where the fighting had occurred. It seemed the rebels had made a stand across a level field from where our road arose from the chasm and when our advance appeared there was a sharp skirmish which ended in a little artillery duel. We saw nothing more of the rebels that evening.

July 11th, 1864. We were upon the road at five o'clock although the First Division was still in front and must have started at four or sooner. The First Division remained in front because part of it had followed the rebels the night before and were left in front over night. We camped last night about eight miles north of Pontotoc and arrived at the town about ten o'clock in the morning. Had several sharp skirmishes during the morning. We passed through Pontotoc and marched about a mile south and went into camp. It rained all the afternoon, sometimes quite hard, which gave us a good excuse to remain in camp the next day, which we did. The rains had made the roads very muddy. We supposed our objective point was Okolona, a town on the railroad about fifteen miles south of Pontotoc. We were led to believe the town was strongly fortified and that the rebel army there numbered from twenty-five to thirty thousand men. We had lots of faith in General Smith and believed he would not undertake what he could not accomplish, yet it looked to us like a pretty big contract to try to capture Okolona. But if General Smith said we could capture the place we believed we could and would do it.

The rebel army was under General S. D. Lee and with him were Generals Forrest, Marmaduke, Price, Chalmers and a number of others. The rebel army ran more to generals than ours did. With us were two colonels doing duty as major generals, and a half dozen who took the place of brigadier generals.

July 13th, 1864. Well, we were surprised this morning when we started on the march to retrace our steps through Pontotoc and as soon as we were through the town to strike out due east toward Tupelo. We had no doubt the rebels were surprised at the move. Everything indicated Okolona to be the objective point. And as we laid over one day it gave the rebels a good chance to concentrate all their force there. Now we were on our way to Tupelo where there was a long string of trestle work in the railroad which we would destroy and prevent the rebels shipping supplies from Tennessee and Kentucky over this railroad. There was scarcely a skirmish line between us and Tupelo. When the battle came, as we knew it was sure to come, General Smith would choose the ground and fight on the defensive. They would attack us and we would defend.

We started at four o'clock this morning and the air was fresh and fairly cool and our boys' spirits were high. They felt that victory was more than half won by this strategy. Frequently the boys would cheer as we marched along. The cheering would begin in front and gradually pass along the line to the rear. We had avoided fighting the enemy behind breast works which was hazardous even when we had equal numbers but much more so when they had nearly double our numbers, which was the case here. Their men were old soldiers, too. Forrest's men were known veterans used to hard service.

I remember we captured a scout soon after we left Wolf River. He was a boy about eighteen years of age. He said he belonged to the army of Virginia and was home on furlough and was sent out to see about how many men we had and where we were going. He was bright for he knew almost exactly how many men we had and had a pretty correct idea of where we were going. General Smith asked him where General Forrest was, and he answered, "If you keep your present course a few days you will doubtless meet him." General Smith said, "I suppose General Forrest is a very good officer." He answered. "He can whip equal numbers every time." All the other officers and men concentrated against us were of those who had been in service since the war began. It was not strange we rejoiced to know we would fight an open battle instead of butting our heads against fortifications as we had expected to do. General Smith would rather beat the enemy by strategy without a battle while General Mower, the next in command, would far prefer to whip them in open fight.

Before noon a light body of rebel cavalry was on our right flank but caused us but little worry. Soon after noon a much heavier body of cavalry struck us on the right wing which produced lively skirmishing at times but did not prevent us marching onward. At four o'clock the rear division had some pretty severe fighting. We went into camp very soon after near the town of Tupelo. It was a hasty march. The roads were good and the air cooler than it had been for some days, so the boys stood the march very well.

Before General Mower came into camp with his First Division we heard severe cannonading in the rear and supposed he was teaching the rebels not to encroach on ground that he was occupying. He was always a little particular about his rights. The camp was quiet till about midnight when there was some cannonading but we were not molested.

July 14th. We had slept in line of battle last night and the battle opened before six o'clock this morning. Our regiment was sent to the rear to guard the train. Our army lay just back of the crest of a ridge and our regiment was in the timber about twenty rods in the rear with open ground between. The rebels came over a wide open place to make the attack. The battle became general at once. They were so strong they attempted to storm our whole line at once and overpower it by sheer force of numbers. But our old veterans did not propose to be run over by anybody. So they held their ground and gave them so hot a reception that they were compelled to fall back. They rallied again and again were driven back. Soon they came again, even more determined than ever to crush our men, but again they were hurled back in confusion. By eleven o'clock the battle was over. The rebels had withdrawn to a timber belt about a mile away and the firing had entirely ceased. The victory was ours.

During the battle the enemy threw their shot and shell at our lines and as they came over or through among them they struck the trees above our heads, for we were on lower ground than our army was, and cut off large branches which sometimes fell upon our men. In this manner we had in our regiment two men killed and a number wounded by falling timber striking them. We fired not a shot from our regiment. Only once did we take active part and that was when the enemy tried to outflank us and stampede our train. We were then sent out to prevent this. But they did not succeed in passing the army flank and we were recalled. In the afternoon we were relieved of guarding the train and marched out on our extreme left flank. We could see the rebel army in the edge of the timber probably a mile and a half away. We lay there and watched them till dark and then were relieved by a colored brigade.

Just back of us the ground fell off very abrupt to a small creek and we were moved back to this creek to cook some supper. We built fires to make coffee and were preparing our bacon to fry when we heard heavy firing in front of us and here came the negroes closely followed by the rebels yelling like Indians and firing as fast as they could load their guns. Quick as thought our boys had their arms in hand and we went up over the bluff and formed line on the level ground. It was so dark we could not see a man of the rebels but the front was full of the flashes of their guns. We fired one volley and then dashed after them as fast as they had come after the negroes. It was our turn to fire and yell and quite lively we did both and the rebels fled before us as fast as the negroes had fled before them. We chased them half a mile where we stopped and lay down and there we lay until morning.

This was the only night battle I was ever in and I can say I did not like it very well. I would rather see the enemy than only see the flash of their guns. In the morning we could plainly see the rebels preparing their breakfast a mile away. Sometimes one of them, I suppose to try the range of his gun, would send a shot over our way. While we were trying to start fires to make coffee young Ingham was on his hands and knees blowing the fire when a ball came with full force and struck among his fire brands, scattering them all about him and filling his eyes with dirt and ashes. A very close call. Probably the rebel soldiers remember some such experience with some of our bullets, for some went from our side over there too.

We were withdrawn from this position about six o'clock in the morning, and took our place again with the wagon train. It was said our cavalry destroyed the trestle work on the railroad but we knew nothing of it. We saw neither the railroad nor the trestle.

We started north with the wagon train about eight o'clock. After we were on our way there was heavy firing in our rear and we understand General Mower with the First Division fought them another battle after the train left. Afterward we learned the rebel loss at the battle of Tupelo, as this battle was called, was twenty-five hundred men killed and wounded, one general and many minor officers being among the killed. Our loss was nothing near that figure, but our men were somewhat protected by the crest of the ledge and were not exposed like the rebels were when they advanced over open ground.

In guarding the wagon train we were obliged to march beside the wagons and not behind or between them. The orders were if we were attacked for all the troops to come to the side upon which the attack was made. This was to prevent the enemy seizing the mules by the head and running them off in the bushes as they did for us a few days later. The main object of the rebels now would be to capture or stampede our train and leave us without provision or ammunition. Our object was to prevent this catastrophe.

Once a heavy body of cavalry came upon an open field to our right, but we opened fire upon them and they withdrew. It was hard marching beside the wagons for the roads there were not like these in our country. Most of the way they lay through timber and the ground was also covered with underbrush so there was scarcely room to march beside the wagon. Where we passed through cultivated land the worm fences on either side left the road so narrow we could hardly keep our places. The most dangerous places were where there were cross-roads in the heavy timber, but our cavalry were on the lookout at these places.

We went into camp before four o'clock that evening. Had just crossed a small stream and camped on the north side. The wagon train was corralled in an open field on the east side of the road and we camped in open timber on the west side. We at once prepared something to eat. Felter and I had managed to get some corn meal and had a fruit can full of hot mush and another full of boiling coffee, when like a clap of thunder from clear sky a shell burst in the tree tops above our heads. We tried to drink the coffee to save it and burned the skin off our lips and tongues. The can of mush I placed in my haversack and we were into line and ready to move.

But by this time half a dozen shells had burst among us and over among the wagon train. The rebel battery was planted on a hill a mile away and our brigade started after it. Just north of the creek was a sharp ridge running parallel with the stream through which the road had been cut which produced a passage about eight or ten feet deep. The rebels could see our train through this gap and now were throwing their shells, at the rate of one about every five seconds, through it and among the wagons hoping to stampede the train. Our officers marched us to the road and then through this gap to the creek. It was a bad move and might have been fatal to many of us. We were among the first who went through. We met a shell just as we entered the gap but it passed over our heads. A few steps farther and we were startled by a heavy explosion and all dropped to the ground thinking it was a shell burst over us, but next instant we understood the cause. It was one of our batteries that had taken position on the ridge just behind the gap and fired their six guns at once. But falling really saved us for the next shell from the rebel guns came an instant after our battery fired and it passed just over our prostrate forms. We were on our feet again and pressed forward. As we cleared the end of the gap our battery gave them another volley and theirs made no reply.

We now deployed line of battle which should have been done in camp, and dashed across the creek below the bridge and went after the rebels. Soon we struck their dismounted cavalry far in advance of the battery that opened the battle. We gave them a volley and charged, they fled to the top of the first raise and turned on us. They had the shelter of the ridge and poured out a fire upon us that was enough to make veterans quail. But on we went. When we got too close they broke and fled down the hill and we peppered them for all they were worth. In the hollow the rain had cut a channel which was sometimes two or three feet deep and as many wide, though in some places these ditches were much deeper and wider. When the rebels dropped into one of these ditches they turned on us and gave us as hot a fire as they were able to deliver, but when we came too close, out they would jump and run up the next raise till they got shelter behind the ridge. We had bayonets and they had none and in close quarters they stood no chance. This running fight was kept up till we came to the hill their battery had occupied, but it had pulled out before we got there.

We were totally exhausted and lay down at the brow of the hill to rest. After resting awhile we took off our clothes and wrung the water out of them, for we had crossed the creek and were thoroughly wet from that as well as from sweat, for it was a warm evening. After that I remembered passing a hat a quarter of a mile back, and Felter had lost his hat the night we camped at Pontotoc and had been wearing a handkerchief over his head ever since. I asked permission of the commander to go back and get the hat. I secured it and returned. It was just a fit for Felter and he was much pleased to get it. It came very good both in sun and rain. We now thought of our mush and took it out and ate it. It was quite warm yet though it had been in my haversack for two hours. This battle we called the "Charge of Towncreek". There were but six killed in our regiment and quite a number wounded among whom were Gallion and McLain. We were recalled at dark and took a position about half a mile from camp. There we stayed in line of battle without fires or supper except such as Felter and I had.

It grew quite cold in the night, or at least seemed so to men with wet clothes, so we had to exercise to keep warm. In the morning the reveille sounded in our camp across the creek half a mile away from us and in a few minutes the rebel camp fully as near on the other side of us sounded their morning call. The clear notes of their bugle followed by the shrill fife and drum seemed just on the other side of the hill from us. We held the heights we were on till our army broke camp and its long line marched across the lowlands and climbed the hills on the other side of the valley and passed out of sight. Our mission was to prevent the rebel battery shelling our army as it was in plain view across the creek and ascending the hills. When they were gone out of sight we quietly moved down the road to the bridge and then at a double-quick up the hills on the other side. There was a small body of cavalry remained in position while we crossed the creek and then followed us at a gallop. It seemed to me it was a risky venture to leave one brigade out so far as we were after our army had climbed the hills. We knew there was a large army near us and how easily they might have intercepted us with either infantry or cavalry and cut us off from the army and captured us. But they did not for some reason.

We were not free of the rebels yet. Several times during the day they made demonstration in such force that we were compelled to deploy in line of battle. This was no small matter. Our army of fifteen thousand men would line up from two to three miles long, and was five to eight miles long as it marched along the road. To turn this army in battle line across the road caused much hard marching. The ground chosen for this line was generally very rough and often covered with brush and timber. Just before night they made a sudden attack at a cross road and attempted to cut our column in two but were foiled in the attempt, but in the flurry they managed to capture two of our wagons which contained nearly all our crackers. From this on we had but a cracker a day to the man till we reached our supplies.

We camped near a town called Ellerton after marching about fifteen miles. If we counted all the deploys we made it would have been at least ten miles farther. It was a custom now with us when we went into camp to plant a battery and as soon as all our men had passed it to shell the timber for an hour to drive the skirmishers back. The boys said it was to tell the rebels we had stopped and they had better stop too. In the morning before we start a battery shells the timber in front of us to tell the rebels to get out of our way for we are coming.

July 17th. Slept without an alarm, the first time for several nights. All went well in our march today. No enemy to be seen. Our cavalry captured two wagons loaded with bacon, which were trying to cross the Tallahatchie River, but we got them. Arrived at New Albany at two o'clock in the afternoon. Rested till near dark and then moved to the top of the hill back of town and lay in line of battle all night. No attack but our officers surely expected one.

July 18th. Started at half past three o'clock this morning on the road to Ripley, but soon changed to a road leading to Holly Springs and again changed to a road leading to Salem. Third Division in front. During the morning the country we were marching over was quite level but as we advanced it became rolling and where we went into camp it was quite rough. For some days we had been short of rations, especially crackers, of which we had only had one a day per man for four days, and marched hard at that. We were expecting to meet supplies every day.

July 19th. Started early as usual this morning and soon came to Tippah River. There was a large drift of logs against which the body of a bridge had lodged. We crossed on this wreck of the bridge and then laid down and slept for two hours. During this time they brought the batteries and the wagon train across the river. This morning we had but a half cracker each. They assured us we would receive supplies by noon.

Started from the river near noon and marched very fast. The country was very rough there. Soon after noon we found the body of a large negro lying in the road. He had been shot or stabbed in the neck and breast and was dead. We had no knowledge how he came by his death. Whether by the hands of the rebels or by our men, but dead he was.

Camp on a beautiful stream of water about a mile below Salem. Our supply of rations met us here and we received our usual five crackers per man, as many as we had for the last five days before. It was pleasant to hear the glad remarks of the boys when they received their crackers.

July 20th. Did not start till late this morning. It was eight o'clock before we were upon the march. Traveled very leisurely along till after noon. About two o'clock we struck the road upon which we had gone out on this raid. Knowing the road enabled us to cut corners where otherwise we were obliged to make square corners. Traveled not over twelve miles and camped about four miles from Lagrange.

July 21st. Started in good time this morning and before noon arrived at the old camp ground near here. We received our mail which was the mail that accumulated during this three weeks we were away. I had a number of letters, and oh, how pleasant it was to get these letters.

This camp ground was arranged for holding camp meetings on. There was plenty of spring water and the underbrush had been cut off and all loose limbs and rubbish gathered out of camp. The timber was principally beech, which made a thick shade and was cool and pleasant.

About one o'clock orders came to prepare to march again. Soon came to Lagrange and expected to take the cars to Memphis, but we were told we would have to march to Colierville, a distance of something like thirty miles. This was so we might guard the wagon train. In our country, which this was supposed to be, this duty was usually done by the cavalry, but our cavalry with the First Division was sent on some other expedition two days before. Left Lagrange soon after three o'clock that afternoon and arrived at our old camp at Moscow at six in the evening. Our Company was detailed for picket guard but when ready to go the order was countermanded, the officers saying we did not need picket guards here.

July 23rd. Started at four o'clock this morning. Marched hard for we were anxious to get through. When about two miles from Colierville we came to the camp of the Forty-Sixth Iowa regiment of one-hundred-day men who were here guarding the railroad. When they saw us coming they came to meet us with pails and pans and kettles of cold water for us to drink. And we were very thankful for this day was warm.

The winter of '60 and '61 I taught school two and a half miles west of Buckingham and boarded at home. A young man from Grinnell, James Ellis, taught the Buckingham school and boarded at father's house. We were very warm friends. He was here, a member of this regiment. I did not know he was in the service till he slapped me on the shoulder and called my name. How very agreeable the surprise of meeting him here. He took me to their tent and introduced me to Mr. Scott and Mr. Cooper who had both taught school in our settlement, after I had gone in the army. He also introduced me to Professor Parker of Grinnell College who was captain of their company. The company was made up of students from Grinnell. We had been marching, fighting and starving for nearly three weeks and these boys knew it for the Memphis papers had given a glowing account of our raid. So they did their best to prepare us a feast. This special mess selected me for their victim. They had so many good things and pressed them on me with such gracious hospitality that I loaded my willing stomach and in consequence was sick that afternoon.

Took the cars for Memphis and arrived there before night. Went to our old camp beside Elmwood cemetery. Captain Gallagher was not with us on this raid. He was left at Memphis sick in hospital. We now learned he was very bad with lung fever. John Dew was also very sick in hospital. For a week we did nothing but rest and write letters. Some of the boys built a bake oven and baked bread for us. When we were within reach of a bakery Felter and I had been in the habit of buying dough ready to bake and make a mess of fried cakes with it. We would cut it into shapes and fry them in grease just as our mothers used to do at home, but did not sweeten but made syrup of our sugar and ate our crullers with the syrup. We indulged in these crullers to our heart's content while here this time.

Colonel Shaw had taken command of the Third Division and Colonel Moore commanded the Third Brigade under him. Bully for Colonel Shaw. It seemed that while he was away he visited St. Louis and there found his commission was issued several days prior to that of Colonel Moore's. Therefore he was senior officer and was by right in command of the division. When he returned to Memphis he was again detailed as Chief of Court Martial and served till we returned. He then came to his regiment and demanded his position as commanding officer of the division, which was accorded him. Again we say bully for Colonel Shaw.

FIRST MISSISSIPPI RAID - Notes:

-- **James I Gilbert** 38 of Lansing, Allamakee County, was appointed Colonel of the 27th Iowa Infantry August 1862 and was promoted Brigidier General in February 1865. He was wounded slightly at Pleasant Hill. He and Moore, who received their first appointments long after Colonel Shaw was commissioned to command the 14th, seem to have worked together to push each other for promotion over Shaw.

-- **Warren C Jones** 33 from Mount Pleasant, Henry County was appointed Captain of Company I in November 1861. He was taken prisoner at Shiloh. He distinguished himself in battle at Pleasant Hill when he assumed command after Lieutenant Colonel Newbold was killed. The roster says Jones mustered out after three years; it does not mention that he remained with the regiment for extra duty after November 1864.

-- **Jeremiah Mills** 25 of Tama County, enlisted October 1861. At the Hornets' Nest of Shiloh Jerry had been wounded slightly in the hand and taken prisoner with the others. Two years after his release from prison camp Mills re-enlisted as noted here and served in the veteran's regiment until August 1865. For the extra bounty and furlough Mills, Josiah Luke, Addison Davis and others agreed to serve beyond the time of their original three year enlistment which would have soon ended in November 1864. These older veterans from 1861 who took this bounty were later formed together with the newer recruits from 1864 into the 14th Iowa Residuary Battalion. Mills was a carpenter in St. Louis after the War; he died there in 1904.

-- "Young" Ingham, who was almost killed beside the fire, may have indeed been young. Roster records say **Melville C Ingham** was 19 when he enlisted January 4 1864 but census records both before and after the War indicate Ingham, who was the son of Toledo's Methodist minister, was probably 16 when he signed up. After the War he lived near Columbus Ohio, where he died in 1897.

-- **Turner McLain** 19 of Nevada, Story County enlisted October 1861. He fought at the battle of Shiloh and survived the POW camp afterwards. He was made First Corporal July 1863 and mustered out with the regiment in November 1864. Unquestionably a brave man, the official roster doesn't record him being wounded at Towncreek. His full name was Ferdinand Turner McLain; BF Thomas and the roster both spelled his last name as "McClain" but census records before and after the War, Story County records, and his gravemarker in Ames spell it McLain. He died in 1910. See Chapter 3.

-- **Elijah Gallion**, John R Felter's 21 year old brother-in-law, was wounded in the hand near Tupelo Mississippi on July 15 1864, during the battle described above. He had enlisted in February 1864 and after this battle he served in the 14th Iowa Residuary Battalion until it was disbanded in August 1865. Before joining the 14th Iowa, Elijah had already served with the 16th Ohio Infantry. He remained in Toledo until his death in 1888.

-- **John Dew** 27 of Howard Township near Toledo enlisted in December 1862; he recovered from this illness and served until the regiment was disbanded in November 1864. A few months before John signed up, his brother **Andrew Dew** 25 had enlisted into the 24th Iowa in August 1862, but Andrew died from disease May 13 1863. Andrew Dew is buried in St. Louis in Jefferson Barracks National Cemetery, Section 5 Grave 40. They were the sons of Thomas and Margaret Dew of Tama County.

-- Educated in Ohio, **Professor Leonard Fletcher Parker** came to Iowa in 1856. It is said he choose Grinnell because the community was strongly associated with the causes of temperance and abolition, and that he was involved in the activities of the Underground Railroad. The roster says he was 38 when he was appointed First Lieutenant of the 46th Iowa Infantry. Company B was comprised of many students from Grinnell College including the three named here. They served from June to September 1864, but there is no indication that Parker served as Captain. After the War Parker remained on the faculty and collected a large archive of local history in the course of writing a history of Poweshiek County. **Charles N Cooper** was 20 and a native of Ohio. **Charles Scott** appropriately enough was born in Scotland; he was 27. New York born **James E Ellis** was made Fifth Corporal when the Company was formed. Even though he was only serving 100 days for the purpose of freeing the experienced soldiers from having to do non-combat duty, Ellis was exposed to the same diseases that frequently killed many hardened veterans. Within a month of hosting this feast for his warm friend BF Thomas, James Ellis died of disease in Memphis on August 15 1864. He was 24.

CHAPTER XIV

OXFORD RAID

August 1, 1864. Orders were given to pack our surplus baggage and prepare for marching. Did not know where we were going but expected it was another raid into Mississippi. Sent our things into storage this evening. Captain Gallagher was still sick in the hospital at Memphis and Lieutenant Presbury of Company E was in command of our Company.

We understood there was a call for carpenters on government work in Memphis so I went to the city and tried to get a detail for Felter, for he was unfit to go on this raid. I easily secured a job for him but there found it was necessary to get a surgeon's certificate to his disability to go on the raid. I saw Dr. Staples and he said he did not know there was anything ailing Felter. He had not been under his care for a long time therefore he could not give the certificate. Felter was a man who would do his duty when entirely unfit and who would not go on the sick list till totally unable to do duty. He was too ambitious and now for this he must suffer. I explained this to Dr. Staples and asked him to make an examination of Felter at this time. But no; he could only go by the former record and Felter had no record in his books. By this rule if a man lost a leg today he must still do duty till he established a record as a disabled man. Many of the men who were much better off than Felter got certificates simply because they had got themselves on the sick list as often as they could and thereby escaped duty. I was very fearful he would not be able to stand the march. Leach, Ingham and Yarham were sent to the hospital.

August 4, 1864. Left camp this morning at half past four o'clock and took the cars and left the depot at Memphis at eight o'clock. Went to Grand Junction and there took the Mississippi road to Holly Springs where we arrived at four o'clock this evening. There had been a large depot and hotel building here and when General Grant was marching down the Coldwater River to get in the rear of Vicksburg two years ago his main supplies were stored here. This the rebel General VanDorn learned through some friends here, so he made a raid on this place and succeeded in burning the depot and other buildings containing these stores. This with some other matters compelled General Grant to fall back. Most of the massive stone walls of these buildings were still standing, but some had tumbled down. We were landed at dusk near these old walls and for some reason there were no orders to camp or do anything. Soon the rain came in abundance and we gathered about the walls for shelter, but there were too many of us to shelter, and besides, the walls were perpendicular.

Soon it was dark. I groped my way through a door in the wall and after some time found a wall at right angles to the one I had been following. I followed this some distance and came to an opening and on entering found I was in a dry place under some kind of cover, I knew not what. I groped my way back and got Felter and some others of our Company and went back to the dry room. While I was away some other parties had also discovered the place and were in it. Still there was room enough for us with them. We lay down and slept but were disturbed many times in the night by other parties joining us. When daylight came we found ourselves packed in like sardines in a box. We were surprised to find we were in the vault where the books and papers had been kept. It was arched over with stone and was a very safe place to retreat from the rain storm. The rain had ceased but there had been heavy rain nearly all night and all our men but the few of us had been in it all night with absolutely no shelter but that of the stone wall.

Next morning we moved about a half mile south from the railroad and pitched the little "pup tents", as we called them. Peaches, apples, roasting ears and berries were in abundance here. As we were coming on the train, we were in box cars, the peach trees grew so close to the track that sometimes the branches brushed hard against the cars and when they would whip past the open door the peaches would be knocked off in the car. Large, luscious fellows, too. Now, we were camped beside a large apple orchard in which was a hand cider mill. You will not be surprised when I tell you this mill ran from early in the morning till late at night. There was always a long line of men awaiting their turn at the mill. I think we made the best cider there I ever drank. We also made all kinds of apple sauce to eat, probably the best of which was to take a whole apple and slice it into a pan of hot grease and fry the slices brown.

August 8th. Orders were to be ready to march at an hour's notice. It was reported that General Mower had taken the First Division out on an expedition against the rebels and might need our assistance. The weather was again very hot. Our veterans who were at home on furlough, except Mills, returned. Rumored that Colonel Gilbert with his Twenty-Seventh Iowa would remain in command of the post.

August 10th. Was in the city today. It was a very pretty place with many costly residences. There was no business done here now. It was said there had been no train over this road for more than a year. There was about one thousand inhabitants here before the war. Talked with a negro man of about forty years of age. He was a slave and was coachman for his wealthy master. He was well dressed and felt his dignity. Said the North was wrong in the war; that the slaves were used well and were much better off than if they had their freedom; that he would never leave his master and wanted no better freedom than service to him.

August 13th. Our First Brigade was ordered on the march some days ago and marched out about five miles and was then ordered to return to camp.

One day two regiments of the same brigade marched back toward Memphis. The next day one of the cavalry regiments came back from the front and they said the other cavalry regiments were coming. The First Division had joined us again. We hardly knew what this meant.

August 15th. We had division inspection by a regular officer. Our arms and clothing were in poor condition. After inspection we moved our tents to another plat of ground. This was our way of cleaning house. It was very effective and did away with a deal of scolding and unpleasantness. Move the house away from the dirt instead of trying to drive the dirt out of the house. It was not only more effectual but much easier done.

On picket south of the city. Felter was with me. We went to a farm house but it was vacant. Visited the garden and found nothing but some very black round beans that grew on a little bush instead of vine. They grew like small trees about eighteen inches high and were full of beans. We gathered them and started to camp. Met a negro and asked him about our black beans. He said they were beans and made the nicest kind of bean soup. We took them to camp and cooked them but failed to get them in edible condition. They were too coarse grained and strong flavored. Found we had orders to march at two o'clock this afternoon, August 16th, but did not start at that time. In the evening got orders to start at six o'clock next morning.

August 17th. Started on time and arrived at Waterford about one o'clock in the afternoon, about nine miles from Holly Springs and about the same distance from the Tallahatchie River. Soon we had our tents up and just in time for it began to rain and rained hard for an hour or more.

August 18th. Started at six o'clock. Soon reached the Tallahatchie River which we crossed on a bridge and marched about two miles farther near a village called Abbeville where we pitched our tents about one o'clock in the afternoon. It rained nearly all the evening. The roads were getting almost impassable by so much raining.

August 19th. This morning took down our tents and were ready to march. The cavalry and some infantry passed us to the front. It began to rain and there we stood in the rain with no protection till ten o'clock when we were ordered to put up our tents again. We soon had the tents up and were into them again. It rained till after dark. It seemed to be almost impossible to move our artillery and train over such roads as we now had. We lay still all the next day. We had no communication with the Union lines; having dropped that at Waterford. Every day lost was serious to us as we barely carried rations enough to last the trip. As soon as we cut communication with the Union lines we were put upon half rations. This was also the case on the other raid. We were now in the enemy's country and unable to move a wagon because of so much rain. I found a wash boiler and secured a sheet of tin from it which I punched full of holes with a nail. This made an excellent grater upon which we grated the new corn that was now just right to make golden meal for boiling into mush. My grater was much in demand. They spread a rubber blanket on the ground, cloth side up, and grated their meal on this blanket. It went from mess to mess and from company to company so it kept busy all day and often in the night also.

August 21st. Marched this morning at six o'clock. Roads were much better than we expected. It was a very pleasant day. Went into camp at eleven o'clock in the forenoon. Our division was in front which made it much better for us. We only traveled about eight miles and camped near the railroad track. Got plenty of salt pork. Some of the nicest smoked hams I ever saw. Took them from a smokehouse we passed on the way. As the boys were taking them down an old lady at the house watching them remarked, "You Yanks may as well take these hams for we will not eat them. The hogs were fatted on General Sturges' men." This was a fling at the defeat and rout of the men under General Sturges. It made no difference to the boys or the hams, they took them just the same. Corn was plenty and my large grater was putting in its best licks. Company E had a grater like mine this evening. I do not know whether it was patterned after mine or not.

August 22nd. We understand we were within about five miles of Oxford and that was the point at which we were to strike. Started at eight o'clock this morning and halted after marching but a short distance, then started again and again halted. It seemed the head of the column had reached Oxford and found no rebels there. We lay along the road without marching again till afternoon. Then a messenger came from Memphis with word that General Forrest with his rebel cavalry had passed by us and pushed into Memphis and captured the city. Of course he could not hold the city, but he could carry off all the supplies he was able to handle and destroy the balance of the military stores there. He would also parole all the sick in hospital and the numerous officers and men on duty there. Besides the prestige would go over the land both north and south as well as to the rest of the world that Memphis was captured, although he could not hold it two hours. Our purpose was now to counteract this as much as possible by capturing him and his men, or in recapturing the supplies he had taken from the city. There was a council of the officers held at once and after a half hour's parley the cavalry was all sent back toward Memphis under General Mower to try to intercept General Forrest and destroy him. As the cavalry galloped past us, some of them carrying boxes of crackers on their horses, we cheered them lustily.

About five o'clock in the evening the infantry faced to the rear and started back to Memphis. We learned that the town of Oxford was entirely destroyed by fire set by our men. We only marched about four miles and went into camp.

August 23rd. Started this morning at six o'clock and when we got to the Tallahatchie River found the bridge washed away and the river spread all over the bottom lands, so we camped for an indefinite time. It would be necessary to build a bridge before we could cross the river. That might take several days. Soon after we went into camp the rebels made an attack upon us, driving in our pickets and were nearly in our camp before we could get into shape to repel them. The fighting lasted nearly two hours and sometimes it was quite lively. They finally withdrew. Their object evidently was to surprise us and capture our train if possible. But this they did not succeed in doing. This was called a skirmish but was really quite a brisk battle.

We were at a great disadvantage. They knew all about us and the ground we were on, while we had no cavalry and therefore had no means of learning much about them. We felt sure they purposed doing us all the mischief they could while we were here. There were many surmises about who these rebels were. Some thought General Forrest and his men with large reinforcements were here and would either capture us or drive us into the river. Many of our men thought that our officers had been outwitted and that our defeat was certain. Our own boys did not think this. They thought it was a brilliant dash of General Forrest to go into Memphis, but that he most likely would pay dearly for his hardihood. We believed General Smith was much more than a match for him.

The pioneer corps and a heavy detail of men were hard at work building a bridge. The water in the river was falling fast and it soon would be within its banks. Felter was detailed for picket this evening and was not fit to go. I wanted to go in his place but he would not consent. I cautioned him not to expose himself needlessly. If there should be an attack at night, which was very probable, not to hold his post too long for fear he might be captured, but to fall back on the main line which I knew would be formed at the first alarm. He was a very brave man and altogether too reckless at times. We knew they were close about us but had no means of knowing about their number. But the night passed without an alarm being sounded.

The bridge being built was a very primitive affair. They made huge trestles of logs about a foot through and twelve or fifteen feet long. They put two mortises in each end of these logs and then in these put poles from ten to twenty feet long for legs. These trestles were then stood in the river about fifteen feet apart and logs laid from one to the other for stringers. Upon these stringers the floor of poles and split logs was laid and this completed the bridge. They tried to conform the length of the trestle legs to the depth of the river but did not succeed entirely, so the floor of the bridge was quite uneven in places. The timbers would spring and tremble under the load as we crossed but everything held safely together and so we crossed as soon as the bridge was completed. The last two days were miserable and we were glad to end the suspense. We expected the rebel batteries to get position so they could shell the bridge as we crossed but for some reason they did not do it and we crossed over unmolested, although as the last of our men were coming on the bridge the rebel cavalry dashed onto them and captured several of them.

This day proved very warm. We marched out some distance toward Waterford and camped. Many of the men were overcome with the heat. We were camped by a beautiful stream of water so I gave my clothes a washing as did most of our boys. In the evening I was detailed on picket guard. The camp was in a beautiful valley that was under cultivation. Surrounding the valley the hills were covered with timber. The picket line occupied this circle of hills. Our post was at the head of a ravine through which the water had washed a deep and wide ditch that started where we were and ran down more than half way to camp, which was about a mile away from us. It was a very favorable situation for pickets. In case of attack we were on lower ground than they and could see them toward the sky over the hill while we had the ground for background and therefore were invisible. Then if hard pressed we could drop into this ditch where we were safe from bullets and had a safe passage nearly to camp. In this manner we could have held a large body of men at bay while we slowly fell back to camp.

There was one lieutenant and two sergeants and twenty men on this post. We had four vidette posts at some distance in front and on either flank, so we felt pretty secure. I had just changed the guards at the vidette posts at midnight and returned to main post when I heard a low rumbling noise at some distance in front. It sounded like troops marching. The noise seemed to come closer for awhile and then bore off to our left. It sounded like soldiers marching, tramp, tramp, tramp, but so faint we could hardly feel sure of the sound. The lieutenant was asleep and at first I feared to wake him because it might be a false alarm. As the sound seemed more clear I awoke the lieutenant but by the time he was fully awake the noise had died down so he could not hear it. He said we were excited and heard only the breeze in the branches of the trees and imagined it was men marching. He sat up a few minutes and then laid down again and at once began to snore.

As soon as he slept I started out to visit the videttes again to learn what they knew of the noise. As I came to each one he told me he had heard the noise plainly and felt sure a large body of men had passed within a short distance of us. I charged each one to be very vigilant and by all means to not be taken by surprise. I had again returned to the main post when there came a sharp, clear challenge from the first vidette: "Halt! Who comes there?" I sprang to my feet and hastened to the vidette and asked in a low whisper what was the matter. He told me there were some men in the bushes just in front of him. He heard them talking as they came toward him but since his challenge they were still. Just then I heard one speak low to the others and I told them if they spoke again we would fire on them. I then commanded them to raise their hands above their heads and stand upon their feet. We were on lower ground than they and I knew if they stood up we could see them towards the sky. Again came a low murmur and I told them to arise at once or we would fire. Then three men arose about two rods from us with their hands above their heads. I then ordered the first one to approach us, which he did. When he came near us I halted him again and asked who they were. He said they were negroes who belonged to a colored regiment that had been in camp about eight miles from here at a mill; that these three men had lived in this settlement and took the opportunity to visit their friends. While they were away the regiment marched away. They followed as best they could. When they struck the ridge above us and saw our camp-fires in the valley they thought it was their regiment camped there and started directly for the fires and next they knew they were challenged by our vidette. At first they thought they had struck a rebel camp but by our language they soon were convinced we were Yankees. I then ordered the other two men to come in and bring their guns with them. I took them to the lieutenant who was now awake, and told him the mystery of the noise was solved. It was the negro regiment marching by us. The laugh was on the lieutenant this time sure.

Next morning started at seven o'clock, the First Division in front. While it was a very hot, sultry day we took the march very easy and arrived at Holly Springs at three o'clock in the afternoon. The next day we did not march but August 28th started in the morning at half past five. It still was very warm and we marched slowly. At twelve o'clock we stopped in a shady beech grove. I was completely overcome with the heat. If we had not stopped I verily believe this narrative would never have been written. As soon as we stopped I fell into a sound sleep and slept for two hours. In fact I knew nothing till I was aroused by the boys to fall into line for marching. I was very much refreshed by the shade and sleep.

This evening as the head of column was going into camp just out of sight around a hill some of the boys stopped at a house about a half mile back along the road. As soon as the rear of the column passed the house a body of rebel cavalry dashed up and captured the boys and carried them off on their horses almost within sight of our camp. Our old Colonel conceived an idea that some of the people of the house had influence over the rebels so he sent an officer with twenty men back to the house and they told the people if our boys were returned to us before daylight all would be well, but if they were not here then their house, barn and other buildings would be burned at sunrise. The prisoners all returned long before daylight. We were glad to get them back and leave the people in their house.

Some of our boys straggled off in squads or even singly to forage, although it was strictly against orders, and many of them were captured or killed and we only knew at night when the roll was called that they were missing. Many were so left that we were unable to tell what became of them.

At this place the First Division left us and the next day we started at eight o'clock and marched only about ten miles and went into camp. Weather still warm but cloudy. Next day crossed the Coldwater River and at evening heard the evening gun on the fort at Memphis.

August 29, 1864. Started at five o'clock and soon after we started we struck the old plank road called the "Pigeon Roost Road". The order had been that two men from each company might take a number of canteens and go to a house and fill them with water from the well. It seems that this order was changed that morning and orders given that no man must leave ranks under penalty of being shot. This forenoon as we were stopped in front of a large farm house, Gideon Hate asked permission of Lieutenant Presbury to go for water. The Lieutenant not having received the above order gave permission. Hate gathered a number of canteens and passed through the gate and around the house. Colonel Shaw rode up at this instant and jumped off his horse and followed Hate.

As the Colonel passed out of sight around the house we heard a revolver shot. Some moments after the Colonel and Hate came back both as pale as death. The Colonel asked Lieutenant Presbury if he had given

Hate permission to enter these premises for water. Lieutenant Presbury said he had. The Colonel then said, "Lieutenant Presbury, you may thank your God that you are not a dead man now." He then turned to his aide-de-camp, Lieutenant Gilbert, and said, "Lieutenant Gilbert, take Lieutenant Presbury back to the wagon train and tie him up behind one of the wagons." The Colonel mounted his horse and rode forward. The two lieutenants were close friends. There was not a word spoken for some minutes. Then Lieutenant Presbury said, "Gilbert, are you going to do it?" Lieutenant Gilbert answered, "It is the Colonel's orders." "Well, let us be going then." So they passed to the rear toward the train, Gilbert on his horse and Presbury walking by his side. Sometime after, Gilbert rode past us on his way to the front. Soon he returned to the rear and again returned to us with Lieutenant Presbury who again took command of the Company.

Hate said as he passed around the house he heard the revolver shot but had not thought he was the target. The well was an open one and a windlass was used to hoist the bucket. He had cast the bucket loose and held his hand on the roller to restrain it from running too fast, with his head over the well watching the descending bucket when something cold touched his temple. He looked up and there stood the Colonel with a cocked revolver staring him in the face. "Who gave you permission to come here?" "Lieutenant Presbury." "Well, b- G-- I will shoot him anyway." And they came out together. I cannot account for the ungovernable fits of temper the Colonel fell into. Several times we had seen him as mad and as reckless in language and action as in this case, and soon again saw his great warm heart open to take all the boys in. They were very strange moods.

August 30, 1864. Arrived at Memphis and went to our old camp ground near the cemetery in time to get everything snug before night. Next day we were mustered for pay. I had six months' pay due me which amounted to one hundred and fourteen dollars at nineteen dollars per month, which was my wages at this time. I also had thirty-one dollars due me on clothing account. Had on hand but thirty-five cents. At the first of this month had just one dollar but during the last month had been where money was of no use to us.

September 2nd. Captain Gallagher came out to our camp yesterday and was here again today. He was very weak yet and not fit for duty. He expected to start for home the next day on sick leave. While here today he told me he thought he ought to recommend a man to fill Shanklin's place as Second Lieutenant and asked if I was willing to have Wilson's name sent in. He said he knew Wilson was in prison and probably would not get out till our time had expired and would never be mustered as lieutenant, but it would show our regard for him to have him appointed. There was something touching to me for the Captain to come and ask if I was willing to have Wilson appointed to the office he had defrauded me of. It proved to me that he thought I should have some voice as to who should now fill the place. I answered him that nothing would please me better than for him to give the place to Wilson. I felt if there was an honor to be conferred Wilson was the man who at this time deserved it. He said he would send in the recommendation to the Governor at once, and so he did. Wilson had stood by me truly when I aspired to the place and I felt I could repay his loyalty no better than by now giving him my earnest support.

The First Division was going up the river, rumor said, to join General Sherman at Atlanta. Had not received our pay so I borrowed five dollars of Pap Edwards and loaned two of them to George Shiner.

September 5th 1864. Went to the city to express some clothing home and as we went we heard there were orders for us to march this evening. Came back to camp at noon. It rained hard soon after. About five o'clock struck tents and started for the river and soon went aboard the steamer "Bostonia Number Two" and ready to move before dark but were told the boat would not go till ten o'clock tomorrow morning. Was weighed this evening, and weighed one hundred and thirty-seven pounds.

September 6th. Left Memphis at one o'clock today. Signed the pay roll and as the paymaster was aboard our boat we were likely to be paid before we reached Cairo. I hoped we would so I might express my money home from Cairo. Rained hard today. The "Bostonia Number Two" was a very slow steamer and many of the other boats had passed us but we kept steadily pounding our way up the river.

September 7th. Received our pay. I got one hundred and fourteen dollars. Major Thurston of the regular army was paymaster. Passed New Madrid about four o'clock in the evening and soon after there came a severe wind and rain storm. The wind was so strong the pilots could not control the boat so they tied up to trees on shore till the storm was over. This was just below Island Number Ten. Started again about midnight and arrived at Cairo about ten o'clock next morning. Here we landed and expected to remain a few days till arrangements could be completed for us to go to Atlanta. But General Price was said to be advancing on St. Louis and this diverted us from the Atlanta trip. Not long since I saw it stated that the General Sturges raid and the two raids under General Smith were planned to keep General Forrest from joining General Johnston at Atlanta. I would rather believe that General Forrest and General Price were especially active to keep General Smith from joining General Sherman. Let this be as it may, all the generals on both sides were very busy along the Mississippi River during the summer and fall of 1864.

While at Cairo we saw Peter Quinn, West McDowell and John Wilson. They were recruits on their way down the river to join the First Iowa Cavalry then at Little Rock, Arkansas. Expressed ninety-five dollars home from Cairo and still I have plenty left for my present needs.

September 10th. Still at Cairo. Weather quite warm in the day time but quite cool at night. Many of the boys were intoxicated yesterday and some are still so today.

Last night I was detailed with nine men as extra patrol in the city. Went the rounds and found everything quiet and then went to the theater and asked to be passed in to see if any of the boys were in without passes. Searched through the theater and found none so I thought this a good time to rest awhile and told my men to sit down and they did so. It was a very pleasant place and we stayed there till the play was over, which was near midnight. After the theater we went to headquarters and I was detailed to go the grand rounds. That was to visit every post in the whole city and see that all was quiet and in order. This service I did in a manner pleasing to the officer of the day.

The next day at noon got orders to be ready to go aboard the boats at a moment's notice. Had no idea where we were going. Even rumor was quiet now.

Our camp was just above the city between the railroad and the Ohio River. It was a beautiful piece of sod ground about ten rods wide with the railroad above us and a gentle slope to the river below. Along the river were many coal barges tied up to the shore and steamboats frequently stopped there to coal. One afternoon as a steamer was coaling, two of their deck hands got into a fight. In a short time the mate made them stop fighting on the boat, telling them if they must fight to go on shore and finish it. A half dozen of them started ashore over the coal barges quarreling as they went. Lieutenant Ditto of Company A was officer of the day in our camp and as the roughs came over the barges he walked down toward them. Now Lieutenant Ditto was a dressy fop of a fellow and we had not thought much of his fighting qualities and the whole regiment was watching the outcome. Ditto met the men just as they were about to leave the barge for the shore and ordered them to keep off of our ground. He told them this was our camp and they should not come off here to fight. They all began to banter and swear at him but he took out his revolver and cocked it and told them they would die as fast as they stepped ashore, and the little man cowed the half dozen bullies so they turned back to their boat again. As they went one of the pugilists took a lump of coal nearly as large as his head and struck the other on the head with it and knocked him down. Then he took a large piece in both hands and was about to crush the other's head with it when his companions interfered. So ended the fight. We all cheered little Ditto.

That night there was a large fire in Cairo. Quite a number of buildings burned among which was the United States Hotel and the Brown Hotel. The estimated loss was a half million dollars.

I told Sergeant Ford how I went to the theater the other night so last night he had the detail of patrol guard. When he had patrolled the city he went to visit the theater but the manager met him at the door and told him to take one of his men and patrol the theater but leave the other men outside. So as soon as he patrolled the theater he came out and away. He should have demanded admittance for all of his men. The managers were generally very courteous about letting the guards in to see the plays.

OXFORD RAID - Notes:

-- **George Yarham** 19 of Toledo enlisted December 1863; Melville C Ingham 19 of Toledo enlisted January 1864; William Leach 34 of Buckingham enlisted January 1864. All three served in the Residuary Battalion until August 1865 after the 14th disbanded in November 1864.

-- **Gideon Hate**, who was almost shot for seeking water, was 17 [the roster says 18] when he enlisted in October 1861. He was the son of a blacksmith from Tama County. He fought at Shiloh and lived through all the hardships of prison camp. On May 18 1864 he was wounded in the left leg at Bayou de Glaize, Louisiana. He mustered out with the regiment at the end of his three years and after the War he ran a blacksmith shop near Toledo. BF Thomas spelled the name both as "Hoyt" and "Hait" The roster spelled it "Hait". The census, wedding license, and Gideon's gravemarker at Jordan Cemetery, West Des Moines spell it "Hate". See Chapter 2. Hate and Yarham both had brothers who enlisted from Tama County and served three years in other Iowa regiments. **William W Yarham** 21 served from July 1861 until September 1864 with Company C of the 10th Iowa Infantry while **Henry Hate** 18 was in Company F of the 24th Iowa Infantry from August 1862 until July 1865.

-- **George Presbury** 27 of Wapello enlisted into Company E September 1861 and was promoted to First Sergeant March 1862 after the Donelson fight. He is listed as missing after the Shiloh battle most likely as a prisoner of war. He was made First Lieutenant August 1863 and mustered out with the regiment in Davenport in 1864. Thomas spelled his name "Presberry". Shaw's Adjutant, **Joseph B Gilbert** 28 of Anamosa (Shaw's hometown), enlisted November 1861 into Company K. He then was appointed to serve as Quartermaster Sergeant. He seems to have not been captured at Shiloh but in April 1863 he was promoted to Second Lieutenant of Company H. He mustered out November 1864 with the regiment.

-- "Little Ditto" was **Lieutenant William T Dittoe** 29 of Davenport. Enlisted in August 1862, as First Sergeant of Company A, he was promoted Second Lieutenant February 1863. He mustered out with the regiment November 16 1864 at Davenport Iowa.

-- **Peter Quinn** 27, **West McDowell** 18, and **John Wilson** 21, all from the Buckingham-Crystal area, enlisted August 1864 into the 1st Iowa Cavalry Company M. They all mustered out June 1865 from Memphis. Twenty years after war's end they were all still farming in Iowa. John Wilson Junior was Peter Wilson's younger brother. Young John, who is remembered as jolly, good-natured and generous, enlisted while his brother Peter was still being held captive in the Texas POW camp. John mustered out about the same time Peter was finally being released. John is buried in Buckingham cemetery just north of Traer with his brothers Andrew and David. West McDowell was the Wilson brothers' first cousin, the son of Gilbert McDowell and Margaret Wilson, sister of Peter Wilson's father, John Wilson Senior. Before the War, the Quinn family lived in Crystal Township as close neighbors to the Felters.

CHAPTER XV

GENERAL PRICE'S RAID IN MISSOURI

September 14th. Yesterday I was detailed to take charge of the guard at division corral where our mules and horses were kept. When I left the regiment they had orders to go aboard the boat early this morning. When the men came and took the horses and mules away they had no orders to relieve the guards. I knew our boat had gone and my men were still on duty. Colonel Shaw was in command of the division with headquarters on board the steamer "*Longworth*". I went to him and reported the condition. He swore a little at his adjutant for not tending to business better and then ordered me to bring my men on board the "*Longworth*". I went to the corral and brought my men onto the steamer. There were thirty-one of them. The Colonel assigned us a location on the cabin deck on the guards just in front of the left-hand wheel-house. This for us was a very choice place, about the pleasantest place on the boat. I inquired of the Colonel about rations. He said go to the division quartermaster and draw rations. I found the Quartermaster but he said he could only issue rations on a written order from a commissioned officer. I told the Colonel and he swore some more. Then he went with me to the Commissary and ordered him to issue rations to me for self and thirty-one men, and when he issued rations to the Fourteenth Iowa again to make proper allowance for this. So we received our rations.

Left Cairo at three o'clock in the afternoon. The river was very low and our boat was heavily loaded. It struck bottom frequently and sometimes was difficult to get afloat again. Traveled all night but next morning found we were tied up at Cape Girardeau. We went ashore to find some bread and learned we could get a good breakfast at the Missouri House for twenty-five cents, so I and some others enjoyed a hotel breakfast once more. The boat we were on supplied rations to two other boats while here and then started up the river again. Came to the steamer "*Decatur*" which was sunk so the boiler deck was below water. The soldiers had been taken off of her and for the present she was helpless and abandoned. Soon after we came to an island where the boat pulled to the shore and all the men were ordered off to lighten the boat so it could pass over the rapids. We were ordered to march to the head of the island and then wait for the boat. The island was about four miles long and there were a number of improved farms on it. At these farms we found water melon patches and got many good melons. Arrived at the upper end of the island before the boat did. It must have had trouble crossing the rapids.

When it came we went aboard and it started and had gained a couple of hundred feet when one of the soldiers appeared on shore calling to us that he did not want to be left. He had found liquor on the island and was so drunk he could not stand alone. Colonel Shaw ordered the boat to return for him and when he was helped aboard he ordered him to stand on the bow of the boat and a man on either side to dip and pour water on his head till they had given him a hundred pails. At first he had to he held to steady him but soon the water began to have its effect and he stood alone. When a pail of water was poured upon him it would take his breath but he would look up at the Colonel who stood on the upper deck, and say, "Now, (*hick*), another (*hick*), Colonel." This he would repeat after each pail till he became exhausted with the cold douche. When they were done with the punishment the man was strictly sober.

Some farther up the river were landed on the Missouri side and marched across a neck while the boat went around a bend in which were rapids. Soon after going aboard again the boat tied up for the night because of the low water. During the day we have passed three boats that were sunk but none so the cabin deck was under water. We understood we were about eighty miles below St. Louis.

Next morning started early and pursued our course up the river. The day was pleasant and all went well. Arrived at Sulphur Springs at nine o'clock in the evening and found our division going into camp here. Soon found our regiment and company. Was glad to be at home with the boys again. The regiment had orders to go to Jefferson Barracks. The next morning went aboard the "*Bostonia*" early and at ten o'clock were at Jefferson Barracks. Went ashore and camped about a half mile above the barracks between the railroad and river. Soon after going into camp John Scott of the Twenty-Eighth Iowa came to see me. He attended the school I taught the winter before I enlisted. Was wounded in the foot at Pleasant Hill and was still unable for duty. He was here in convalescent camp. This was a very pleasant place to camp and the weather was fine.

September 19th. Went to Carondelet this morning where they were still at work on armour clad vessels but there were not nearly so many men employed as when we were here before. There was a slight frost that night.

September 23rd. Felter, Shiner and I went to St. Louis yesterday to get some books to read and some to send home. Visited the Mercantile Library and the museum in connection with it. Visited the old book store where we had often bought books before and got some more this time, then returned to camp. The next day got orders to be ready to move at once but soon the order was countermanded.

There was a hard rain with much wind that afternoon and it turned quite cool at night. Next day was bright and pleasant. Received a letter from home stating that my sister Rebecca was very sick.

The evening of September 24th our division had a grand time. The officers and men were assembled together and a sword was presented to General A. J. Smith by the officers of the Third Division. The presentation speech by General Ewing was fine, as was also General Smith's reply. Then a sword was presented to Colonel Shaw by the officers of the brigade. The presentation speech by Lieutenant Calkings of Company H was very witty and entertaining. When the Colonel took the sword he merely thanked them for the gift and sat down. There were calls for "Speech! Speech!" but the grim old Colonel sat still. General Smith arose and placed one hand on the Colonel's shoulder and said, "Boys, you all know Colonel Shaw never makes a speech, but by God he fights." Then the cheers arose and echoed and re-echoed through the grove. Several other swords were presented and many bright speeches made by the recipients and others. Just after the meeting closed we had orders to be ready to move at any moment, and at eleven o'clock that night we were aroused from our slumbers and started. Went aboard the cars and down the river.

At daylight next morning passed DeSoto, Missouri. There was a heavy frost that night. After leaving DeSoto passed through a long tunnel. Soon after Company I was left as guards at a bridge. The next bridge we came to was called Deck Bridge and our Company was left at this place. The stream was called Mill Creek and was twice as large as Wolf Creek. The bridge was Number Forty-one. There was a well built block house here which could stand a siege of infantry or cavalry till starved out but would be useless against artillery.

Arrived here at eight o'clock this morning and supposed the balance of the regiment would be parceled out along the road as guards as we had been. We were under command of Lieutenant Presbury of Company E. When we left Vicksburg we were to join General Sherman at Chattanooga. When we arrived at Memphis the defeat of General Sturges made it necessary to raid the northern Mississippi country and so we made two raids. This was to prevent the small rebel bands under Generals Forrest, Chalmers, Price, VanDorn, Marmaduke and others joining General Johnston in front of General Sherman. We started from Memphis to join General Sherman and when we got to Cairo the rumor came that General Price was advancing to raid Missouri and we were sent there to oppose him. General Rosecrans was in command at St. Louis and General Smith reported to him. We were now on the Iron Mountain railroad guarding the bridges so that our army might pass down the road to meet Price.

September 26th. Lieutenant Presbury ordered me to take ten men and scout through the country and learn what I could of the rebels. Visited a number of houses within ten miles of our camp but heard nothing of any secesh scouts in the neighborhood but everybody seemed to think they were near. When they first saw us they thought we were secesh. Stopped at last with an old farmer who claimed he was a Whig and neither Union nor Secesh. He would not believe the Whig party was dead. Had twice been presidential elector on the Whig ticket. He insisted we should stay to dinner with him, which we did. I feared he was setting a trap for us and kept strictly on guard but saw no evidence against him. He used us as well as he was able. I believed he was secesh but had not found it out himself. Got back to the block house before dark. Although we heard nothing definite of the rebel army we felt sure it was not far away by the symptoms manifested by the people.

The next morning another train loaded with troops went down the road. George Shiner and I went out for a walk without our guns. The country was very rough and among the gravel in the gullies there were many fine lime crystals. These we gathered till we had our hands full of specimens. We then sat down to look them over when we were startled to hear several rifle shots and then a volley and a few moments after a cannon and ten seconds after another. Then all was still. The firing was south of us along the line of railroad and seemed not more than half a mile from us and we were about two miles from the block house. We dropped our specimens and ran for the camp, fearing our men had not heard the firing and might be surprised by the enemy. When we arrived at the block house all our boys were there and much excited at our absence. They had also heard the firing and supposed we were involved in the scrap. At once we made disposition of our men so if we were attacked we could make the best defence possible.

We heard nothing more for an hour when the train came back that had gone down in the morning. We were ordered to get aboard the train which was already heavily loaded, so we abandoned the bridge and boarded the train. They told us they ran into a nest of rebels just below here and found a party was behind the train tearing up the track. They attacked this party and drove them off although they had two mountain howitzers with them. Then they relaid the track and came back. The road evidently was cut behind the train we came down on and our Companies B, C, D, E, F and part of H were either captured or had succeeded in reaching Pilot Knob, which was fifty miles down the road. We were soon on our way but moved slowly. Whenever we crossed a wide open piece of ground we would wait on the other side to see if the rebels were following us. When we came to high peaks of hills some of us would climb them to survey the surrounding country. When we reached the bridge that Company I was guarding we left the train and took a strong position on the north side of the river and stayed there during the night. While we remained there the train ran back to DeSoto and left much of its load and came back for us again next morning.

During the day some of our men captured a man they believed to be a spy. He was dressed in citizen's clothes and within our lines and seemed to be learning all about us he could. When first arrested he was quite boisterous but soon became sullen. He was among us in the box car I was in. When we stopped in the evening it was dusk. Several of us had jumped out. The ground was steep for we were on a grade of probably ten feet. In the door of the car Sergeant Treat Company G Twenty-Seventh Iowa was standing eating an apple which he was slicing with his knife. Suddenly the prisoner grabbed the knife and cut the Sergeant' s throat and jumped from the car. We outside did not know there was anything wrong till several men from the car fired at the man who had just jumped out and called us to catch him. We caught him, still not aware of what he had done. He fought like a tiger but soon was overcome. We bound him hand and foot and placed him in the car again where he was thrown upon the floor and bayonets were thrust through his clothes into the floor to hold him fast. The Sergeant was dead. I was well acquainted with him as he had been with the squad sent home recruiting and was with us for some time at Columbus, Kentucky. He had been a very nice, sober, candid man. The prisoner went to DeSoto with the next train and we were told was tried and executed next morning. At his trial he said he hated all Union men and was glad he killed the Sergeant. He only desired to do one more deed and that was to kill his own brother who he said was a Union man, then he could die happy. He seemed to be thoroughly crazed by excitement.

We remained in our position at the river and in the night we heard two distinct explosions one immediately after the other like cannon shots far away. We supposed they were signal guns of the rebels communicating one body with the other. But long after we learned that it was the report caused by the blowing up of the powder magazines at Pilot Knob which our own men destroyed when they abandoned the fort. It was sixty miles from us and we heard it very distinctly.

The train came for us in the afternoon and we boarded it and arrived at DeSoto at seven o'clock in the evening. It was fourteen miles from the bridge we were guarding to DeSoto and we retreated this fourteen miles in two days and traveled by railroad at that. We left the train as soon as we arrived and cooked some supper and laid down to sleep in the open air. The night was cold and our clothing was wet for it had rained on us hard during the day and we suffered with the cold.

Got breakfast next morning, September 29th, as best we could, and then mounted the cars and started for St. Louis at ten o'clock in the forenoon. Took all the government stores and the citizens shipped much of their goods to St. Louis and they also came away. General Price with a large army had invaded the state of Missouri and many feared he would be able to capture St. Louis. Everything in the way of troops and state militia were concentrated there for the city's defence. We arrived at our old camp at Jefferson Barracks in the evening. Everything was quiet there but we learned that in St. Louis all business was suspended and every man had to enroll and drill so as to assist in the defence of the city.

September 30th. We learned that the part of our regiment that was driven into Pilot Knob had about five hundred militia with them. The fort was immediately surrounded by the rebels who demanded its surrender. Our men asked time to consider the matter, but the rebels demanded its immediate surrender. This was refused and the battle opened. The enemy kept up a brisk fire on the fort and our men answered as best they knew how. Every rebel that exposed his form to sight received a bullet if within reach of the fort. Our men also used the artillery in the fort to good advantage.

The second day our men turned all the guns as far as they could in one direction and shelled the timber, furiously. They expected this would cause the rebels to abandon that line, and they also laid a slow match to the powder in the magazines. As soon as darkness came the men set fire to their slow match and marched out over the track they had scathed during the day. They carried with them one small cannon, wrapping blankets around the wheels and over the horses' feet to prevent making a noise. As expected, there was not a rebel to interfere with their march. After they had gone several miles the fort blew up with a very loud noise as I have noted before. Then the pursuit began and for seventy-two hours our men marched northward, fighting and skirmishing without an hour's rest till they came to Rolla and then took the cars for St. Louis. A more daring feat was never planned or more brilliantly executed than this of Captain Campbell with his two hundred soldiers and five hundred militiamen. In the face of General Price's army of twenty-five thousand men who were sure he must surrender, he destroyed the fort and brought off his little handful of men in safety. All hail Captain Campbell.

Captain Gallagher returned to the Company today from sick leave. We got a great many letters today. Our mail had been held here for us. What joy it gave us to get letters from dear ones. We read them over and over again. The letters informed us that J. C. Wood and Nelson Read had been drafted in Buckingham. Very sorry. Had hoped there would be no draft at home. Afterwards we learned that they hired substitutes to enlist from the township and the drafts were cancelled.

October 1st. Had orders to be ready to move this morning at seven o'clock. It began to rain at four o'clock and kept it up pretty much all day. Stored our things ready to go but did not go. The Third Brigade went out last night and heard they have had a skirmish with the rebels at Franklin, driving the rebels out and occupying the place. General Price evidently did not intend to attack St. Louis but now seemed to be heading for Jefferson City. It was the purpose of General Rosecrans to follow the rebels and harass them all he could till more troops joined him so he could give battle. Evidently General Price's purpose was to raid Missouri and carry off all the supplies and recruits he could. We expected to follow him as closely as possible and prevent all the damage to the Union people we could.

Sunday, October 2nd. We stayed last night on our old camp ground but without tents or fixtures, they having been stored. Started this morning at nine o'clock and marched through Carondelet and thence along a graveled pike road some distance to Kirkwood. The telegraph was cut between here and Franklin. Had traveled about fifteen miles. Stayed over night near Kirkwood and started next morning at nine o'clock and marched along the Franklin pike which was a broad, smooth road covered with gravel. Soon it began to rain but on we went. Passed through Manchester about noon and Baldwin soon after. Did not camp till after six o'clock and it still was raining. Marched twenty-two miles and my feet were very sore.

October 4th. Not raining and we started at eight o'clock. We were in front yesterday and in the rear today. Soon after we started we left the pike and followed a very poor country road. The country was quite hilly and rough, covered with jack oak timber. Arrived at Summit about noon and went into camp. Soon after it began to rain again and for three hours we had a heavy down pour of rain. The wind turned from the northwest and it became quite cool. General Price and his army passed here two days ago.

October 6th. We are still at Summit. On picket with Lieutenant Tomlinson of the Thirty Second Iowa. Were surprised that we were not marching. Some thought we would go no farther. Two of our boys who were captured at Pilot Knob were paroled and came to us today. They said General Price had a large army and was pressing on to capture Jefferson City before we could get enough men together to oppose him.

October 7th. Was relieved of picket duty by an officer who told us there was no detail to take our place for we were to change camp ground. When we arrived at camp found the boys ready to march but did not start till two o'clock in the afternoon.

Marched very fast till six o'clock and then went into camp on the banks of the Merrimac River which was quite a large stream of beautiful, clear, cool water. We had marched twelve miles and still felt fresh and willing to march on.

October 8th. Did not start till nine o'clock this morning. Marched four miles and came to Union which was a county-seat town. The rebels had been here and robbed the stores and destroyed the public record. We found many loose leaves of record books scattered over the country. Here we found a camp of militia which was to go with us. They were loaded with overcoats and knapsacks and blankets and other useless things such as we usually deposited in time of marching. We took the lead and they followed. For sometime they kept up with us but as the day grew warmer they lagged behind and by and by we lost sight of them altogether.

During the march today passed the body of a negro whom the rebels had killed and left laying in the road. We marched till near nine o'clock that night and then camped. I was so tired before we stopped that I could hardly get my feet along and was very glad when we stopped for camping. Had very poor water where we camped and it was quite a distance away. As soon as we camped I got to work to start a fire and Felter went after water. I had a rousing fire before he got back with the water. Soon we had hot coffee and fried bacon and crackers. Good enough for any man. Then we built large fires, for the night was cold, and lay near them to keep warm. The militia did not come into camp with us that night. We had marched thirty-five miles, four miles of which we marched before they joined us.

Next morning the militia were not with us and we had orders to await their coming. It was not strange they did not keep up with us. They were too heavily loaded. No man can march wrapped up in his overcoat and carrying a loaded knapsack and blankets. They were too much hampered. About two o'clock in the afternoon the militia came marching into camp. They were about the worst jaded lot of men I ever saw. The commander then ordered that we should not march till next day.

October 10th. Rained nearly all night last night, and was still cloudy and very windy. Started at seven o'clock. The road was very muddy. The people we met seemed to be very loyal. There were flags displayed from nearly every house. Most of the inhabitants here were Germans or of German descent, and Germans were nearly always Unionists.

Passed the body of a citizen lying dead in the road, whom the rebels had killed. Saw also many horses and cattle they had killed. The dead man still lying in the road indicated that we were close upon the rebels, for the citizens would have buried the man as soon as their terror had subsided, and he was still unburied.

That evening we came to the Gasconade River about four o'clock. Where we crossed the river was shallow, not more than three feet deep in the deepest place and probably a hundred yards wide. Water very cold. We heard the boys a long way ahead of us shouting and hallooing but had no idea what caused it till we came on the bluff just above the river and saw the water full of men wading and shouting. When I came to the water's edge I took off my shoes because they were badly worn and I feared they would go to pieces if soaked wet, but before I got far in the water I found I had made a mistake for the river bottom was composed of coarse gravel and stone and many of them had sharp edges which cut my feet so I could hardly walk. I tried to put my shoes on again but with my gun and accouterments on I was unable to reach to my feet in the depth of water, so I slowly and carefully picked my way across. Then I found my feet bleeding in many places from cuts from stones or shells. When we got into the deep, cold water we learned what made the boys shout so and we shouted too. Camped as soon as we crossed the river.

October 11th. Started at six o'clock this morning and arrived at Linn at noon. This was the county seat of Osage County. Arrived at the St. Mary's River at five o'clock in the evening. It was a very small river. Traveled twenty-five miles that day and were very tired. We met General McNeil with a small detachment of cavalry, here, on his way to St. Louis. He told us the rebels had been repulsed at Jefferson City and had departed due west from there.

It rained on us hard at night which gave us a good wetting, for we had no protection. We cared less for the wetting than for the muddy roads it would make.

Started at eight o'clock the next morning and arrived at the Osage River at noon. This like the Gasconade was a wide, deep stream and the water was also very clear, cold and swift. I was more fortunate in crossing here than at the Gasconade. I chanced to make the acquaintance of a sergeant of the Twenty-Seventh Iowa at Columbus, Kentucky. After we joined our regiments he was promoted to a lieutenancy and now was Quartermaster of this regiment. Just as I was going into the water he called to me and told me to get on his horse behind him and he would carry me over. It was a kind offer and I gladly accepted it. I crossed the river dry shod and dry clothed thanks to the Quartermaster.

The Osage was much larger than the Gasconade. They head in the Ozark Mountains not far apart and empty into the Missouri close together. Cold, clear, swift water in both rivers. Marched to within four miles of Jefferson City and camped for the night on a small stream of water, having marched about twenty miles that day.

October 13th. Did not start till ten o'clock although the Third Brigade had gone on the night before. Passed through the city before noon. We saw the marks of war here. All the fences of every description were thrown down so as to prevent the rebels getting shelter behind them. Large apple trees were cut down and piled in the ends of the streets. They being a very bushy tree made good barricades. This prevented cavalry or infantry passing in through the streets. Many small fortifications had been hastily built, rifle pits and breast works thrown up. In fact they had used every means they could invent to defend the place and succeeded in holding the rebels at bay. There had been some fighting but the rebels had not attempted to storm the place. After we passed through the city we halted for two hours and then marched about eight miles farther and camped. Had soft bread issued to us here. The boys for a joke said we waited two hours to give the baker time to bake this bread.

October 14th. Started before seven o'clock and marched eight miles to a small town called Salt Lake and about as much farther to a larger place called California. Here we joined the Third Brigade again which had gone on ahead of us. This was quite a nice little city and had the marks of business and prosperity. It was supposed General Price was at least two days ahead of us here. For some cause the pursuit had not been pressed as fast as it might have been but it may be there were good reasons for that. The militia have been a detriment to us from the start.

Our three years' term would expire on the second of next month and the men were eager to drive General Price to a finish before that time. The men out on detail in the pioneer corps and other details had been ordered to the regiment. The boys all looked forward to the home coming, that must be near us now, with much satisfaction.

We remained at California all day but next morning, Sunday, October 16th, we started at seven o'clock and still our course was due west. About two o'clock in the afternoon we arrived at Tipton where our regiment was left and the rest of the division followed on after General Price. There was a large pond just east of the town and the railroad company had a water tank there. It was the only one west of Jefferson City and we were to guard this for a time. The orders were to defend it at all hazards.

October 18th. There was a rebel flag reported flying from a house four miles south of town and a squad of men were sent out to capture it, and although they completely surprised the people, they either had no rebel flag or succeeded in concealing it for our boys found nothing. But they did capture two horses with saddles and bridles and brought them into camp. The whole country was over run with bushwhackers and they and our cavalry were continually skirmishing.

Teams under strong escort started to take material out to repair Lamine Bridge. They had not gone far till they returned badly scared. They again started with a much heavier escort and went through. We were quartered on the people of the town, that is, apportioned to private houses to board. While this was in a sense arbitrary, still we made a bargain with them and gave them our rations and paid them something beside for board. At first four of us were sent to a very aristocratic house. They were people who had owned slaves and while they claimed to be Union they expressed themselves very sore at the manner in which the government treated the slavery question. Their intercourse was constrained. They seemed glad to keep us for the pay it brought them but shunned us socially. They had visitors come whose whole stock of conversation was in regard to General Price's successful raid. Several of them had near relations in the rebel army. Our squad asked permission to change boarding place and went to a German family where we got probably a more common bill of fare and also more congenial surroundings.

One day four of us went to a farm house and I noticed they had sheep and spinning wheels. I asked if they had any woolen socks they would sell. The lady of the house turned to her daughter who was probably twenty years of age and asked her if she would sell the ones she had. She hesitated a while and then went and brought out two pair of splendid home-knit socks and tossed them to me saying, "I will sell you them if you want." I asked the price and she said fifty cents per pair. I handed her the money and she burst into tears and said, "I want you to know these socks were knit for a young man in General Price's army. I knew he was coming and knit them myself for him. As he and his company were coming here they met your cavalry in Tipton and fought in the streets and he was killed there almost in sight of our house. He will not need them and I would rather they would go." And she hurried from the room. One of the many sad incidents of the war.

The weather had been very changeable for the last week. Rain, snow, wind and cold. One evening several hundred men came in from Glasgow, whom the rebels had captured and paroled. They were sent on to St. Louis. When we went to Tipton there was a steam mill to grind corn there. It was broken and out of repair. Two young boys who understood an engine went to work on it. They soon had the broken part mended and repacked the cylinder and fired up and the mill was going as well as ever. The corn was nearly all cut for fodder and was in shock and dry. The boys would go to the fields and husk what corn they wanted and then take it to the mill and have it ground and so provided the household where they boarded with plenty of meal. In our case the German lady made most generous johnny cakes, also flap jacks and mush. The mill ran day and night, for the citizens from near and far brought their grists to have them ground. The boys who run the mill adopted two rules. One was that whenever a soldier came with a grist his turn came next no difference how many citizens were waiting, and his grist ground free. The second rule was citizens must pay cash to have their grists ground. This was done to defray expenses.

Had a grand scare Saturday night, October 22nd. Just after dark a courier came in who was badly frightened. He said there was a large body of rebels marching on us intending to surprise and capture us. Our pickets were doubled and warned of the danger. A strong skirmish line was formed inside the picket line. The regiment was formed and informed of the tactics that would be employed if the rebels came, and then we lay down in the public square in the center of the town to catch what sleep we could before the rebels came. The night gradually wore away and the new day came and no rebels had put in an appearance. Whether there was an attack planned and when they found us prepared it was abandoned or whether our informant was frightened at some fodder shocks or loose colts, will never be known to us.

The German family with whom we boarded had three children, two boys and a girl. The oldest boy was about eight years and the girl about four years old. They were very fond of our crackers and it was quite amusing to us to see them try to eat them. Probably they never had anything but corn bread before this. It took a sight of gnawing for them to get flakes off the crackers even with their sharp teeth.

October 29th. Received orders for a detail of one hundred men to guard the telegraph construction corps to Brownsville. Companies A, B, and K went.

October 30th. An order came at ten o'clock last night relieving us of duty here and ordering us to return to St. Louis. Captain Jones immediately sent an order to Brownsville for our three companies that were there to return to us at once. It was expected that we were to start as soon as another regiment came to relieve us. We learned at this time that General Smith had received an order from Washington to dismiss Colonel Shaw from the service in disgrace. The charges had been preferred against him by General Banks in which he stated that Colonel Shaw had written an account of the Red River Expedition and had it published in an Anamosa paper over his own signature in which he had severely condemned General Banks, Emery and Dwight as being drunken and incompetent officers and entirely to blame for the disastrous expedition. The court to which this was presented never summoned Colonel Shaw to their presence nor gave him a chance to defend himself, but issued the order of dismissal. Colonel Shaw said the letter they presented to the court was one he wrote privately to a friend who published it without his knowledge or consent. But he also said that everything in the letter was true.

At the time General Smith received the order, Colonel Shaw was far from us at the head of the Third Division of the Sixteenth Army Corps which he had commanded since the raids in Mississippi. He was chasing the fleeing army of General Price. Instead of General Smith promulgating the order as his orders were, he simply put it into his pocket and wrote an order relieving Colonel Shaw of the command of the Third Division and ordering him to report to his regiment at St. Louis and transport it to Davenport to be mustered out of the service because of the expiration of their term of service. This saved him of any disgrace that General Banks intended to place upon him. The Colonel came in on the train that we were to go to Jefferson City on and also the Thirty-Third Missouri Infantry came to relieve us of our duty here. All was joyful and happy for now our service was over and we were homeward bound.

Stayed over night at Jefferson City and visited the State House and saw Governor Hall. About ten o'clock next morning the steamer "Enterprise" came in and was immediately pressed into the service to take us to Hermon. It seemed there was a piece of railroad destroyed between this place and Hermon and we were obliged to make this part of our trip by river boat. The boat had to be unloaded and our men were anxious to be off so they all set to work at unloading the boat. The state penitentiary was located here and many of the convicts were at work at the landing. Our boys did not like the idea of working along with the convicts but were so anxious to be going that they only grumbled at this but did not strike. Had the boat unloaded soon after three o'clock and all went aboard and the boat was soon on its way to Hermon but it had not run half a mile till it struck a sandbar and did not float again till after dark. When we got loose ran a short distance farther and a heavy fog came on and the boat was tied up to the shore because of the fog.

November 1st. We had a great time boating that day. Started early in the morning and soon were fast on a sandbar. Off again, it was repeated and repeated over and over again.

Arrived at Hermon about four o'clock in the afternoon. Governor Hall came on the boat with us. We remained on the boat all night. It was raining the next morning but we went aboard the cars about eight o'clock and without an unusual incident arrived at St. Louis about sunset. Here we were joined by the companies that had been separated from us on the Iron Mountain Railroad. I do not think I ever saw men better pleased at meeting each other than our men were. There were a thousand questions on either side to ask and answer. We here received a number of letters from home and how glad we were to get them although we expected to soon be at home to remain always. Davis, who had been at home on veteran furlough, here joined us and was mustered as Second Lieutenant. This was to give him that rank in whatever organization he may be placed after we are mustered out.

November 3rd. We were quartered in Winter Street Barracks. There was snow, rain and cold weather. We drew clothing preparatory to being mustered out. Expected to start for Davenport the next day as we had orders to be ready to start at six o'clock tomorrow morning.

November 4th. Started for Iowa this morning at eight o'clock. About two inches of snow on the streets of the city. Went aboard the steamer "David Tatum" and started at ten o'clock for Alton and when we arrived there took box cars for Joliet. It was a strange coincidence we should go back through Alton the same route we came when we first came to St. Louis and not the usual route of travel.

Left Alton just at sunset. It did seem to us that after traveling all over the south in box or flat cars or cattle-cars that the government might have sent us home through the loyal northern States in passenger coaches. But we were so anxious to get home that we never stopped to protest against the means of transportation.

Arrived at Joliet at noon, Saturday, November 5th. Had passed through Springfield during the night and Bloomington at daylight. At Bloomington there was fully two inches of snow and at Joliet there was none. Changed cars there and by some lucky chance were put into passenger coaches.

Left Joliet at seven o'clock in the evening and it was wonderful how well we enjoyed the luxury of cushioned seats. They were so delightfully soft and warm that we curled up and slept sweetly, calmly and dreamlessly in them. If any poetic thought entered our heads that night it must have been "Soldier, sleep, Thy warfare's o'er." And sleep we did. During the night something happened to the engine or the officials thought there was no hurry about getting us to Iowa, for when we awoke in the morning we found our train on a side track without an engine in sight. By and by an engine came and coupled onto our train and again we sped away for Davenport, which place we reached about noon November 6, 1864. We were conducted to Camp Roberts and given very good quarters. The next day all who could be used were put to work making out our muster rolls. Everything had to be entered up and then balanced so the sheet made a clear record in each man's case. It seemed there was no end to this work.

November 8th. Was election day. It was heavy, foggy weather and very rainy. In fact, rained all day and so dark we could hardly see to write. We held our election as usual. For President there were three hundred and sixty-seven ballots cast of which Abraham Lincoln received three hundred and twenty-five and George B. McClellan forty-two. Nearly all our democrats were in Company D. I think there was but one in our Company and he was a recruit.

There was a rumor that we would not be mustered out till the twenty-sixth of this month. This we could not understand as our time had expired the second of the month, and we were here where we would do no more duty.

November 11th. By order of the mustering officer all of our boys whose time had expired took their guns and accouterments to town and turned them over to the government. This of course did not include the veteran nor recruits nor the three new companies, A, B and C, though it was reported they were to exchange their guns for better ones as soon as we were discharged. There was also a rumor afterward that Companies E and I would be mustered out tomorrow.

November 14th. Have completed all the muster rolls and have the accounts of each one of the men balanced showing the amount due him and have everyone signed these rolls and have nothing to do but await the pleasure of the mustering officer to get our pay and discharges.

Was at Davenport and saw Mr. McCosh. I was glad to see him and he seemed well pleased to meet me again. He was anxious to have me go home with him but I could not leave here, not knowing when we might be discharged. Tried buying some clothing but did not succeed. Picked out a suit of clothes but did not feel well pleased with them. Must look farther.

Companies D and F were mustered out today and there are rumors that other companies are to go at once.

November 17th. There was an order promulgated to muster us all out at once and again we were busy completing the muster rolls. Worked nearly all night that night to finish the four copies necessary for our discharge. These rolls have every man's name, office, age, complexion, weight, height, nativity, etc. Also the time he was last paid, the amount due for service, the amount due on clothing account and the total amount due him. The four copies must agree in every particular. Then each man signed his name after his account as a receipt of payment. There were present to be discharged of our Company one captain, three sergeants, five corporals, one musician and fourteen privates. One lieutenant, one sergeant and several privates were in prison at Tyler, Texas. Several of our boys were in hospitals at Memphis, Cairo and St. Louis.

November 18th. We were marched to Davenport in the afternoon and were mustered out and given our discharges about four o'clock in the afternoon and were paid after dark at the United States Bank. Felter and I then went to a clothing store and bought our clothing and a trunk each. My overcoat cost twenty dollars, dress coat twenty-five, pants ten, vest eight, cap five and shoes five, besides other clothing. We packed our clothing and our money in our trunks and carried them to the Burtis House and checked them there. Then we went back to camp to spend the last night with our soldier comrades. There was not much drinking or rowdyism there that night, but they quietly discussed the situation from the standpoint of free men. For some days there had been men in camp offering a bounty to the boys to re-enlist and credit themselves to certain localities so as to prevent a draft there, for which service they freely offered a thousand dollars as soon as the man was mustered in, but so far not one of our boys had accepted the offer. Their answer was, "We did not go for money before and we will not go for money now. We will go home first and then if we think it necessary we may enlist again, but not for money." I now believe that was a mistake. We should have accepted their offer and secured the thousand dollars. The great goal with us then was to go home.

Next morning we were up early and had breakfast together and then bade each other a final goodbye and each one wended his way homeward. Several of us took the nine o'clock train on the Rock Island Railroad for Marengo and arrived there at two o'clock in the afternoon. Had dinner there and took the stage for Blairstown where we arrived at twenty minutes to eight. The train was due at five o'clock but was far behind time and we were told it might not come that night. "But all things come to those who wait." And so the train came at last after eleven o'clock and carried us to Belle Plaine where we arrived at twelve o'clock, midnight. We found a hotel and aroused the landlord and told him we wanted a bed for the rest of the night. He showed us a room and we told him we would pay him then as we wanted to start as soon as daylight next morning. One dollar paid the bill and soon we were rolled in the warm blankets and were probably snoring. Only Felter and I were here. We left the other boys at Marengo.

As soon as the first glimpse of light came next morning we left the hotel with the inmates all asleep as far as we knew, and trudged off with light hearts through the snow, for there was about eight inches of snow on the ground. It was Sunday morning. Cold and clear with a sharp breeze in our faces. At Irvington lived Mr. Selva who carried the mail three times a week from Belle Plaine to Buckingham, and we aroused the people in the first house we came to and inquired for his place. We found him and gave him the checks for our trunks and told him to bring them to Buckingham for us the next day. I had met him when at home recruiting and he knew me and insisted on us staying over till the next day and going up with him. Our thoughts did not run in that channel. We thanked him for the offer but told him we must be on the march. When we reached Redman where Overturf, one of our boys who had been discharged two years before, lived, we found the family at breakfast, for they were early risers. They soon had places prepared for us and we had a hearty breakfast with them. We did not tarry long with Overturf after breakfast but soon were pressing northward.

We thought we knew the road, and did know the road that had been used three years before, so when we left Redman we took the left-hand road and crossed Salt Creek. Soon we found the travel on this road went to Toledo, and the road we expected to travel north had not been broken since the snow fell. The traveled road north was on the east side of the creek. We followed the unbroken road for ten miles, snow eight inches deep with some crust on but not enough to bear our weight, and now a very strong cold wind from the northwest. Tramp, tramp, tramp, till we were nearly exhausted. When we came to a house we stopped and tried to hire the man to take his team and carry us to West Union. He said we must have dinner first. So his wife prepared dinner, after eating which the man hitched his team to a sled and we started about three o'clock in the afternoon. He had the wagon box filled with hay and we laid down to keep warm for the wind was stronger and colder than before. After going about three miles we became so chilled we told the man we had better walk so as to keep warm and he had better go back. So we got out and he went back. When we came to the Norman Rice farm where the Bunker family live now, we stopped and borrowed shawls to wrap about our heads to keep our faces and ears from freezing. Then we went on to West Union and there stopped for a few minutes' discussion as to whether we should separate and Felter go to father's house where Rebecca was, and I go to Stoakes' for the night, but decided I was too cold and tired to spend the evening there, so we went together to Buckingham and home where we arrived a little after seven o'clock, cold, hungry, tired but happy men. Our service was over and we were home again with those we loved.

The next evening I went to the Stoakes' home where I received the kindest welcome by one who had been my guiding star through all these three years of war. A thousand things I had to tell Stoakes of our comrades and our ventures, though I had but one story to tell Sarah -- the old, old story that is ever new.

Of the ten of us who first messed together Robert Clark, John Gaston, Ed McClaury, Espy McKune and Dewitt Southwick were dead, all having died before we had served ten months. Eleazar Stoakes was discharged for disability when in the service one year. Peter Wilson was in prison at Tyler, Texas, and remained there till the close of the war. Mat Clark, J. R. Felter and I had just been discharged. Some of the boys had been in two battles. I had been in five and Wilson the same number. Felter and Clark had been in ten battles. All had been captured and in prison. Wilson had been captured twice and the last time spent fourteen months in prison. McKune was the only one that had been struck by a rebel bullet. At Donelson a bullet struck his belt buckle and bent it nearly double. It knocked him down. No doubt the buckle saved his life.

November 20th. We arrived at home and I urged Sarah to name the earliest day possible for our marriage. She said December 22nd. The twenty-second was chosen in preference to Christmas because Christmas occurred on Sunday that year.

Father built some addition to his house, making another bedroom and kitchen, and when married we were to occupy part of his house till we were able to build for ourselves. We have been told that the 22nd of December, 1864 was a cold and dreary day but our recollection of it is that it was the brightest and happiest day we ever knew, for at seven o'clock that evening Reverend Bennett Roberts, Congregational minister at Buckingham, pronounced the words that made us forever man and wife. There were present at the ceremony only the bride's family.

And so my story ends.

GENERAL PRICE'S RAID INTO MISSOURI - Notes:

-- The prison camp at Tyler Texas where Peter Wilson and others from Company G were still being held as prisoners of war, was Camp Ford. Taken during the battle at Pleasant Hill Louisiana April 9 1864, they still remained prisoners long after the rest of the regiment had ended their three year term of service. BF Thomas' former student from Company F 28th Iowa was **John H Scott** 20 of Tama County. Scott was 20 years old when he enlisted in August 1862. He was made a First Corporal, was later "reduced to ranks" in October 1863, then quickly rose again to Second Corporal. On April 8 1864, at Sabine Crossroads Louisiana, he was severely wounded and taken prisoner, according to the roster record. This was the day prior to the Pleasant Hill battle. If Scott had been taken prisoner he may have gone to Camp Ford Texas with those captured at Pleasant Hill the following day, yet he met BF Thomas in September as noted above. With the chaos after the Pleasant Hill fight some men were thought to have been taken prisoner when they had in fact been evacuated for wounds. Whatever his true status as a POW, the roster says Scott was discharged for his wounds May 23 1865.

-- **Lieutenant Vincent Tomlinson** was 37 in August 1862 when he enlisted from Nevada, Story County, as a First Sergeant of Company K, 32nd Infantry. He was promoted to Second Lieutenant in December 1863 but disability forced him to resign in February 1865. A carpenter by trade, he moved to Boone after the War.

-- The two men from the 14th Iowa who were captured at Pilot Knob and then paroled, were most likely **John Nerge** ("Nergo" in the roster) a 27 year old from Maxfield, Bremer County Iowa and **William Mofield** (the roster spelled it "Mowfield"). Both men had enlisted in December 1863 but Mofield 18 was a Kentucky native who had signed on from Columbus Kentucky. Mofield was taken prisoner on September 27 1864 and Nerge was taken two days later on September 29. Both recruits later served with the Residuary Battalion with Nerge mustering out in late June 1865 and Mofield out in early August. Nerge, who was born in Germany, returned from the War to farm and raise a family near Waverly.

-- Sergeant **Lewis J Treat** 28 of Floyd County, who was killed with his own knife, enlisted into Company G of the 27th Iowa Infantry in August 1862 and rose in rank to Fourth Sergeant in July 1864. The company roster says he was killed on guard duty by a rebel prisoner September 27 1864. He is buried in Jefferson Barracks National Cemetery in St. Louis, Section 38 Grave 134.

-- Lieutenant "Calkings" who made the memorable speech when the regiment presented Colonel Shaw with the ceremonial sword, probably was **William H Calkins** 21 of Jones County who had been appointed First Lieutenant of Company H November 1861. Calkins was among those taken prisoner at Shiloh and held until late October 1862 in the POW prison for the officers. The official roster reports that in January 1863, a few months after his exchange, he resigned, probably for illness. He must have regained his health and rejoined the regiment to have been present to make this speech. The ornate sword, crafted by Tiffany Jewelers, can be seen on exhibit at the museum of the State Historical Society of Iowa in Des Moines.

-- Rebecca Thomas Felter, sister of BF Thomas, recovered from her illness. While home on parole JR Felter had married Rebecca on December 10 1862, changing his friend and brother-in-arms "Frank" Thomas into a brother-in-law.

-- **Jacob B Overturf** 21 of Redman, Tama County, enlisted October 1861. Captured with the regiment at Shiloh, he survived the terrible conditions of POW camp in Georgia. Still suffering from the effects of his captivity he was discharged for disability March 27 1863 at St. Louis; luckily he seems to have regained his health at home. Redman was once a small village located west of the Tama-Benton countyline, north of Irving, along today's Highway 21, and north of present Highway 30. Thomas spelled it "Redmond". Like so many of the men who had fought and bled and died in this War, and whose bravery and sacrifices have been mostly lost to memory, the tiny hamlet of Redman paid a high price to preserve our Union, and the town is all but forgotten today, marked only by a graveyard. It was once home to Overturf's cousin Simon Eccles, and the Dykeman brothers. All three had given their lives for their country. Several more of Redman's patriotic sons volunteered for service then returned to live simply and quietly and anonymously afterwards, but the collective dreams of the once promising village were lost forever, shattered by the War.

-- The story of Benjamin Franklin Thomas actually ended in 1912. After the War he returned to the Traer area where he and Rebecca raised their family. For a time he ran a hardware store in downtown Traer with his grown sons. Any visitor to Traer's business district can easily find the clearly marked brick "Thomas" building. BF Thomas is buried in Buckingham cemetery just north of Traer. Nearby are the graves of his companions Peter Wilson and Eleazar Stoakes and a memorial marker for John McKune.

THE WOLF CREEK RANGERS

ROBERT FISHER CLARK and **MATHEW CLARK** were the Canadian-born sons of William Clark and Nancy Straker. William and Nancy Clark, both born in England, migrated to Quebec Canada where their ten children were born in the area south of Montreal, north of the New York border. The entire family came to the United States in the middle 1850s and settled onto a farm near today's LaPorte City, Black Hawk County, Iowa, north of the Wolf Creek settlements of Tama County. Rob and Mat signed on together. At the time of their enlistment Robert Clark was 23 years old, and stood half an inch over six feet tall, which made him the tallest of his tentmates. Robert had blue eyes, light hair and was light complected. His younger brother Mathew was 21, and stood five feet, ten and a half inches tall. Mathew had light hair, blue eyes, and a "sandy" complexion. Mathew Clark remained a farmer in the LaPorte City area after the War, married, and raised a family of five daughters and one son. Mathew survived longer than any of his messmates, living until 1918.

JOHN ROCKEFELLER FELTER was one of six children of Nelson Felter and Calpurnia Powers from the area of Schoharie New York where John was born. The Felter family migrated first to Cook County Illinois before coming to Tama County Iowa. Nelson Felter and his family were the first settlers of Crystal Township, west of Traer, living in a log cabin near the north bank of Wolf Creek. John had a stutter but loved to play the violin, "fiddling" at dances for the neighborhood. The Felters were close friends to the McKunes before the War. During the War John married BF Thomas' sister Rebecca. John and Rebecca were the parents of one daughter, Clara. John was the shortest of his messmates at five foot, six. He was 24 years year old when he enlisted, having light hair, gray eyes and a dark complexion. John died in 1876.

JOHN GASTON's parents were James Gaston and Elizabeth Kilgore of Columbiana County Ohio. The Gaston family operated a mill that is today an Ohio State Historical Park called Gaston Mills. John's brother Hugh Gaston married Elizabeth Stoakes, sister of Eleazar Stoakes, in Ohio. Hugh Gaston then came to Tama County with his in-laws, the Stoakes family, and operated a sawmill at West Union a mile east of Traer. John Gaston came to Iowa before the War broke out to help his brother Hugh. John had black hair and grey eyes. He was dark complexioned, stood five feet, nine and half inches tall, and was 25 years old when he enlisted in early October 1861 along with BF Thomas and Peter Wilson, who called John Gaston the best friend he ever had. John Gaston's sad death left behind a widow and an infant son.

EDMUND McCLAURY, born in Meredith New York, was the son of Robert McClaury and Margaret Rowland. Robert and Margaret McClaury were from Delaware County New York and were the parents of eleven children. The whole family moved to Benton County Iowa and in the middle 1850s lived on a farm south of the village of Irving, just north of the present city limits of Belle Plaine. The McClaury farm was situated right on the Tama-Benton county line along today's Highway 21. The family also owned land in Salt Creek Township of Tama County on the Tama side of the county line. Edmund was five feet, nine inches, light skinned with dark hair and dark eyes. He was 21 years old when he signed his enlistment papers. Although he lived across the county line in Benton County, Edmund signed on with the Wolf Creek group from North Tama when they all enlisted in early October 1861. Edmund bunked with BF Thomas.

JOHN ESPY McKUNE was born in Susquehanna Pennsylvania, the youngest son of John W McKune and Frances Stewart. Young John came to Iowa with his whole family: his parents, his older brother George, and his two sisters. The McKune family lived for a time with the Nelson Felter family while the McKunes built a log cabin and broke ground for their own farm west of Traer near the Crystal village. John's two sisters, Hannah and Augusta, married the Wood brothers, Joshua Clark Wood and Lyman Edo Wood, and all remained in the Traer area. In October of 1861 John was 21 years old. He had a dark complexion, grey eyes and dark hair. He was five foot, nine and a quarter inches tall. John was known as "Ep", short for Espy, by his closest friends. At training camp, in sight of the Mississippi, John wrote that he missed seeing the prairie. John McKune and John Felter enlisted at the same time.

DEWITT CLINTON SOUTHWICK's parents were Nathan Southwick and Susan Guy of Crawford County Pennsylvania, living near Sparta, and Guys Mills. A few weeks after the family learned of Dewitt's death, Dewitt's younger brother Guy Southwick enlisted in the 16th Pennsylvania Cavalry. When Guy was killed six months later at the battle of Gettysburg, the Southwick family had lost two sons to the War. Dewitt was born in Pennsylvania and had come to the Traer-West Union area of Tama County before the War to join his married cousin John W Southwick, who farmed near West Union. The youngest of his tentmates, Dewitt was 20 years old, and five feet, seven. He was light complexioned with grey eyes and light hair. He was said to have a light-hearted disposition as well. Dewitt Southwick, the youngest of these Wolf Creek men, signed up the same day in late October 1861 with Eleazar Stoakes, who was the oldest of their group of ten.

ELEAZAR STOAKES was one of eleven children born to John Stoakes and Jane Vantilburg of Jefferson County, Ohio. Eleazar's father was born in England but came to Ohio as a child. After many years in Ohio John and Jane Stoakes brought their family, including married children, to Perry Township, Tama County, arriving around 1855. In late October 1861 when he signed into the Iowa Volunteer Infantry, Eleazar was 26 years old. At five feet eleven and a half inches, Eleazar was blue eyed with sandy hair. He had a "florid" complexion. After the War, Eleazar and his wife Eliza Granger had three daughters and three sons, one son named Dewitt C Stoakes, in memory of his close friend and messmate Dewitt Southwick. Both Hugh Gaston and BF Thomas were brothers-in-law to Eleazar. Eleazar died in 1911.

BENJAMIN FRANKLIN THOMAS was 24 when he enlisted. He was dark complectioned, blue eyed and dark haired. Like Peter Wilson, he was five feet ten and a half inches in height. "Frank", as BF was known to his friends, was born in Ohio, the son of Leonard Thomas and Lydia Phillips. Frank's father ran a pottery shop in Preble County Ohio and upon arriving in Iowa, Mr. Thomas established his shop at old Buckingham village near today's cemetery north of Traer. Frank assisted his father in the manufacturing of all types of much needed earthenware goods before the War. Frank's oldest brother, John R Thomas, a cabinetmaker and married man, also enlisted into the 14th Iowa Volunteers the year after Frank, serving in the Red River Expedition. When the War was over Frank came home to marry Sarah Stoakes, younger sister of his friend Eleazar; they became parents to seven children. Frank Thomas was brother-in-law to two of his fellow soldiers: Eleazar Stoakes and John R Felter. Frank loved to write poetry. BF Thomas died in 1912, five years after the publishing of his Civil War memoir, "Soldier Life".

PETER WILSON enlisted at age 24, the same age as his friend "Frank" Thomas. Both men were five feet, ten and half inches tall but Peter had hazel eyes, light hair, and light skin coloring and Peter spoke with a Scottish accent. Wilson was born in Ayrshire, Scotland, coming to the United States as a boy. His family lived in Connecticut for a time before coming to Iowa. Peter was the second child of a large family of 14 children, some born in Scotland, some in Connecticut, and the rest in Tama County Iowa. Their parents were John Wilson and Jean McCosh. Peter's oldest brother was James "Tama Jim" Wilson who later became the longest serving United States Secretary of Agriculture. Both James and Peter wished to serve their adopted country during the War, but one needed to stay and care for the farm they had begun together. James ended up staying home while Peter fought for his country. After the War their roles reversed, Peter stayed close to home while James served his country in peacetime, as a public servant. Peter was a father to seven children before he died in 1887.

B. F. THOMAS

Author B. F. Thomas, 1907, from the photograph published in his book *Soldier Life*.

SERGEANT B. F. THOMAS   CORPORAL JOHN R. FELTER
CAPTAIN WM. GALLAGHER   LIEUTENANT H. A. SHANKLIN
COMPANY G, 14th REGIMENT IOWA
INFANTRY VOLUNTEERS

From a tin-type taken at St. Louis, February, 1863

Four men of Company G, 14th Iowa Volunteer Infantry, as published in the original *Soldier Life*.

COLONEL WM. T. SHAW
14th Regiment Iowa Infantry Volunteers
From a photograph taken in 1862

Colonel W. T. Shaw, as published in the original *Soldier Life*.

Edmund McClaury, courtesy of family.

B. F. Thomas, from the original group photo, cropped and reversed for accuracy.

John Gaston, courtesy of Parker Historical Society of Clay County, Spencer, Iowa.

Peter Wilson, courtesy of grandson Evan Wilson.

John Espy McKune, courtesy of Tom L. Sawyer.

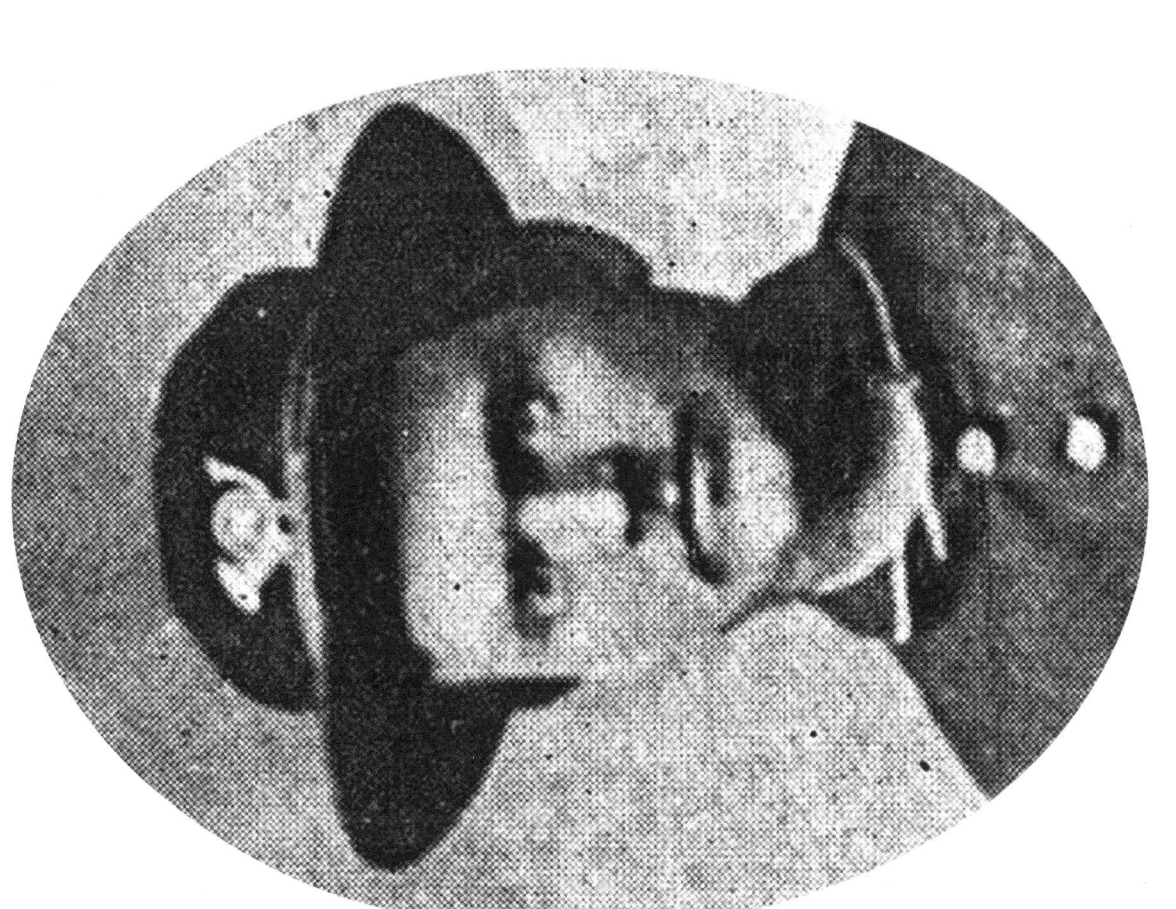

John R. Felter, cropped from original group photo and reversed (note bugle on cap).

Dewitt Southwick headstone at Jefferson Barracks.
Note, the regimental numeral "4" should be "14."

Eleazar Stoakes, photographed for his February 1866 wedding to Eliza Granger, courtesy
of Russell Reigle. His suit and her dress are now on display at the Traer Museum.

Clark family headstone, with Robert Clark memorial, LaPorte City, Iowa. Mathew is buried up the hill to the right.

Mathew Clark as an older man, courtesy of Marlene Bown.

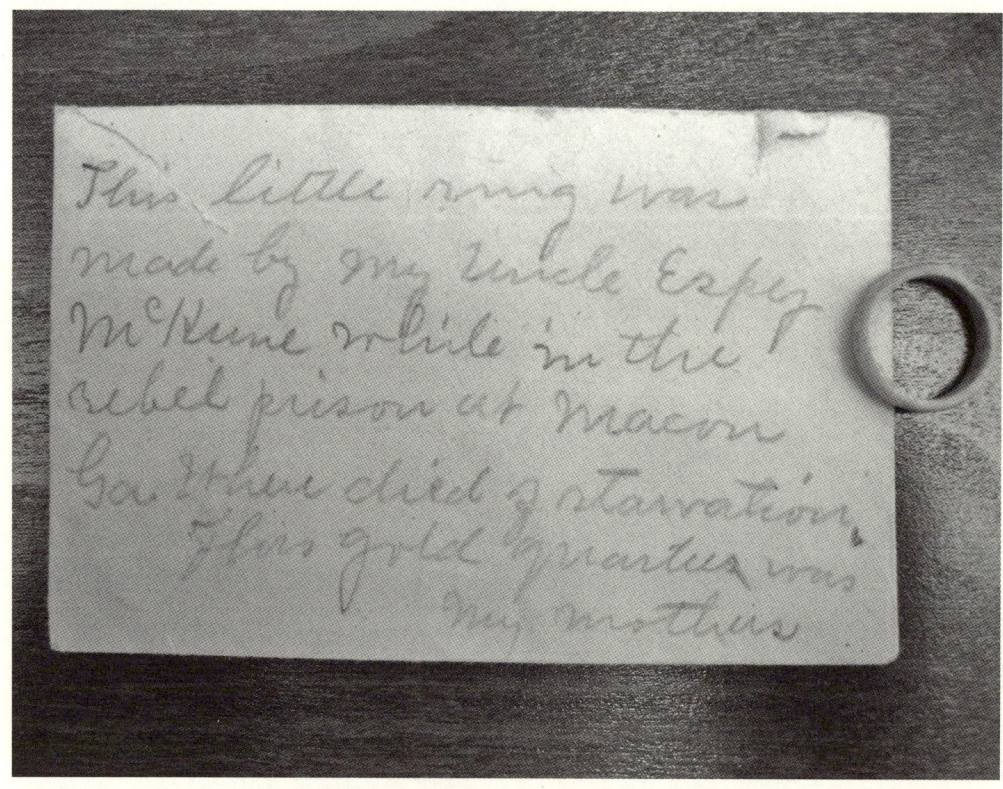

This book is presented to
Mrs L E Wood as a memorial
of the affectionate remembrance
I bare to her brother John Espy McKune
Who served with me and
Died at Macon Georgia prison 1862
Yours &c
B F Thomas

Inscription by B. F. Thomas in a copy of *Soldier Life* given to John McKune's sister,
Augusta McKune Wood.

This little ring was
made by my uncle Espy
McKune while in the
rebel prison at Macon
Ga. where died of starvation.
This gold quarter was
my mothers

Bone ring carved by John McKune while a prisoner, given to his niece Abbie Wood Sawyer,
daughter of Augusta.

John Wilson's letter to General Canby concerning Peter's needs in the Texas POW camp.
(National Archives, Washington, DC)

General N. B. Baker's letter to Daniel Connell of Buckingham, informing him of recent local battle casualties.
(State Historical Society of Iowa, Des Moines, Iowa)

Key Locations

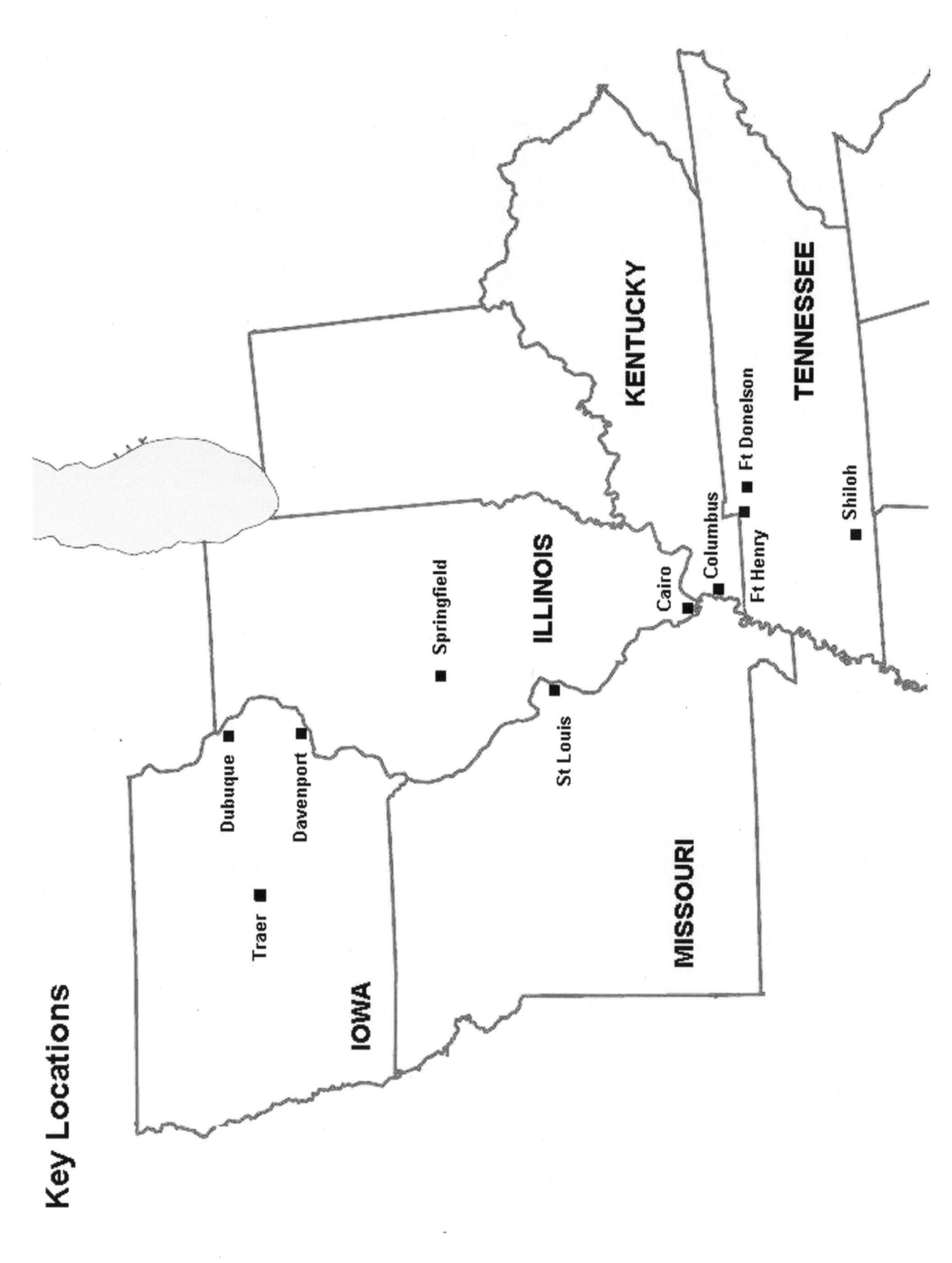

POW Route Through Dixie

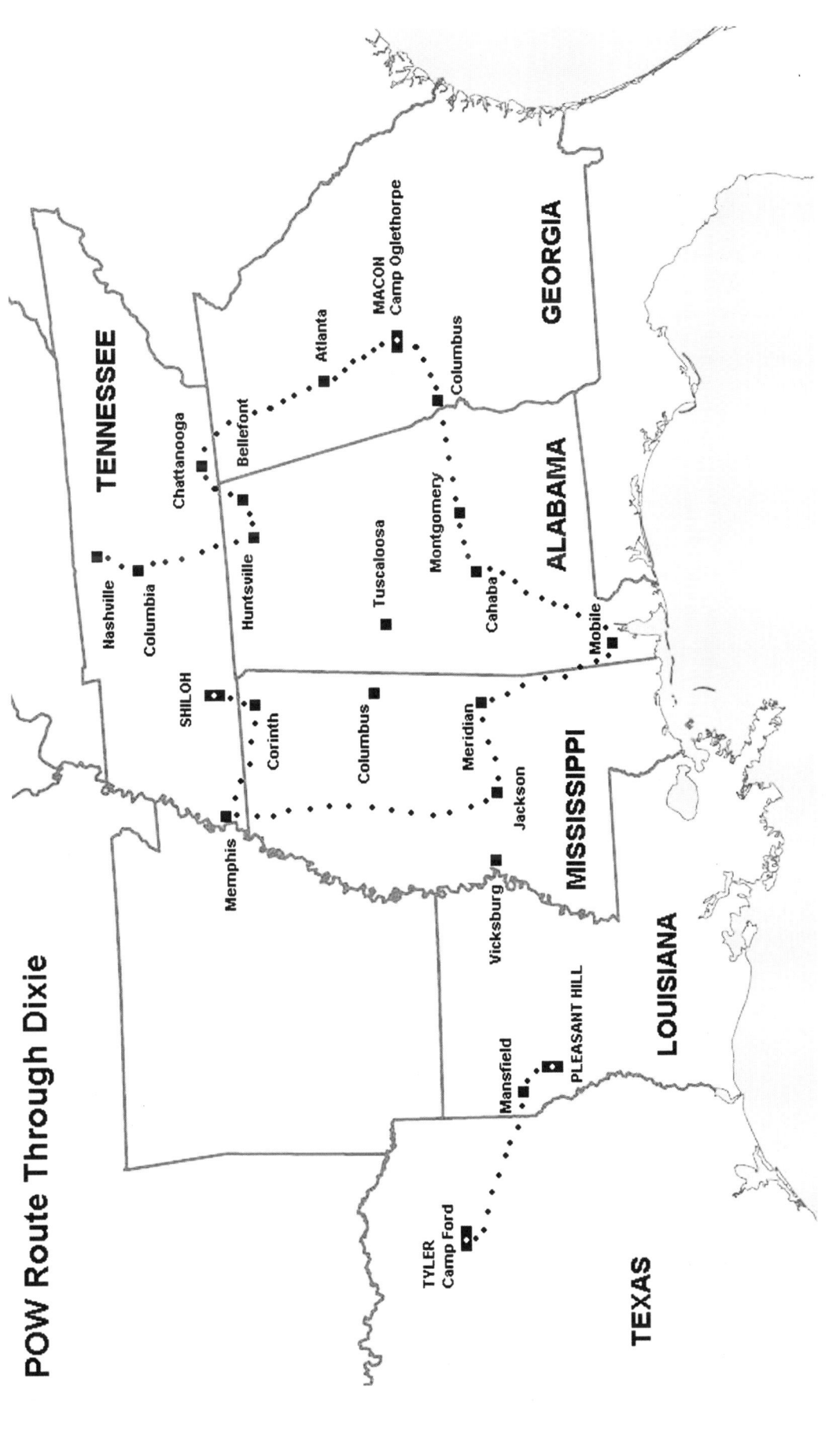

Peter Wilson, whose collected letters are included here under the new title *Many Must Fall*. Image has been reversed to show correct orientation. (Courtesy of Evan Wilson)

MANY MUST FALL

Correspondence from the Civil War

THE LETTERS OF

Peter Wilson

Sergeant Company G, Fourteenth Regiment Iowa Volunteer Infantry

October 1861- May 1865

PREFACE

In frequent letters to his family Peter Wilson related many of the events he observed as a soldier during the Civil War. The Wilson family kept his letters to serve as a narrative of the War and to preserve a personal history for his descendants. The family later permitted them to be published by the State Historical Society of Iowa in their Journal of History and Politics. They are re-printed here for the first time in book form, along with additional letters from his companions.

THE TRAER MUSEUM

DEDICATED TO THE MEN WHO SERVED

"I see no reason to dread the future. I think the war will go on and many must fall, perhaps without doing much good."
-- Peter Wilson

TABLE OF CONTENTS

It has never been my lot to lose any very near relative but the time will come for us all to go to another world. It matters little, if we are ready, how soon. Here in the Army we are often reminded of the uncertainty of life and the certainty of death.

If half of us come home when the war is over it will be better than I expect. But I need not continue on the dark side of the picture. If the cause of justice and liberty triumphs over that of slavery and wrong, those that die have not died in vain.

I presume you have not thought much about the merits of the war or rather you may doubt whether it is right for us to go on at the rate we have, sacrificing so much life, but I take it for granted you would like to see America as it was before the war commenced, with the exception of slavery. I think the time is coming when that will be the case. For my part I want to see the war go on until we are completely successful.

The fall campaign will perhaps decide the long struggle. If we have as good success as we have had this summer it certainly will. I don't know when I will come home but I think some time before winter. We soldiers see a good many places and a great deal of the country but I have not seen anything down this way to compare with Tama County, Iowa.

From the Peter Wilson Letters

PART ONE

THE TRAINING PERIOD (1)

INTRODUCTION

In a letter dated March 19, 1861, Robert Young, one of the Scotch settlers who had come to Tama County in 1851, wrote to his parents in Scotland of conditions in the new homeland. The clouds of disunion and war were already apparent, but the young Scot reassured his family already making preparations for emigration to Iowa. "You need not be afraid of the secession movement", he wrote, "you seem to take the affair far worse on your side of the Atlantic. The western people treat the matter pretty coolly. The thing will blow over in a little while. The people here hate slavery as badly as they do in Britain. It is evident that they can't get along in the same Union, the fire eaters of the South and the people of the North. " (2)

But Robert Young was wrong in his prediction that the war cloud would soon blow over. Only a few weeks after his letter, the guns roared at Fort Sumter and then came the call for volunteers. The Scotch in the settlement along Wolf Creek felt the thrill of allegiance to the new land. The young men began to enlist. Two brothers, James and Peter Wilson, already farming for themselves, entered into an agreement that Peter, then twenty-four, would volunteer. James, a year older, was to take over Peter's farming interests and both were to share alike at the end of the war. This co-partnership to exist during the war was a not uncommon arrangement between brothers at that time.

Accordingly, Peter enlisted on October 9, 1861, at a meeting in the Buckingham schoolhouse. Nearly every man in the settlement was there. North Tama with scarcely one hundred and fifty men of military age sent eighty recruits. After a dinner in Toledo served by the church ladies, the men started by wagon for Marengo where they entrained for Davenport. Here the Fourteenth Iowa Regiment was mobilized, with only seven companies. (3)

The roster of Iowa soldiers gives the following skeleton record of Peter Wilson, the soldier: "Age 24. Residence Wolf Creek, nativity Scotland. Enlisted Oct. 9, 1861. Mustered Nov. 2, 1861. Missing in action April 6, 1862, Shiloh, Tenn. Promoted Fourth Sergeant April 12, 1863; Third Sergeant, July 1, 1863. Missing in action April 9, 1864, Pleasant Hill, La. Returned from missing July 1, 1864. Mustered out June 12, 1865, Davenport, Iowa." (4)

From the camps Peter Wilson wrote letters to the members of his family. Those preserved in this collection were chiefly to his father, John Wilson, his brother James, and his sister Flora. These letters reveal the hardships of the soldiers in the Union army, the life in the camps, the psychological reaction to danger and battle, and the terrible conditions in the military hospitals. Interspersed with these grim descriptions, are allusions to affairs at home.

At the battle of Shiloh early in April 1862, the Fourteenth Iowa lost heavily in killed, wounded, and prisoners. Among those taken prisoner on the sixth of April was Peter Wilson. He spent some time as a prisoner in a Memphis hospital suffering from fever, and later, with others of the Fourteenth Iowa, took an oath not to fight again until regularly exchanged and was permitted to return to the Union lines. Bound not to take part in the war as a combatant and not being permitted to return home, Peter Wilson spent some time working in an army hospital at Monterey near Corinth. Later in the summer the young soldier went home on a furlough and then returned to Benton Barracks to await a formal exchange. When the exchange was finally completed he returned to active duty.

Peter Wilson fought throughout the war and lived to raise a family in the Scotch settlement in Tama County. Of his seven children four are still living in Traer: Miss Mary W. Wilson, Mr. Sheridan S. Wilson, Mrs. Nellie Wilson Currens, and Mr. Peter L. Wilson. There are also six grandchildren. (5)

----

1 The State Historical Society of Iowa is indebted to Mr. Sheridan S. Wilson of Traer, Iowa, for permission to publish these Civil War letters written by his father, Peter Wilson. Letters to Ruth A. Gallaher, dated March 12 and 14, 1942. The letters included in this installment cover the period of training at Camp McClellan

and Benton Barracks. Letters written later will, it is planned, be published in later issues of this volume. Only minor changes in spelling, punctuation, and capitalization have been made in the letters.

2 This information from the letter written by Robert Young was taken from a manuscript containing sketches of the lives of various residents of the Scotch settlement in Tama County compiled by Janette Stevenson Murray (Mrs. Frederick G. Murray) of Cedar Rapids. Her father, William Stevenson, was one of the Scotch settlers in Tama County.

3 From data included in Mrs. Murray's manuscript on the Scotch settlers in Tama County. For another account of the enlistment and mustering of this company see Benjamin F. Thomas's "*Off to the War*" in The Palimpsest, Vol. XXII, pp. 161-177. Thomas and Peter Wilson enlisted at the same time in a company raised by William H. Stivers.

4 Roster and Record of Iowa Soldiers in the War of the Rebellion, Vol. II, p. 851. [It should be noted that the phrase "Returned from missing July 1, 1864" in this record does not mean that Wilson actually returned to his Company on that day. He had been taken prisoner on April 9, 1864 and was held in a POW camp in Texas until May 28, 1865. The word "returned" here merely reflects that his status as "missing in action" had been changed in the Company records on July 1st when it was confirmed that he was in fact a prisoner of war for the second time.]

5 Information in a letter from Mr. Sheridan S. Wilson to Ruth A. Gallaher, March 14, 1942.

THE LETTERS:

Camp McClellan Davenport, Iowa

Camp McClellan Oct. 25th, 1861

" Dear Father: I take this opportunity to write a few lines to let you know how we are getting along. We had a busy time that afternoon when we started, we stopped at Irving and the next day we arrived at Camp. We were welcomed with the rousing cheers of some 3000 men. We were marched into our quarters and I was rather struck with the appearance of them. Our shanties are made as tight as a good barn, bunked up like a ship two in a bunk. We have plenty of straw and we are very comfortable. Our fare consists of beef, bread, beans, potatoes, rice & coffee, we get plenty to eat and good enough. We are all satisfied with our camp arrangements.

In order to get into the 13th Regiment (6) we had to double with another company. Their Captain is a first rate drill master and we had to take him for First Lieutenant which throws our officers down one step. I don't know what my position will be. If we had had men enough of our own I should have had what Stivers promised me but it is a very troublesome post & the hardest work in the company. (7) We drill 3 hours per day and it is different from our old drill in the guards. I could hardly believe how much we learn. We have the best drill master in the camp and we make as good an appearance in two days practice as some of the companies that have drilled two weeks. Our camp is situated up the river just above east Davenport. It is a very pleasant place, we have a splendid view of the river, the bridge, and Rock Island. We are up in the morning at daylight and march down to the river to wash. The sentinels are posted around the camp at short intervals muskets in hand and no soldier can get out without a pass or with a commissioned officer. If any one gets on the spree or misbehaves in any way he is put into the guard house; one got in tonight for stealing a pipe and another for stealing a pie. There is a great variety of character among 3000 men. At present some are writing, some are fiddling, dancing, fifing, drumming, playing cards, singing hymns, songs &c, some are reading the Bible, some the newspapers, some studying tactics, every one to his fancy, everything goes on very agreeable. I have not seen a quarrel since we came into camp. The Vinton boys are our next neighbors, amongst them I find several old friends. There are a great many splendid looking men in camp, the majority are stout good soldiers. There are ten or 12 teams hauling wood, water, beef, bread, potatoes, and all such things. I think if some of the Wolf Creek boys knew [how] well off we are they would not hesitate to come and join us right away.

As near as we can find out our destination is Leavenworth. (8) If so we will start in 3 or 4 weeks. The prospect of going there is satisfactory to the whole Regiment, we will have good winter quarters and time to drill before we are brought into service. I wrote to Uncle David (9) to come and see me. I shall probably see him before we go from this place. I can't get out until we get our Regiment full which will be a week or more. I shall write weekly to some of you. Give my love to all. Write to Camp McClellan, Davenport, care of Captain Stivers. (10) Your affect(ionate) Son Peter Wilson "

----

6 There was much confusion in the organization of volunteer regiments and companies and the Fourteenth Iowa Infantry seems to have been very unfortunate in getting started. Too many companies were organized with too few men. The Tama County contingent hoped to get into the Thirteenth Iowa Infantry, but was finally crowded out. Indeed it was only by high pressure recruiting and consolidation that **Captain William H. Stivers** succeeded in getting his group mustered into the Fourteenth Iowa as Company G. See also Thomas' "*Off to War*" in The Palimpsest, Vol. XXII, pp. 168, 169.

7 The First Lieutenant of Company G was **George Pemberton**, thirty-five years of age, a resident of Scott County. His selection for this position was part of the plan for the consolidation of various groups. The officers of the Tama County company, designated at first as the "*Tama County Rangers*", were to have been: William H. Stivers, Captain; **William Gallagher**, First Lieutenant; **Simon F. Eccles**, Second Lieutenant. In the consolidated company Gallagher dropped to Second Lieutenant and Eccles became First Sergeant. What position Peter Wilson was to have had is not stated. His description of it as "a very troublesome post & the hardest work in the company" suggests that he might have been promised the position of First Sergeant. Lieutenant Pemberton had been a soldier in the Mexican war and in experience had the advantage of Captain Stivers, whom he succeeded on January 25, 1862. Roster and Record of Iowa Soldiers in the War of the Rebellion, Vol. II, p. 833; B. F. Thomas' "*Soldier Life A Narrative of the Civil War*" (Manuscript).

8 Companies A, B, and C of the Fourteenth Iowa were sent to Fort Randall, Dakota Territory. For an account of their service see Iowa Troops in the Sully Campaigns in THE IOWA JOURNAL OF HISTORY AND POLITICS, Vol. XX, pp. 364-443.

9 This was apparently David McCosh, a brother of Mrs. John Wilson. Benjamin F. Thomas says that he, Peter Wilson, and John Gaston visited at the McCosh home in Long Grove early in November, 1861. Long Grove is a community center some twelve miles north of Davenport.

10 William H. Stivers, Captain of Company G, Fourteenth Iowa Infantry. He is described as an attorney, thirty-one years of age, and a resident of Tama County. His enthusiasm for military activities seems to have declined steadily and he resigned his commission on January 24, 1862.

Camp McClellan Nov. 23rd 1861

" Dear Father: We are still in this place although expecting to leave soon. This is the first snowy blustering day we have had since we came to camp. We got our overcoats yesterday so we can brave the coldest weather. I have got the best suit of clothes that I had in my life, we have an overcoat, fatigue coat, and uniform coat, and plenty of other clothes. We packed such things as we did not need and sent them home this morning. We Wolf Creek boys put our things in a barrel and sent them to James (11) care of Graham of Toledo. Among other things I sent four pairs of shoes, three pairs tied to my carpetbag and one pair with my name in them. They are a very easy shoe to walk in. I bought three pairs for two dollars, the fourth I received when I got my clothes. They will be useful with you, they were of no use to me. My expected trip to Toledo fell through and I am not sorry, it would have been rather an unpleasant trip. Since the 11th and 13th left, things are more quiet. There are not more than 1000 men in camp at present. The lines have to be guarded all the same, it makes the boys stand guard oftener. It don't make any difference to me as I don't have to stand. My work comes very near being nothing as my health is good, plenty of amusement. I need not grumble but times will not always be so. There are some of the soldiers that won't be content to stay at home in the evening, they run the guard and go down town on the spree.

When there is a good many out, we sometimes have to go after them and have some fun bringing them back. They are not very severely punished, generally being put in the guard house until morning. Our Company has behaved well so far. The restraints put upon us are none too strict and for my part I have no disposition to break them. Since writing this the report is that we leave Monday or Tuesday for Cairo but there is no certainty about it.

You will not hear from me again from this place. Write to the care of Capt. Stivers, Company G 14th Reg. Iowa Volunteers. Our letters will be sent after us, so you may write any time. Your affect Son Peter Wilson "

----

11 James Wilson, later Secretary of Agriculture. Unless otherwise addressed, letters to "Dear brother" were written to James. [James Wilson, nicknamed "Tama Jim", was head of the USDA from 1897 to 1913 serving in the cabinet during the administrations of Presidents McKinley, Theodore Roosevelt, and Taft.]

Camp McClellan, Nov. 24th, 1861

" Dear Sister Flora: I have written several letters home this week, and therefore I have nothing new to write. I went to town the other day and had my likeness taken. The uniform don't look so well in a picture as it does on the individual but I will send it just as it is. It will give you some idea how a soldier looks. I will send one to mother, one to Long Grove (12) as my aunt requested, and the third you will hear from. We do not expect to be in this place much longer. We have orders to be ready to go at three hours warning, the probability is that we will leave this week. I have sent such things home as I did not need. I would send some more of my clothes if there was any way to send them. I have so many clothes and blankets that I scarcely know what to do with them. I would like to hear from James. When we go down the river I probably won't have time to write so often but I will write as often as I can. Write to the care of Capt. Stivers, Company G, 14th Reg. Iowa Volunteers. If we go down the river that would find us when we get to our destination. I will give you my address the first letter I write. Give my best wishes to all, Horace in particular, Bob Young not excepted.
   Your affect(ionate) brother Peter Wilson "
----
   12 Apparently Peter Wilson had recently returned from his visit to the McCosh home although he does not mention it in the letters preserved. [Flora was 22 in the 1860 US Census; other sisters were: Jane 20, Janet 18, Agnes 11, Margaret 8 (David's twin), Elizabeth 6, and Sarah 4.]

Camp McClellan, Nov. 27th 1861

" Dear Brother (13): We leave today at ten so I will have time to scratch but a few lines. We got our letters from home Tuesday night so letters that are now on the way won't find us in this place. I have not heard from you since I left home. Our letters will be sent after us if properly directed. We have packed our things in our knapsacks and some more things that we don't need we have packed in another barrel and sent to you the same as the first. There is nothing of mine in it but your old overcoat which I either had to send home or throw away. I think from what I can learn we are yet going to Leavenworth but there is nothing certain. For my part I don't care which way we go. We are all glad to leave this place although we have been very comfortable and well used. We were drilled yesterday afternoon by the Adjutant. (14) He was greatly pleased with us and unhesitatingly pronounced us the best drilled Company in the Regiment, so much for our First Lieutenant's pains in drilling us. Capt. Stivers is good enough as a man but as a military man he is not as good as he ought to be. Galager (15) is a first rate fellow and one of my particular friends. I think our Regimental Officers are all we could wish both as men and officers so that we have the satisfaction of being used as we ought to be. Our Colonel (16) is said to be worth 600,000 dollars. You would think he was a farmer just come in to sell a load of wheat, he is so plain. He has been through the Mexican War and got his kneecap shot off which makes him walk a little lame. But I must conclude. You will hear from me as soon as we get to our destination. Your brother Peter Wilson "
----
   13 Apparently addressed to his brother and partner, James Wilson.
   14 The Adjutant of the Fourteenth Iowa was **Noah N. Tyner**, apparently one of the officers contributed by the Scott County contingent. Roster and Record of Iowa Soldiers in the War of the Rebellion, Vol. II, p. 731. [Noah Noble Tyner from Davenport was wounded and taken prisoner of war at Shiloh. After the War he lived at Fort Scott Kansas, Des Moines Iowa and Augusta Illinois.]
   15 William Gallagher, Second Lieutenant of Company G, was described as twenty-seven years of age and a resident of Toledo, Tama County. He became First Lieutenant on January 25, 1862, and Captain on January 7, 1863. Roster and Record of Iowa Soldiers in the War of the Rebellion, Vol. II, p. 807.
   16 The Colonel of the Fourteenth Iowa at this time was **William T. Shaw**, forty years of age. He was born in Maine and was a resident of Anamosa. He commanded the Fourteenth Iowa throughout the war. [Colonel Shaw has been described as a "colorful and brilliant leader, strong willed and energetic". Educated in the Maine Wesleyan Seminary, as a young man he went to Greencastle Indiana to teach in a private school which later became DePauw University. Teaching school in Kentucky when the war with Mexico broke out, he enlisted in the Second Kentucky Infantry. He fought Indians in the southwest after the Mexican War, yet is said to have lived among the tribes in Oklahoma. Noted for his reputation for courage and determination, he was chosen captain of the first party to cross the uncharted territory between Fort Smith, Arkansas, and Santa Fe, New Mexico. His company left the mouth of the Little River in April and arrived in Santa Fe thirty-six days later. He then crossed into the gold fields of California where he mined and engaged in lumber businesses. About 1851 he returned to the east by ship through Nicaragua. He again crossed the plains in

1852, starting from Council Bluffs accompanied by just one man. Finally settling down to married life in Anamosa Iowa, he farmed, invested in commercial real estate, built hotels, schools, churches, and banks and started a local railroad company. $600, 000 in 1860 might be roughly equivalent to $6 million today, by any standards a wealthy man.]

Benton Barracks, St. Louis, Missouri

Benton Barracks Dec 1st 1861

" Dear Sister: We left Camp McClellan on the 26 [November] and part of our Regiment came down the river on a boat, the balance among whom was our Company took the cars and went round within a little ways of Chicago. We had a pleasant trip, passing through a great many towns and villages amongst which was the home of old Abe which is a very pretty town with many splendid buildings. We arrived at Alton about midnight where we went on board a boat where there was already a regiment of Illinois troops with part of a regiment of Cavalry. They being first on board had filled the cabins so we had to take a deck passage. The night was cold and the change from the warm cars to the open air was not very pleasant, but thanks to my own number one propensities I slipped into a stateroom which privilege might be had for fifty cents. However I had not the money to spare. I slept as sound as if I had paid for it. We started at daylight and as it was only 25 miles we were in Saint Louis about nine o'clock. There is a large fleet of steamboats lying at the wharf with gunboats getting ready for the move down the river. We [dis]embarked about noon and took our line of march through the town. We passed through the principal, that is the most business, part of the town.

Saint Louis is a very large town but where the buildings are 4 or 5 stories high the streets are only about 30 feet wide which makes it terribly crowded most of the time. It was easy to see by the reception the immense crowds gave us that we had got into the land of Secesh. The cheers that we were accustomed to everywhere we go were not forthcoming. If it were not for the presence of so many Union soldiers Saint Louis would be against the Union. As it is they have to keep quiet. The camp is some five miles from the landing, it is just outside the town so you have some idea what size Saint Louis is. We arrived about two in the afternoon. We were welcomed heartily by the other Iowa regiments nine of whom are stationed at this place. There are some twenty thousand men here at present including three or four regiments of Cavalry. They are nearly all armed, those that are not, will be immediately. Everything indicates speedy preparations for the winter campaign. Our camp is two miles square. It is on high level ground originally fitted up for fair grounds, the barracks are ranged from east to west and also about one mile across the east end leaving the center for drill and parade ground. We had a review today and the sight of so many fine regiments was very inspiring. The Iowa 7th is here in camp. They have suffered severely in their recent fight (17) there are only some 250 left. Such is the fortune of war. We don't know when we may leave this place. It will take us some time to drill sufficiently to be fit to take the field. As part of our Regiment is at Leavenworth* we may be sent there. However we are well off where we are. I feel thankful that so far our lines have fallen in pleasant places and I am not fearful for the future. I will write to father and James soon. This leaves the Wolf Creek boys all well and in good spirit. Skuse bad ritin & spelin. Your affec brother Peter Wilson "

----

17 The Seventh Iowa Infantry had just returned from the battle of Belmont. It was at this time commanded by Colonel J. G. Lauman. He reported that the Regiment had only a little more than four hundred men and thus it lost almost one-half. (Colonel **Jacob Gartner Lauman** was himself severely wounded at Belmont Missouri in November 1861, but was well enough to command a brigade during the successful assault on Fort Donelson in February 1862. His personal courage and skillful leadership at Donelson immediately earned him a promotion to brigadier general. After participating in battles at Shiloh, Vickburg, and Jackson, General Lauman returned home to Burlington Iowa where he died in February 1867 still suffering from this Belmont wound.)

* Companies A, B and C had been sent to Leavenworth before going to the Dakotas.

Camp Benton, Dec. 2nd 1861

" Dear Brother: Everything is so new and exciting that I scarcely know what to write about. We have just come in from a three hours drill in the snow. There was just enough snow to make us slip and slide and tumble. There were so many companies drilling all around us that we could scarcely mind our own business.

There is an incredible amount of maneuvers going on in drill hours. The drill ground is some two miles square and in Company drill there seems to be scarcely room for the exercises. There is Flying Artillery which as near as I can describe looks something like Klingiman's (18) big wagon with six splendid horses hitched to it, the nigh horses mounted, the gunners sitting on the box on the front axle where the ammunition is kept. The cannon is mounted on the hind axle. They gallop from one place to another, firing blank cartridges at the Cavalry to get the horses used to the noise. There are some splendid Cavalry regiments in camp, their horses are generally light, fiery, prancing nags. They are well fed and ridden very hard. They mostly stand in the open air but they have good blankets. There seems to be plenty of food and clothing for man and beast. I was perfectly surprised to find such good accommodations. Where there are so many men everything goes on like clock work. They are getting all the Iowa regiments into this place with the intention of forming a Brigade. So far the Iowa boys have proved themselves second to none and we rejoice at the prospect of being brought together. I think we will go down the river together sometime this winter.

Benton Barracks was laid out by Fremont (19) and does credit to the man. They are comfortable and convenient. The place is well adapted for a camp of instruction. A good many of the regiments have got so far along with their drill as to use the bugle in giving commands. That is what they use on the battle field. It is a splendid sight to see a well-drilled regiment drilling with their commander so far away that his voice could not be heard. I saw a company of Sharpshooters going through their exercises this morning. They were a good-looking lot of men and seemed to understand their drill which is entirely different from ours. I would not say anything against Capt. Stivers in the Company as that is against the rules but if ever we come to the field of battle we will send him to stay with the women where he spends most of his time now. He has not drilled us once since we enlisted, in fact he don't seem to care how we get along. Our Lieutenants are very different, they take pride in having us the best drilled Company in the Regiment which we are said to be. When we go out on Battalion drill, Stivers has to take his place as Captain where he is so awkward that he makes himself a laughing stock for his own Company. He has either got to do better or the First Lieutenant will be elected over him. We Wolf Creek boys saved him from such a fate once but we won't do it again. He has broken too many promises to keep friends a great while. There are three women with us ostensibly to sew and wash but they are rather loose characters. They may be useful if many of our men get sick. For my part I wash and sew for myself. I have been writing you and others a series of rambling letters scarcely knowing what I have said and left unsaid.

Flora has been my most punctual correspondent. I have not heard from you yet. If you have not written, on receiving this please do write soon, a letter from home is the most desirable thing we soldiers get. I am one writing against many and so far I have done my share. I suppose I have more time but not so good accommodations. At present I am sitting in my bunk with our music book on my knee using it as a desk, the boys as usual carrying on several amusements amongst which is dancing and boxing. The latter is the best amusement we have in which we all participate. I can hoe my row at it with most of the boys and can put the gloves on with our teacher to as good advantage as any one with the same practice. It teaches one to guard himself which is likely to be useful before the war is over. There is no more running the guard as it was in Davenport, any soldier that goes to town does it at the risk of his life. There are so many Secesh in Saint Louis that they take advantage of every straggler they can find, so the boys have to keep inside the lines. My letter, such as it is, is long enough, give my best wishes to all our friends and at present I shall conclude.

Your brother Peter Wilson "

----

18 This reference was to Stephen Klingaman, who ran the mill in the Scotch community and was one of the important men in the county.

19 John C. Fremont was for a time in command in Missouri. He had married Jessie Benton, a daughter of Thomas H. Benton.

Camp Benton, Dec. 3d, 1861

" Dear Father and Mother: As I have written several letters since our arrival I don't know that I have anything new at present. I have been rambling through the camp when at leisure and after seeing the complete arrangements of such an extensive military school I begin to believe that if every other camp is as well regulated and getting their regiments as well drilled the country must be getting on a very warlike footing. The camp includes the fair grounds of which you have some idea from the picture four months ago. Then there were no barracks in this place, now there are good accommodations for twenty thousand men. The barracks are built in rows about a mile on each side with sundry others across the ends. Each barrack contains two companies. They are about 40 feet wide and seventy feet long, one large stove in the center which keeps the place quite comfortable. The front door opens on the parade ground which is perfectly level and about a mile square, the back door opens on the row of kitchen buildings. The dining room is roofed but not sided up, the cook houses are the next row. Each company does their own cooking, some hire darkies to cook for them. We pay three of our own boys to cook for us, we pay them 12 dollars per month each. They have pretty hard work and we would rather have it so than take turns as some do. Behind the cook houses are the Cavalry horses. They mostly stand in the open air but they are well fed and have warm blankets. They are generally good horses and make a splendid appearance when drilling. The Cavalry boys have more work than we do, it takes them all their time to keep their things in order while we are generally with the exception of drill hours spoiling for something to do. We fill up the time pleasantly enough. I would like to know what kind of weather you have in Iowa at this time.

It looks like May here. We had slight fall of snow but it did not stay long. We went out into the country the other day some five or six miles, we were uncomfortably warm with our coats off. We went to get some persimmons. They taste something like raisins and are about the size of figs. They grow on trees something like hackberry. The country around Saint Louis is very beautiful, the farms have good houses and good fences and orchards. The most of them have slaves and are Secesh in principle. The soil seems to be good by the looks of the corn stalks but it is very poorly watered as far as I have seen. The camp is watered from the Missouri river, it is brought some distance in pipes. It is pretty good.

Friday Dec 6th. Our Barracks have been overhauled and fixed to suit the Colonel's notions which has prevented me from finishing my letter. In the meantime I received a letter from Jane (20) and also one from James. I am glad to hear that you are all getting along so well. They also inform me that Sloss's (21) little girl is dead which was rather a sad affair. If we stay away three years there will doubtless be a good many such changes. I am also informed that Uncle Gilbert McMillan still trades a little and that John Glen still keeps his health &c &c. If we stay long in this place I will write to Uncle West, (22) Andrew, and the McDowall boys. There are so many to write to that I have not got around [to]them all yet. We soldiers have no idea when we have to march, in fact we don't know as much about war matters as those that are out of the camp. We have received everything but our guns. There are plenty of them here but our Colonel don't like their pattern so we wait for something better. We drill in everything but the manual of arms, I think on looking at some of the old regiments going through Battalion drill it will take us two or three months before we are fit for service. Most of the regiments have brass bands some of which play splendid. The Cavalry bands go on horseback and between one band and another the drill ground looks like a continual holiday rather than preparations for war. There are some splendid looking field cannon in this place. I should suppose from the way they are managed on drill that they will be heard from some time if they ever get into the fight but I will conclude my disjointed sentences. You must consider the place I have to write in. You might as well try to keep your thoughts collected in bedlam, if there is such a place, as to attempt such a thing in this place.

Your affect Son Peter Wilson "

----

20 Jane was a favorite sister, mentioned frequently in Peter's letters.
21 This refers to a daughter of George Sloss who lived north of the John Wilson farm.
22 West Wilson, known as the "Squire", was a brother of John Wilson, the father of Peter. [In the 1860 US Census Peter's Father, John Wilson, was 48 and his Mother, Jean McCosh Wilson, was 45.]

(Probably Camp Benton) Dec. 7th 1861

" Dear Brother James: I received your letter yesterday and shall answer it as quick as possible. I am glad to hear how well you are getting along. At the date of your letter you were not aware that we had started for Missouri. Probably before this reaches you we will be on the way to Leavenworth. The reason why I think we are going there is that three of our Companies (23) are out there now and our Colonel says we must either have them back or go to them. The Colonel is an old hand and knows his rights and looks like a man that will have them. You wish to know what kind of material the 14th Regiment is composed of. It is rather hard for me to say with my limited experience of military matters. I think our Colonel, Major, Adjutant, and Lieutenant Colonel (24) are all men that understand their business and as far as I have seen are men in the highest sense of the word. They come among the boys occasionally, use us like equals. When in the ranks they of course show their dignity. I have never seen an officer insult a private since I enlisted. Some of them probably would if they dared to do so but it is all day with them if they lose the good will of the men. As a proof of this our boys got to thinking Stivers was paying more attention to his women than he ought and neglecting to drill us as much as he ought. They got up a petition requesting him to resign or tend to his business; he took the latter course double quick time. If he is not very careful our First Lieutenant will be in his place before long. There are several other green Captains in the Regiment, with some firstrate drill masters. There is not any of them can beat our First Lieutenant. Gallagher is also getting to be a good drill master. He is also a very sociable companion. I have made a good many friends and I think no enemies since I came into the Company. I think when the 14th gets well drilled they will compare favorably with any of the Iowa regiments, which are composed of the stoutest men on an average that I see in this place. There are some fine regiments from Illinois in this place and some Missouri regiments that look very well.

The First Iowa Cavalry are a splendid regiment. They seem to be well drilled and daily practice the sword exercise. They have fine horses and ride like Jehu. The government teams are rigged like Klingiman used to rig his. They mostly use mules. They drive from four to six with the single line. There is some fun breaking mules and horses but they do it up in business style and I believe there are some of the best teamsters here that I have seen. They teach a pair of mules how to pull and go with the single line in a few days. Speaking of climate the warm rain falls steadily today. We will have it very muddy when we go out to drill again. We have nothing to [do] when it rains except the guards. They of course have to stand in all kinds of weather. I have only been Corporal of the Guard once since I enlisted. When the boys are absent at roll call they are put on double duty so that those that are on hand all the time seldom come on guard duty. Among so many men there are generally some that won't conform to the regulations so they have to do the sweeping in the barracks and such little chores. Everything is kept clean and neat and in good order in the barracks. We have to keep our clothes clean and our brass fixins bright. We are inspected once per week. Some of the boys are continually losing their things. They are furnished with what they lose at their own expense. Some of our boys have spent their first wages and are running on tick with the Sutler. They have to pay very dear for what they get. I don't believe the Sutler can collect his bills and I hope he can't. It would be a good thing for the boys if there was no such establishment. Things have passed on quietly the last few days. There has been no disturbance on the lines which is generally the place for some shooting. However the reports that we heard on our arrival were somewhat exaggerated. I don't think this country is as healthy as Iowa. I believe this is a great place for the ague and bilious diseases generally. I would rather have frosty weather than such warm, muddy, disagreeable weather as this is.

The parade ground is empty today for the first time since we came here. The boys are all in the barracks which present a lively scene of confusion. We have some very waggish characters in our Company. The[y] of course run the rig on their more simple brethren. We have over a month's wages due but probably won't receive any money before the first of January. I have enough to do me for a month or two. When we get our next pay if there is much prospect of going into the field I will buy a revolver. Some of our boys can shoot with wonderful accuracy now. Gaston **(25)** got a very good seven shooter for fifteen dollars but I don't much think there will be any chance to use them. When you write let me know whether you received the barrels and how you like Uncle Sam's shoes. I have more clothes now than I need. If we go into the field I will have to throw some of them away but I must conclude. Write soon to Peter Wilson Co G 14th Reg. "

----

23 Companies A, B, and C of the Fourteenth Iowa Infantry were mustered into service at Iowa City and later were sent to Fort Randall in Dakota Territory. They did not join the Regiment, but later were replaced by three other companies.

24 Colonel William T. Shaw, Lieutenant Colonel **Edward W. Lucas**, Adjutant Noah N. Tyner, and Major **Hiram Leonard**. Lieutenant Colonel Lucas resigned on March 12, 1863, Major Leonard on February 26, 1862. [Before his promotion to Major, Leonard originally was appointed Captain of Company K. At this same time, Leonard's 19 year old nephew **Howard D. Leonard** enlisted into Company K as a private under his Uncle's command. Both Leonards were from the Burlington area, Des Moines County.]

25 John Gaston, one of Peter Wilson's friends both at home and in the army. [Gaston most likely was Wilson's bunkmate; they enlisted together along with B.F. Thomas. See *"Soldier Life"*, Chapter 1]

Camp Benton Dec. 8th 1861

" Dear Sister Flora: I have been writing a good many letters since we came to camp and receiving so few answers makes it rather discouraging. No one has seen fit to write without my writing them first and then they seem slow to answer. But I did not intend to grumble, my luck may be better by and by. This being Sabbath it is not hardly right to be employed writing but although we have preaching, the Sabbath is not kept very strict. We do not drill but we have to fix up our knapsacks and go out to be inspected. While we are being inspected outside, our bunks are inspected to see that everything is in good order. Feeling slightly indisposed I was excused from going out today and after reading until I got tired I changed the program to my present occupation. The Iowa 11th and the 52nd Illinois left for Jefferson City. The Iowa boys were much the stoutest men. I stood where I could see each platoon as they passed. The Iowa boys were evidently from the farm their unshaven faces considerable dirty and being well armed and having plenty of ammunition they looked as independent as could be. If they don't fight well I am much mistaken. Since writing so far I have been to preaching. The Chaplain treated more on the laws of health today than would suit in some congregations. His remarks however suited the occasion very well and will probably do as much good as a more orthodox sermon.

The weather is so pleasant that we go about in our shirtsleeves. The ground dries very quick after rain. Two days ago it was very muddy but it is already comfortable getting about. It is certainly much pleasanter to live in a climate like this in the winter than in Iowa, however if we pass the summer in the South we may not like it so well. Frank (26) has got some new guttapercha pens and has me trying them, hence my mixed looking letter. We generally spend half of our evenings or more writing. I have written to Uncle David and to Six Mile Grove and intend to write to all my old friends. If they don't see fit to answer me I will soon forget them.

I believe if the society was congenial to my tastes I would like the life of a soldier better than anything else, but there are too many men that I despise, that is their manner of life, for me to think of staying any longer than the war is over. We Wolf Creek boys are much attached to one another. I could not have better comrades. We spend our evenings together and at present are all writing to our friends. The more noisy amusements of other evenings are rejected for singing, writing, and in some of the quarters they hold prayer meetings which are generally well attended. I had a letter from Jane a few days ago, the second since I became a soldier. She gives me more encouragement than any of my correspondents which is something I shall always feel grateful for. She seems to get along well with her studies and always looks on the bright side of the picture. But I must conclude. You will get tired of reading so many jumbled harem scarem letters.

Your letters directed to Camp McClellan have found me here the postmaster knowing where to send but the proper direction is Co G, 14 Reg. That will find us wherever we go. Your Affect Brother Peter Wilson "
----
26 The friend referred to as Frank was **Benjamin Franklin Thomas**, who described his visit to the McCosh home at Long Grove. B.F. Thomas' "*Off to the War*" in The Palimpsest, Vol. XXII, p. 170.

Benton Barracks Dec. 9th 1861

" Dear Brother West: (27) I had intended to write some of you boys some time ago but have postponed it until the present. I sent home the picture of the camp ground but it gives but a poor idea of this place. There are so many men and horses here it would make you wonder where they all found accommodation. There are some regiments going out and some coming in every day. There are some splendid horses and some good riders also. I was looking at the Cavalry going through squadron drill this afternoon. In wheeling from column into line the outside horse has to gallop about as fast if they were trying to head off a steer that did not want to be yoked. They are four deep and come around in better line than the Infantry can on a double quick. The Cavalry are armed with carbines, sabres, and revolvers. The revolvers are carried in the saddle, the sabre is carried at the left side. The carbine is something about half way between a gun and a pistol in size. It is strapped on the right shoulder. Their blankets and knapsack are strapped behind the saddle. They have much the pleasantest way of travelling but they have more chores to do while in camp than we do. We have not received our arms yet, we could get muskets but the Colonel would rather wait and get rifles.

Dec. 10th 1861. I have been out this forenoon for the first time with the officers on officer drill. They form the Regiment with strings in place of the men. The Colonel takes command and every one can hear the orders so much better than the other way. The Captains or Lieutenants that don't know their business are corrected as well as the rest. The noncommissioned officers have a chance to learn just as much as the commissioned officers. A good number know more now. But such news won't interest you much. If you will write, you can mention any thing you wish to know. Have John and Andrew also write. You can make up a pretty interesting letter among you. Let me know how you get along with your school and how your colts get along, your cattle, and so on. Give a general description of all your separate charges. I don't know that I have much more to write. I shall expect a letter from you in a week or two.

It is getting near drill time so no more from your brother, Peter Wilson "
----
27 Peter Wilson mentions six brothers in these letters - James, John, West, Andrew, David, and Allen. [In the 1860 US Census, Peter was 23. His brothers were James 24, John 17, West 15, Andrew 13, David 8 (Margaret's twin), and Allen 2.]

Benton Barracks Dec. 11th 1861

" Dear Uncle: I suppose it is time that you should hear from me but I scarcely know what to say to you. After being out with the officers of the Regiment several times on officer drill I begin to see how deficient some of them are in regard to the most simple movements of Company drill as well as Battalion. There are a good many men in the wrong place which time will probably remedy. There is an old Dutchman that holds the position of Major (28) in the Iowa Twelfth that drills the officers of the 14th. He is the best drill master in Battalion movements that I have seen. It pleases me immensely when he corrects some of our officers and shows them their ignorance which mortifies them as much as it pleases the sergeants and corporals. We form companies without the men, that is the pivot men have a string between them instead of the men. The officers then take their proper places and the old Major puts us through Battalion and Brigade drill without anything but the officers. I think it is a very good idea and is certainly much needed in our Regiment. We understand Company drill pretty well and that is about as far as our officers can take us. This morning as usual we went out on officer drill at eight o'clock. Our old Dutchman not arriving, some of them made a motion that we should fall in and have Company drill as there were so many commanders. There was some time spent in contending about who should take command, each one putting it onto the other. Finally our First Lieutenant agreed to take command for the time. He is an old Mexican soldier and is the best drill master in our Regiment*. We found that what they had been teaching others they could not do themselves much to the amusement of the non-commissioned officers who of course had no difficulty. Some of them will learn and keep their places, others will be thrown aside in the course of time if the war goes on long enough. Some time ago we invited Stivers either to tend to his business or give up his place. He of course chose the former and since has been doing firstrate. If he don't keep his eye peeled he will lose his place sooner or later. For my part I like him very well but he has a good many enemies in the Company. The Thirteenth Regiment leaves early tomorrow morning. They don't know where they are going. I have just been up to their quarters and bid my old acquaintances in the Vinton Company good-bye. They were in good spirits and did not seem to care where they went. They are pretty well drilled, but their muskets are not firstrate. When we came here we were offered the same kind. Our Colonel said they might go to h--1 with their old muskets that would kick a man over a fence and kick at him through the rails after he was over, so we have not got our arms yet.

Dec. 12th. The Thirteenth left today, also part of the Iowa 3rd Cavalry and a Company of Sharpshooters called the Missouri 13th. One of their numbers slipped through the guard last night and got into a brawl in a saloon close at hand. He was stabbed so that he has since died. On learning the above his comrades went out and as they could not find the assassins they burned the house [and] started squads in pursuit. They found them in a house close by and as it is the place where several soldiers have been killed they will doubtless be hanged or shot. Where there are so many men such things are not to be wondered at. I did not expect to see the soldiers so well disposed to one another. Any one that has on Uncle Sam's clothing and gets down town on the spree they are all right if any of the same stripe finds them. If not they sometimes have trouble in getting back to camp. There are lots of sneaking Secesh in and around St. Louis who lose no chance of shooting the soldiers. For my part I feel as safe as if I was at home and with few exceptions those that lose their lives have themselves to blame.

Dec 14th. We have been so busy for the last few days that I have not had time to finish this letter. There are some of our men sick with the measles and I suppose there will be more of them soon. It is very disagreeable where there are so many men hardly sick enough to go to the hospital and not well enough to be on duty. We got out into the country yesterday after persimmons and hickory nuts. We found plenty of both. The country is very beautiful around St. Louis and the woods abound with the former commodities. The persimmons are as good to the taste as raisins and grow on trees something like hackberry. I will send you some of the seed in this letter. You can try if they will grow in Iowa. We are progressing steadily with our drill and I think by the way they put us through they intend to give us something to do by and by. It can't come any too soon as far as I am concerned. I believe it would be healthier in tents than in the barracks but I am well enough where I am and don't care much which way the wind blows.

I don't know that I have any thing more to write at present. I have written a good many letters such as they were and received very few answers so far but I may have better luck by and by, so I will finish by requesting you to write me a few lines at your earliest convenience. Peter Wilson "
----
28 The Major of the Twelfth Iowa Infantry at this time was **Samuel D. Brodtbeck**, a native of Switzerland. [*The First Lieutenant was Pemberton who proved to be an excellent drill master but perhaps not so good as an officer in the field.]

Benton Barracks, Dec. 16th 1861

" Dear Brother: I received your letter dated Dec. 5 and one from father also. It is needless to say how glad I am to hear from you all. We are getting along very well, but if I go more than a week without getting a letter from some of you I get very impatient. You inform me that the Buckingham ladies are raising money for the soldiers. I think they had better use it about home. Dewitt Southwick (29) had a letter from Murdock the other day who proposes to send him some socks and so forth. Dewitt who is one of our most jolly good natured boys thinks if he wants to send us any thing he had better send us some money or Sutler tickets, that being the only thing we have any use for. As far as clothing and blankets are concerned we have more than we know what to do with. When we go into the field and have to march a good deal we will throw away probably half of what we now have. When a regiment goes out I could buy all kinds of clothing for almost nothing so that the good ladies of Tama County must be under some mistake in regard to our wants. We expect to get our pay in a week or two and then we won't have a want of any kind. I have some money yet but it is not much. Our real wants above what we are furnished are trifling, writing materials and tobacco are about all. There is a system of trade carried on between the Sutler and the soldiers on the plan of the milk pedlars of Greenville. They sell one dollars worth of tickets and charge them to the receiver who gives his name and Company. The Sutler has to get his pay the best way he can. If the boys don't see fit to pay him they have to pay two or three prices for everything they get. However they intend to regulate that when they pay him. For my part I pay as I go and shall do so as long as possible.

The next time you write let me know whether you have received the barrels with our old clothes. The shoes were the most that was worth looking after.

I am sorry for Jany's misfortune but accidents will happen sometimes. Whatever you find best to do in regard to the management of our stock, trading &c do just as you see best. I think it is the safest way not to make any calculations on my help at present. The chances are slim for my being home in time for doing anything next summer but that remains to be seen.

I am in good health and spirits so for the present good bye, from your affect brother, Peter Wilson "

------

29 Dewit or **Dewitt Southwick**, aged twenty. He enlisted with the Tama County boys, was taken prisoner at the battle of Shiloh and died at St. Louis soon after he was paroled. [Before the War Dewitt lived and worked on the farm of Evander Murdock of Buckingham, close to the Thomas pottery works.]

Benton Barracks Dec. 17th 1861

" Dear Sister: I received your letter and shall scrape a few lines in reply. I forgot to state in writing to Jane that the song Frank composed while at Long Grove is lost but if you take the Toledo paper you will see something of his in it some of the time. The piece is about his leaving home and is very good*. My friend from Long Grove* is gone down the river again. He wanted to go home for a short time but he could not get away so he had to go with his Regiment. I think they went to Cairo. The 13th Iowa is at Jefferson City. I expect to hear from one of the Vinton boys some of these days. I may have been a little too impatient on account of not hearing from home as often as I could wish but I shall be content in future if I hear from home as often as I have since I came to this place. See that you and Jane are on hand with your next as soon as possible. I expect to hear from Six-Mile Grove, Long Grove, and various other places soon, so I am in good spirits on that subject at present as I am on every other at all times. I felt somewhat anxious about the future when we first enlisted but now I don't care much whether school keeps or not as the saying is. The worst trouble is that we are getting so lazy we will be spoiled for any use if we ever happen to have to work for our living but that don't disturb us much. But I must quit this nonsense. We are at present seated in our tent the candle in the middle and each one at his own business. I never lived in a house that I liked so well as our tent. If you ever saw an Indian's wigwam you have something like our palace*. We lie around to suit our own fancy with no man or woman to say what doest thou. One of the boys belonging to Co. F died today*. Some one or two of ours are very sick and will probably die. John Felter has the measles but was not very sick and is getting better. His folks won't know that he was sick until he is well again. He is very anxious to be well before we go away so that he will be able to go with us and I think if we stay this week he will be all right next week. The Buckingham (30) boys are as much attached to one another as if they were brothers and are as kind and as accommodating as can be. There are some good sociable fellows and also some hard cases in our Company but we get along very agreeable all round. But I must finish, so bidding you good by, I remain your affect brother, Peter Wilson "

-----

30 Buckingham was a townsite north of Wolf Creek not far from the present town of Traer. It was named for Governor William A. Buckingham, who had been Governor of Connecticut. Annals of Iowa (Third Series), Vol. XVI, pp. 136-142. It is still a community center. [Buckingham was Governor of Connecticut from 1858 to 1866. Nothing remains of "old" Buckingham village except the cemetery a mile north of Traer. Other remnants were later relocated several miles to the northeast, site of today's "new" town named Buckingham.]

* This might be the poem "*To My Friends*" which appeared in the Toledo newspaper *The Iowa Transcript* January 16 1862.

* The friend from Long Grove might be **Mark L. Thomson** of the Second Iowa.

* The Sibley tent was cone shaped much like an Indian tipi. It was twelve feet tall and eighteen feet in diameter, and was supported by a single pole mounted upon a tripod. Ventilated in warm weather by a circular hole in the top, in the winter a stove or fire could sit in the middle of the tent under the opening, and a kettle could be hung over the stove. It is said they had enough room for up to a dozen men to live comfortably.

* **George W. Pitt**, twenty-six, died December 16, 1861 of measles. George W. was one of four members of the Pitt family from Western (or Western College), Linn County, who all served in Company F. He enlisted with **Philip Pitt**, twenty-one, in October 1861. Philip also became very ill and was discharged February 1862. **George L. Pitt** and **William A. Pitt**, both twenty-six, enlisted in February 1862 and served until February 1865. William was wounded at Pleasant Hill.

Benton Barracks Dec. 24th 1861

" Dear Father and Mother: I received your letter since writing you the last time. I also had letters from James, Flora, and others. I am happy to hear that you are all well and are getting along as well as usual. The weather has been rather more like Iowa for the last few days. We had another slight fall of snow with something of a bluster when it ceased falling. The next morning was pleasant and during the day it thawed considerably. Today the snow is pretty much gone, another day will finish it. Things go on as usual in camp only there are a good many regiments going out. I think there are brisk times expected soon down the river. You have doubtless heard of the late affair in western Missouri. The prisoners are now in St. Louis. The Iowa 2nd went down last night to guard them. Yesterday we followed the remains of our first comrade that has died to the grave*. He first took the measles and was moved to the hospital. The doctor said it was lung fever that caused his death. There are two or three others very sick of the same trouble. The measles went through our Regiment in such a manner that out of 560 men only some 250 are on duty. At present John Felter is well again, so are some of the others that were first taken sick but there are some new cases every day. The chance is not good for taking care of a sick man in this place and the doctor is, in my opinion, not worth much, so that some that die would live if they had good care and skill. Our prospects are not very encouraging at present. We expect marching orders soon and half of the Regiment sick. I have reason to be thankful that while so many of my comrades have been sick and some have died my health has been good and spirits also. The burying ground is some three miles from camp. In going to and coming from it we had a chance to see some of the forts by which St. Louis is protected from any hostile movement of the Secesh. There are forts every mile or so on the most prominent position to sweep the roads and so it is all around St. Louis. Three hundred in the fort could keep out 3000. They are constructed in such a way it would seem almost impossible to take them. There were some three hundred soldiers' graves that had never been rained on where we buried our comrade. The graves are as close together as can be and are only about three feet deep. They have a good plain coffin and are decently buried. There being so many men in the various camps in the vicinity of St. Louis and all their dead being buried in the same place accounts for so many graves newly filled. I have not the least doubt but the climate will kill more men than the rebels will. Such has been the case so far as much as ten to one.

Dec. 25. Today is Christmas so we are not doing any thing. A good many have gone down town to spend the day. They will doubtless spend considerable money at any rate. I have not been in St. Louis since we came here. I intend to go down some day to see the sights but I thought it would be as well to wait until a more quiet time than today. We are not very strictly looked after in this camp and have as much to interest the curious as there is out. There are so many artillery companies in this place at present it is very interesting for me to see them when on drill. It is a splendid sight to see a well drilled artillery company going through their exercises.

Things are as convenient in this place as can be. Anything can be got for money that can be got in St. Louis. The morning papers and evening also containing the latest news are sold by thousands night and morning. I said that anything could be got here but there is one article that is forbid within half a mile of camp that is strong drink of any kind which is strictly attended to, which is one good thing. Sometimes the boys get tight when they get to town. As soon as they come back they are marched to the guard house. There is no admission except at the gate and there are men stationed to see who comes in or goes out. If the officers don't do their duty they lay themselves liable to be punished so there is seldom any favor shown in that respect, not so in others however. A great many favors are shown in some respects however more of that when I come home. For my part I have no reason to grumble.

I will send you some of our St. Louis papers once in a while. The news will be old when you get them but there are some very good daily papers published in St Louis. John Gaston is not very well at present. I can't tell what ails him. It is not measles. I think it is something about his lungs. I hope it won't be very serious. He is my best friend and I could not have a better one. All the boys from Wolf Creek have a partiality for one another and are as kind and accommodating as can be. The probability is that as soon as the Regiment is in a condition to go we will be sent out to guard the North Missouri Railroad. The Secesh along it have been burning bridges and so forth and have to be attended to. I suppose we will be as well there as any other place. For my part I don't care where we go. It would not make any difference if I did. We would be apt to be healthier out in small squads than where there are so many together. Any thing like the measles, mumps, or any such thing getting into such a place as this is apt to go the rounds giving them all a call that has not before made their acquaintance but I must stop as I have some washing to do this afternoon.

The sun shines out so nice for drying so I will close for the present your affect son, Peter Wilson "

-----

* This "first comrade" Wilson refers to might be **Leroy Bowen**, eighteen, of Toledo who died December 22, 1861. He is buried in Jefferson Barracks National Cemetery, St. Louis Missouri.

Camp Benton (St Louis) Dec. 29th, 1861

" Dear Brother: I received yours of 17th some time ago and would have answered it immediately had circumstances permitted it. There are so many of our boys sick, amongst whom are John Gaston and John Felter, that we have spent all our leisure time waiting on them. They are some better now and I think they will get along. It is the hardest part of our new mode of life seeing so many of our boys down at the same time. Only one has died so far but one or two are very low. We have not received our arms yet. We might have had some old Austrian muskets belonging to Fremont, but upon trial our officers condemned them as not being fit for use. I was one of the party detailed to try them. Some forty men with 20 rounds of cartridges went outside the lines. We fired at a tree some forty rods off and about one shot in ten hit it. There was a fence a good distance beyond the tree. Most of the balls that missed the tree hit the fence. We all fired at the word and, it being the first time, some of the boys did not take very good aim. The guns kicked some of them over at the first fire so they took care how to hold them the next time. I happened to get a pretty good one. It did not kick much so I could fire it safely. Some of the locks broke in different places, so after a good deal of fun we concluded Uncle Sam would have to get us something better. They carried up strong enough, but seemed out of repair. We will probably get something better soon. We have some old muskets borrowed to practice the manual of arms so that we are in no hurry for our own guns.

We expect to get our pay this week. It is two months since we were mustered into the United States service so we will get two months wages. They keep two dollars per month until we are discharged which is a good plan as most of the boys spend their money as fast as they get it. I am glad that [you] are taking hold of things so energetically and seem to get along so well in my absence. I shall save as much money as possible and send it to you as I get it. If the war ends sometime next summer and we get our bounty it will help some. If it continues longer and I keep my health I look for promotion but it is useless to speculate much in such things. I don't care much how it goes. I have no fears for the future. I intend to do my duty let things go as they may. There are ten chances for dying in the hospital for one by rebel bullets but I think when we get used to the climate our health will be better. Frank has written to his father about the barrel so it won't be worth while for me to say anything about it. It is worth going to Marengo after. You can get some chance to send for it. I will not add more but remain your affect brother, Peter Wilson "

(Undated, probably from Camp Benton)

" Dear Sister Flora: I received your important and highly interesting epistle and shall not endeavor to reply in the same style as I have not much of the same kind of news. We have no girls to talk with in camp for which we ought to be thankful so we have no such doings as is going to happen with you on New Years Day. So Margret is married at last. Some of the rest of you had better be following in her steps. She has made a start. There are a good many to follow. Of course such things don't occupy my mind much at present whatever may have been the case in times gone by. Frank got the portrait of a certain young lady by mail the other day which is a great consolation to him. I don't mean to say that he needed any such consolation, he keeps his spirits firstrate. I think a great deal more of him since we left home than I did before.

I received a letter from Jane the other day. She was well and in good spirits as usual. She wanted to know my opinion in regard to our difficulty with England. (31) Of course I don't know any more about [it] than others that read about it in the papers. I guess it won't amount to much. For my part I am as willing to fight against England as any of our country's enemies but don't think it will have to be done at this time. I would like to see the rebels whipped first, which will be accomplished in a few months if things are managed as they ought to be. However I won't fret if it takes three years. I have got somewhat behind hand with my writing for the last few days so I will conclude for the present hoping to have time to write you a longer letter next time so no more from your brother, Peter Wilson.

[PS] Since writing the foregoing John Gaston is much better, John Felter is also better. Another of our boys has died* which I hope will be the last at present, as there is good hope of the rest. "
-----

31 The Wilson family had come from Scotland only ten years before the outbreak of the Civil War. The event referred to was probably the Trent Affair, involving the seizure of two Confederate agents on an English ship. [See B.F. Thomas, "*Soldier Life*", Chapter 2, specifically the entry for December 19 for his comments on this matter.]

* Perhaps Wilson is thinking of **Joseph J. Alldredge**, nineteen, of Nevada, Story County who died December 29, 1861, a week after Bowen, and was buried in Jefferson Barracks National Cemetery.

Camp Benton Jan. 1st 1862

" Dear Father: I received your letter today. I think I have received all that you have written. There is such a continual hubbub in camp that when I sit down to write I am apt to overlook some things that I ought to mention, so I neglected to mention the receipt of your letters. I am very thankful for your good advice and although there is very little religion in this place still we have two or more sermons per week. Our Chaplain (32) is a very good man, he is also a good preacher. He preaches only once on Sabbath but he generally preaches in the evenings in some of the barracks. There is prayer meeting in some of the companies frequently. I see no reason why a man can't be a Christian here as well as at home. There is so much swearing in this place it would set any one against that if from no other motive but disgust at hearing it. As for drinking I will not taste any thing intoxicating while in the army. I see the effects of it too plain. If I ever come home I will come home at least as good as far as morals is concerned as when I started. I am well aware of the uncertainty of life and the certainty of death and shall try to be ready to meet my fate whatever it may be. There are two of our boys dead since we came to this place. There are over 400 of the soldiers from different states, over one fourth of which are from Iowa, whose graves have never been rained on yet. The deaths of our boys were a week apart. They bury each state by themselves numbering the graves so that if their friends should want them they can be found. Our first comrade's number was 100. In one week the second was buried, his number was 139. (33) So many of the Iowa boys in one week was rather startling but there are a good many men in the army that have not common sense enough to take care of themselves. I think with common prudence there is not much danger of being sick, at least no more here than in other places. For my part I have been in excellent health ever since I left home. But I have written long enough in this strain.

We have not drilled much since Christmas, as they keep a good many holidays here in Missouri. We have been offered some old muskets but have rejected them and expect to get something better soon. We have some borrowed ones to drill with. I begin to see how little the Buckingham drillmasters knew. It takes a long time to learn the whole rigmarole but we are getting along very well and by the spring will be a good regiment, judging by others that have been in the service since last July. You may tell Mr. Gaston that John will be able to write to him soon. I don't know any thing more worth writing. If times were not so hard I would like to have you send me a few postage stamps. We have to pay as high as 15 percent for them here. It seems too much of a shave. I have money enough but hate to be cheated in such ways. I will write you once per week most of the time when I have as good a chance as I have at present.

No more at present but remain your affect Son, Peter Wilson "

-----

32 The Chaplain of the Fourteenth Iowa at this time was **Samuel E. Benton** of Anamosa. [Reverend Benton only served during the month of November 1862.]

33 This number might be 129.

Camp Benton Jan. 1st, '62

" Dear Brothers John, West & Andrew: As I have so much writing to do this week you will excuse me for writing you all together. I received five letters today and was glad to hear from you all. There has been considerable sickness here lately but they are mostly getting well again. We have been rather idle since Christmas but will [be] drilling as usual after today. Andrew asks me how I like living in a t[ent] & so forth. Since we moved into our tents the weather has been very pleasant. It is so much more quiet in the tent than in barracks and healthier that we like it much better. We have not [sic] but we get along very well. He asks how I like to be a soldier. That is more difficult to answer. There are a great many things connected with the life we now lead that I like very well and some things that I don't like so well. We are well used in every respect and our officers are generally well liked but there are a good many very hard cases to associate with. That is the only thing that would keep me from following the profession.

They had a good deal of excitement in St. Louis last night. They have some rebel prisoners in town. They tried to get away but failed. It was supposed some of their friends were going to help them. It was reported that Price (34) would soon be upon us, our pickets or guards stationed some five miles out being driven in by some small party of Secesh. Some of the more credulous believed we would be attacked right away, the more mischievous that like a joke raised all sort of rumors and some of the green ones were badly scared but it is all passed off quietly. There are a good many jokes played in this place. There are some of our men tired of being in the army already but some men can't be content any place. They will find it is not so easy to get out as it was to come. If they were ill used in any respect I would have more sympathy for them. There are some just as good fellows in our Company as I ever knew any where. I think we will be apt to stay in this place some time yet but we don't know and as far as I am concerned I care less. I like to be on the march so as to see the country if nothing more. We may yet go to Leavenworth but it is somewhat doubtful. There is no telling where nor when we may go from this place. Now boys I must finish. Tell me the next time you write how the Charley colt's leg is, how many steers you are going to work next spring and so on. Tell Allen when I come home I will get him his drum. There are lots of drummer boys in camp not bigger than David. (35)

Good by, your brother, Peter Wilson "

-----

34 Probably this reference is to General Sterling Price, who had been one of the Confederate officers at the Battle of Wilson's Creek and was still trying to swing Missouri into the Confederacy.

35 David and Allen were the two youngest of the Wilson boys.

Benton Barracks Jan. 8th 62

" Dear Brother: As this is the day that we usually get our letters from home I will begin before they arrive to answer them. We were paid off the other day receiving all that was due up to the first of January. I will send you fifteen dollars in this letter. I will try and spare more the next time. I had to spend money for a good many things that won't be wanted every pay day.

We buried another of our boys yesterday being the third in three weeks*. In that time over 100 of the Iowa boys have died. It is principally lung fever that proves fatal. I would rather fight a battle every month than idle away our time where there is so much sickness. Lung complaints prevail more than anything else. Any one that has not good health has no business in this climate. There is not more than one-third of our Company able to be on duty at present. The Buckingham boys fare no better than the others. None of them has been seriously ill but John Gaston. He is still very low, he don't seem to make much headway for the last week. It will be some time before he is well enough to be up. Dewit & I have been well all the time. Frank is mostly pretty well. The others have been more or less sick for some time. I have been waiting on the sick for the last two weeks. It takes four to keep them right. We sit up all night in turn. It is not a very pleasant job but there are so few that will do it as it ought to be done. The probability is I will be one of the waiters for some time. I think the change of climate has something to do with so much sickness (36) besides there are a good many bring on their own trouble by eating too much trash of one kind and another. Let that be as it may, the mortality in this camp is more than in the City of St. Louis.

There are five or six recruiting officers gone to Iowa to raise three more Companies for this Regiment and to fill up the present Companies to the fullest extent. (37) They have been trying to get us to take some old condemned muskets but our officers are determined not to take anything but the best of arms. They have got hold of the wrong man when they try to impose on Col. Shaw. We have not received marching orders yet but expect to go to Leavenworth within a week or two. The prospect of going to a healthier place is very encouraging but there are so many orders countermanded and so many false rumors that we may not go very soon. But I will quit for the present. If I receive your letters this afternoon I will probably write some more.

At present good bye your affect brother, Peter Wilson "

------

36 Peter Wilson seems to have had no suspicion of the Missouri River water piped into camp and apparently used without treatment of any kind.

37 The Fourteenth Iowa still lacked Companies A, B, and C, which had been sent to the Dakota frontier.

* This third burial in three weeks must be **Charles R. Whealen**, eighteen, of Marshall County. His remains seem to have been later retrieved by his family for reburial at Marietta cemetery west of Marshalltown; his marker can be seen alongside that of his parents.

Benton Barracks Jan. 10th, 62

"   Dear David: (38) I received your letter a day or two ago and would have answered it sooner had circumstances permitted it. I forgot all about telling you not to write as I am likely to forget such things. I have a good many correspondents and a very noisy place to write so I seldom think about what I have written after the letter is gone. You seem to think I have been a little severe on the ragged Lairds of Tama. Perhaps I have but you must take it as the boy did when the long eared animal kicked him. I guess I have been rather slow about writing home the last week or two. I have been waiting on the sick and as I have been very busy both day and night I kept putting it off from day to day. We have had three deaths in so many weeks in Co. G. There is one or two more not likely to get well. It is hard to see men die through neglect and bad nursing which has been the cause of three-fourths of the deaths in our Regiment. The average of deaths in the Iowa boys is about thirty per week. John Gaston has been sick some three weeks. He is getting better rather slowly. If he had had the same care as some of the rest his chance would have been rather slim for getting well. There have been some of us at his bedside ever since he got sick.

I think the general health will be better pretty soon. The change of climate generally has to be paid for. Yesterday I got a pass and spent the day sight-seeing in St. Louis. There is a railroad from the camp to any part of town. They carry passengers so cheap no one thinks of walking. I visited all the most popular places amongst which is where the Secesh prisoners are kept, the Arsenal, Museum, &c&c. It would take a good many days to see all the interesting places in town but I won't be apt to get out again very soon. Only one can go from each Company per day so it takes some time to get round again. The probability is we shall go to Fort Leavenworth in a week or two. You will see by the papers that Gen. Lane is going to take thirty of the western regiments for his expedition. (39) The 14th is to be filled up but whether we will get to go or stay at Leavenworth remains to be seen. If the wishes of our officers have anything to do with it we will be sure to go down the river. For my part I am tired of doing nothing and hope we may get a chance to show what stuff the 14th is made of. That box sent by the Buckingham folks arrived the other day. It was very welcome, pillows and such things are very comfortable things for sick men. I put one of the pillows under Gaston's head as soon as the box was open. It has done him a great deal of good.

Jan. 13. We have got our guns today. They are not very good but they will do to drill with. They say we will get something better if we ever have need for them. We are all things considered pretty well rigged out. There is little chance for our seeing any fighting this winter. If the war continues we may get a chance next summer. Several regiments left this morning for Cairo. Camp Benton is getting pretty well thinned. I don't think there are more than 8 or 10,000 altogether here at present. They still keep going for one place and another. I get letters from the 13th. They are guarding railroad bridges. I will send you one of the letters so you can see how they get along. I had intended to give you a general description of Co. G some time or other. We have got the name of being the best Company in the Regiment as far as drilling goes. We have the most and loudest swearers. We are said to have more quarrelling among ourselves, which is probably the case, than any other Company in the Regiment. We have some men that Stivers found in Davenport that ought to be in States prison or some such place. They shirk every duty they can, break guard, and go to town. When they come back they have to carry a stick of cord wood sometimes one and two days opposite headquarters.

It is a very humiliating punishment to any one that has any pride but our boys take it as cool as can be.

We have half a dozen Dutchmen, one of which makes us more fun than any other 10 men in the Company*. He is hardly sensible. He is very spunky. The boys have plagued him so much he is out of patience with everything. The other day a stranger came up and asked him some questions. He did not understand what the stranger said so he did as he always does, that is to pitch in with all his might. It was very amusing to us to see the astonishment of the stranger at such usage. But I need not write about such things. If the war is soon over I can tell you all about it when I come home. If it lasts long I will have plenty of time to write. I think the next time you hear from me we will be at Leavenworth. We are sure to go sooner or later. We expect to go in a few days but may not so soon. But I must finish at present.

Give my respects to all so no more at present but remain yours &c Peter Wilson "

------

38 Peter had a brother David, and a cousin, David Galt. [Peter's brother David, however, was only nine years old, this letter seems directed to an adult; also Peter always signed letters to his brothers with "your affect(ionate) brother"; finally, Peter soon mentions that he had received two letters this week from David Galt.)

39 This reference apparently refers to the "Great Southern Expedition" which was to have been led into Arkansas by General James H. Lane. It did not materialize.

* The only true Dutchman in the Fourteenth Regiment, not "half a dozen" as Peter thought, was **Cornelius Joor**, born in Holland. Joor was thirty-eight when he enlisted from Story County, where he was a farmer for many years both before and after the War. He was captured standing with the bravest at Shiloh but following his release from POW camp, he was discharged for illness in December 1862. Joor's career after enduring Shiloh, imprisonment, and the illness that caused his disability discharge, indicates that he was certainly determined, if not outright "spunky", for he enlisted into another regiment as soon as he was well enough to be accepted. In Chapter 12 of "*Soldier Life*", Thomas described Joor as well-meaning and earnest, but unintentionally a source of amusement for the other men. Perhaps he was Wilson's funny Dutchman, but he was also a very brave man, who served his adopted country well.

Benton Barracks Jan. 20th 62

" Dear Brother: I received a letter yesterday dated Jan. 1st. I received one last Wednesday dated Jan. 9th so you see letters sometimes get delayed. It usually takes 4 days for a letter to come from Wolf Creek to this place. The letters you post on Saturday we generally get on Wednesday afternoon. I guess you don't get our letters so soon. You tell me in last nights letter that the barrels we sent are as good as lost. The stuff that I sent in the first one was worth ten or twelve dollars that in the second was not much of mine. We sent them to Marengo in care of Graham of Toledo. Frank Thomas has been writing to the freight agent at Davenport. He don't get much satisfaction. They may turn up yet. If they don't let them go. I have received a good many letters lately one from Doe. Daniel among the rest. It is getting to be pretty hard work for me to answer them, that is I am somehow getting out of the notion of writing.

We expected to have been at Leavenworth before this time. The reason they say why we are still here is they are full out there at present while here we are getting so much thinned by the troops going down the river that they need us where we are at present.

We shall probably be here some time yet at least I won't believe we are going any more until we start. The boys are mostly well again. Gaston is doing first rate. There are a few grunting around with the mumps but they are doing well enough I had almost made up my mind the first month we were here that I never would winter in Iowa again. However I have changed my mind somewhat the last two or three weeks. It has not rained much but the mud is awful. I suppose it is worse in camp where there are so many men and horses. The parade ground is about the consistency of mud when it is ready for making brick. It is very unpleasant, but we have no women to scold us when we come in so we don't get into difficulty on that score. We are inspected every Sunday. We have to keep things in pretty good trim. I sent you some money in my last letter if you have not said any thing about receiving it when you get this, please to lose no time in doing so. If it gets lost I will be more careful next time. I don't know that I have any more to write at present I must say a few words to Flora or rather write a few lines. So at present good by from your brother, Peter Wilson "

Benton Barracks Jan. 20th 62

" Dear Sister Flora: I have received several letters since I last wrote you so I am getting somewhat behind hand with my writing but you must not expect that I can answer all your letters. Sometimes I can get a chance to write and sometimes I can't. At best it is very poor, but I will write as often as I can and let it go at that. I don't know whether those that have left Wolf Creek had any influence to keep things quiet. It seems however since they left there is a great change in their behaviour. I suppose it is all right. I am glad to hear you are enjoying yourselves. We that have left have had better times than we could have expected. We have been rather quiet for some time for reasons already stated but we intend to make that up by and by.

I received two letters from D. Galt (40) in as many weeks. I was much surprised at getting the second one. However I am pleased greatly to think that he is making up for lost time. I was beginning to think he had forgotten all about us. I have written as much as twenty different individuals that have not answered me. Of course they will not be troubled with any more of my letters. You need not think that I am out of humor at present. If you could just take a peep at me as I sit writing this you would at once conclude that I am in good humor as usual. But I am writing a great deal about myself this time. I will now state how the other boys are getting along which can be done in a few words. John Felter after getting better of every other trouble has got the mumps. He is doing well and will soon be all right. The rest of the boys have not been sick to amount to any thing so they are at their usual duties and in their usual spirits. We have some men in Co. G that are terribly homesick so much. However it is not any one that you know so it would not be interesting to say much about them. There are some men that have no idea of going through with what they undertake. Such men had better not join the army. There is no getting out when they are once in. There are some ill-behaved rascals that Stivers got at Davenport that are continually kicking up rows and getting themselves into trouble. They are dealt with pretty severely now. They have been up before the Colonel so often he puts them through and no one pities them. But I must finish, not having any more news.

Give my respects to old Mrs. Young and the rest, your affect brother, Peter Wilson "

-----

40 Possibly this is the David to whom Peter Wilson wrote on January 10, 1862. [It is interesting to note that in his account of the events of this week, B.F. Thomas mentions that Peter Wilson was "taken sick" on January 15. Since Peter makes no mention of it himself, either it did not amount to much, or Peter wished not to worry his family at home. See "*Soldier Life*", Chapter 2.]

Benton Barracks Jan. 21st 62

" Dear Father: I take this opportunity to write a few lines to let you know how we are getting along. We generally get our letters from home on Wednesday evening so tomorrow night I will be apt to get several letters. I guess it takes much longer for a letter to go home than it does for one to come from home to this place. We generally get a letter from home in four days. You know how long it takes to get from here home. However it matters little so as you get them some time.

Things go on pretty much as usual here, the same old routine every day. It is and has been very muddy for some time, the most so of anything I ever saw. So many men and horses plunging round keep the mud very deep. It has banished all my thoughts of making Missouri my future home. The sick boys are mostly well, all out of danger but our Lieut. Gallagher. He is very low, his chance is slim of getting well (41). It is a different thing to be sick here to what it is at home. Some of the boys that died, with proper and good care, would have lived but it is useless to fret about such things. It can't well be otherwise in such a place as this. Our Regiment is fitted out with all necessary fixins. We expect to go [to]Leavenworth sometime between now and spring. We are doing tolerable where we are but we would be healthier out there which makes us anxious to leave this place. I suppose the reason we did not go there before this time is Lane's expedition is gathering there, so the place is full while this place is almost empty compared with what it was when we came here. Gaston is doing first rate now. He will soon be all right. The other Wolf Creek boys are all well at least as well as usual.

I did not intend to write much this time, I have not much to write. I suppose from the prices times are pretty hard with you. Money is plenty here but we soldiers have to submit to a great many shaves. The only way is not to purchase anything but what is absolutely necessary, which is my plan as far as possible. If we should leave this place soon which is not unlikely I will write when we leave and when we get to our destination. At any rate I will write next week, so at present I will finish from your affect son, Peter Wilson "

------

41 Lieutenant Gallagher did, however, recover.

Benton Barracks Jan. 23rd, 62

" Dear Brother: I received your letter dated Jan. 16 last night and among other things received the intelligence that the barrels had got home at last. You seem to get along first rate in all your arrangements which gives me pleasure although my time is taken up with other matters. I am glad to inform you that the Company is fast getting well and begins to look respectable on drill once more. Since we got our guns I like drilling much better although I liked it well enough before. Now however we look more like business. Our muskets would kill a man pretty certain at 20 rods. The bayonet on it makes it about all the weapon that is necessary. I have got out of the notion of getting a revolver as they cost so much and are so unlikely to be of any use. A good many have got them but they are more bother than profit. If I stay long in the army I will get a watch as that is indispensable while on guard duty. We have to be punctual in relieving the guards. The officers both commissioned and noncommissioned have to keep their eyes peeled or they get put through. One of our corporals has been reduced to the rank for a very small offence and the Captain* is now under arrest for three days for not obeying orders. Being under arrest means simply stay in the quarters, not going out any where. It is rather galling for the Captain but Captains have to obey as well as other folks.

We have a good many shines to relieve the monotony of camp life. There is an old big Dutchman that has been furnishing some of the lovers of something good to drink with lager beer. The other day as he was passing along behind our quarters our Major stopped him, got into the wagon which contained some fifteen or twenty kegs of beer. He took out the end board and rolled the kegs out on the ground. The old Major was jumping mad and went into the cook house to get an axe to hack the ends out of the kegs. By this time a great crowd had collected and the kegs by some unaccountable means began rapidly to disappear. By the time the Major got ready to smash the kegs there was none to be found. He immediately began to search for the lost kegs. Some of them he found, mostly empty by this time. He was determined to make an example of some one and continued his search. He came into our quarters and found a keg to all appearances full. He pulled out the plug and strange to tell instead of beer pure water gurgled out. The Major left, amongst ill suppressed laughter. The beer had been drunk and the boys, liking some fun, filled the keg with water hiding it where he would be sure to find it. We have some good jokes but they won't hardly pay for writing.

But I must finish at present as you will be tired of this nonsense so no more from, your affect Brother Peter "

------

* The next day, January 24, 1862, Captain Stivers resigned his commission and returned to his law practice in Toledo. Pemberton became Captain on January 25. Peter Wilson only casually mentions Stivers' departure in the following letter. Also on January 25 Gallagher became First Lieutenant and Simon F. Eccles took Gallagher's place as Second Lieutenant.

Benton Barracks, Jan. 30th, 62

" Dear Brother: I received your letter dated Jan. 23 today. As usual I was glad to hear that you are all well and getting along well as usual. We are all well and are getting along firstrate. The health of the Company is greatly improved. The most of the men are on duty again and things begin to look more promising. There is a good deal of sickness in the Iowa 2nd Cavalry. They came from Davenport some time after we did and have gone through about the same kind of trouble. One of their men told me today that out of their Company that was full when they came here, 10 had died and all the rest but 11 were off duty. Their Regiment has suffered worse than we have. Their duties are much harder than ours, they are out in almost all kinds of weather and are kept busy all the time so we may thank our stars that we don't belong to the Cavalry. I hear no more about our leaving this place at present. There are only some two or three regiments of Infantry here at present with ten or twelve of Cavalry so we seem to be as much needed to garrison this place as any thing. On the whole I don't know that we need care. We are passing the winter pretty easy and if we stay here much longer the spring will soon be on hand. If we go into active service we will have better weather to be moving around than it now is.

Although our work is about the same day after day, still for my part I never get tired of it. There is always something interesting going on. The other day I was on guard. I had quite an interesting time and in order to make you understand something about it I will try and give you an idea what standing guard is. In the first place there are so many men detailed from each company every morning to stand for the next twenty-four hours. The Adjutant of each regiment sends the number of men wanted to the Orderly who details the men in turn.

Guard mounting, as they call it, comes off at nine in the morning. The guard is divided up into three divisions, each division is divided into three reliefs. Each relief has one corporal & one sergeant. There is one commissioned officer to each division. He is called the Officer of the Guard. Then over all there is a Colonel or Major who is Officer of the Day. His business is to ride from one place to another and see that things are done right. Besides the outside guard there is a prison guard. I had frequently been on line guard, but never until the other day had the luck to get on prison guard. I got on the first relief and stationed my men at their respective posts, then according to rule went around and took their name, company & regiment. That is done so that if they leave their post they can be found and punished.

I then took a look into the prison to see what kind of a place it was and what kind of inhabitants it contained. There were some thirty or forty prisoners, some of the most hardened, degraded wretches that I ever saw or expect to see. They were loose, running around something like a nest of hornets, fighting with one another, cursing and brawling. There were four guards stationed inside of the door, four on the outside, so they could not expect to get out, so we had no trouble with them on that score. The four that were inside the [prison] were immediately attacked, first with all kinds of abusive language and any thing that could be found to throw at them. They did not happen to be very plucky and the prisoners soon found it out. They called for me as the guards always do when they get into trouble. If the corporal can't decide the case he calls for the sergeant and he in turn for the Officer of the Guard. I told the boys to use their bayonets if they did not behave so they quieted down for a time cursing me for everything that was bad and worse. The second relief came on at twelve and the third at two, the first again at four. Before I posted my relief that time I called for volunteers to stand inside the door and four of the best jumped at the chance for fun. The prisoners however could see the change and kept quiet as mice until the second relief came on.

Being relieved at six, we went home for our supper and, returned about the time the third relief was going on so we had to wait two hours before our relief came on again. The day and night was very wet so we were lucky in getting on prison guard, as we were in the house all the time. During the time the third relief was on, the prisoners got up a row among themselves. The sergeant going in to make peace, the lights were knocked out and some one hit the sergeant on the head and felled him to the floor. I heard the fuss and taking a light hurried in in time to see the sergeant getting up and drawing his revolver. He was just in the humor to use it, but he did not know who knocked him down so he had to content himself with putting a ball and chain to the feet of five of the worst. It would have been a hard job but for the revolver. They knew that if they made any resistance they would get a ball through their body. After getting them quiet once more we let the fire go out and as they had the windows all broke it got cold so they went to bed. I thought I would get along quiet for the rest of the night. My relief came on after due time and I had just lain down to take a few hours sleep when the Officer of the Day came round and called for one private and one corporal to go with him on the Grand Round and again I must explain a little.

Sometime during each night the Officer of the Day with a noncommissioned officer and a private go all round the camp and see that all the sentinels are at their post and understand their business. We went clear round the camp, only four miles. It was raining hard and very muddy. I had to go ahead and do the talking. When within ten or fifteen yards of the sentinel, he calls loudly, "halt, who comes there?" My reply was, "Grand Rounds." "Advance, Sergeant of the Grand Round, and give the countersign", which I had to do over the point of the bayonet or sabre as the case might be. We found some off their beat which is a guard house offence. We found another drunk and brought him with us to the guard house. The Officer of the Day was a colonel, in the Second Ohio Cavalry. He was not very strict so those that were anything near their post were let go as the night was too dark and wet to make it an object for anyone to run the guard.

But I guess I may as well stop writing about things that you can't have much interest in. I thought I would give you some thing of an idea of what kind of times we sometimes have in camp. There is not a day passes but we have some shines of some kind. I can't describe things so you can understand them as you are unacquainted with all parts of our business. However you can take it just as it is. What you don't understand you can let it go as it is not much difference. We have had Regimental inspection today and Co. G, heretofore hated by the field officers, has beat all the rest in having every thing in the best order and the most men out and making the best appearance generally. We have the fewest number of men and always have the most men on duty. We have been looked after very strictly for some time by the Major to see if he could catch us in some scrape. I guess we will get along firstrate now that Stivers is gone. If he had not resigned he would have been court martialed for insulting his superiors. But I must finish. We are all well, Gaston and all. There are four of our boys in the hospital, two have lost their health and will be sent home, the other two will soon be with us again. Give my respects to Mr. & Mrs. Young and the rest of the neighbours and bidding good bye for the present I remain your Affect brother Peter Wilson "

Camp Benton, Jan. 31st, 62

" Dear Sister Flora: I received your letter the other day and was as usual glad to hear from you. It is all that I need to make me as content [as] can be to know that you are all well and getting along well. I have not any thing to write about that I can think about that would interest you but I must write something. We are getting to have merry times once more and getting to understand ourselves as soldiers pretty well. It takes close attention to get into all the forms of our various duties but if men will attend to their business they soon learn to do all that is required of them in a soldierlike manner. The better behaved a man is the better his officers like him and his comrades also. The 14th is said to be the best behaved regiment in camp. There is only one of our Regiment in the guard house which can't be said of any other regiment in Camp Benton. There are some regiments in camp that were got up in large cities such as Chicago that have a great many rowdies in them. One or two such in a Company keep up a continual disturbance but I need not write about such things as they won't interest you much.

Since the boys got sick we have mostly been in the barracks again and we have not moved into the tents as John is hardly well enough to stay out. So the boys have got into the old practice dancing in the evening. They are going ahead at present so that it is up hill work for me to keep my mind on what I am doing. The Lieutenants are going through a cotillion with the rest of the boys. We are fortunate in having officers that are all we could wish. When not in the ranks they are just as much in for fun as any of the boys. The[y] put on no airs but use us like men which is not always the case in the army which I have seen to my satisfaction since we came to Camp Benton. Lieut. Gallagher has been very sick but is getting well again. He is much respected in the Company for his manly qualities. I think if his Sis is single when we come home I will call and see her but I may forget all about it before that time. I have received but one letter this week from Buckingham but my luck may be better next week. I have begun to keep a list of all the letters received and sent so that I won't forget to answer any of them. Give my respects to Margret McDowall and tell her to send me a few lines sometime soon. I would like to hear from Robert Young. I was much pleased to get a letter from Jane Young but I may as well quit as there is so much fuss I can't think of any thing more to write, so good bye for the present. Your Affect brother Peter Wilson "

Benton Barracks Feb. 4th, 1862

" Dear Father: We expected to have left this place today but we will not start until tomorrow. Some three or four weeks ago we got some very poor muskets. We came very near getting into difficulty with our officers about taking them, but we received them under promise that we would get better before we left this place. According to promise we gave up our first guns and today we have received the very best, lightest, and altogether the best rifled musket in use so we are in good spirits with everything, knowing that if we ever get in sight of the enemy we have got something fit to fight with. We are cooking three days rations so that we conclude we are either going down to Cairo or some point down the river or Fort Leavenworth. We care little which way we go. We consider ourselves fit to go any where that any other regiment is able to go but there is so much confusion it is impossible to write.

As soon as we get to our destination I will write again (42) Your affect Son Peter Wilson. "
----
42 The next letter was written from Fort Henry, Tennessee. Actual war service had begun. [The uncertainty was over. Peter Wilson's Company was among those sent south downriver toward Cairo; they never did rejoin with that portion of the Regiment at Leavenworth. Those three companies in Kansas were now considered more or less permanently detached from the Fourteenth.]

This first installment of Peter Wilson's Civil War letters was published in APRIL 1942 in **The Iowa Journal of History and Politics** -- Published Quarterly by The State Historical Society of Iowa; Iowa City, Iowa

DONELSON

Two articles about the new regiment of volunteers from Tama County appeared in *The Iowa Transcript*, the newspaper of Toledo Iowa; the first one from October 24 1861:

" **Volunteers Leaving**. The volunteer company which has recently been forming in our county under Wm. H. Stivers, left town last Tuesday. Quite a number of their friends were in town to witness their departure, and take perhaps the last parting hand.

There were about fifty in the company when they left this place, and it was expected this number would be increased by ten or twelve upon their arrival at Irving, where they intended to rest the first night. A few others intend to join the company shortly at Davenport. The people of our town very kindly furnished them an excellent dinner upon the occasion of their departure which we fancy was highly relished, especially by those who had been fed by Uncle Sam.

We have not witnessed the drilling of this company, so that we are unable to bestow any compliments in this direction. It contains however some very good recruits who when thoroughly drilled will make first class soldiers. ---- We wish them all as pleasant a time as can be afforded to a soldier, and a safe return to their numerous friends. "

The second was published in *The Iowa Transcript*, January 9 1862:

" BENTON BARRACKS
 Dec. 23, 1861

Mr. Editor,
Below I send you the roll of the Tama County Rangers:

Wm H Stivers, Captain, Tama Co.
G Pemberton, 1st Lieut, Scott Co.
Wm Galligher, 2nd Lieut, Tama Co.
Simon F Eccles, 1st Sergt, Tama Co.
Addison Davis, 2nd Sergt, Story Co.
E G Oldroyd, 3rd Sergt, Tama Co.
George W Walroth, 4th Sergt, Tama Co.
Andrew H Hazlett, 5th Sergt, Johnson Co.
Peter Wilson, 1st Corporal, Tama Co.
Joseph H Shanklin, 2nd Corporal, Tama Co.
B F Thomas, 3rd Corporal, Tama Co.
Wm Breese, 4th Corporal, Tama Co.
S B Betts, 5th Corporal, Cedar Co.
John A Pope, 6th Corporal, Tama Co.
S W Jenks, 7th Corporal, Story Co.
Wm C Hafar, 8th Corporal, Tama Co.
H H Williams, Bugler, Tama Co.
W S Goit, Wagoner, Tama Co.
Stewart Burright, Musician, Tama Co.
Cornelius Burright, Musician, Tama Co.
Joseph Burright, Musician, Tama Co.

   The following are Privates:
Arbuthnot Daniel   Tama Co.
Aldridge J J   "
Brannon Leonidus   "
Bowen Leroy *   "
Clark Samuel +   "

Clark Mathew	"
Clark R F	"
Chambers S H	Cedar Co.
Cheney Alexander	Scott Co.
Casady David	"
Dykeman Edgar	Tama Co.
Davis I J	Story Co.
Edwards J B	Tama Co.
Edwards Charles	Scott Co.
Evans John	Story Co.
Fox James	Tama Co.
Fitch Robert	"
Ford Charles	Cedar Co.
Felter J R	Tama Co.
Fingle Peter	Scott Co.
Grubbs Martin	Tama Co.
Gaston John	"
Hunnicutt Isaiah	"
Heimlich George	"
Heath Wm	Benton Co.
Hait Gideon	Tama Co.
Hastings Leander	"
Holland F F	"
Has Henry	Scott Co.
Jordon Thomas	Story Co.
Joor Cornelius	"
Jespersen Peter	Johnson Co.
Klien Francois	Scott Co.
Kellogg Anson	Tama Co.
Luke Josiah	"
Larew J M	Benton Co.
Loomis Henry	Tama Co.
Lawrance Jeremiah	Des Moines Co.
Mills Jeremiah	Tama Co.
Miller David	"
Moyer J R	"
McClaury Edmond	Benton Co.
Martin J L	Story Co.
McClain Turner	"
McKune J E	Tama Co.
Maholm John	Benton Co.
Overturf J B	Tama Co.
Powel Leander	"
Pierson J A	Des Moines Co.
Shopshire Joel	Cedar Co.
Snelling Thomas	Story Co.
Stoakes Eleazer	Tama Co.
Southwic Dewit	"
Taylor Robert	Scott Co.
Willis Eugene	Marshall Co.
Woodward Rezin	"
Whealen C R	"
Walker Isaac	Story Co.
Wineman J B	Tama Co.
Williams J D	Benton Co.
Woodard L D	Marshall Co.
Young D S	Tama Co.
Young Elijah	"

Young William   Des Moines Co.
Zehrung David   Tama Co.

* Since making out the above roll Leroy Bowen of Tama County departed this life of Lung Feaver.

\+ This very interesting young gentleman a member of the company after taking the oath to serve his country for three years or during the war, disregarding the same deserted his company at Camp McClellan, Iowa on the 10th of November, 1861, for which thirty dollars reward will be paid for his delivery to the Company.

S. F. E., Orderly   "

Notes:

-- The editor of the *Transcript* was Nathan C. Wieting.

-- Simon F Eccles was the Orderly Sergeant who sent this letter to the newspaper. **Samuel G Clark**, a twenty-one year old Kentucky born resident of Toledo, ended up enlisting into Company F of the Twenty-eighth Iowa Infantry. He served honorably and bravely from August 1862 to July 1865 and was wounded at Vicksburg. He later lived in Oxford Kansas. Before this list had even been printed in the newspaper, Joseph J Alldredge and Charles R Whealen died of the same disease that had already taken Leroy Bowen.

-- This is one of the earliest published rosters of Company G (Eccles was still calling them the "*Tama County Rangers*") and it is notable for differences with other rosters published long after the War. Missing is the name of **Andrew H Harcutt**, age 24. Harcutt is found in later rosters listed as born in Germany and a resident of Davenport, Scott County. He is said to have enlisted October 13, 1861 and to have mustered out November 16 1864, after serving three years. There seems to be no military service records for Harcutt on file with the National Archives. His absence from the above list suggests that Harcutt's inclusion in a later roster may be nothing more than a simple clerical error since Harcutt's name almost exactly matches that of Andrew H Hazlett. Another possibility is that perhaps "Harcutt" might have been a POW alias used by Hazlett when he was taken prisoner a second time.

-- Three men on this list whose names are not found in other places within the pages of this compilation deserve recognition for their service. **Leander F Hastings** from Davenport, Scott County was 25 when he enlisted in November of 1861. He was discharged for disability in September 1862 and later lived near Russell Iowa. **Jeremiah H Lawrence**, born in Canada, and Kentucky born **William Young** were both 28 and residents of Burlington, Des Moines County, when they volunteered in October 1861. They both mustered out in November 1864 at the end of three years service. After the War both men moved to Kansas where they spent the rest of their lives raising families on farms in Sumner County.

-- Finally, also not mentioned elsewhere, is **Anson Kellogg** who, together with his brother **Chester Kellogg**, went to Davenport to sign on into the 14th Iowa in October 1861. Both men were married men with children, farmers from the area near Butlerville, the site of the modern town of Montour. Anson, age 33, was accepted into service but Chester, who was 42, was turned away. Anson was discharged for illness from Corinth Mississippi in July 1862. When Chester volunteered, two of his sons, **Amos H Kellogg** 22 and **John C Kellogg** 18, had volunteered together into the 10th Iowa Infantry. Amos was wounded in action at Charleston, Missouri, but John, who was first rejected and later accepted into service, died from illness October 1862. Several other members of this Kellogg family served the Union, including three more of Anson's brothers who enlisted from Illinois; **Dennis Kellogg** enlisted twice and served in two different Illinois regiments; **Lewis Kellogg** and **William Kellogg** signed on together into Company H of the 86th Illinois Infantry. Lewis and William later moved to Tama County after the War, coming to Montour where their brothers Myron and Calvin were among the earliest settlers. Descendants of the Kelloggs still reside in the area around Montour, Legrand and Toledo, but Anson Kellogg moved his family to Parsons, Kansas where he died in March of 1878. The Kelloggs were not unique. Many of the patriotic families in Tama County sent multiple members of their family to the War. Quite a few men on the list above had brothers, cousins, nephews, fathers, in-laws, step-brothers and in-laws serving in other Iowa regiments.

-- For readers of wider histories of the Civil War, like those written by Bruce Catton, Shelby Foote, James McPherson and others, the 14th Iowa served in the divisions of C. F. Smith at Donelson, W.H.L. Wallace at Shiloh, and under A. J. Smith at Pleasant Hill.

-- Articles and letters from period newspapers re-printed in this collection are reproduced pretty much as they appeared in print originally, without many corrections of spelling errors etc.

These two letters from William Gallagher were published in *The Iowa Transcript*, on the same day, November 21, 1862:

" Camp McClellan Nov 3 1861

Mr. Editor,

If you deem these lines of sufficient importance to occupy a place in the columns of your paper, I would be obliged, and perhaps it would not be wholly without interest to the general reader. By this means, perhaps I may be able to comply with those numerous requests for letters, made by friends at home.

Our journey from your place to Davenport was as pleasant as need be, boys bearing the parting from "friends at Home" bravely. They all expressed great satisfaction with the bountiful dinner so kindly furnished us by the citizens of Toledo, and thankful indeed for that lot of eatables stowed away for our use by the thoughtful ones of Toledo; had it not been for this precaution, we would have had to went hungry to bed on our arrival at Camp McClellan.

The night after leaving Toledo we put up in Irving, where we gathered up the balance of Capt. Stiver's men. And next morning at daybreak ere "old Sol" had sent forth his warming rays, frosty though it was, we were on the march for Marengo, in which place we arrived at 12 o'clock, and at 1 o'clock, p.m. took the cars for Davenport, arriving there safe and in good spirits at about 7 o'clock, p.m. We were immediately marched for Camp McClellan and on our arrival there, were greeted with a perfect storm of hurrahing and yelling and whooping such as you do not have exceeded often, for rest assured that the continuous yells of two or three thousand as stout boys as Camp McClellan contains is not easily excelled by anything short of an equal number of men possessed of the same vocal powers, and the "will" to exercise them; add to this the long line of bright "blazing camp fires" glittering in the midst of pitchy darkness, accompanied by hurrahs, such as Volunteers only can make, and you have an idea of our introduction into camp life.

Camp McClellan is situated about 1 1/2 mile east of Davenport and about one fourth of a mile from the Mississippi river, on the summit of one of those gradual sloping River Bluffs, in the midst of "barren or scrub timber" thus rendering it as pleasant and healthful a location as could be selected; this is attested by the small number of men on the "sick list".

As to the scenery, we have a view from the Camp standing in front of our "barracks" away off in the distance. On the opposite bank of the "Father of waters" lays the City of Rock Island, encircled on the left by sloping banks of Timber; on the right the Mississippi flows silently on in one of its grandest curves, still nearer resting upon Rock Island, rises the "Great Rail Road Bridge", on which has been expended so much labor, anxiety and treasure, and to enliven us the busy steam works of East Davenport and Moline whistle forth their shrill notes, reminding us through all the busy throng they do still live.

There is now in Camp McClellan the 11th and 13th Regiments full and the 14th has its compliment of Companies except that one or two companies are not yet full, in all probability it will be filled this week. After a good deal of changing, and a great deal more hard work, we have been assigned permanently to the 14th Regiment. We expected to be placed in the 13th and would have been could we have raised our minimum number of 83 men for the company, but in this we were not successful until too late. Yesterday Nov. 4, we were sworn in as a Company and assigned to the 14th Regiment. Col. Shaw of Anamosa being the Colonel. We go on "Dress Parade" this evening as a separate regiment.

I have had the opportunity of seeing several men "drummed out of camp", for refusing to take the oath and such poor pitiful looking objects as they are seldom appear; it is really a hard sight; to think men should bear such an amount of disgrace, rather than support as good a government as ours. In fact I do not care to behold that sort of drumming process again and I hope I may never hear of a friend who will run that gauntlet. The Tama Co. boys "face the music" finely; all taking the oath without hesitation, except those that were rejected and they were "chapfallen" because they did not get through.

We now have 84 men in the company all good hearty fellows. One would have thought them so, if you could have heard the three cheers that went up for the ladies of Tama County when the Captain distributed those nice "needle cases" or whatever you call them, sent by the good ladies of Toledo. A thousand thanks to the donors! long may they live to encourage and cheer the soldiers who may muster to the call of our country.

Three cheers were given by the boys for the "ladies of Tama Co." and they were given with a will, by one and all, strangers as well as those from Tama County.

God bless the ladies, for loyalty to the stars and stripes is a strong element in their natures.

Government furnishes us plenty of food, the legal rations are sufficient. As yet we have not drilled very hard not averaging over 4 hours per day.

The programme of the days work is about as follows, to wit: Reveille at day break, all hands must then get up, breakfast at 7 o'clock, officers drill 8 1/2 o'clock, orderly call at 10, regular drill 10 1/2, recall from drill

11 1/2, drill again at 2 p.m., recall from drill 3 1/2, dress parade at 5 o'clock, supper at 6 p.m., at 9 o'clock tatoo beats, all hands go to bed, 9 1/2 the drum tap. Lights then must all go out and every thing made quiet. Thus you see everything goes by rule; even in walking about camp, men keep in step.

We are well satisfied with camp life, enjoying good health and fine spirits with plenty to do, so much that we have scarcely time to write a careful letter to anyone, which added to lack of mental calibre may account for all errors and discrepancies in this which I hope you will have the kindness to pass over lightly and believe me to be yours,

Most truly,   W.G.   "

" Camp McClellan, Nov 18, 1861

Mr. Editor:

Sir: Again the Pen is tasked with the chronicling of a few of the passing events of Camp McClellen. And in making this chronicle it requires considerable of an effort amidst the noise and "hurrying to and fro" of camp to shape even an ordinary letter correctly. But to-day perhaps we are a little more lively than usual on account of receiving the new uniforms. The 14th Regiment of Infantry received their coats, pants, hats, haversacks &c., to-day; the muskets are expected shortly. The uniforms are of dark blue cloth of good quality, with Black Hats.

The 11th regiment Col. A. M. Hare took their long looked for departure last Saturday at 10 o'clock A.M. Cheerfully and in their best style they past out of camp. Strong goodlooking fellows they were, and as they passed the lines, the opinion was expressed that wherever they go to do battle for their country they will be sure to make their mark.

The 13th and 14th and a few squads for the 16th regiments are now in camp. The 13th and 14th regiments are expected to leave this week, it is now rumored that their destination will be "southward" perhaps Missouri or Kentucky. This will suit the boys better than any other movement; they all feel anxious to go south and Beard the Lion in his Den, rather than lay cooped up idly in Ft. Leavenworth or any other frontier Fort. Yet if the course pursued by the 11th is to be a precedent for us, we may stay here for three or four more weeks yet.

So it goes in camp; to-day the hopes are high, imagination builds numerous plans for the future, tomorrow they lay torn and shattered a worthless mass of ruins. This is the case not only with the soldier, but also with those "Gentlemen" aspirants for the "feathered nest" who "log roll and wire work" until one is almost driven to the conclusion that "love of money" is taken for "love of country" and papers for the Genuine Coin.

But lack of time prevents me from further remarks, which perhaps you will not be sorry for.

Yours truly,   W.G.   "

Notes:
-- A day before this first letter was written, **William Gallagher** 27 of Toledo, was elected by the men as Second Lieutenant November 1861 when the 14th Iowa Volunteer Infantry Regiment was formed. He was promoted First Lieutenant in January 1862. On April 6 1862 Lt. Gallagher was captured with his regiment holding the line at the "Hornets Nest" during the battle of Shiloh, Pittsburg Landing, Tennessee. As an officer he was not paroled with the privates and remained a prisoner of war until October 1862. When the regiment was reassembled in January 1863, Gallagher was promoted Captain of Company G. He survived battles, and POW camp, and the War to muster out with the regiment in Davenport Iowa November 1864 but then died in Denver Colorado in 1872 from the lingering disease he had contracted as a POW. Captain Gallagher is buried in Crystal cemetery, Tama County Iowa. Peter Wilson called William Gallagher a "first rate fellow and one of my particular friends".
-- Many years after the War, Captain Gallagher's son William, a lawyer from Tama City, donated a trunk containing his father's Company G record books and papers to the Tama County Historical Society in Toledo Iowa. Among the items found in Captain Gallagher's papers are monthly rosters, recruiting records, records of equipment issued to the company, some final inventories of deceased soldiers, and ledger books containing each soldier's personal description. Uniform items like hats, shoes, and coats given out to the men were deducted from their pay and required a signature. A ledger of these clothing items issued to each soldier, with the soldiers' signatures, was also in the trunk.

A descendant of the McKune family has provided two letters for this collection; the first was written from Davenport, November 2, 1861, swearing-in day for the regiment:

" Camp McClellan, Nov. 2 (Village of East Davenport, Iowa)

Augusta,
   You know very well that I am the poorest hand in the world to write a letter so I suppose you will not criticise it very closely. We are all enjoying good health. I believe there is only nine sick in the whole camp and that I call pretty healthy, there being two thousand five hundred men in Camp. I enjoy myself better than I expected to before I left home. I expected to (find) old shabby, dirty huts not fit for any human being to live in but it was not so. We found pretty good shanties at first but did not have to stay in them long. We went to work and built new barracks that are very comfortable and clean and we are all together. Yesterday we elected the non-commissioned officers of which Peter is first Corporal and Frank third. Today we are sworn into the US service so we are fast. Now we are in the thirteenth regiment but it took pretty hard scratching to get there. We probably shall go to Leavenworth but we are not certain of it and don't care where we go so that we do some good. I can not tell you when we shall leave, perhaps not for one month or we may start in one week. There is no telling anything about this kind of business. There is as many stories as there is men in camp.
   Lem Kile was discharged as well as two others not being considered fit for service for which I am very thankfull. I wrote all the particulars when I wrote home that were worth telling and I suppose you have seen that. I intend to write home as often as once each week and you must mak(e) one letter do the whole family.
   Would like to see the prairie once more. The camp is situated on a high hill surrounded by timber so that we cannot see the prairie in any direction. It seems almost like summer, the ground is covered with blue grass as green as it ever was. You must not expect a very connected letter for such a fuss you never heard. Some singing, some dancing, some talking, some reading aloud.
   There is one thing I have to remark, I have not seen one bit (of) quarrelling or fighting since I have been here and take it all around. I think it is not so corrupt a place as people generally think. Tell Hannah the next letter I write will be to her. I bought a package of paper that had a little shield on it which I enclose for Abbie. Write soon, please direct to Camp McClellan, Davenport care of Capt. Stivers.
                                                                        J.E. McKune   "

Notes:
-- John McKune's sister Augusta had married Lyman Edo Wood in the first marriage recorded in Crystal Township. John's other sister, Hannah, was married to Lyman's brother, Joshua Clark Wood, after Joshua's first wife, Elizabeth Kile, died. Elizabeth's brother, Lemuel Kile, John McKune's friend, bravely volunteered with the other men from north Tama County but he was rejected for health reasons. Abbie was Augusta and Lyman's only child, Abigail. The Woods brothers and their McKune wives remained in north Tama for the rest of their lives. Members of their families reside there still today. Peter is Peter Wilson; Frank is BF Thomas.

The second McKune letter was sent from St. Louis on New Years Day, 1862 (the date below is an error):

" Jan. 1st, 1861 Benton Barracks

Dear Sis,
   I received your letter today and two from Hannah and they made (me) so happy that the boys thought I was crazy. It was the greatest new years treat that I ever had. I began to think that I was not going to hear from Hannah but I see it was not her fault for one of her letters was on the road ten days. I got a letter from you some time ago but owing to my having the quinsy and tending the sick, I did not get time to answer it. We have passed a pleasant new years day but I keep thinking what it might have been if I had been at home with my own connections. We had a holiday feast today. I will tell you what it was. For dinner we had coffee, boiled pork and beans and about seven ounces of bread. I tell you that was pretty nice wasn't it. Well supper beat that. We had bread, coffee, fried pork and rice. So you see we have nice dinners if we are in the army. Uncle Samuel don't forget his boys if he does work them pretty hard some times.
   We have lost two of our boys with the measles. They caught cold and they settled on their lungs and took them. Their names were Leroy Bowen and Joseph Aldridge. I rather guess if you could see the expense of this war just what there is here, perhaps 15 thousand men and such an awful as it is to keep that many. What

must it take to keep six hundred thousand. Now to think that the government will allow this war to go on is rather preposterous. The soldiers generally and almost universally think the war will be ended in six months. I think in six months you may look for me for I am coming home just as soon as I can get there.

We have had the most beautiful weather since we have been here. There has (been) some snow since we have been here, but not much and that did not stay on long. The twelfth of Dec. we were out in the country and saw men ploughing. Oh, by the way, it is said that this camp is situated on a tract of land belonging to that Shaw that was sued for breach of promise by (--?--) Carstang. He is Secesh and his property was confiscated. I hope it is a fact but I am not certain. Write soon and every little while kiss Abbie for me.

Yours Truly, John E. McKune   "

Notes:

-- Eighteen-year-old Leroy Bowen of Toledo, Tama County, died of measles December 22 1861. Nineteen-year-old Joseph J Alldredge of Nevada, Story County, died December 29 of lung fever. Both men are buried in Jefferson Barracks National Cemetery in St. Louis. "Quinsy" is an old term for tonsillitis.

The Iowa Transcript, Toledo Iowa, published this letter from William Gallagher Thursday February 27 1862:

" **FROM OUR BOYS**

' Fort Henry Correspondence   Fort Henry, Tenn., Feb.10

Mr. Editor,

So fine a day and fair an opportunity for writing I cannot let pass, and as my health is good enough at present to allow me again to give you an item or two, relative to our position and recent movements, although the noise and confusion of so large a camp as this is not the best place for composition, and to-day there is unusual noise as new regiments are continually arriving.

But to begin at the beginning; on the 4th day of February, while we were laying at Benton Barracks Mo. thinking that our stay there would be still of four or five weeks duration, we received orders to be ready to march in 24 hours, the news creating considerable stir; the sick were removed to the hospital, and all got in readiness. February 3d at 7 o'clock P.M. we all were safely stowed on board the Government boat *Empress*, and soon thereafter we shoved out into the river steaming away for Cairo. We were compelled to leave two of our men in the hospital, one subsequently receiving a discharge.

The ice ran rapidly in the river until noon when a warm sun aiding a warm climate succeeded in clearing it all away, and from whence forward we had but little ice to combat with, thus giving our good boat a chance to increase her speed.

Our first night out we tied up in consequence of a cold rain which rendered travelling very disagreeable. Started early the next morning ran into a sand bar which took us some time to disengage from, as we had a very heavy freight on board, the river being low and boats had to run slow. The banks of the river for 30 or 40 miles below St. Louis are low, and covered with a poor quality of bottom timber. Passed Cape Girardeau Feb. 6th at 5 o'clock. This town is situated on the Missouri side of the Mississippi river, on a high point of the river bluffs, yet how it received the name of "Cape", I cannot say, for the resemblance to a Cape is not very striking. It appears to be a healthy locality, abounding in mud of the most sticky kind, an article by the way that abounds in all the country down in this direction.

There is stationed at Girardeau about 3,000 troops. The sentiment of the place is strongly Union.

At the next wooding place some 18 or 20 of the boys got ashore and ere the officers were aware of what they were at, they had fired an old Cabin inhabited by a contraband and burnt it to the ground, whether this had anything to do with our leaving the shore I cannot positively say, only I understood we were to remain at that place until morn, and I know about 11 o'clock we pushed off passing Commerce, the station of Jeff Thompson, in the night, and the next morning at 8 o'clock we quietly steamed our way up to the landing at Cairo. As to the looks of this place we cannot speak very favorably, only that that disgusting feature of all southern cities, sticky mud, is here unusually abundant. I saw a mule team forcing its way through the streets in mud nearly knee deep; while you folks in Iowa are plunging through snow 18 or 20 inches deep, your more fortunate Southern Brethren are wading the mud nearly of the same depth.

Cairo was our point of destination, but like everything else, military movements are subject to changes, and here we were changed, or at least our destination was. While laying at Cairo expecting to land, 1 or 2 gunboats came in from Ft. Henry with the news that the fort had surrendered, and as we were already on Board it was determined that we should go there. I will just state here that we were honored with the presence of Capt. Stoddard, T.S. Free, and several others of the Iowa 10th. The Capt. and Mr. Free look fresh and hearty and appear to stand the rough and tumble of camp life very well; several of Com. C are sick, I was informed.

The gunboats have proved a success. Nothing baffles the skill of rebel artillerists so much as these gun boats; the "*Essex*" came into Cairo considerably disabled, her boiler had been shot into by the 124 pounder here in the fort, thereby emptying her boiler and scalding some 30 of our men. This boat suffered the greatest damage from the Rebel guns. We left Cairo for this place at 1 o'clock on the 7th. Our passage up the Ohio was unimportant, no events worth recording transpiring save a trial of our new muskets, and the usual amount of cheering, all was quiet.

The river is very high and on the rise, its muddy waters and great amount of driftwood indicate a heavy fall of rain, or melting snow, far up towards its head waters. The Tennessee river empties into the Ohio river a little above Paducah. We halted an hour or two at Paducah; here is stationed a large force of Federals the number I do not know.

On arriving at Fort Henry we found a heavy force already there; two Iowa regiments were there, viz. the 7th and the 12th; the force already on the ground was 17,000 men and the arrivals of the last few days I suppose will not fall short of 12,00 more, and in this is included a heavy force of artillery, so we have quite an encampment.

I will give you a few of the particulars concerning the fight. The ground on this side of the river is not as high as on the other, there is perhaps 400 acres surrounded by a breast work to protect musketry, and perhaps there is in the neighborhood of 150 acres of timber cut down to impede the progress of troops that there sharpshooters might have a chance to pick off the advancing foe. On the river bank on a slight eminence is the Fort, enclosing perhaps 4 acres, the wall is earthen work of perhaps 18 or 20 feet in thickness at the base, sloping gradually from the outside, the inside of the wall rests against a fence consisting of stout poles into the ground and interwoven with Hickory withes; this prevents the dirt from falling in; the whole is surrounded by a wide and deep ditch. The Fort mounts 17 guns, one an immense Columbiad bearing on the carriage the name "Gen. A.S. Johnston, Nashville" -- a 24 pounder, and close on either side is two 32 pounders; the others differ in size. There was 5 Rifled Guns, one of them has busted. The guns and gunners were protected by piles of sand bags. The Fort is said to be one of considerable strength; and then on the opposite bank of the river was another fortification commanding this one. Nevertheless all this proved too weak, our gunboats proved too hard for them; it was they that took the Fort and they that did the fighting. The Infantry on account of the excessively muddy roads did not arrive in time to co-operate and consequently the main body of the rebels escaped, some 15,000. We secured one Brig. Gen. and the gunners; some 70; among these is a Capt. Jones, son of Gen. Jones of Dubuque Iowa. A good many of the rebels were killed, how many is uncertain as they were buried as fast as possible.

It is quite an interesting sight to pass over the grounds and Fort. Near the large gun is two spots of clotted brains still adhering to the sand bags. Here some of the gunners were blown to atoms by the explosion of a shell; another is wounded in the leg. Several of the wounded are still in our care. Logs are knocked from the "low log cabins" and many a tall tree in the vicinity has been skinned and limbs torn from them, all this shows plainly that war has been here.

The amount of ammunition taken is great. Both of the Forts were well supplied with provisions and ammunition. The clothing is principally home made; and the guns are of all description, from a 10 inch Columbiad to a single barrelled shotgun. Several shot guns have been found in the path over which the rebels passed.

Contrabands are coming in, several came in to-day, they say their masters don't like the movements of the "Bean eating Yankee" as they call us.

I saw a "Secesh" letter and song. It is quite a singular relic; they talk strongly of the justice of their cause. But in all their movements and meetings the one predominant feature, "Cotton Is King". This is the matter of interest, the Alpha and Omega of the whole thing.

But I must close shortly as all is stir around me, preparing for an onward movement. All this tends to increase rather than diminish the fury, and then the prospects of a fight looms up in the near future. Fort Donelson on the Cumberland river is to be taken. Bowling green and several others. All I would ask is good health, which I am gaining daily. Our present locality is a healthy one; it is a hilly and heavy timbered country. At present I can say but little more. We are in TENNESSEE in the centre of Secessiondom, and we are to-day disposing of all unnecessary baggage, Hospital stores &c. The health of the company is pretty good and the friends of Company G in Tama County can rest assured that we will strike hard and strong for the cause of freedom and our country wherever we be.

Yours truly,   W.G. '   "

Notes:
-- **Daniel Arbuthnot** of Irving was discharged for illness from St. Louis on February 16, a week after this letter was composed. The other man from Company G who was left behind in the hospital has not been determined.
-- **Albert Stoddard** 31 was appointed Captain of Company C of the 10th Iowa Infantry, in September 1861. Most of the men of this Company were recruited from Tama County. Albert served the full three-year term, mustering out in October 1864. His younger brother **William H Stoddard** 22 served with him and rose in rank from private to corporal to lieutenant and ultimately became Captain himself after Albert mustered out. William served until August 1865. **Thomas S Free** 22 joined them and was promoted Sergeant Major before his discharge for disability in June 1863. Free later accepted a commission as Major of the 49th US Colored Infantry. All three men were from Toledo where they lived the rest of their lives. Two more Stoddard brothers from Toledo served during the War. **Lyman H Stoddard** 21 signed up with the 47th Iowa Infantry, serving from June to September 1864. After enlisting into the 24th Iowa Infantry in August 1862, **Corporal George Henry Stoddard** 29 was killed May 16 1863 during the bloody battle at Champion Hill Mississippi.
-- Before the Emancipation Proclamation, Federal officers often took a politically neutral stand on the issue of slavery. Taking slaveowners at their word that blacks were property not people, however, some Union commanders "confiscated" slaves, or passively allowed them to pass into Federal hands, under the guise of "property". Since the work of slaves contributed to the rebel war effort, they could be seen as legitimate spoils of war. Losing them weakened the enemy. In Union camps their labor on menial tasks permitted more men to carry guns. The self-emancipated slaves were designated as "contraband".

Two letters from Lt. Simon Eccles concerning the taking of Fort Donelson have been preserved; the first letter was sent to the editor of *The Iowa Transcript*, and was published March 6 1862:

" Fort Donelson Tenn., Feb. 17

Mr. Editor,
   Sir: I seat myself down to write a few lines for your paper for the gratification of the friends of the company residing in Tama County.
   The cannonnading commenced Feb. 13th 8 o'clock A.M. At 10 o'clock our Brigade composed of the Iowa 2nd, 7th, 12th and 14th, the Indiana 25th and Sharp Shooters; commanded by Col. Lauman, Col. of the 7th Iowa, made a charge on the breast works! We marched up in line of battle until we came to the fallen timber which is sixty rods wide; we then scattered, and took the trees for it, for the rebels poured a volley down on us thicker than hail stones and played on us with their battery; the bomb shells bursting over our heads and flying in all directions. At this point of the fight Thomas Snelling private of our Company fell, a musket ball passing through his head & killing him instantly; also Charles Ford of our Co. was wounded, but not bad, he is now with the Co. There were three killed in our regiment and several wounded.
   We lay under their fire about five hours; during this time the greater portion of the 25th Indiana advanced within 30 rods of the breast works concealing themselves behind logs and stumps, shooting at the rebels, even when they stuck their heads over the breast works. The 14th Iowa with the Sharp Shooters were popping away at them the same time. We worked away at them in this way until we silenced their battery, with which they were firing on us. The battery was silenced by shooting their men when they went to load; this saved us from being cut all to pieces by their shells & balls for they had their guns ranged on us and were firing very rapidly. After this the 25th Indiana raised a stampede, and all retreated back down the hill when the rebels shot them down by the dozen. While they were retreating the 14th Iowa and Sharp Shooters made them take their heads down behind the breast works. They shot about 25 of their regiment while they were retreating, after this the 14th Iowa retreated man by man, and did not lose a man in retreating. We then formed our regiment in line and retreated back over the hill, broke ranks and lay down on the ground for the night. We had nothing but one blanket a piece. Each man slept on his musket, so that he might be ready at a moments warning. It rained on us in the fore part of the night, and topped off with snow towards morning; we were nearly frozen.
   We took a cracker and water for breakfast, dried our blankets, and were ready to fall in at a moments warning. We stood around our fires until nearly evening, during which time the Sharp Shooters were around the breast works, behind trees shooting nearly every secesh that stuck his head above the breast works. We

were then formed in line of battle, there being a line formed all around the breast works. We expected the secesh to break out, but we stood in line until dark; we then put out pickets, broke ranks and lay down by our fires. It snowed on us all night and we nearly froze.

The next morning, being the 15th, the gun boats commenced firing on them, eight in number, but the Fort lay so high they could not do much damage, so they had the river filled with trees. Their guns disabled one of our gun boats: the rest played on them until about 4 o'clock P.M., when our Generals, Grant and Smith, made a charge on the breast works on our side. The Iowa 2nd went first, the Indiana 25th next, the Iowa 12th next, and the Iowa 14th next. We gained the first breast work, and the 2nd Iowa ran them back to their first battery, when the order came to retreat behind the breast work which we did and formed behind them. I had to call Co. G and form them in the regiment for our 1st Lieutenant got struck with a spent ball and had to leave the field and our 2nd Lieutenant, being sick, was left behind. They sent the shell and grape shot around our heads. Two horses fell within about two rods of me struck with shell. We ran one of our batteries up to the breast work and returned their firing; they planted it within two rods of our company. When they fired, some of our men had to help run the cannon up to its place. They kept up firing until dark when we threw out our pickets and the Brigade lay behind the breast works with guns in hand all night expecting an attack from them, but they did not attack us. We lay in silence all night with dead men all around us, among which was our Sergeant Major who was shot in the head. There were none of our men killed in the charge. J. Fox of Toledo was slightly shot through the shoulder, but not hurt bad; he and 1st Lieutenant are both with the Co. at present.

The long looked for dawn of a Sabbath morning approached, and the rebel bugle sounded. We then expected them to open fire on us so we waited and looked with patience, but presently they run up the white flag and came to meet our officers. They met in the hollow and Smith gave them one hour to surrender unconditionally. We waited the hour and the white flag was run up which made glad hearts on both sides, we marched then into the Fort. The Iowa 2nd first, Indiana 25th next, the Iowa 14th next, and the rest following by thousands, with music in abundance; and never did music sound sweeter. The morning of the 15th General Floyd broke out through the line of McClernands Brigade and escaped with several thousand men.

I took a ride out through the battle ground to day and the dead men lay very thick, they had buried quite a number of them. Our men had thirty seven in one pit. The secesh were burying their dead. The woods was full of graves. The ground was covered with blankets, knapsacks, arms and cooking utensils of all kinds. There was not a bush as large as my arm that was not struck with four or five musket balls. I counted the balls in several small trees and there were from 15 to 20 balls in each tree shot in from both sides. There were trees cut off as thick as my body by canon balls. Every house within reach is used for a hospital. It is hard to tell the number killed and wounded. I have some reports which I will give. 8th Illinois 54 killed, 150 wounded; 18th Ill. 50 killed; 11th Ill. 70 killed; 34th Ill. 40 killed; 25th Indiana 25 killed; the Iowa 2nd, 7th, 12th and 14th 57 killed, 237 wounded; besides these there were several other regiments which I have not heard from but I suppose 400 will cover the killed on our side, of the wounded I can not give any idea of the numbers. Their loss is not known, but I think it was as great as ours, although they had the breast works to protect them. We took fifteen thousand prisoners, but I think several of them made their escape. I think they will ship about ten thousand; Floyd and Pillow made their escape.

We took 15 pieces that commanded the Fort. Amongst these was the old peace maker pointing down the river, a 120 pounder; besides these we got several batteries of artillery, and all their muskets with which the ground is covered. The main Fort encloses about seven acres well fortified with earth breast works on three sides and the river on the other. The outside breast works, as near as I can judge, is eight miles around, bounded by the river on one side. It is one of the strongest places in Tennessee. There was a large number of horses, but no wagons taken, also a large amount of provision and ammunition. It is the report here that Tenn. is in the Union now. We have very comfortable quarters here now in log cabins. The secesh built them for winter quarters.

Our Tama county boys are all in good spirits since the fight.

S. F. ECCLES   "

Notes:
-- Lieutenant Simon F. Eccles 27, son of Jacob and Minerva Overturf Eccles, was a teacher at the village of Redman, Tama County. The census of 1860 lists him as a farmer living with his uncle, Simon Overturf. Simon Eccles's cousin **Jacob Bonham Overturf** 21 and their neighbor **Robert Fitch** 18, along with **Edgar Dykeman** 24 who also lived close by, enlisted with Eccles in October 1861. Eccles was elected as First Sergeant by the men and was later promoted Second Lieutenant of Company G in January 1862. A month after the above letter was published, Eccles, along with Overturf and Fitch and Dykeman, was reported missing in action, all

four having been taken prisoner at the battle of Shiloh, April 6 1862.

-- The officers like Eccles were not paroled when the privates, including Overturf, Fitch and Dykeman, were released on parole to await official exchange. Lieutenant Eccles died while still a prisoner of war August 26 1862, at Madison Georgia and is now buried in Andersonville National Cemetery, Georgia, Grave 13560. From his deathbed, Eccles sent one final letter, "should death overtake me in this strange land", to his brother Allen to be delivered by fellow prisoner William Gallagher. A copy of this letter, a brief personal message of farewell to his family, was found with Gallagher's papers at the Tama County Historical Society.

-- After their release from the prison camp Eccles' companions were not well; Fitch was discharged in December 1862 while Overturf was discharged the following March of 1863, both men disabled by illness. When the War ended Fitch became a rancher and a school principal in Laramie Wyoming where he died in 1908. Overturf settled in Darby Montana. Dykeman remained in the service but died July 19 1863 never having fully recovered from his time as a prisoner of war.

-- **Stillman H Smith** of Anamosa was the Sergeant Major who was killed in action at Donelson. He was widely praised as a very courageous man.

-- The published roster makes no mention of **Charles Ford** or **James Fox** being wounded at Donelson but Captain Gallagher's records at the Tama County Historical Society in Toledo confirm that both men had been shot although not hurt badly. Ford 21 of Tipton, Cedar County, and Fox 17 of Toledo both enlisted October 1861. Ford eventually became Second Sergeant of the Company in July 1863 and was wounded in the right shoulder at the battle of Pleasant Hill in April 1864. James Fox, who was only five foot two, was later taken prisoner at Shiloh. Fox was sent with the other privates to the prison camp "Oglethorpe" at Macon Georgia until he was released on parole. Both Ford and Fox lived to muster out with the regiment in 1864 after serving three years.

-- **Thomas Snelling** 26 of Nevada, Story County, enlisted October 9 1861. Killed in action at Donelson on February 13 1862, he was buried on the battlefield, but his grave today is currently unknown. He was the son of Alex and Agnes Snelling of Story County. He was the first man of Company G to die in battle.

The second letter from Eccles was written to his friend, James Henry. It is now held in the archives of the Pearce Civil War Collection, Navarro College, Corsicana, Texas, and is reprinted here with permission.

" Mr. James Henry   Ft. Donelson Tenn
   Redman   Tama Co Iowa
   Feb 25th 1862

Mr. James Henry
   Sir I hear you are at home on furlow & have been very sick but getting beter I am glad to hear that you were fortunate enough to get home to recruit up in health for it is no place for sick people in the army Our company is in very good health at present Jacob B Overturf & John Maholm are with the company now they were left at Ft Henry during the fight Our 2 Lt Gallagher is in good health: I am fortunate enough to have good health at present I weigh one hundred & sixty pounds ten pounds more than I ever weighed in my life before: Well James I have been in the greatest of victories & never got a scratch: The first day I was perfectly cool not withstanding the bullets whiseled around me in all directions one of our men fel dead from a shot through the head killing him instantly. I was acting Lieutenant as one of our Lts was sick at Fort Henry & we had no Capt: The last day I was considerable excited our Lt getting hurt and was obliged to leave the ground So I had the company to manage
The fight comenced the morning of the 13th and lasted untill the morning of the 16th being three days & three nights the last night we had a hard time standing in the ditch behind the breast work but we stood untill morning when The rebels sounded their bugle & we all expected them to open fire on us imeadiately but instead of that they run up the white flag & I never saw more glad hearts in my life: my heart leaped with joy for the times indicated a verry bloody time that day if they had not surendered & the ground was covered with ded bodies then so it made me glad to see them come to termes we then marched into the Ft. The Iowa 2nd first because they stormed the breast workes the 25th Ind nex the 14th Iowa next the 7 next Iowa next and the rest by the thousand for we had about 40 thousand men to suround the breast works: The Breast works being about 8 miles around bounded by the River on one side with an inside breast workes around the Ft enclosing above acers. The buildings are log cabbens covered with shakes without any windowes in we ocupy them now.

We took 12 thousand seven hundred prisners with one General We took 15 large guns amongst which was two large rifle canon and one large columbia With several pieces of artilery and a thousend head of horses with a large amount of amunition and provisions: I think our boys was 400 hundred kiled & one thousand wounded I think their loss about the same: The place where they broke through was hard fighting I was out on the ground the next day after we came in to the Ft and the ground was covered with ded Bodies the trees shot all to pieces with muskets balls this Brigade was composed of Illnoise troops our brigade was composed of the 2nd Iowa 7th 14th Sharp Shooters & 25th Ind commanded by Col Lauman General Smith & Grant was at the head of our forces: We was ordered to Nashville but it has surendered & Buell army is in there at present so we stay here: Robert Fitch is well & he stood the fight bravely Some of the boys backed off a little when the bullets commensed flying The Gun Boat did not do much good in the fight the Inft: deserves the praise the gun boats only kiled two men: It is the report that Abraham has granted the rebel ten days armistis to consider and make up their minds: The Rebels say that the Backbone of Rebledom is broken and I think it is: I think we will see home about the first of July to spend the fourth of July with you we have plenty to eat Well James no more at present   please write Soon

Simon F Eccles Orderly

To Hellen, well Hellen you must excuse me for not writing to you I am kept verry buisy being orderly of the company: but I expect to have easier times pretty soon for I have been appointed 2 Lt but have not got my comishion from the Govener: but expect it in eight or ten days then I will have easy times for the 2 Lt hasn't much to do: Jerry is well at present Edgar Dykeman is rather under the weather the rest of the Salt Creek boys are well: The weather is verry pleasant here it is coming Spring here the grass is Starting and every thing looks like Spring: The cuntry is verry roling here and verry heavy timbered: The buildings are log cabbens with plenty of Darkies around them I think we are in a verry healthy place here: We will all come home to Spend the 4th of July with our friends I hope & Rebeldom will be put down: Write when you get this Direct (to)

<blockquote>
Simon F Eccles
Co G 14" Inft Reg Iowa Vol
Ft. Donelson Tenn   "
</blockquote>

Notes:

-- James Henry, the recipient of the above letter, very probably was **James P Henry**, the 28 year old resident of Toledo who had enlisted into the 10th Iowa Infantry in July of 1861. The roster of the 10th Iowa merely says James Henry was discharged from St. Louis, giving no specific date or reason. This letter suggests Henry may have been discharged because of a serious or lingering illness. It seems to show that he was sent home on furlough to recover and was later given a discharge.

-- The full identity of Hellen is not clear at this time.

-- Before the War began **John Maholm** was a 21 year old day laborer and his 18 year old brother **Cyrus Maholm** was a farmhand, both from the area around Redman. They had come to Iowa when their sister married GW Sheets and moved with Sheets to the Redman-Irving area that straddled Tama and Benton counties. In their rosters and the census the family name "Maholm" is frequently misspelled as "Mahlon" or other variations. Cyrus enlisted into the 10th Iowa Infantry in July 1861, the same day James Henry signed up. John Maholm soon followed by enlisting into the 14th Iowa in October on the same day that Eccles and their other friends from Redman [the "Salt Creek Boys"] joined what became Company G. Cyrus was wounded in battle in Missouri in January 1862. At the same time Cyrus was recuperating from his injury, John became very ill at Benton Barracks in St. Louis from one of the diseases like measles and mumps that had weakened and even killed many of the men in their winter barracks before they ever even saw combat. John continued to serve but never quite recovered his health; he was eventually discharged in April of 1863. Cyrus, who had been shot in the arm and hand, mended from his wounds and even volunteered for extended service when his three year enlistment was coming to an end. Cyrus was finally mustered out from Little Rock Arkansas in August 1865. After the War John opened a boarding house and restaurant in Montour and then lived in Reinbeck for many years. He owned at least one boarding house there and maybe other rental properties, making his living as a landlord. Cyrus became a lawyer and soon expanded into banking. By 1880 Cyrus Maholm was the president of the Belle Plaine bank.

-- "Jerry" is **Jeremiah Mills** 25 of the Irving area of western Tama County, who had enlisted for three years in October 1861. Salt Creek ran through the Redman - Irving area so the men of that neighborhood -- like Eccles, Overturf, Fitch, Dykeman, Maholm and Mills -- identified themselves as the "Salt Creek Boys" much as men from the Buckingham - Crystal area called themselves the "Wolf Creek Boys". At the battle of Shiloh, several weeks after this second letter was written, Mills was wounded in the hand. Sent to the rear for medical attention, he was not captured with the others. He continued to fight as a member of the Union Brigade until his companions being held prisoner were exchanged and the 14th regiment was reunited. In December 1863, with two of his three years complete, Mills and a few others signed fresh enlistment papers committing themselves to a longer term of service in exchange for an extra bounty and furlough. These men formed the core of the 14th Iowa Residuary Battalion in which Mills served until August 1865. Mills married after the War, raising his family in Illinois and St Louis Missouri, where he was a carpenter. He died in April 1904 and is buried in St. Peter's cemetery in St. Louis.

The letter below was sent to **Edmund McClaury**'s sister Mary. The original is in the possession of a member of her family. "Eb" was Edmund's oldest brother, Ebenezer. Extra spacing has been used here in place of missing punctuation.

" Ft. Donaldson, Tenn. Feb 21st, 1862

Dear Sister,
   I received your very welcome letter today and was glad to hear from you. I suppose that you will be surprised at the heading of this letter but Ft. Donaldson is ours and the 14th Regiment played a prominent part in helping take it   at least we had two hard battles to get it   but that is over and we are very tired for, you see, we started from Fort Henry early wednesday morning and marched over here a distance of twelve miles   it was a hard march on me for I am very weak with the diareah   we arrived within a mile of the breastwork just dark   I was completely tired out
   after laying in the fencecorner for about two hours we were marched up to within a mile of the(m) and a breastwork and about one mile farther North the rebel pickets and ours were within speaking distance of each other all night   in the morning about nine o'clock the order came for us to go forward and for the works   accordingly we marched forward to within about five hundred yards of the works when all at once the bullets commenced to fairly hail upon us and we could not see a man to shoot at   and from there to where we were to the breastworks the rebels had fell(ed) trees with the tops towards (us) so that it was impossible for us to go any farther   so the Colonel gave the order to push forward to a hollow a fiew rods ahead and drop down and get behind the logs and take care of ourselves and (he) turned around and (went) to get orders to withdraw us for he did not dare to withdraw (us) himself   and there we lay for about five hours
   when we first went in there they had two cannons that they played upon us from in front and off to one side and the way they made the shots and shells fly over our heads was a caution   but before they got them low enough to do us much harm there was a regiment of Sharpshooters attached to our brigade   they are armed with long shooting rifles   they will, some of them will, kill a man a half a mile off   they don't fight in any order but their officers tell them where to go and what to do   they go behind trees and logs and that day and finally all through the siege they could not get to us, (get) their artill(ery) on us, at all for the sharpshooters would step up and shot off their gunners   on thursday one of them shot thirty one
   about five o'clock we got order(ed) to retreat one by one   we got off with the loss of four men killed and about 20 wounded   we were then marched back on the hill about twenty rods and ordered to lay down and keep our guns dry   a very sensible order for it had rained about an hour then at least   my blanket was wet through   then we had to lay down with our blankets around us and guns under us   it rained untill two o'clock when it turned and snowed for two hours
   the next day we done nothing but dry our blankets and keep our arms ready to fall in at any moment and that night we lay down in our blanket again and it snowed again as usual that night
   in the morning the sun came out and the snow nearly all went off during the day   about noon we were called into ranks and marched a mile north   when we had gone about a quarter of a mile we heard a quick sharp fireing and then directly after, a loud shouting   and just then one of the general's aides rode up and said that the Iowa Second was inside the works and for us to hur(r)y up   so we started on a run and in a fiew moments we began to meet men shot in the arms, legs, breast, head and finally all over   we were the fourth regiment in the breastworks but it took some hard fighting   about eighty rods from the first breast is

another, but the other regiments did not come up to support us and we were obliged to fall back behind the first breastwork   the rest of the brigade layed down on their arms while the Fourteenth Regiment stood behind the breastworks in line of battle for we were expected to be attacked before morning and we after wards learned that they expected an attack as much as we did   as soon as it was light enough to see, the pickets came in and said that there was a white flag on the fort and in a fiew moments a man came out with a white flag and in about two hours they got the papers signed and they surrendered   we got General Buckner and about twenty thousand prisoners   General Floid [*Note: Floyd*] and Pillow but they escaped in the night but I must close

write soon as you get this and tell Eb to write   Edmund McClaury "

Another letter from William Gallagher letter was printed in *The Iowa Transcript* Thursday April 3 1862:

" Camp McClernand, Iron Landing, Tenn.,
March 9, 1862

Sir,

This fine Sunday morning finds us again at the above landing on the Tennessee River about 4 miles above Fort Henry; halting for the present, for want of transportation, as there is so many troops here for the same purpose. We came here yesterday about 10 o'clock and now lay cooped up between hills of dangerous height and steepness, patiently awaiting further orders. Destination unknown, perhaps Florence Alabama. There is just at this time, here a moment of considerable magnitude, some say one hundred thousand men are collecting at any rate, there is a large "fleets of Steamboats" collecting at and near here.

Preparations for our departure from Donelson were perfected on Thursday 6th, we were all packed, Tents struck, and all the "Camp Traps" aboard the Wagons. Patiently we waited for the order "forward march"; the whole day was thus spent in anxious waiting; and as a matter of course, the boys, for lack of better employment, the meanwhile went to turning up things, yelling, scuffling and smashing up things generally. By the way, the 14th bears the name of caring for No. 1 and a regardlessness for what may come after them.

The other Regiments of the Brigade left on Thursday, and as they did not get started soon enough, we could not move until they had gained marching distance, which kept us another night. Friday morn at an early hour we got under way, passing out at the rear of the main Breastworks of the Fort, taking about the same course that we came into the Fort, striking the "outer earthworks" at the Point where Laumans 2nd Brigade made the brilliant charge on Saturday the 15th and where the 14th Iowa and 25th Indiana on Thursday previous, for 5 hours, lay under a most galling fire from musketry and a "Brass Battery" posted inside the Breastworks. Had it not been for the "sharp shooters" "picking off" the Gunners as they ran from the guns to the caisons a greater number of our brave men would have "bit the dust".

Outside of the Embankment we filed through a belt of timber that bore many marks of the heavy cannonade; here we struck the road leading to this place, fording as usual, plenty of mud. We encamped for the night in a deep ravine surrounded by hills, high and covered with the stumps of a heavy forest taken away to supply fuel for an Iron Furnace, some 2 miles further back on the road. The weak, sick and weary came struggling in after the main body, some three fourths of an hour; for at this time we are afflicted with Diarrhea. Otherwise the health is good. Saturday at sunrise we took up our line of march, the roads growing better, as we now travelled along the Creek Valley. The Country Oh! The principal features besides the lonely good-for-nothingness, is the high stony hills bearing nearer resemblence to mountains then anything of smaller dimensions. Its only redeeming feature is its "clear sparkling" streams of water, and fine forests of Timber. Chestnut, Poplar and other valuable varieties are here seen in abundance.

My impressions of Tennessee will not bear in comparison with our "own beautiful Hawk Eye State". Hilly and rough, the soil is a combination of Clay, Gravel, and redish sand compounded largely with Iron. Thus giving the soil its red color.

As an agricultural country it is worth little, the tillable land is in the valleys along the streams of water, here the soil is good. As to improvements, it appears as though man here did not wish to alter nature's work with any improvements of his. Everything in this line appears to be twenty years behind the age. Here you see the old fashioned Log House; fences overgrown with Briers and Brush; "Old shabby stables", and the farms do not exceed 35 or 40 acres in extent; the most charming feature is the orchard; the size of the trees indicate and ancient date of settlement. Farming utensils, what they have, are of a Pattern that in more"civilized" States were long since thrown away as utterly worthless.

The people are not capable of coping with Yankees in shrewdness; many men and women here of middle age and even of old age have never seen the country outside of their own county.

It is not then to be wondered at, that they have espoused the cause of Jeff Davis & Co., ignorant of the principles of our Government. In fact the majority of the "Secesh" to-day do not understand the doctrine of "Secession", and hence being ignorant of the principles of their own, as well as our form of Government, it is an easy matter to delude them, with such trash as "Southern Rights" Total emancipation &c.

If I had time and space I would perhaps give you a few items in regard to the Battle of Fort Donelson, yet I suppose the "papers" have given all the necessary information, after erasing the misrepresentation, which I know to be numerous, especially is this true of the "Chicago Tribune". History perhaps will purge the records of impurities and those engaged in the Battle of Donelson will live in the memory of posterity when such correspondents as the Chicago Tribune and others of like ilk have long been consigned to forgetfulness and oblivion.

Yours truly   W.G.   "

Notes:
-- The taking of Fort Donelson was a crucial early turning point of the War. Union forces under Ulysses S. Grant had encircled the hilltop fortress commanded by Confederate General John Floyd. The fort was made up of two rings of earthen walls overlooking the Cumberland River. The big guns of the fort had prevented the Union army from using the river as a means to easily transport troops deep into Dixie. As the Union men settled in around the fort the weather suddenly turned to freezing rain and snow which caused them much misery throughout the long night.

With his fort surrounded, Floyd attempted to break out with a pre-dawn attack against the Union forces on one side of the fort. As the rebels poured out of that end Grant boldly sent his men against the opposite end. This assault by the Union army, which included the 14th Iowa Infantry, seized the outer defenses on the left while the Confederates' almost successful escape attempt against the right suddenly collapsed. Grant's army huddled down again for a second miserable night in the snow unable to light fires that attracted rebel sharpshooters.

Overnight Grant prepared his forces for an all out attack as Floyd, concerned for his personal safety, turned his command over to General Gideon Pillow and fled under cover of darkness. Pillow in turn, passed the command over to General Simon Buckner and then he too fled, joining Floyd. In the dark the two rebel generals separately made it to the river and escaped by boat. The next day Buckner, a personal friend of Grant before the War, attempted to negotiate a surrender, sending an emissary out under a flag of truce.

General Grant refused any negotiations, sending a terse message back to General Buckner, who was compelled to accept Grant's ultimatum: "No terms except an unconditional and immediate surrender can be accepted. I propose to move immediately upon your works." It was this famous reply which instantly brought U. S. Grant into nationwide prominence and earned for him his reputation as "Unconditional Surrender" Grant. He had become a national hero. News of the fall of Fort Donelson was met with stunned silence in the South and wild jubilation throughout the North. It was the North's first major triumph of the War, an important victory that opened the way into the very heart of the Confederacy. In celebration of the wonderful news, the Iowa legislature marked the festive nature of the occasion by passing a special resolution temporarily suspending the state liquor laws.

-- Another Company G casualty from the siege of Fort Donelson was **Frederick F Holland** 27 of Marshall County. During the march from Fort Henry, the weather had been unseasonably warm. Tents, overcoats and extra blankets were left behind with the non-essential equipment and supplies. When the weather suddenly turned to freezing rain the first night of the siege, the men were forced to sleep out for two nights on the snowy ground in wet frozen blankets without fires, which could attract enemy sharpshooters. They suffered terribly. Men who had barely recovered from mumps and measles now caught pneumonia. Many had to be evacuated by riverboat and hospitalized. **Elijah Young** 38 of Toledo was discharged for disability from the military hospital in Cincinnati but Holland died there April 1 1862. He is buried in Cincinnati's Spring Grove National Cemetery.

PART TWO

IN BATTLE AND ON PAROLE

INTRODUCTION

The installment of Civil War letters written by Peter Wilson published in THE IOWA JOURNAL OF HISTORY AND POLITICS for April ended with a letter written from Benton Barracks on February 4, 1862. The collection published in this number includes the letters written in the midst of the battles of Fort Henry, Fort Donelson, and Pittsburgh Landing. Peter Wilson was taken prisoner on April 6, 1862, and there are no letters in the collection after March 24th until May 17, 1862, when he wrote from Monterey, Tennessee. He was then a paroled prisoner, having given his word not to fight against the Confederates until exchanged.

His experiences during the time he was a prisoner in the Confederacy are briefly told in his first letter written to his father. For the next seven months Peter Wilson was a paroled prisoner, neither a civilian nor a soldier, and his letters reflect the uncertainty of his status. -- The Editor.

THE LETTERS:

Forts Henry and Donelson, Tennessee

Fort Henry, Feb. 10th, 1862

" Dear Brother: The last time I wrote we were under marching orders. At present we hold ourselves in readiness either for marching or fighting. But to go back a little, we left Camp Benton last Wednesday and got aboard a steamboat with all our baggage, teams, ambulances, &c. The boat was pretty well crowded but we had a very pleasant trip. We came to Cairo under sealed orders. When we got there we heard of the capture of this place (1) and were immediately steaming up the Ohio. I suppose you know where this place is better than I do so I will not say any more than it is some 50 miles up the Tennessee River. We arrived about nine o'clock Saturday morning and got ashore as quickly as possible. As far as we could see in all directions from the river the woods were full of tents and multitudes of soldiers. As soon as we got ashore we went up to the fort where we could see Secesh blood and brains. I don't think there were many killed. I will try and give you an idea of the plan of the fight and how it came out. I don't know how many Infantry and Cavalry there were. It don't matter as they did not get a chance to do any thing. The gunboats were some four or five miles down the river and the Cavalry and Infantry on shore just opposite. The gunboats were to go ahead and shell the fort, while the land force went around to capture them [the garrison] as they ran out. The plan was all right but instead of hours, 1 hour and ten minutes cleared out the nest so the land force was too late. The Cavalry pursued and took some prisoners. The woods were full of clothing, guns, knapsacks, &c thrown away by the frightened Secesh. You have heard a good deal of the Secesh being poorly clad and fed. It has not been so in this place. Some of the Companies had the dinner on the table and so sudden was the stampede they left it all in order for the hungry Yankees. They had about ten acres covered with log cabins and tents enough for five or six thousand men. The fort had 17 cannon from 64 to 124 pounders. They have thrown up breastworks enough to make five miles of railroad. They have cut down a great amount of timber to keep us from getting at them from the land. They have done an immense work and thought that fifty thousand men could not whip them.

There was an Irishman in the fort who would not run with the rest. He said when the action commenced the first shot from their heaviest gun struck one of the gunboats and bounded three hundred feet high without doing any damage. The gunboats are such a shape that they can't be hit so as to do much damage. They slant from the water up so that the balls will glance. The only damage to the gunboats was a ball from a rifled cannon entered through one of the portholes and entered the boiler. Some of the men were scalded to death by the hot steam. As soon as the Secesh saw what effect their guns had on the gunboats they gave up all hope. To add to their trouble the gunboats threw their shells so accurately they could pick off the gunners like a rifleman at fifty yards. One shell hit their rifled cannon and glancing under exploded in the carriage tearing it to pieces. Another fell in front of their 124 pounder throwing a quantity of dirt into it. They were in so much hurry they crammed in the cartridge on top of the dirt and it would not go off. It was found so when our men entered the fort. But you will have all the details in the newspapers so I need not add.

There are somewhere near 40,000 men here at present and still they come at the rate of five or six thousand daily. There are six batteries of Field Artillery close to our encampment and doubtless more in other parts of the camp. This is what has a right to the name of a camp. It is three miles long by a mile and a half wide on our side of the river and as the land is high on both sides of the river we can see thousands of tents on the other side. The first regiment that arrived got all the clothes, guns, pistols, &c. The first thing that took my attention when we landed was one of our boys in a full suit of a Captain's uniform with something like a hedge knife dangling by his side. The clothes were good but not so fine as our officers wear. The sword was heavy enough to chop wood with and must have been made many years ago. The most of their arms were flint lock muskets, shot guns, &c &c.

We have struck our tents on a pleasant hillside. The weather is very pleasant, the country abounds with cattle, sheep, hogs, geese, ducks, chickens, &c. Our Regiment killed two good big fat oxen yesterday. A number of our boys go out daily and bring in all they can carry of the feathered tribe so we are having good times. What the design of bringing so many men to this place is I cannot tell. There is another fort (2) some fifteen miles from here over on the Cumberland that will doubtless be attacked within a few days. My opinion is that they are going into the Secesh in good earnest now. If they don't fight any better than they did this time they will soon be played out as the saying is but time will tell. You need not expect to hear from me very often for some time. We don't expect to stay here many days, we may leave tomorrow. If we get to marching overland which is very probable my chances for writing will be few but I will write as often as possible. I received three letters while on board the boat at St. Louis. Your letters directed to Camp Benton, St. Louis, will find us here but I think they would come more direct by Cairo, Illinois. It don't make much difference if the Company & Regiment is correct which way you send. It would not be best to direct to this place as we may be gone soon. I think they will dismantle this place and leave it to itself pretty soon.

But I must finish, give my love to all and at present no more but remain your affect brother, Peter Wilson "

----

1 Fort Henry was captured by Federal forces on February 6, 1862.
2 Fort Donelson.

Fort Donaldson [Donelson] Tenn. Feb. 18th, 62

" Dear Father: I wrote James before we left Fort Henry and now that another opportunity presents itself I shall write a few lines again to let you know how we fare in Dixieland. We left Fort Henry on Wednesday last and marched over here a distance of twelve miles. We left our knapsacks so as not to have any trouble with them in the battle. The fight commenced the next morning although but few of the regiments had come up. The 14th was the first to begin. We were expecting to find a masked battery and to feel the enemy's strength at a certain point without getting into a general engagement. As soon as we came in sight of the breastworks some eighty rods distant the balls began to whiss [whiz] around us. We had only some ten or fifteen rods further to go to get under the brow of the hill where we were out of range. In going that distance which did not take long we lost 4 killed and 15 wounded. One of the killed belonged to our Company*. Six of our boys were hit in various places but none of them seriously. Espy McKune (3) was hit on the buckle of his cartridge box which saved his life. When we got out of range of their musketry we began in their own style to fire from behind trees, stumps, &c. Pretty soon the shells from their batteries began to fall amongst us, with a sprinkling of grape, canister, &c. The place was getting very uncomfortable when a party of Sharpshooters of which the woods was full, seeing our danger, got to a position where they could pick off the gunners. In a short time the battery was silenced and one of the prisoners told me since that the Sharpshooters had killed their gunners all but two or three and they were wounded.

I need not give you a detailed account of the battle as you will hear it more correctly than I can give it. I will only speak of what came under my own observation. The 25(th) Indiana on our left retreated hastily and got pretty well cut up. We saw the way it was going and retreated round the hill about dark without losing any more men. Considering all things we did well for the first time. It commenced raining about the time we retreated and in the course of the night turned into snow and in the morning was freezing hard. We had no tents and nothing most of the time but crackers to eat. The booming of artillery was kept up most of the time. We lay quiet all day Friday and Saturday afternoon the Iowa Second & the Indiana 25(th) and Iowa 14(th) were again brought into it. The Iowa 2nd (4) stormed the breastwork in gallant style. We came up over the same ground and the sight of so many dead and wounded was shocking. The smell of powder was strong and seemed to have the effect of making me [the men] feel as though they did not care. The regiments got mixed up in going over the breastworks. For my part I got ahead from our Regiment which was ordered to halt and hold what those ahead had gained. The rebel cannon from the second breastwork was raking us fearfully while we could not shoot for our own men of the 2(nd)& 7(th) were all mixed up. For the same reason they directed their guns on us. All those inside were ordered behind the breastworks out of the fire, the 2(nd) & 7(th) retreated and formed behind us and took their station on our right along the breastworks. Our cannon were soon playing against the rebel batteries with good success and towards evening the battle ceased and we stood to our guns another night expecting an attack. The wounded were taken off the field. Some forty or fifty dead lay on the hill where we had came up. Only one* of our Regiment was killed that day, a good many were wounded. While I was inside the breastworks there were a good many killed and wounded all around me. I cannot understand why so many of us escaped. The balls flew so thick, sometimes within an inch or two of my head, it seems astonishing how I escaped. I have great reason to be thankful for health and preservation from the many dangers through [which] we have passed.

Sabbath morning preparation was made to storm the entire fort. Everything was in readiness for the attack when the white flag was run up and the fort surrendered & we were glad to have it end so. For my part I expected to see the hardest fight that day. I don't know how many have been killed as the fortifications are some five miles long. The hardest fighting was done between some Illinois regiments and the enemy on the left wing. Some of our boys that visited that part of the battle ground saw as many as 60 in one pile laid out for burial but I may as well finish. All the Wolf Creek boys are unhurt and there are not better or braver soldiers in the Army, that we have had a chance to prove. Some of our boys got frightened and ran like sheep but they were not many. I will write more as soon as possible, so no more from your affect son, Peter Wilson.
 [PS] The number of prisoners taken was about 15 or 16000. "
----
3 **John E. McKune**, aged twenty-one, from Tama County, is listed on the roster of Company G. He died at Macon, Georgia, on August 9, 1862, while a prisoner of war. Roster and Record of Iowa Soldiers in the War of the Rebellion, Vol. II, p. 824.

4 A brief account of the Second Iowa at Fort Donelson is given in Cole's "*Iowa Through the Years*", pp. 291, 292.

* Tom Snelling from Nevada, Story County was the one man killed of Company G. He was the twenty-six year old son of Alex and Agnes Snelling. The location of his grave is not known at this time. Captain Gallagher's Company books archived at the Tama County Historical Society show that **James Fox** of Tama County and **Charles Ford** of Cedar County were among the wounded.

Fort Donaldson [Donelson], Feb. 19th, 62

" Dear Brother: I wrote to father yesterday but as this is a rainy day and we have nothing to do I will write a few lines more to give you some idea what kind of a place this is. The country between Fort Henry and Donaldson [Donelson] is as rough as Connecticut and the soil very poor. The timber is good both in quantity and quality. There are not many houses and the slaves have all been carried off. We passed several plantations that had been vacated. We had quite a pleasant nights rest in the timber the first night, thinking what scenes the next day would bring forth. We supposed the hardest fighting was done by our Brigade but after the battle we found that much the hardest fighting was done on the right some three miles from our position. The breastworks & rifle pits extend about six miles along the heights back about two miles. The country is very bluffy about here. I was much surprised at the surrender of so strong a place. If they leave as many of our troops here as we had to fight we can hold it against any thing Jeff [Jefferson Davis] can send against us. We received the thanks of General Grant last evening on dress parade for taking the largest number of prisoners ever taken on this continent.

There were only two brigades engaged in the principal part of the fighting so it is likely we will get to stay here for the present to garrison the Fort. Our Brigade is composed of the Iowa 2(nd), 7(th), 14(th); Indiana 25th & Col. Burges Sharpshooters*. We all had a hand in taking the Fort. The Iowa 2nd led the charge on the breastworks. They did it in gallant style. They are an old regiment, they have been in the service since last April and have been all over Missouri. My friend, Thomson, (5) from Long Grove was the second man on the breastworks and came out safe. The incessant cracking of musketry and roar of cannon, whizzing of balls of all kinds, the dead and wounded, made a scene I shall never forget. There were a good many killed and wounded within a few feet of me. We can tell by the sound what kind of balls are being fired at us. For my part I dreaded shells more than any thing else. I had no fear of being hit myself but every time a shell fell among us it was sure to kill some one or more. We had not gained the heights more than half an hour before we had four Parrott guns playing on the rebel battery. Our Regiment was ordered to take their stand to support the batteries. The enemy's guns poured shell, grape, canister, and every other kind of missiles amongst us but we had a sheltered position so they could not hurt us much.

We knew we had gained the key to the fort when we had taken the heights and expected they would try to retake them in the night and as we could not be reinforced before morning we expected a hard time but we were agreeably disappointed. I guess they were as much afraid we would attack them in the second breastwork as we were that they would attack us in the first. The battle on the right was fought in the forenoon. The rebels came out five or six thousand strong and charged on a battery supported by some Illinois regiment. They were successful in taking it but it was retaken and a furious battle was fought. The rebels had all the advantage in the ground and numbers but were finally driven back with a loss of not less than 400 killed and three times that many wounded. The loss among the Illinois regiment was full as much as theirs. Any one going over the battlefield cannot form a very correct estimate of the number. You will see in the official report how many were killed and wounded on both sides.

I have had my curiosity satisfied as far as being in battle is concerned and have no wish to be in another but I guess we have only made a beginning. However we must take our chance. We may be in a good many battles before we get into as hot places as we have been in. The first time we got into the bullets we were not expecting it so we had no time to get scared. The second time I was somewhat excited before we got into the battle but when we got among the balls my nerves were as calm as they are at present. I did not know whether I had pluck enough to go through but now I have no fear but I can do my duty, although I know the danger is great. I would rather now be in a soldier's grave than to have acted as some of our boys did. It is disgraceful to see some of our greatest fist-cuff rowdies running away into the timber and not coming back until the battle is over, then hold up their heads and try to make a joke of it. They will not hear the last of it very soon. I am proud to tell you that all the Wolf Creek boys did their duty bravely, not one of them showing the least fear. We are glad that our little party are all alive yet and in good health considering the hardships we have gone through.

Since we left St. Louis we had no accommodations fit for a human for about two weeks, but we were more concerned about taking the fort than we were about our personal comfort. For my part I feel firstrate after lying in the timber in very rainy, snowy, mean weather and eating hard crackers. Now we have got into good quarters and have plenty to eat. The Secesh had log cabins enough and tents to accommodate fifteen thousand men. We stepped right into their shoes and are doing first rate. I received two letters yesterday, one from you and one from D. Galt. I understand Stivers (6) has been telling we were homesick and out of health and spirits. It is just as I expected. He knew we did not like him so he takes the only way left to spite us. I weighed myself yesterday and found I am as heavy as usual. I believe the other boys, Frank (7) in particular, are stouter than when we left home. However it don't matter. Campaigning in the winter is pretty tough business but when I left home I made up my mind to take things as they come and so far I have not grumbled. But I may as well finish. You must overlook bad writing &c as the chance for writing is poor. Write to Co. G 14th Reg., Cairo, Ill., that will be the most direct route. No more from your brother, Peter Wilson "

----

5 This was, apparently, Mark L. Thomson, born in Scotland and a resident of Long Grove, Scott County. He later became Captain of Company C, Twentieth Iowa Infantry.

6 W. H. Stivers had resigned his commission as Captain on January 24, 1862, just before the Regiment moved into battle. He was later a member of a law firm at Toledo.

7 Probably Benjamin Franklin Thomas.

* Lieutenant Colonel **John M. Birge** of St. Louis commanded a regiment of skilled marksmen armed with deer and target rifles who fought as individuals scattered out behind logs and stumps, treetops and foxholes rather than as companies working in lines in unison. Known as Birge's Western Sharpshooters, they had been brought together from many midwestern States under the special patronage of Major General John C. Fremont. Designated to be used as skirmishers, they wore distinctive caps decorated with squirrel tails and sometimes wore green uniforms. Their rifles were equipped without bayonets but usually with telescopic sights that gave them a very effective range of 500 yards or better. Extremely informal, the Sharpshooters were often deployed with the simple command, "Hunt your holes, boys". With sharp eyes and steady hands, the Sharpshooters at Donelson picked off the rebel artillery crews who were shelling the Union troops encircling the fort. By forcing the Confederates to keep their heads low, they rendered many of the rebel cannon useless during the siege, winning the gratitude and admiration of the regular line-of-battle soldiers.

Fort Donelson, Feb. 22nd, 1862

" Dear Sister Jane: Since I last wrote you we have seen some stirring times. We left St. Louis some three weeks ago and after a pleasant passage of four days arrived at Fort Henry the day after it was taken from the Secesh. We stayed there a day or two and then marched to this place, some twelve miles. We took our stand something about a mile from the enemy's rifle pits and the first night passed away quietly. We slept on the ground and as there were plenty of dry leaves we spent the night quite comfortably. The next morning we got into a fight with the Secesh for the first time, we lost four killed and twenty wounded. The next night was very unpleasant, first rain then snow, and finally pretty hard frost. We had no tents and spent a sleepless night. The next day we had no fighting but we were prepared for an attack. The next day, Saturday, the battle became general on all sides. Our Brigade stormed the heights on the left while a furious battle raged on our right. The enemy tried to break out and get away on the right but were driven back after some four or five hundred were killed on each side. There was some fifty of the Iowa 2nd killed on the left, they being the advance regiment in storming the breastworks. There were generally ten wounded where one was killed so you have some idea of the horror of such business. I hope we may be spared the necessity of seeing any more such sights.

The dead on our side are all buried so are most of the enemy. The prisoners are all sent off and we are making ourselves comfortable in the enemy's log huts and tents. We found plenty to eat when we got into the Fort and satisfied our hunger after four days on hard crackers and no rest at night. Nothing but the excitement could have kept us up through such hardships as we endured. The artillery kept up an incessant roar through the day and skirmishing by the pickets went on briskly every night. None of our little party from Wolf Creek has got hurt. Espy McKune got hit on the buckle of his cartridge box belt. The buckle is about two inches square and a quarter of an inch thick. The ball hit it, glancing off, tearing his coat and bending his buckle considerably. The little piece of brass saved his life. Only one of Co. G was killed and none seriously wounded. Some six or eight were hit in various places through their clothes but a miss of an inch is as good as a mile. Some of the balls came pretty close to my head but I never got touched.

We are under marching orders again and expect to go up the river tomorrow as far as Clarksville. We don't know how it will go at Nashville. There may be some hard fighting there but I guess we will be successful. I think now we have got started the war will soon be finished one way or another. It is more satisfactory than laying round idle. But I must finish. This leaves us all well. I have written several letters home since the Battle (8) and got several letters every week. I am glad to hear that they have such good times in my absence. I hope to be with them in the course [of] the summer if I have the luck to get through safe. If it is my fate to die the soldier's death I will try and be found doing my duty to the last. I am proud of the bravery shown by the Wolf Creek boys in the time of battle. They knew their danger and like brave men faced it. But my letter is long enough, so good bye, your affect brother Peter.

[PS] Write to Co. G 14th Iowa Vol., Cairo, Ill., that is the most direct route to this place. Fort Donelson is in Stewart Co., Tennessee. "

----

8 These letters reveal the psychological effects of the first battle on the young soldier from a peaceful community. Like many other serious-minded young men, he seems to have wondered how he would react to personal danger. He also sought for an explanation of his excitement under fire.

Fort Donelson, Feb. 24th, 1862

" Dear Sister Flora: It is some time since I wrote you. I did not expect to have as much leisure after our first battle as we have had. We expected to march on Nashville some days ago, but it seems we are not to have any fighting at that place. The news from all points seem to be encouraging to our side. I see the Chicago papers give all the praise to the Illinois troops. They scarcely mention the Iowa regiments. However the mistakes will probably be corrected when the truth becomes known. The Illinois boys fought on the right and had by far the hardest battle. While they were engaged on the right our Brigade stormed the works on the left. There were some fifty or more of the Iowa 2nd and 7th killed in getting up to the breastworks and some 200 wounded. Our Regiment was the fourth inside the works. We had only our Sergeant Major (9) killed and a few wounded in getting that far.

We were then ordered to fall back behind the breastworks and give room for the artillery which had just come up. It was our good fortune not to get into as hard fighting as some other regiments. If we had we would have done as well as they did. There was not a regiment in our Brigade but would have been willing to have taken the lead in storming. The Iowa 2nd being an older and better drilled regiment than any of the rest was chosen and nobly did they sustain the credit of Iowa soldiers. I talked with some of the prisoners that had fought them. They said they lost all hope when they saw that no matter how many fell in coming up the hill they never wavered. As soon as the boys got near enough to use the bayonet the Secesh broke and ran and many a Greycoat got a bullet in his back in the race. But I may as well quit writing about the battle as the more I explain the less you will understand, so I will write a little about how we spend our time.

At present some of our boys live in tents and some in log cabins. Our mess live in one tent. We have not done any thing since we came into the Fort but cook and eat. We appropriated flour, rice, molasses, sugar, &c when we came into the Fort and get our rations as usual from the Commissary. We make flapjacks, biscuits, cook rice, have plenty of all that is necessary to eat and tea & coffee to drink so we have great times cooking and fare sumptuously every day. We had all our clothes dirty when we came here but now we have our washing done up again. There are some of the best springs of soft, clear water here that I have seen. The soil is gravely and soon dries after rain of which there is no lack here at present. Today it is very pleasant something like May. It is very different from the weather we experienced the time we lay before the breastworks. I suppose the spring begins about this time in this part of the country.

We don't know how long we may remain here. The way thinks look now I think there is more likelihood of our going down the Mississippi than up the Cumberland. For my part I am not particular where we go, only as we get a chance to do as much good as has been done this time. I can't say that I like such times as we have gone through lately but I would rather they would pitch in and finish what is so well begun. I am not tired of soldiering yet, but I don't care how soon the thing is decided, only so as the rebels are completely brought under. Some of them, after being so badly whipped here, did not hesitate to say that one of their soldiers was good for half a dozen of ours. I think they will begin to lose conceit of themselves by and by. They look more like a colony of Irishmen just come over than they do like soldiers. Their clothes are all homespun, mostly Kentucky jeans. They all carried heavy clumsy knives made out of files. I guess they did not do much execution with them. Some of their best regiments were armed with six-shooting rifles. They are a splendid gun and they used them with deadly effect on the Iowa 2nd as they came up.

I had not intended to write so much about the Battle but it seems to run in my head more than anything else at present. We have gone all round where hardest fighting was done. Some places where the brush was very thick it is mowed off by the bullets. It is surprising that so many of the men came out alive as did. There is not more than one man killed out of 500 shots fired. I know that hundreds of balls came within a few feet of me the first day, but they could not get a fair shot at us after we got under the brow of the hill. We carried on the fight in bushwhacking style for several hours as we could neither advance nor retreat until the Sharpshooters silenced the guns by picking off the gunners. We had come over an open space of some ten rods where we were exposed to their fire while we could only see by the smoke where they were. It was rather an uncomfortable predicament we had got into but as soon as we got into as good a position as they had we had a more equal time. As soon as a head raised above the breastwork it was the mark for a dozen shots. In that way we kept things safe until we got out of our unpleasant situation. Few of the Regiment had yet come up and it was not the calculation to make an attempt to go into the works. It was supposed there were some masked batteries in the vicinity and we were sent down to find out so we blundered ahead a little too far but we got out pretty safe considering the place we had got into. But I must finish. There is much that I might write but I can't get it down in a way that it could be understood, so no more from your affect brother, Peter Wilson "

----

9 Stillman H. Smith, Sergeant Major of the Fourteenth Iowa, was killed in action at Fort Donelson on February 15, 1862. His residence was Anamosa.

Fort Donelson, Feb. 28th, '62

" Dear Brother: It is not long since I wrote you but as I received yours of the 13th yesterday and the mail is not carried regularly to this place I again take my pen and sit down not to a desk or on a chair but on the ground with my portfolio on my knee to scratch a few lines because I have nothing else to do and no disposition to do it if I had. The weather is just warm enough to lie in the shade through the day and sleep good at night. We were inspected today for to be in readiness to receive our pay which we expect to get in a few days. There is no express office here and I don't know how safe it is to send money from here in a letter. However I will see in a few days and send you what I can spare when I get it. We do not get the news here as we used to in St. Louis so we are not posted in what is being done in the other Divisions of the Army but I would rather live here than up there as it is more healthy here and a very pleasant place.

The Sutlers have no opposition here and they run up prices accordingly. Still there are not as many ways of spending money as there were in St. Louis. We have not done any work or drilling of any kind since we came here to amount to anything. We spend our time in cooking, washing, and lounging about. If there was any chance for mischief we would be into it. It is against the rules to go out into the country so we have to content ourselves in the Fort. There is room enough to tramp around considerable. We have been all round over the various battle grounds and discussed the various merits and demerits of Secesh and Union soldiers until the subject is worn out. It seems a wonder that we got into this place without more fighting than we did. I see the Chicago papers give the Illinois boys all the praise not wishing to admit that some of their regiment, though having done their best, were cut to pieces and driven back. The Chicago Tribune says it being necessary to do something to change the fortunes of the day Col. Lauman's Brigade was ordered to make an attack on the left and storm the breastworks which was done with a will every regiment coming up the hill on a double quick cheering loudly as they went over. I believe that the advantage then gained discouraged the enemy more than their heavy losses on the right. However I don't intend to take any honours from the Illinois boys that justly belong to them but the Iowa boys first planted the Stars & Stripes on the Fort and they don't like to see the fact overlooked. I guess the Iowa papers will not pass us by if the Illinois papers should. Governor Kirkwood is here at present. I guess it does the old chap good to find us getting along as well as we are in this outlandish place. Your brother Peter Wilson "

[Fort Donelson] March 2nd, 62

" Dear Sister: I don't recollect whether I have written you since we came here so I will scratch a few lines now to keep our correspondence from falling off. We have had an election of officers to fill the vacancy occasioned by the resignation of our Captain. The Lieutenants & Orderly (10) were promoted in order and the Company then elected Joseph Shanklin (11) Orderly, and John Gaston to his place of Second Corporal. Shanklin was not the choice of the Wolf Creek boys but the Salt Creek party beat us by only one majority. It don't make much difference as Shanklin is fully qualified to fill the office. There are men in the Company that are nothing but privates that could fill any office in the Company. But you will not take much interest in such things.

The weather is very rainy here, at present it rains about every other day. The river is very high and steamboats are going up every day with troops. As much as ten regiments went up today. I cannot even guess what is going on that so many troops are wanted up the river as it is understood here that the fighting is about over in this State. However we don't know much about what is going on and we must content ourselves to wait and get the news three or four days old. After all we are getting on very comfortably. I sometimes think we are getting spoiled for something to do. We have had the most glorious do nothing time imaginable. When it don't rain the sun shines warm as it does in Iowa in May, the hillsides where they are not tramped too much are getting green so you see it is pleasant to be out of the snows of Iowa for one winter.

It would amuse you some to see us getting our meals cooked. Ep* and Frank are our chief cooks. The rest help according to their strength, skill, and disposition. We get along very agreeably and set a good example to some of the more quarrelsome messes. We have more than we can eat furnished by the Commissary and sometimes add some little luxury from our own pockets. It is about all we have to attend to at present and we get up some grand feasts. I understand from James' letter and others that Cousin Margret (12) is married and also my old friend W. Spencer. The former did not take me unawares but the latter did. Billy will probably find it is easier to get a wife than to get quit of her if they don't agree. I believe I would not swap positions with him. My term is only three years or during the war, his is rather a different arrangement. However I wish them all happiness in their new relations. Give my respects to Margret's husband if you should see him and for the other it is not particular.

March 3d. You will see by the dates that I make rather slow progress with this letter. I just write a piece when I feel like it as the saying is but I will finish today and get it started. The probability, from the appearance of things at present, is that we will not remain here much longer but I will write to father before we start as it is not likely I will have much chance to write for some time after we leave if we go where we expect to. But my letter is long enough. Give my respects to all the girls first and the boys afterward or let it go just as you please. Good by, Your affect Brother Peter Wilson.

[PS] I received two letters from home today, one from father and one from Agnes McMillan. (13) Father seems to think things move very slowly in the War Department. I guess if he had come through as tough times as we did from the time we left St. Louis until we got into Fort Donelson he would get over some of his hurry for having things go off before they are ready.

I am of the opinion that things will be all right before long. I have confidence in General Grant after seeing the way he managed things here. However time will tell. It is much easier for those at home to talk than it is for those in the field to surmount the difficulties of a campaign at this time of the season.

Your brother Peter. "

----

10 Under this plan of promotion First Lieutenant George Pemberton became Captain, Second Lieutenant William Gallagher became First Lieutenant, and First Sergeant Simon F. Eccles became Second Lieutenant. The First Sergeant was then referred to as the Orderly Sergeant.

11 Joseph A. Shanklin became Second Lieutenant about a year later. [For more on the voting see B.F. Thomas, "*Soldier Life*", Chapter 9.]

12 This was a common name in the Wilson clan. The letters do not indicate to which family Margret belonged.

13 Agnes McMillan was one of the Wilson cousins, her mother being a sister of John Wilson.

* "Ep" is John Espy McKune.

Encampment in the Woods near Fort Henry March 11th, 1862

" Dear Father: We have been in our present encampment several days waiting for a chance to get transported to some other point. There are such crowds of soldiers going up the river it keeps the steamboats busy to get us all moved around. It is impossible to make any speed going by land in such a country as this, the roads are so bad. Report says we are going to Alabama. What the prospect is when we get there we know little about. Of one thing we may be pretty sure that is if there is fighting to be done the Iowa Brigade will get their share of it. General Lauman **(14)** is bound to get his own name up if his men do pay for it. He is a very brave man and runs more risk than any of his men. He seemed to be as much at home when the battle was at its heat as if he had been in no danger. Such a man can see what ought to be done in any emergency. The river is so high the gunboats are getting much further up than they expected to have done. I guess if we have good luck there will be something important done here before long.

Savannah, March 16, 1862: You will see by the date that it is some time since I commenced writing this letter and also that it is some further into the wilderness as we call it. As much as we have [seen] of Tennessee it is more like a wilderness than anything else. We left our encampment down the river two days ago and ran up to this place. Here we find a good many boats full of soldiers waiting for further orders. Part of our Brigade is further up the river and the probability is that we will join them if the rebels in this part of the country show fight. But I need not even guess what place we will go to, for things change so quick there is no telling where we may be ordered. The 2nd, 7th, 8th, 12th, 13th, and 14th Iowa Regiments are here at present so that in the next battle if one should come off in this part of the country Iowa will be largely represented.

I received a letter from Mr. Hier today dated Feb. 5th, also one from W. A. Daniels dated March 2d so you see our mail don't find us very regularly. I have not received any answers from home to my letters from Fort Henry or Donelson but from Daniels I suppose it is owing to the irregularity of the mails. Frank Thomas received letters from home today. They say you were very uneasy when it was rumored the 14th was cut up. You must not believe rumors that are always circulated at such times. I have been astonished to see how far wrong the newspapers get in giving the details of the taking of Fort Donelson. They got the thing considerably mixed up. The first rumor is never correct. However if you feel as unconcerned in regard to our safety as we do ourselves you will get along.

I am glad to see the way the Army in this part of the country is being pushed along. If things are as brisk in every other Division the Secesh will have to do better than they have done or they will soon be used up. Going through the country, sometimes on foot sometimes on the steamboats is, although our accommodations are pretty rough, very much to my liking. I have enjoyed myself more since we left St. Louis than I could have expected. The rainy weather is the only uncomfortable weather we have. I got a good oil cloth Secesh blanket at Fort Donelson so it don't trouble me much. The weather is quite warm, the leaves are coming out on the trees. I went on a ramble through the fields today and going through a peach orchard I plucked some blossoms which I will put in some of my letters and send home. We were not paid last pay day but I have money enough and can get anything I want except postage stamps. I have ten or twelve yet. When they are gone I don't know how I will get more without they come from home.

The change of climate and irregular living has given a good many of the boys the diarrhea which has pulled them down some, otherwise the general health is good. The Wolf Creek boys are all in good health and spirits. I could not be in a more sociable, well behaved crowd than I am in at present which is something when far from home. I have excellent health all the time which is the greatest blessing where there [is] little chance of taking care of the sick.

I believe I have not mentioned that our Major (15) thinking discretion, turned and ran down the hill out of harm the last day of the Battle. He was not present the first day. He has since resigned and has gone home. Probably one or two others will follow his example if they think we will soon get into another fight. It is the privilege of commissioned officers to do so at any time while the rest of us have to take it as it happens. Their places will be filled by better men. I am glad to state that our Colonel is all we could wish both in the battle and in the camp. He takes good care of his Regiment and gives them all the privileges consistent with strict discipline. Our Company officers are as good as we could have, so that we are used like men. The officers don't get any more respect while off duty than any other [men] while on duty their orders are obeyed with good will. There is scarcely any quarreling and no drunkenness, so we are all things considered getting along very well. So I will finish, wishing you as well and as happy as I am.

I remain your affectionate son Peter Wilson. "

----

14 Colonel J. G. Lauman of the Seventh Iowa Infantry commanded the Fourth Brigade, Second Division. (Lauman's personal bravery at Donelson earned him a promotion to general, and the respect of the Iowa soldiers.)

15 Hiram Leonard was Major in the Fourteenth Iowa at this time. He resigned on February 26, 1862. There seem to have been many officers unprepared for leadership. [Major Leonard resigned shortly after the siege of Donelson. Many men, including Leonard's young nephew Howard, became gravely ill from exposure after two nights sleeping in the wet snow without shelter or fire. Howard was evacuated to the hospital at Mound City Illinois but did not recover. Howard D. Leonard died in Mound City March 19, 1862.]

Pittsburg Landing (Shiloh Battlefield) Tennessee

Pittsburg Landing, March 24th, 1862

" Dear Brother: I received your letter today dated Feb. 28. One week ago I received a letter from W. A. Daniels dated March 2nd so you see the mail is not very regular up this way. Today we have plenty of letters and newspapers, the first for ten days. We are at present getting ready as near as we can guess to make an advance on the rebels a short distance from this place. (16) The possession of the railroad some twelve or fifteen miles from this place is doubtless the next object in view. There are various rumors of the force of the enemy. The Cavalry bring in some prisoners nearly every day some of which say we will find strong opposition others say they are not confident [of] being able to hold out against us.

It is very slow getting a large army moved while the roads are so bad. There has been so much rain the streams are all very high and the teams often get fast in mud on the highest ground. You can imagine the times where the roads [are] full of teams for four or five miles, mostly six mules. Sometimes I have seen three or four of the mules down and the wagon hub deep besides. We are at present camped about a mile from the Landing. You can go down any time of the day and see any amount of runaway teams and all kinds of sprees among the mules and their drivers. There is more waste in all kinds of property belonging [to] Uncle Sam than would break up any other uncle in the country. However if we do make sad work among mules, horses, &c, the necessity of the case requires it. We got some splendid mules at Fort Donelson, enough to put in the place of those that were worn out. Our teamsters were not slow to exchange their worst for the best they could find. The other day some of the scouts came across a planter who had his crop of cotton on hand yet. The teams went out and brought in 24 bales. They help themselves to corn, hay, beef, cattle, &c, where the owners are Secesh which is mostly the case in this vicinity, although [in] some places the people seem to be for the Union.

We have been very idle for some time, laying on the steamboat and in camp one place and another but probably it will all be made up before long. When we leave this place we will very likely have some irregular times both in eating and sleeping but it won't be as cold as when we were at Donelson which is one advantage although the spring advances very slowly. It is not so warm now as it was some weeks ago. We got along comfortably without stoves which owing to the roads we could not haul any farther. We always camp in the timber and build rousing fires when it is cold. We have plenty to eat such as it is. The only thing we would like that we can't get is bread. As a substitute we have crackers, something like we used to eat in the "Cora Linn". (17) They would do very well if we ever got hungry enough but we have so little to do it gives us a poor appetite for such hard "shingles", as they are called. When we go on a march they have a different taste altogether.

I came across George Conor* the other day and had a long talk with him. He told me Steve* went to Texas after he left Ohio and he is of [the] opinion he is somewhere alive yet. George was in the three months service in Virginia and at present belongs to the 2nd Ohio Zouaves. He likes soldiering firstrate but has not been in any battles yet. Robert Kirkpatrick* is here. His regiment as they came up the river the other day was fired into by some straggling Secesh, two were killed and two wounded, which is their first experience although they have been through a good part of Missouri. They think they are some pumpkins. I guess they will get their hand tried before long. As a general thing the regiment that has had the hardest fight has the least to say. Some of the regiments that never lost a man at Donelson do some very tall bragging. It is fun for us to hear some of them tell us about things that we knew a little about ourselves. Lauman's Brigade is willing to give the privilege of attacking to some other the next time but chance has more to do with that than anything else.

The 2nd, 7th, and 14th would, if consolidated, make one full Regiment*. The 8th and the Sharpshooters are with us. The 8th is about nine hundred strong. It is likely they will give us as much to do as if we were all full regiments. The other Iowa brigade is all full regiments with the exception of the Third. I guess some of the best or at least as good troops as the country affords are in this expedition. We have the same artillery used at Donelson besides some other batteries. They may be of more use the next time than they were at that place.

I see by the papers that we received today that the Ninth Iowa has been badly cut up and Frank Heath* among the mortally wounded. It will be more than we could reasonably hope for if he is the only Buckingham boy that loses his life before the war is concluded. It is the general opinion among the soldiers that two or three months or perhaps less will finish the fighting so the tale will soon be told. We are within a short distance of important events up this way but we are confident of success. I think our generals intend to move cautiously and surely. It will take a good many Secesh, more than we are likely to find in this part, to beat us but there is no telling who may get killed in the coming contest. There is something in getting used to anything. We look forward with as much indifference as if we were at home probably more.

I am glad you get along so well with your work and your other affairs. We were not paid last pay day. I don't think we will get paid off until the war is over if it looks like coming to a conclusion. Send me some stamps when you write. We can get any thing here from the Sutler but them. Give my respects to the Hartshorns and as my letter is long enough I will finish for the present. Your affect Brother, Peter Wilson "

----

16 The Confederates, however, were making plans of their own and did not wait for this attack. During the battle which followed the attack on Pittsburg Landing and Shiloh, the Fourteenth Iowa lost heavily in killed and wounded and even more heavily in prisoners. Among the prisoners was Peter Wilson. (He and the rest of his messmates, except John Gaston, were taken prisoner on April 6, 1862.)

17 Possibly the boat on which the Wilson family came to America in 1851. Both James and Peter would have remembered the crossing.

* **Franklin H. Heath**, twenty-two, enlisted into Company G of the Ninth Iowa Infantry on August 20, 1861. At the battle of Pea Ridge Arkansas, March 7, 1862, Heath was shot in the chest. He died several days later at Cassville Missouri on March 28, 1862. Two years later Franklin Heath's younger brother **William Heath**, of Peter Wilson's own Company, was mortally wounded at Pleasant Hill Louisiana, in the battle where Wilson was taken prisoner for the second time.

* **George Conor** has not been identified. "Steve" is probably Steven Klingaman, who once owned the mill at Buckingham. "They think they are some pumpkins" is an interesting expression. See note 42 for more concerning Robert Kirkpatrick

* In camp at Pittsburg Landing, the Fourteenth is still only a partial regiment; with three companies gone to Dakota there is already talk of consolidating with other regiments, even before the battle of Shiloh which occurs two weeks after this letter was written.

Monterey, Tennessee

Monterey **(18)** May 17, 1862

" Dear Father: After being six weeks in the Southern Confederacy so called I have so much to write I scarcely know what to begin with. In the first place the most of our Regiment were taken prisoners after fighting hard all day at the Battle of Pittsburg Landing. I was sick with some kind of a fever when the battle commenced so that by the time we got to Memphis I was about used up. I was taken to the hospital while the Regiment was sent to Tuscallusca [Tuscaloosa]*, Alabama. The Wolf Creek boys were all taken but Gaston. They were in good health and as good spirits as could be expected. I spent three weeks in the hospital. I found many friends and was well treated. There are a great many Union men in Memphis and women too. The latter brought me many good things and gave me considerable money, clothes, &c. As soon as I was well I was removed from the hospital to the guardhouse where I staid two weeks when I, in company with 30 more prisoners from Arkansas, was started for Columbus, Mississippi. We made the trip in five days only, some 500 miles. We had a good chance to see the country and its inhabitants.

We staid only two days at Columbus, when an order came from Beauregard (19) to parole all the prisoners. We took an oath not to fight any more until regularly exchanged. We then started for Corinth and in due time arrived at that place. We were passed through the lines with a flag of truce and conducted to General Halleck's quarters. Here we were told that we would be exchanged in a few days and were sent to this place some five miles from the army and 8 miles from Corinth. This place is being fitted up for a hospital to put the wounded in after the battle which is expected every day. I don't think the exchange of prisoners will take place until after the battle so I will not be in this time. I am not very well satisfied with the way they have done in my absence. The sneaking, runaway cowards of four regiments have been put together consisting of the 8th, 12th, & 14th Iowa and the 58th Illinois. The new Regiment* is made up of the poorest fighting men in the said Regiments. The best part of the Regiments were taken prisoners.

May 19, 1862: There is heavy skirmishing going on every day. Our forces are advancing every day. The heavy siege guns are planted. There is no doubt but the battle will come off soon. The result is pretty certain in my mind. I have had some opportunity of guessing at the resources of the rebels and my opinion is that if they are defeated at Corinth the fighting is pretty much over. Time will soon tell. It is more than likely if we whip them this time we paroled prisoners will be sent home or discharged. However it is impossible to tell how things will go. I have not had a chance to go to my Regiment to get my letters that might have arrived after we were taken nor have I much prospect of getting there. Things are conducted very strict here at present and will be until the battle is fought.

I need not say much about the Battle of Pittsburg Landing as you have seen the accounts of it already. My opinion is that if we had not been surprised we would not have suffered so terribly. On Sabbath, our Brigade being camped some two miles from where the fight commenced, we formed and marched out quickly to the scene of action. We formed in line of battle just in time to meet the enemy. The first regiment we fought we exchanged about 20 rounds when they ran pell mell leaving many dead, wounded, guns, and their flag. We were equally successful with three other regiments. Our loss was not heavy owing to our having the advantage in the ground. Our great mistake was in not falling back in line with the other regiment. Just about sundown there came up another regiment in front of us. We had exchanged 12 or 15 rounds with them when another opened fire on us from behind and a third advanced from the direction of our own lines. Our retreat was cut off, our men were falling fast, so we had to surrender.

I don't know that I may be here long enough to have a letter directed to this place. I will write again soon, you need not write until you hear from me again. It is not very pleasant to be in the position I am in at present but as soon as the battle is over I will know how it will be, so I must wait patiently which I took lessons in while in the land of Dixie. Give my best wishes to all and as my letter is long enough I will finish for the present your Affect Son, Peter Wilson "

----

18 In Tennessee, eight miles from Corinth. Peter Wilson mentions six brothers in these letters: James, West, John, Andrew, David, and Allen.

19 This was General P. G. T. Beauregard, who succeeded General Albert S. Johnston as commander of the Confederate army at Shiloh.

* Note the nearly two month gap between this letter and the one preceding. Peter has become separated from his companions. The men captured at Shiloh were scattered in various towns on the way to prison camp. Most of the Fourteenth Iowa men, including most of the men from Wolf Creek, were taken to Macon Georgia. Some who had been detained by illness in Memphis, like Peter Wilson, were later forwarded on to Columbus or Tuscaloosa and then paroled to Corinth. Other men were hospitalized in Mobile, in Cahawba, in Montgomery and elsewhere along the way to Macon. They were paroled from there, going by train to Huntsville Alabama to be released. It is interesting to note that Wilson says he was well cared for in Memphis by Union sympathizers even though the rebels were holding him there as a prisoner of war.

* This "new" regiment would become the "Union Brigade". It was primarily assembled from the remaining men of the Eighth, the Twelfth, and the Fourteenth Iowa Infantries, and the 58th Illinois with a few from other regiments as well.

Monterey, May 31st, 62

" Dear Sister: It is but a few days since I wrote you but as I am not very busy I may as well scratch a few lines occasionally. I hardly know what to write that would be of interest. The papers give you the war news and [as] I am six or eight miles from Corinth I can tell only by the sound of the cannon and the reports of the ambulance drivers how the times are over at Camp today. We are told that Corinth is taken but how much bloodshed there has been we have not learned. I guess from the fact that few wounded have been where preparation has been made for a great many, the fighting has been light compared with Pittsburg Landing. But as I have no more to write I will finish. Be sure and write and I will be prompt in answering. Give my respects [to] inquiring friends and wishing you good bye I remain, your Affec Brother, Peter Wilson "

Monterey, May 31st, 1862

" Dear Father: I again take this opportunity of sending you a few lines to let you know how I am getting along. I believe I wrote that I had been over to see Gaston and the rest of the boys. (20) When I returned I found it so tiresome to have nothing to do that I thought I would go and help take care of the sick and wounded in the Hospital so for the last week I have spent my time in making the occupants of one tent comfortable. There was one man in the tent shot in the leg that was very badly off. He lingered some three weeks from the time he was wounded and then died. The rest of my charges, 13 in number, are all doing firstrate. We have the very best of physicians here. There are some six hundred patients and the deaths have only been two or three per day while in Memphis the deaths in the same number of patients averaged from 20 to thirty, sometimes 35 daily.

Our men seem to stand the Southern climate better than the natives. I don't think the weather is much warmer here than in Iowa. Since I have got my liberty and had a chance to exercise I feel that I could work here as much as in Iowa but as we have been looking for thousands of wounded at the great expected Battle of Corinth I may as well give all that we know about the last few days proceedings. Several days ago the big guns commenced booming and kept it up almost constantly day and night. Yesterday the breastworks of the opposing armies were only 80 rods apart. Our men had made the last advance in the night and threw up their breastworks. Today the enemy is in full retreat beyond Corinth and our men in full pursuit. How the race will end is impossible to tell. At any rate Corinth is taken and I think Beauregard will have hard work to keep his army together for another stand. I wish the rebels had fought at Corinth. They would have got defeated and the war would have been brought to a close sooner than otherwise, but my sheet is most full.

I did not like to stay here when I first came. Halleck promised to exchange us in a few days but I don't believe we will be exchanged at all. I now feel pretty much at home here. It is much more comfortable here than with the army. My pay is now 20 dollars per month and we have things as comfortable as we could wish. I would rather not be in the service, since I cannot be a soldier any more, but although the Government has no claim on me until exchanged no one can go down the river without a pass so I must stay here until Halleck gets time [to] attend to our case. While over to the Regiment I received a letter from Flora that had been written after you knew I was a prisoner. That was the only letter I have received since the battle and there was little in it. I don't know whether my letters get home but if you get the half of them you will do [well]. So for the present I will close, from your affect Son, Peter Wilson "

------

20 The letter telling of this trip is not included in this collection. John Gaston was not captured and was probably with the part of the Regiment still in service. [John Gaston had been detailed to deliver ammunition during the battle at Shiloh and was not captured with his companions. Still very ill after the battle, he was with the remainder of the Regiment near Corinth. As prisoners, Peter Wilson, Robert Clark, and John McKune had been separated from the other captives when they were hospitalized along the way to Macon. Wilson was taken to a hospital in Memphis then later moved to Columbus Georgia where he was released on parole. Clark could go no further than Mobile, Alabama, where he died as a prisoner in a hospital May 5 1862. McKune fell ill at Cahawba, Alabama and was hospitalized there. The other six of their original mess were taken to Camp Oglethorpe on the fairgrounds at Macon Georgia.]

Monterey, June 3rd, 1862

" Dear Father: Although I have written several times since coming from the land of cotton and slaves and have not yet received an answer still I suppose you will be pleased to hear from me pretty often. I have got somewhat content to stay here although I would much rather be in the old Regiment as it was before the battle but knowing that our Regiment is not likely to be exchanged there is no use in my making any calculations of ever taking a musket again. Here we get 25 cents per day extra for taking care of the sick and wounded. If a man is very sick or severely wounded when brought in he soon dies nine times out of ten; if not very sick he is not troublesome to attend to. There are two of us to attend to 14 men. When I commenced ten days ago two were very low from the severity of their wounds, now they are both dead and the others are doing very well. Some are well enough to go to their Regiments.

I see by the papers that the Federal prisoners captured at Bull Run and other places in McClellan's department and paroled by the rebels have been sent home. Why those in Halleck's department are detained I cannot understand*. The oath we have taken keeps us from doing any duty but I don't think the oath is understood as broken until we go into the ranks again. It would be impossible to even go to farming without assisting in an indirect way to carry on the war. At any rate if I have to stay here it is as well to be content and make the most of it. A soldier is liable to mishaps of every sort and when compared with others my luck has been good. There are so many that started from home in good health and spirits that will come back if at all ruined in health or crippled or something of the kind. I have great reason to be thankful that through so many dangers so far I have been spared. My health is as good as when I left home and I see no reason why it is not as healthy here as in Iowa.

June 5th 62: We have been so busy for two days in consequence of the arrival of so many more sick that I have not had time to finish. The army is doubtless soon to follow up the rebels. They have sent back all their men unfit for duty. There are a good many here that are worn out with diarrhea and such like that will soon be all right again. Then there are a good many that are playing off, as they call it, so as to shirk, and keep out of danger. There must be some 2000 patients here in all but as much as 1500 of them are able to wait on themselves. There are a good many legs and arms taken off every day, but most of the cases die this warm weather. The head surgeon is from Ayrshire and he is the most skillful surgeon in this place. He does all the cutting of legs and arms &c. It is hard to see the destruction of human beings that goes on from day to day, but one gets used to almost any thing.

Part of the released prisoners now at this place start for home tomorrow morning. Why we don't all go at present I don't know. I think it is the intention to discharge us all sooner or later, but there is no telling when. I am quite willing to take a discharge seeing I can't be a soldier any more, but it may be months before I get it if I have as good health as at present. I don't care whether I get it or not at present. I guess it would be rather tough to go to work again at this time of the year. I hardly know where to have my letters sent to. The Regiment is getting so far from here it will take a letter a long time to get to me from there and I may not be here long. I suppose you may direct as before and Gaston will send them to me.

I have not received any yet but it is hardly time. I don't know that I have anything more worth writing so for the present I will close your affect son, Peter Wilson "
------

* Prisoners paroled in the East, which was under McClellan's command, were sent home to await exchange, the idea being that it was too costly for the army to feed and house men who were not available to fight. On the Western front however, thinking that such furloughs might encourage more men to surrender in the future, things were done differently. Halleck's policy was to keep the paroled men waiting idle in the Union camps, held as virtual prisoners, unable to go home on leave as the men had been promised, until they were officially exchanged. This lack of faith in Western loyalty, and the unequal treatment applied to the paroled men from the regiments of different States, caused some very hard feelings, from the common soldier clear up to the Iowa Governor's office. Adjutant General Baker strenuously objected to this practice in correspondence to General Halleck and to the Secretary of War Edwin Stanton.

Monterey, June 9th, 62

" Dear Brother: I again take my pen to write a few lines, not that I have any thing worth writing but it is so long since I have heard from home I would like above all things to get a letter. The Regiment is getting so far from this place that if at all it will take a long time for a letter to reach me by going that way. There is no telling how long I may be here. This is the General Hospital now and a letter will come here quicker than the Regiment. I did not expect to be here long when we came here but now I expect to be here perhaps all summer. I would as soon be here as any other place if I only knew where to have my letters sent to. C. W. Burright (21) is here with me. We tent together and attend to the same lot of sick men. Corniel and myself keep a kind of a grocery. We have tobacco, lemons, &c, and sometimes do quite a prosperous business on a small scale. Small profits is the custom of the country. We sell 10 cent plugs at 25 cents. The next time I go to war it will be as a Sutler. They make more money in one day than D. Connell (22) does in a year.

It is not likely that any of the letters sent [to] the Regiment will get here as soon as the answer to this if sent direct to this place so you will please write me how you have got along for the last three months and whether you received the money I sent, how the crops, cattle, &c, get along, and how all the folks are. I don't think that we will be sent home although it is what is our right. There are so many of the soldiers getting used up they are bound to keep us at something. They talk of sending us north to guard prisoners when they can spare us here. There is no use in guessing what they will do with us. For my part I don't care. I don't think we will be sent to our Regiment any more as we won't be exchanged. If the old 14th was in the field again I would like to be with it.

I have heard that there has been a large number of prisoners paroled at Huntsville, Alabama*. That would be the place our boys would be likely to be sent to from where they were. If any of them have written home let me know where they are and what they are doing. Give my love to all and as I have nothing more worth writing at present I remain, Your Affect Brother, P. Wilson.

[PS] Please write to Peter Wilson, Co G, 14th Iowa, General Hospital, Monterey, Tennessee. "

-----

21 Cornelius W. Burright was also from Tama County. He was nineteen and a musician. [Cornelius was one of three Burright brothers who all served in Company G with Peter Wilson. Brother **Stewart Burright** farmed next door to the Felter family; he was twenty-six. Brother **Joseph Burright** was twenty-eight and lived in Toledo before the War working as a brick maker. Joseph had been taken captive at Shiloh and was one of those held at Macon. The Burright brothers were the sons of Orrin Burright of Crystal, a close neighbor of the McKune family.]

22 Daniel Connell kept a store at Buckingham. [Connell was also the first postmaster at Buckingham. During the War Connell's store naturally became an important gathering place for anyone anxious to learn the latest news from the front. On April 25 1862, following the battle at Pittsburgh Landing, Connell wrote a letter to **Adjutant General Nathaniel Bradley Baker** on behalf of many worried members of the Buckingham community asking for any information Baker may have had concerning their missing sons, husbands and brothers. On May 3 Baker penned his reply addressed to Daniel Connell, Jr. Esq., of Buckingham, Tama County: *"Sir I have received your letter of the 25th ult. In reply I have to state that Franklin H. Heath, Company G, 9th Iowa Infantry is reported at this office as mortally wounded at battle of Pea Ridge, but I have received no report of his death. B.F. Thomas, Peter Wilson, John R. Felter and J.E. McKune, Company G, 14th Iowa Infantry, are reported missing and were probably taken prisoners at Pittsburg Landing April 6 1862. Very Resp'y Y'r Ob't Serv't, N.B. Baker, Adjt. Genl. of Iowa."*]

* Huntsville Alabama is where Peter Wilson's captured messmates B. F. Thomas, John Felter, Eleazar Stoakes, Mathew Clark, Dewitt Southwick and Edmund McClaury were taken by train after their May 24 release on parole from Macon's prisoner of war camp. After reaching safety in Huntsville, Southwick and McClaury were taken directly to the hospital while the other four were sent away by Union General Orsmby M. Mitchel to walk to Nashville with the other released prisoners. John McKune also had reached Huntsville on a second train but it was heartlessly turned back from Huntsville by Mitchel. This second trainload of released prisoners from Montgomery was taken back to prison at Macon Georgia [Camp Oglethorpe] after Mitchel refused to allow them to be received into his lines. Many, like McKune, needlessly died in prison as a result of Mitchel's actions.

G(eneral) H(ospital) Monterey, June 25th, 62

" Dear David: Your very welcome letter came to hand a few days ago. It was nearly three months since I had heard from home. I got tired of waiting here for letters, so I went to the Regiment two miles south of Corinth and found only four of Co. G remaining. I got three new letters and a lot of old ones. The boys have been marching and doing so much duty since they left Pittsburg Landing they are now dirty, ragged, and lousy, but they may have more time to get fixed up now. The Union Brigade* is not much like the old 14th was but it makes little difference to me as I never expect to belong to it. I came back to the Hospital which is about broken up. The sick have been sent home, most of the tents have been pulled down. We get our pay tomorrow. The most of the prisoners that came here have gone home. What are left have to report to their regiments, get their pay, and I think get a furlough until exchanged. We may not get it but we will do no duty in the Regiment until we are exchanged. I think there is little doubt that you will see me home in a week or two. If I go by Long Grove it may be longer but it may be things will turn up so I don't get home at all at this time.

It is rather a poor place here to make any calculations but I have learned to take things just as they come so it makes little difference to me how it goes. I have been doing little since I have been [here] with the exception of a week or so when there were so many sick here. Since I got rid of my sick boys have been acting Wardmaster that is to see that the nurses (23) attend to their respective charges &c. There have been about 160 deaths here within a month. I often assist in digging graves and burying. They bury them without a coffin sometimes as many as ten in one grave, two or three deep. It looks rather hard but it is the best that can be done under the circumstances.

I don't know of anything more worth writing, so I will finish and go out with Corniel and get some plums this afternoon. [This] is a good country for fruit. Apples and peaches are nearly ripe and there are large orchards of both all over Tennessee and Mississippi. It seems there are some new settlers coming near father's. I am afraid there won't be grass enough for all their cattle but I like to hear of more settlers if they are the right stripe. Give my best wishes to all and bidding good bye I remain, Peter "

------

23 The nurses were apparently all enlisted men assigned to that duty with no training for it.

* When many of the defenders of the Hornets Nest were finally surrounded and taken prisoner, some members of the Iowa regiments had not all been captured. Some men had been on leave, some had been ill, some had been performing duties elsewhere, and some had slipped through the Confederate noose as it tightened around their position at the time of surrender. These "orphaned" remnants were temporarily consolidated into a single unit called the Union Brigade to serve as a combat unit until the time when their fellows would be released from the prison camps and the original regiments reunited.

General Hospital, Monterey, Tennessee, July 5 [1862]

" Dear Father and Mother: Contrary to my expectations we are still in this place. The sick and doctors have gone, the tents have been pulled down some time ago, and no one is here now but the guards and about 20 of the paroled prisoners. We have nothing to do but I suppose they want to keep us here until the tents and hospital stores are hauled away. This place is about 12 miles from Corinth and the same distance from Pittsburg Landing. There would be nothing to hinder a party of the enemy from making a sudden attack and destroying a considerable amount of government property so they keep us here so as to make the surrounding Secesh think there is considerable force here. However a few days at farthest must finish our stay in this place. Whether we have to stay for any length of time at any other point we don't know but we won't do any more duty until exchanged. I understand by the papers that we will be mustered out of the service but although that may be the intention it may be a good while before we get through.

It is sometimes provoking to be obliged [to] spend the summer in total idleness while I know you have so much to do at home. I suppose I might as well [have] come home long ago (24) but I believe now that I have waited so long I will go according to orders, if that don't conflict with my parole. If it does I will raise a row for the first time since I have been in the army but I don't anticipate any trouble. The mail don't come here any more, but I will go over to the Union Brigade and get my letters if we stay here much longer. If we get to Corinth in a few days I will then go to the Regiment at any rate for a few days.

We spent a very quiet 4th of July yesterday. After partaking of a good breakfast (and here let me state that we have the very best living, with good ale three times per day which is very healthy as far as my experience goes) we started as usual for a walk into the country. We took along a pail and filled it with blackberries. This is the best fruit country I have seen but that is about all it is good for. We brought home the berries and spent the rest of the day as usual in playing checkers, pitching horseshoes, &c.

It is surprising how easy it is to get used to doing nothing. The most of the boys that are here have got completely used to loafing. I am still in hopes of getting home in time for to help in harvest time but I may be disappointed. It is better to stay until they see fit to discharge us than to have the expense of coming back again. I want an honorable discharge if it don't come for some time but I think this is the last letter I will have to write from this place. I will write again when I find what is the will of General Halleck in regard to us. I think a week at most and by that time we will know just what is to be our destination. This is such an out of the way place we don't get much reliable news. The report now is that Richmond is ours but we don't know whether it is true. The troops at Corinth are in very good health, the men look better than hard working men in the north. For my part I don't suffer any more inconvenience from the heat than in Iowa. The nights are cool and there are no mosquitoes. A tent is a splendid thing to sleep in, much better than a house. Instead of sleeping on the ground here we have cots which is of course much better.

I don't know that I need prolong my letter. There is nothing going on here to make it interesting. The returning farmers have kept quiet so far, but it is easy to see that the most of them are still Secesh at heart. It is only because they know the consequences that they keep quiet. They have suffered enough now to learn them a lesson they will not soon forget. The fences between Pittsburg Landing and Corinth have been used for wood by the soldiers, most of the stock has been killed, everything looks forlorn and desolate. I guess the government will have to feed the inhabitants next winter or they must starve as they are raising nothing this season. But my letter is long enough. I should have written sooner but I expected to have been gone from this place and still look for it every day, for the present I will close, Your affect Son, Peter Wilson "
------

24 The army authorities did not, it seems, know what to do with the paroled soldiers. They were unwilling to compel them to do combat service, but they did not wish to encourage surrender and parole by sending such paroled prisoners home, while others were fighting. Officers, however, seem to have generally connived at visits home by paroled men and punishments were light if any were imposed.

CAMPLIFE (25)

A soldier's life is very gay,
Time passes pleasantly away.
Of one thing he gets his fill,
That is, "boys fall in & drill".

A common game is that of cards,
To pass the time in all the wards.
But dinner hour only means
"Fall in boys and get your beans".

When it rains we lie and sleep
Or closely in our bunks do keep.
Five times a day they call the roll
And put on guard each absent poll.

We sometimes dance while others sing,
No female form to fill the ring.
We boys are gay and faces bright,
The tap sounds, out goes the light.

We have fought some great sham battles,
Around our head no bullet rattles.
We have prayed to have a tramp,
If only to some other camp.

Reveille, guard mount, morning drill,
Then battalion whether we will,
Then dress parade is sure to come -
We might as well be guards of home.

Months have passed, in camp we stay,
The same old routine every day,
We brush our clothing just for fun,
For a change we scour our gun.

If Uncle Sam would send in orders
To march us to the rebel borders,
We would be anxious for the fight
And not stay here another night.

If all winter we stay here,
Uncle Sam will pay full dear.
We'll shoulder arms, draw our pay,
And never fight a single day.

-- One of Uncle Sam's boys.

------

25 These verses were included with the Peter Wilson letters and were in his handwriting but there is nothing to indicate that he composed them. (Possibly they were written by B.F. Thomas who sent several poems to newspapers during the War)

Corinth, Mississippi

Corinth, Miss., July 12 [1862]

" Dear Brother: We have got through at Monterey and have reported at Corinth. We don't know yet what disposition will be made of us. It is published in the papers that all paroled prisoners are to report at different stations, those of Iowa, Illinois, & Minnesota at Jefferson Barracks, Missouri. Probably we will be sent there to do duty of some kind. I have not concluded to do duty, as they want us to, until exchanged but I don't like to go against orders. I believe it is best to take things cool for the present. They cheated us out of part of our hospital pay at Monterey, but I don't mind that much as we did not earn our board while there. At present we are not doing anything so we are not getting any thing but our regular pay.

John Gaston has got his discharge on account of ill health. He will start for home tomorrow. I have sent my dress coat and a coat and cap for Andrew, also two likenesses found by a dead Secesh at Pittsburg Landing. One of the likenesses has the case broken. I would like you would get a new case put on it. John has been sick a long time and has lost most of his clothes. I gave him one of my blankets and an overcoat. You will see what kind of clothes we have when he gets home*. The coat I gave him was one that some soldier threw away. Thousands of such were thrown away between Pittsburg and Corinth. You will know when he gets home and can get the things I have sent by him. I have no use for my dress coat here as I have coats enough without it.

I don't know at present when I will get any more pay. There is two months pay due the 1st of this month but we may not get paid for another two months. I have fifteen dollars now so I guess I can spare 50$ next pay day if the[y] don't pay us for four months. It don't make much difference how long they put it off. The pay is sure to come sometime. I don't know of anything more worth writing. I will let you know where we are sent next or whether we are kept here. There is no use of making any calculations of going home. That don't seem to be the order of the day. I would like very well to get home for a time but I am not homesick by any means. I think I can stay my time out quite content if I keep my health as well as I have done. Just ask Gaston how I look and I guess he will report favorably. I have never felt as well in Iowa as I do at present, but I will not add. Give my love to all and for the present I remain, your affect brother, Peter Wilson. "
-----
* John Gaston was discharged for chronic illness the week of July 11-17 from Corinth, Tennessee. He never made it home. Gaston's brother Hugh of Buckingham received an urgent message that John was very ill in a hospital in Dubuque, Iowa. Arriving in Dubuque, Hugh Gaston found his brother had died July 21 1862 and had already been buried. His grave is in Linwood cemetery, Dubuque.

Benton Barracks, St. Louis, Missouri

Benton Barracks, Sept. 5th [1862]

" Dear Father and Mother: It is needless to make excuses for not writing sooner. (26) I just arrived today and nothing is wrong on account of my absence although some of the boys have been punished for going home, and all that are now absent will be when they come. We are not exchanged yet and there is no telling when we will be. We have nothing but guard duty to do and very little of that, only being on duty about once per month. The boys are in good health and spirits. I was sorry to find that Dewitt Southwick* was dead and another that you were not acquainted with is also gone.

I spent a week at Long Grove, being assured when I got to Davenport there was no use for hurry. The folks are well and Aunt has another little girl*. I got acquainted with Mr. Allan & his family, spent a very pleasant week. My health is good again and all things considered I have no reason to complain. I don't know of anything more worth writing so for the present I remain your affect son, Peter Wilson "
-----
26 Peter Wilson had been home in the interval between the letter dated July 12 and this one dated September 5. [See B.F. Thomas, "*Soldier Life*" Chapter 7; Peter's return is noted. * Peter's cousin Williamina McCosh, daughter of David and Isabel, was born August 15 1862 at Long Grove.]

* Dewitt Southwick had been hospitalized with Edmund McClaury on May 28 in Huntsville after their release from the prison camp at Macon, both being too ill to walk with the other paroled prisoners to Nashville. McClaury was sent home on parole from Huntsville, still very ill. Southwick was later transferred to the hospital at Benton Barracks in St. Louis where he died August 19 1862. Dewitt is buried in Jefferson Barracks National Cemetery in St. Louis. The identity of the other soldier that Wilson's parents were "not acquainted

with" who had recently died is unknown. However, two men, who were both wounded severely at Shiloh, may have lingered for months in military hospitals before both died in July, a day apart if the published roster is correct. **Robert Taylor** died on the 11th of July from a terrible wound in the hip after a long stay in the hospital at Cincinnati. The published roster says **Alexander Cheney**, shot in the head at Shiloh, died on July 10, but Captain Gallagher's Company records show Cheney actually died on April 10, a few days after the battle. Another good choice may be **John Pope** from Toledo, a paroled prisoner, who had survived the prison camps only to die in an army hospital July 11 of lung fever. However, the best choice might be **Robert Clark**, Wilson's friend and messmate from Black Hawk County just north of Buckingham, Tama County. Robert had died as a prisoner in a rebel hospital in Mobile, Alabama in May, but perhaps Peter had just learned this news. Robert's grave is currently unknown but his name is remembered on a marker shared with his parents in Westview cemetery, LaPorte City, Iowa.

Benton Barracks, Sept. 18th [1862]

" Dear Brother: It seems hardly worth while for me to attempt to write a letter seeing there is absolutely nothing worth writing but as I have nothing else to do I will try and fill up with something. A fellow will get tired playing marbles, chequers, and so forth and will go and vary the routine of games by writing even if he hardly knows who to write to or what to write. It seems strange that the government keeps so many men here doing nothing. If they had been mustered out at first they would mostly have gone into the new Refits. Now I don't know whether it is because I did not notice it, but I never saw so many green officers as are in some of the new Regiments. There is fun for us to see them go through their maneuvers. It is rather a funny operation for one man to teach another what he don't understand himself but time will improve officers as well as men.

My friend, Mark Thomson* of Long Grove, originally of the 2nd Iowa, wounded at Pittsburg Landing, [was] sent home and as his arm was slow in getting well, General Baker gave him a Recruiting Commission. He raised a Company, was elected Captain, and is the only Captain in [the] 20th Iowa that had any experience. His Company is Co. C. He has acted Colonel on dress parade and sometimes drills the Regiment on battalion drill. So much for getting wounded instead of being taken prisoner. There are hundreds of men here on parole that are every way qualified for company officers, but their hands are tied. In the meantime there is one consolation, if they have no chance for advancement they have little chance of getting hurt if they don't break one another's necks in some madcap row. So many idle men must have some vent for their mischievous propensities and nightly until late the quarters of the paroled men are noisy with all kinds of fun, music, and dancing. We have plenty and to look at our boys enjoying themselves so well one would think they had never been on half rations in Dixie at least. But we get no word from, or of, those yet in the hands of the rebels*. They may come around by Washington and you may hear of them before we do. Today is a regular Missouri rainy day and as we can't get out most of the boys are at their usual games. It is a great way to keep men but I guess we can stand it, although when we get paid a good many will skedaddle for home again.

I received a letter from Long Grove today. They are all well although the letter had little that would interest you however much it might interest me. One thing I must say you need not repeat, there are plenty of young ladies round the Grove and to think that I might as well [have] stayed there two or three weeks longer and did not is rather provoking. But let it go, I may profit by past experience and take more time at my next visit. Benton Barracks is being put in order for the new regiments so we look for more Iowa boys before long. The news from Maryland is cheerful*. I think the rebels have done their best and the tide must turn against them soon. Uncle tells me that a good many men heretofore sound in wind and limb have suddenly picked up a hilch. (27) I suppose from what Frank tells me such things happen nearer home. I hope some such may get drafted and do their share of fighting. I don't for a moment doubt their abilities; just put a Regiment of Volunteers behind them with orders to shoot them if they run. Poor souls, theirs is a hard lot, I pity them from the bottom of my heart.

I see in this morning's paper the prisoners at Camp Chase are being organized to go against the Indians. The Wisconsin men that were here have gone home today for the same purpose. I would not be surprised if they would send us the same way. They could not please us better than by forming us into regiments and giving us something of the kind to do. I would like very much to see the country up that way and that would be a good opportunity. Although there would very likely be long marches and so forth to encounter, I would much rather go there than lay here idle, much as I like to have nothing to do. I have not received any letters from home since I left, but look for some soon.

The 22nd Iowa has just come in and I find the Tama County boys are not in it. It is like the other new regiments from Iowa, composed of as good material as the country can furnish. Like the others they have Enfield rifles. I believe the Iowa men are as a general thing better equipped than any other troops that visit

Benton Barracks. But my letter is already too long so I will close for the present. I will write to some of you as often as once per week, Your affect brother, Peter Wilson "

-----

27 A hilch was a Scotch term for a hobble or limp.

* Mark L. Thomson, twenty-six, born in Scotland, enlisted April 1861 in the Second Iowa. He was wounded April 6, 1862, and was discharged the following August to become Captain of Company C, Twentieth Iowa. He mustered out in July 1865 with his regiment at Mobile Alabama.

* At this time the officers taken at Shiloh were still being held. They would be exchanged in late October at Aiken's Landing, Virginia.

* The "cheerful" news from Maryland might be the costly Union victory at Antietam, September 17, 1862, but that might be timed too late for the date of this letter unless it was written over several days; Antietam was hardly cheerful despite being an extremely crucial victory for the Union. Perhaps Wilson is referring to McClellan's success against Lee at South Mountain, which forced Lee to withdraw from the high ground to make a stand along Antietam Creek at Sharpsburg several days later. Some newspapers exaggerated Lee's retreat and trumpeted it into a "glorious victory" for McClellan prematurely saying that Lee had been "shockingly whipped". McClellan's unexpected aggressive action certainly would have been good news. Just a few days later came the battle of Antietam, the bloodiest single day of the entire War.

Benton Barracks, Sept. 24th, 1862

" Dear Father: The mail came in from Buckingham today and as yet no letter for me. I had expected one this time but the disappointment is lessened by hearing the news from the boys. I have letters from Corinth & Long Grove. I have written to Scotland and requested them to write to you instead of [to] my address, not knowing where we may be by the time a letter would get here. The prospect of being exchanged seems to grow less while the prospect of anything but staying where we are is dubious enough. There is some prospect of being sent against the Indians but that is not certain. The boys are in good health and of course their spirits are ditto. We have been mustered for pay and expect to be paid soon. There will be a general stampede for home after pay day of those that have not been home, but I guess I will stay this time as there will doubtless be something done with us before long. I think if they have any use for us on the frontiers there we will go sooner or later, but it is all guess work on my part. We may be here six months for any thing I know or care.

It is well that I came here when I did as we settle up for our rations while prisoners and clothes lost in battle & besides it might be a long time before we get any more pay. The names of those absent at this muster have been sent to headquarters. I don't know how it may be with them. I think if I had not come this time I would not [have] gotten my pay for the time I was absent*. There is little of interest going on here. There have been several new regiments from Iowa here but they have gone. There was a Missouri regiment here that had preachers for field officers. In a speech their Colonel made when they received their colors the men pledged themselves not to swear or drink whiskey until he set them the example. I guess some of them will fail in the promise although they are a fine regiment with such good officers. I don't know of any thing more worthy of note. My health is good as it ever was. I believe I can go farther at a double quick than I could last winter. I think the southern climate will agree with me first rate now. John Felter is fatter than he was when he left home, the other boys are as usual.

Direct to Paroled prisoner B(enton) B(arrac)ks St. Louis, Missouri good bye your affect Son, Peter Wilson "

-----

* "The time I was absent" might refer to Peter's Wilson's implied trip home in July -August. It is possible he had taken what others have called "french furlough". At first the paroled men had been promised they'd be sent home to await exchange, later that was denied and they were kept uselessly waiting in St. Louis. During this extended idleness many soldiers on parole decided to "skedaddle for home" anyway, unauthorized; there was usually little punishment if they then returned in a timely manner.]

Benton Barracks, Oct. 22nd, 1862

" Dear Brother: I received your letter today and your being so busy is sufficient excuse for not writing sooner. For my part I have nothing to do but follow the bent of my own inclinations and certainly I keep myself going at something. The most of our time is spent to but little purpose as we are hardly warranted in making preparations for a long stay. I see by the papers our officers are released on parole and gone home on thirty days leave of absence*. I don't know what to think about our prospects of getting exchanged. Sometimes we think one way and sometimes another. There is no certainty of either one thing or another. There are but few of the paroled men here at present, the most of them have gone home. Their names have been stricken from the rolls and they are reported deserters. I guess they will be all right if they stay away long enough. If they should come back now they would be fined as that is the penalty now instead of the guardhouse.

Since writing so much I learned that the 24th Iowa was down at the Levee on their way down the river. I immediately started to see the boys. I found Capt. Clark (28) at the gangway. He had the interesting post of Officer of the Day and was busy about one thing and another. He showed me where to find his Company and I proceeded to the place. There I found A. Felter, John Gross, W. Wilber, John Mulki, Snow. (29) I spent but a short time with them as it was late before I knew they were in town. The boys were in good spirits and in good health. Ward looks as though he would stand it well and make a good soldier. William Beattie* was left at Keokuk in the Hospital. The boys are pleased with Capt. Clark. They have Enfield rifles and as far as appearances go they are a good Regiment. Somehow I could not help thinking I had seen some of them for the last time. It is all before them, they will learn something of the fortune of war before long. The 28th (Iowa) is expected soon. I will try and see them if they stay in town long enough. When I got back to Camp I found John and Frank (30) had just gone to see the boys so they changed their mind since I went out. We expect to get paid soon again as our first year is soon up. I will send you some money this time. My trip home cost me the most of my last four months. I could have sent you twenty or twenty-five this time but I had some notion of coming home so I thought best to wait. I need hardly write to father this week as this is about all I have to write. Give my respects to inquiring friends and for the present I remain your affect brother, Peter "

------

28 This was **Captain Leander Clark** of Buckingham. He was in command of Company E of the Twenty-fourth Iowa Infantry.

29 Abram H. Feller, **John Gross**, **Ward Wilbur**, **John Mulcahy**, and **James M. Snow** are listed as members of Company E, Twenty-fourth Iowa. All were from Buckingham. Roster and Record of Iowa Soldiers in the War of the Rebellion, Vol. III, pp. 826, 830, 860, 882, 895. There is a possibility that this should have been **Abram H. Felter**, as Peter Wilson wrote it. [These men all enlisted August 21 1862. Wilbur, twenty-one, was discharged for illness a year later in August 1863. Mulcahy, thirty-two, who was born in Ireland, mustered out in June 1865 from Trenton New Jersey. Felter, thirty-seven, and Snow, eighteen, mustered out with the Regiment a month after Mulcahy in July 1865 from Savannah Georgia, having served the full three-year term. German born Gross, twenty-nine, was killed in action at Champion Hill Mississippi May 13 1863. ***William W. Beatty**, twenty-two, from Toledo, also of Company E, Twenty-fourth Iowa, died of disease at Keokuk November 13, 1862. William Beatty is buried with his parents at West Union cemetery near Traer.]

30 Probably **John R. Felter** and **Frank Thomas**.

* The officers of the Fourteenth Iowa captured at Shiloh were finally released through exchange on October 17, 1862, at Aiken's Landing, Virginia, and most were immediately sent home on leave.

Columbus, Kentucky*

Columbus, Ky., Oct. 25th [1863 ?]

" Dear Brother: As the time of the week for writing home has come round I take the opportunity of letting you know that we are still at Columbus. There seems to be some wire pulling as to where we may go. Col. Shaw don't want to go to Cairo as he cannot take command of the post but perhaps part of the Regiment may go there and part stay here. If you have not sent that box, send it to Cairo. Anyway I can get it from there. John brought 25 lbs. [of] butter and some other fixin's with him. Frank will get some when ours is used. John is keeping well. I think he may get along now. When you send the box write and let me know as I will go to Cairo and get it. I will make arrangements to send you some dried apples and peaches from Indiana by and by. We have had some cold frosty weather here but we are pretty well fixed to keep comfortable.

I have only been on duty once per week since I returned. It seemed rather dry the first week but it is like old times now. You may expect short letters this winter as there is not enough in our local paper, the War Eagle, to fill one letter. I will send a Columbus War Eagle occasionally so you can see the kind of editors they have in the army. I see there are to be 300,000 more men called out. Bully for that. Put it through is the word. If the Democrats had carried the elections there would be opposition to it but now it will work. It seems Rosecrans (31) is superseded. I thought he was sure to win all the time, but let him go, if he proves unworthy. Every dog has his day and Rose has had his. Frank tells me Mrs. Wm. Provan is dead. Young's folks have had severe trials since they came to Iowa. Lose no time in letting me know how Uncle West comes on in his new harness. Please write soon. Give my respects to Esther. (32)

Wishing good bye I remain, Your Brother Peter Wilson "

------

* This undated letter seems to have been placed a year out of order in the original *Iowa Journal* publication. See PART THREE, October 1863.

31 General William S. Rosecrans. [Rosecrans was relieved of duty in October 1863 following the battle of Chickamauga, giving this letter the probable date of 1863.]

32 James Wilson married Esther Wilbur on May 7, 1863. [Sister of Ward Wilbur, from the previous letter.]

Benton Barracks, Oct. 28th, 62

" Dear Father: Since writing my last I have received letters from you and James. It had been so long, that is it seemed so long, I was almost out of patience but I guess you have not so much time to spare as I have so in future I will make allowances for such things. I am glad you are getting at the house at last. If it is with you as it is with us you must have had a taste of winter already. We had a slight fall of snow but it is now gone and leaves pleasant weather again. It has been fine weather here for a long time, just enough rain to keep down the dust. This climate is very pleasant when it don't get to raining too much. I had a letter from Jane this week. The girls after the old fashion urge the necessity of my studying so I have commenced Grammar. I don't know as I will make much progress but I can try. This is not the best kind of a place to study. There is so much nonsense going on it takes up the attention, at least mine was always easy taken from any kind of study.

It is reported here that the 24th Regiment was fired into below Cape Girardeau and some killed. It may not be true* but the boys expected to have some such scrap before they reached Helena. The 30th Iowa is here at present. It is surprising how many fine men are coming from Iowa. The new regiments are ahead of the old as far as good-sized men go. I had a letter from a friend* in the 20th Iowa the other day. It is down in Missouri near the Arkansas line. He tells me they have had hard times. They have some four hundred sick in the Regiment. It is only some five weeks since they left Iowa so you see how camp life takes down the men at first. They don't know how to take things to the best advantage yet and hard marching on hard crackers and sowbelly, as we term pork, is rather more abundant than anything else on the march. I guess if they put us in the field again, which there is no apparent prospect of, they won't feast us on such if there is any Secesh on the way that has any thing that is better. I hear from our boys at Corinth occasionally. The Union Brigade fought well this time. They lost 115 men killed and wounded*.

There is one circumstance worthy of mentioning. There was a farmer near the camp of the Union Brigade, a pretended Union man. The Union boys guarded his property all summer. Well after the Battle of Corinth and the whole army with the exception of a few sick and some teamsters were gone in pursuit of the rebels this said farmer gathered some 150 citizens and pitched into the deserted town, but his treachery was short lived. One of the boys that knew him sent a ball through his head at the first fire. Seeing their Major fall, as he was styled, the balance skedaddled for home leaving 5 of their number dead and some more wounded. The resistance was made by some ten or twelve muskets. On the body of the Major was found a muster roll with most of the citizens of the vicinity of Corinth. I guess some of them will swing for their pains. They buried the Major with his hands sticking out: rather hard but he deserves his fate hard as it seems. Such is the kind of men that in nine cases out of ten have had their property guarded so far. I will send you the weekly Democrat. We like it very well here. It is one of the first papers in the country and I suppose it tells truth as much as any. Besides it gives the news from the western army better than any of the eastern papers. Our first year of enlistment will soon be up. There is a list of the Shiloh prisoners that died in the South in one of the St. Louis papers. Among others John E. McClure, Co. G, 14th Iowa, is printed. As there was no such man in our Company, I fear it is John E. McKune (33). The other boys think so, but perhaps some of the released officers will know. I understand that Frank's partner Ed McClaury (34) that lived below Toledo is dead. That is four out of our old Mess of eight*. I guess it is about as bad all through the Company and Regiment.

I was out in the country today getting some apples and engaged with a woman, her husband being absent, to come back and help work a week or so at making cider, gathering apples, &c. I don't know how I may like working but I think I will like to make cider. Anyway if I get lazy I can come back to camp. There is no trouble about getting out of camp for a few days at a time as the officers need not know anything about it. We know how to forge passes and never think of getting out in the regular way.

Quite a number of paroled men came in today. They were paroled at Vicksburg. They have the old report of hard fare with the rebels. They passed through some of the same places that we did and say the crops are very poor. The rebels are ragged and hungry but they have been so for so long it seems to agree with them.

I need not add as my letter is too long now for anything it has that is worth while. Your affect son, Peter "
-----
* This probably was not an accurate report, as Wilson guessed; an examination of the roster of the 24th Iowa indicates only one man was wounded, possibly by sniper fire while boating to Helena, Arkansas, on October 15, 1862. This man was **Joseph Conway**, twenty-nine, of Van Buren County, who had enlisted in August 1862. He was later killed in action two years later at Cedar Creek, Virginia, October 19, 1864. He is buried in Winchester National Cemetery in Virginia. The battle at Cedar Creek took a heavy toll on the 24th Iowa.

* The friend in the Twentieth Iowa is probably Mark Thompson. The Union Brigade fought at the battle of Corinth October 3-4, 1862.

33 John E. McKune was the soldier who died. See note 3. [McKune was one of the men on the trainload of prisoners shamefully turned back from the Union lines, and freedom, by General Orsmby M. Mitchel. Returned to Macon, McKune died as a prisoner of war at Camp Oglethorpe, Macon, Georgia August 9, 1862. He is now buried in Andersonville National Cemetery.)

34 Edmund McClaury, a paroled prisoner, died at his home in Benton County on October 18, 1862, of disease contracted while a prisoner of war. Roster and Record of Iowa Soldiers in the War of the Rebellion, Vol. II, p. 824. (*McClaury's was the fifth death from the original group of 10 tentmates giving their messgroup a 50% casualty rate. Robert Clark, John Gaston, John McKune, Dewitt Southwick and Edmund McClaury died in service to their country while Peter Wilson, Benjamin Thomas, John Felter, Eleazar Stoakes, and Mathew Clark --Robert Clark's brother-- survived combat, prison camp, and disease. Wilson says there were eight "Wolf Creek Boys" but B.F. Thomas names ten men in their mess and sharing the tent. In his count Wilson probably is omitting the Clark brothers from Black Hawk County, whom he never specifically mentions in his letters. Perhaps Peter's family wouldn't have recognized the Clark brothers' names.)

Camp of Instruction, Benton Barracks, Nov. 3d, 1862

" Dear Brother: I received a short letter from you today. Your prospects seem good and for my own they seem to be after the old fashion. We had a visit from Col. Shaw a few days ago. The old Colonel has proved himself to be as good a man as we always supposed him to be. He has seen Governor Kirkwood, got him to use his influence at Washington to get us up to Iowa to stay until exchanged and organised. We don't think that they will succeed in getting us to Iowa as General Curtis **(35)** is opposed to it and the Secretary of War is opposed to it on account of the influence it is supposed to have on others in the field if they knew paroled men were sent home.

The Colonel tells us the Shiloh prisoners stand second to no troops in the service in the estimation of the military authorities at Washington and the officers are in consequence furloughed until exchanged. I might inform you that part of the 23(rd) Missouri have been here acting as outside guards round the camp. The fighting part of the Regiment was taken when we were, the runaways sent here to do guard duty as they were fit for nothing else. The Colonel took pains to arrange so they would have no more to do with us. He put a stop to [incomplete] He gave them his mind at Headquarters in his old way about having such d- - - - -d cowards over his boys. The Colonel says we must not think ourselves disgraced in the least if we should stay here to the end of the war.

He maintains that if others had maintained their position as they ought [at Shiloh] the victory would have been ours and no prisoners taken. He advises us to stay here and take things cool as in the way we are situated he can't send [us] home in direct violation of the law but those now at home he advises to stay for the present as he will do his best to keep them from being punished. If he cannot succeed in getting us to Iowa and the officers here in charge of us insist on punishing the boys for going home he is coming to take charge of us himself so that he is bound to see that we are well used. He says the prospect of being exchanged is not very flattering, still it may come some time. I had a letter from D. Gallagher*. He had a letter from his brother and I guess you were wrongly informed about his being the only surviving officer in the Regiment. He is all the officer in Co. G however. Our Second Lieut., S. F. Eccles, is dead and Capt. Pemberton **(36)** is trying to resign to get clear of being court martialed. The remainder of the Shiloh prisoners are at Annapolis, Md. Those of the 12th Iowa arrived here today. We expect the balance of our boys in a few days.

I sent some papers to the boys containing a few persimmon seeds. Frank sent some home last year that they succeeded in growing. You put them out in the spring in time to freeze some. The fruit is very good and is plenty not far from camp. We have good weather here yet and unlimited freedom of rambling. Our boys seem to remember their old tricks yet as many a goose and chicken find their way into camp. For my part I can't justify myself in plundering here. It seems too much like stealing, as farmers give us fruit as much as we want and we have plenty to eat of everything we require. I think the way the case now is I won't come home after this pay day as I had intended. The river must soon freeze so it would be expensive coming back again and perhaps we may be ordered home by and by. At any rate I will let well enough alone and try to improve my time as I best can. It is not so unpleasantly cold here and it seems to me I won't much like the Iowa winters again, although snow is no worse than mud. I don't know as I need to write any more at present. My health is very good. I weigh 189 in light clothes, something more than usual with me.

I will write to some of you once per week. Give my respects to inquiring friends, and for the present good bye, Your affect brother, Peter "

------

35 Samuel R. Curtis of Keokuk, Iowa. For a sketch of his career, see Gallaher's "*Samuel Ryan Curtis*" in THE IOWA JOURNAL OF HISTORY AND POLITICS, Vol. XXV, pp. 331-358.

36 Captain George Pemberton resigned his commission on July 10, 1862. No explanation of the charge against him is given. Roster and Record of Iowa Soldiers in the War of the Rebellion, Vol. II, p. 83. [See B.F. Thomas, "*Soldier Life*", Chapters 3 and 5 for more on Pemberton; Simon F. Eccles had been taken at Shiloh and died as a prisoner of war. He was from Redman, a small village on the Tama-Benton county border. In 1863 Redman's post office, store, hotel and tavern burned to the ground ending its existence as a viable townsite.]

* Daniel K. Gallagher, who farmed north of Toledo, was the brother of Lt. William Gallagher. The Lieutenant had just been released from his long captivity after the Shiloh battle and was on his way home on leave. While on leave, Lt. Gallagher married Mary Crawford in Tama County, December 2, 1862. Gallagher was made Captain of the Fourteenth Iowa upon his return to duty.

Camp of Instruction Benton Barracks, Nov. 12th, 62

" Dear Father: I again take this opportunity of letting you know how we get along. There is little of interest to communicate, the same old nothing over again. If we should be paid this time I would come home but the prospect for being paid this time is not very good, so I will put it off to the next pay day, that is the first of January. If nothing happens before that time I will come then, as there is little or nothing being done in the way of punishment to those that are coming back. The 28th Iowa Regiment has just gone down the River. We went down and spent the day with them. We saw Connell **(37)** and the rest. They were in good spirits and quite glad to see us.

John Connell seems to make a good officer as the men speak well of him. He said he would like to have us go along. I would have no objections if we were exchanged but as it is I believe I will let well enough alone. If the 14th is organised again I would not leave it for any new regiment let who will command it. Col. Shaw is as good a man as need be and when we take the field again we expect to have a full Regiment. The chances for taking the field again are not very promising. The 28th have the old musket. It is good enough at short range but is too clumsy. I think likely they will have something to do before long the way they are sending troops to Helena puts me in mind of the time we went to Pittsburg Landing. Frank had a letter from Abe Felter. **(38)** He says they are fortifying and their pickets were driven in the day he wrote. I see by the papers Grant has moved on Holly Springs with the old army from Corinth. It is situated about 25 miles from Helena across in Mississippi. Perhaps the army at Helena may cross the river and act in concert with Grant. At any rate there is likely to be fighting in the West soon. I hear little from the East. I guess it will be as it was last winter, all quiet on the Potomac. I have begun to think if something decisive is not done this winter, the Southern Confederacy will become fact. Let it go as it will I hope it may be decided this winter. If they keep us on parole I guess we can stand it as long as any of them. Still while I am a soldier I would as soon be in the field as here. The Colonel is gone to bring the remains of the prisoners from Maryland. We expect them in a few days*. Stoakes **(39)** is discharged and will leave for home soon.

I need not continue as news is scarce so no more at present from your affect Son, Peter "

----

37 Lieutenant Colonel John Connell is listed as from Toledo, Iowa. [John Connell was born in Scotland in 1823, coming to the United States as a young man with his parents and several related families including the family of Peter Wilson. These families of Scottish immigrants settled first in Connecticut and later came to the Traer area. In Connecticut Connell was employed by Governor Buckingham, whose name was memorialized by these Scotsmen when the village and township of Buckingham was first established in Tama County. Connell was a farmer, served in the State Legislature, helped establish saw and grist mills, and opened a mercantile store in Toledo with John Zehrung. In September 1862 he was commissioned Lieutenant

Colonel of the Twenty-eighth Iowa Infantry, receiving a promotion to full Colonel of the Regiment the following March. On April 8 1864 at Sabine Crossroads, Louisiana (the day before the battle of Pleasant Hill) John Connell was terribly wounded and taken prisoner. His left arm had practically been shot away and had to be amputated above the elbow. After his release from prison camp Connell served on court-martial boards in Washington D.C. before finally returning to Toledo where he served as the District Tax Assessor for the Department of Internal Revenue.]

38 See note 29.

39 The Roster and Record of Iowa Soldiers in the War of the Rebellion, Vol. II, p. 840, records the discharge of Eleazer Stookes of Tama County on November 8, 1862. The name, apparently, should have been Stoakes. [**Eleazar Stoakes** had not recovered from serious debilitating illness that lingered long after their release from the POW camps. It had already killed several of their companions. Eleazar was finally discharged but his recovery at home was slow going and a matter of some concern to his close friend B.F. Thomas. See "*Soldier Life*", Chapter 7. It is interesting to note that Thomas implies that Peter Wilson was also not feeling well at this time, while Wilson says in the following letter that his failure to come home was more a matter of economics.* "The remains of the prisoners" refers to the remaining prisoners from Shiloh that had been held until October, released at Aiken's Landing, Virginia and then taken to Maryland.]

Camp of Instruction Benton Barracks, Nov. 14th, 62

" Dear Brother: As the boys have concluded to go home you will wonder why I did not come with them. In the first place I think we will be sent to Iowa before long and I can come then without so much expense. If we are not sent I want to get paid once more before I come up. I have lent some money to the boys and I must be on hand at pay day to get it. We expected to have been paid before this time or I would not have lent any money but as it is there is little difference as my time would not be worth much at home now.

General Prentice (40) visited us yesterday. He told us the reason we were not exchanged was because the rebels outnumbered us in prisoners and consequently they have no men to give for us, something we suspected before. He says he is going to have the right version of [the] Battle of Shiloh published so as to justify his course on that day and clear up the lies that have been to some extent in circulation. He says we will be the first exchanged and he wants to command us again. I guess he was puffing us a little.

Few of us are anxious about getting into the field again. For my part I care but little how it goes. I am ready for anything, even to put for Iowa as soon as I finger some more greenbacks.

Charles Baily (41) has just got back. He got the Governor to intercede for him and his pay is all right. That is what they propose to do with those that are at home, stop their pay. I don't much think they will, however.

I need not write any more as you can talk to Frank so no more from your Brother Peter "

------

40 This was probably Major General Benjamin M. Prentiss, who had also been captured at Shiloh and had been exchanged in October, 1862. He had been ordered to report for duty to General Grant.

41 The roster of the Fourteenth Iowa does not include the name of Charles Baily. There was a Charles L. Bailey from Toledo in the Tenth Iowa Infantry, but he is not recorded as a paroled prisoner of war. [**Charles L. Bailey**, twenty-two, from Toledo, born in Ohio, enlisted July 1861 in Company D of the Tenth Infantry and then transferred to Company C. In the US Census in 1860 Bailey is listed as a schoolteacher in Toledo. He was wounded severely in the leg at Champion Hill, near Vicksburg in May 1863. Re-enlisting in February 1864, he later reached the rank of full corporal and served until mustering out in August 1865 at Little Rock Arkansas.]

Camp of Instruction Benton Barracks, Nov. 20th, 62

" Dear Brother: I sent you a few lines by Frank and as the time of the week for writing home has returned I will scratch a few lines more not that there is much worth writing but I suppose it is as well to write, news or not. I am not making much progress in grammar as there is too much mischief going on in which I am easy induced to join. Then my teacher is gone and perhaps I may soon follow. Sometimes I think I will come home but it seems hardly worth while considering the probability of being suddenly called upon again. I begin to wish more than ever for the organisation of the Regiment as then a fellow will know his destiny that is he would not be in uncertainty of how he should act.

If the boys are content to stay at home it is more than I think they will. For my part I think I can stay here more content than if I was at home considering the circumstances but for all that I may start as soon as pay day is over. I received your letter today and some letters that were dated Oct. 29th. They must have laid by somewhere. I am glad to know that you get on so well. You must be very busy. Here it is not so. We have adopted the system fashionable among the upper ten of breakfast at nine, dinner at four, so you see we are somewhat late up in the morning.

I had a letter from Lieut. Gallagher. He says he thought I was dead, as he never heard from me after they left Memphis until he got home. He promises to come and see us soon and says he is ready for Dixie as soon as we are organized. I am glad to hear of our having one officer left in the Company, the best one at that. I need not write any more as you can talk to the boys. Your affect Brother Peter "

Camp of Instruction Benton Barracks, Dec. 5th [1862]

" Dear Brother: I thought to have been on my way home before this time but they seem to be slow about getting ready to pay us. We have been expecting pay and still expect it. I would not have waited so long but for the expectation of getting it in a few days. Robert Kirkpatrick (42) and myself are coming together. I have a half fare ticket for three (43) that Frank sent us. It has made two trips to Iowa already and is good for another one. Some of the boys, tired of being at home, are coming back every few days. There is no punishment and no hindrance going or coming. I suppose the weather is cold in Iowa now. Here it is very pleasant, no snow on the ground, slight frosts at night, and pleasant days. I believe I have tramped within 5 or 6 miles of camp in every direction & begin to be familiar with a good part of St. Louis. We generally spend most of our time rambling round or reading, playing some game or other. It is surprising how little it takes to keep us busy or rather kill time which is the most object. I don't know what effect it will have on our after life, so much idleness. I must admit it suits very well at present. I have been rather opposed to coming home on account of the uncertainty of staying even for a month but if I come I will not be in so much hurry as last time. If my health keeps as good as it has been for some time I will enjoy a trip better than before. I have so many girl correspondents it will be quite a round to see them all, which of course I must. But of this keep mum.

I might better keep quiet myself, but I guess it is not particular. If the girls write I must answer hence I have as much writing as a store clerk. I guess it won't amount to much only it takes money to buy postage stamps &c. There are good prospects of being paid soon. If all is right I will be up in a week or two.

I need not write any more at present, your affect Brother Peter "

------

42 The roster of the Fourteenth Iowa does not list a Robert Kirkpatrick. This friend was probably **Robert H. Kirkpatrick** of Vinton. He was in the Eighth Iowa and was taken prisoner at Shiloh and paroled. Roster and Record of Iowa Soldiers in the War of the Rebellion, Vol. I, p. 1143. [See B.F. Thomas, "*Soldier Life*", Chapter 5.]

43 Peter Wilson gives no description of his trips home, and there is no explanation of this "half fare ticket for three". [Thomas says soldiers were sometimes given discount fares. See "*Soldier Life*", Chapter 6.]

Benton Barracks, Dec. 10th, 62

" Dear Sister Jane: I don't know whether I may come home this winter or not. Some of the boys just returned from Iowa tell us that the Colonel told them they were exchanged & sent them here. If so I will not come. It is a long trip and hurry back again. I would like very well to come up provided I could stay a month or two but if the 14th is organized and sent to Dixie it will suit better. I see in this morning's paper an account of the battle in Arkansas*, in which several of the new Iowa regiments have distinguished themselves, while we are idly spending the time in Benton Barracks. I may be wrong but I think this winter finishes the war. I would like to see the end before I come home, then and not before I can content myself to stay. I wrote to you just before you left Grinnell or after I don't know which. I have not heard from there since. I have not again heard from Sue. I was somewhat curious to know more about her but I am not particular. If she don't write it will save me some postage stamps, paper, &c &c.

Since writing so much we have signed the pay rolls and we will receive pay tomorrow. If this report of our being exchanged proves untrue I will come up soon. Ten days or less will be sufficient to decide. I need not write any more this week. Write soon if I don't come up. Your affect brother, Peter "

------

* Wilson is probably thinking of the battle at Prairie Grove Arkansas, which was statistically a near stalemate on the actual field of battle. However, by causing the Confederate forces to withdraw from northwest Arkansas, this battle was an important and decisive strategic victory for the Union. Neither side "won" the battle, but important areas of Arkansas ended up firmly under the control of the Federal forces. The scene of the battle is now a well preserved national park.

Benton Barracks, Dec. 18th [1862]

" Dear Brother: A blundering Dutchman is talking to me so I have some bother to write sensibly. I have concluded not to come home at present. The reason is this. There is to be a general muster soon and all the boys are coming so I have concluded to be here and be mustered with the rest. We will be paid up to the first of January. Some time in January, if there is no exchange, I may come home then. We received two months pay a few days ago. I intended to have sent some home. Several sums were coming to me and I still owed ten dollars that I borrowed when I came home. That I paid, but those that owed me could not get pay this time on account of their descriptive rolls not being right, so for this time my luck has not been good. I think it will be all right next time.

I received a letter from Frank today. He informs me of John Felter's marriage and of his coming back soon*. I hope he will stay, as there is no exchange that we know of. I think Col. Shaw merely wants to get the boys paid. So there is no trouble about his future. If Frank is at home yet tell him he need not hurry as there is no exchange yet and he need not believe there is until I send him word. Letters from the Toledo boys say they are coming here soon. There will be merry times when they all get here. The general opinion is that we never will be exchanged. I am of the same opinion myself although of course we don't know. For my own part I am indifferent as to how it goes. I am ready to go to Dixie any time. I am confident that I would stand the hardships now better than formerly and the life in the field is more exciting but here we are very comfortably situated, good quarters, nothing of consequence to do. I think but few families in the country live better than we do. Groceries & meat & vegetables we have in abundance. We can live as well as the hotels in St. Louis, as far as substantial living goes. It is quite different in the field, but I never read of important military matters but I wish to be into it again.

I need not add let me know how you get on at home. Give my respects to inquiring friends.
Your brother, Peter "
------
* While home on parole John R. Felter married Rebecca Thomas, sister of B.F. Thomas. The wedding took place December 10, 1862.

Benton Barracks, Dec. 23, [1862]

" Dear Father: I take this opportunity to inform you that I am in good health &c thought from the letters from the boys at home that they would have been at Benton B(arrac)ks by this time but they are not here yet. It is currently reported here that we are coming up to Davenport to recruit & organize. I think if we come it will be in January, as we will be mustered the last of this month at this place. If we come up I will be home for a short time at least. We have been so often deceived in regard to our being exchanged I can not put much confidence in it this time, although perhaps it is so. A good many of the officers of the 14th are here but none of them has reported for duty yet as none of the officers that were prisoners has been called to duty. It seems doubtful about their being exchanged.

There is not anything of interest going on here. It seems the Army of the Potomac is again defeated*. I much doubt their ever taking Richmond. There are some splendid gunboats almost finished here. I have been on them several times. If we were certain that we were exchanged I would try my hand on the gunboats. The 11 1/2 inch guns throwing a 180 pound ball and protected by 2 1/2 feet solid oak covered by 2 thicknesses of iron and one of India rubber everything is so strong and so well arranged it seems almost impossible to damage such boats. I suppose they possess advantages over anything that has gone before. I have visited most of the forts about St. Louis as well as foundries, machine shops, &. There is much of interest about the city. I have rambled round it much and always felt well paid in seeing the different curiosities about such a city as St. Louis. I was much astonished at seeing the steam press roll out the newspapers. The Democrat press turns out the papers printed & folded much quicker than bundles go through a threshing machine. You have not mentioned whether the Democrat comes regularly and how you like it.

I need not write any more this time. I suppose if we come to Davenport the same direction will find us.
Your affect son, Peter " (44)
------

* Peter may be referring to the battle of Fredricksburg December 13, 1862, an enormously costly and unnecessary defeat for the Union Army.

44 The next letter in this collection is dated January 13, 1863, and was written from Rolla, Missouri. In it Peter Wilson says indirectly that the paroled men had been exchanged and he tells of being on a military expedition. His second period of service had begun.

This second installment of Peter Wilson's letters was published in JULY 1942 in **The Iowa Journal of History and Politics --** Published Quarterly by The State Historical Society of Iowa; Iowa City, Iowa

_____

_____

SHILOH

The day before the Shiloh battle, William Gallagher mailed this letter to the Editor of *The Iowa Transcript* in Toledo. It appeared in the paper April 24 1862 along with alarming accounts of the battle that described the incredible numbers of casualties, including the terrible news that most of the men of the 14th Iowa were missing in action.

" Pittsburgh Land., Tenn., April 5

Mr. Editor,

Well we are yet alive, and are encamped at the above named place, a point some 130 miles above Fort Henry and 7 miles above Savannah on the Tennessee River. It is a place of no importance, otherwise than furnishing a landing for troops and stores. There is no town here, nothing but a house or two, and here a slight engagement took place between our Gun Boats and the rebels directly after the fall of Fort Henry, which resulted in the death of 10 or 12 secesh.

Last night at dark the drums pealed out the long roll, far and wide along the lines you could hear the roll of the drum, and cracking of caps, and other preparations for an immediate fight, the batteries were all in readiness at short notice and we looked for an attack ere another morning sun. But it was only an alarm, a body of rebel cavalry had made a dash at our pickets, and a Brigade near the lines being on drill the Cavalry dashed among them, and ere our men were aware of what was doing, they (the Rebels) bore off 9 of our men including a Major and Lieutenant. At first it was rumored that Beauregard's forces were marching to attack us; but this proved to be untrue. Our forces gave chase to the rebels and captured 13 prisoners and a brass gun. Thus ended the alarm, and we are all quiet again to-day.

There is now collected here some 100,000 men under General Grant, the ostensible object being to gain possession of the Memphis and Charleston R. R. at Corinth Miss., some 23 miles distant. Arrangements are being made for a severe contest, as the rebels are said to be at Corinth in heavy force, with a good supply of heavy ordnance, commanded by Beauregard and Johnston; if such is the case we may have to fight hard. We cannot retreat as the Tennessee river would cut off that, and hence with us it is victory or annihilation. Buell's forces are expected to join us, shortly. Gen. Grant had a grand review on Thursday last, so you can see we can follow the Grand army on the Potomac in one Point of Military Manouvers, if we do discard the Wooden Gun arrangement.

We have been laying here about two weeks; we lay at the Iron landing, where I wrote you last, about 5 days, and as is generally the case, on the rainiest and most muddy of days we marched aboard the boat. We had some 2 miles to go, over swampy roads, where our freight trains were lugging through. Our company wagon fortunately escaped by performing one summersault, scattering trunks, blankets &c. far away into the liquid mud; and the remainder of the teams fared about the same, only some stuck so fast in the mud that all the mule power, and strength of "horrid oaths" failed to extricate them from their oozy bed, until Old Sol gave more light and Humor on the subject another day, as it was dark and raining murderously, a regular North Easter; this is one of the phases of soldiering.

The next day at noon we were all aboard, and soon wheeled out into the stream, and soon were coursing our way in the wake of the great Expedition. We arrived at Savannah undisturbed, no hostile Rebels felt in the mood to send their Ball and Buck among the boys of the bloody 14th. Savannah is not prepossing in looks, a few Dingy old Black looking Stores and Dwellings, with here and there a negro shanty, rearing its head in solitary grandeur, thus rendering it quite unique and southernlike in appearance.

Still it is strongly Union. Our Division gained here about 1,000 Recruits. The weather is fine; roads now are good. The woods is green, and the dogwood, with its white blossoms, make it look almost like a Garden of Eden, for beauty and fresh breezes.

We are under marching orders. Our health is good with the exception of Diarrhea, which is not serious however.

                                                              W. G.   "

Notes:
-- Lieutenant Gallagher was captured with the regiment the following day at the Hornets Nest and spent many months as a prisoner of war. The staggering cost of the battle at Pittsburgh Landing shocked the entire country, North and South. Even in victory there were serious calls for the dismissal of both Generals Grant and Sherman whose lack of adequate preparation for a possible Confederate attack, despite several warnings,

was blamed for adding greatly to the amount of Union casualties. A decisive defeat at Shiloh would almost certainly have ended the careers of these two most effective Union Generals, which in turn must have drastically changed the outcome of the entire War. Whether the long delay at the Hornets Nest was caused by Southern miscalculation or Northern bravery, the result was the same: a second chance for Grant. The stubborn stand of the Union men along that old road stalled the momentum of the rebel advance and bought for Grant an opportunity to re-organize his scattered army, bring up reinforcements overnight, and win the next day. It was a pivotal moment. These brave men didn't win the War that day but at the cost of their own lives and their freedom they prevented a terrible disaster. In doing so they may have saved the Union itself.

This wonderful letter, recently discovered in the files at the National Archives, was turned over to the government in 1884 in order to help substantiate the application for pension of Nancy Clark, Mathew and Robert Clark's mother :

" Pittsburgh Landing Tennessee April 4th, 1862

Dear Father, Mother, Brothers and Sisters
    it is with much pleasure I again take my pen in hand for to answer your kind letter which I received yesterday dated March the 15   we both was very glad to hear from you and home and that you was all well and doing well   we are both pretty well   not as well as we used to be but we are still gaining and we hope soon to be as well as ever and at home with you all again for I think I like home better than soldiering but never the less I go with heart in hand for to put down rebellion and protect the Union   why should I stand back and see my fellow men just as good as I bleed and die to save our Country?   then ought not I be willing to share my lot with them?   certainly I ought and will and then I can come home and know that I have done my duty to my Country   it never will be any disgrace to me
    we have been here in camp some 2 weeks and a few days   it is longer than I expected to stay when we first came as there is a large body of rebels but a few miles from us and they gave us but ten days to leave in, but the ten days has past and gone and we are here yet and I think if we do not before they come and drive us away we shall stay here some time yet for they will never attack us   but we will them in a short time I think   we expect a hard fight with the secesh for there is where they have concentrated their forces and we expect that is where they will fight   if they will fight at all
    we do not know their number as there is so many camp reports   some times we hear that there is two hundred thousand at other times that there is 80 thousand   I guess the last is about the number   I have no doubt but what you at home know more about what is going on in the line of war than we do   we never hear of any battle until (it) is all over with   we have got a large number of men here some 80 or 100 thousand and if Buell comes with 75 thousand men more we will then have a pretty good force   if we gain this expected battle I shall then think that the back of secession is broke but we cannot tell (when)   but I hope soon to hear that peace is proclaimed but that will take time before we can hear such news   but I have no reason to complain for we have plenty to eat such as it is   I will tell you what we get for bread   we have crackers or shingles as we call them   They are made of flour and water and then dried as hard as (they) can get them   they are so hard that you can hardly bite them   for meat we get sow belly that is side meat   it is sometimes smoked   we have ham some time too   we also have had fresh beef 3 times in the last 2 months   we have coffee sugar rice beans potatoes   when we get all this if we want any thing more we can get it by buying them
    now I will tell you what we have to do in regard as to work   we have roll call four times a day   we drill half an hour in the fore noon   some times (we) have battalion (drill) in the after noon   we will form in line of battle and then march a short distance strike arms and lay round a little while then come home   this is all we do   we have got (a) firstrate colonel the best one that I know of   we are in the 1 Brigade 2 Division
    our Division was out yesterday on grand review   it was a pretty sight for to see them all out at one time there are 2 batteries with us   the 12 Iowa Regiment is with us   also the 7 (Iowa) and 2 (Iowa) is in our brigade besides some Illinois regiments   you wanted me to send you word when I wrote whether I got your letter that you mentioned the price of stock we did   we will not be able to send any money until we get our pay as we have not had any since the 1 of Jan(uary) and we spent considerable when we was sick but we could not send any from here if we had ever so much   we would be glad to do it if we could but I suppose we will get our pay after the fight is over with
---

5 Ap(ril) --- last night about 9 o'clock we were ordered for to cook up 2 days rations and have it ready at 5 o'c(lock) this morning   Mathew and I went to work and baked some biscuits and boiled some meat and went to bed   I understand this morning that there was some 8 hundred rebels came in the out skirts of our camp   they killed 6 of our of our men and we took 50 prisoners but they was driven back   there was a deserter came to the 6 Iowa   he says that they intend to attack us in 3 days if we don't before (they do) he says that their supplies is cut off   there was 3 deserters joined our regiment last week and 3 in the 12 (Iowa)   I saw James Stewart a few days ago he sends his best respects to you   Mathew was out to the 13 (Iowa) the other day they was all well   I have not had any letters from Roxham since last winter nor sent one nor I don't know when I can for postage stamps   we can neither for love or money   I hardly know what I will do quit writing I guess but I will do the best that I can   you must write (as) often as you can and I will

I suppose you would like to know what kind of weather we have in Tennessee   it is most beautiful tho grass is growing fine and the timber begins to look thick with leaves and all the royal (*man -- crossed out, perhaps manner?*) family of birds, bumble bees, butter flies, and frogs can be heard and seen

O yes I must not forget little sister Hatty and brother Nock   they sent me some kisses   I tell them both and James too to be good children and I will come to see them some day   tell Hatty that I put her kisses in my pocket

I suppose this battle will be over before you get this letter   the peach trees is in blossom they look pretty

Give my Love to all inquiring Friends and tell some of them that I would like to hear from them   I would like to (be) at home and go to Origon with them that is going this spring   I guess that I will not write any (more) at present   you must excuse bad writing for I have got a bad place to do it in   when you write to Roxham send my (love) to them all   Good bye for the present still send your letters to Cairo

From your sons Mathew and Robert F Clark "

Notes:

-- Mathew and Robert, born in Canada, were the oldest sons of William and Nancy Clark whose farm was near LaPorte City Iowa. James, Edwin and Harriet were the three youngest children in the William Clark family; their ages were approximately ten, eight and six when this letter was written. "Nock" seems to have been a family nickname for Edwin. The other unnamed Clark children were Elizabeth, William, Mary and Rachel.

-- Roxham is the village where the William Clark family lived in Canada before moving to Iowa. It is south of the city of Quebec, just north of the New York border. Mathew and Robert's paternal grandparents, Matthew and Phillippa Clark, remained in Canada as did some of Mathew and Robert's aunts and uncles. Rob and Mat were teenagers when they became to the United States. A few short years later they both put their lives on the line for their adopted country.

-- This letter was started on Friday, April 4 1862, two days before the Sunday morning attack that opened the battle of Shiloh. The Confederate army was already on the march. Robert continued the letter the next morning, Saturday April 5, and it was probably sent off down river with a mail packet that day. Robert and Mathew were taken prisoner at the Hornets Nest late Sunday afternoon April 6, and Robert died as a prisoner of war in Mobile Alabama on May 5.

-- James Stewart from Company E of the 12th Iowa Infantry must have been a close friend of the Clark brothers. He did not survive the War, according to this entry in the roster: **Stewart, James.** Age 25. Residence Waterloo, nativity Ohio. Enlisted Sept. 23, 1861, as Fourth Sergeant. Mustered Oct. 19, 1861. Promoted First Sergeant April, 1 1862. Missing in battle April 6, 1862, Shiloh Tenn. Promoted Second Lieutenant March 6, 1863; First Lieutenant May 28, 1863. Died of wounds July 4, 1864, Memphis, Tenn.

-- The 13th Iowa Infantry had many members from neighboring Benton County and the town of Vinton which was not far from the Clark home, so there may have been many friends for Mat to visit. Jacob Woodley of Company E especially may have been well known to the Clarks. After the war he remained a resident of the LaPorte City area the rest of his life and is buried in Westview Cemetery not far from Mathew Clark: **Woodley, Jacob A.** Age 19. Residence LaPorte City, nativity Ohio. Enlisted Aug. 21, 1862. Mustered Oct. 21, 1862. Discharged for disability March 5, 1863, Lake Providence, La.

For several Thursdays after the battle on April 6, the Toledo weekly paper carried stories of carnage and disaster at Pittsburg Landing, the location on the banks of the Tennessee River where General Grant's army had been camped before the pivotal battle now remembered as "Shiloh". For weeks after the battle Iowa newspapers were full of terrible accounts in general, but there was no specific word on the fates of the soldiers from Tama County. The anguished families finally learned the news of their men through this letter, written by a resident of Toledo, which was printed in *The Iowa Transcript* on April 24 1862 :

" CORRESPONDENCE FROM PITTSBURG

The following letter, written by Sergt. Oldroyd to his relatives in this town, giving the fate of the Iowa 14th, will be found quite interesting.

' Pittsburg Landing, April 10 '62

Dear --------,

I have at last found a little time which I gladly embrace to pen you a few lines and let you know that I am still alive and well. You have no doubt ere this heard of the hard and bloody battle which was fought here on Sunday and Monday last. I could not, even if I had the time, give you a full detail of what transpired under my own observation, and you would not wish to hear it --. But I have sad news to break to you and to the friends of my Companions and brother Soldiers. Last Sunday morning as we were preparing for inspection as usual, we heard a noise in the distance resembling very much a heavy shower of rain, and would have thought it such, but the continual booming of the cannon in connection, told us too plainly that the rebels had attacked us, and that a bloody contest was ensuing. The long roll was heard beating in every direction; and now the order was "to arms boys and form in line".

This was quickly done and we were soon marching on to the scene of action which was about two miles or more distant. We were then formed in line and ordered to lay down and await further orders. Our position was in the rear of the 8th Mo. battery, which we were to support. One of our Generals (I have forgotten his name) rode along our lines speaking encouraging words to the Boys "Boys keep cool, aim low! and remember you are from IOWA", in reply to which was given one long hearty cheer. But our battery was by this time playing upon the enemy pretty briskly, which would as a matter of course, draw a fire from them in our direction. Shell and grape flew over us thick as hail and we hugged the ground closer and closer. The enemy then made a charge on us. We waited till they got in good range, then jumped up and the way we put cold lead at them was a caution. We drove them back some three or four hundred yards and advanced on their grounds; we then fell back, formed our lines and waited for another charge.

They rallied and come on again, we pushed them back the second time and held the ground, lying down or standing behind trees to load, jump up and fire, then down again. I was standing by a tree taking as good aim as I could when whiz came a ball through my hat, wounding me slightly on the head. The ball produced such a shock that it fell me to the ground --. I heard someone halloo "Oldroyd is shot". Several of the boys came to me and asked me if I was much hurt. Said I "no but a pretty close call though". It did not hurt me very bad but made me very dizzy. I finally got up and went back to a large tree and sat down; how long I sat there I don't know, but soon a couple of our boys came up and told me to go to our tent. I started and soon heard heavy firing in the direction of our regiment. I went to camp and got some boiled meat to take back with me for the Company, it was only half cooked when we heard our Regiment was all cut up and taken prisoners. The enemy was advancing on us very fast and their shell began to fall around our fire.

I helped to get our sick boys out of range of them and then went back to look for the Regiment, in hopes that the report was a false one; but they were no where to be found. It was now getting dark and the firing ceased except for an occasional shot from one of our large guns.

Monday morning came and the battle began to rage terribly. By this time reinforcements came to our aid and our men began to regain their former positions, and took some guns back which they lost the day before. As our Regt. was gone, I went and assisted in carrying off the wounded in prefference to going into the field in some other strange Regiment.

I worked all day on Monday and Tuesday, the hardest work I ever did. Some men were very heavy and being badly wounded were hard to handle. There appeared to be no end to their cry for water. I might set here and write all night about the poor fellows, but I must forbare as I wish to send a report of our Co., to let their friends know their fate. Our loss in killed is not very heavy. Our Capt. was hurt by a limb falling from a tree. He fell back, this is all that saved him from being taken. He is the only commissioned officer in the Regt. that is left --. We had 73 men able for duty in our Co. We now have 23, eight of which are able for duty.

The following is a list of the killed, wounded and missing, in Company G.

Wm Galligher	1st Lt.	Missing
S Eccles	2d "	"
J Shanklin	1st Sergt.	"
A Davis	2d "	"
A Hazlett	5th "	"
P Wilson	1st Corp'l	"
B F Thomas	3rd "	"
J A Pope	6th "	"
S Jenks	7th "	Killed
Wm C Hafar	8th "	Missing
H H Williams	Private	"
Joseph Burright	"	"
Wm Goit	"	"
L Brannen	"	"
M Clark	"	"
R F Clark	"	"
A Cheney	"	Killed
E Dykeman	"	Missing
J B Edwards	"	"
James Fox	"	"
R Fitch	"	"
J R Felter	"	"
M Grubbs	"	"
I Hunnicut	"	"
Wm Heath	"	"
G Hate	"	"
H Hass	"	"
C Joer	"	"
P Jospeison	"	Wounded
F Kline	"	Missing
D Zehrung	"	"
Jos Luke	"	"
Jas Larue	"	"
H Loomis	"	Wounded
Jerry Mills	"	Missing
D Miller	"	"
J R Moyer	"	"
E McClary	"	"
T McClane	"	"
J E McKune	"	"
J B Overturf	"	"
J A Pierson	"	"
J Shopshire	"	"
E Stoaks	"	"
D Southwick	"	"
R Taylor	"	Wounded
J B Wineman	"	Missing
J D Williams	"	"

To the friends of the missing ones, I would say that they need give themselves no uneasiness, fearing that any of them are killed; for I have searched the battle field over faithfully and nothing is to be seen of them except some of their guns and cartridge boxes. One thing I would say in compliment to the 14th Regt. (if I may be allowed to compliment) I could stand in one position, not move my feet, and count from 13 to 20 dead secesh. The ground was literally covered with them.

It is hard to tell what will be done with the balance of us. I have heard some talk of the sick and wounded being sent off to the Hospital, and those fit for duty be attached to some other Regiment.

We are expecting another attack here. Two prisoners made their escape from Corinth during the excitement there by our men being taken in. They report the rebels making a strong effort to raise 200,000 men to clean us out.

But I must close at present as my sheet is full, I should like to write much more but have not time, as I have all the business of the Company to attend to, and the condition we are now in, it requires a great deal of writing, making out reports &c.

Give my love to all enquiring friends.

Yours Truly, ELMORE ' "

Notes:

-- **Sergeant Elmer G Oldroyd** 25 was living in Toledo, Iowa when he enlisted. Oldroyd was married to Sarah Bunce of Toledo, Iowa and this letter may have been written to her or to another member of the Bunce family. Wounded slightly in the head April 6 1862, at Shiloh, Tennessee, Elmer's record states he was discharged in June 1863 at Toledo, Ohio, but that may be a clerical error. Oldroyd was from Ohio however, having grown up on a farm near Wooster, next door to his cousin, Osborn H Oldroyd. After his discharge Elmer returned to Wayne County Ohio where he was a dealer selling watches and clocks in the town of Shreve. In 1867 Elmer was elected Shreve's mayor. He was an enumerator in Shreve for the US census in 1880. He died in 1926 at the age of 90.

The same month Elmer enlisted in Iowa, his 19 year old cousin Osborn enlisted into the 20th Ohio Volunteer Infantry. When the war ended, cousin Osborn published his diary of the siege at Vicksburg and began collecting memorabilia of the martyred President Abraham Lincoln. In time Osborn Oldroyd became one of the country's top experts on Abraham Lincoln, helping to establish museums at Lincoln's Home in Springfield Illinois, and the Peterson House in Washington DC, where Lincoln died. He lived for years in both houses. Osborn Oldroyd wrote a best selling book about the assassination and much of his collection can be seen today at Ford's Theater, where Lincoln was shot.

-- Most of the men on Oldroyd's list of the missing have been noted elsewhere in this compilation. Four men not specifically mentioned are cited below.

-- **Isaiah Hunnicutt** 19 of Toledo, Tama County enlisted October 1861. **John A Pierson** 18 of Burlington enlisted November 1861. At Shiloh both of these men were missing in action and taken prisoner and both survived the Southern prison camps. At the end of their three year enlistment they mustered out in Davenport with the regiment. Before the War Isaiah worked as a laborer burning lime for mortar; after the War he and his family farmed for decades in Tama County. Some of his children, sons Benton and Clifford, lived in Toledo into the 1970's. Sometime around 1910 while oldest son Frank continued to farm, Isaiah, in his late sixties, headed for the Devil's Tower area of Wyoming with his wife and youngest son Samuel. Isaiah died in 1935 and was buried beside his wife at Pine Slope cemetery, Belle Fourche, South Dakota. Pierson farmed, raised a family in Kansas, and died at the National Soldiers Home in Hampton Virginia in 1928.

-- Two others on this list of Shiloh prisoners were born in Germany. They were **John B Wineman** 42, a native of Wurtenburg, who enlisted from Tama County October 1861 and **Henry Hass** 19 of Davenport who enlisted in November 1861. Both survived the POW camps. Wineman and Hass served the full three-year enlistment and mustered out with the regiment. Hass was later a policeman in Davenport where he lived for the rest of his life. He died in January 1914. He is buried in Davenport's City cemetery. Wineman (sometimes spelled "Weinman") had attempted to enlist with the 10th Iowa in August 1861; he was rejected as being too old. Determined to serve, Wineman waited two months and then tried to enlist again, this time successfully with the 14th. He is buried in Rose Hill cemetery northwest of Toledo, having farmed in the area for almost forty years after the War.

This article appeared in *The Iowa Transcript* May 22, 1862:

"The following letter from Mr. Joseph Shanklin Orderly Sergeant of Co. G 14th Iowa Regt. was not intended by him for publication, but his friends in this place, thinking it might be interesting to those having friends in the same company, have permitted its publication.

" MEMPHIS, Tenn., April 12, 1862

Dear Father:

I write you now not as a freeman, but as a prisoner of war, and for that reason I write to let you know that I am safe, and came through the battle safe, although I am a prisoner.

We have no reason to complain of the treatment we get, for they use us as well as they can. We were in the fight all day Sunday, and were surrounded about 5 o'clock and were taken prisoners.

We marched to Corinth and arrived there the next evening, and then took the cars for Memphis, and arrived here Tuesday evening, and are still here, but expecting to be taken away this evening or to-morrow morning. Destination not known to me.

I hope you will not have any serious apprehensions about David and myself, for I think we will get along very well, although we cannot write letters home nor receive any from there. But please do not let the thought of our being prisoners trouble you. We will take care of ourselves as well as possible, and trust to Providence for our safe return home again.

Among the prisoners from Toledo and vicinity are: Lieut. Gallagher, Joseph Burright, Goit, L Brannen, Fox, Hazlett, Josiah Luke, J R Moyer, David and myself, and a few others.

I will have to close for I have not much to write, and I do not know whether it will go or not after it is written; but thought I would write a few lines to let you know that I was not killed nor wounded.

From your son, J A SHANKLIN '   "

Notes:

On this list of prisoners:

-- Joseph Shanklin of Toledo was 19 when he enlisted. He had been a student at Grinnell College before the War. Captured at Shiloh April 6 1862, he survived his time as a POW but was later killed in action April 9 1864 at Pleasant Hill Louisiana, almost two years to the day from the heroic stand at Shiloh's Hornets Nest. The Toledo newspapers gave a lot of attention to his death; he was well liked, well known and widely mourned. Joseph's name is inscribed on a marble plaque in the sanctuary of Herrick Chapel on the Grinnell College campus. The memorial plaque honors the Grinnell students killed in the line of duty during the War, including BF Thomas' friend, James Ellis. See "*Soldier Life*" Chapter 13.

-- "David" most likely is **David Zehrung** 28 of Toledo, Tama County. David Zehrung was married to Joseph Shanklin's sister Sarah. Before the War he was a carpenter in Toledo. David enlisted October 1861 and was listed as missing in action at Shiloh. He lived through the trials of the POW camps but on March 31 1863, like many of the men who came out of the prison camps, he was discharged for disability; he had acquired a serious and chronic eye infection that defied treatment and rendered him unfit for duty. After the War he farmed in Nebraska. The 1880 US census shows Eliza Shanklin, David's mother-in-law, living with his family in Clay County. David died in October 1888 and was buried in Grandview cemetery near Anselmo Nebraska.

-- Lieutenant William Gallagher, later Captain, of Toledo, was 27 when he enlisted in October 1861. He survived POW camp and the War but died a few years after the War from the lingering effects of disease from the POW camps. The same time Gallagher was joining the 14th Iowa, his younger brother James signed on from Cedar Rapids into Company D of the 12th Iowa Infantry which fought along side the 14th at Donelson and in the thickest of the Hornets Nest fight. The 12th later helped secure important Union victories at Vicksburg and Nashville. **James S Gallagher** 22 served out his full three year term but then died at home in January 1866, within a year of the War's end. He is buried with his parents in Crystal cemetery, near the town of Garwin. (A different **James S Gallagher** 23 from Story County enlisted into the 14th Iowa in January 1864.)

-- Joseph Burright 28 enlisted in the 14th Iowa along with his brothers Cornelius Burright 19 and Stewart Burright 26 who were not taken prisoner. All three brothers had enlisted together as musicians when the Company was first formed in October 1861. Joseph survived his time as a POW and all three lived to see the War's end. The Burright brothers were from the Traer and Toledo area. Joseph, a stone mason, died in Guthrie Oklahoma in 1920. Cornelius died in 1910 in Independence Oregon. Stewart was buried in Sawtelle National Cemetery in Los Angeles in 1916.

-- Wagoner **William L Goit** 29 of Tama County, survived his captivity but was not well. He was discharged from St. Louis in December 1862. Returning home alive but very ill, he died the following month on January 22 1863, leaving a widow and four young children. His widow Esmeretta later remarried and moved to Nebraska. William is buried alone in Woodlawn cemetery in Toledo, a soldier's stone marks his grave.

-- **James Fox**, Toledo, was only 17 when he enlisted in October 1861 as a drummer. He made it through the prison camp and mustered out with the others at the end of his term in 1864.

-- **Andrew Hazlett** survived the Georgia prison camp; captured a second time in April 1864, he was held POW in Texas. He made it through the War and later became a physician.

-- **Josiah H Luke** 20 of Toledo, the popular fiddler for Company dances at Benton Barracks, also lived to serve until the end of the War signing up for extra time with the Residuary Battalion. After farming in Nebraska for many years he retired to Los Angeles where he became a well known fixture at Memorial Day ceremonies; every year for a decade the 80 year old veteran inspired new audiences with his recitation from memory of Lincoln's Gettysburg Address. His violin and his voice were finally silenced in August 1930. He is buried in Inglewood Park cemetery in Los Angeles.

-- **Jackson R Moyer** 19 Tama County, enlisted in October 1861 and mustered out with the regiment in November 1864 at the end of his three year term. After the War Jackson raised his family in Nebraska and later moved to Falls City Oregon where he worked as a skilled carpenter. He died in Oregon in June 1924 and is buried in Salem's City View cemetery.

-- **Leonidas H Brannen** of Toledo, said to be 18 on his enlistment papers, also survived the prison camp and the War. He lied about his age when he enlisted. In the 1860 US census there is a 13 year old LH Brannen living in Toledo. In 1880 Leonidas H is listed as 33 years old, running a hotel in Tama city. He was 14 when he signed up, not 18. Brannen's true age was not a secret back home: at the time of his enlistment the Toledo newspaper proudly reported: " ….*If there is a soldier in the United States army that can beat one of the boys of this town in Co. "G" 14th Iowa Regiment, we would like to have his parts measured and published. We speak of Leonidas H Brannen who when last heard from was five feet, eleven inches high, weighed one hundred and seventy pounds, and was only fourteen years old last June. The Soldier of these years that can present greater height and depth, length and breadth, must belong to a race of giants; and his corporosity would be a strong claim upon the office of General Corporal.*" Leonidas was still living in Tama city in 1900, aged 53. He is buried in Oak Hill cemetery east of Tama. Brannen's son Legrand at age 18 was an "automobile machinist" in Waterloo in 1910.

After the privates from the Iowa regiments captured at Shiloh were released from the southern POW camps on a conditional parole, Andrew H Hazlett sent the following letter from Benton Barracks to Samuel J Kirkwood, the Governor of Iowa:

" SAINT LOUIS, MO., July 11, 1862

Governor S. J. KIRKWOOD

RESPECTED SIR:

Perhaps I am presuming too much in troubling you with matters which may not concern you, but however I will have to ask a hearing and your aid if such you deem necessary.

Our condition has been and is as follows: On the 6th of April at the battle of Pittsburg Landing we were taken prisoners and released on parole the 25th of May. We were kept at Nashville until the 29th ultimo. While there every plan which they could devise was taken to get us in service again as a Tennessee regiment, but all their schemes proved of no avail. They found us as firm as the Secesh found us on the battlefield. We are now here and the same proceedings are to be acted over again. They want us to do guard duty notwithstanding our parole of honor. Now if we are not to be exchanged why not be called to our own State and not be here to be bamboozled by a colonel that is intoxicated the greater part of the time.

I have always considered a parole honorable for any prisoner to take, at least most people think so when lying in Southern prisons nearly naked and their flesh raw from the effects of vermin.

But the officers here and at Nashville act as though they thought differently. We have been treated but little better since our release than we were while in the South. We have not had much over half-rations and these of the poorest quality, having sour bread and rotten meat. This remark is not entirely applicable to our treatment here for it is some better.

I have now given you an indefinite idea of our condition, and if you can lend us any assistance we will consider ourselves much indebted; if you cannot, at least write me, with your advice with regard to our duty as paroled prisoners.

Respectfully, your obedient servant,   A. H. HAZLETT "

Notes:

-- The prisoners held in Alabama were released under this oath: *I do hereby solemnly swear and pledge my most sacred word of honor that I will not during the existing war between the Confederate States and the United States of America bear arms or aid and abet the enemies of said Confederate States or their friends, either directly or indirectly in any form whatsoever, until regularly exchanged or released.*

-- Those held at Macon Georgia were given this oath: *I do solemnly swear that I will not take up arms against the Confederate States of America or form any alliance to defeat them until regularly exchanged or otherwise honorably discharged.*

-- From the moment he learned that Iowa men were taken prisoner at Shiloh, Adjutant General of Iowa Nathaniel B Baker sprang into action on their behalf. He sent out a flurry of letters in May to Governor Kirkwood, General Halleck, and others to inquire about how to arrange for the prisoners' exchange or parole. When the men were then paroled, Baker sent out telegrams by the handful trying to arrange for their transportation home by rail or riverboat. When the parolees still didn't arrive back in Iowa, he sent out more urgent messages to anyone he could think of: *"Are not the 600 paroled Iowans to be forwarded at Government expense to Davenport?"*. He urged hospital commanders in several western posts to immediately forward home to Iowa any invalid ex-prisoners under their care, if the men were able to travel.

Then in early July, Baker discovered (perhaps from the visit by Thomas, Felter and Stoakes) that the men were being detained, first in Nashville and then in St. Louis, and were not being allowed to come home on furlough. Upset, Baker sent his protests to the War Department in Washington DC. Baker and Governor Kirkwood next learned (perhaps from the letters of Hazlett and others) that not only were the Iowa men being kept from furloughs, but that the paroled men had been ordered to do guard duties and other tasks around the barracks where they were being detained. The 23rd Missouri, which had been previously assigned these routine barracks duties, was then free to be sent into active duty against the rebels. The Iowa men felt that by doing duties which allowed another regiment to fight, they were violating their Oath of Parole. This could possibly subject them to summary execution if they were ever taken prisoners of war again; it was a very serious business. The Iowa men grew angry and refused to do the barracks duty; they were not active duty soldiers, they had falsely been promised furloughs, and they were being held against their will under guard in the North in almost the same conditions under which they had been imprisoned in the South. In response to their protests, Halleck released this harsh order: *"Paroled prisoners are obliged to do Guard, Police, and Fatigue duty for the proper order of their own Companies. Those who refuse are mutinous."*

Having these brave men, who were all willing volunteers, called "prisoners" rather than "released soldiers", and having them threatened with the guardhouse, sent Baker into renewed action. Baker wrote another long letter to the Secretary of War saying, *"I object to Iowa soldiers who are on parole doing anything which by implication or indirection may make them violate that parole"* urging Stanton again to *"allow these brave and gallant men to be furloughed to their homes"*. Baker told the Secretary *"it is a mistake to treat brave and willing men as mutineers"*. Baker also wrote again to Governor Kirkwood saying that the men were being treated outrageously. Baker personally commissioned retired Major Charles Bodfish to embark on a diplomatic mission to investigate this incident fully, and intervene on behalf of the men to get them returned to their homes to await exchange. Baker asked Bodfish to meet with the army officers in charge at St. Louis, and the Iowa soldiers being detained, and, if he could do nothing else, get the men spared from any further punishment. Bodfish was further ordered to personally visit all other western posts and hospitals for the purpose of arranging for any parolees found in these other places to be sent quickly home to their families in Iowa to recover. (Edmund McClaury may have reached his family specifically because of this effort by Major Bodfish.) See *"Soldier Life"*, Chapter 6.

This matter reached all the way to the desk of President Lincoln, who finally resolved the issue in favor of Halleck and the regular army. The Iowa volunteers were placed on duty, but they slipped away on "french leave" to go home whenever they could, and never forgot Baker's labors. When Baker died years after the War, the grateful veterans of Iowa took up a collection and had a tall monument to Baker's memory erected over his grave in Woodlawn cemetery in Des Moines.

From the *Dubuque Times*:

ANOTHER YOUNG HERO DEAD

We understand that Mr. John Gaston, of Tama county, in this State, belonging to the 14th Iowa, died very suddenly in this city on the morning of the 21st instant. Mr. Gaston had lately been discharged from the service at Corinth in consequence of permanent disability incurred in the service. At the battle of Pittsburg Landing he escaped capture with his regiment in consequence of being detailed to serve as powder carrier on that day. The surgeon of the regiment, Dr. Staples, and others who were acquainted with him, speak in the highest terms of him as a brave patriotic and Christian young man. Although he died and was buried among strangers, he was surrounded in his last sickness, and carried to the grave, by kind and sympathizing hearts. Many a tear of heartfelt sympathy was shed at the grave of the departed young hero, for hero he was in the truest sense of that term. Although occupying a very humble position in the service, no one discharged his allotted duties with more zeal, promptitude, energy, and fidelity than this young man. We understand he has a brother and other relatives at Wolf Creek in Tama county in this State. May the green sod of his mother earth rest lightly upon the heart of the brave one who has gone to his last long rest from the battle fields of his country. Rev. John C. Holbrook of this city kindly volunteered to attend his burial and perform the last sad rites that mortals can confer upon departed ones, whether friend or stranger.

Thus has another of the brave young men of Iowa been offered up to the accursed Moloch of this rebellion. How long -- oh! how long shall this sacrifice of the young, the brave, the true continue before the country shall arise in its might, and smite to the earth this rebellion and extirpate it's cause?

From the National Archives:

" State of Iowa
 County of Dubuque

I, GM Staples, late Surgeon of the 14th Iowa Infantry Volunteers, hereby depose and say that within the soldiers' lot in Dubuque, cemetery of Linwood, there is a grave with a headstone marked as follows:

"John Gaston, died at Dubuque, July 22, 1862, of disease contracted while in the service of his country, in the 14th Iowa Volunteers, aged 25. Was at Fort Donelson and Shiloh."

And I further depose and say that to the best of my knowledge and recollection, the said John Gaston left the command after the battle of Pittsburgh Landing, or Shiloh, on board a hospital boat, which proceeded down the Tennessee River, and he probably found his way into the Ohio, and up the Mississippi to the City of Dubuque, where he died having been cared for by the Sanitary Commission of said place.

I also further depose and say that I have no interest whatever in the prosecution of the claim for pension by the widow of said John Gaston.

> (Signed) GM Staples
> Late Surgeon 14th Iowa Vols.
> + Bvt Lieut Col

Subscribed and sworn to before me by said GM Staples this 26th day of October, 1888
> JR Lindsay
> Notary Public
> Dubuque County, Iowa "

Notes:
-- Before he left to fight for his country, John Gaston, Peter Wilson's close friend and bunkmate, had married Sarah Jane Moore of Beaver County Pennsylvania. They had a son, Oliver. As the Shiloh battle opened, Gaston had already been very ill. Despite his sickness he refused to stay behind safely out of the fight. As a result of his brave determination, he spent months in the hospital afterwards. When John arrived in Dubuque barely

clinging to life, Regimental Doctor **George M Staples** had been home on leave from the front and was on hand to offer John his personal services. When peace was finally restored, Dr. Staples returned to his medical practice in Dubuque, and was still there decades later to once again offer his personal help, this time to aid John's widow in obtaining a pension. Found in the National Archives one hundred and forty-five years after John's burial, Dr. Staples' deposition preserves forever the lost inscription of John's now badly eroded and broken headstone. Gaston's worn out marker was replaced recently with a new military marker and his original headstone is now in the collection of the Traer Museum.

This article appeared in *The Iowa Transcript,* Toledo, Iowa on November 6, 1862:

" We have been kindly furnished with the following letter by the brother of Mr. Wm Gallagher Jr. to whom it was addressed. Mr. Gallagher was 1st Lieut. of Co. G 14th Iowa regiment, taken prisoner at the battle of Shilo or Pittsburg Landing.

Annapolis, Maryland
Oct. 14, 1862

' Dear Brother,

It has been quite a season since my pen has traced a line to you, so long has it been that I have almost lost the power of constructing a letter.

If hard treatment and hard living could weaken man I am, we all are, weak and worthless as men can be. I cannot write you an account of our treatment tonight, I will have to reserve it for a verbal one, which I may soon. I will say this, it was such as no civilized people ought to bestow on humanity. Half-starved, filthy, bare and ragged as beggars having no change of clothing &c. &c.

I have been sick or unwell a great part of the time of my imprisonment. I have had chronic Diarrhea of which I have not entirely recovered. I had typhoid fever in Macon, Ga., and nearly died yet the thought of laying my bones in Dixie stimulated me and I stubbornly held on to life. I have been in 8 or 10 different jails or cottonsheds, have been in nearly all of the Southern States, have seen enough to make me clamor for revenge, vengeance equal to an incarnate devil and my fellow prisoners feel the same.

I am as well as could be expected. We arrived at this place via Fortress Monroe and Richmond, Va., this evening about 4 o'clock. What disposition will be made of us I know not, when I get localities I will write again.

I will give a list of the sick and dead among the boys.

Dead - R F Clark in Mobile, John Williams, John E McKune in Macon, Ga., David Miller, Montgomery, Ala., Lieut. Simon F Eccles died at Madison, Ga., after a long illness. They were all of my Co. Mortality at Macon this summer was great, of 1200 as high as 27 have died in one week, 7 in 24 hours. Joseph Shanklin had the ague when last heard from. Wm. Heath had bilious fever. Gen. Prentis and Crittenden and all the non-comissioned officers and privates were exchanged long ago and not gone by some means, they will all come too this week, tell the friends that they will be in our lines in a day or two, they were to start the next day after us. I hope to see you soon and I can give you a short history such as you do not often hear.

From your brother,
Wm. Gallagher, Jr '

LATER- We received a communication from the writer of the above dated at Washington DC, Oct. 19th in which he gives the following additional particulars: Lieut. Eccles died Aug. 26 of Chronic Diarrhea, David Miller in May of fever, R.F. Clark in May of lung fever, John D. Williams May 27 of fever, John E. McKune Sept. 9 chronic diarrhoea. He speaks very highly of all the Tama County boys and adds that he will be in Toledo in the 1st week of November next. "

Notes:
-- This letter, written to Lieutenant Gallagher's brother, may be the same letter written to Daniel Gallagher that was mentioned by Peter Wilson on November 3, 1862. Gallagher was later promoted to Captain of the 14th Iowa. His health was never the same, however, and he was hospitalized again later in the War. Captain Gallagher completed his three-year term of enlistment, but he died in Denver while still in his thirties a few years after peace was restored. His untimely death left his young widow Mary to raise two small children alone, their daughter Cora and son Willie. His son William S Gallagher later became an attorney practicing in Tama City at the turn of the new century.

-- After peace was restored, the Federal government tried to locate the burial places of each of its fallen soldiers, those whose remains had not been returned to their families, and to move their bodies to national cemeteries for burial as heroes. In many cases it was no longer possible to properly identify each soldier. Simon F Eccles, **John D Williams**, and John E McKune, who all died as POWs, are now buried in Andersonville National Cemetery. The gravesites of their fellow prisoners, **Robert F Clark** and **David Miller**, have not been located. They may have been among those unnamed men whose remains were also later taken to Andersonville and re-buried under individual headstones marked "Unknown". McKune and Clark have memorial markers alongside their parents' graves in their family plots in cemeteries near Traer and LaPorte City Iowa.

Edmund McClaury's father Robert sent the handwritten notarized statement below to the Office of Pensions in 1884. It is now preserved with the pension files kept by the National Archives. This is Robert's first-hand account of his son's condition after Edmund's release from the prison camp in Georgia:

" Edmund McClaury was born August 1st 1840 and enlisted in August 1861 & was in perfect health till he took the measles while on duty from which time he enjoyed no more good health but grew worse but continued in actual service through the siege of Fort Donelson & at Pittsburg Landing was taken prisoner on the 6th of April after fighting all day & was held a close prisoner til June when he was paroled after being carried in open or flat cars without food for 4 days at a time & exhibited and represented as all the Northern army

& having acquired the chronic dysentery til he was so reduced that he could not get up nor walk with out assistance & when he was sent to me by General Baker he required that he should be moved by short stages I took him & nursed [him] under the direction of Doctor Foursithe & Doctor Boldey two of the most skillful physicians we had [been] as careful as if he had been an infant till October 14th 1862 on that day he died he was the most emaciated looking object I ever saw

the Doctors & medicine bill amounted to over two hundred dollars those Doctors I am told are both dead I will here state that Edmund McClaury was never married nor never had no child or children but had lived with me & worked the farm I could not find their books of account they treated him for chronic diarrhea caused by exposure & fatigue and abuse while a prisoner "

Notes:
-- It should be noted that the prisoners were exposed not only to dangerous organisms like Salmonella and E.coli in their food and water, but were victims of unscrupulous war profiteers as well. Unethical contractors would grind the cobs along with the corn to lower cost, add weight, and cheat the army buyers, North and South. The prisoners complained of the low quality of the cornmeal provided to them but it was more than just the taste. The presence of the roughly ground corncobs also caused injuries to the men's stomachs and digestive systems, scouring and scratching their intestines and bowels. The result would often be bleeding and infection. This coarse meal, often also invested with weevils, mold, and rat droppings, made the men even more vulnerable to terrible long term and frequently fatal diseases. Sleeping in the rain without blankets or shelter only added to their misery and their chronic inability to recover any strength. Robert McClaury's moving description of his son's broken health, severely underweight and unable to stand without assistance, reflects upon the condition of many of the men who left the prison camps on both sides, so far gone that no amount of care, even at home, could restore them.
-- "Dr. Boldey" probably should be "Dr. Baldy". Dr. Henry T Baldy practiced medicine and farmed in the Salt Creek area of eastern Tama County, near the McClaury homestead just across the Tama-Benton county line. Henry Baldy later relocated to Toledo where his older brother, Dr. Peter L Baldy had also been an esteemed local physician for several years. It is also possible that Robert McClaury was referring to the more experienced Peter Baldy, a close neighbor of David Appelgate, the popular and well-known county clerk who was married to Edmund's sister Margaret. It is not certain whether Edmund died at his father's farm near Belle Plaine, or in Toledo at the home of his sister.

PART THREE

RETURN TO WAR 1863-1865

INTRODUCTION

This is the final installment of letters written by Peter Wilson during his service in the Civil War. [Following his release from his capture at the battle of Shiloh April 6 1862, Wilson was "on parole" awaiting an official prisoner exchange before he could return to active duty. This period was covered in the previous installment. This third group of letters covers that period of time when he had reported for duty but still was forced to wait in idleness for his scattered regiment to be re-united and re-organized and sent into action. The very existence of the regiment as a whole was uncertain, up in the air cloudy with rumor. This reunion, at first expected to take place in Davenport, was postponed by side missions, and then finally came about in St. Louis at Benton Barracks. Peter's reunited regiment hunted for rebel partisans in southern Illinois and then became stalled by the routine of garrison duties at Columbus Kentucky where the men settled into cabins for the winter of 1863-1864. Finally headed back into combat in the spring, Wilson was captured a second time at the battle of Pleasant Hill Louisiana, April 9 1864.] For the last thirteen months he was a prisoner of war in Texas and only two notes seem to have been smuggled out during this period.

THE LETTERS:

Rolla, Missouri

Rolla, Mo., Jan. 13th, 1863

" Dear Brother I take this opportunity to let you know how we come on. We are so far on the way to Davenport. We have been looking round this town since yesterday morning and I think it is time to put some of what we have seen on paper. It won't make much difference to future generations but for my own satisfaction I will note down what I think of Rolla. We left Camp Benton Sunday evening and marched down to the depot. We left St. Louis the same evening and rattled along over the roughest road imaginable. Daylight found us 70 or 80 miles from St. Louis. The train stopped at a farmhouse where there were plenty of chickens. The boys commenced firing out of the car windows making some commotion among the feathered tribe but little damage was done.

We arrived at Rolla a little after sunrise, got out of the cars, took breakfast, and then came here to our present camp, a little east of town, beautifully situated among scrub oak timber. I promised to describe this magnificent town. The situation is high and dry like Fort Donelson, the homes mostly new, not painted yet. There is "Saloon" written on the door of every other house. There are a good many log houses. The town is something like the size of Toledo. It is the present terminus of the Pacific Railroad and like all little towns of the same kind has plenty of speculation going on. There are a good many government buildings, storehouses, hospital, &c. There are a great many government teams getting ready to start to the frontier with supplies for the army. The recent troubles at Springfield were the cause of our being sent here. The citizens got scared and requested the commander of the post to send for more troops. There seems to be no cause for alarm as the rebels have been unable to accomplish anything and are reported falling back. I don't know how long we may stay here. Perhaps if things get quiet we may soon start for Davenport.

The country in the vicinity of Rolla is something like the country below Toledo, the settlers much the same as in Dixie. Rambling round this morning with a comrade we called at a house to get some water. A girl came to the door, looked at us, then shut the door, and peeped out the window at us. We knocked again but got no satisfaction. I concluded it was rather singular conduct but perhaps the ladies were too much Secesh. Perhaps if we stay a week here we may call again and have the matter explained. Fresh pork, turkeys & chickens are continually coming into camp. The chance for jayhawking* is not very good owing to the fact that so many have been here before us but we will glean up what is left.

We have 23 men in Company G. The Colonel is not with us. We have little restraint put on us. We have the small tent, five men in one. I like to be in tents much better than in barracks. They are warm enough for the climate and more quiet than in the barracks. I don't anticipate much fighting out this way. This being the depot for supplies for the frontier army has to be carefully guarded. The trains must be guarded against Bushwhackers*. The road to Springfield is about 140 miles and sometimes the rebels capture the trains. I suppose there will be a heavy escort sent this time. I think that is why we are here, to guard the place in the absence of the regular troops who will go with tomorrow's train. The teams are the usual six mules and heavy covered wagon. It makes little difference to the drivers whether the mules are trained or not. It is amusing to see the monkey shines going on among the teamsters getting their mules hitched up. Six new mules make some motions at their first go off. Government teamsters get 25 [dollars] per month. They have rough times but their work is not as hard as those that work on a farm. This place is 100 miles from St. Louis. The railroad is graded some of the way to Springfield but the cars have not run beyond this place.

I was amused this morning at the appearance of the farmers that were in town selling their produce. One old fellow and his boy had eggs, butter, rabbits, squirrels, possums, turkeys, chickens, and two nice large fat deer. Commodities sell [at] a good price. There is generally a good market where there are plenty of soldiers. Saloon keepers seem to have the majority in all towns in slave States. I think if I was led blindfold into a strange town I could tell as soon as my eyes were open whether I was in a slave State or not. Here in Rolla the pigs and cows have undisputed possession of the front yards. The farmers round here wear the everlasting butternut. I hate that color ever since Donelson & Pittsburg. The women say that our soldiers have taken nearly everything they had. One old lady lamented her last old hen yesterday. One of our boys came along and killed it. He would have done the same had it been the last in Missouri. For my part I seldom prowl after chickens. I think the people are to be pitied that live in this State. While I am writing one of the boys came in and reported having found a flock of sheep. About twenty are just starting. They will be apt to have mutton for supper. I am writing on my knee so I will finish, not being used to it. You may direct as usual only keep off "Paroled", as we go by that no longer. Benton Barracks, St. Louis, Mo., Co. G, 14th Iowa, will find us here or wherever we may be. We did not receive pay yet, I think we will not get any for two months. I will not write any more this time. I will write from our next stopping place if we go anywhere else.

For the present good bye, your brother, Peter "

----

* Jayhawkers were anti-slavery, pro-Union guerrillas operating in Kansas and Missouri. Bushwhackers were their counterpart: pro-slavery marauders that favored the Confederacy. Both were gangs of pillaging bandits and destructive raiders with a quasi-military excuse for vengeful ambush, robbery, plunder, arson and murder. Jayhawking and bushwhacking soon became widely used terms to describe soldiers foraging for supplies, as well as looting, scavenging and stealing, often with a sporting connotation.

Columbus, Kentucky

Columbus, Ky., Jan. 20th, 1863

" Dear Brother: I received your letter a few days ago and take the present opportunity of answering. The only news of importance is that we are all ready to leave Columbus and expect to start tomorrow morning. We go down the River (1) rumor says to Texas but we only conjecture. The 6th Division is all going from this vicinity. Gen. Smith (2) commands the Division. Col. Shaw (3) will command our Brigade. We will most likely see some active service this spring. The Regiment is in fine order as far as health is concerned. It is a severe time to leave our cabins as the snow is quite deep but no doubt we will go far enough South to get out of the cold. I send home my extra clothing; it is only some shirts and my coat. The shirts are in J. Felter's box. The coat is in a box sent to your address at Toledo. There is another coat in the box. You may leave it at Mr. Thomas's so the man can get it some time when he comes to Buckingham. We are leaving a good place to take the chances in the field.

We have fared sumptuously every day for a long time. We may look forward to hard tack as our principal stand by now. I am glad we are going. I want to see some more of the South before our time is up. There are ten of Company G enlisted in the Veterans and some more intend to go in. There are only about thirty old soldiers in the company. I suppose we will have a fine lot of recruits before long. They will see the elephant in full size before they are long in the service. (4) I will write from our first stopping place.

Until then good bye. Your brother, Peter "

------

1 The Mississippi River.
2 Possibly Brigadier General Andrew J. Smith.

3 Colonel William T. Shaw commanded the Fourteenth Iowa Infantry throughout the war. [Shaw had been captured with the Regiment at Shiloh and was kept as a prisoner of war until his exchange in late October 1862. While he was held captive his two-year-old daughter Nannie, his youngest, died at home. After a short home leave to Iowa he returned to take command again of the Fourteenth.]

4 The meaning of this statement is not clear. Perhaps Peter Wilson refers to the story of the blind men who tried to determine what an elephant was like by feeling various parts of its body, such as the trunk, leg, tail, and side. [Actually, "seeing the elephant" was a common slang term for experiencing combat by seeing the "beast" of war firsthand. It also meant enduring any hardship and was used by travelers on the Oregon Trail to describe the "beastly" rigors and unusual sights they found on the journey west.)

Benton Barracks, St. Louis

Benton Barracks, Jan. 21st, 1863

" Dear Father: We have just arrived at Benton Barracks. I found your letter dated Jan. 8th upon arriving. I received one from James just before we left Rolla. I am glad to know that you are all well and getting your house up &c . . . I think you will tire of keeping a negro. There are plenty of them here, shiftless, good for nothing as may be.

It must be you jump at conclusions in thinking the first soldiers will all die or be killed. Of course bullets are no way particular who they hit but I am convinced that we stand much better chances of keeping our health in the South now than formerly. We have been out ten days in the worst kind of winter weather, we lost two nights' sleep in going and coming, I was up two nights on picket guard, we had rough times in all respects, but none of the men were sick during the time. Such a trip last winter would have been very different. There are but few of the 14th now, only 60 men were with us this time. I will put them against any men in the service for standing hard usage or fighting. I might as well say for jayhawking too. The people of Rolla will remember us for some time. The amount of goods taken from the groceries yesterday would be worth at least 200 dollars. I don't justify such conduct nor have anything to do with it. I can't say that I pity the losers much. They are a lot of unprincipled suckers that make fortunes in a short time by selling goods at exorbitant prices to the soldiers. I think if they make much of the 14th they deserve it.

The country, what we saw of it between St. Louis & Rolla, is rather hilly but the land is pretty good. We had merry times coming in this morning. Having plenty of ammunition we sometimes took a shot from the car windows at dogs, sometimes at chickens round the houses, &c. Although we had rough times we liked the trip very much. I don't know what will be the next move. We will either come to Davenport or the Union Brigade will come here. If we come to Davenport I will most likely be home for a short time. If we stay here I cannot come home, but it is not much difference. This is a good place. My health is good. I have nothing to complain of in any way. Frank (5) is much improved since he came here. John R. Felter is with us. He is looking well but not so well as when he left. The snow that fell a few days ago is melted and Benton Barracks is very muddy but we have little to do in muddy weather. It seems almost like home to be back in this place.

I see no reason to dread the future. I think the war will go on and many must fall perhaps without doing much good. I trust that the Almighty Hand that has kept me in health thus far will keep me still in safety although much danger may be before me. If it is God's will that I find my grave in the South I hope to be ready. Let it come when it may, I am determined to do my duty and come home honorably or never. Still I do not anticipate losing my life. I have strong hopes that I will go safely through. After what we have come out of already I think we should be more hopeful under difficulties in the future. There is not much prospect of the 14th being filled very soon (6) and we are likely to be at some unimportant place for some time. I think if I had my choice I would prefer going to Dixie with a full regiment to staying in Benton Barracks the way we have been. The prospect of staying in Dixie perhaps for years I don't much like but if we have a good Regiment I am willing to go South and see the war ended before coming back. We might be taken prisoners again but we might not in a long time. If we get a fair chance there is not much danger. I need not write any more now. If we come to Davenport I will be home soon after we arrive, if not I will write as usual.

Your affect Son, Peter.

[PS] I expected to have sent home some clothes but it seems we cannot get our lost clothing now. "

------

5 Frank was probably Benjamin Franklin Thomas, who was an old and close friend of Peter Wilson's.

6 The placing of newly enlisted men in old regiments was hindered by the desire of influential men to form new regiments and thus secure for themselves commissions as officers. Usually old regiments had few places for newly commissioned officers. [Beyond the men lost through illness and battle, the Fourteenth was still short the three full companies which had been detached and sent to the Dakota frontier when the regiment was first formed. These companies would have to be replaced with new recruits in order to make a full regiment.]

St. Louis and Carondelet, Missouri

(Benton Barracks) Jan. 28th, 1863

" Dear Brother: It is not long since I have written all that seemed worth writing but we have just been paid this afternoon and for once I must send some money home. I find that to keep my money is poor policy as there are so many ways of spending money here. There was only two months' pay due me up to the first of January. The boys here owe me 20$ all of which I will get this time. C. Burright* owes me 10 dollars. I will find him some time. I will send as much as I can spare this time.

We have not been paid more than two hours and a good many of the boys have gone to town to have a spree. Some of the green ones may come back without much money. Some have left their money in safekeeping until they come back. I have about 200$ belonging to different ones. It is needless to explain the kind of places the majority of soldiers frequent whenever they have money. More of the soldiers are ruined at such places than killed in battle. Gambling prevails to some extent; after payday I have seen a dozen or fifteen banks in full business at the same time in Benton Barracks. Dice is used more than cards for gambling but both are used. There are some sharp customers among the soldiers sometimes too sharp for the regular gamblers. I have sometimes watched the game long enough to see how it goes.

It is reported that we start tomorrow for Carondelet some ten miles from St. Louis to guard the Navy yard or properly speaking the new gunboats that are being built there. Only two companies are going. Co's G & H are the ones. I hear no more of going to Davenport but still we may come after all. It looks as if we are to be cut up into small detachments to do small kind of business. It is just as well for us perhaps but somehow I would prefer being filled up and try it in Dixie. The boys are spoiling here. They hardly know how to behave any longer. One good thing there are no brawls among ourselves. The boys stand up for one another in all scrapes that any member may get into so that if some one does something that is against all rules such as knocking the lights out in a grocery in the evening and taking whatever is handy or taking a milk pail from a pedlar wagon, any kind of stealing whatever is never reported. If any one gets drunk the orders are to report him so that he may be sent to the guardhouse. Instead of doing so we stow them away in some quiet place until sober. We have some hard cases in the Company. There is nothing too bad for them to do and they are seldom out of mischief of some kind. Some of the worst will desert as soon as we are ordered into the field again. How long before that time shall come I cannot guess.

I think we have some reason to fear that traitors in the North are going to trouble us. I see in today's paper that the 119th Illinois is under arrest for disloyalty and quite a strong party in the North is in favor of ending the war on any terms. (7) I hope the government will severely punish northern traitors. If half of that regiment were shot it would be no more than they deserve. After all the blood that has been spilled it is too bad to give it up. It is poor comfort to the Illinois soldiers now in the field to see how the traitors at home are trying to undo all they have done.

To be sure little has been done, but if the war is carried on the western men will open the Mississippi and keep it open. I have not much hopes of the Eastern Army taking Richmond but I want to see the war go on some time yet and if we must acknowledge the Southern Confederacy let them sue for peace. Then and not before could a peace be made that would be honorable and fair in case of a separation. We must have Kentucky, Missouri, and Maryland or nothing has been gained by the war. If the North concludes to stop fighting the South will claim all the border States. I have often heard the Secesh say they must have all the slave States and they will if they possibly can.

I suppose there are some of the people not ten miles from Buckingham that would indorse the treasonable speeches made in the Illinois legislature this winter. If they lived in Missouri instead of Iowa they would suffer for their opinions.

Jan. 31st: We are now in Carondelet, comfortably settled in a stone schoolhouse something like the one three miles from Cedar Rapids. Co. G in the house and Co. G in the barn. (8) We like this place the best of any place we have ever been in. Carondelet is about twice as large as Cedar Rapids. It is pleasantly situated on bank of the river. The Navy yard is at the lower part of the town. I have spent considerable time inspecting it but I cannot give much idea of the extent of it in this letter. There are five gunboats being built there. One will be launched Tuesday, two are afloat and almost finished.

I will finish by giving you some idea of our duty here. In the daytime we have nothing to do. We have to do our duty in the night. We will be on duty about four hours every third night. The first comes on at six and is relieved by the second at ten. They are relieved by the 3rd at two and the third stand until six. Then the workmen commence for the day. There are five or six hundred men working on the boats. It sounds something like a boiler manufactory. The noise is intolerable. Of course we need not stay in longer than we please. There is so much machinery it is quite a treat to spend a few hours looking at it.

I need not write any more this time. I will try in my next to describe some of the gunboats.

Your brother, Peter "

------

7 The term "appeasers" was evidently understood although it was not then in use. ["Copperheads" may have been the 1860 term for what the 1942 editor called "appeasers". "119th Illinois is under arrest for disloyalty" may be an error. The 119th seems to have served bravely and honorably to the end of the War. However, the 109th Illinois, which was formed in September 1862, was plagued by desertion. Several officers were dismissed in February 1863 for "utter incompetence" and many of the men were later transferred to other Illinois regiments and the regiment was completely disbanded in April 1863.]

8 This is apparently a slip in writing. The two companies were G and H.

* Cornelius Burright was one of the men not captured with the regiment at the Hornets Nest. Musicians often performed other duties such as nursing, rather than combat. He was one of the men assisting Peter Wilson at the hospital in Monterey. They tented together and ran a "grocery".

Benton Barracks, St. Louis, Missouri

Benton Barracks, Feb. 11th, '63

" Dear Father: As it is time to write so as to give the letter time to get through in the usual time I proceed to write a few lines although there is nothing worth mentioning without it is the state of the weather, roads, and Benton Barracks in particular. Missouri against the world for mud and Benton Barracks against any part in the State. One good thing we can keep out of it as we have little to do. The winter has been unusually mild and but very little frost but plenty of rain. There seems to be more sickness this winter than there was last not in our Regiment but in the new, and among citizens. There is considerable small pox both among soldiers and citizens in St. Louis. No cases that I have heard of have been known in this camp but in the hospitals in the city and in some parts of town. The small pox hospital is far enough out of the way to be safe and all who take it are sent there. I have visited some of the large hospitals to see acquaintances and found them very well conducted and good care taken of the patients.

Since coming back to the Barracks (9) we have not done much nor made any move towards filling or reorganising the Regiment. I think there is no particular line of action marked out for us yet. It seems to me there is a good deal of uncertainty in the most of Uncle Sam's affairs at present and small hopes of their getting better. Still we must carry on the war, hoping to have more success in future. The men that want to make peace now are nothing but Secesh and ought to be dealt with as such. I see no way but stick to the President in all his measures and if they agree to arm the negroes so much the better. But I need not discuss such affairs. The subject is too extensive to go into. The unsettled state of affairs in the Regiment makes it an easy matter to get discharged from the service now if any thing is the matter. Quite a number have been discharged this winter that were in good health and some on pretence of being unfit for service. If I should have a spell such as I had in Memphis I could easily get a discharge but I have not seen a sick day since I was home and hope I may continue so. I would much rather see the war ended before I come home than be discharged for disability. I need not add your affect son, Peter "

------

9 No explanation is given in the letters preserved of the return to Benton Barracks. (It is probable the return was for the purpose of bringing the separated parts of the Fourteenth back together which had been originally planned to take place at Davenport.]

Benton Barracks, Feb. 18th, 1863

" Dear Brother: I have just received your letter and proceed to reply, though nothing new is to be the subject. We have been here since coming from Carondelet and we neither drill nor any thing else. Sometimes it is whispered that we will be consolidated with the 8th & 12th (Regiments) and commanded by Col.

Geddes (10) of the 8th but whether such will be the case we can't find out. If the three Regiments could be brought to the arrangement peaceably they would make a first rate regiment but there are too many aspirants whose hopes of a commission would vanish to make the thing comfortable, so it will be against the wishes of most of the men. But I don't know as it will be done so I will not write any more of the matter. In any case it won't matter to me. It will bring us sooner into the field and I would just as soon go there as any other place. The spring is coming and it will be more pleasant now camping than in the winter.

You must be in good spirits at home getting so much for wheat. I don't expect to save much money in the army as it is almost impossible to do so being paid regularly and in company all the time but if I keep well it won't make much difference.

I received a letter from Uncle David today. He says they have expected us at Davenport for a long time and meant to have roast turkey &c when we came. Perhaps we may come yet and if so we will have good times at the Grove, but I have but small hopes of coming this time somehow. For the short time I spent there I took quite a fancy to the place or the people I don't know which. The Union Brigade is still at Davenport and we hear nothing of their being sent here. It seems to me we must get together sometime. I want to see C. Burright to get what he owes me. You may pay Gaston 11$ dollars although I had only agreed to pay John when Corniel paid me. There are some things Frank, John, and I sent in company to Mr. Thomas. I had intended if we received our lost clothing to send home all I did not need, but we have not got it and some things I did not need I sent among Frank's things. I have no more to write this time. Give my respects to inquiring friends &c. Your brother Peter Wilson "

----

10 James L. Geddes, of Vinton, had commanded the Eighth Iowa during most of its service. [The life story of James Lorraine Geddes would fill an incredible biography. He was born in Scotland in 1827 and emigrated with his parents to Canada at the age of ten. As a young man he served with the British Royal Horse in Calcutta India and fought in the Punjab campaign, in Afghanistan at the Khyber Pass, and in the Himalayas. Returning to Nova Scotia he married then soon left, in 1857, for the United States. Choosing to settle in Vinton Iowa he farmed and taught school until the War broke out. In August 1861 Geddes enlisted as a private in the Eighth Iowa Infantry but swiftly rose in rank to Captain. He led the Eighth Iowa in standing firm alongside the Fourteenth Iowa at the Hornets Nest of Shiloh, where he was wounded and taken prisoner. He was held prisoner in Georgia and at Richmond's notorious Libby prison. He spent his time in prison camp writing patriotic war songs that later became widely popular. Upon his exchange he served at Vicksburg, Jackson, Brownsville, Memphis and Mobile accomplishing some very notable and important successes; his distinguished service earned him a brevet rank of brigadier general at war's end. Coming back to Vinton he served as County Auditor, a Judge, and head of the Vinton School For The Blind until he finally moved to Ames to serve in many capacities for the Iowa College of Agriculture, today's Iowa State University. Among his positions at the College were: professor of military tactics, treasurer, librarian, vice-president, and acting president. James L. Geddes died February 1887 in Ames, and is buried in Vinton.]

Benton Barracks, March 4th, '63

" Dear Father: I neglected to write last week because I had nothing to write and it is not much better yet, but I will send a few lines this week to let you know that we are still in Benton Barracks working at the same trade and in good health. We have almost come to the conclusion that the War Department has forgotten us. I have not heard a whisper of what we are going to do or whether we are to take any more active part in the seemingly endless war. It seems the longer we fight the less success we meet with. If we lose a few more gunboats the rebels will have as good a fleet as we. I think the North is in rather a ticklish place. They can't honorably give up the struggle and there is not much encouragement in carrying it on. I think the best way is to put it through right or wrong until some side says "enough", as the saying is in common terms. The number that fall in the struggle must be very great. Take for instance the 3rd Iowa Regiment. They were in this camp last September, 950 men as good looking as ever came from Iowa. They are here now and have only 100 men fit for duty. They were only in one battle, that of Arkansas Post, where their loss in killed was but slight. They have perhaps 100 men dead and 150 deserters; the balance are in the hospitals. I think that is the worst state of affairs in any of the Iowa regiments. Some of the others are not much better. The old regiments seem to have a better sort of men in them. I think the aggregate of deserters from the 14th would not amount to more than twenty and we have now been 16 months in the service. We have at present very few sick men but we may account for that in having good winter quarters and not undergoing the privations of soldiers in the field.

If we went to Dixie where the common chances of war would give some chance for advancement I think my prospects would be good. As it is there is nothing going on. I think in filling the vacancies that are now in the Company I can get only one step higher but the next, if ever that comes, my chance is good for a commission. So the sooner we go into active service the better it will suit me, but I am only hoping that we may go South without any probability of our going. Governor Kirkwood is trying to get us to Davenport and if he succeeds he will then have us sent to the frontiers. This would be all very good if he can accomplish it. I received a letter from James today. I need not answer it this week as this is sufficient. I think the boys might go at it and write me how all the business in their charge is progressing. I am mostly idle and a letter from the boys would be very acceptable. I need not write any more this time. Your affect Son Peter Wilson "

Benton Barracks, March 12 [1863]

" Dear Brother: I will send a few lines this week as usual but I don't know what to write. The prospects of filling the vacancies in the Company is all over for the present. I think after all our waiting we will go to Dixie just as we are. Of course there must be an organization of some kind. They will most likely make three companies of the 14th and attach us to something else. The law is to consolidate regiments that number less than 505 men. If we get no more recruits and go south now we will soon get below that number so we may as well expect to be consolidated sooner or later. If they would fill us up and send us to active service and as quick as vacancies [occur] in the commissioned officers fill them from those entitled to promotion there would be more encouragement in the business. There is a surplus of commissioned and noncommissioned officers now so of course there is no promotion at this time.

It seems too bad to keep those that came out in the first call in the ranks and give them no chance to get up and so many more regiments raised since they came out. I don't know how they mean to officer the conscripts. I hope they will fill the 14th with them. I suppose they will make new regiments with them and do the same in all respects as with volunteers.

How do you like the conscript law and what do you think of the prospects of the war for the Union? I think it looks uncertain but I hope it may go ahead for years rather than stop without accomplishing the desired end. Sometimes I see letters to the boys in this Regiment so full of Secesh notions that if the writers were exposed they would be severely punished, letters encouraging desertion &c. It seems there are numbers of Copperheads in Iowa. I hope the conscription will find some of them. I respect an open enemy that will fight for what he believes in but those in the Northern States that can find nothing better to do than work against us in every mean sneaking way ought to be put into the service and made to toe the mark. It would at least get them where they would get less in numbers. Frank, John, and myself will send a box in company. I will send my overcoat and one of my blankets. I know now what is necessary in Dixie so I will not take anything more than is necessary with me, one rubber blanket and one government blanket are all that I will carry besides some shirts &c.

There is some talk of our starting down the river soon. Our Lieutenant Colonel has resigned. (11) He is not much force so no one cares. Our Major is ditto. (12) Somehow our field officers always were of the poor sort with the exception of old Shaw (13) and he is fishing for a brigadiership. Governor Kirkwood gives his friends appointments in the army without knowing how they are qualified. So it goes, but I must finish for this time. I enclose a list of Co. G. It may be of use to refer to if I wish to do so at some future time so I will send it where it can be kept safe.

I will write next week. Perhaps we may know how soon we may start by that time. You might write a longer letter and give me your opinions on matters and things. I have dropped most of my correspondents so I don't get so many letters now as formerly.

March 13th: I have just received a letter from Flora (14) enclosing one from Scotland. A letter from Scotland is so much out of my line it don't interest me much but still I was pleased to get it. I would like to know their sentiments on the Secesh question. I suppose they are not particular how it goes if they only have good times in Scotland. Quite unexpectedly we received orders this morning to elect a First Lieutenant. Sergts. Hazlett & Shanklin (15) were the candidates. Hazlett was elected by a large majority. I think if we fill any more it will be done according to seniority*. If so Shanklin will be Second Lieutenant. Gallagher (16) is Captain now. All the troops here now except the 14th have marching orders.

According to a recent order from the War Department if a Company has less than fifty men they can't have more than two commissioned officers so there is no telling whether we will get the number or not. I think if Col. Shaw stays with us we will be all right. It is not certain whether we will leave this place soon or not. The Union Brigade has not joined us yet and of course they will before we leave. I am in good health and spirits. Let things go as they may I mean to keep a stiff upper lip, but I must finish as my letter is too long for anything there is in it.

I forgot to mention that we are becoming adept in the bayonet exercise. Your Brother, Peter   "

----

11 This was **Edward W. Lucas** of Iowa City.

12 The name of this officer has not been found. [**William W. Kirkwood** was appointed Major September 8 1862 and resigned March 4 1863.]

13 Colonel William T. Shaw.

14 Flora Wilson, an older sister and one of Peter's faithful correspondents.

15 **Andrew H. Hazlett** of Shueyville and Joseph A. Shanklin of Toledo.

16 William Gallagher of Toledo. [* Geography and politics, in the army and at home, also played a part in promotions besides seniority; even family ties were taken into consideration. After the men voted on their choice, all promotions had to be then approved in turn by Capt. Gallagher, Col. Shaw, Adj. Gen. Baker, and Gov. Stone. Correspondence from the Company to the Adjutant General, now preserved by the State Historical Society Of Iowa, reflect how much controversy entered into some decisions. There was an effort to balance the candidates geographically within the Company; nominations from Tama County were often paired with nominees from another area. After the battle of Pleasant Hill, Lts. Hazlett and Shanklin were both thought killed; Capt. Gallagher recommended Addison Davis and Peter Wilson to take their places. When Hazlett later turned up still alive, only one position was available. According to surviving correspondence, Capt. Gallagher then chose Davis over Peter Wilson for promotion to Lieutenant because Davis was planning to remain in the service beyond their three year term of enlistment. Also see Chapter 9 of B.F. Thomas, *"Soldier Life".*]

Benton Barracks, March 19th [1863]

" Dear Father: The time for receiving letters from home this week has gone by and none has come so I must write now or you will not get this next week. I scarcely know what to write as little is going on here. There is no immediate prospect of leaving Benton Barracks. It is rumored that Pope (17) is bound to get us into Iowa. He keeps the Union Brigade and perhaps he may succeed in getting us into his Department. Of course we would prefer going to the frontiers to going South but as it is not certain I need not write about it. How do the folks like the conscript act? It seems to me if the Copperheads* mean to kick up a fuss in the North their time has come. There may be some resistance to the conscription but I think if Jeff Davis can make it work we can.

There is no use in thinking of peace until the South or the North is conquered. The South has all their available force now in the field and if we get 500,000 more men and go ahead I don't feel uneasy as to the result. We must do it and we must have men, so the soldiers indorse the conscript act and the sooner we get 500 of the rankest Northern Secesh into the 14th Iowa the better we would like it. Of course many of the conscripts will make as good soldiers as volunteers but there will be some that would not fight at all if they could help it and if they had their choice would fight against us. They will have to toe the mark to atone for their disloyalty if they get into the old regiments. It seems as though war matters must come to an end in this year. The South cannot be conquered at all if another year goes by and nothing accomplished. The longer I stay in the Army the more I hate the South and worse still their friends in the North. Perhaps if we had been in the field this winter I might feel differently on the subject but we have long wished to be organised and sent into the field. As long as we are obeying orders we are not responsible for our idleness.

There is one thing sure if we were in the field it would be better for a majority of the men. There are some of the boys that are completely spoiled by being so long in a city with plenty of money and nothing to do. It is getting fashionable to steal anything they can. A few nights ago the post sutler's store here in camp was broken into and several hundred dollars worth of revolvers, watches, &c taken out. The thing was done in a reckless manner and the Provost Guard was soon on the ground but I think they will not succeed in proving any one guilty. There is any amount of mischief going on all the time and if we were sent to Dixie such work would come to an end. But I must finish this scribble. The weather is fine here and the fields begin to look green. If you have such weather in Iowa I suppose you are sowing wheat. Your Affect Son Peter Wilson "

----

17 Probably Major General John Pope.

 * The Copperheads were a faction of Northern politicians, columnists, protestors and agitators, mainly Democrats, who opposed the War, sympathized with the South, opposed Lincoln's policies, or wanted an immediate peace settlement with the Confederates. When events on the battlefield went badly for the Union, the people wishing to make peace with the Confederacy, or to simply end the War, grew in number and loudness. When things went well for the Union on the battlefield, they became more quiet and less

influential. Copperheads were dismissed by the Unionists as defeatists, the poisonous snakes in the midst of the Union. No matter how the War progressed, pro-peace activists constantly had to defend themselves against charges of disloyalty. Most Northerners believed, perhaps with good reason, that the Copperheads prolonged the War by encouraging rebels to continue the bloodshed in the vain hope that the North would become discouraged and abandon the struggle. When the "endless" war finally ended, the Northern anti-war factions were completely discredited.

Benton Barracks, March 27th, '63

" Dear Father: I received your letter this week too late to answer it but as I write to some of you every week I suppose you hear from me often enough. As long as we stay in Benton Barracks I can have nothing new to write. We expect from time to time to leave for some point down the river but there is no time set to leave yet. The latest reports we have had is that as soon as the Union Brigade comes from Davenport we will report to General Grant at Vicksburg. There is no telling when the Union Brigade may come. We don't much expect to leave for some weeks at least, perhaps longer. We will get paid and exchange our Austrian muskets for Enfield or Springfield rifles before we go. If we have to wait for conscripts to fill the Regiment it will be two months before we get them.

The arrangement made for giving furloughs to the soldiers has not been used here yet. I suppose they will give some furloughs this summer but if we go three or four hundred miles down the river it would take so long to come home it would not pay to take a short furlough. I think there is not much chance of my coming home this spring. As long as I am in good health it don't matter much.

If we are paid I will send the boys some books before we go down the river. I can get books very cheap in St. Louis, if they let me know what kind to send. The History of England in five volumes costs only two dollars. Byron, Shakespeare, Scott, Pollock, or any such can be had for reasonable prices and I can send them in the trunk we send our surplus clothes in. We have had plenty of time to read this winter and I have improved it to some extent. I found it more to my mind than studying grammar. I guess I was not meant for a student so I must not go against what seems to be ordained.

It is surprising that Uncle Dodd (18) would come out at a time like this. It must be he has more pluck than some of our relations that preceded him. I suppose he will find a hearty welcome and no doubt he will like Iowa. If the war was carried on in the North instead of the South there would not be much immigration to it. The South will be reduced to a wilderness in a few years if they keep on fighting. If accounts are true they begin to be in straits for provisions now and they will get worse. The loss of Vicksburg if they do lose it and with it the Mississippi will stop them from getting supplies from Texas. If they can hold out much longer I think they will learn to live on short rations something that few soldiers can tolerate.

But I will change the programme and write a little about raising garden vegetables in the vicinity of St. Louis. This morning John R. Felter and myself went out of camp to take a ramble in the country or rather the suburbs of St. Louis. Among the various objects of interest we noticed on a hillside a good many glass houses or rather frames covered with glass roofs and fronts and looking so much like Uncle West's cabbage plant houses we thought we would go in and look at them. There was something like half an acre in beds of different plants all in good condition, cabbage plants of the early Oxheart kind just big enough to set out looking very thrifty and healthy. All kinds of plants generally raised by gardeners were there in tens of thousands. They were setting them out today and they have some twelve or fifteen acres of very good land.

I think from the prices of their produce they must have a good business. He told me he had his cabbages into market about the first of June. He is selling some of the early stuffs already, such as lettuce, radishes, &c, at prices not profitable to the consumer. He says the war hurts his business and particularly the blockade of the river. There is not so much business done in St. Louis now as when the river was open to New Orleans. Still there seems to be a great amount of business going on. I have just received a letter from D. Galt, so I must finish and write a few lines to him. So no more from your affect Son, Peter Wilson "

------

18 This was, apparently, Andrew Dodd, who had married Christine Wilson in Scotland.

Benton Barracks, April 6th, 1863

" Dear Father: You have heard before this time that we had gone from Benton Barracks so I will give you a short account of our trip. We went to Memphis to guard the Paymaster and some seven millions of greenbacks down the river. We had a pleasant trip and had no mishap of any kind. The boat had a valuable cargo of government stores besides the money to pay the soldiers. We stopped at Cairo, Columbus, Island No. 10, Fort Pillow, and other places of note on the way down and arrived at Memphis and deposited our charge in the bank all right, then spent 24 hours in the city. It pleased us to visit our old prison* under such different circumstances. Memphis is strongly fortified and I think it will stay in the Union if fifty heavy guns in one of the best forts I have seen is any argument. The city could be demolished in a short time and a small force in the fort could hold the place against a host.

Contrabands were coming in by the hundred, little wooly darkies looking more like a new species of monkey were piled up on the wagons, men and women walking by the side. They must have brought their masters' best furniture along judging by the bureaus, bedsteads of the best quality, feather beds, &c, that were piled on the wagons. I wonder what is to be done with them. They are a kind of people I would not like to have for neighbours.

The soldiers down at Memphis and other points on the river are in very good spirits. They are more than ever in for fighting to the end. The general health is good. They think the time is not far distant when the Southern Confederacy will be numbered among the things that were. We found the Union Brigade* at the Barracks on our return and we are under orders for Vicksburg. I think we will start in a few days. I will send some books to the boys if I can get time to go to St. Louis tomorrow or before we start. I need not write to Janet this time. I will write when we get to Vicksburg. You may not get my letters very regular now as it will be so far, I suppose it will take a week to get there. I may write from Cairo or Helena on the way down. I will write to Grandfather before we start. Your affect Son, Peter Wilson "

----

* Memphis was one of their first places of imprisonment after Shiloh. Peter remained hospitalized there as a POW while the others moved on to Mobile. The Eighth Iowa under Geddes is credited with keeping Memphis from later falling back into rebel hands.

* While their captured companions were taken to camps deep in the Confederacy, the Union Brigade continued to fight during the siege of Corinth, and elsewhere. After their time of captivity, and then their idle parole period waiting for their official exchange, the former prisoners had to wait again until April 1863 to be finally rejoined with the other members of their regiments. The Union Brigade was then disbanded and dispersed back into their original regiments. At this time the command structure of the regiments was reshuffled to fill the positions of men who had been lost in battle or discharged for illness. Also complicating matters was the fact that some men of the Union Brigade had been promoted to take the places of their fellow regimental lieutenants, corporals and sergeants, who as prisoners and parolees had been held temporarily out of action but were now ready to resume their former positions. When they all came together again there was a lot of "dust" to be settled. See B.F. Thomas, *Soldier Life*, Chapter 9.

Benton Barracks, April 8th (1863)

" Dear Brother: I take this opportunity of sending a few lines just before we leave. We start tomorrow morning for Memphis. We know not whether we may go farther than there at present. I have sent some things home by David Zehrung. (19) My overcoat, one blanket, and my cap are all that were worth sending. I sent some books. You will see what they are. The whole cost only seven dollars. I think the boys will like Scott's works. For my part I think Pollock the best work of the kind that ever has been written but if they had sent for any particular book I would have sent it. We have been paid two months' wages and I must keep considerable as it may be some time before we get any more.

Joseph Shanklin has been promoted to Second Lieutenant without being elected by the Company. I don't much like it, ditto Frank, as either of us might have beat him. Gallagher is Captain now and he seems to have taken matters into his own hands in regard to promotion. The vacancies in the Sergeants will be filled in a few days. If we could have an election I could get nine tenths of the votes for first Sergeant. Still I am not certain if Gallagher appoints them himself that I will be promoted at all. There is some mischief kicked up in the Company almost every day, that is the boys will rob pedlars, saloon keepers, &c, and some sneak told Gallagher that I took no pains to prevent such things. He believes it, I suppose, but as he never mentioned the matter to me I have not attempted to clear myself. One thing is I am satisfied of having done my duty to the letter. I will not curry favor with any officer, as I consider myself as good either as a man or a soldier as any of them. I feel somewhat vexed that I cannot get what the boys would give me now as the next step from that is a commission. You see it is not all smooth sailing in the Army. However I can get along, if I must remain in my present place, so I mean to go ahead and do my duty let things go as they may. I enclose a likeness for Aunt McCosh with my respects. I got sunburnt black as the picture on the trip to Memphis.

I enclose ten dollars. It is not much but I have given up the notion of saving money soldiering at thirteen dollars per month. I will write from Memphis in a few days. Give my love to all. Agnes must excuse my not answering her letter this time. I will do so before long. Direct as usual. Your Brother Peter Wilson "

----

19 David Zehrung was from Toledo, Tama County. [He was a brother-in-law of Joseph Shanklin. A survivor of the prison camps, David was discharged for disability at the end of March 1863. Peter Wilson used this as an opportunity to send some items home. In 1880 Zehrung was farming in Clay County Nebraska; Eliza Shanklin, his sixty-seven year old mother-in-law, lived with his family. David, who died in 1888, is buried in Grandview cemetery near Anselmo Nebraska.]

Cairo, Illinois

Cairo, Ill., April 12th, 1863

" Dear Brother: I take this opportunity of sending a few lines to let you know where we are and how we are. It seems that the 14th is elected for good times yet awhile. We left St. Louis calculating to soon be in front of the enemy but on arriving here we found that we had to relieve the 35th Iowa from duty at Cairo and let them have a chance to show their mettle at Vicksburg. So we are now stationed here as Provost Guards. We have to patrol the levee, guard the fort, prison, &c. We have good quarters and though Cairo is an unhealthy place, low and swampy, we are better off than at any point below. I have little fear of ill health now and I don't much mind where we go. As a general thing the boys are not particular where we go or stay. If we stay here we will have good times. The Lieutenant Colonel (20) is in command. Old Shaw is on duty at St. Louis. The Lieutenant Colonel is recently promoted from Captain. He is very strict. He puts the men in the guardhouse for missing one roll call or stealing an apple from a pedlar. If he continues he will get something like discipline in the Regiment. I am glad to see it. I am tired of the system of plundering that has been in fashion for some time.

As I expected we have had no election for Orderly Sergeant. The system of regular promotion has been introduced. Some of the Union Brigade were appointed Sergeants while we were on parole and Gallagher leaves them above Frank and myself, something unfair, as an election would have made us all right. I am Fourth Sergeant, Frank Fifth. There may be a change in the program sometime. If election should ever be the order of the day to fill a vacancy in the commissioned officers I think I can come in. If regular promotion is the way, I think there is small chance of my ever getting a commission particularly if we stay in places of safety like this. But I will not mention this matter any more. At present numbers of the old officers of the 14th have resigned since the Battle of Shiloh and their places are filled, some of them by smart men and some by the stupidest greenhorns in the Regiment. Some that were commissioned in the Union Brigade are of that kind that cannot smell powder without getting faint and falling to the rear. I am glad that Co. G has officers of good pluck and common sense, if some are not the choice of the men. Capt. Gallagher is the best officer in the Regiment, if he has used partiality in filling vacancies. From your affect brother, Peter Wilson "

------

20 The Lieutenant Colonel of the Fourteenth Iowa Infantry at this time was **Joseph H. Newbold**. He was killed in action in Louisiana on April 9, 1864. [See B.F. Thomas, "*Soldier Life*", Chapters 10, 11, 12.]

Jonesboro, Illinois

Jonesboro, Ill., April 29th, 1863

" Dear Brother: I take my pen to scribble a few lines to pass the time this afternoon as I am not busy. Yesterday and the day before we had hard marching and today we are resting. The raid by Marmaduke (21) into Missouri caused some stir up that way. As we are only 25 miles from the Cape (22) of course we had orders to go and help but we were too late to have a chance to fight from behind breastworks. A small force of Infantry, some Cavalry, and the Artillery had no trouble in keeping the rebels out. Reinforcements from above and below enabled our men to assume the offensive and at last accounts the rebels were getting enough of it ten miles from the Cape. I have not heard how the battle terminated. I think the rebels have had poor success this time.

We have been longer in this place than we expected to be, still it is something new bushwhacking in Illinois.

The country near the river is very hilly and the river bottoms heavily timbered. There are some fine farms on the bottoms, the land is said to be the best in the state. The country is full of deserters and Secesh. We have arrested a good many of both kinds. We found 15 barrels of whiskey and a quantity of powder near the Cape this trip on the premises of a disloyal citizen and confiscated the same. I think if we stay here long whiskey will be scarce as it is mostly owned by Copperheads and we spill it if we can [not] bring it in to the Quartermaster. I have seen four barrels spilled and not a man wish to drink any. Beer is the universal drink in the 14th now and there is seldom any drunkenness. We must respect private property here in Illinois though if they did not board [us] we would not be so honest.

It seems the rebels are coming into us at all points just now. I am glad of it as it is easier to fight them up this way than to hunt them in Arkansas. I think it is useless to hope for the restoration of the Union as it was or in any way, still I think it is best to go ahead and fight the rebels until there is some show for peace. I don't think that time will be very soon. There seems to be as much fight in the South as ever though they are said to be hard up. Well I must finish and go and eat supper at (------) well I guess they will have something good to eat and I will spend the evening with the girls. The men are so disloyal they cannot stay at home so we must tend to their women folks as much as possible in their absence.

I have not seen Frank or John R. Felter for a week. I guess they are all right. I expect to ride forty or fifty miles tomorrow. As we have borrowed horses we put them through. We mean to visit some adjoining counties before going to Cairo. I think it will not be necessary for me to write from here again. I would not have written now if we had not the prospect of being so busy. I may not write for some days.

Your affect brother, Peter Wilson "

------

21 Brigadier General John S. Marmaduke, of the Confederate Army, led a raid into Central Missouri in the spring of 1863.

22 Probably Cape Girardeau was the place meant.

Jonesboro Courthouse, Union Co., Ill. May 6th [1863]

" Dear Father: It is some time since I have had any letters from you but I suppose you are very busy at this time. It is not so with me so I can afford to send more letters than I get. James has been very prompt about answering my letters for the last while for which I feel very grateful. Our letters go to Cairo to the Regiment and then are sent here as opportunity offers. We generally send a squad of prisoners to Cairo every few days and those that take the prisoners down bring the mail and such things as we need.

We have extended our researches into the neighbouring counties and are doing a good business among Copperheads & deserters. We go in small parties of six or eight and generally find our prisoners in the night when they don't expect us. I think our operations will have a good effect on the traitors in this part of the State. A good many deserters after living in the woods until they got tired of it come and give themselves up. The Copperheads are very quiet here now. I think they are the best neighbours we have ever had. We have had one public dinner and a ball and next Tuesday is appointed for another of the same. I suppose there are some of the people that treat us well because they like us but the majority do it because they fear us. They know they are guilty and they think by using us well to gain our good will and make us believe they are good Union men. Of course we will accept their hospitality but if anything is found out on any of them that will send them to prison they must go after all their kindness to us.

Some that we have arrested have been sentenced to six months imprisonment and 500 dollars fine for harboring deserters, hurrahing for Jeff Davis, and such like. I think that is paying for their whistle but it is no more than is necessary to cure them of their disease. There are only some six or eight Union men in this place. Still nothing can be laid to the charge of most of them. Perhaps after the lesson they are receiving is past those that have escaped this time will keep out of mischief hereafter.

It seems as though good fortune follows the 14th now as we could not find a better place than we are now in if we had our choice. The detachment that is here has the advantage of those in Cairo as our propensity for rambling is gratified and we are more at liberty but the whole Regiment is very well off, and the General in command at Cairo has spoken highly of us on several occasions. He is well pleased with our success up here and I see our doings here have been mentioned in the Chicago papers. To be sure this is unimportant business that we are engaged in but it is right for us to do well what we find to do.

They are so strict now at Cairo that one of the boys was sent to the guardhouse for wearing a white hat on dress parade. It is easy enough to conform to the rules in dress and everything else and while we stay at Cairo where the General is we must do it. For my part I like to see everything go off in a soldierlike manner. There are some soldiers from the Army of the Mississippi at home here on thirty days furlough. There will be two from each Company of our Regiment furloughed this week. As soon as they return others will go. I think my turn will come in time to be home about the first of July, if we stay in Cairo that long which is very probable. I must finish as I have nothing more to mention. Your affect son, Peter Wilson "

[Jonesboro Courthouse] May 7th [1863]

" Dear Brother West: I must pen a few lines in answer to yours so you will excuse my doing so on this sheet. I have nothing particular to write only that I wish you would write oftener. I am always interested in hearing from you boys, how your business prospers &c. Well I will try and write something that would interest you. As you are interested in hunting I will mention that we have some sport after wild turkeys. There are plenty of them in the woods round here. This is not the proper time to kill them but we don't mind that. It is not easy to kill small game with an Enfield rifle but some of the best marksmen do very well. The best shot I ever saw was on the River. One of the boys killed a gull over half a mile [away]. As we were going along the road one day we saw a flock of buzzards, some eight or ten on a tree about three-fourths of a mile distant. There were twenty of us and the Captain gave us permission to shoot at them. We gave them a volley all together and killed three at that distance so you see our guns carry a long distance. There are plenty of fish in the creeks round here, mostly catfish. Down at Cairo the boys catch some very large ones. We catch them with hook and line. I think if Mr. Quin were here he would enjoy himself. Now West write again and I will write you a longer letter. I remain your affect brother, Peter Wilson "

Cairo, Illinois

Cairo, May 19th, 1863

" Dear Brother: I received your letter of May 14th this morning and send a few lines in reply though there is nothing new at present. I was sorry to hear of the sudden death of your brother-in-law and of the continued sickness of Ward. (23) I know a little from experience how it goes to be sick in the Army and can understand how he is situated. If he had six months good health so as to get somewhat at home in the Army it would not be so bad. I am happy to state that the health of the 14th was never better than at present. If Ward could get to some of the hospitals up this way or at Memphis he would get the best attention possible.

I think the field hospitals must be in good shape judging by the stores that are taken down the river. There are immense quantities of ice shipped from Canada to Cairo on the cars and from here to Vicksburg in barges. All kinds of hospital stores are abundant. Still the best of care cannot save all. We have as recruit in Co. G one of the Doo's (24) from Crystal. He received a letter from home this morning informing him of the death of his brother in Co. E, 24th Iowa. The new regiments have had more sickness last winter and this spring than the old but after they get used to the climate they will not be so much sick.

I had hoped to see the Tama County boys in the 10th, 24th, and 28th Iowa in Grant's Army this summer but since we are scattered in southern Illinois it is not likely that we will see them. The Paymaster is here paying the 14th. I will send what I can spare by letter as usual. I guess it is best to send it in two letters as if one should get lost the other might not. There is only two months wages due this time. If I should get furloughed before another payday I may be short of cash but I can make it some way. It seems to be a slow business getting a furlough. They have been more than two months trying to furlough the first squad and they have not gone home yet. It puts me in mind of the Circumlocution Office that is mentioned in some novel (25) I will be in the second squad but I don't know when that may be. I don't expect to be home but once until my time is up so it don't matter for a month or two. It seems after all the good and bad news from Hooker's Army that another defeat* is added to the former ones in the east, but still I think the time is coming that will see the Grand Army of the Potomac victorious over those that have so often driven them from the field. I must finish for the present with best wishes to yourself and Esther I remain, your affect. Brother.

[PS] I enclose fifteen and will send ten or fifteen the next time. Peter"
------

23 This was **Ward Wilbur**, a brother of Mrs. James Wilson. He was discharged because of illness in August, 1863. [Ward Wilbur, twenty-one, of Buckingham, enlisted August 1862 into Company E Twenty-fourth Iowa and was discharged from Carrolton Louisiana.]

24 This was apparently **John Dew**. His brother was **Andrew J. Dew**. [Andrew J. Dew, twenty-five, of Howard Township near Toledo, enlisted August 1862 into Company E of the Twenty-fourth Iowa with several of the men from Buckingham. He died May 13 1863 and is buried in Jefferson Barracks National Cemetery, St. Louis in Section 5 Grave 40. John Dew, twenty-seven, also of Howard Township, enlisted into Company G of the Fourteenth Iowa December 1862, was promoted to 6th Corporal and mustered out November 1864 with the regiment.]

25 Peter Wilson had evidently read Little Dorrit, by Charles Dickens.

* Wilson must be thinking of the battle of Chancellorsville of May 1863, one of the costliest battles of the War, and a pivotal defeat for the Union. Hooker's loss opened the door for Lee to take his Confederate offensive north into Pennsylvania, bringing on the terrible battle of Gettysburg.

Cairo, Ill., May 23d [1863]

" Dear Sister Flora: I have just received your letter and proceed to reply though I have nothing particular to communicate. In the first place I will mention that it is somewhat uncertain what time I may come home. I may be home at the first of July and I may not be home for three months. My furlough is due about the first of July but if some of the boys are sick I will let them go in my place, as it don't make much difference. I like Cairo first rate now and if it was not for seeing father and mother I would not come home this summer. I had a letter from Allan Sloss a few days ago. He gave me James Soils's address and promised to come and see me as he went to Chicago this summer. If I had known of his being in Memphis I would have called on him when we were in Memphis. Allan has heard of the weddings on the Creek and thinks I will be the next, judging from what he heard while up there. I think he is mistaken for once but time will show. I think being away from the girls so long will insure my being an old bach(elor).

If I keep my health I will stay with Uncle Samuel as long as we can agree and he needs soldiers. Perhaps when my time is up I may feel like coming home for good, still I have no idea that I will be satisfied to stay. I hardly know anything more to write. I think you might write a little oftener and longer letters. I have dropped a number of my correspondents from my list partly because I did not care much for their letters and partly because I did not get answers to half the letters I sent them. D. Galt is the most punctual correspondent I have outside of home. He is the first to give me the details of any important event.

There is a good number of churches in Cairo. I attended the Episcopal last Sabbath. I think once will do me for that kind of mummery. We generally attend the Presbyterian, sometimes the Methodist. As a matter of course the theater is largely attended every night in the week. I have seen Uncle Tom's Cabin acted. I think it is the best subject they could get and they do better than in St. Louis. I generally go to the theater twice per week as I am on guard that often and the guards can go where they please. We generally have some fun on patrol guard as we have to visit all places of amusement to see if any disorder is going on. There are so many gunboat soldiers, steamboatmen, &c in Cairo it takes a few guards to keep order.

With love to all I remain your brother, Peter "

Cairo, Ill., June 8th, 1863

" Dear Father: It is some time since I have written to you but as I had nothing of consequence to write I must be excused. It is little different yet, but I will send a few lines anyway. Up to this time we have had excellent health in Cairo and as long as that is the case we will enjoy ourselves. The weather has not been very hot yet for longer than a few days at a time. Within the last few days the Army from Missouri and Burnside's old command has passed enroute for Vicksburg. It looks as though there are to be extensive operations down the river. I think there is no likelihood of the 14th being there. It was almost certain we would go last week but now it is the reverse.

I see the Tama County companies at Vicksburg have suffered pretty severely in the late battles*. Some boys that I was acquainted with have been killed. I saw some of my Long Grove friends in the 20th (Iowa) the other day as they stopped a few hours at Cairo. The 20th (Iowa) was at Benton Barracks last fall while we were there. Since then they have been marching through Missouri and Arkansas. They were in the battle of Prairie Grove. The Army of the Frontier has done more hard marching than any other in the service. They are now on the way to Vicksburg. The men look well and are willing to join the Army of the Mississippi and quit bushwhacking in Missouri. Now that we have nothing but State Militia in Missouri it is likely there will be an invasion from Arkansas and as we are not far off we may be sent to that State before long. But I need not speculate on the subject.

I had a letter from Uncle David (26) a few days ago. His folks were well as usual and crops looked unusually well. He is coming up this fall to see you. Perhaps I may come at the same time. I cannot come before August now and perhaps not then. I have nothing more to write. Good by, your Son, Peter Wilson "

------

* The Twenty-fourth Iowa had fought at Champion's Hill near Vicksburg May 16, 1863, suffering many casualties.

26 This was, apparently, David McCosh, a brother of Peter Wilson's mother. [At the start of the War Peter's Uncle David McCosh and his wife Isabelle Brownlie lived at Long Grove near Davenport but later moved their family to a farm in Powesheik County. Peter mentions several times that he sent his "likeness" to his Aunt Isabelle McCosh.]

Columbus, Kentucky

Fort Halleck, Columbus, Ky. June 18th, 1863

" Dear Brother: We left Cairo rather suddenly a day or two ago. The troops had mostly left this place and gone to Vicksburg. The enemy, knowing how it is, are said to be preparing to attack this place. Five companies of the 14th have been spared from Cairo to reinforce the few that were here. There are about 1500 men here and the place is so strong we can hold it against 5000 or more. We don't expect such good luck as to be attacked here. There is plenty of heavy artillery and a couple of gunboats to keep them from getting into the town so let them come. They will find us ready. Fort Halleck is situated on the bluff above the town. The bluff is very high and the view up and down the river is splendid. It was called Fort Beauregard when in rebel hands.

There is a Coloured Regiment in the other fort at the lower part of town. We will have a high time in case we are attacked, but the belief is now that they will not come. They were 25 miles from here yesterday and I don't know whether they are coming on or not. We have pickets out five miles and scouts beyond. It is all right to keep on the lookout. The first two boys that went home on furlough will be back today. The next two will start as soon as it is quiet. I will not promise any more about coming home.

It seems the rebels are putting their threat of invasion into practice in the East. (27) Perhaps if they burn a few of the large cities it may wake up that part of the country. They have plenty of men and if they don't choose to meet the enemy half way I hope the Secesh will learn them something of how an invading army destroys where they go. Price and Marmaduke have tried to get to St. Louis several times and have never been able though. There were not many soldiers in their way. If Hooker cannot take care of his part of the frontier I don't know what his Army is good for but it is not for me to have an opinion in such matters. I have no doubt but you at home take more interest in the progress of events than we soldiers. If we knew for certain that tomorrow we would be in battle we would sleep as sound tonight. We don't know what changes an hour may bring and we have learned to take every change with indifference.

The rain has been falling fast all day and all our mess are on picket but Frank and myself. We have been fixing hammocks sailor fashion in the tent. If you could step in and see us and how nicely we have fixed up you would be surprised. I need not write any more now. There is no telling how long we may be here. The Headquarters of the Regiment is at Cairo. This detachment is commanded by Capt. Crane. (28) The most of our officers are here on Courts Martial. Give my love to all. Good bye your affect brother, Peter Wilson "

----

27 General Robert E. Lee had started north on the campaign which was stopped at Gettysburg.
28 Captain LeRoy A. Crane was at this time Captain of Company H of the Fourteenth Iowa. [Crane, from Anamosa, was Colonel Shaw's brother-in-law. After the War Crane practiced law in Pueblo Colorado where he died in 1917. He is buried in Pueblo's Mountain View cemetery. See B.F. Thomas, "Soldier Life", Chapter 10.]

Fort Halleck, Columbus, Ky., June 27th, '63

" Dear Brother: Your letter of June 20th arrived this morning. I was glad to hear of your continued prosperity and of the welfare of all our friends. I have no doubt but you find yourself very busy. I am happy to state that since we came here we also have been busy though there has been no particular reason for so much vigilance. The rebels are between here and Memphis but we have no reason to suppose they are in force sufficient to trouble us much. They have fired on the boats with Light Artillery and they threaten to stop boats from running. The boats that went down yesterday had a gunboat in company.

We go out on picket about two miles and scout nearly every day from ten to thirty miles. The Cavalry do most of the scouting. Since we came here no considerable force has been nearer than thirty miles. They don't run the cars regularly to Jackson, Tennessee, now. When they go they take a strong guard. There are plenty of orchards out on our picket line and apples are ripe here now. We enjoy ourselves better while on duty than when we have nothing to do. For my part I like to ramble round the country much better than loafing in the city. I think we have done with doing guard duty in cities now. If we stay here this summer our business will be to keep the rebels quiet in this part of Kentucky. There are some three thousand men at this post. Some of them are drafted men. Their nine months is almost up, when I suppose they will be mustered out.

The remains of the 128th Illinois is temporarily attached to the 14th. They have only about 150 men. Their commissioned officers have been mustered out. Desertion is the cause of their being so much reduced. We have a pretty large Regiment now, more so than when we left the State. I will mention that Col. Shaw owns 80 acres of prairie south of Sprole's place. Sprole knows the lines or Eleazar Stoakes* could show you the land. You might look at it sometime when you are over that way. It can be bought cheap, a trifle more than the original cost perhaps. It is not best for me to buy land until I come home but there might be some advantage in this. It can do no harm to find how it is. I could pay for it in a year at any rate if I don't come home and the prospect now is that I won't. Furloughs are not given now in this Division owing to the threatening attitude of the rebels.

D. Connell has written to B. F. Thomas that he is a candidate for State Senator. I need not express my opinion as I am not much of a politician. If the Republican Party is for him he will be apt to be elected. We will be mustered for pay in a few days. Please mention in your next whether you received two letters with 15 dollars in each from Cairo. I think of nothing else at present but remain your affect Brother Peter Wilson "
------

* Eleazar Stoakes of Wolf Creek, Wilson's friend and messmate from the beginning had been discharged for lingering illness after their return from the Southern POW camps. William Sprole, who was a hired hand for John Gaston's brother Hugh Gaston, also farmed his own land nearby.

(Columbus, Kentucky, undated)

" Dear Brother Andrew: I received your letter last night and thank you very much for writing. I can stand almost anything better than to be disappointed in getting letters from home. You boys must have busy times to get your work done this season, but you will get through some way. You must have had good hay weather this season to have put up so much yourself. The little stumpy fields in this part of the country look something like Connecticut. (29) They have no reaping machines here, but negroes and most of them belong now to the Coloured Regiment here in Columbus. They raise good corn here and good hay but the country is rough, the timber heavy. If you had some of their timber and orchards it would be a fine thing. I think plenty of apples is the best thing to keep healthy in the summer. Perhaps they may be plenty in Iowa some time. They have plenty at Uncle David's now. So much horse trading has been done since I came away I don't know what kind of horses you have now. If you had some of their big Kentucky mules you could make things gingle.

I would like very much to see our cousins just come from Scotland. Perhaps I may by and by. I need not tell you boys to be kind to them and make them feel as much at home as possible. I guess they will soon learn to like Iowa. Now Andrew if you will write about once in two weeks, John and West also, I think among you you might do it. I will always answer. It would improve your style of writing and I would be your debtor. I have not many correspondents but those at home and you know it is sometimes a good while between letters. If we had more to do we would not care so much about letters, but I am happy to say we have plenty of time to do anything we please. I have forgotten whether I answered West's letter. I think not so I will do it soon.

So at present good by from your brother, Peter Wilson "
------

29 The Wilson family had lived for a time in Connecticut before moving to Iowa.

Columbus, Ky., July 1st, 1863

" Dear Father: Once more I send a few lines to let you know that we are in good health and like we always have done enjoying ourselves. Our duty here is something like it was at Cairo, only there are more men here and more to do. There are men enough to make a brigade but each regiment is commanded by its own colonel. I suppose none of us is permanently established here. Col. Shaw will have command of the post as soon as he is relieved from Court Martial duty that he is on at present. He is the oldest colonel at this place and perhaps he may be a brigadier before long. We are on guard about twice a week, the rest of the time is mostly at our disposal with the exception of a few hours drill each day.

The weather has been pretty warm with heavy rains nearly every day. We may thank our stars that we have no marching to do. Yesterday we went out about a mile to be reviewed by the General. Before we finished a heavy shower came on us and there were at least two thousand of us came back drenched to the skin. I think it can rain in this State at the shortest notice. The only consolation we had was to see the officers get their nice uniforms wet.

It must be raining up the river. The river is rising rapidly. What little crops I have seen here look well. There is a fine corn field over the river where the Battle of Belmont was fought. The soil is good in this part of Kentucky but the timber is very heavy and like other parts of the South they have been farming among the trees. The most of the farms are deserted and left to ruin. There are some splendid orchards a few miles from camp and we begin to use the apples now.

There is plenty of game in the woods and plenty of hogs, but pork is not much in favor with us. We had a box of dried peaches, apples, and a quantity of butter sent from Indiana. We got it cheap and have not found it worth while to forage any for some time. We sold our fishing boat and lines before we left Cairo and we don't know that we will be here long enough to pay us for getting another.

July 4: We are just returned from our picnic and I will give an idea of how it went off. The ground was fixed up in good style for having a good time, a large floor was made for dancing, ropes were fixed for tight rope performers, all kinds of folks from the General to the contraband were there. Well there were some good speeches made, plenty of music from the bands, and some songs sung. Then we were dismissed for dinner, ah there's the rub. We had marched three miles in the hot sun, listened to the speakers, and then there was nothing to eat except by paying for it, ten cents per glass for lemonade and other things in proportion. You may guess we were not in the best of humor. There was plenty to eat and drink on the ground, but it was not for nothing. The citizens of Columbus make plenty of money from the soldiers to enable them to give us a free dinner. Instead of that they took advantage of the occasion to make some more out of us.

Well there was but one opinion among us, to pitch in and clean out every stall on the ground. The officer in command saw that things began to look squally, he mounted the stand and called "Attention". We know so well what that means that he had attention immediately. He then told us that no doubt we had come there with the intention of eating two or three oxen &c but there was not even a fatted calf, nary chicken nor anything else, so we would go home and eat hard tack and pork as usual and invite our entertainers to come and eat with us.

We gave three cheers for dinner at camp and fell into line and started leaving, those that had intended to sell us something to eat looking rather wistful. If the Colonel had not marched us off when he did we would have made a clean sweep of the place. There was plenty of beer, whiskey, wine, &c. and we had both the will and the power to take it. The Colonel touched us on the only weak place we had when he told us we will show them that western men are too well disciplined to raise a row even when we have been provoked.

There is some trouble over in Tennessee and perhaps we may be sent out to Jackson before long. It is said the Rebs are conscripting out that way. Most likely we will go and see how they prosper. I am only guessing at it but I hope we may run around and if there are such things going on have something to say on the matter. I will finish this scribble. I think some of the folks might write as often as once per week. I get very few letters now and the longer the fewer. Give my respects to the rest, your affect son, Peter Wilson "

Columbus, Ky., July 10th, 1863

" Dear Brothers John, West, & Andrew: I am going to tell you the kind of times we had when the news came that Vicksburg was taken. We had a general permit to go to town and enjoy ourselves. Since the 4th the boys have only been waiting a good opportunity to take vengeance on the Secesh of Columbus and by common consent now was the time. General Asboth issued an order for all loyal men to illuminate their houses in the evening. Some of the saloon keepers did not comply, saying they did not care about Vicksburg's being taken. There were perhaps two thousand soldiers in town and this was a good case to begin with. They rushed in and smashed everything to pieces, drinking all the liquors, taking tobacco, cigars, &c, and making short work with it. Every saloon in town was visited and they had to shell out what was called for on pain of losing all. Soon half of the crowd was drunk, officers as bad as the men, considerable fighting going on.

General A. was said to have made good use of an empty whiskey bottle in a row with one of the boys. He was in citizen's clothes, having a jolly time with the others. About midnight most of the men returned to camp.

The next morning strange to tell nearly every tent had something in it that was not the previous day. Some had liquors, some tobacco, some dry goods, some furniture. One had a large quantity of snuff, enough to keep Uncle McDowall in snuff for five years. Every thing that could be carried away was brought to camp. If they had given us something to eat on the Fourth nothing of the kind would have happened. Nothing of the kind has happened since. We were out at Rolla last winter. If we get on another spree when Richmond is taken I think Columbus will be reduced to the ranks. Nearly all the business of Columbus is supported by the soldiers and they pay two prices for everything. It is no more than right that they confiscate a little sometimes.

It has a bad effect on a regiment, such plundering, and I hope it may not happen any more. Now boys you will please each of you to write. Let me know how all your affairs, agricultural, nonsensical, &c, are. John R. Felter and Frank get six letters from home to my one and I write almost or quite as many as they.

At any rate I will write next week, so at present I will finish from your affect brother, Peter Wilson "

Columbus, Ky., July 11th, 1863

" Dear Father: I received your letter last night with one from Uncle Andrew and was glad to hear from you. I would write oftener to you but when I write to James you can see the letters so it is not worth while to write to you both in one week. I hope Uncle Dodd's folks will soon be well and at home in Iowa. I would like to see them, but for the present there is not much likelihood of my being home very soon. There is generally a big scare here once per week. The Rebs are reported coming this way now and are said to be within a few miles of this place. We were under arms all night last night.

I will just mention that we of the 14th don't believe they will do us the favor of attacking us. If they do they will get whipped the worst kind. They have been too strong for our scouting parties but it don't follow that they will commit suicide by running against the guns of Fort Halleck. They would place us under lasting obligations if they come on and pitch in.

Now that Vicksburg is taken Port Hudson must soon follow. General Herron is going to Texas with the old Army of the Frontier. He wrote to Col. Shaw that if he chose to go along he might. I don't know how the Colonel will decide. If he pleased us he would go to Texas. Col. Shaw can keep his Regiment pretty near where he chooses. I think he will stay where he is for the present. He knows how to logroll as well as the next one and he knows where we are best off. I think Col. Shaw has more respect for his men than any officer from the State and he cares nothing for his superior officers. If they don't please him he has a very plain way of speaking his mind. I think we have more reason to hope now for the end of the war than we ever had before*. If Lee don't manage to take his Army back to Virginia their case seems hopeless. I think Lee will get back but he must have made a poor spec[tacle] in Pennsylvania this time. I will write to Grandfather soon. I think Uncle Andrew don't understand it when he says we must have some other government before we have peace. He says the sympathy of the Scotch is with the South. That seems strange but our recent victories will shut up intervention for a time, so it don't matter. I think jealousy and a wish to see our country go to pieces has something to do with the sympathy for the South. Well I sincerely hope that the time is near when the restoration of the Union is no longer doubtful. I have written some to the boys so for this time I will finish.

So no more from your affect Son Peter "

------

* Two decisive battles were won by the Union on the very same day: on July 4, 1863, Vicksburg surrendered to Federal control and Lee was turned back at Gettysburg, where Dewitt Southwick's younger brother **Guy Southwick** was mortally wounded serving with the 16th Pennsylvania Cavalry.

Columbus, Ky., July 20th, '63

" Dear Sister Jane: I received your letter last night. I did not know you had gone home so I wrote to Grinnell last week. I have written twice since I got any letters from you. As soon as I get a letter I answer it forthwith if practicable. I generally write two letters for every one I get, but no matter. I hope you may like harvesting. If it was possible I would come and help. There is no doubt but considerable inconvenience is experienced in Iowa on account of so many being away but they know comparatively nothing compared with any of the Southern States or in any part of the North where the raids have been made.

One of Co. G died yesterday. His brother belonging to the 24th died last week. Their name was Dykeman. (30) Their folks live on Salt Creek. There has been no deaths in the old soldiers of the 14th since November until now. Some of the recruits have died. We buried him with military honors. He died very suddenly, though his health had been poor for some time.

There seems to be a general feeling of security here now among the citizens. Sometimes squads of the enemy come within a few miles, but for the last few days everything has been quiet. There is little to write. We went out a few miles today after blackberries and apples and though it was very warm we brought in enough to last some days. Some of the boys make very good pies, dumplings, &c. Kentucky is a good fruit country. Every farm is well supplied with all kinds of fruit trees.

I should write to West but you must let him read this and I will write to him before long. I hope he may get well as soon as possible. I hope his trouble may not be serious. It is rather hard for Uncle Dodd's folks to be sick in their new place, but the folks around will do their best to make them like Iowa. I think the prospect of the war coming to an end was never so bright. A few more victories will finish the Southern Confederacy. I hope the time is not far distant when we can leave the land of Dixie forever. Perhaps things may take a turn in favor of the South again but if they don't soon they cannot hope to fight to any purpose much longer. Uncle David's folks and some of the Brownlee girls are coming up this fall. I hope they may have a pleasant visit, as they take pains to use me well when I go there. I may have something to write next time, for the present good bye. I remain your Affect brother Peter Wilson "

------

30 Edgar Dykeman was in Company G. His brother, **Simon Dykeman**, died in St. Louis. [See B.F. Thomas, "*Soldier Life*", Chapter 11.]

Columbus, Ky., July 23d, 1863

" Dear Sister Flora: It is time for me to get a letter from you, but I don't expect it knowing how slow you all are about writing. Perhaps I don't write as often as I ought, but staying so long in one place gives us nothing to write. Everything is quiet here, so quiet as to make it uninteresting. Our regular turn of guard once or twice per week and a few hours drill every day is all our duty. We go out a few miles for fruit and vegetables two or three times per week. Peaches are pretty plenty and just beginning to be ripe. Apples are very plenty and have been ripe for some time. Blackberries are very plenty everywhere. All kinds of vegetables are very dear, but we find a way to get enough. The most of our time we have nothing to do and it comes very good this warm weather.

There is a good deal of chess playing in Co. G now. John and Frank are both very good players. I don't know whether you ever saw the game. It is the best I ever saw. Of course we must introduce it at some future time among the folks at home. I don't think there will be anymore furloughs given in the 14th. There has not been any for the last month, so I don't expect to be home until our time is expired or the war ended. I think the prospect for a successful termination of the war is getting no longer doubtful. There is no doubt but the South will fight until they cannot raise another regiment but their efforts must be in vain. Their case is getting no better very fast as the record of events in the last month will show.

Another of Co. G's boys died a few days ago. With that exception the health of the Company is very good. Our duty is regular and not hard enough to hurt our health. I guess they must be very busy at home this harvest. West being unwell will make it more so. One thing they ought to be glad of is that they don't happen to live in the part of the country overrun with opposing Armies.

The folks in Iowa will never know anything about the miseries an invading Army brings on the inhabitants of the country they occupy. I hope the draft will not fail to bring out some of our neighbours that think more of their interests than of their country. Now is the time to increase our Army when we are getting so much advantage over the rebels. If the whole power of the North was given to the prosecution of the war, six months would end it. I don't think the men drafted this time will have long to serve if they go into it with a will. So it is no great calamity to be drafted at this time. I have nothing more to write.

Your affect Brother Peter "

Columbus, Ky., August 1st, 1863

" Dear Brother and Sister: The mail came in last night bringing letters for John and Frank but none for me. Such is often the case. I suppose the reason is one is a married man, the other expects to be, so their letters come as regular as the day of the week. I must admit that in that they have the advantage. It is very pleasant to hear from home regularly, though I don't care as much about it as formerly. Time will get us used to most anything.

I may report all quiet in our department, nothing more exciting than drumming a deserter through camp before he goes to serve his time out in the Military Prison at Alton, Illinois. They begin to punish desertion pretty severe now. If they had done so sooner it would have been better. They must come down pretty severe to keep the drafted men from deserting. I wonder who of the Wolf Creek men will have the honor of carrying a musket. I see in the papers the regiments on the Potomac are to be filled with drafted men. I hope they may do the same in the West. Let the men choose the regiment they will serve in and it will make them useful right away and make them more satisfied.

We have been paid two months' wages. I would rather have waited another month and received four months' wages and pay for clothing that I did not get. I send ten in this, the next time I write I will send more. For the present I will not make any arrangement with Col. Shaw about his land. I think 120 dollars cash would buy it but as I have not the cash I can't do it and I guess it is not worth while to buy it on time. Money will buy land some other time, perhaps not so cheap but no matter. The troops that left this place to assist in the reduction of Vicksburg have returned. I don't know whether any of them will stay here. I hope we may go next time. We have had good times here this summer but I would like to go somewhere else, now it is quiet. Likely we may stay here all the fall though there is nothing certain in the Army. Don't you think things begin to look like a war with England or France or both? I think in a short time we will be able to defy them. If my time was up today and either England or France recognizes and helps the South I will enlist again. Esther will please write this time. Your Affec Brother Peter "

Columbus, Ky., August 3d, 1863

" Dear Parents: I have been putting off writing till I would get a letter from home. I got one from Andrew last night or rather this morning as I was out on picket yesterday and did not come in till ten o'clock this morning. I think I killed ten thousand mosquitoes last night. They are more trouble than the Rebs. They are not bad in camp but out in the woods they are as the sands of the seashore.

It seems you have had busy times to get your harvesting done this season. The measles is something that everyone ought to have while they are young so it is well to be through with them. To have the measles in the Army is as bad as anything, particularly for men rather old. I hope by the time the next letter comes you may all be well again. There is not much sickness here though among the new companies there is some. There are some of the boys that never have nor never will get entirely over the diseases contracted while in prison. I have not been sick an hour since I was home. I have not even had a cold though we sleep in the open air, sometimes every other night. This is election day in Kentucky and there have been squads of soldiers sent to the different points of this district to keep order. I presume they will elect a Secesh in this county as the most of the people belong to that persuasion.

There are some Union men round here. I will mention an incident that happened at the Provost Marshal's the other day to show you how it is in Dixie. Two men living not ten miles from Columbus and on adjoining farms, the one Secesh the other for the Union, both leading men in the county, both men of great strength and pluck, mortal enemies of course. At a political meeting a short time ago the Union man made a speech and as usual was opposed by the Secesh. The Union man was, it seems, too much for him so Secesh threatened to kill him. The parties next met on the porch in front of the Provost Marshal's. Secesh says very blandly "how are you", Union man answers with a smasher in the face that knocked his opponent down. Then the fight commenced in earnest. The Provost Marshal and his peacemakers kept out of the way until Secesh was used up sufficiently then came and stopped the fight. When it was over Secesh was so badly beaten his folks would not know him and could get no redress. The Union man was presented with a revolver and encouraged in well doing. I will finish by writing a few lines to Andrew. Your Affect Son Peter Wilson "

Columbus, Ky., Aug. 19th, '63

" Dear Uncle and Aunt : (31) Though I don't remember much about you, as it is so long since I have seen you, still I hope the time is not far distant when we may become better acquainted. Your experience in Iowa must be rather melancholy, owing to the sickness and sad bereavement in your family. May He that giveth and taketh away be your consolation in your time of trouble. It has never been my lot to lose any very near relative but the time will come for us all to go to another world. It matters little, if we are ready, how soon. Here in the Army we are often reminded of the uncertainty of life and the certainty of death.

If half of us come home when the war is over it will be better than I expect. But I need not continue on the dark side of the picture. If the cause of justice and liberty triumphs over that of slavery and wrong, those that die have not died in vain. I presume you have not thought much about the merits of the war or rather you may doubt whether it is right for us to go on at the rate we have, sacrificing so much life, but I take it for granted you would like to see America as it was before the war commenced, with the exception of slavery. I think the time is coming when that will be the case. For my part I want to see the war go on until we are completely successful.

The fall campaign will perhaps decide the long struggle. If we have as good success as we have had this summer it certainly will. I don't know when I will come home but I think some time before winter. As there have been a good many changes since I was home I am quite curious to see the place. Of course I should mention the folks before the place as I am most anxious to see them. I shall be happy to see my new friends from Scotland as the more of them come the more it is like home. We soldiers see a good many places and a great deal of the country but I have not seen anything down this way to compare with Tama County, Iowa. Your Peter Wilson"

------

31 This letter was apparently written to Mr. and Mrs. Andrew Dodd who had come to Iowa from Scotland after Peter Wilson enlisted. [Johnnie Dodd, six-year-old son of Andrew and Cristina Dodd, died August 8, 1863. The cause of his death is unknown but three months later their ten-year-old son Thomas passed away on November 7. See Peter's letter of November 12.]

Columbus, Ky., Aug. 20th, 1863

" Dear Brother West: I hear you have been quite unwell for some time and not making much progress towards getting well. There is one thing in your favor, you are where you can be taken care of. That is an important item. Perhaps one-half of the men that are sick in the Army get very indifferent attention, many of them that die would have lived if they had had any care. I hope to hear of your getting better soon. I have had the ague but I am as well as ever now. The ague is very plenty just now. It comes all at once. Such a time I never saw.

The Doctor don't excuse a man from duty if he is shaking but he can cure the ague in a short time. Our Doctor is a hard old sinner. He would put a man on duty if he was three-fourths dead. He once sent one of our Company to load some commissary wagons in the forenoon. The man had been very unwell for some time previous and died in the evening of the same day so you see the ague is not much with such a man. I am lucky in not being much in his power. A Doctor has much power in the Army. If he says a man is fit for duty his decision cannot be appealed from. He has much power for evil if he sees fit to use it. I think we have a good Doctor in serious cases but he is too severe if there is not much the matter.

I must write of something else now so for want of something better I will tell you about the kind of folks that live in this part of Old Kaintuck. I have been to most of the houses in the vicinity of the picket line, sometimes five or six miles out. The farms are generally small something like Connecticut. When you are on one farm and look around you would think it was the only clearing in the country. The thick tall trees shut up the place and make it look isolated and lonesome. A good orchard, a cornfield, garden, a patch of a few acres of tobacco, sometimes a few acres of cotton, a log house generally of inferior quality the chinking out in summer to let the air circulate, two or three cows, ditto oxen or mules, with a yoke made after the pattern of the last century, and the harness for the mules one-half chain the other old ropes. The wagons are like the one Mr. Nungesser brought to Iowa.

The men and boys dress either in butternut or common tent cloth. The women smoke, quite often make corn dodger without salt and solid enough for cheese. The men wear long hair and are generally a rough, hossier, (32) sickly, lazy, and mostly drunken set. There are of course exceptions to all this, but I mention the common farmers that work for their living like we do in Iowa. Every farmer keeps a lot of hounds or curs of some kind. When you go up to the house you would think there was a general invitation to all the dogs in the country and they were there to have a general barking when any one came. Now West I hope you may feel well enough to write by the time you get this scribble. Your Affect. Brother, Peter "

------

32 This word has not been found. Possibly the term meant was "hoosier" meaning "uncouth".

Columbus, Ky., Sept. 1st, '63

" Dear Parents: I take this opportunity of sending a few lines to let you know how we prosper down this way. The most attentive visitor we have at this time is the ague. At least one-third of the men in camp has it at times. I happen to be among the number myself. I was in hopes it would not come back on me but in that I was mistaken. I have broken it up the second time and mean to keep it off if there is any virtue in dogwood bark, Peruvian bark*, and Old Rye Whiskey. That is the kind of Bitters the Doctor gives us.

I cannot account for so much ague here. The place looks healthy, the ground is high, the water we use mostly from the river and river men say it is as healthy as any water in the U. S. I think being out in the night (33) so much has something to do with it but whatever may be the cause there is plenty of it. I think a short time will bring cool weather and good health. The weather has been quite cool for the last few days. One of the boys that was up to Chicago with prisoners says they have frost up that way. I presume you have the same in Iowa. Rather early for frost, but nothing is surprising in Iowa, it can freeze there most any time.

The newspapers tell us of the fall of Sumter and Wagner. Charlestown must follow sooner or later. Also Jeff Davis has called out 500,000 Africans. Who would have thought it? They must be changing their opinions in Dixie pretty fast to think the chivalry would be brought so low as to fight their battles with slaves. I think between us the Negro will get his freedom. I am not prepared to give an opinion as to the result of Jeff's new policy. I will venture that it is too late now. If he had done so in the first place he would have made it win. I think before he gets his armies in shape we will have pushed farther into the South and what we get we can keep.

Yesterday being the last of the month, we had review. Besides the white regiments out there was one colored regiment. I must say they both looked well and marched well. A review is conducted something after the following manner. In the first place the troops are formed in line with open ranks. Then the reviewing officers ride along in front, the band of each regiment plays a short strain as they pass. They ride round the left and along behind to where they started, then take their station opposite the center and some distance in front. The ranks are then closed, wheel by company and pass in review. If a company of 100 men can keep a good line and keep step it looks well. Our negroes did splendid, considering the short time they have been in training but for the present I must close. I will write more next time. Your affect Son Peter Wilson. "

------

33 Peter Wilson, like others of his time, saw no connection between the thousands of mosquitoes and the epidemic of malaria. [*Quinine, used to fight malaria, is derived from the bark of the Peruvian chinchona tree.]

Columbus, Ky., Sept. 5th, 1863

" Dear David: I take this opportunity of penning a few lines to let you know how we prosper down this way. In the first place I will mention that Frank and I were expecting to have started home today, but just when our furloughs were to be sent in, furloughing has been stopped. Nothing but sick furloughs are given at present. John R. Felter started home this morning. His health has not been good for some time and we hope a month at home may help him. Perhaps Frank and I may have a chance by and by, but there is no certainty of it. If I cannot come before cold weather I will not come in the winter and it is not worth while to come next summer. You may look for us in fourteen months at farthest.

You will likely see John about the time this reaches you. From him you can get all the news that happened up to the time he left but though he has not been gone a day we have seen the execution of three American citizens of African descent. They belonged to the party that murdered a family of whites at Compromise Landing near Island No. 10. Six more will be executed next week, so you see there is to be considerable performing on the tight rope yet before justice is done.

There was a large crowd of soldiers and citizens, women and children present. A hollow square was formed round the scaffold and after waiting a short time the prisoners, escorted by a company of Regulars and the band playing the Dead March, arrived at the scaffold. The prisoners mounted the ladder with a firm step and took their places, the ropes dangling at their heads. Fifteen minutes of religious exercises by a colored preacher and they were ready. The ropes were put round their necks, they shook hands, then the caps was pulled over their faces, the drop fell, and they were dangling between Heaven and Earth. One died instantly, the next struggled a few minutes, the last about 15 minutes. One was a small man, the other two were upwards of 200 lbs. They died game. It is said their officer told them to commit the murder but I don't know how it is. The spectators looked on like as if so many cattle were being killed and rough jokes were passed on all sides. But I must change the subject and tell you about something more civil than hanging darkies.

One of the boys found a bee tree in the woods the other day and we made up our minds to have some honey forthwith. So the same evening we started well supplied with axes and a good supply of something to take. We arrived at the tree just at dark and built fires to see to cut the tree. It was a large poplar four feet in diameter. We were not long in bringing it down, when we proceeded to chop open where the bees were. This was not so nice as the bees would sting and buzz at a furious rate. Finally we got to where the honey should have been but it was mostly comb. We got about fifteen pounds of honey. There are plenty of bees in the woods if we had time to hunt them. It is too early in the season to get much honey. There has been so much ague among us for a few weeks that we have had no drill, so we are having pretty good times as far as work goes. We have a regimental library now and preaching every Sabbath. There are some histories &c in the library. It helps to pass the time agreeably. This part of Kentucky is as quiet now as Tama County, Iowa. The same precautions are taken to keep in readiness for the enemy as if there was one in the vicinity. There are some negro troops here that are already well drilled. They go through the maneuvers on battalion drill in a style that no troops need be ashamed of. There is one reason why they learn so quick, they will obey orders and give their attention to what they are doing much better than we will. They are used to being ordered round, we are not nor never will be. We obey our officers because we know there must be discipline but as a general thing we don't hold them much in awe.

The discipline in the negro regiments too is very strict and they have a funny way of punishing offenders. They have a large pole laid up on crotches and every morning a number of darkies are taking a ride on the pole. The offenses generally consist of running the guard, being absent from roll call, &c. The court martial is still in operation here. Some time ago the remains of the 128(th) Illinois was temporarily attached to the 14th. They deserted almost to a man. Most of them have been retaken and sentenced to work out their time under guard at Memphis. The deserters are generally sentenced to finish their time at hard labor and their pay is all stopped. The way of the transgressor is hard in military life.

I suppose the draft is postponed in Iowa once more. I wish they would give us a chance to recruit some way. We have only some thirty men in our Company. If we should be sent to the field we would amount to but little. Politics run high here. If Tuttle (34) had come out Independent he would have had a good chance for the soldiers' vote. As it is nothing but those that have been Democrats without the possibility of change will vote for him. I presume he is just as good as Stone (35) but being in bad company is what we don't like. Now David you must excuse the want of news in my letter, as there is nothing going on here. Please write soon and let me know how matters and things are about Buckingham. Give my respects to all the folks.

Your Peter Wilson "

------

34 **James M. Tuttle** was the Democratic candidate for the office of Governor of Iowa at the 1863 election. [General James Tuttle was born in Ohio in 1823 and settled in Van Buren County Iowa in 1846. As a Colonel, Tuttle commanded the Second Iowa Infantry and was a very brave leader during the heaviest fighting at both the assault on Donelson and the defense of the Hornets Nest at Shiloh, where he commanded the brigade that included the Fourteenth Iowa. He certainly had the admiration of his soldiers; it was his only affiliation with the anti-Lincoln Democratic party that many soldiers found troubling. Personally, Tuttle completely supported the war effort and the goal of maintaining the Union. He was later made a brigadier general; a monument in his honor stands in Vicksburg National Military Park.]

35 **William M. Stone**, the Republican candidate, was elected. [See B.F. Thomas, "*Soldier Life*", Chapters 8 and 11. Some accounts of the imprisonment of the officers taken at Shiloh say that Stone and the Fourteenth's Colonel Shaw entertained the other officers with lively, sometimes heated, debates that lasted hours, sometimes late into the night, on a wide variety of topics from politics, history, religion, philosophy, and war strategy, among other subjects.]

* The letter dated October 25th from Columbus Kentucky concerning General Rosecrans from PART TWO most probably should have been placed here chronologically.

Columbus, Ky., Oct. 31st, 1863

" Dear Parents: I take this opportunity of informing you of my welfare. There is little else to mention. We have not left Columbus yet nor are there any signs of it. We have fixed up our tents so as to keep comfortable while here and on the whole are doing very well.

I was on prison guard yesterday and as there are some queer chaps in prison sometimes I will give you some incidents that came under my notice last night. There are about 100 Secesh prisoners in the guardhouse at present, besides half as many Union soldiers, citizens, negroes, &c. About nine o'clock in the evening two butternut chaps were added to the number and soon another, all three pretty drunk, that being the cause of their incarceration. When a new one gets into the guardhouse he hears nothing but taunts on all sides. If he is spunky it comes to blows right away. The first two that got in last night had a serious time of it as they would not put up with the insults that were offered and got sundry knocks and bruises into the bargain. No. 3 came in like as if he was at home. He answered all comers in such a witty good-humored way we saw there was fun ahead.

After introducing himself as an uncompromising rebel and being congratulated on finding good winter quarters he proceeded to take a seat and came down to the tune of 250 lbs, on a man sleeping on the bench by the stove. The sleeper waked up swearing loudly. "He's only a Copperhead", says one, "A Copperhead", says the big man. "Where are you from, you durned reptile, get up and give me a seat and let us have a chat."

Q. How do you like Governor Yates? (36)
A. I don't like his politics.
Q. How do you like Old Abe?
A. They say he made good rails.
Q. Do you know if military law can divorce a man from his wife?

The general opinion was that it should, as a man in military prison was cut off from all society. The bigman says if he can get a divorce by staying in prison six months he will be content. "So Mr. Copperhead, you're from Illinois. Durn you. Hope they'll hang you. I'm a Reb out on the square, you are a half Reb, half anything and too much of a coward to fight for either party" &c &c.

Thus poor Copperhead is abused even by drunken Rebs. Citizens are charged 5 dollars for a night in Uncle Sam's Hotel, if nothing more than drunk and disorderly is the charge. There are some getting in and some getting out every day. One of Co. G got in since I was home (37) and has been sentenced to three months hard labor and imprisonment, charges sleeping on post.

The health of the men is good now. Co. G has not a man on the sick list. There are only three or four in the hospital. John R. Felter is improving and if nothing unfavorable happens he may have good health now. This is muster day. There is four months pay due me now. One of our boys has bought Col. Shaw's 80 for 150 dollars to be paid in installments of ten dollars per month. I think he has a good bargain. I would have taken it myself if it had not been inconvenient to go so far to improve it. If we pay more nearer home the advantages in being near it will more than overbalance. I have not got any letters since I was home, please write soon.

Your affect Son Peter Wilson. "

------

36 Richard Yates, Governor of Illinois.

37 This suggests that Peter Wilson finally got a furlough and was home some time between September 5th and October 31st. [See B.F. Thomas, *Soldier Life*", Chapter 11 for information on Wilson's furlough and Heimlich, the Company G soldier in the guardhouse.]

Columbus, Ky., Nov. 12th, '63

" Dear Parents: I take the present opportunity of informing you of my welfare. There is nothing of much importance going on at present. We are busy building log cabins to live in this winter. I have been in the woods every day for some time and I find that work is not so intolerable as I thought it would be. However I don't mean to do much more till I quit soldiering.

For some time back there has been general license for all the boys to go and hunt on the river bottoms, the game is plenty, deer, turkeys, and small game in abundance, also hogs and cattle which belong to the farmers. But no matter who they belonged to there have been so many of them killed that hunting is forbidden altogether. That is generally the way it goes. The boys get to killing private property, then they must quit hunting till the offense is forgotten. Perhaps in a month there will be as much liberty as ever.

I had a letter from Uncle David. He has offered his farm for sale and he says there are some of his neighbours in the notion of moving to Tama. I guess if they get Section 17 there is no doubt but they will come. Aunt is as much in favor of it as Uncle*.

I think if James can get a reasonable bargain he should buy 160 acres from the man that owns the land south of his place. I can pay for 80 acres before my time is up, so there is not much doubt but we can pay for it.

It is nearly a month since I left home and no letters yet. I will expect one soon. There is little to write from here but I will write once in two weeks to you and the same to James so you will hear from me every week. I have written to Cairngaan since I came back. I will write to Pinmore some time soon. Give my respects to Uncle Dodd's folks*. Excuse my short letter. Your affect Son Peter "

------

* Peter's Uncle David and Aunt Isabelle McCosh did sell their farm at Long Grove but did not end up on a new farm in Tama County; they ended up farming in Powesheik County instead, just south of Tama County near today's town of Brooklyn.

* See Peter's moving letter above to Uncle Dodd dated August 19, Note 31.

Columbus, Ky., Nov. 23d, 1863

" Dear Parents: I take the present opportunity of letting you know that all is well with us as usual. We have moved into our cabins and fixed up in good order for winter weather. Our cabins have not cost the government much as the roof is made of shingles of our own making, most of the floors are made of boards taken from deserted buildings about town, windows from the same place, stoves ditto. We have plenty of room. There are nine of us in (a)16 x 16 square. We like our prospects for passing the winter first rate. The only war news from here is the capture of fifty-five rebels by a party of our Cavalry. The Rebs were just from Mississippi. They came to operate along the River, burn steamboats, &c. They came within five miles of this place when our Cavalry got after them and gobbled the most of them, killing some ten or twelve. None of our boys was hurt.

The prisoners are here in the guardhouse. Some of them are glad of their capture, but most of them are regular cutthroat Bushwhackers. Not long ago the rebels captured L. Anderson, the Congressman just elected from this district. Our forces took some of his neighbours and kept them as hostages for his safety. They have effected his exchange so he can take his seat instead of lying in some Southern prison. Gen. Smith is very successful in keeping order in his department by his stringent measures of holding citizens responsible for any mischief done in their neighborhood. Some time ago a bridge was burned on the road between here and Union City. As the citizens took no pains to put out the fire he made them build the bridge as good as it was. The recent order from Gen. Hurlbut (38) pressing all the citizens of Memphis and throughout the department into the service is very popular among the soldiers.

Private Peter Fingle* a member of our Company is condemned to be shot next December for cowardice at the Battle of Shiloh and desertion from the service June 1862. There are measures being taken to have him reprieved and the sentence mitigated. His sentence is according to military law but he is the first Iowa soldier that has been sentenced to death for that offense. I hope he may be reprieved as it is hard to see an old comrade shot, though he is a worthless fellow.

If James has not sent the box hurry him up, as John's butter will soon be gone. The Paymaster is here and will pay us this week. I will have considerable to spare this time. I hope to hear from home soon. You might all immigrate to California and get there before I heard of your going. Don't forget me altogether. This leaves us in good health. Hoping you enjoy the same blessing, I remain your affectionate son. Peter "

------

38 General Stephen A. Hurlbut, commander of Union forces around Memphis.

* For more on Fingle, see "*Soldier Life*", Chapter 11.

Columbus, Ky., Nov. 24th, '63

" Dear Brother: I received the box this morning all right. Frank also got a box of chickens, butter, pickles, eggs, &c. There are nine of us in a mess and the program is for each one to get something from home as long as we stay at this post. So we will live this winter. I think the Q. M. (Quartermaster) has been making a speculation of our rations, or we have got more appetite than formerly, as we have been scant of bread and groceries for some time. But if there is any cheating it will be found out pretty soon. We have generally had something to sell, but now we buy. However there is no danger of our going hungry as we have learned how to help ourselves when there is any need.

Our comrade that is under sentence of death has been reprieved one month. It will be the 4th of January now. The President will be petitioned to pardon him or mitigate the sentence. The effect of his sentence has done a great deal of good by way of restraining unruly men. They think military law is not to be trifled with where they put on the string as they do here. One of our boys that has spent most of his time in the guardhouse and has twice deserted* is just returned to the Company after being in prison all summer. Col. Shaw told him if he gets into the guardhouse any more he will have him shot. He means it. I forgot to send the likeness last time. I will try and not forget this time.

Mr. Wambaugh is still provost guard. He likes it very well and is in good health. I will give him some butter as I guess that is the instructions though I have not got any letter in regard to it. We will have a Thanksgiving dinner as Frank and John have lots of chickens. It is almost too far to send such things as they can be had here at reasonable rates. I received a letter from father a short time ago. It was time as I began to think I was quite forgotten. I keep an account of how many letters I write and how many I receive. Since I was home I have written twenty and received five, so I am getting on nicely. Have you heard from the owner of Section 17? If so let me know how he proposes to sell or if at all.

There is some talk of enlisting in the Veteran Corps. Quite a number of the 14th will go in. For my part I will not until I finish my present term. The Colored Artillery offers more inducements than the Veteran Corps but I believe it is best to get out of the old first, then I can keep out if I choose.

I need not prolong my letter as news is scarce. With love to all I remain, your affect brother Peter Wilson. "
------
* David Casaday. See B.F. Thomas, "*Soldier Life*", Chapter 11.

Columbus, Ky., Dec. 12th, [1863]

" Dear Brother West: Yours of Oct. 27 is just arrived so you see it has been mislaid somewhere a month or more. I should have answered it promptly if it had come direct but now that it is here I will send a few lines to let you know how we wave down this way. There has been considerable stir here for some time. There have been six or eight regiments of eastern men passed through Columbus. They stayed a few days, just long enough to see what kind of chaps they were. There was a New York City regiment mostly Dutch and Irish, fond of lager and whiskey, consequently fond of fighting among themselves and spreeing generally.

One regiment was from New Jersey. They belong to the Zuave [Zouave] persuasion. The only difference between them and other soldiers is in dress. Being comically dressed they think they should be comic all through and as a general thing they are a harum scarum set. Then there was Pennsylvania Cavalry, riding the poorest horses imaginable and if a cavalry regiment has poor horses they make a poor appearance and I think they cannot hurt the enemy much. We think it is the intention to clean out the Rebs in this part of the country and open this road to Corinth. Perhaps we may be sent out, but we hope to stay in our comfortable cabins till spring. The weather has not been much cold yet but it is rather rainy and disagreeable for camping now.

I don't think there is much chance for a fight out on the road as there cannot be much of a rebel force out there. There are plenty of guerillas, however, and some of them are brought in every few days. We send them to Rock Island now. Some of our boys went up there this week with a lot that were captured last week.

It is hard to get on a trip of that kind as so many want to go. Well, West, there is nothing more only that we are all well and having very good times. Please write again. Perhaps your letter may come sooner next time. I need not write to Father this week as this will do for all. I will write a longer letter next time. I am on guard today and it is nearly time for my relief to go to duty. So no more from your brother Peter "

Columbus, Ky., Dec. 19th, 1863

" Dear Parents: I have been writing to one and another pretty often lately but it is nearly a month since I have written to you, so I will send you a few lines this time though I have nothing of importance to mention. We have had some rough weather lately almost as bad as in Iowa. There is no snow but there was plenty of rain and now quite hard frost. The regiments that were passing through had very uncomfortable times in their little shelter tents. I think there is force enough gone out into Tennessee to clean out all the rebels in this part of the country. The most of the troops that have gone out are eastern men and perhaps they may get the worst of it. If the Army of the Potomac is like the eastern men that are in this Division no wonder Richmond is not taken but they may do in this district as the Rebs that they will find are of the guerilla mixed with conscript breed and don't make a very hard fight as a general thing.

There was some talk of putting the 14th in a Brigade with the eastern men but I think it will not be done now as they have gone and we will likely stay in Columbus. I never want to have anything to do with such men as they are. They mostly came out for the large bounties paid in New York and Jersey and care little about anything else.

How is it about the draft in Tama? Will there be enough of volunteers to keep it off? It seems land is looking up as the owner of 17 wants $3.50 for the unbroken and $6.00 for the broken. I presume Uncle David has concluded to stay where he is. It is not likely land will get cheaper as the prospect for a peace is becoming brighter and no doubt Iowa will soon settle up when the war is over. It don't seem possible for the Rebs to hold out more than till next summer. Don't you think the Abolitionists are having things as they want them now? They will soon pay negro soldiers the same as white and level things generally. There are some furious debates between the Democrats and Republicans about it. I see the white officers of the 2nd Tennessee Colored Artillery are as much respected here as any other officers and put on as much style as Regulars.

There are some Democrat soldiers very much opposed to Negro equality. Still they think they may as well grin and bear it. They sometimes cuss old Abe &c but there are four of our strong Democrats of Company G reenlisted for three years*. It seemed at one time as if the 14th would go in as a Veteran Regiment. That would require two-thirds of the men. Perhaps they may get that many but they have not yet. For my part I mean to finish my present term and then quit the business if I keep in my present way of thinking.

I see they agitate the question of giving us the same bounty as those that are enlisting now. I hope they may as we deserve it as much as the rest. There is nothing more worth writing so I will close.

Your Affc Son Peter Wilson "

----

* The re-enlisted veterans of Company G were Samuel Chambers, Addison Davis, Charles Edwards, Josiah Luke, Jeremiah Mills and Joel Shropshire.

Columbus, Ky., Dec. 28th, 1863

" Dear Father: I take this opportunity of sending a few lines to let you know that we are all well and putting in the time as agreeably as possible. We are having a wet time just now but our camp is on high ground so the mud is not bad only in town. Columbus, though not as low as Cairo, is on a flat piece of ground and in wet weather is muddy enough. Our camp is almost as high above Columbus as Balcary was above the Fishhouse. If there was anything to look at the view would be good from the bluff but nothing only an occasional steamboat or gunboat disturbs the sameness of the prospect.

Negro sentinels walk their beat on the fortifications, which no one would have thought of a short time ago but now is looked upon as indifferently as if it had been so from the first. Everything goes on with as much regularity as in times of peace. The colored men do all the heavy work such as unloading boats and putting the goods on the train to be sent out to the Army at Union City. The darkies save us some hard work in that line besides taking care of the Fort. They could not be spared from here without the same number of troops of some kind taking their place.

You seem to have but a poor opinion of soldiering. There is no mistake but the majority of soldiers are a hard set. It would be hard for you to imagine anything worse than they are. They have every temptation to do wrong and if a man has not firmness enough to keep from the excesses common to soldiers he will soon be as bad as the worst. If it were not that the Army is principally made up of such men I would like it much better. I have no serious intention of remaining any longer than my time is up, unless I can make it pay [something]. Sometimes I think if I come home I cannot stay but I can try. I know there are sometimes circumstances that make a man wish he never had enlisted, but there are trials and troubles other places besides the Army. There is one thing certain, the Army will either make a man better or worse morally speaking. There are men in Company G that have reformed greatly in regard to drinking, swearing, &c. Others have become confirmed drunkards, thieves, &c. As you seem to wish it I will promise to come home if spared till my time is up unless something unlooked for comes up. I must answer Jane's letter so goodbye. Your affect Son Peter "

Columbus, Ky., Dec. 28th, 1863

" Dear Sister Jane: I have been a little slow in answering your letter, but there is so little to write it don't make much difference. Writing letters is dry work when one is situated as I am. If you were acquainted with this place as I am at home there would be more to tell but as that is not so you must make allowance for the dullness of my letters. There is little change in our duties or drill or anything else. Since we came to Columbus it has generally been light, two days per week is the average time on guard and an hour's battalion drill in the afternoon is about all we have to do. There is a good deal of time to read, write, or anything that suits the fancy. I have read considerable ancient history this winter. I have tried to study grammar but something is sure to turn the attention from anything like study. It is impossible to keep long at any one thing, there is so much noise and bustle but there is always some in every family that won't learn. The fact is I don't like to study and never can hope to overcome the dislike I have to any kind of study, except Hardee's Tactics and Army Regulations. I don't like them but must study them so as not to be behind the times.

If I leave the Army in ten months it will not be necessary for me to get very well posted on military matters.

I suppose by this time you have a recruiting sergeant among you. We may look for some of our neighbours down here before long, if they don't put the draft farther away. It was a fortunate thing for Frank to get home so as his expenses are paid and he wanted to go very much*. One of the boys got more butter from home today. We have quite a fund ahead now from the rations we sell. We are pretty economical in our household affairs and make the most of everything. We had a very fine Christmas dinner principally chickens.

The boys went out a few miles one night on a chicken expedition and were mistaken for guerillas by the Cavalry. They had to take to the woods until the Cavalry was gone. They came in with full hands but tired of being chased by our own Cavalry. I think it is not the first time mistakes of that kind have been made. Every thing is laid to guerillas no matter who does it. I must finish for this time so good bye.

Your affect. Brother, Peter "

------

* B.F. Thomas, "Frank", went home on a recruiting mission, see Chapter 12, "*Soldier Life*". The Fourteenth needed more men while Tama County hoped to have enough volunteers sign up to avoid an enforced draft in the county. Some of the original records of that recruiting mission were found with Captain Gallagher's papers at the Tama County Historical Museum in Toledo.

Columbus, Ky., Jan. 12th, 1864

" Dear Parents: I take the present opportunity of letting you know how I get along. There is still the same report to make, all quiet at Columbus. The snow is beginning to melt today. Kentuckians say they never saw so steady freezing weather so long as it has been this time. It was not very uncomfortable for us but the troops that are in tents must have suffered considerably. I suppose the 6th Division will leave this district in a month or so, at least so goes the report. If we stay a little longer the worst of the winter is past and we can get along anywhere in summer. But it is time enough to speculate about leaving. One of our guardhouse recruits that is a Secesh soldier enlisted from the guardhouse into our Army. There are a good many* such in the 14th. Well last night one of them deserted and tried to steal a horse from the Cavalry pickets. There are three pickets at each post. The one on duty saw him slip up to the horses and fired at him. He turned to run but had not ran far before he fell. The picket shot him three times. Either shot would have killed him.

I got a letter from Frank Thomas last night. It is the only one from Buckingham for some time. I don't hear of Perry's recruits this time. I hope Perry may do their share without drafting. It seems recruiting is not quite useless yet in Iowa. It will be quite a difference to see so many in our Company. The 14th will be a mixture of Kentucky recruits*, Iowa recruits, and Veterans. There won't be many discharged when the three years is expired if the bounty is still offered. There is nothing of importance to write so I will finish for this time.

Your Son, Peter "

------

* When the Fourteenth Iowa was first formed, Companies A, B and C were detached and sent to the Dakota frontier to guard against Indian attack. Eventually three more companies were later recruited to fill their places. Some of these men, especially in Companies C and H, came from Kentucky and Tennessee after those States were more firmly secured for the Union by Grant's campaign to Corinth. Most of these Southern born men remained loyal and fought bravely alongside their Iowa companions. They endured the same campaign hardships, contracted the same debilitating and often fatal diseases. They were killed in the same battles, suffered the same terrible wounds, and often found graves far from their homes just as the Iowa men. Many of them remained to serve in the Residuary Battalion after the rest of the Regiment disbanded. But a study of the roster shows that the Kentucky and Tennessee men of the Fourteenth Iowa had higher rates of desertion, several leaving within a month of their enlistment; perhaps these were recruited direct from the guardhouse as Wilson describes above. Tennessee born Seth Cason, a thirty-six year old recruit from Columbus, Kentucky, enlisted into Company H January 7, 1864. The roster says he died a week later, on January 14, of "wounds received while attempting to desert".

Memphis, Tennessee

On board the Steamboat "*Fanny* " Memphis, Tenn., Jan. 24th, 1864

" Dear Parents: I take this opportunity of letting you know that we are so far on our expedition. We have not learned our destination but the rumor is that we are going a visiting to Mobile. If so I presume we will join a large force down the river, but I need not anticipate, time enough when we get there to see. Our Brigade came down on four boats and there was exciting times to see which boat would get to Memphis first. We started last and passed two of the boats on the first evening. We overtook the third in the morning and tried to pass but could not do it. The two boats ran within speaking distance for half a day and got in, in 20 hours from the time we started. It was the best time I have seen. And we enjoyed it very much. Our fleet is anchored out in the river to keep the men out of mischief. If we could go ashore here the citizens would suffer, so to keep the peace they keep us on the boats.

You need not expect to hear from me often now. I will try and send a few lines from N(ew) Orleans.

Your Affect Son, Peter "

Vicksburg, Mississippi

Vicksburg, Miss., Jan. 29th, 1864

" Dear Father: I take the earliest opportunity after getting a peep at the places of interest to let you know that I am well. We left Columbus on the 21st and landed yesterday, the 28th. We had fine sunny weather and enjoyed the trip very much. I might make an attempt to describe the places along the river but the chance to write is so poor owing to the confusion of fixing to move the camp that I will pass over with a glance at one or two places.

There is very little to see along the river now. Most of the plantations are deserted and destroyed. Some places the rows of brick chimneys standing where the houses were burned are the only mark to guess at the size of the plantation. Helena is the only place of consequence between Memphis and Vicksburg. Like most of the river towns it is too low to be healthy. Colored soldiers seem to be the principal part of the population.

Vicksburg is the best location I have seen since we left Columbus. It has the merit of being high and dry. It is very bluffy where the fighting took place, so much so I don't see how they could hurt one another much. The rebels had their holes to get into from the shells and no other kind of balls could touch them in their works. It is quite interesting to see the places of safety the people had fixed. I presume when traveling on the river becomes safe curiosity seekers will visit Vicksburg and find it the most interesting place on the river. There is an endless amount of fortifications. It is stronger now than it was when the rebels held it. There has been a great amount of fortifying done since it came into our hands. There is one Iowa brigade here besides ours. They have reenlisted in the Veterans, and mean to stick to Uncle Samuel to the end of Rebellion. There were eight Infantry regiments, three Batteries, and four Cavalry regiments in this force that came down the river. The Infantry and Artillery are here, the Cavalry is coming by land. It is likely all the troops up that way are on the move. We don't know whether we go out to Jackson or farther down. We expect to stay here a week or two. The roads are dry now, rivers low, and perhaps we may move on immediately. The Regiment is in good health and fine spirits. I mean to enjoy myself if I keep well through this campaign. I will write as often as convenient but you need not expect regularity in my letters.

Your affect Son, Peter Wilson "

Canton, Mississippi

Canton, Miss., Feb. 27, 1864

" Dear Parents: I take the earliest opportunity since we left Vicksburg of sending a few lines to let you know that I am well. We left Vicksburg and marched to Meridian, Mississippi, by way of Jackson, Brandon, Hillsboro, & Decatur. We tore up railroads at all points along the route, burned cotton and other Confederate property. We lived upon the country and have lived well. There is no enemy of consequence in this State. I have been with the foraging party of our Brigade all the way and only in one skirmish and no one was hurt. We had some brisk skirmishing every day from Black River to Meridian. The rebels retreated all the way before us and seldom had time to burn bridges, we kept so close to them.

I am writing by the camp fire and you must not expect a decent letter till I get time to write. I think we will come to the River in a few days. We have any number of darkies, mules, horses, &c. There is some party going to Big Black tomorrow and I take the chance to send this. We have had fine weather, good roads, and marched near three hundred miles and are in good trim, no sick nor none wounded. Some few of the Regiment have been taken prisoner but I must finish.

You may hear from me soon and it may be some time but I am doing well and will write again as soon as possible. This is Confederate paper. Your affect son, Peter "

Red River, Louisiana

On board the Steamer " *W. L. Ewing* ", Grand Echo *, Red River, La.,
April 4th, 1864

" Dear Parents: I don't know as you will know by all the above just where we are at present. If you look on the map you will see a place called Natchitoches. It is a few miles from this place on the old bed of a river now called Cane River. Well I may as well begin by saying that since the little affair at D. Rucy (39) nothing of importance has been done unless it is being done now. There has been some skirmishing for the last two days and this morning a force went up to engage the rebels if they still wait. I know nothing of the prospect for a general battle up here but I think it is very unlikely. Banks (40) is with us now and I presume we outnumber the rebels too much to get them to give us battle. The probability is that as soon as Banks can safely spare our Division we will join our Corps at Vicksburg or Memphis. Then rumor says we may go to the East or into Georgia, but time enough to go there when we finish this expedition. The 28th and 24th Iowa are in this Army, but I have seen none but A. Felter yet. I may see Col. Connell before we come down the River.

I like field service much better than I did garrison. We have marched part of the way on this trip and sailed the rest. We don't burn and destroy as on the Mississippi raid but take only such things as we need to eat. This is the finest country I have seen in the South. The land is good and all the planters are or have been wealthy. There are some few Union men still in the country and I think there is some chance of restoring order to this country by keeping some gunboats along the River and letting those who will go ahead and raise cotton, sugar, &c. There are few men but will mind their own interest and certainly the Red River farmers can make money by coming under the protection of Uncle Sam.

I received a letter from James the 26th of last month, dated March 6th and have heard nothing later. There are few chances of sending mail and few of getting it. John Thomas has been down with fever for a few days but I think he is past the worst*. The rest of us are in good health. I might go on and write a long letter but the deck hands are chopping rails below and jarring so I must finish. I will try and write again when there is another chance to send a letter. Your affect Son Peter "

------

39 The Union forces had captured Fort DeRussy, Mississippi, on March 14, 1864. [Ft. DeRussy actually was in Louisiana near Marksville.]

40 General Nathaniel P. Banks. There was much criticism of his handling of the expedition and he was soon afterwards replaced. Details of the capture of Peter Wilson are not given.

 * Probably Grand Ecore, in northwest Louisiana on the Red River. "Grand Ecore" means "Big Bluff" in Old French. Rising over 100 feet along the Red River, Grand Ecore is said to be the steepest river bluff in Louisiana.

 * **John R. Thomas**, brother of B.F. Thomas, did not recover. He died April 9, 1864; see "*Soldier Life*", Chapter 12.

Camp Ford, Prisoner of War Camp, Tyler Texas

Texas, April 25th, 1864

" Dear Parents: I take this opportunity of informing you that I am a prisoner of war, (41) in good health, well treated, and hoping to get out in due time. You need not write to me at present. Your affect Son, Peter Wilson

List of prisoners of Co. G, 14th Iowa, taken at Pleasant Hills, April 9th, 1864:

Lieut. A. H. Hazlett	H. Brownell	
Peter Wilson	C. Vimpeny	
Joel Shopshire	Hiram Aurner	Co. B
W. S. Townsend	[Meroni] Clark	" "
D. C. Vail	John A. Kleber	" D
George Loucks	Joseph Gillet	" F
P. J. Cook	W. D. Goben	" K
Wm. Nance	W. B. Gray	" "

Please send a copy of this list to the Regiment. "

------

41 Peter Wilson was captured at the battle of Pleasant Hill, Louisiana, on April 9, 1864. How this letter was gotten out of the Confederate lines is not explained. It was written on a small piece of paper. [This letter also helped prove that Lt. Hazlett was still alive and ironically cost Wilson a chance for an important promotion. Peter Wilson, even though he was a prisoner of war, had been nominated by Capt. Gallagher to take Hazlett's position as Lieutenant, a nomination that was withdrawn when word was received that Hazlett had survived. However, Gallagher's choice of Wilson to be promoted even as a prisoner shows his esteem for Peter Wilson.]

* **William D Goben**, twenty-five, and **William D Gray**, eighteen, both of Kossuth, Des Moines County and **John A Kleber**, twenty-five, of Franklin, born in Germany, and **Joseph Gillett**, thirty, of North Liberty, all enlisted October 1861, and all survived their Texas captivity and mustered out at war's end. Goben and Gillett had earlier been taken POW at Shiloh and then taken again at Pleasant Hill. **Hiram Aurner**, twenty-seven, of Bremer County, and **Meroni Clark**, twenty, of Jefferson, both enlisted August 1862. The roster lists Aurner as killed in action at Pleasant Hill while Wilson lists him above as a fellow prisoner at Tyler. Aurner was still alive in Denver, Iowa in 1902, and is buried in Janesville. Meroni Clark died July 15, 1864 as a POW in Texas from wounds he suffered at Pleasant Hill.

Jan. 10th (42) (1865, probably from Camp Ford, Tyler Texas)

" Tomorrow they start for our lines. Two months from this time I can hear from you if all goes well. Tell Frank I would write to him if I had paper and I want him to write and let me know how many of the old part of the Company were discharged with him and how they spent the summer &c. I may not be here to get the letters but if I should not the loss is not great. You have concluded by this time that I won't get home in time to farm this summer. Perhaps I may get home by harvest time. You must be your own judge of how to manage with reference to my absence. If I get out this spring I will have four or five hundred in Greenbacks. If I must stay longer I will have more. If you buy land or anything else, whatever you do it will be all right as far as I am concerned.

When you write, if there is anything you wish to say that would not do to be seen by the rebels, write with onion juice on the last page. It can be read by the fire and is invisible by daylight. Send me some spare paper so I can write again and do your secret writing on it. Let me know something of war matters if you think it can be done in the way I mention. They only publish such things as suits their fancy in the Texas papers. We don't know how Grant is progressing at Richmond, but we know that Sherman and Thomas have done well, also that Pap Price (43) came back from Missouri in a used up condition.

Give my respects to inquiring friends and love to Father, Mother, Brothers, and Sisters, and hoping to soon get on the soil that is not cursed by the presence of a rebel, I remain your affect Brother Peter "

----

42 This letter has no place given and the year is omitted, but it appears to have been written in 1865 while Peter Wilson was still a prisoner of war in Texas. It was apparently written to his brother and business associate, James Wilson. From his instructions about secret writing it seems that this letter was uncensored.

43 The Confederate leader, Sterling Price.

New Orleans, Louisiana (Freedom)

New Orleans, La., May 28th [1865]

" Dear Father: I take the first opportunity of informing you of my return to the land of the living, for I have been in all respects dead for the past 13 months. Well thank God it is past now and as I have seen the Confederacy go to pieces it is some satisfaction for my long imprisonment. It seems almost a dream that we are really out of Texas and the war over, but perhaps I will get used to it in a short time. We just got out of Texas in time as the rebel authority is gone and we had some difficulty in getting rations on the way out. Everything is confusion up Red River. There is likely to be trouble among the rebels if our forces don't go up soon and take charge.

It is astonishing to see the change that has taken place among the people in regard to the Union. It is the universal talk. We are glad that the thing is over and they generally express satisfaction that the Union is restored. I will not write much this time. Perhaps in a few days we will be on the way up the River. I will lose no time in coming home as soon as I get my discharge. We will likely remain a few days at Davenport, and you may write to me in care of D. McCosh, Long Grove &c. Tell James also to write. If we don't get away from here in a few days I will write again. Let me know Brother John's address and how he is getting on. I am in good health and hope to be fit for duty when I get home.

   With love to all I remain, your Affect Son, Peter Wilson "

WELCOME HOME TO IOWA FROM BROTHER JAMES

Perry, June 12, 1865

" Dear Brother: (44) It was with feelings of joy and thankfulness that we received your letter last mail. I cannot imagine the feelings that daily possessed you in your dreary confinement. Probably you cannot imagine our feelings while you were there. I wrote you several letters not expecting much you would ever get them, but hope induced me to try. Once I sent you ten dollars. Folks said it would be surely lost but I considered it my especial business to leave no stone unturned. Father and Mother have suffered a great deal on your account. Father especially bore suspense in silence. In fact your detention has been common talk in the neighborhood, "any word from Peter", "any word from Pete", " any word from your brother " &c &c was the continual question. The prayers of your friends, of our Minister, the desires of all your friends was that you might be spared to return and who can tell what effect the effectual fervent prayers of righteous man may have had at the source of all our blessings. But it is over and I hope that in some way it may work for your good.

   There has been a great many changes since you left, a great many folks have come into the place. The face of the prairie has been considerably changed, new houses on some farms, new breaking, new fences, some that you were acquainted with are dead, though God has spared those who are near and dear to you. Grandfather Wilson and Grandmother McCosh are gone, several in this place, Mrs. Bywerth, George Shiner's wife, John Leffler. W. Hough has sold & gone to Kansas. D. D. Wartson has sold to a relation of Uncle McMillan's and bought the old Connell farm. Hiram Klingaman has sold to Pearson & left. A family of Stevensons have moved around Collins grove. A Mr. Wilson from Illinois has bought the land west of Uncle West's and is improving [it]. George Sloss & John Tenan talk of coming back to this place from Shell Rock. A Scotch family named Lawson* have bought Fox's place and nearly all those mentioned have connected with the church. We have just had a very edifying communion season. Mr. Fulton from Cedar Rapids preached for us.

   If you got my last letter you will have some idea of our financial affairs. I bought ten acres of timber from Jonas Wood. It is young and for future use. Then I bought forty acres in Four Mile Grove, half pretty good timber. Then I bought a tract of timber from Uncle McMillan that will fence up all our land. The timber is all paid for. Last winter after a great deal of trouble and expense by finally going to Illinois I bought the quarter section south of our old eighty. I borrowed the money (800) to pay for it. I have got the house finished upstairs and down. Uncle Andrew and I bought a mowing machine and paid for it. I built a two-horse cultivator this spring on wheels so you can ride or walk. Have 20 head of cattle, 7 head horses, 36 head hogs, plenty of corn, and half last year's wheat. I am building the pasture fence. I told you I have Robert Dodd hired till harvest. Finally have just succeeded since you went to war in getting the place ready to pay well, your Affectionate Brother James   "

------

44 This letter, written by James Wilson to Peter Wilson in reply to the letter announcing Peter's release from the Confederate prison, was included in the collection and is printed with the Peter Wilson letters because it gives briefly the conditions at home. Peter returned to take up work on his farm. In 1870 he married Miss Emma Lawson*. Seven children were born of this marriage: John L., Mary W., Sheridan S., Andrew C., Nellie (Mrs. John Randolph Currens), Grace G., and Peter L.

This third installment of the letters of Peter Wilson was published in OCTOBER 1942 in **The Iowa Journal of History and Politics** -- Published Quarterly by The State Historical Society of Iowa; Iowa City, Iowa
All three installments are reprinted from "Peter Wilson in the Civil War", IJHP # 42 (1942), 153-203, 261-320, 339-414. Copyright 1942 State Historical Society of Iowa. Used here with the permission of the publisher.

PLEASANT HILL

From *The Iowa Transcript:*

" **CORRESPONDENCE**
 Camp near Rolla, Mo., Jan. 20, '63.
 Editor Transcript

Dear Sir!

One week ago yesterday we came to this place, then it was warm and pleasant, to-day we have about 4 inches of snow and the dusty rain now settling down upon us this morning gives us fair warning that for the next three or four days we will have regular Missouri weather, mud, sloppy, splashy roads, and a disagreeable time generally.

Last Thursday it was cold and stormy and our men in their frail and tattered wedge tents suffered greatly from the effects of the sudden cold, no stoves and crowded together in these small tents with barely room to squeeze in, and when they wished to turn over, the command "about face" was given and all turned together executing the movement with the same precision as though drilling in ranks or parade.

Our transit from Toledo, Iowa to Benton Barracks, Mo., was agreeable and prosperous. We reached St. Louis on Christmas and reported immediately to the barracks. Our regiment had removed to the barracks occupied the year before, and the meeting of the members of the regiment once more was one of gladness and pleasure.

Our first dress parade was one long to be remembered by us. Many absent members told of the heavy mortality and the heavy loss in the changes of one year. Indeed it was rather sad to see the thinned ranks, and then consider what had made it so. Many brave men, and true, of Iowa's noble sons, were resting quietly in a soldier's grave, some in the land of Dixie, and others on the fields of Donelson and Shiloh.

We were ordered to this place to reinforce it in case our troops at Springfield should meet with a defeat which place we understood was attacked by a rebel force under "Marmaduke". But as the rebels have been repulsed at Springfield we will go back to St. Louis and perhaps Davenport, Ia. I understand by latest news that we leave this afternoon for St. Louis.

Rolla is a place of but little importance aside from its Government stores, and these at present are quite an item. There is a great deal of Government property here at present, as this is the depot for stores of all kinds sent to the army of the southwest. The army at Springfield receives all its supplies from this post, this being the terminus of the railroad from St. Louis.

Take away the Government stores here and you would have a town about one half the size of Toledo.

The town is situated on one of those points of land remarkable for nothing save barren scrubby oaks, hazelbrush and rabbits, the very place above all the guerillas and bushwackers would conceal their carcases in. East of town is an earthwork or fortification commanding the approaches to town. North and west are encamped the 22nd Iowa, 27 Mo. and the detachments of the 14th, 8th, and 12th Iowa Infantry regiments.

But I must close as orders have come to strike tents, and then ho! for St. Louis. The snow flakes are settling quietly down covering everything in a sheet of white; and the muddy roads proclaim that previous to this we have had rain.

News to-day confirm the report of the capture of Arkansas Post with four thousand eight hundred prisoners.

My haste is my excuse for errors.
Yours truly   WM. GALLAGHER   Co. G, 14th Iowa Regt.   "

Notes:
-- Of the men from Company G who died in service, some, like Eccles, Cheney, and McKune, are now buried in well-marked graves in national cemeteries. Fifteen men of the Company "rest quietly" in soldiers' graves in unknown locations. Most were probably exhumed after the War and buried in a national cemetery without any confirmed identity, placed under headstones bearing the simple inscription "Unknown". Some have memorial markers in their local cemeteries with their families but the location of their actual grave is not known with certainty.

Unless new information on their burial sites comes to light, these men are:

Thomas Snelling -- Killed at Donelson 1862
Samuel W Jenks -- Killed at Shiloh 1862
Robert F Clark -- Died as a POW in Mobile Alabama after Shiloh 1862
David Miller -- Died as a POW in Macon Georgia after Shiloh 1862
Edgar Dykeman -- Died of disease at Columbus Kentucky 1863
William B Wade -- Died of disease in New Orleans Louisiana 1864
John R Thomas -- Died of disease near Fort DeRussy Louisiana 1864
William Heath -- Killed at Pleasant Hill 1864
Enos Kern -- Killed at Pleasant Hill 1864
Sephman F Martin -- Killed at Pleasant Hill 1864
Joseph Shanklin -- Killed at Pleasant Hill 1864
John Shumaker -- Killed at Pleasant Hill 1864
Henry Spangler -- Killed at Pleasant Hill 1864
Philo H Brownell -- Died as a POW in Tyler Texas after Pleasant Hill 1864
William Nance -- Died as a POW in Tyler Texas after Pleasant Hill 1865

This letter, from Joseph Shanklin, written in March, was printed in *The Iowa Transcript* April 14 1864.

" ALEXANDRIA, LOUISIANA March 17th, 1864

DEAR FATHER,
    Perhaps you are wondering by this time where I am and what I am doing. When we were at Vicksburg I hardly had time to let you know that I had returned safely from the Miss. expedition. And since leaving on Board the transports I have had no opportunity of sending a letter.
    We left Vicksburg the evening of the 10th arrived at Red River landing the 11th started up the next morning. After going up the river a few miles we struck off into the Achafalaya Bayou, went as far as Simsport. Next morning (Sunday) nearly all the troops disembarked expecting a little fight, as they learned the Rebels were fortified out about two miles from the landing. Our regiment was ordered across the other side of the river to go foraging, and to drive off a few rebels that were reported to be on that side engaged in taking away some rebel commissary stores. We returned to the landing about 5 P.M. without seeing any rebels, but they left in such a hurry that we got five hogsheads of sugar, which they left behind.
    When we returned, we received orders to cross the river immediately and disembark with five days rations, as the rebels had evacuated the fort and we were to follow them. The expedition had returned to the river to prepare the rations, and we were to start at 7 o'clock. We marched 7 miles that night after marching 18 in the day time; rather a hard tramp on our new recruits. Next morning we started at 5 o'clock; our brigade in the advance the 27th Iowa 1st regiment, 14th Iowa 2nd. After marching 14 miles we came up with their rear guard, and a few shells from our battery soon convinced them that they were not in a safe place, consequently they burned the bridge and then skeedaddled. The 27th, 14th and 32nd crossed the Bayou in an old flat boat that happened to be there, and by that time the Pioneers had a kind of Pontoon bridge made to cross the artillery and the wagons on. After crossing we did not see any more of them and suppose we were pushing them so close they took off on another road.
    The country through here was all settled by the French and all of them claimed protection. During the day we passed through three towns and in each one they had a French flag flying. The prettiest country I ever saw in the Southern Confederacy lays between Simsport and Red River near where we came to it. The last town we came to was Marksville; here the white flag was floating in token of surrender. What they intended to surrender was more than I can tell for I did not see anyone there but citizens.
    This town is about three miles from the river and fort, where the rebels thought themselves safe from all harm. When we came to the town the 27th Iowa being in the advance were left behind to guard the town while the troops passed through. That brought us in the advance. Companies I, D & G were ordered in front of the battery as skirmishers; but our company having so many recruits not drilled were ordered to act as reserve for the other two. After marching about two miles and a half we saw the rebels pickets and were ordered up on double quick; also the whole brigade soon after. We double quicked up within 300 yards of the fort and the two companies were deployed. By this time our regiment and the battery was up; our company

took it's place in the regiment and the battery opened the fire. We were ordered to support the battery; and the 32d to support the skirmishers.

A brisk cannonading was kept up by the 3d Indiana's 6 and 12 pounders, and the rebels 32 pounders for two hours, neither doing any particular damage, and then a charge was ordered by our brigade, which resulted in the capture of the two forts in short order. I say two forts for there was one built to protect the river and another, the one we stormed, about 1/2 mile back to protect that passage. Our batteries in firing had both in range and when they shot over the 1st they shot into the 2nd, which owing to the incompleteness of the forts caused them to evacuate the river fort and seek shelter in the other. If we had let them alone for 3 or 4 months longer we would not have had such an easy time taking it, or even if they had had troops there sufficient to man the works it would not have been an easy task. But Gen. Walker had left the fort the day before with the intention of checking our advance with his brigade of 4 or 5 thousand men, and had also sent a courier back to tell them that he could hold us in check 4 days where he burned the bridge and in that time they expected reinforcements from Alexandria, but he was not aware that we were able to cross some where else in a short time. We went so fast after that we beat him to the fort, which was left with a small force. When the charge was ordered owing to the distance to be traveled, the 24th Mo. was the first to plant their flag on the fortifications and the 14th 2nd. The result of the victory was 10 siege guns and from 4 to 5 hundred prisoners. I have not learned the exact number.

The loss in the 14th Iowa was five wounded, none killed. The only casualty in Co. G was Corporal McLain scratched on the finger a very little. Our Sharpshooters, from our regiment, kept them so close that they scarcely dared show their heads above the works. What our entire loss was I do not know but I think it is not more than 25 wounded and 5 killed.

The next morning after the fight our boats were all up waiting for us, they having come round the river, under protection of the gun boats. What was most remarkable in the affair was that we marched 53 miles, had a fight and gained the victory, besides sleeping 7 hours in 32 hours, which was something of an item. The fort was almost completed and was the strongest fort I have seen built by the rebels. The one next the river was not so near completed. But when complete would have been almost impenetrable, for it was being double plated with Rail road iron.

The next day we embarked again and started up the river, expecting a little fight here, but we just arrived in time to find that the rebels had left as usual; where they have gone is more than I can tell, we arrived here yesterday and are in camp just below the town. Alexandria is a very nice place, and I suppose in time of peace would be quite a lively place. We have just received orders to be ready to go aboard again, any minute, we are called upon I suppose up the river when we go again. Oh! I forgot to tell you the name of the fort we captured, it was Fort DeRussy, a French name. Please give my respects to all and write often to your son.

J.A. SHANKLIN "

Notes:
-- At the time this letter appeared in the newspaper, Joseph Shanklin, of Toledo, age 19 when he enlisted in October 1861, had been killed five days earlier at the battle of Pleasant Hill April 9 1864. It is possible that his body may have been later recovered and returned to Toledo for burial alongside his sister and two brothers in Toledo's Woodlawn cemetery, but most likely his marker is only a memorial over an empty grave.
-- Even though the Red River campaign failed to achieve its objective (the taking of Shreveport) because of decisions by Grant, Sherman, and Banks, the victory at Pleasant Hill again staved off a terrible, almost certain defeat for the Union army that may have had very serious long-range consequences. Almost two years to the day of the Shiloh battle, once again the men of the 14th Iowa helped hold a crucial line in a fierce fight, saved the bulk of the army behind them, prevented a disaster, and then paid a terrific price with their own lives and freedom.
-- Corporal McLain is Ferdinand Turner McLain.

Addison Davis sent three letters to *The Iowa Transcript*; the first was printed on May 5 1864:

" FROM THE 14th IOWA INFANTRY
GRAND ECORE, La., April 15 (1864)

Editor Transcript,

For the benefit of the friends of Co. "G" 14th Iowa, I send you an account of the action in which it was engaged and the losses it sustained in the hard fought battle of Pleasant Hill April 9th 1864. We reached the town on the evening of the eighth after the battle of that day had been fought and lost. On the morning of the 9th, Col. Shaw's Brigade (2nd brigade 3d division 16th Army corps) took up a position nearly three-fourths of a mile in front of the town to the left and around which the main portion of the 16th and 17th Army corps were massed behind thirty pieces of artillery with a converging fire. Skirmishing continued throughout the day until 4 P.M., when the rebels opened a heavy fire on our advance lines, and for nearly two hours we were under the most destructive fire I have ever witnessed.

Co. "G" were drawn up in line across a road upon a level plain and in twelve hundred yards of the enemy's batteries, the fire of which was principaly directed upon this road. Here we sustained two charges; of the first battalion, which charged across this plain, some six or seven wheeled to the right and escaped. Of the second battalion which seemed more determined and some of whom come within a few yards of our lines, but two escaped and one of them without his horse. The enemy then charged with his whole force. Bravely did our little brigade sustain the shock and held in check the masses in front until by passing our flanks the rebels had obtained our rear when flight {became?} a necessity to some, the same {disaster?} as fell to us at Shiloh.

The enemy rapidly pursued {--?-ss} until they reached the concentrated fire of all our batteries and massed forces. Their loss was terrible; such a fire as was directed upon them no force could withstand. They broke and fled in confusion. Our forces followed but a short distance as darkness rendered it impossible. We camped upon the battle ground during the night and spent most of the night in gathering up our wounded. Though a dear bought victory as it was, it was lost as soon as won. For early the next morning a want of supplies compelled us to retreat.

Lt. Col. Joseph H. Newbold, Adjt. W.H. McMillen, & Lt. J.H. Logan were killed upon the field. Below I will give you a list of the killed, wounded and missing of the company with their whereabouts as near as ascertained.

1st Lt. Andrew H. Hazlett, killed.
2nd Lt. Joseph A. Shanklin, killed, shot through the heart.
Private Enos Kern, killed.
Private Henry Spangler, killed, shot in head.
Private William S. Townsend, killed, shot in head.
Sergt. Charles Ford, wounded in right shoulder by shell, slight.
Private George W. Bates, severe wound in right knee.
Private Philo H. Brownell, severe wound in leg.
Private Perry J. Cook, severe wound in head.
Private Isaac J. Davis, severe wound in right shoulder and left hand.
Private John B. Edwards, severe wound in left leg.
Private Wm. Heath, right leg cut off by shell.
Private Shepmen F. Martin, severe wounded in thigh, hip, groin and shoulders.
Private Jacob Nauerth, severe wound in thigh.
Private John F. Shumaker, severe wound in abdomen and thigh, died on the morning of 13th.
Private Daniel C. Vail, severe wound through the hips.
Private James H. Wilkins, slight wound in thigh.
Private Johnathan Morton, slight wound in thigh.
Sergt. Peter Wilson, missing supposed to be wounded and a prisoner.
Private George Loucks, missing.
Private William Nance, missing.
Private Joel Shropshire, missing.
Private Charles Vimpany, missing.

Six killed, twelve wounded, and five missing. The missing are supposed to be killed or wounded and taken prisoners.

C. Ford and J. Morton are with the company. George W. Bates, I.J. Davis and John B. Edwards have been sent down the river to Alexandria. The remainder of the wounded and missing are in the hands of the rebels.

The health of the company is good considering the low swampy country.

Since leaving Columbus, Ky., we have travelled over one thousand six hundred and fifty miles, of which we have marched five hundred and eighty.

A.D. "

Notes:
-- Davis names three officers killed in the field. Joseph H Newbold 25 from the Henry County town of Hillsboro, was appointed Captain of Company F November 1861. Promoted Lieutenant Colonel March 1863, he was in command of the regiment during the battle at Pleasant Hill when he was shot from his horse and killed. **William H McMillen**, 20 enlisted into Company E in September 1861 together with his 22 year old brother **James E McMillen**. At Shiloh, James McMillen was badly wounded in the thigh and was discharged later that year in October 1862. A third McMillen brother, David 18, joined Company I in July 1863. **David McMillen** was killed in action at Pilot Knob Missouri September 27 1864. Promoted Second Lieutenant in April 1863, William was mortally wounded during the Pleasant Hill fight and died three days later. The McMillen brothers were from Vandalia, Jasper County. **George H Logan**, of Bloomfield, Davis County, was 28 when he was appointed Second Lieutenant of Company I in November 1861. He was killed in action at Pleasant Hill April 9 1864. Two years before their deaths in battle in Louisiana, Newbold, William McMillen and Logan were among those captured in the fight at the Hornets Nest of Shiloh and all three were held for several months as POWs.
-- About Addison Davis' list of casualties from Company G:
Of the killed: Hazlett and Townsend were actually alive, but taken prisoner at Pleasant Hill; Townsend later died in Texas as a POW; Kern was reported killed, then reported alive but recovering, then later reported dead from his wounds; Shanklin was killed outright during the battle. **Henry Spangler** 27 of Nevada, Story County Iowa had enlisted January 1864; he was killed in action in this battle April 9 1864.
-- Of the severely wounded: Heath died a week after having his leg severed. **John F Shumaker** 33, and **Sephman F Martin** 26, were both of Nevada Iowa and enlisted the same day with Spangler in January 1864. Three months later they were both mortally wounded at Pleasant Hill. Some reports say Shumaker was killed in action, rather than living until the 13th as stated above. Martin may have died the day of the battle, other sources say he died April 16. Martin was married to Addison Davis' sister Mary; his first name is frequently misspelled.
-- Of the wounded: Addison Davis' brother **Isaac J Davis** 18 of Nevada, also enlisted October 1861 but was not captured with the regiment at Shiloh. Wounded severely in the right shoulder at Pleasant Hill, he survived to muster out with the regiment at Davenport the following November. **Charles Ford** 21 of Tipton, Cedar County, enlisted October 1861. He is not listed among those captured at Shiloh. In July 1863 he was promoted Second Sergeant. At Pleasant Hill he was wounded in the shoulder by shrapnel from an exploding shell but he continued to serve until the end of the War.
-- **George W Bates** 21 of Toledo enlisted January 1864; by April he was severely wounded in the knee, and in November he mustered out when the regiment was disbanded at Davenport. He farmed near Toledo for many years after the War before moving to Ashland Nebraska, the home of Peter Jesperson, a Company G man who had been wounded at Shiloh. Two decades later Bates relocated to Guthrie Oklahoma, home of Joseph Burright, another Company G survivor of Shiloh who had been taken prisoner. Bates had enlisted after both these men had been discharged, so it may have been merely a coincidence. Bates died in Guthrie in 1932 and is buried in Summit View cemetery.
-- Also from Toledo, both **James H Wilkins** 18 and **Jacob Nauerth** 27 are listed as prisoners of war in some rosters but the above letter makes it clear they were both still with the Company a week after the battle. Wilkins enlisted December 1863, recovered from his wound at Pleasant Hill, and served until August 1865 with the Residuary Battalion of the 14th. In 1910 Wilkins retired to Tacoma Washington where he is buried. Nauerth [Wrongly identified as "Manerth" in the roster] was born in Germany. He enlisted in January of 1864 and was wounded by April. He too continued to serve with the Residuary Battalion but discharged in January 1865 still disabled by his wounded thigh. Nauerth farmed near Blaine Nebraska before retiring to Wichita where he died in May 1937. Jacob Nauerth is buried in Highland cemetery in Wichita and may have been one of the last members of Company G still alive in the late 1930's.
-- **John B Edwards**, of Tama County, the Company cook, survived his leg wound. He had fought at Shiloh and was taken prisoner there, but survived his imprisonment to fight again at Pleasant Hill. Despite his wound he

stayed on with his regiment and mustered out with the 14th at the end of his three years of service. In Chapter 11 of "Soldier Life" BF Thomas says Edwards was commonly known as "Pap" among the men. "Pap" is buried east of the bandstand in Buckingham cemetery near Traer.

-- **Jonathan Morton** 25 of Crystal, Tama County, was enlisted December 1863. Some records report he was not only wounded but also taken prisoner as well at Pleasant Hill, but Davis says he was still with the Company a week later when this letter was written. BF Thomas met Morton and Ford not long after the battle. See BF Thomas, "Soldier Life" Chapter 11. Jonathan's sister Persis Morton married John R Felter's brother Matthew. After the rest of the regiment was mustered out in November 1864, Morton continued to serve in the 14th Iowa's Residuary Battalion serving until June 1865. When he returned home to Crystal after the War, Jonathan was still suffering from his wounded leg and still struggling to regain his health from illness contracted during his time as a soldier. The coming of winter only made his condition worse. On February 24 1866 his long slow decline came to an end; he had only been home just over six months. He is buried in Crystal cemetery. Members of the Morton family lived in the Traer and Toledo areas for decades after Jonathan's death.

-- Despite winning the actual battle, the regiment was immediately ordered to retreat. Under orders from the Union officers directing the campaign, the bodies of the men killed in this fight were left behind and even some of the wounded men, if they were unable to walk, were left to the mercy of the enemy. The whole situation left many soldiers, including Colonel Shaw himself, feeling disgusted, bitter, and with little respect for their commanders. Brownell, Cook, and Vail, named above as wounded, were captured with Hazlett and Townsend and the five men that Davis listed as missing: Loucks, Nance, Shropshire, Vimpeny, and Peter Wilson. These men were taken to Camp Ford at Tyler Texas where they were held until the rebellion finally collapsed fourteen months later. Vail, like Townsend, died at this Texas POW camp. Nance also died, but it is unclear when and where. Brownell's ultimate fate is also not known with any real certainty. Of the ten men captured from Company G, Hazlett, Cook, Loucks, Vimpeny, Shropshire, and Wilson made it home alive.

Two more letters from Addison Davis appeared at the same time in *The Iowa Transcript* on June 9 1864 :

" Vicksburg, May 24, 1864

MR. EDITOR,

We left Grand Ecore April 20th, and covered Banks retreat to the Mississippi river, with the exception of one day, when there was a fight ahead, we were sent forward and the 13th corps sent to the rear out of danger. This was on the 16th of May. We passed the enemy that night, when we were again thrown in the rear and on the 18th of May the battle of "Old Oaks" was fought by the command under A.J. Smith, and without either the 13th or 19th Army corps. For a while the contest was doubtful. With the fire of 20 guns, they had silenced our rifled battery, blowed up one of the caisons with a shell, killed eight or ten of the horses and several of the men. One of their shells burst in one of our ammunition wagons and set it on fire. They had outflanked us on the left and were pressing us in the rear.

The 14th Iowa were thrown forward in the center and charged impetuously into a heavy timber with dense undergrowth, broke their center and thus endangered their flanks. In this we captured over two hundred prisoners, with a loss of less than two hundred in killed and wounded on our side. The 14th Iowa's loss was fourteen in killed and wounded. None of Co. G were hurt enough to keep them from duty, except six, who fainted from the intense heat and scarcity of water.

We reached the Miss. on the 20th and embarked on the 21st arriving here this morning and are bound for Memphis.

Yours truly
A DAVIS
Co. " G" 14th Iowa   "

" Vicksburg Miss., May 25, 1864

MR. EDITOR,

In my letter of April 15th I communicated to you a serious error, and I take this earliest opportunity to correct it. Enos Kerns was not killed as was reported. He was seen to fall, shot through the breast and thigh, and was supposed to be dead. But was afterwards picked up and taken to the hospital, and was still alive on the 29th of April as reported by one of our men who escaped at this time.

William Heath died of his wounds on or about April 15th 1864, the date not definitely ascertained. William Wade is also reported to have died in New Orleans, sometime in April, of fever.

As the request has been made of me that I should mark the graves of those who fell, with a view to the recovering of their bodies, I am sorry to say this is impossible. All of our dead and a majority of our wounded were left to the care and mercy of the enemy.

In that "one red burial bent" their ashes will rest unknown and undisturbed and the green and shady spot marked only in our memories where it shall remain forever as fresh as the verdure on which they fell.

A. DAVIS "

Notes:
-- Addison Davis 21 of Nevada Iowa enlisted Oct. 9, 1861. Taken POW at Shiloh with the regiment, he survived prison camp in Georgia. When the regiment reorganized in April 1863 he was made First Sergeant; a few months after these letters were written he was promoted to Second Lieutenant. He mustered out at the end of the War. Addison was one of the three men who volunteered to join BF Thomas to recover Tom Snelling's body while under enemy fire at Donelson. Addison Davis is buried in Goleta cemetery Santa Barbara County California. The phrase "one red burial bent" is from "Childe Harold's Pilgrimage", by Lord Byron.
-- Serving in Company G with Addison were his younger brother Isaac J Davis and his brother-in-law Sephman F Martin. Martin enlisted in January 1864, a few months before he was mortally wounded at Pleasant Hill, but Sephman's younger brother **John L Martin** had enlisted earlier with Addison and Isaac Davis in October 1861. John Martin died April 24 1862 less than three weeks after Shiloh. The Davis and Martin brothers were from Nevada, Story County
-- **William Heath** 21 of Buckingham, Tama County enlisted October 1861. He also had survived the prison camp after Shiloh (April 1862) but two years later, at Pleasant Hill, in April 1864, he was severely wounded in the right leg. The leg was amputated but he did not survive, dying on April 15, 1864. Other reports have his leg taken off by a shell rather than amputated. His gravesite has not been determined. His older brother **Franklin H Heath** 22 of the 9th Iowa Infantry was mortally wounded two years earlier at the battle of Pea Ridge Arkansas. They were the sons of David and Lydia Heath of Buckingham Township, neighbors of the Thomas family.
-- **Enos Kern** 21 of Toledo enlisted January 1864. He was wounded (and mistakenly reported as having been taken prisoner) April 9, 1864 at Pleasant Hill Louisiana. His death is officially recorded as occurring on April 15, 1864, although Addison Davis believed Kern was still alive. Enos was the son of long time Toledo area farmer William Solomon Kern and his wife Maria.
-- **William B. Wade** 25 was born in Canada but was a resident of Crystal Township when he enlisted December 1863 [The official roster says September but BF Thomas recruited him in December]. He died April 1 1864 in New Orleans and is said to be buried there.
-- The confusion in the records about the casualties at Pleasant Hill reflects how badly damaged and scattered Company G was after this battle. Determining who had lived, who was taken prisoner, who was injured, and what had become the fate of the injured, was very difficult at that time and under those circumstances. Accounting for everyone proved to be very difficult with wounded men scattered, and prisoners taken, and bodies left on the field when the Company was forced, under orders from General Banks, to withdraw despite winning the battle. After the span of almost a century and a half, it still is hard to sort out and determine with any real certainty now. Most of the dead from Pleasant Hill were probably taken to Alexandria and hastily buried, although some may have been buried where they fell in the field. After the War they are all thought to have been exhumed and placed in graves in Alexandria National Cemetery but the individual identities of the remains are probably lost forever. They share a common designation, "Unknown".

The following notice appeared in *The Iowa Transcript* June 16 1864:

" The following list of names was furnished to Mr. John Wilson of this county by his son Peter Wilson of Co. G of the 14th Iowa Regt. They were taken prisoners at the battle of Pleasant Hill in Ark., and some of them reported killed. They are still held as prisoners in Texas. The news that they are still alive will be most joyfully received by their friends:

Lieut. A. Hazlett,
Peter Wilson,
Joel Shropshire,
W.S. Townsend,
D.C. Vail,
George Loucks,
P.J. Cook,
Wm. Nance,
H. Brownell,
C. Vimpany "

Notes:
OF THE TEN CAMP FORD PRISONERS, 14th IOWA INFANTRY, COMPANY G, CAPTURED AT PLEASANT HILL LOUISIANA, APRIL 9, 1864, SIX MEN SURVIVED:

-- Peter Wilson and Andrew Hazlett both survived the Camp Ford prison camp. Wilson is recorded as mustering out from Davenport on June 12 1865, while Hazlett mustered out on the 19th, also from Davenport.
-- Joel Shropshire 18 of Cedar County enlisted October 1861; He was taken prisoner the first time after Shiloh, and again after Pleasant Hill. He survived both prison camp experiences, first in Georgia, and then the longer later period in Texas. Like Wilson and Hazlett, he served out his full three-year term of service while still a prisoner. He became an attorney after the War, practicing in Omaha Nebraska and Butte Montana. When he applied for a pension twenty years after Pleasant Hill Shropshire described the long forced march from Pleasant Hill Louisiana to Tyler Texas, and their first month in Texas. He recalled that it seemed to have rained on them almost every day and every night for the first three weeks of their captivity and that they had no shelter or protection of any kind. He spoke also of the fear many of the veterans had about being recaptured a second time after their original exchange. They thought they might face extra punishment or reprisals if the Confederates learned that their new captives were previously released prisoners of war. Having been captured in battle a second time, these men feared they would be considered in violation of their earlier parole, with possibly very severe consequences. Therefore, when questioned by the rebel officers, Shropshire gave his name as "Joel Spence", using his middle name. When they were finally exchanged again on May 27 1865, at Red River Landing Louisiana, Shropshire was listed in the official exchange documents as "Joel Spence". The anxiety he felt and his use of an alias during his captivity and release may explain why the records of many of these prisoners are so unclear and confusing today. The records say he was mustered out from Davenport Iowa on June 20 1865.
-- **George Loucks, Jr** 28 of Story County, born in Canada, enlisted January 1864 and was captured three months later in April. He is listed like the others as "returned from missing July 1864" but probably he was exchanged in late May 1865 and released in early June 1865. He survived Camp Ford, and according to the roster was mustered out from Clinton Iowa on June 21 1865. After the War he spent many years farming in Nebraska. He then retired to Santa Ana California and died there just after Christmas 1919.
-- **Perry Cook** 18 of Mount Pleasant, enlisted January 1864. He was a 15 year old boy living on his grandfather's farm when the War began. After three years the War still continued and Cook decided it was his time to join "old" veterans like Joel Shropshire; within three months he too was a prisoner of war. Listed as "returned from missing July 1864", Cook survived his time at Camp Ford. The roster says he was mustered out June 21 1865 with Loucks and Vimpeny at Clinton Iowa. He spent the rest of his life in the Linn County town of Central City Iowa where he died at his home in May 1922 after an extended illness.
-- **Charles Vimpeny** 27 of Toledo enlisted December 1863; listed as "returned from missing July 1864". Born in England, he survived the prison camp and was mustered out June 21 1865 at Clinton Iowa. After the War he raised his family in Joliet Illinois where he made his home for several decades. In October 1912 while crossing a street to attend a political speech at a theater in Quincy Illinois, he was suddenly and accidentally run over and killed by an automobile. His name is frequently misspelled, even in the Company roster and records.

TWO MEN OF COMPANY G DIED AT CAMP FORD, TYLER TEXAS:

-- **William S Townsend** 18 of Toledo, enlisted December 1863. He died as a POW at Camp Ford Sept 1 1864 and is now buried in Alexandria National Cemetery, Pineville Louisiana. A marker with his name is placed with his parents' graves in Crystal cemetery in Tama County. Members of his family were still farming in Tama County fifty years after the War.

-- **Daniel C Vail** 29 of Nevada, Story County enlisted December 1863, He died as a POW at Camp Ford Sept 26 1864 and is buried in Alexandria National Cemetery, Pineville Louisiana not far from his friend William Townsend. The roster, his widow's pension, and gravemarker list his name as Daniel. Some Story County and Vail family records list his name as "David", as does the 1860 US Census for Linn County Iowa, perhaps because of bad handwriting. He left a widow, two sons and a daughter.

TWO MEN OF COMPANY G PROBABLY DIED AS PRISONERS AT TYLER:

-- **Philo Brownell** 30 of Indiantown [Montour] Tama County enlisted January 1864 and three months later was listed as missing after the battle at Pleasant Hill. There is no "returned" notation in his roster information. The roster then says he mustered out with the regiment on the 16th of November 1864, but that hardly seems likely if he was a prisoner in Texas. Peter Wilson verifies that Brownell was with them at Camp Ford. The military records at the National Archives state that Brownell was wounded at Pleasant Hill, taken prisoner, left in the hands of the enemy, and died a few weeks later as a POW of disease about the 1st of May 1864. His burial place is not known.

-- **William Nance** 28 (enlisted February 1864) of Irving on the Tama-Benton county line, is listed as "returned from missing July 1864". Some roster records list Nance in Company F, but he was actually in Company G. Existing records are also unclear as to his ultimate fate at Camp Ford. The regimental roster says he mustered out August 8 1865 in Davenport, almost a full two months after the other men of Company G had been released from Texas. The pension records of his widow say William died as a POW in Tyler. It is clear that he died either as a POW, or very soon after returning home to Iowa, perhaps in Davenport. His gravesite is also unknown. His brother **David Nance** 39 from Tama County died of disease June 30, 1862 while serving in Company F of the 28th Iowa Infantry. David had enlisted in August 1862. He is buried in Jefferson Barracks National Cemetery in St. Louis.

-- "Returned from missing" in the Company records for all of these prisoners merely indicates the date they were taken off the Regimental "Missing" list; obviously they were still prisoners of war several months after this July date. The notation of July 1864 only reflects the date the Company officially recognized them in the records as being accounted for officially, still alive and prisoners, rather than merely "missing". The six who survived were probably officially exchanged together at the same time with Joel Shropshire in late May 1865 and arrived home sometime in June although some men seem to have been discharged from Davenport Iowa, others from Clinton, and not all on the same dates.

-- While Peter Wilson and his companions were being held as prisoners in Texas, the 14th Iowa Volunteer Infantry, and Company G, ceased to exist. The rest of the men of the Company mustered out with their regiment in Davenport. The 14th Iowa Residuary Battalion was then formed into three Companies: A, B and C. Therefore it not surprising perhaps that records for men of Company G after November 1864 have several errors: the original Company clerks were long gone by June 1865.

-- Philo Brownell and William Nance may be buried as "Unknown" in Alexandria National Cemetery where the bodies of many of the men who died at Tyler were later taken after being exhumed for reburial with honor in a national military cemetery. Both these men from Tama County have not ever been previously recognized as casualties of war in the official Iowa Roster and Records. In the future, justice perhaps requires that their names should be listed among all those brave men who are to be remembered and honored for giving "the last full measure of devotion" while in the service of our country.

From the Compiled Military Service Record files of the NATIONAL ARCHIVES, Washington DC:

" Perry Township, Tama Co. Iowa

General Canby,
Sir I have a son a prisoner at Camp Ford one of the 14th Iowa Vol, would you be so good as inform me if there is any way of sending him a little money or any thing else   we have heard they have no cloths and no medicine
            Your answer will oblige me and others
                                        John Wilson
                                        Adress   Buckingham
                                        Tama Co. Iowa "

Notes:
-- Peter Wilson's father John wrote the above letter to Union General Edward R.S. Canby, commander of the Union forces operating in Texas at this time, seeking information about his son. The original eventually became part of Peter Wilson's Complied Military Service Record now kept at NARA.

The two letters below were published in *The Iowa Transcript*, Toledo Iowa. Each letter is from William Gallagher quoting excerpts of other letters he himself had received which were written to him by Andrew Hazlett from POW Camp Tyler.

" **COMMUNICATED**
 Officers Hospital, Memphis, Tenn. August 19th, 1864

Friend Wieting;
    A few days ago I received a letter from my 1st Lieut. now a "prisoner of war" in Texas, and thinking that the friends of those of Co. "G" 14th Reg. Infty. whose friends, husbands, and sons are with him, might be gratified to hear what he has to say concerning their health and welfare, I append a few extracts from his letter, and give what information may be interesting to them hoping that you will give it space in your paper.
    Lieut. Hazlett writes under date of "Camp Ford, Texas July 5th, 1864", and from his statement of the manner of his capture, he seems not to have heard the order to "fall back", but tried for some time to hold his Co. in line and again to reform in the rear on a new line.
    By superior numbers he was over powered and driven back, and for a time kept up a fire from the protection of a large log. Where the rebels turned the flanks and came in the rear, and he and a few others who had delayed too long, were now surrounded and captured. Of Lieut. Shanklin he speaks as follows:

' *When we were talking our position under cover of the log, Lieut. Shanklin was shot, and from everything that I could learn, I concluded was killed immediately. He was struck when he was passing around the root of the tree and fell against it, but regained his equilibrium and passed on toward the top of the tree to where I stood; when he was again hit and fell dead without a struggle. I did not see this latter but give it as reported by C. Vimpany "from Toledo". Here follows a list of fellow Prisoners, members of Co."G". -- Peter Wilson, J. Shropshire, C. Vimpany, D.C. Vail, G. Loucks, Wm. S. Townsend, P.J. Cook. Of these Loucks and Nance have been sick; the former is recovering but it will keep Nance busy to get out of this; he is still able to go about, and draw his full rations however.*
    There is 4,000 prisoners here, 1,000 of whom leave to-morrow, we expect to go next trip.
                                        Yours truly, A. H. HAZLETT '

    No news of importance here. A.J. Smith's command is out on a raid, and I am, and have been for several weeks a denizen of this Hospital, trying to regain lost health and strength, am improving gradually. The boys at last accounts were enjoying good health generally. It is wet here and river low, with plenty of mud in the streets and more making.
    I remain yours truly,
            Wm. GALLAGHER   Capt. Co. "G" 14th Regt. Io. Infty.   "

Notes:

-- William G. Nance and Philo Brownell's names are missing from Hazlett's list above, at least as printed in this paper. The letter then does go on to say that Nance is very sick. Nance died soon after this letter was printed, but whether in Texas as a prisoner, or shortly after his release, is unclear. From records in his military file at the National Archives, Brownell seems to have died soon after their capture and his name was left off this list by some error of Hazlett, Gallagher, or the newspaper, or perhaps because, already released by death, he was no longer considered a "fellow prisoner". Loucks survived his illness but Vail and Townsend were dead a few weeks after this letter was sent. Notice, no one named "Lowell" is mentioned.

" COMMUNICATED
  Camp Kinsman, Davenport, Iowa, Nov. 11, 1864

Editor of Transcript.

Dear Sir, for the gratification of friends of members of Co. G., I here with send copy of Lt. Hazlett's letter just received.

' CAMP FORD, TYLER, TEXAS, (no date)
Capt. Wm. Gallagher;

Dear Sir, I again have an opportunity to send a letter to you from this place, and do gladly improve it.
There are reports continually of our being exchanged but when that will take place is more than we can tell.
From 700 to 900 leave within a few days but we are not of the fortunate number. Col. Dwight being of the
160th N.Y. and 19th Army Corps, nearly all of those who are exchanged are of that Corps.
                    *   *   *   *   *
This imprisonment is not as hard {as} we have undergone. Rations are meal and fresh beef -- change -- beef
and meal; when these luxuries are gone or exhausted (which occurs quite frequently) we receive shelled
corn or "chopped feed", the latter being coarse dirty and musty; worse than I ever saw fed to horses. Have
obtained four shirts for the men of the Regt. since I have been here. We are told that there is clothing from
the S.C. God bless the ladies and all engaged in this! Scurvy is becoming very prevalent, fever is prostrating
many of late. If we remain here much longer the suffering of many will be indescribable, and death will
stalk abroad through this cursed stockade like a mighty warrior going forth to battle.
                    *   *   *
The following are the casualties: S. Townsend died Sept. 1st. Daniel Vail, Sept. 26th, 1864. This is official, if
necessary before I get through.
The S.C. above does not stand for Southern Confederacy. *
        No more. But remain yours,
                    A.H. HAZLETT '

This is the substance of the letter.   Yours,
                    W. G.

We are here to be mustered out.

Lincoln vote in the Reg't.   324
McClellan   29
                              298 Major(ity).

The County Ticket all Republican.
Still in Consequence of having no tickets for Tama County, only as others were altered many did not vote,
only for President and State.
              WM. GALLAGHER   "

Notes:

-- "S.C." probably stands for Sanitary Commission, a Northern charitable organization working to aid the soldiers with food, clothing, and medical supplies. On November 16, 1864, five days after the above letter was written, the 14th Iowa Volunteer Infantry was mustered out after completing the three-year term of service. The *Iowa Transcript* made note of the occasion with this brief observation in the October 20 1864 edition:

"Having served three years the 14th Iowa Infantry will be mustered out of service at Davenport, sometime in November. It is now, however, at the front, under command of Captain Crane, and ready for a brush with Price."

The Company G recruits of 1864:
COMPANY A, THE RESIDUARY BATTALION OF THE FOURTEENTH IOWA INFANTRY
An excerpt from a short memoir by George W. Shiner, who enlisted from Buckingham, January 1864:

" In 1856, May 1, being 21 years old, started out for myself. Tried peddling medicines compounded by Dr. Henry Steel of Linden, Illinois. I did not succeed with that, so I went to Buckingham, Tama County, Iowa, where my two oldest brothers had located. Went into company with Stewert on a hand leaver shingle machine. While working there, got acquainted with Janett Lefler and on the 4th of November 1856, we were married by the Justice of Peace, in Toledo, the County seat of Tama County, Iowa. Went back to the old place in Illinois to settle up Father's business, as administrator.

In 1858, moved to Buckingham, Iowa, where I followed farming and running threshing machines until January 1st, 1864 when I enlisted in the U.S. Service, under Frank Thomas, recruiting Sergeant. Mustered into the service on the 23rd by Colonel Grier, U.S. Mustering Officer at Camp McClellan, at Davenport, Iowa. As a recruit for Co. G. 14th Infantry. Left in a company of about 60 recruits under Captain Campbell for the same regiment, then in the state of Mississippi. Got to Cairo, Illinois on the 3rd of February.

Left on the steam boat "Olive Branch". Got to Memphis on the 6th. Left Memphis on the 7th on the steamer "Adriatic". Got to Vicksburg 9th. Camped on the Black River, 12 miles east of Vicksburg. Waited for Sherman's expedition to return from Meridian. On the 4th of March joined our regiment. Camped at Vicksburg until March 10th. Left under General A. J. Smith to join General Banks expedition up the Red River the 16th. Got to Alexandria April 9th. In the engagement at Pleasant Hill after Banks defeat on the 8th at Sabine Crossroads. The expedition moved slowly down the river in an almost continual skirmish until the 9th May. We reached the mouth of Red River, the 23rd.

Got to Vicksburg June 4th, started up the river, landed at Memphis on the 10th. June 24th, General Smith with a few regiments, including the 14th started out to Tupelo, Mississippi, to tear up the Mobile and Ohio Railroad. Returned on the 23rd of July to Memphis, August 4th, started on a raid through Tennessee and Mississippi. Returned to Memphis on the 30th. September 5th went on board a boat called the "Bostonia". 6th started up the river for Cairo where we landed on the 8th. The 14th started for St Louis. 17th landed at Jefferson Barracks below the city. On the 24th went out on the Iron Mountain Railroad. The regiment scattered out, a company in a place, to guard the bridges to keep the guerrillas from burning them. The 28th moved back to DeSoto, to keep between rebel General Price's command and St. Louis. 29th got back to Jefferson City and guard water tanks on the Pacific Railroad. On the 16th our company detailed to guard tank at Tipton.

On the 29th the 14th Iowa ordered home to be mustered out of the service, which ended our field service. On the 6th of November got to Davenport. Presidential election on the 8th. Our regiment gave Lincoln 325 votes and McClellan 42 votes. After the election the recruits and veterans of the whole company organized into two companies called the Residuary Battalion of the 14th Iowa Infantry.

On the 24th left Davenport for Springfield, Illinois to do garrison duty at Camp Butler, where we arrived on the 26th. Garrison duty means going on guard, on drill, on dress parade, on inspection, something every day. December 13th I am detailed to guard 3 men from Camp Butler to St. Louis to be tried for desertion. Returned on the 16th. From the 16th of December to January 20th on regular camp duty. On the 20th got a furlough for 10 days. Got home on the 23rd, left home on the 28th, got back to camp on the 30th. On regular garrison duty until February 16th. Detailed to help guard prisoners to St. Louis, got back on the 18th. In camp until March 28th. Detailed to guard recruits to Nashville Tennessee. Back to camp on April 8th. On the 12th detailed to guard recruits to Baltimore, where we arrived on the 15th. President Lincoln shot last night at Ford's Theater in Washington, D. C. He died this morning.

We got back to camp on the 18th. On camp duty til May 4th. The Company acted as President Lincoln's funeral escort. In camp till June 19th. Detailed as head nurse in Ward B, Post Hospital, where I remained on duty til August 2nd. Started to Davenport to be mustered out of service. Got my discharge and left camp to go home on the 9th, where I landed on the 10th. In the service one year, seven months and ten days.

Home from the War. Bought a team and rented a farm. 1866 raised good crops of corn and wheat. Bought a threshing machine and run it to good advantage. 1867, farmed and threshed. In 1868, moved to Breckenridge, Caldwell County, Missouri. Bought land from Hannibal and St. Joe Railroad in Caldwell County, 7 miles southwest of Breckinridge where I farmed and threshed and run sawmill until 1873. The first of 13 children was born in Whiteside Co. Ill in 1857, then 4 children were born in Buckingham, Iowa between 1859 and 1866. The next three children were born in Breckenridge, Caldwell Co. Misssouri in 1869 to1873. Sarah Jane Shiner was the first child born in Utah at Mill Creek Canyon, Salt Lake Co. in 1875. Two more children were born in Salt Lake Co. The last two children were born at Dover, Sanpete County, in 1882 & 1884. Dover was near Price, Utah. "

Notes:

-- The men recruited into Company G in early 1864, plus a few of the three year veterans from 1861, all became a part of Company A of the 14th Iowa Residuary Battalion. Among the men who were recruited in 1864 by "Frank" Thomas along with **George Shiner**, who wrote this short memoir above, was Thomas' own brother **John R Thomas**, who died on the Red River campaign, and Shiner's brother-in-law **James Lefler**. See BF Thomas, "*Soldier Life*" Chapter 12.

-- Most of the casualties from Company G, those men killed, wounded, or taken prisoner during the Red River campaign have been discussed in other sections of this compilation except for two men who deserve to be remembered for their sacrifice. **Josephus Brock** 33 of Toledo, who was born in New York, enlisted on January 5 1864. During the campaign he was stricken with fever, perhaps malaria, and died July 21 in Memphis Tennessee. He is buried in Mississippi River National Cemetery in Memphis, Section 2 Grave 358. Canadian born **George Lowell** 28 of Nevada Story County, who had enlisted January 4 1864, is shown in some records as wounded and missing in action at Pleasant Hill but Peter Wilson does not list him among the captured men being held at Tyler Texas. Lowell's description in the roster almost exactly matches that of George Loucks who was taken prisoner, so perhaps "Lowell" is only a clerical error, or an alias. The company roster says Lowell was mustered out with the regiment in 1864 while another published account of the battle lists George Lowell as among those killed at Pleasant Hill; at this date the full truth has not been determined.

-- Other recruits from Tama County into Company G in early 1864 were: Charles Alexander, Hartman Barnes, Joseph Barrett, Harper Cunningham, Elijah Gallion, Preston Greenleaf, George Helm, Melville Ingham, John Krewson, William Leach, Joseph McRoberts, Alonzo Rines, Jacob Rosenberger, William Rogers, William Spear, Philemon Willey, and George Yarham. Dilman Rosenberger, brother of Jacob, enlisted from Henry County where their family had been living, but he settled in Tama County after the War. Company G recruits in 1864 not from Tama County were: John Elwell and Charles Hull of Muscatine County, James Gallagher and Charles Smith of Story County, and Benjamin Williams of Henry County.

-- **Newton J Pilcher** enlisted into Company G in December 1863, giving his age as 18 and his residence as Toledo, yet years later he applied for a pension from North Dakota using the name **John P Buckley**. One version of events says that Buckley was orphaned at a young age. Still underage when the War broke out, he is said to have enlisted into a regiment from Polk County under his own name but was discovered by his guardian and brought back home. He waited a few months then tried again, avoiding detection this time by enlisting from Tama County and using his guardian's own name as an alias. After he was discharged in 1865 from the 14th Iowa Residuary Battalion, "Pilcher", still using his assumed name, enlisted into the U.S. Infantry at Fort Riley Kansas during the Indian wars. He later remained at Fort Rice North Dakota as an Indian trader, married a Sioux woman, and then settled down into farming. At the time of his marriage, he reverted to his original name. He and his wife had several children. Bilingual and courageous, he was widely recognized as one of the first permanent pioneer settlers in the Fort Rice area. Buckley's gravemarker in Fort Rice Union Cemetery says he was born in April 1847. He died in November 1917 after an adventurous and active life.

-- Samuel Chambers, Addison Davis, Charles Edwards, Josiah Luke, Jeremiah Mills, and Joel Shropshire were the Company G veterans from 1861 who signed on for additional time. Except Shropshire, who was still a prisoner of war in Texas, these veterans remained with the recruits when the other three-year men of the 14th Iowa Infantry mustered out. With the regiment disbanded, all the men left in Company G were placed into Company A of the 14th Iowa Residuary Battalion until the end of the War. Headquartered at Camp Butler, Springfield Illinois, the Battalion, as mentioned by Shiner above, performed mostly non-combat duties as the War ran down. The Battalion mustered out in the summer of 1865.

-- The presence of the Residuary Battalion at Camp Butler in April and May 1865 placed them at the forefront of one of the saddest events in American history, the burial of President Lincoln. After Lincoln's assassination in Washington DC, his body was brought back to his home in Springfield for entombment. The men of the 14th Iowa Residuary Battalion became part of the escort taking Lincoln's body to the statehouse and stood guard at the capital building for the funeral. They marched with the funeral procession to the cemetery, and some later acted as guards at Lincoln's tomb. **Charles E Edwards**, who was 19 when he enlisted from Tama County in October 1861, is said by family sources to have been chosen to be one of members of the honor guard who stood watch over Lincoln's bier as the President's body laid in state at Springfield before the burial. After the War Edwards returned to farm in Indiana where he had been born. He died in Indianapolis in 1931.

PRISON LIFE EAST AND WEST   By Lieutenant A H Hazlett

It has been said:

"Our nimble souls
Can spin an insubstantial universe
Suiting our mood, and call it possible,
Sooner than see one grain with eye exact
And give strict record of it."

This, probably is true, in a degree, in people of all stages of civilization; but if civilization's successive stages are compared we find untruthfulness and credulity decreasing together, until we reach our era of historical criticism; when it is becoming more and more necessary for the historian to be exact in his statements, and critical respecting evidence, from the fact that every sentence is examined and verified if true, if not, it is contradicted and expunged. It is in this way that we reach the truth, and the result becomes common property. That which stands verification remains the enduring heritage of mankind.

During all the ages of historic times, it has been the supreme ambition of aspiring men to erect some durable structure to perpetuate their names. If the desire to perpetuate a name has been deemed worthy of so much effort, how much more laudable the endeavor to perpetuate a principle. While the ostensible purpose of this Order is sociability, it has an object far more commendable, as expressed in its by-laws, which provides for the reading and publication of articles of an historical character. This, then, is the prime object: to perpetuate a principle, to leave landmarks for the guidance of coming generations, to record the history pertaining to an important epoch in the life of our Republic, the history of which stirring period we, here assembled, helped to make; and this history has become a part of our personal creed to which we are willing to swear unwavering allegiance. As a slight addition to this general fund, I offer, by request, the views and impressions received from the point of observation which I unwillingly occupied for a period of sixteen months. My sketch is wholly from memory, all data having been lost; my diary, along with my blankets and other personal effects, having been stolen on our northward trip after leaving prison. The actual *depiction* of these sixteen wretched months of my army life, as I lived them, becomes comparatively easy, however, aside from the little daily occurrences; but in order to compress it in proportion to the time at command, I can only hope to touch some of the more salient points.

On the morning of April 6, 1862, we were formed into line and hastily marched to the front to take part in that memorable battle of Shiloh, in which the Fourteenth Iowa Infantry, of which I was a member, was under a murderous fire the greater part of the time from ten o'clock in the morning until six in the afternoon, when we were compelled to surrender. As rapidly as possible, all prisoners captured were gathered together and moved to the rear. This proceeding consumed more than an hour, giving the remainder of our army time to reform. There is not a doubt that our holding the center so stubbornly, with the excitement and delay incident to our removal from the field, together with the elation of the Rebels under the impression that they had captured our entire army, saved the day for the Union forces. We were taken a short distance to the rear and went into camp for the night. As soon as we got started the guards plied us with questions. The answers to many would prove most amusing, but would hardly look well in print. They first wanted to know, "What did you'uns all come down here to fight we'uns for? We'uns don't want to fight you'uns." They also inquired where are we from. Upon being told "from Iowa", they asked, "where is that, -- is it in Cincinnati?" I presume the most unlettered Southerner knew of Cincinnati simply on account of its being a prominent station on the

Underground Railway.

After a night of refreshing sleep, with the earth for our couch and heaven for our canopy, we were formed into line, without any breakfast, and started on our way to Corinth. The first sight that greeted us was about a dozen forlorn looking Rebs standing in single file beside the road, exposing their wounds for our benefit, and looking as if they thought we had done a mean thing in thus playing havoc with their anatomy. I had studied medicine for two years before enlisting, and glancing critically at their wounds I noticed that many were shot in the right hand or arm -- their right arm being most exposed in loading their muzzle loaders. Thinking of the grit of our own mangled boys, the hurt expression of these fellows amused me considerably. One big fellow, with his shirt drawn up, exposed a bad gash over the short ribs and left side of his stomach, and he presented such a woe-begone appearance that I remember wishing the ball had carved open his bread-basket. Our own bread-baskets were yawning vacuums, and continued so until we reached Memphis on the night of the next day, for not a mouthful was served us on the entire route.

To the oft repeated question along the way, "How many are you?" the reply was invariably, "Forty Thousand". Before ten o'clock, on the first day out, the jubilant expression of the Johnnies changed to one of doleful anxiety, a fact we did not fail to note, deriving much comfort therefrom, as we knew the tables had turned. We reached Corinth after dark, in a drizzling rain, and were loaded into cattle cars and started for Memphis, which we reached next night. Here we were huddled into a warehouse, so closely there was scarcely standing room. After much importunity we were given "a bite to eat" at about eleven o'clock at night, the first since Sunday morning at Shiloh. Here the officers and privates were separated. We were kept in the place for several days, and not permitted to go outside the building for any purpose, so that it is not difficult to imagine the condition of our quarters.

Three of our boys were shot here while sitting in an open window on the second floor, simply because some fiend of a Rebel wanted to shoot a Yank. My blood boils while I write of the dastardly act. This was Southern chivalry, to shoot an unarmed prisoner.

We were next packed into cattle cars and started to Mobile, by way of Jackson. They still continued along the route to report the number of prisoners "forty thousand".

The train stopped at Jackson long enough for the citizens to take in the show. We were surely a curiosity. Some said, "Them be'n't Yanks, they haint got no tails". The young ladies were anxious to see if there were any good-looking fellows. One pointed toward myself and my corporal, Frank Thomas, the poet of our company, and remarked, "There is one good-looking fellow". Frank insisted strenuously that I was the favored one. Judging by their lively interest they had been lightly impressed by Beauregard's famous order, the purport of which was to excite the fears and incite the hatred of the people, and eventually to cause every man to enlist. "Beauty and booty are the sole objects of the invasion of the Northern hordes", proclaimed this chivalrous Rebel, on conspicuously displayed placards throughout the land, calling upon the men to rise and drive us from their soil, and upon the women to compel the men to do so. Their eagerness in flocking to see us suggested Byron's reference to the women after the siege of Ismail.

When we arrived at Mobile, the train was surrounded by as many "natives" as could get within seeing distance, and we received the same curious scrutiny as elsewhere. Many of the better class, who had traveled and were somewhat cosmopolitan, were inclined to discuss the war question. A polished old gentleman made the remark that he did not blame *us*, but our leaders.

Corporal John A. Pope, my messmate, who had been nearly blind ever since leaving Camp McClelland, but always reported for duty, was lying in the end of the car, and upon hearing this he sprang to his feet, picked his way among the boys until he reached the door, when he called out to the old gentleman, "See here, my short-haired friend, because you are all fools down here, you mustn't think we are up North. There isn't a ten-year-old boy up there who doesn't understand the whole matter thoroughly". I wish here to pay tribute to John A Pope, a native of Vermont, who died at Mound City, Illinois, soon after being released, as being as brave a soldier as ever lived and one of the most upright men I ever knew.

Some of the citizens here were inclined to be abusive. The guard at the door of our car pushed them away, using his bayonet, and remarked, "If you had fought these men you wouldn't abuse them now". We were kept at Mobile in a tobacco warehouse for eleven days, when we were taken up the river to Cahawba and put into a new warehouse, in which there was a pipe from an artesian well, so that we had clean quarters and pure water, although too warm to be palatable. The ladies of the place sent in a good, square meal for all, which considerably elated us, but the unaccountable streak of generosity ceased to *inflate* us when we were compelled to wait twenty-four hours before receiving anything more in the way of rations, and then but a modicum of poor corn meal. We remained at Cahawba about a week, when our journey was resumed, continuing up the river to Montgomery, where we disembarked, got aboard cattle cars, and soon concluded our tour of exhibition by reaching Macon, Georgia, where we were put into a stockade, remaining until paroled. Here we were strongly importuned to take the oath of allegiance to the Southern Confederacy. One old preacher made daily visits, and in response to the boys' assertion that they would die first, he retorted, "When Yellow Jack comes up through the swamps you'll be glad to do anything".

Major Hardee, a relative of General Hardee, was in command of this camp. Under favorable circumstances we might have esteemed him a gentleman. Our treatment here was the ordinary abuse of most Southern prison pens; not so bad as Andersonville, but the fare was a pint of unsavory corn meal, loathsome to the smell, nauseating to the taste. A very little salt was doled out with it. Most of the meal we got in Southern prisons was of this grade; made of damaged corn, heated and musty from exposure to the weather in open pens. But hunger whetted the appetite into acceptance of anything under the name of food. We suffered the usual prison discipline, with its regulation "dead line" claiming its usual number of victims. The best of these Southern prisons were a disgrace to modern civilization.

After taking the parole, we started for our lines, the jolliest lot of men you ever saw. Passing through Chattanooga, we came within General Mitchel's lines at Bridgeport, but were not received until the next day, at which time all the food I had had for three days was a handful of parched corn. Notwithstanding the vacuum in my stomach which nature abhors, I never slept better than on my last night in Rebel hands, three rails constituting the luxurious couch whereon I rested. Five hundred sick prisoners subsequently followed us, but under Secretary Stanton's unaccountable orders, General Mitchel was not permitted to receive them. Many of the men died when they learned that they were to be returned to prison. Joyful anticipations had buoyed them up on their journey northward. Deprived so suddenly of all hope, they sank beneath the terrible disappointment. I have often thought that if Stanton could have been subjected for one month to the torture he so ruthlessly meted out to helpless prisoners, he would quickly have renounced his mistaken policy.

From Bridgeport, we were taken to Huntsville, and after a delay of a few days marched to Nashville, an arduous task in our stall-fed condition, as the following incident will illustrate. The last morning before reaching Nashville, one of our men was found sitting bolt-upright, against a tree -- dead. Most of us felt as if we could have gone the same route with little effort.

At Nashville we received tents and went into camp for about two weeks; from there to Cairo, next to Benton Barracks, where we felt at home and remained till our officers reached us, some time in December, after their parole. During the winter of 1862, we did some campaigning in Missouri, but our regiment was not recruited nor fully re-organized until the spring of 1863, when I received my commission as first lieutenant, was formally discharged and mustered as such, April 9, 1863, and placed in command of Company G, Captain Gallagher being on detached service [note: recruiting in Toledo]. After a little of all kinds of service, including the guarding of a railroad back of Columbus, Kentucky, the Meridian campaign, and capture of Fort DeRussy, Louisiana, my narrative brings me to the ill-starred Red River campaign, which every soldier of A.J. Smith's Division mentions with indignation. Our division reached Pleasant Hill, Louisiana, April 8, 1864, to which place Banks retreated, after the battle of Mansfield, with his troops considerably demoralized. After talking over the battle and their retreat, and seeing their condition, we knew that we would bear the brunt of the engagement next day; and we were in no wise deceived.

On the morning of the 9th of April, our line of battle was formed at the edge of timber skirting an open field, but my company was placed across the main road, in the most exposed position that could have been selected. Whether this was a blunder or intentional on the part of Lieutenant-Colonel Newbold, I cannot say. My impression at the time was that it was the latter, and in consequence I resolved, in most emphatic thought, that I would hold the position till ordered to retreat or be blown to Hades in the attempt. It seems that we were flanked on both our right and left, which rendered our exposed position something terrible. I don't understand yet how any one could live a minute, much less several hours, under such a fire. In recounting this to a lady, she wittily remarked, "The immediate atmosphere was undoubtedly so *blue* that the bullets melted". When our regimental ranks broke, I formed a line not thirty paces to the rear of our original line, facing to the right, and I saw my men kill at least three Rebs within ten feet of us; but in less time than I can tell it we were entirely surrounded and escape impossible. Lieutenant Shanklin was killed just as we surrendered, and fell against me, nearly bearing me down. I was reported killed, and so considered by my friends at home for about six months, when I got a letter through the lines to them.

When I realized that I was again a prisoner my feelings may be better imagined than described. We were taken seven miles to the rear that night, and every step of the way I watched for a chance to escape. The Rebel army retreated the same distance. Banks thinking *he* was whipped, ran in the opposite direction. Next day we were taken to Mansfield and put into a large brick building, where the guards manifested their usual valorous and high-toned, chivalrous character by shooting two of our boys who were sitting in a second story window -- one, a mere boy; I shall never forget the pitiful expression upon his pallid face as he was carried out, while not a sound escaped his lips. Our march from Mansfield to Tyler was uneventful, but occasionally some incident occurred showing some amusing characteristic of our captors. We met a wagon load of natives, among which were a number of women, about whose appearance one of our boys made some remark not very complimentary, when one of the guards drew up his gun saying, "You'uns can make all the fun of we'uns you've a mind to, but you cain't make fun of the *other race*". Their military tactics were strikingly original. We plodded along under such commands as, "Flank down along that 'ar fence"; "Fall in two lines like the regulars". There was a Captain Preston in our guard who was a versatile liar of the first water, and a braggart devoid of sense. He nauseated us by a relation of his wonderful exploits and the number of "Yanks" he had killed, amounting, on an average, to seven per day for two weeks. It is safe to say he had never been in a battle. Some of us swore we would shoot him, if we ever met him on an equal footing, at any time or place.

Finally, we reached Camp Ford, a stockade containing about eight acres. We found we had an advantage over eastern locations, from the fact that the climate was more healthful, and there was an abundance of good water. The diet consisted of a pint of corn meal with part of the cob ground in, and from two to eight ounces of wretched meat per day. This became disgustingly monotonous, to say the least, before the expiration of fourteen months, while the men on the whole were continually hungry.

After the retreat of Banks, the Rebels concentrated all their available forces on General Steele in Arkansas, from whose army many more prisoners were taken, so that at one time there were about 6,000 men in the stockade. We were allowed to go out in squads of twenty, under one or two guards, for wood and timber to build "shacks", so that most of us were finally housed, with a fireplace in each shack. We would cut down trees, then cut them up, and "tote" the loads into camp, a distance of from one to two miles, on our backs, so that we finally became tolerably fair pack mules. There was but little occurred at Camp Tyler different from the usual round of prison life. There was the dead line claiming its number of victims. There were hundreds of escapes, very few of whom ever got through, owing to the great distance to our lines, the character of the country, and the fact that it was constantly patrolled for deserters and runaway slaves as well as prisoners. To escape from the stockade was not difficult. A darkey who hauled out the refuse every morning in a mule cart, took out a number of men covered up with the trash in his cart. There were many men from Northern states among the guards who would let any of us out when it could be done in safety to themselves. In fact, getting out was a weekly pastime, but the undertaking was practically useless, as nearly all who tried it were brought back, and generally badly treated on the way. Several were badly mangled by bloodhounds. Nearly all were punished in some way, after being brought back. One day there were five, who had been recaptured, hungry and worn, standing on stumps in the stockade. Senator Twiggs, I think it was, who was passing through, seeing them, inquired the cause of punishment. Upon being told, he ordered Adjutant McCann to release them, saying that it was our business to escape and theirs to prevent it.

A German, whose name I have forgotten, was recaptured, and the guard tied one end of a long rope around the prisoner's body, and the other to the pommel of his saddle. In this way he would run his horse, and when the prisoner could not keep up, but fall forward to the ground, he would be dragged some distance, then allowed to regain his footing. This was repeated many times. He finally shot him before bringing him in -- three buck-shot entering his body, one passed through his lungs, another through the abdomen, and the third was not found. The strange part of it is that he lived through it all, and was released with us.

A tunnel some sixty feet long was about completed, extending away down into a ravine outside the stockade when some misguided villain betrayed the secret. He was one of a few who should not have been allowed to encumber the earth. One of these took the oath of allegiance, and married a girl in the neighborhood. Two others were detected stealing from fellow prisoners. A court of justice was instituted, they were tried, convicted, and sentenced to be thrown into the sink [*Note: trench latrine*]. The sentence was executed in the presence of the whole camp, who wished to witness it, and in they went, up to their necks, getting out as best they could.

As to our commandants here. A Colonel Allen, who had been a regular, was our first; but we learned that he was removed on account of the kindness of himself and wife toward the prisoners. Then an Englishman was put in charge, who did not trouble himself about our condition; but his adjutant -- a brute, and as Bill Nye would say, a boneless coward, by name of McCann, mentioned before -- exercised full authority. It was a part of his daily business to beat some soldier over the head with a navy revolver, when attending roll call. He was, one day, having a game of keno with some of our officers. Not being an expert, and finding it a losing game, he waited till there was considerable money on the board, when he raked it in, at the same time jumping to his feet and whipping out his revolver, and backed away. "Keno" was his only name from this time on, and he could hear it from every quarter of camp whenever he came in sight; but with all his efforts he never could catch the man that called it. The word "Keno" is still a means of recognition between former Camp Ford men at reunions. It was reported that some of the released prisoners who returned to Shreveport with their regiments, met and recognized McCann there, and that he denied his name. I have heard two stories in relation to the treatment he received at their hands.

General Steele's men, who were transferred to Camp Ford, after a season at Camden, Arkansas, said that at that place the prisoners were daily punished by being placed in the stocks -- a favorite method and imposed upon the slightest pretext.

Their heads were thrust through an aperture, at a painful angle with the body, and in this position they were often confined so long that they fainted from exhaustion. Other brutal inflictions, common at both places, were indicative of the vindictive feeling toward helpless and unarmed men. This characteristic Southern trait was fully shared by the women. The burial place of the boys who died in prison lay in plain view facing the stockades. One day we saw several young ladies (?) on horseback, galloping about over the graves. Sacred ground it was to us in every saddening sense; sacred to the memory of many a departed comrade, suggestive of many suffering ones to follow. Often their horses stumbled and nearly fell over the freshly mounded earth, but this did not prevent a full exhibition of their heartless disrespect toward the silent dead.

While exchange was the ever present subject of conversation, and was discussed in all its phases, we had some means of diversion, cards being a popular one. We had a few books which, by interchange, became a medium for passing many profitable hours, to such as felt inclined. I became a tolerably fair reader of French, under the tuition of a native Frenchman, and I also taught algebra to Joel Shropshire, a member of my company. He is now a practicing lawyer in Butte, Montana. But above all else, our minds were ever busy trying to devise some effectual means of escape. At a secret meeting of the officers, we discussed the practicability of trying the bold plan of capturing the guards and securing arms at the arsenal at Tyler, but it was decided adversely.

We voted on the presidential election, using beans furnished us by the authorities for the purpose -- white for Lincoln, black for McClellan. Lincoln received twenty-seven hundred, and McClellan four hundred; the latter polled principally by Irishmen from New York. The Rebel authorities angrily pronounced the majority, "d----d fools".

We celebrated the "Fourth of July", having numerous speeches; some very good. A few Rebel officers were present. There was quite an excitement at first, owing to the flag of the United States being hoisted. Being seen by the Rebels, they demanded it and tried to secure it, but it was nowhere to be found. Among the speakers were two chaplains who, contrary to the rules of civilized warfare regarding noncombatants, were held as prisoners of war with the rest of us. They held regular Sunday services during our entire time of imprisonment.

Few of this generation can realize the frightful amount of disease and death suffered by armies in the field. Marching and sleeping in cold rains; often fed on insufficient and inferior provisions, and this in connection with the forced march; lying upon the damp ground, and in malarious localities; exposed to extremes of heat and cold; all these induce a debilitated condition rendering the soldier doubly sensitive to the exhausting efforts and intense excitement of battle. To two and a half years of this experience, add sixteen months imprisonment, with worse exposure, the scantiest and most wretched of fare, and the unavoidable filth, producing an atmosphere burdened with foul odors and laden with disease. Imagine, if you can, the swarms of graybacks [*Note: lice*] which, like Banquo's ghost, would not "down", but preyed like vampires upon the hosts of physical wrecks, many of whom were mere breathing, putrid carcasses from scurvy induced by prison fare. To the horrors of brutal confinement, add the monotony of a life which, in the less hopeful, engendered a mental condition bordering on despair.

One among the worst annoyances to many during the last six months of confinement, with nerves more and more unstrung, was the sentry's call. Every night from 9 to 6 in the morning he called out in loud and drawling tone the number of his post, the half hour, and the time-worn watch call, "All's well". I am safe in saying that I heard every call during the last six months. It is in accordance with the eternal fitness of things that the *new* finally wears off from every fashion, fad, fancy or custom; but this call was just as new our last night in the stockade as it was at first. The hoarse reverberation of the infernal trumpet in Tasso's Pandemonium could not have more grating to sensitive nerves, nor more conductive to wakefulness than this monotonous twang of the sentinel.

The recital of these events of the past has been to fight one's battles over again. The lengthened and weary train of incident, privation, disaster, disease and death, amid ever alternating hopes and fears, did not leave a misty impression upon the mind, but is eaten into the imagination as if by an acid -- etched indelibly upon the mind.

Notes:
-- The article above is taken from: WAR SKETCHES AND INCIDENTS as Related by Companions of the Iowa Commandery, Military Order of the Loyal Legion of the United States, Published by the Commandery, Volume 2, Des Moines: The Kenyon Press 1898.
-- The opening poem is taken from "*The Spanish Gypsy*" by Mary Ann Evans, the poet better known as George Eliot.

-- Andrew H Hazlett of Shueyville, Johnson County, was 24 years old when he enlisted. Like Peter Wilson, he survived two separate periods as a POW, first after Shiloh, April 1862, and then again after Pleasant Hill, April 1864. After the War, Hazlett was a physician for over three decades in the western Iowa town of Dunlap. Late in life he resettled in Chattanooga Tennessee where he died in May 1926. Hazlett's messmate, **John A Pope** 22 was originally from Danville Vermont but enlisted from Toledo. Released from the Macon Georgia prison camp, Pope was hospitalized in Mound City Illinois where he died of fever in July 1862. He is buried in the family plot in Danville. Joel S Shropshire 18 of Tipton, Cedar County, enlisted in 1861, and mustered out in 1865, having also survived twice being held as a prisoner of war. Both times he used the periods of captivity to increase his education. He was later an attorney in Butte Montana and Omaha Nebraska. He died in November 1906 and is buried in Omaha. [See BF Thomas, "*Soldier Life*" Chapter 7.]

" A TRIBUTE TO HIS BROTHER'S MEMORY by James Wilson
(An obituary taken from the files of the Traer Iowa *Star-Clipper* of 1887)

Peter Wilson is dead! This startling announcement spread rapidly over our town last Saturday evening. It circulated through the community on Sabbath and into every part of the country. It was so unexpected and so painful that it brought a cloud of sorrow over the country as perhaps the death of no other man has caused.

* * * * * * * * * *

Peter Wilson was born fifty years ago in Ayrshire, Scotland. He came with his father's family to the United States about thirty-six years since, thirty-two of which have been spent in Iowa and Tama County. He was a representative of the neighborhood, a man who quietly takes upon himself the duties of life and deals faithfully and generously with his country and his neighbor. Should you ask Tama county people of his life they would tell you it was a great success. Beyond his county he was little known, as the men upon whom the Republic leans are not much heard of outside of the range of their life work. Within the sphere of their usefulness those neighborhood men are the marks set up by advancing humanity to see how far it has got.

When Peter became of age he was adopted by the United States and given all the privileges of a citizen. Up to this time he had his way to make among fourteen children, and his cases to look after in the family court where his mother presided. He was not reputed as a saintly little fellow in whose mouth butter would not melt, but was so sunshiny that he kept the nursery well warmed up. It is said that when his mother had company Peter was also likely to entertain in the orchard or haymow, and pies and cakes and jellies and fruits would be missing, and the burden of proof would be on him to prove what had become of them. The prosecution by brothers and sisters was always vigorous until conviction looked likely, when leading witnesses would modify and take back, and Peter would get clear. So family stories ran when he was absent and his life in jeopardy.

His majority had not long been reached when a terrible test was put upon him and his family. The country was threatened with dissolution. Tama county families were offering their best boys as pledges of patriotism. The native born American descended from revolutionary families and familiar with public affairs saw his duty as his fathers saw it a century sooner. The emigrant family to which Peter belonged considered the matter. Its family traditions were different only as the Covenanter differs from the Puritan, but they were cut off. The new relation with the United States had given shelter in distress, a home in adversity and citizenship with no return or equivalent unless help were given the country in national danger. Father Wilson was very clear regarding the subject in dispute and concerning the gratitude he and his family owed the protecting nation. The boys had to settle for themselves who should be the first. Peter enlisted in Company G, 14th Iowa infantry, in 1861, This was an Americanizing process for the family. It had more than ever at stake now, besides it brought fellowship and sympathy from other families that had made like offerings--and there were few that had not. Bonds of sympathy between families that had boys in the army became very strong. The father and mother of a soldier were venerated. Lifting one's hand to anyone was not a western habit in those days, but the whole-souled western man made his approval and gratitude evident to fathers and mothers of soldiers in other ways. Since 1861 the great magnitude of the war has seemingly blunted the correct sense of what is due to the survivors of the republic, but it was lively then, and it will revive when in the future we measure our heroes with common men.

Peter was at the taking of Donelson, in the battle of Shiloh, in the Hornets Nest, was captured with the regiment, and being too ill to march to prison with the rest was left at a wayside hospital and paroled or exchanged soon. He was with Sherman in his Meridian expedition and up the Red River. He helped to capture

Fort DeRussey, and fought under A. J. Smith at Pleasant Hills, where he was captured with most of his company. Orders had been sent to it to retreat, but the orderly was killed while carrying them, and the company surrounded. Peter observed afterwards that "the old 14th boys never retreated until they were commanded to do it." He was sent to Camp Ford, Tyler, Texas. The rations on the way consisted of one ear of corn each a day. He was kept prisoner fourteen months. Holes were dug in the ground for quarters. Texas beef and corn were the rations. The boys made saws out of barrel hoops with which they made combs out of the horns of the cattle. These they traded with visiting Texas farmers for vegetables. They generally had enough to eat at that prison--such as it was: Peter was liberated in the spring of 1865, at the close of the war. A lieutenant's commission had been made out for him, but he could not be mustered in under it. At the close of the war he returned to civil life and gradually assumed the duties and responsibilities, in all of which he has made the reputation that can be made in quiet life that is more enduring than public notoriety.

There are rewards in farm life if one makes the farm the prime object. It develops men peculiarly. Reflection is more prominent than activity. Purposes are only accomplished after sustained effort for years, and this gives power to intelligent minds. Peter Wilson was not only an excellent farmer, leading in the improvement of his acres, the superiority of his animals, the success of his feeding and breeding, the public spirit he showed in associations that extended the knowledge of this field, the crop and the herd, but he was in demand in every laudable neighborhood undertaking. The Grand Army Post, where veterans plan to smooth the downhill path of life to those in need of help among them, will miss him; the agricultural societies will miss him; the Sunday school, of which he was superintendent, will miss him; his neighbors who liked to meet him will miss him; needy people, who wanted little favors will miss him; his father, who has been so often proud of him, will miss him; orphan children he was raising will miss him; brothers and sisters, four boys and two girls of his own all under fifteen years of age, will miss him; and the brave wife, who must now fill her place and his at home and abroad, will sadly miss Peter.

The wide expression of sympathy with his family on his sudden death showed the place he filled in the hearts of his neighbors. As much as a death-bed can be robbed of its horrors, his was robbed-- family and friends about it, and the Christian's hope assured. The old metrical Psalm that tells of "the widow's stay and the orphan's help" came readily to his mind. It had been committed to his memory forty years ago against this trying hour, and was his greatest comfort. His life has been a joyous, sanguine, happy life. It has been very clear of selfish effort. He could have been a wealthier man but not without being a narrower man. His period of army hardships curtailed his life many years. The veteran misses the nervous expenditure of army life after middle age. A year in the army shortens every man's life five years on the average. The lives of these good men are family and neighborhood heirlooms that act as object lessons. These lives do not cloud over and sink in oblivion like transient notoriety.

There is power in the influence of such a life, for whoever lives a life so notable as to hold the confidence and love of the people who mourn his loss, traces the marks of his own character on the characters of those by whom he is surrounded. There is promise in the end of such a life, for it has the pledge of all the blessedness which eternity is able to bestow. "

Notes:
After his release from Camp Ford, Peter Wilson returned home to his farm where he raised a family, bred livestock, and improved his land until his death on April 23, 1887. He is buried in Buckingham Cemetery, just north of Traer, Iowa. Nearby are the headstones of his wartime companions, John McKune, Eleazar Stoakes, and Benjamin Thomas. The Wilson farm, west of Traer and just north of Highway 96, including the brick home built by Peter after the War, has continuously remained in the Wilson family ever since and is currently operated by Peter's great-grandson.

A SPECIAL NOTE ABOUT PETER WILSON'S BROTHER JAMES WILSON

Peter's brother, James Wilson, nicknamed "Tama Jim", was the recipient of many of the letters printed here, and the author of Peter's obituary on the previous page. James was born in Ayrshire Scotland in August 1835, the oldest of John and Jean McCosh Wilson's fourteen children. The Wilson family came to the United States when James was sixteen, settling first in Connecticut and then moving to Tama County, Iowa in 1855. Taught to read by his father, James also attended college in Grinnell Iowa for a short time. He then taught school at old Buckingham village north of Traer, worked at local sawmills and gristmills, and started farming in partnership with his brother Peter. When Peter went off to defend their adopted country in the War James agreed to stay home to care for their joint farming operations; when the War ended and Peter came home, it became James' turn to go forth to serve their community. Their Buckingham neighbors chose James Wilson to represent them, first in the State Legislature, and then later in the U.S. Congress. While with the State Assembly he was selected as Speaker of the House. Returning to Iowa from Washington DC, James spent the next six years as a professor of agriculture at Iowa State College in Ames, where he also was Director of the Agricultural Experiment Station. He was heavily involved with organizations like the Farmer's Alliance, and the Dairy and Stock Breeder's Associations, and the Extension Service, tirelessly working for the benefit of farmers and the advancement of agricultural progress.

In 1897 President William McKinley appointed James Wilson to be the Secretary of the U.S. Department of Agriculture. He was then retained in that cabinet position in the administrations of Presidents Theodore Roosevelt and Howard Taft. Serving until 1913, it was the longest term served by any cabinet official in U.S. history. As head of the USDA James Wilson was instrumental in supporting increased meat inspection, food and drug laws, forest and soil conservation methods, rural road development, irrigation programs, and scientific weather forecasting on a national scale. He heavily promoted cutting-edge agricultural techniques by recruiting leading agricultural scientists and genetic researchers to help develop and encourage the use of new high yield crops and more productive breeds of cows, hogs, hens and horses. He worked to improve market conditions and crop reporting; boosted agricultural industries like making sugar from beets. Under his leadership the Department helped introduce vaccinations and serums to cure animal disease; sent experts across the country and the world to discover innovative and practical ways to defeat insect pests. He then invented and administered programs to teach all these new methods to farmers across the entire country. His energy and long tenure at the USDA, and the programs he helped initiate, still influence the quality of all our lives even today, and in many ways they touch so deeply that we take them completely for granted.

James Wilson also served as Railroad Commissioner of Iowa for a number of years and was editor of the Traer *Star-Clipper* newspaper for a time, writing a popular and widely distributed column on scientific and practical farming. He was a close personal friend of George Washington Carver who was a frequent guest at the Wilson farm and who often traveled with Wilson on lecture tours to educate farmers' groups on new discoveries and ideas. James and his wife Esther Wilbur, who are buried in Buckingham cemetery, were the parents of seven children.

A BRIEF SUMMARY OF HIS TRAVELS IN THE WAR BY ELEAZAR STOAKES:

Long after the War, Eleazar Stoakes' adult son Theodore decided to write down the details of his father's life. As his father spoke, Theodore made notes concerning his father's childhood, the War years, and the years on the farm following Eleazar's marriage to Eliza Granger. Eleazar drew a rough map and told his son about the War. Provided by Theodore's grandson Clair Stoakes, this is an excerpt from Theodore's notes:

"When the Civil War broke out he (father) sold his 80 (acres) to 2 of his brothers. He & Uncle Frank Thomas enlisted in the Army for three years, in Co. G 14th Regiment Iowa Volunteer Infantry, at old Buckingham the later part of October 1861, then went to Toledo, Tama County, where the company was formed, there being several Tama County boys enlisting.

From there they went to a camp near Davenport were they were mustered in, and received their uniforms. Nov 28th they left the camp, went to Davenport took train for the south riding in passenger cars arrived at St. Louis Nov 30th. Feb 5th 1862 Left St. Louis on steamboat down the Mississippi River to Cairo Ill. Up the Ohio river then up the Tennessee River to Fort Henry where they landed Feb 8th (which was captured the day before Feb 7th by the Union troops). There they camped, then on Feb 12th they started to march to Fort Donelson & camped within a mile of the hostile forces. On the morning of Feb 13th the battle of Fort Donelson began lasting three days when the rebels surrendered Feb 15th 1862 with heavy losses on both sides. The Union forces camped on the battlefield that night using the log cabins, which the Confederates had left, for tents as far as they went. (note: meaning "as far as the limited supply of cabins were available until all were full")

They left Fort Donelson March 7 1862 arriving at Savannah Tennessee Sunday morning March 15th. Left Savannah arriving at Pittsburg Landing March 19th and went into camp. On the morning of April 6th began the battle of Shiloh a few miles from the river. About 5:30 P.M. the first day they were taken Prisoners of War.

Next day were marched south, that night camped in a cottonfield without any tents, it rained and they were soon ankle deep in mud. Next day marched on to Corinth Mississippi arriving at 5 P.M. Next morning April 8th were put into boxcars & sent to Memphis Tenn, went on south to Canton then to Mobile arriving the morning of April 16th 1862. On April 19th marched to Alabama River put on a steamboat & started up the river arriving at Cahaba Alabama, were put in prison there for 2 weeks receiving scant & unwholesome rations. May 2nd left Cahaba by boat at sunrise up the river past Selma & arrived at Montgomery at 6:30 P.M. the same day. Next morning put in box cars and sent east across Chattahootchie river arrived at Columbus, thence to Macon Georgia, arriving Sunday May 4th 10 A.M. at Camp Oglethorpe also short of rations & spoilt meat, after 20 days in camp there, left May 24th by train arrived at Atlanta Georgia at 1 P.M.

Left Atlanta 7 P.M. the same evening and arrived Chattanooga May 25th 8 P.M. took us out of town to a cotton shed were held under guard until May 26th were issued half rations. Then marched back to the river put on steamers went down river past Lockport & Bridgeport and farther down the river landed on the shore for the night. Then by boat up the river landed on an island. Left there May 28th. Marched to Belfont took train to Huntsville Ga at 7 P.M. (note: Huntsville, Alabama)

Next morning received full rations of good wholesome food, first in two months. Stoakes (as Eleazar Stoakes was called from a boy) came up missing, when by chance the rest of his squad was sent to the 3rd Ohio regiment & when they arrived, there sat Stoakes as he had heard some of the boys he knew from Wellsville Ohio were there. From Huntsville marched to Columbia put on cars & sent to Nashville Tenn. then taken to Fairground & camped there about 20 days.

Stoakes, Thomas & other comrades started home via Smithland Tennessee, went to Cairo Ill. Then to Clinton Iowa, then to Otter Creek, that was as far as trains came. Stayed all night with a farmer next day went to Toledo arriving home that evening with much joy. Aug 1st received orders for all paroled prisoners to return to Benton Barracks, St. Louis, not later than August 20th. They started Aug 11th by way of Clinton, then to St. Louis arriving Aug 17th.

Received his discharge Nov 8th 1862 for disability. One week later started for home. Thomas and Felter accompanied him home via Davenport by boat then to Marengo by rail, then by stage coach to Blairstown then by rail to Toledo, next day arriving home in the evening very happy."

INDEX

The Soldiers of the 14th Iowa, Company G:

Soldiers from other companies or regiments:

Aurner, Hiram W- 106, 107
Bailey, Charles W- 61
Baker, NB, Adjutant General T- 3, 8, 50, 52, 53, 56,
   69 / W- 49, 50, 55, 73, 76, 84
Banks, NP, General T- 66, 70, 87, 89, 117, 118 /
   W- 106, 111, 114, 115, 120, 124, 125
Bartholomew, Robert T- 80, 81
Beatty, William W- 57
Benton, Samuel, Chaplain T- 9 / W- 15
Birge, John T- 20 / W- 39, 40
Boyd, Richard T- 86, 94
Bridges, James T- 28
Brodtbeck, Samuel T- 13, 18 / W- 10
   -- Otto T- 18
Burke, Orville T- 71, 81, 90
Calkins, William T- 113, 121
Campbell, William T- 83, 91, 94, 98, 114
Carmean, Joshua T- 88, 89, 95 "Carmine"
   -- Pearson T- 88, 89, 95 "Carmine"
Cason, Seth W- 104
Churchill, Elias T- 88, 94
Clark, Meroni W- 106, 107
Connell, John W- 60, 61, 106
Conway, Joseph W- 59
Cooper, Charles T- 103, 104
Crane, Leroy T- 67, 70, 74, 79, 80 / W- 91, 120
Crocker, Marcellus M, T- 7, 9-10, 13
Crowhurst Henry T- 85, 93, 94
   -- Seth T- 93, 94
Curtis, Samuel T- 35, 63 / W- 59, 60
Dillman, Sylvester T- 87, 94
Dittoe, William T- 110, 111
Dodds, William T- 74, 81
Duncan, Nathan T- 32, 33, 46
Elliot, Nathan T- 87, 95
Ellis, James T- 103, 104
Emerson, Richard T- 63, 64
Free, Thomas T- 90, 95 / W- 29, 30
Gard, Burtis T- 46
Geddes, James T- 14, 29, 30, 95 / W- 82, 86
Gentzler, Martin T- 25, 28
Gilbert, James, Colonel T- 91, 97, 104, 105
Gilbert, Joseph, Lieutenant T- 109, 110-111
Gillet, Joseph W- 106, 107
Goben, William W- 106, 107
Grant, US, General T- 10, 17, 21-23, 26, 30, 46, 78,
   89, 90, 105 / W- 31, 33, 36, 39, 43, 60, 61, 65,
   66, 68, 85, 89, 104, 107, 111
Gray, William W- 106, 107
Gregg, John T- 25, 28
Griggs, Luther T- 13, 18
Gross, John W- 57
Halleck, HW, General T- 13, 22 / W- 47-49, 51, 73
Henry, James W- 32, 33
Irwin, James T- 58
Jennings, Alexander T- 25, 28
Jones, Warren T- 70, 97, 104, 117
Kiner, Frederick F T- 9
Kirkpatrick, Robert T- 32, 46 / W- 46, 62

Kirkwood, William T- 7, 63-65, 69, 70 / W- 84
Kleber, John W- 106, 107
Lauman, Jacob T- 22, 23, 26 / W- 5, 30, 33, 35, 43-
   46
Leonard, Hiram T- 8, 9, 15 / W- 8, 45
   -- Howard W- 8, 45
Logan, George T- 22 28 / W- 112, 113
Lucas, Edward, Lt. Colonel T- 9, 65 / W- 8, 84
Lucas, William, Lt. T- 7, 9
   -- James T- 9
   -- Parker T- 9
McDowell, West T- 109, 111
McMaken, William T- 7, 9, 43, 44, 46
McMillen, William W- 112, 113
   -- David W- 113
   -- James W- 113
Messmore, Isaac T- 72, 76, 81
Mitchel, Ormsby T- 40, 45, 48, 49, 53, 58
Mofield, William T- 115, 121
Moore, David T- 29, 88, 89, 91, 93, 95, 97, 98, 104
Moore, Robert T- 49, 53
Moorehead, John T- 83, 94
Morton, William T- 75, 81
Mulcahy, John W- 57
Nerge, John T- 115, 121
Newbold, Joseph T- 65, 67, 70, 72, 77, 78, 80, 90,
   104 / W- 87, 112, 113, 124
   -- Cyrus T- 70
   -- Jacob T- 70
   -- Joshua T- 70
Parmenter, William T- 89, 96
Parker, Leonard T- 103, 104
Peyton, Absolom T- 88, 94
   -- Micaiah T- 88, 94
Pierce, Samuel, Doctor T- 56, 57, 65, 66
Pitt, George W W- 11, 12
   -- George L W- 12
   -- Philip W- 12
   -- William W- 12
Prentiss, BM, General T- 29, 30 / W- 61, 75
Presbury, George T- 105, 108-110, 113
Quinn, Peter T- 109, 111
Rhodes, Isaac T- 87, 94, 95
   -- Milton T- 94
   -- Wesley T- 94
Rogers, Elliot T- 89, 95
Roland, William T- 33, 34, 46
Root, Elisha T- 75, 81
Runyon, John T- 87, 95
Savage, Joel T- 22, 28
Schaeffer, Theodore T- 84, 94
Scott, Charles T- 103, 104
Scott, John (32nd Iowa) T- 81
Scott, John (28th Iowa) T- 112, 120, 121
Shaffer, George T- 33, 46
Shannon, Joseph T- 8, 9, 15, 25, 26, 28, 34, 63
Shaw, William T, Colonel T- 7, 15, 26, 33, 56, 62,
   63, 65, 67, 70, 88, 91, 93, 95, 97, 98, 104, 108,
   110, 112, 113, 117, 118, 120, 121 / W- 4, 8, 16, 25,
   28, 57, 59, 60, 63, 78, 79, 83, 84, 87, 91, 92, 94,
   96, 99-101, 112, 114
   -- Robert Gould T- 70

Note:
Andrew Whalen T- 13 has not been identified.

T = THOMAS , *Soldier Life*
W = WILSON , *Many Must Fall*

TRAER HISTORICAL MUSEUM

The Traer Historical Museum would like to acknowledge and thank those people who helped make this book possible.

Original copies of *Soldier Life* were made available by the Traer Public Library and by the State Historical Society of Iowa. Sharon Avery, Susan Jellinger, and Sherri Stelling of the State Historical Society Research Library were extremely helpful, offering wonderful assistance locating other important documents in their extensive archives of original Civil War material. Copies of *The Iowa Journal of History and Politics* containing Peter Wilson's letters were found at the Traer Museum and at the Tama County Historical Society Museum/Genealogical Library in Toledo, Iowa. We received a tremendous amount of help and support from Joyce Wiese, Karlene Foreman, Chris Daisey, and the entire staff at Toledo who often went above and beyond the call of duty whenever asked for assistance. They have a large collection of books, files, microfilms, and newspapers about the family genealogy, cemeteries, and history of Tama County. We thank the State Historical Society of Iowa for permitting us to reprint the Wilson Letters.

Thanks also to Eleazar Stoakes's great-grandchildren Mary Sievers and Dennis Stoakes for their contributions in making this publication possible. In honor of John Espy McKune, Tom L. Sawyer, McKune's great-great grandnephew, also very generously donated to the start-up costs of the publishing of this book. Tom provided photographs, letters, family information, and shared with us the wonderful ring carved by McKune while confined in the POW camp and sent home as a gift for his young niece Abbie, Tom's great-grandmother.

Evan Wilson, grandson of Peter Wilson, not only furnished Peter's photograph, but offered a great deal of helpful background information. Photographs, letters or valuable family information were also provided by Russell Reigle, who is another great-grandson of Eleazar Stoakes; Sarah Meyer and Norm Hopkins, of the Felter family; Harriet Pedelty, Patricia Marsh, and Marlene Bown.

Others who contributed pictures, letters, advice, encouragement, inspiration or support in some way are: Navarro College in Corsicana, Texas; the Vinton Public Library, Linwood Cemetery in Dubuque, and the Parker Museum in Spencer, Iowa, which provided the photograph of John Gaston. We constantly relied on Ellen Young and Judy Robb; and of course, we could not have gotten far without the knowledge and expertise of our publisher Clark Kenyon of the Press of the Camp Pope Bookshop.

A special thanks goes to Sara Kay Stoakes for designing the cover of our book. She is the great-great granddaughter of Eleazar Stoakes. J. A. McCann, who edited the text from the original edition, did a tremendous amount of research and compilation of material. His love of this subject is infectious. A great deal of thanks is owed to Sharon Stoakes, the "General Grant" of our project, for pulling all the different pieces together and pushing it through to the end despite many obstacles and upsets along the way. We are grateful for all the assistance these people, and others too numerous to name, have given, helping us to preserve these histories of these ordinary but heroic men from North Tama and their companions.

Finally we especially remember and thank the Soldiers, and all who served their Country along with them, almost 150 years ago, in their "War of the Rebellion." Our deepest gratitude goes to all these men, and to all the men and women who have ever fought and sacrificed themselves to keep this Nation strong and safe throughout the entire history of our County. May God always bless America, and may God forever watch over our Soldiers wherever they serve.

Traer Historical Museum
514 2nd Street
Traer Iowa   50675
Phone 319-478-2346